JUVENILE JUSTICE IN AMERICA

FOURTH EDITION

Clemens Bartollas
University of Northern Iowa

Stuart J. Miller
Washington & Jefferson College

Upper Saddle River, New Jersey 07458

Library of Congress Cataloging-in-Publication Data

Bartollas, Clemens.
Juvenile justice in America / Clemens Bartollas, Stuart J. Miller.—4th ed.
p. cm.
Includes bibliographical references and index.
ISBN 0-13-112326-2
1. Juvenile justice, Administration of—United States. 2. Juvenile delinquency—United States. 3. Juvenile delinquents—United States. I. Miller, Stuart J., II. Title.
HV9104.B34 2004
364.36′0973—dc22 2004008593

Executive Editor: Frank Mortimer
Assistant Editor: Korrine Dorsey
Production Editor: Brian Hyland
Managing Editor: Mary Carnis
Design Director: Cheryl Asherman
Senior Design Coordinator: Miquel Ortiz
Director of Production & Manufacturing: Bruce Johnson
Manufacturing Manager: Ilene Sanford
Cover Design: Steve Frim
Cover Image: Ghislain and Marie David de Lossy, Getty Images/The Image Bank

This book was set in Palatino by *The GTS Companies*/York, PA Campus. It was printed and bound by RR Donnelley-Harrisonburg. The cover was printed by Phoenix.

Pearson Education Ltd.
Pearson Education Singapore Pte. Ltd.
Pearson Education Canada, Ltd.
Pearson Education—Japan
Pearson Education Australia Pty. Limited
Pearson Education North Asia Ltd.
Pearson Educación de Mexico, S.A. de C.V.
Pearson Education Malaysia Pte. Ltd.

10 9 8 7 6 5 4 3 2 1
ISBN 0-13-112326-2

Dedicated to Kristin, Kathryn Leigh,
Andrea Lyn, and Laura Ann,
our children

CONTENTS

PART III: COMMUNITY-BASED CORRECTIONS

PREFACE

Juvenile justice is part of a broader human rights movement that is concerned with far more than society's response to juvenile lawbreaking. Indeed, as globalization, urbanization, industrialization, and worldwide communications increase, the world's attention increasingly is directed to the plight of all children, regardless of circumstances. This concern is extremely late in coming. Approximately one-half of the world's population today is age fifteen or younger, and the magnitude of the problems these youths face is staggering. Poverty, racism, sexism, ethnocentrism, and religious differences all influence how children are treated. The reality is that in many societies, children are considered to be economic hindrances and expendable. Local, municipal, state, provincial, territorial, and national governments often lump together the needy, the dependent and neglected, the status offender, the mentally ill, the violent, and the victim of abuse. These children are discriminated against, victimized, persecuted, and sometimes executed by citizens, police, and paramilitary forces. The problems youths face go to the core of cultural thinking, far beyond the needs of societies simply to fine-tune agencies and rules for the handling of youths in need.

English-speaking countries such as the United States provide many of the ideals that are behind current world efforts to reform the world's approach to juvenile justice. Unfortunately, even world leaders often fall far short of their own ideals. In this regard, the United States is an excellent case study of what is and what could be in juvenile justice in the world today.

Our primary purpose in this text is to explore and define the important components of and debates over juvenile justice in the United States. Some believe that juvenile justice involves only a study of the early processing of juvenile offenders; others state that the processing of any or all who come through the juvenile justice system should come under the purview of juvenile justice. Because the authors regard the basic focus of juvenile justice as the control, correction, and treatment of both juvenile offenders and the other groups mentioned, we have accepted the latter definition.

We judge that the history and philosophy of juvenile justice, the processing of youths, the detention of juveniles, and the diversion of youths from the juvenile justice system should all be included in discussing juvenile justice. We are committed, moreover, to depicting the fascinating and sometimes tragic world of the juvenile offender, to describing the jobs and problems of practitioners in the justice system who work with youths, and to addressing important issues inherent in juvenile justice. This new edition includes two new chapters, Chapters 3 and 13. The former focuses on explanations for why juveniles become involved in illegal behaviors; the latter, on juveniles' participation in youth gangs and urban street gangs. Other important new features of this text are more emphases on the balanced and restorative justice model, on updating juvenile sentencing structures, on expanding prevention programs for juveniles and boot camps, on developing an understanding of and treatment for sex offenders, and on revealing more on how participants in the juvenile justice system do their jobs. There continue to be frequent glimpses into the mind and perspective of the youthful offender, a portrayal of the emerging trends of juvenile justice and an examination of the risk control and crime reduction measures in probation and aftercare.

This book begins with an overview of the juvenile justice system, with a special emphasis on the challenges facing juvenile justice in the twenty-first century. Chapter 2 presents an empirical profile on youth crime, derived from the main official and unofficial measurement of crime. Chapter 3 examines the causes of juvenile crime, ranging from the perspective that the origins of delinquent behaviors arise from rationality to that of viewing juveniles as biologically, psychologically, or sociologically determined in what they do. Chapter 4 discusses the role of the police in preventing and controlling youth crime. Chapters 5 and 6 are concerned with the background, legal norms, stages of decision making, trial process, and personnel of the juvenile court. Chapter 7 shifts to the types of experiences that await the juvenile who is transferred to the adult court. Chapters 8, 9, and 10 focus on community-based corrections, including probation and aftercare services and residential programs. Chapter 11 presents the structures and programming of short- and long-term confinement of juveniles. Chapter 12 examines treatment of youthful offenders in both community-based and institutional settings. Chapter 13 presents a portrayal of the juvenile who becomes involved in a youth gang or in an urban street gang. Chapter 14 discusses the various types of youthful offenders. In Chapter 15, we introduce the *Beijing Rules*, the model juvenile justice code for the world, which provide a basis for the chapter. We discuss how juveniles are handled in three English-speaking countries, Canada, England,

and Australia, as well as juvenile justice in four countries from other areas of the world with distinctive problems. Chapter 16 summarizes the text and predicts what juvenile justice will look like in forthcoming decades of the twenty-first century.

Although no one is totally value-free, every attempt has been made to be fair and provide a balanced presentation of the juvenile justice system. Before juvenile justice can develop more just systems and a more humane present and future for juveniles, its characteristics, procedures, policies, and problems must be carefully examined. This is the task of this text.

ACKNOWLEDGMENTS

Many individuals have contributed to the writing of this book. We are profoundly grateful to our wives, Linda Dippold Bartollas and JoAnn Miller. Both were constant sources of support and encouragement throughout the many phases involved in the publication of this fourth edition. Linda Bartollas also conducted interviews with juvenile offenders in three states.

We are grateful to those participants of the juvenile justice system who were willing to be interviewed, who contributed materials for this edition, or who assisted us in replicating scenes from the halls of justice for photographs for this volume. Special thanks are due to North Franklin, Pennsylvania, former Police Chief Roger Cuccaro; current Police Chief Mark Kavakich; Sgt. Richard Horner; Lt. Kirk Hessler and Officer Jerry Cavanaugh; Claysville, Pennsylvania, Police Chief David Danley and Patrolman Donald Cooper; Pennsylvania Magistrate Jay Dutton; Probation Officer Steven Tkatch; Washington County Correctional Facility Treatment Supervisor Dave Talpus; Mall Managers Richard Conrady and David Graham; Mall Security Officer Rich Keys; Willard (Buzz) Holbert and Shane Bane; and Mel Blount Youth Home Directors Mel Blount and Carol Lockett. Special thanks are also due to Trevor Onest and David Kraueter, current and past reference librarians at Washington & Jefferson College, as well as to those students who were willing to be models for various photographs throughout this book: Mary Murphy, Jessica, Melody, and Thomas Butterfield, Tommy Suitek, Anne Moore, Damille King, Tanya Terchanik, Jeffrey Pollack, Azzorrahhnove Livingstone, Andrea Miller, Robin Cook, Nelson Downey, Richard Kelley, and Alanna Santee. Katie Miller and Heather Dengle provided photographs for this and past editions.

At the University of Northern Iowa, we thank Betty Heine for all the tasks that she and her staff performed to keep the manuscript moving without interruption. Bridget Welch, Karla Davies, Katie Sorrell, and Alison Reicks were especially helpful. At Washington & Jefferson College, Emily Bloom, Rachel Guyton and Alanna Santee diligently performed research and sent out permission requests to sources. Alanna Santee also typed, developed questions for the test manuals, and assisted in writing several boxes. Debbie Trent, Margie

Mahramus, Sunny Sefzik, and Barbara Rea provided invaluable assistance in preparation of the text, instructor's manual, and index; as did Katie Miller, Andrea Miller, and Laura Miller. Willie T. Barney, Robert Quirk, Hanna Bengston, Jamie Miller, Matthew Beals, and Domenick Lombardo also played key roles in the development of the manuscript. We would also like to thank the following reviewers: George Evans, William Raney Harper College, Palatine, IL; Janice Joseph, Richard Stockton College of New Jersey, Pomona, NJ; and Al Marstellar, Drury University, Springfield, MO. Finally, we are grateful to Neil Marquardt and Kim Davies, our former editors at Prentice Hall; and Frank Mortimer, our present editor, and his associates, Sarah Holle and Korrine Dorsey.

1

JUVENILE JUSTICE: AN OVERVIEW

OBJECTIVES

1. To reveal the historical themes that have guided the development of juvenile justice in the United States
2. To examine the various philosophies of and strategies for correcting juvenile offenders
3. To discuss several social challenges currently facing the juvenile justice system

KEY TERMS

adjudicatory hearing
aftercare officers
balanced and restorative justice model
commitment
crime control model
dangerous poor
detention
dispositional hearing
just desserts
justice model
juvenile court officer
least-restrictive approach
medical model
minor
parens patriae
petition
petitioner
respondent
status offenders
taking into custody
treatment model

Juvenile justice reform has always been more rhetoric than anything else. . . . Juvenile justice has always been, and continues to be, neglected, demeaning, frequently violent, and largely ineffective. Permissive treatment of delinquency is reserved for middle- and upper-class adolescents who are not likely to enter the juvenile justice system, which is reserved for children of the poor. Nearly 90 percent of the inmates of juvenile detention homes and reform schools come from fragmented and damaged families which live at or below the poverty line. Even the meager rehabilitative efforts directed at these youngsters have been twisted to meet the demands of political expediency.

—Jerome G. Miller[1]

Jerome G. Miller's 1991 publication, *Last One Over the Wall: The Massachusetts Experiment in Closing Reform Schools,* provides a fascinating commentary of the time in his life when he served as commissioner of Youth Services in Massachusetts and closed the training schools of that state. But in addition to taking the reader through those stormy days, with the punch and counterpunch from both supporters and antagonists, Miller sharply critiques the performance of the juvenile justice system. Miller found that the juvenile justice system, especially training schools, is "impervious to reform." According to Miller, training schools have a hidden task of holding a society together, which makes leaders of society reluctant to embark boldly on a policy of mass deinstitutionalization. Innovation, then, cannot threaten institutional survival, because "reform strategies" must absorb existing staff, must add new institutional staff, and must bolster he institutional plant. He adds that the training school all too frequently dispenses punishment and calls it treatment.[2]

Since the 1960s, the juvenile court, as well as its rehabilitative ***parens patriae*** ("the state as parent") philosophy, has confronted massive criticism from all sides. Indeed, one characteristic of juvenile justice in the 1980s was the proposal, from both liberals and conservatives, to reduce the scope of the juvenile court's responsibilities. Conservatives wanted to refer more law-'violating youths to adult court, while many liberals recommended divesting the juvenile court of its jurisdiction over **status offenders** (juveniles who have engaged in behaviors for which adults would not be arrested). There are also those who believe that the adult court could do a much better job than the juvenile court with youthful offenders. Juvenile offenders, according to this position, would at least receive their constitutionally guaranteed due process rights.

It is not surprising that few are happy with the performance of juvenile justice today. As a police chief told one of the authors, "The juvenile justice system is in a real mess in this nation."[3] To express this in another way, there is precious little support given to keeping the juvenile court and the juvenile system the way it is now.[4] The fact is that the juvenile justice system will experience major changes in the next few years. How it will change and whether the changes will be helpful to the youth of this nation are critical questions yet to be answered.

Juveniles arrested for serious offenses would occasionally have to spend at least short periods of time in the "hole" in the Old Washington, Pennsylvania, County Jail. The facility was open until approximately April 1996. Many crime control advocates argue that the use of such cells for juveniles is appropriate. (Photo by Stuart Miller.)

The juvenile justice system is responsible for controlling and correcting the behavior of troublesome juveniles. What makes this mission so difficult to accomplish in the twenty-first century are the complex forces that intrude on any attempt either to formulate goals or to develop effective programs. Juvenile violence remains a serious problem, although homicides committed by juveniles began to decline in the mid-1990s. Even though juvenile gangs declined in numbers and members across the nation in the final four years of the twentieth century, these gangs continue to be a problem in many communities. Juveniles' increased use of weapons have also became a serious concern, and there are those who believe that "getting the guns out of the hands of juveniles" is the most important mandate that the juvenile justice system currently has. The use of drugs and alcohol among the juvenile population declined in the final decades of the twentieth century, but beginning in the mid-1990s and continuing to the present, there is evidence that the use of alcohol and drugs, especially marijuana, is rising in the adolescent population. Furthermore, the fact that there are conflicting philosophies and strategies for correcting juvenile offenders combines with the social, political, and economic problems that American society faces today to present other formidable challenges to the juvenile justice system.

Beginning with several historical themes, this chapter provides an overview of juvenile justice in the United States by describing the organization and structure of juvenile justice agencies and by examining several challenges that the juvenile justice system faces.

WHAT ARE THE HISTORICAL THEMES OF JUVENILE JUSTICE?

Throughout history, there has rarely been an emphasis on the special needs of juveniles. Adults and juveniles who violated the law were typically processed in the same manner and were subject to the same types of punishments, including whippings, mutilation, banishment, torture, and death.[5]

In the fifth century A.D., the age was fixed at seven for determining whether youths would be exempted from criminal responsibility under certain conditions. With the onset of puberty at the age of twelve for girls and fourteen for boys, youths were held totally responsible for their socially unacceptable behaviors.

This understanding of children and criminal responsibility was continued in medieval Europe. For example, during the entire period between A.D. 700 and 1500, children were not viewed as a distinct group with special needs and behaviors. Although little is known about the peasant families of the Middle Ages, it is clear that children were expected to assume adult roles in the family early in life and apprentice in crafts or trades to wealthier families. The landowners of the country, then, assumed control over children and their welfare and, at the same time, lifted the burden of child care from their parents.

These early medieval traditions eventually influenced the shaping of juvenile justice in England. Both the Chancery court, which eventually became responsible for overseeing the general welfare of the citizenry, and the concept of *parens patriae,* which focused on the sovereign as the one who protected his or her subjects, played a prominent role in the shaping of English juvenile justice.

Because children and other incompetents were under the protective control of the sovereign, it was not difficult for English kings to justify interventions in their lives. With the passage of time, the concept of *parens patriae* was increasingly used to justify interventions into peasants' families.

The common law tradition in England eventually concurred with earlier law that children under seven should not face legal penalties. Children between seven and fourteen were deemed another matter, and their responsibility was determined by other considerations: severity of the crime, maturity, capacity to distinguish between right and wrong, and evidence of blatant malice.

A sad page in the history of English juvenile justice is that some 160 to 200 capital offenses were listed in the statutes for which children could be executed. Although many juveniles sentenced to die were later pardoned or transported to another country, some children were executed. For example, eighteen of the twenty people executed in London in 1785 were under the age of eighteen.[6] The executions of children continued but only occasionally into the 1800s.

The history of juvenile justice in America receives considerable treatment in this text. In this first chapter, the historical themes of juvenile justice are discussed: the declining authority of the family, the repression and reform cycle, the "get tough" approach for serious offenders, the "go soft" approach for minor offenders, the threat of the "dangerous poor," and the unsolvable nature of youth crime. The importance of history in this text is further documented by the fact that nearly every chapter examines some aspect of the history of juvenile justice in the United States.

Declining Authority of the Family

The history of juvenile justice in America began in the colonial period. The family, the cornerstone of the community in colonial times, was the source and primary means of social control of children. The law was uncomplicated; the only law enforcement officials were town fathers, magistrates, sheriffs, and watchmen; and the only penal institutions were jails for prisoners awaiting trial or punishment. Juvenile lawbreakers did not face a battery of police, probation, or **aftercare officers** (the juvenile equivalent of adult parole officers), nor did they have to worry that practitioners of the juvenile justice system would try to rehabilitate or correct them. They only had to concern themselves with being sent back to their families for punishment.[7]

Ever since the colonial period, society has gradually taken authority away from the family and given it to the state for correcting the behavior of children. The house of refuge, the first juvenile institution, was proposed as a better solution than the family in the early nineteenth century. Then, at the end of the nineteenth century, the juvenile court was created to save wayward children by assuming parental responsibility and care. This court was based on the legal concept of *parens patriae,* a medieval English doctrine that sanctioned the right of the crown to intervene in natural family relations. The development of the juvenile court in the twentieth century was supplemented by the rehabilitation model, training schools, and community-based programs.

There is little reason to believe that the three-hundred-year-old legacy of *taking authority away from the family* is likely to change in the near future. Even if the state were receptive to relinquishing some of its power (all indicators point to the fact that the state wants to increase rather than decrease its power over citizens), the American family is under greater pressure than ever before. Its mounting problems include high rates of divorce and single-parent families, alarming rates of abuse and neglect of children, problems with drug and alcohol abuse among both parents and children, and increasing numbers of adolescent out-of-wedlock births.[8]

Reform and Retrenchment

It is sometimes claimed that the history of juvenile justice has been a steady march toward more humane and enlightened conceptions of childhood and democracy, but a more reliable reading of history shows that a period of reform has inevitably led to a period of retrenchment.[9] To express this another way, the history of juvenile justice appears to go through cycles of reform and retrenchment.

Thomas J. Bernard's *The Cycle of Juvenile Justice* is a perceptive analysis of what drives these cycles of reform and retrenchment. According to Bernard, a cycle begins when both juvenile officials and the general public believe that youth crime is at an exceptionally high level and that many harsh punishments are used but few lenient treatments exist for youthful offenders. In this context, many minor offenders avoid punishment because justice officials believe that harsh punishment will make them worse. A period of reform arrives when the solution is seen as introducing lenient treatments for youthful offenders.[10]

Justice officials and the public, according to Bernard, always believe that (1) youth crime is "at an exceptionally high level, (2) present juvenile justice policies make the problem worse, and (3) changing these policies will reduce juvenile crime."[11] It does not take them long, however, to conclude that lenient treatments are the reason for the remaining high levels of juvenile crime. With that awareness, a period of repression begins to replace reform. Responses to serious youthful offenders are gradually "toughened up" so that these youths receive harsh rather than lenient punishments. The response to less serious forms of youth crime is also toughened up so that they too receive harsh punishments. When juvenile officials are forced to choose between harshly punishing juvenile offenders and doing nothing at all, the cycle has returned to where it started (see Table 1–1 for further explanation of these cycles).

S. I. Singer examined juvenile justice policy during the 1980s and 1990s by analyzing effects of the 1978 New York State Juvenile Offender Act (1978 N.Y. Laws). In the late 1970s, legislators responded to several highly publicized murders committed by youths in New York City by increasing sanctions for violent juvenile crimes. According to Singer, these changes reflected the desire of society and its policymakers to "recriminalize" delinquency. Recriminalization is characterized by increasing punishments to juveniles, including waiving more juveniles to adult court. Singer argues that the acceptance of treatment and punishment-oriented policies is contingent on political attitudes and beliefs about adolescent law-violating behaviors.[12]

The period from the 1960s to the mid-1970s was characterized by a liberal agenda. This reform agenda emphasized the reduced use of training

Table 1–1 *The Cycle of Juvenile Justice*

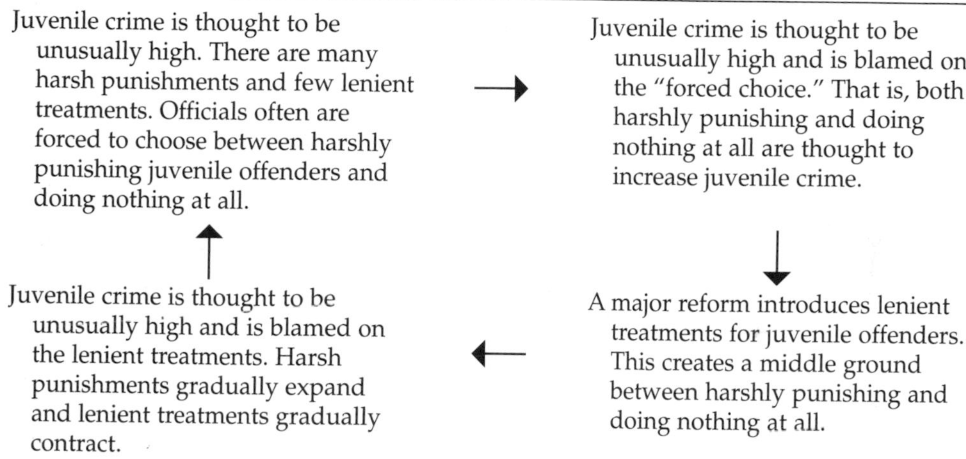

Juvenile crime is thought to be unusually high. There are many harsh punishments and few lenient treatments. Officials often are forced to choose between harshly punishing juvenile offenders and doing nothing at all.
Juvenile crime is thought to be unusually high and is blamed on the "forced choice." That is, both harshly punishing and doing nothing at all are thought to increase juvenile crime.
A major reform introduces lenient treatments for juvenile offenders. This creates a middle ground between harshly punishing and doing nothing at all.
Juvenile crime is thought to be unusually high and is blamed on the lenient treatments. Harsh punishments gradually expand and lenient treatments gradually contract.

Source: Thomas J. Bernard, *The Cycle of Juvenile Justice*. Copyright © 1992 by Oxford University Press, Inc. Used by permission of Oxford University Press, Inc.

schools, the diversion of status offenders and minor offenders from the juvenile justice system, and the reform of the juvenile justice system.

The liberal agenda ended in the 1980s and was followed by a get tough approach. One of the contributing causes of this shift from reform to repression was the failure of the reform agenda of the 1970s to address violent youth crime and repeat offenders.[13] Thus, the inability of the reformers to provide meaningful programs and policies aimed at persistent and serious youth crime proved to be the Achilles heel of the reform process.[14] The get tough approach continued into the 1980s. The main thrusts of the Reagan administration's crime control policy for juveniles were preventive detention, transfer of violent and repeat juvenile offenders to the adult court, mandatory and determinate sentences for serious and repeat juvenile offenders, increased long-term confinement for juveniles, and enforcement of the death penalty for juveniles who commit "brutal and senseless" murders.

The get tough attitude toward youth crime led to a number of federal juvenile justice initiatives in the 1990s that went beyond those implemented in the 1980s. These initiatives consisted of (1) establishing curfews, (2) passing parental responsibility laws, (3) increasing efforts to combat street gangs, (4) moving toward graduated sanctions, (5) creating juvenile boot camps, (6) maintaining and strengthening current laws restricting juveniles' use of guns, (7) opening juvenile proceedings and records, (8) transferring juveniles to criminal or adult courts, and (9) expanding sentencing authority over juveniles. The popularity of the get tough approach is reflected in the fact that in the 1990s nearly every state enacted legislation incorporating these federal initiatives into the social policy for handling juveniles.[15]

As we continue the first decade of the twenty-first century, evidence in at least a few states suggests that the nation is coming out of a period of retrenchment and is in the initial stages of a wave of reform. This new wave of reform is characterized by increased use of community-based corrections for less serious offenders; by growing public awareness and concern about the plight of children; and by greater commitment from governors and state lawmakers to children's issues such as educational reform, child care, infant mortality, child physical and sexual abuse, substance abuse among young people, and teenage pregnancy. The more severe punishment will probably continue to be given to violent offenders, especially minority ones, but minor offenders and status offenders nationwide will likely be the recipients of reform.

In sum, the cyclical relationship between reform and retrenchment in juvenile justice seems to hinge upon society's dissatisfaction with the ill-fated promises of reform, followed a generation or two later by rejection of retrenchment's lack of benevolence. Perhaps the key to this shift is that society and its policymakers want social order, but, at the same time, they want special treatment for children.

Get Tough and Go Soft Approaches

Although reform and retrenchment alternate as official policies for juvenile justice in this nation, the get tough approach for serious juvenile offenders and the go soft strategy for minor offenders and status offenders have characterized the sentencing practices of juvenile courts in recent decades. The **least-restrictive** (or go soft) **approach** first became popular in the 1960s. When professionals and students became aware of the extent of youth crime, the negative impact of delinquency labels, and the criminogenic and violent nature of juvenile institutions, many of them began to reappraise what should be done with juvenile lawbreakers. Studies on hidden delinquency and middle-class lawbreaking also taught a valuable lesson—nearly all juveniles break the law, but only a few are caught.

David Matza, Edwin Schur, and others developed a theoretical framework for the least-restrictive approach.[16] The philosophy behind this approach is that fate and chance are the only reasons that many juveniles are caught. The lucky break the law and get away with it, but those who are caught are labeled and processed through the juvenile justice system. A great many of these offenders, according to this viewpoint, begin to live up to their labels, which then become self-fulfilling prophecies. Offenders become committed to delinquent behavior, particularly when they are placed in juvenile institutions or detention facilities with youths who have committed much more serious crimes.

For these reasons, supporters of this approach urge a least-restrictive philosophy—do not do any more than necessary with youthful offenders. If possible, leave them alone.[17] If their offense is too serious to permit this course of action, use every available resource before placing them in detention or in institutions. Keeping status offenders (juveniles who run away, violate a curfew, are ungovernable at home, or are truant from school) out of the juvenile justice system is one of the predominant concerns of proponents of this philosophy. Providing juveniles with all the procedural safeguards given to adults is also a vital concern. Adherents, of course, urge the use of community resources in working with juvenile offenders, an approach believed by many to be the best for juvenile justice.

On the other end of the spectrum, however, juveniles who commit serious crimes or continue to break the law are presumed to deserve punishment rather than treatment because they possess free will and know what they are doing. Their delinquencies are viewed as purposeful activity resulting from rational decisions in which the pros and cons are weighed and the acts that promise the greatest potential gains are performed.

Threat of the Dangerous Poor

Early in the history of this nation, crime was blamed on the poor, especially on those who were newcomers to America. The fact that these individuals came from different cultural, ethnic, and religious backgrounds also made them appear dangerous. It was reasoned that institutions were needed to protect society against the behavior of these so-called **dangerous poor.**[18]

Significantly, until the late nineteenth century, each succeeding wave of immigration that brought impoverished newcomers was perceived as threatening a new crime wave. Anthony Platt's classic work, *The Child Savers,* makes the point that the behaviors the child savers selected to be penalized—sexual license, roaming the streets, drinking, begging, fighting, frequenting dance halls and movies, and staying out late at night—were found primarily among lower-class children. From the very beginning, according to this interpretation, juvenile justice engaged in class favoritism that resulted in poor children being processed through the system while middle-class children were more likely to be excused.[19]

The association of poverty with dangerousness has continued to the present day. It is expressed, especially, with the fear of violence and gang behaviors from African-American and Hispanic underclass children. Elijah Anderson describes the fear that young African males create in others:

> An overwhelming number of young black males in the Village [in Philadelphia] are committed to civility and law-abiding behavior. They often have a hard time convincing others of this, however, because of the stigma attached to their skin color, age, gender, appearance, and general style of self-presentation. Moreover, most residents ascribe criminality, incivility, toughness, and street smartness to the anonymous black male, who must work hard to make others trust his common decency. . . .
>
> When young black men appear, women (especially white women) sometimes clutch their pocketbooks. They may edge up against their companions or begin to walk stiffly and deliberately. On spotting black males from a distance, other pedestrians often cross the street or give them a wide berth as

> they pass. When black males deign to pay attention to passersby, they tend to do so directly, giving them a deliberate once-over; their eyes may linger longer than the others consider appropriate to the etiquette of "strangers in the streets." Thus, the black males take in all the others and dismiss them as a lion might dismiss a mouse. Fellow pedestrians in turn avert their eyes from the black males, deferring to figures who are seen as unpredictable, menacing, and not to be provoked—predators.[20]

The Unsolvable Nature of Youth Crime

The get tough and go soft policies illustrate that the United States has a history of seeking cure-alls to solve the crime problem. Unfortunately, no simple solutions to this age-old problem exist. The search for a panacea began in the early nineteenth century—the Jacksonian period—when the young American nation was thought to have an unlimited capacity to solve its social problems.[21] The institutions that emerged to create better environments for deviants represented an attempt to promote the stability of society at a time when traditional ideas and practices seemed to be outmoded, constricted, and ineffective.

Legislators, philanthropists, and local officials all were convinced that the nation faced both unprecedented dangers and unprecedented opportunities. It was hoped that the penitentiary for adults and the house of refuge for juveniles, as well as the almshouse for the poor, the orphan asylum, and the insane asylum, would restore a necessary balance to the new republic and, at the same time, eliminate long-standing problems. The fact that these institutions eventually came to be viewed as failures did not prevent another generation of reformers from seeking new ways to cure the crime problem.[22] Ysabel Rennie aptly summarizes this history of seeking a cure-all for crime:

> There is nothing more disconcerting than the realization that what is being proposed now for the better management of crime and criminals—to get tough, to increase sentences and make them mandatory, and to kill more killers—has been tried over and over again and abandoned as unworkable. It is sad but true that the reformation of criminals through education, psychology, and prayer has not worked either. As for that great rallying-cry of the positivists, the individualization of punishment, its chief, if not its only, effect, has been an unconscionable disparity in judicial sentences. Thus, we are left to contemplate the evidence that we have for centuries been going in circles.[23]

WHAT ARE THE JUVENILE JUSTICE AGENCIES AND FUNCTIONS?

The police, the juvenile court, and corrections make up the three subsystems of the juvenile justice system in the United States. Corrections in turn has divided into community-based programs and juvenile correctional institutions.

These subsystems have between ten thousand and twenty thousand public and private agencies, with annual budgets totaling hundreds of millions of dollars. Many of the forty thousand police departments have juvenile divisions, and more than three thousand juvenile courts and about one thousand juvenile correctional facilities exist across the nation. More than thirty thousand of the fifty thousand employees in the juvenile justice system are employed in juvenile correctional facilities; sixty-five hundred are juvenile probation officers, and the remainder are aftercare officers and residential staff in community-based programs. Several thousand more employees work in diversion programs and privately administered juvenile justice programs.[24]

The functions of the three subsystems are somewhat different. The basic responsibilities of the police consist of enforcing the law and maintaining order. The law enforcement function requires that the police deter crime, make arrests, obtain confessions, collect evidence for strong cases that can result in convictions, and increase crime clearance rates. The maintenance of order function involves such tasks as settling family disputes, directing traffic, furnishing information to citizens, providing emergency ambulance service, preventing suicides, giving shelter to homeless persons and alcoholics, and checking the homes of families on vacation. Police–juvenile relations require the police to deal with juvenile lawbreaking and to provide services needed by juveniles.

The juvenile courts must dispose of cases referred to them by intake divisions of probation departments, make detention decisions, deal with child neglect and dependency cases, and monitor the performance of juveniles who have been adjudicated delinquent or status offenders. The *parens patriae* philosophy, which has undergirded the juvenile court since its founding at the end of the nineteenth century, charges that juvenile judges treat rather than punish juveniles appearing before them. This treatment arm of the juvenile court generally does not extend to those committing serious crimes or persisting in juvenile offenses, however; such hard-core juveniles may be sent to training schools or transferred to the adult court.

Correction departments are responsible for the care of juvenile offenders sentenced by the courts. Juvenile probation supervises offenders released to probation by the courts, ensuring that they comply with the courts' imposed conditions of probation and refrain from unlawful behavior in the community. Day treatment and residential programs have the responsibility of preparing juveniles for their return to the community.

Training schools have similar responsibilities, but the administrators of these programs are generally also charged with deciding when each juvenile is ready for institutional release and with ensuring that residents receive their constitutionally guaranteed due process rights. Aftercare officers are delegated the responsibility of supervising juveniles who have been released from training schools so that they comply with the terms of their aftercare agreements and avoid unlawful behavior.

Juvenile justice agencies, as suggested in later chapters, do differ rather significantly across the nation. The structure of the juvenile court, as well as its administrative responsibilities, has little in common from one state to the next. Most juvenile probation departments emphasize restitution and community service programs as conditions of probation, but some juvenile probation departments provide intensive supervision programs and may even have house arrest and electronic monitoring programs. Some states hire private agencies to implement community-based programs, and most states are increasingly using private institutional placements for status offenders. Finally, a number of organizational structures are used to administer juvenile correctional institutions and aftercare services.

Much similarity exists between the juvenile and adult justice systems. Both consist of three basic subsystems and interrelated agencies. The flow of justice in both is supposed to be from law violation to police apprehension, judicial process, judicial disposition, and rehabilitation in correctional agencies. The basic vocabulary is the same in the juvenile and adult systems, and even when the vocabulary differs, the intent remains the same.

Note the following terms that refer to the juvenile and adult systems:

Adjudicatory hearing is a trial.
Aftercare is parole.
Commitment is a sentence to confinement.
Detention is holding in jail.
Dispositional hearing is a sentencing hearing.
Juvenile court officer is a probation officer.
A **minor** is a defendant.
Petition is an indictment.
A **petitioner** is a prosecutor.
A **respondent** is a defense attorney.
Taking into custody is arresting a suspect.

Both the juvenile and adult systems are under fire to get tough on crime, especially on offenders who commit violent crimes. Both must deal with excessive caseloads and institutional overcrowding, must operate on fiscal shoestrings, and face the ongoing problems of staff recruitment, training, and burnout. Focus on Practice 1–1 further describes the common ground and differences between the juvenile and adult justice systems.

HOW ARE JUVENILE OFFENDERS PROCESSED?

The means by which juvenile offenders are processed by juvenile justice agencies are examined throughout this text. The variations in the juvenile justice systems across the nation make it difficult to describe this process,

FOCUS ON PRACTICE 1–1

GENERALIZATIONS ABOUT THE JUVENILE AND CRIMINAL JUSTICE SYSTEMS

Juvenile Justice System	Common Ground	Criminal Justice System
	Operating Assumptions	
Youth behavior is malleable. Rehabilitation is usually a viable goal. Youth are in families and not independent.	Community protection is a primary goal. Law violaters must be held accountable. Constitutional rights apply.	Sanctions are proportional to the offense. General deterrence works. Rehabilitation is not a primary goal.
	Prevention	
Many specific delinquency prevention activities (e.g., school, church, recreation) are used. Prevention is intended to change individual behavior—often is family focused.	Educational approaches to specific behaviors (e.g., drunk driving, drug use) are used.	Generalized prevention activities are aimed at deterrence (e.g., Crime Watch).
	Law Enforcement	
Specialized "juvenile" units exist. Some additional behaviors are prohibited (truancy, running away, curfew violations). Limitations exist on public access to information.	Jurisdiction involves full range of criminal behavior. Constitutional and procedural safeguards exist. Both reactive and proactive (targeted at offense types, neighborhoods, etc.) approaches are used.	Open public access to all information is granted. *Discretion:* Law enforcement exercises discretion to divert offenders *out of* the criminal justice system.

Diversion: A significant number of youth are diverted away from the juvenile justice system—often *into* alternative programs.		
	Intake—Prosecution	
In many instances, juvenile court intake, not the prosecutor, decides what cases to file. Decision to file a petition for court action is based on both social and legal factors. A significant portion of cases are diverted from formal case processing. *Diversion:* Intake diverts cases from formal processing to services operated by the juvenile court or outside agencies.	Probable cause must be established. Prosecutor acts on behalf of the state.	Plea-bargaining is common. Prosecution decision is based largely on legal facts. Prosecution is valuable in building history for subsequent offenses. *Discretion:* Prosecution exercises discretion to withhold charges or divert offenders out of the criminal justice system.
	Detention—Jail/Lockup	
Juveniles may be detained for their own or the community's protection. Juveniles may not be confined with adults without "sight and sound separation."	Accused offenders may be held in custody to ensure their appearance in court.	Accused offenders have the right to apply for bond.

Adjudication—Conviction		
Juvenile court proceedings are "quasi-civil"—not criminal—and may be confidential. If guilt is established, the youth is adjudicated delinquent regardless of offense. Right to jury trial is not afforded in all states.	Standard of "proof beyond a reasonable doubt" is required. Rights to a defense attorney, confrontation of witnesses, to remain silent are afforded. Appeals to a higher court are allowed.	Constitutional right to a jury trial is afforded. Guilt must be established on individual offenses charged for conviction. All proceedings are open.
Disposition—Sentencing		
Disposition decisions are based on individual and social factors, offense severity, and youths' offense history. Dispositional philosophy includes a significant rehabilitation component. Many dispositional alternatives are operated by the juvenile court. Dispositions cover a wide range of community-based and residential services. Disposition orders may be directed to people other than the offender (e.g., parents). Disposition may be indeterminate—based on progress.	Decision is influenced by current offense, offending history, and social factors. Decision is made to hold offender accountable. Victim is considered for restitution and "no contact" orders. Decision may not be cruel or unusual.	Sentencing decision is primarily bound by the severity of the current offense and offenders' criminal history. Sentencing philosophy is based largely on proportionality and punishment. Sentence is often determinate based on offense.

Aftercare—Parole

Aftercare is a function that combines surveillance and reintegration activities (e.g., family, school, work).	System allows monitoring behavior upon release from a correctional setting. Violation of conditions can result in reincarceration.	Parole is primarily a surveillance and reporting function to monitor illicit behavior.

Source: Howard N. Snyder and Melissa Sickmund, *Juvenile Offenders and Victims: A National Report* (Washington, DC: Office of Juvenile Justice and Delinquency Prevention, 1995, 1996 Reprint), 74–75.

Critical Thinking Question:
Do these generalizations make the juvenile justice system seem more or less like the adult justice system? How?

but Figure 1–1 is a flowchart of the juvenile justice system and the criminal justice system that shows the common elements of these systems. The process begins when the youth is referred to the juvenile court; some jurisdictions permit a variety of agents to refer the juvenile, whereas others charge the police with this responsibility. The more common procedure is that the youth whose alleged offense has already been investigated is taken into custody by the police officer who has made the decision to refer the juvenile to the juvenile court. Figure 1–1 shows that after adjudication, a youth is placed in juvenile detention or moved out of detention and into probation, residential placement or the adult system, and then released.

The intake officer, usually a probation officer, must decide whether the juvenile should remain in the community or be placed in a shelter or detention facility. A variety of options exist for determining what to do with the youth, but in more serious cases, the juvenile generally receives a petition to appear before the juvenile court.

The juvenile court judge, or the referee in many jurisdictions, hears the cases of those juveniles referred to the court. The transfer of a juvenile to the adult court must be done before any juvenile proceedings take place. Otherwise, an adjudicatory hearing, the primary purpose of which is to determine whether the juvenile is guilty of the delinquent acts alleged in the petition, takes place. The court hears evidence on these allegations. The *In re Gault* case (see Chapter 5) usually guarantees to juveniles the right to representation by counsel, freedom from self-incrimination, the right to confront witnesses, and the right to cross-examine witnesses. Some states also give juveniles the right to a jury trial.

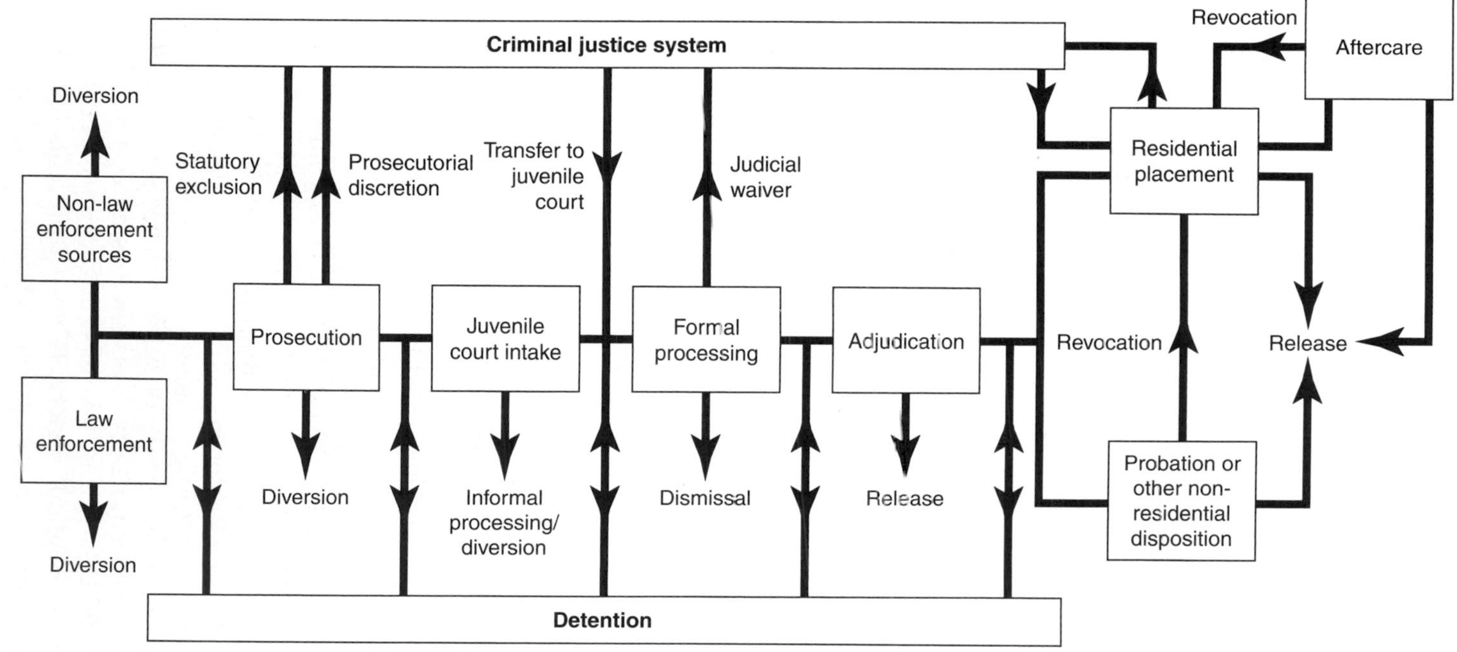

Figure 1–1 *What Are the Stages of Delinquency Case Processing in the Juvenile Justice System?*

Note: This chart gives a simplified view of caseflow through the juvenile justice system. Procedures vary among jurisdictions.

Source: Howard N. Snyder and Melissa Sickmund, *Juvenile Offenders and Victims: 1999. National Report* (Washington, DC: Office of Juvenile Justice and Delinquency Prevention, 1999), p. 98.

A disposition hearing takes place when a juvenile has been found delinquent in the adjudicatory stage. Most juvenile court codes now require that the adjudicatory and disposition hearings be held at different times. The number of dispositions juvenile judges have available to them varies from one jurisdiction to the next. In addition to the standard dispositions of warning and release, placement on juvenile probation, or adjudication to the department of youth services or corrections, some judges can place juveniles in a publicly or privately administered day treatment or residential program. Some jurisdictions even grant juvenile judges the authority to send a juvenile to a particular correctional facility.

A juvenile adjudicated to a training school is generally treated somewhat differently in small and large states. In small states with one training school for males and usually one for females, a youth adjudicated to a training school is usually sent directly to the appropriate school. But large states that have several facilities for males and perhaps more than one for females may send the youth to a classification, or diagnostic, center to determine the proper institutional placement. Training school residents currently are not confined as long as they were in the past and are frequently released within a year. Institutional release takes place in a variety of ways, but a juvenile released from a training school is generally placed on aftercare status. To be released from this supervision, the juvenile must fulfill the rules of aftercare and must avoid unlawful behavior.

WHAT ARE THE MAIN CHALLENGES TO THE JUVENILE JUSTICE SYSTEM?

Three basic challenges are faced by the juvenile justice system today: (1) the confusion caused by the conflicting philosophies on and strategies for correcting juveniles, (2) the social injustice that exists in the juvenile justice process, and (3) the fragmentation of the juvenile justice system.

Conflicting Philosophies and Strategies on Correcting Juveniles

Four basic correctional models exist in juvenile justice: the treatment model, the justice model, the crime control model, and the balanced and restorative justice model. These conflicting strategies handicap juvenile justice and are a major reason that no single policy or set of policies presently guide the handling of offenders. Indeed, nearly everyone has an opinion on what can be done to correct the behavior of law-violating youths; pet theories and folk remedies abound throughout society. Table 1–2 presents the philosophies of correcting juveniles in the various juvenile codes.

Table 1–2 Juvenile Code Philosophies

Some juvenile codes emphasize prevention and treatment goals; some, stress punishment; and others seek a balanced approach.

Philosophical Goals Stated in Juvenile Code Purpose Clauses, 1997

Prevention/ Diversion/Treatment	*Punishment*	*Prevention/Diversion/ Treatment and Punishment*	
Arizona[a]	Arkansas	Alabama	Nevada
Dist. of Columbia	Georgia	Alaska	New Hampshire
Kentucky	Hawaii	California	New Jersey
Massachusetts	Illinois	Colorado	New Mexico
North Carolina	Iowa	Connecticut	New York
Ohio	Louisiana	Delaware	North Dakota
South Carolina	Michigan	Florida	Oklahoma
Vermont	Missouri	Idaho	Oregon
West Virginia	Rhode Island	Indiana	Pennsylvania
		Kansas	Tennessee
		Maryland	Texas
		Maine	Utah
		Minnesota	Virginia
		Mississippi	Washington
		Montana	Wisconsin
		Nebraska	Wyoming

- Most states seek to protect the interests of the child, the family, the community, or some combination of the three.
- In seventeen states, the purpose clause incorporates the language of the balanced and restorative justice philosophy, emphasizing offender accountability, public safety, and competency development.
- Purpose clauses also address court issues, such as fairness, speedy trials, and even co-ordination of services. In nearly all states, the code also includes protection of the child's constitutional and statutory rights.

[a]Arizona's statutes and court rules did not contain a purpose clause; however, the issue is addressed in case law.

Source: Adapted from Melissa Sickmund, Howard N. Snyder, and Eileen Poe-Yamagata, *Juvenile Offenders and Victims: 1997 Update on Violence* (Washington, DC: Office of Juvenile Justice and Delinquency Prevention, 1999 National Report), p. 87.

The Treatment Model

Parens patriae, the philosophical basis of the treatment model, emerged with the founding of the juvenile court and is aptly described by the following statement:

> The fundamental idea of the juvenile court law is that the state must step in and exercise guardianship over a child found under such adverse social or individual conditions as to encourage the development of crime.

> . . . The juvenile court law proposes a plan whereby he may be treated, not as a criminal, or legally charged with crime, but as a ward of the state, to receive practically the care, custody, and discipline that are accorded the neglected and dependent child, and which, as the act states, "shall approximate as nearly as may be that which should be given by his parents."[25]

The state, represented by the juvenile court, was to deal with children differently than it did with adults by substituting a more informal and flexible procedure. In the juvenile court, a fatherly and benevolent juvenile judge would gently, and in a friendly manner, probe the roots of the child's difficulties. According to Warren H. Dunham, the court's purposes were "to understand the child, to diagnose his difficulty, to treat his condition, and [to] fit him back into the community."[26] The court, acting in lieu of a child's parents, was to engage in individualized justice; delinquency was viewed as a symptom of some underlying personality problem.

The juvenile court, then, was to serve as a social clinic. Its task was to call up the scientific expert to provide the necessary treatment for the child. *Child saving reformers,* a term used by Anthony Platt, were confident that the combination of *parens patriae* philosophy and the treatment provided by the scientific expert would lead to the salvation of wayward children.[27]

The **medical model,** the first treatment model to develop from the *parens patriae* philosophy, argues that youth crime is caused by factors that can be identified, isolated, and treated as though they were a disease. Punishment is to be avoided because it gives youths a negative image and does nothing to solve their problem. By diagnosing the causes of youths' behavior, advocates believe that they can cure youths and prevent them from committing additional crimes. Most supporters of this model also assume that juvenile lawbreakers do not have the ability to exercise freedom of choice or to use reason.

The **treatment model,** including the medical model as well as the methods treatment described in Chapter 15 is based on the belief that the basic mission of juvenile justice is to rehabilitate youthful offenders. The treatment model also proposes that the legal definition of delinquency should be broad and that victimless crimes and status offenses, as well as crimes against victims, should remain on the books. Proponents of this model do not believe in the frequent use of detention facilities; these facilities should be reserved for children who need special care and custody. Since the treatment model is much more concerned with the psychological and social conditions of offenders than with their crimes, it holds that the juvenile court's decisions should be based solely on the needs of the child.

The treatment model has diminished in popularity in juvenile justice as the other models have gained acceptance. But the rehabilitation of offenders is still the official goal of many juvenile justice agencies and is the approach most widely used with middle- and upper-middle-class offenders and with youths who appear to have emotional problems.

The Justice Model

The *parens patriae* philosophy was challenged by due process philosophy from the very founding of the juvenile court. Those promoting the due process approach wanted to give juveniles better protection through due process provisions and procedural safeguards. In the 1970s, proponents of due process were troubled by the contradictions of juvenile justice philosophy and by the inequities and inadequacies of juvenile justice law, policy, and practice.[28] These reformers turned to David Fogel's **justice model** and its concept of **just desserts.** Fogel believes that both juvenile and adult offenders are volitional and responsible human beings and, consequently, deserve to be punished if they violate the law. The punishment they receive, however, must be proportionate to the seriousness of the offense. Fogel also proposed the end of the indeterminate sentence and parole, the initiation of uniform sentencing, and the establishment of correctional programming based solely on the compliance of inmates.[29] Fogel reasons, "If we cannot coercively treat with reliability, we can at least be fair, reasonable, humane, and constitutional in practice."[30]

Judge Charles E. Springer has urged the adoption of the justice model in juvenile justice:

> A number of reasons are advanced in favor of adopting the justice model in dealing with the young people who violate the law. The main idea is that committing a crime, whether as an adult or a child, is wrong and deserves punishment. Most of us understand this; and certainly young delinquents do—except insofar as they have been told otherwise by the juvenile court. . . .
>
> Officially recognizing justice as the legitimate end of the juvenile court process certainly does not mean that every lollipop thief will be brought before the bar of justice; it does not mean a palpable move from "tears to teargas" in juvenile court jurisprudence. The call for justice is not a call for thumbscrews; rather, it is a call for a more certain, prompt, proportionate response to criminal misconduct.[31]

Proponents of the justice model are now advocating a number of changes to bring more fairness to juvenile justice:

- Limit the enormous discretion granted to juvenile justice practitioners.
- Divert increasing numbers of youthful offenders from the justice system to voluntary services.
- Remedy common deficiencies in due process so as to ensure greater fairness in the transactions among the justice system, the family, and the juvenile offender.
- Curb indeterminate sentencing practices of juvenile courts and give juveniles a fixed sentence by the court at the time of disposition.
- Decriminalize status offenses.

- Change the governing principle of sentencing to one of *proportionality,* which means that there must be a relationship between the seriousness of the offense committed and the severity of the sanction imposed.
- Make training schools safer and more humane.
- Allow programs offered in training schools to be of a voluntary nature and to have nothing to do with the release of a youth.
- Require restitution and community service sanctions of more juvenile lawbreakers; these sanctions have the potential for fairness because they give youthful offenders opportunities to atone or make amends for the damage or harm they have inflicted upon others.[32]

Many of these proposed changes are found in the standards developed by the Institute of Judicial Administration and the American Bar Association Joint Commission on Juvenile Justice Standards. These standards are also outlined in the report of the Task Force on Sentencing Policy Toward Young Offenders formed by the Twentieth Century Fund.[33] The mandatory sentencing law for violent juvenile offenders in the state of New York, the determinate sentencing law for juveniles in the state of Washington, and the institutional release policy adopted in the state of Minnesota are other indicators of the increasing national acceptance of the justice model.

The Crime Control Model

The **crime control model** emphasizes punishment as the remedy for juvenile misbehavior. Punishment philosophy actually originated well before the eighteenth century, but it gained popularity in the 1970s because of the assumed rise of youth crime. Although this approach has had different connotations at various times, supporters today maintain that punishment is beneficial because it is educative and moral. Offenders are taught not to commit further crimes, whereas noncriminal citizenry receive a demonstration of what happens to a person who breaks the law; punishment, proponents believe, deters crime.

The supporters of punishment philosophy claim that the juvenile court has abandoned punishment in favor of individual rehabilitation. They argue for severity and certainty of punishment and advocate a greater use of incarceration. Other fundamental assumptions of punishment philosophy propose that those who become involved in unlawful behavior are abnormal and few in number; that this unlawful behavior reflects a character defect that punishment can correct; that punishment can be helpful in teaching a youth to be responsible, diligent, and honest; and that the deterrence of youth crime depends on the juvenile justice system apprehending and punishing youthful offenders with greater speed, efficiency, and certainty.

The crime control model holds that the first priority of justice should be to protect the life and property of the innocent. Accordingly, proponents of this model support the police and are quick to isolate juvenile offenders, especially those who have committed serious crimes, in detention homes, jails, and training schools. The increased use of transfers to adult court and the adoption of mandatory sentencing laws specifying extended confinements for serious crimes are recent crime control policies.

Many states are now using a combination of the crime control and justice models to deal with violent and hard-core juvenile offenders. In a personal correspondence with one of the authors, Donna Hamparian, coauthor of *The Violent Few,* put it this way:

> The important point, I think, is that there is a shift from rehabilitation, or *parens patriae,* to punishment. It is much more difficult to talk about rehabilitating the juvenile armed robber than it is to talk about rehabilitating the status offender. I think much of the shift from the resultant legislative changes can be attributed to the news media, particularly, large newspapers, such as the *New York Times.* At least half of the states have changed the provisions with serious offenders in the last ten years. These changes have not all been more punitive, but certainly the states making major changes have moved to more specific ways to deal with "violent" kids. At the same time, several states have increased the age of juvenile court jurisdiction from 15, to 17, to 18.[34]

Balanced and Restorative Justice Model

A traditional New Zealand approach to juvenile offending, the **balanced and restorative justice model,** is rapidly expanding throughout the United States and, indeed, throughout the world. "Balanced" refers to system-level decision making by administrators to "ensure that resources are allocated equally among efforts to ensure accountability to crime victims, to increase competency in offenders, and to enhance community safety." These three goals are summarized in the terms accountability, competency, and community protection.[35]

Accountability refers to a sanctioning process in which offenders must accept responsibility for their offenses, the harm caused to victims, and make restitution to the victims, assuming that community members are satisfied with the outcome. Competency refers to the rehabilitation of offenders, that is, when offenders improve their educational, vocational, emotional, social and other capabilities and can perform as responsible adults in the community. Community protection refers to the ability of citizens to prevent crime, resolve conflict, and feel safe because offenders have matured into responsible citizens. Subsequently, the overall mission of the balanced and restorative model is to develop a community-oriented approach to the control of offenders rather than rely solely on punishment either by confinement or by individual rehabilitation through counseling. The juvenile justice system, in implementing this model, meets the needs of the community, the victim, and the offender in the most cost-effective manner possible.

How Does the Model Work? The important roles the community and the victim play in this model call for a new framework of community organization

Table 1–3 *New Roles in the Balanced and Restorative Justice Model*

	The Co-Participants
Victim	Active participation in defining the harm of the crime and shaping the obligations placed on the offender.
Community	Responsible for supporting and assisting victims, holding offenders accountable, and ensuring opportunities for offenders to make amends.
Offender	Active participation in reparation and competency development.
	Juvenile Justice Professionals
Sanctioning	Facilitate mediation; ensure that restoration occurs (by providing ways for offenders to earn funds for restitution); develop creative and or restorative community service options; engage community members in the process; educate community on its role.
Rehabilitation	Develop new roles for young offenders which allow them to practice and demonstrate competency; assess and build on youth and community strengths; develop partnerships.
Public Safety	Develop range of incentives and consequences to ensure offender compliance with supervision objectives; assist school and family in their efforts to control and maintain offenders in the community; develop prevention capacity of local organizations.

Source: G. Bazemore, 1997. "What's 'New' About the Balanced Approach?" *Juvenile & Family Court Judge*, Vol. 48, No 1. p. 13.

and a restructuring of practitioner roles throughout the juvenile justice system. The model calls for a new set of values that emphasize a commitment to all—the offender, the victim, and the community. Importantly, offenders are viewed as clients whose crime is a symptom of family breakdown, community disorganization, and community conflict, and these problems must be addressed if juvenile crime is to be reduced. Table 1–3 shows the types of roles the balanced and restorative model calls for from all the components of the system.

Gordon Bazemore provides us with a practical example of the model in action:

> In cities and towns in Pennsylvania, Montana, and Minnesota—as well as in Australia and New Zealand—family members and other citizens acquainted with an offender or victim of a juvenile crime gather to determine what should be done in response to the offense. Often held in schools, churches, or other community-based facilities, these *Family Group Conferences* are facilitated by a community justice coordinator or police officer and are aimed at both ensuring that offenders are made to hear community disapproval of their behavior and developing not only an agreement for repairing the damage to victim and community but also a plan for reintegrating the offender.[36]

What Are Some of the Model's Methods? Bazemore goes on to identify some different techniques generated by the model's values. In some jurisdictions, victim/offender mediation is set up so that victims can express their feelings and the harm done to them. Once this is accomplished, an agreement is signed with the offender on how the victim can be "made whole" again. A second approach involves *family group conferencing.* This process is initiated and carved out by a facilitator who guides the victim, his or her family, and the community in developing the restorative sanction with the offender. A third process is *circle conferencing.* This approach, used in Canada, is a sentencing and problem-solving procedure enacted by a judge or community member. This facilitator calls together for problem solving, the victim, the offender, their families, and local citizens who want to resolve the problem in the community. A fourth mechanism, *community reparation boards,* used in Vermont, consists of citizen sentencing, panels that encourage non-felony offenders recognize the harm the victims suffered and that helps devise a way the offender can help restore the community. Another system is *reparative court hearings.* These are often special hearings implemented by judges in an informal community setting during the dispositional phase of the adjudication process. The hearing's purpose is to determine the type of reparation due the victim by the offender. Many other possibilities exist, but the major difference between the balanced and restorative justice model and other approaches is the model's equal weighing of the roles of the victims, the offender, and the community in preventing and responding to criminal acts.[37]

Comparison of the Four Models

The treatment model is most concerned that juvenile offenders receive therapy rather than institutionalization. But the crime control model emphasizes punishment because it argues that juveniles must pay for their crimes. Proponents of this model support long-term confinements rather than short-term confinements for juvenile offenders. The justice model strongly supports the granting of procedural safeguards and fairness to juveniles who have broken the law. Yet proponents of this model also believe that the punishment of juveniles should be proportionate to the gravity of their crimes. The balanced and restorative model also contends that juveniles have free will and know what they are doing and, therefore, should receive punishment for their antisocial behavior. The advantages of this deterrence model, according to its proponents, are that it includes the punishment approach of the crime control and justice models, supports the due process emphasis of the justice model, and places consequences on behavior to encourage juveniles to become more receptive to treatment.

Each of the models has supporters. The crime control model, or the hard line, is being used with violent and repetitive juvenile offenders. The treatment model, or the soft line, is primarily used with status offenders and minor offenders. Some jurisdictions show support for the justice model in juvenile justice, but the balanced and restorative model is making the most extensive advances. Nevertheless, on a day-to-day basis, juvenile justice practitioners continue to pick and choose from each of the four models in designing how they work with juvenile offenders. These conflicting approaches, as well as the intolerance of those who follow a different course of action, create inefficiency and confusion in juvenile justice.

Social Injustice

One of the most serious indictments of the juvenile justice system is the mounting evidence of unfair treatment of African-American, Native-American, and Hispanic males and adolescent females by the juvenile justice system.

African-American, Native-American, and Hispanic youths, as discussed throughout this text, are overrepresented in arrest, conviction, and incarceration rates with respect to their population base. A serious issue, of course, is whether this disproportionate representation in the juvenile justice system comes from a pattern of racist decision making.

Carl E. Pope and William H. Feyerherm's highly regarded assessment of the issue of discrimination against minorities reveals that two-thirds of the studies found "both direct and indirect race effects or a mixed pattern (being present at some stages and not at others)."[38] They add that selection bias can take place at any stage and that small racial differences may accumulate and become more pronounced as minority youth are processed into the juvenile justice system.[39]

The Coalition for Juvenile Justice (then the National Coalition of State Juvenile Justice Advisory Groups) brought national attention to this problem of disproportionate minority confinement in their 1988 annual report to Congress. In that same year, Congress responded to this evidence of disproportionate confinement of minority juveniles in secure facilities by amending the Juvenile Justice and Delinquency Prevention (JJDP) Act of 1974 by providing that

> [s]tates participating in the Formula Grants Program must address efforts to reduce the proportion of the youth detained or confined in secure detention facilities, secure correctional facilities, jails, and lockups, who are members of minority groups if such proportion exceeds the proportion such groups represent in the general population.[40]

During the 1992 reauthorization of the JJDP act, Congress substantially strengthened the effort to address disproportionate confinement of minority youth in secure facilities. DMC (disproportionate minority confinement) was elevated to the status of a "core requirement" alongside deinstitutionalization of status offenders, removal of juveniles from adult jails and lockups, and separation of youthful offenders from adults in secure institutions.[41] See Table 1–4 for a summary of state compliance with DMC core requirements, as of December 1997.

The JJDP Act was reauthorized in late 2002 and took effect in October of 2003. The first three mandates, for the most part, stayed the same. The fourth mandate was changed from disproportionate minority confinement (DMC) to disproportionate minority contact (DMC). The focus presently is on efforts to

Table 1–4 Summary of State Compliance with DMC Core Requirement (as of December 1997)

- States that have completed the identification and assessment phases and are implementing the intervention phase

Alaska	Kansas	North Dakota
Arizona	Maryland	Ohio
Arkansas	Massachusetts	Oklahoma
California	Michigan	Oregon
Colorado	Minnesota	Pennsylvania
Connecticut	Mississippi	Rhode Island
Florida	Missouri	South Carolina
Georgia	Montana	Tennessee
Hawaii	Nevada	Texas
Idaho	New Jersey	Virginia
Illinois	New Mexico	Washington
Indiana	New York	Wisconsin
Iowa	North Carolina	Utah

- States that have completed the identification and assessment phases and are formulating a time-limited plan of action for completing the intervention phase
  Alabama　South Dakota　West Virginia
- States (and the District of Columbia) that have completed the identification phase, submitted a time-limited plan of action for the assessment phase, and agreed to submit a time-limited plan for addressing the intervention phase
  Delaware　Louisiana
  District of Columbia　Nebraska
- Territories that have completed the identification phase (it has been determined that minority juveniles are not disproportionately arrested or detained in the following territories)
  American Samoa　Republic of Patau　Guam
  Virgin Islands　Northern Mariana Islands
- States that have completed the identification phase and are exempt from the DMC requirement because the minority juvenile population in the states does not exceed 1 percent of the total juvenile population
  Maine　Vermont
- State that has now reached 1 percent minority population (statewide) and will begin conducting the identification phase
  New Hampshire
- Territory that is exempt from complying with the DMC requirement (as it has been exempted by the U.S. Census Bureau from reporting racial statistics due to the homogeneity of the population)
  Puerto Rico
- States that were not participating in the Formula Grants Program in FY 1997
  Kentucky　Wyoming

[a]Pursuant to Section 31.303(j) of the OJJDP Formula Grants Regulation (28 C.F.R. Part 31)

Source: Heida M. Hsia and Donna Hamparian, *Disproportionate Minority Confinement; 1997 Update* (Washington, DC: Office of Juvenile Justice and Delinquency Prevention, 1998), p. 4.

reduce minority contact with the system. Programs geared toward delinquency prevention, as well as a multi-prong approach to DMC, are encouraged.

Studies examining the likelihood of juveniles being confined in juvenile correctional facilities before the age of eighteen were conducted in sixteen states. In fifteen of the sixteen states, African-American youth had the highest prevalence rates of all segments of the population.[42] They represented 68 percent of the youth population in secure detention and 68 percent of those confined in training schools.[43] These figures reflected disturbing increases over 1983, when minorities represented 53 percent of the detention population and 56 percent of the secure juvenile correctional population.[44]

Meda Chesney-Lind and Randall G. Sheldon's *Girls: Delinquency and Juvenile Justice* shows that, historically and as recently as the 1990s, adolescent females have received unfair treatment in the juvenile justice system.[45] This unfair treatment appears to take place at several crucial points.

First, adolescent females who are victims of violence and sexual abuse at home have no rights. Parents have the power to invoke official agencies of social control to keep them at home.[46] If they run away from these abusive environments, they are then defined as status offenders.[47] Second, there is considerable evidence of the unfair processing of adolescent females by the juvenile justice system. For example, Christine Adler's analysis of referral patterns in evaluations of diversion programs across the nation found that adolescent females constituted 40 percent of the populations in these programs and that more adolescent females than males are in these programs because of "noncriminal" behavior.[48]

Third, in an attempt to continue institutionalizing status offenders, some juvenile judges across the nation have been "'bootstrapping' status offenders into delinquents by issuing criminal contempt citations, referring or committing status offenders to secure mental health facilities, and referring them to 'semi-secure' facilities."[49] A Florida study of these contempt proceedings found them to be disadvantageous to female status offenders. Adolescent females who were referred for contempt were more likely than boys referred for contempt to be petitioned to the juvenile court. Females also were far more likely than males to be sentenced to detention.[50] This study concluded the following:

> The traditional double standard is still operative. Clearly, neither the cultural changes associated with the feminist movement nor the legal changes illustrated in the JJDP [Juvenile Justice and Delinquency Prevention] Act's mandate to deinstitutionalize status offenders have brought about equality under the law for young men and women.[51]

Fragmentation

The lack of cooperation and communication among some practitioners exists on a large scale within the juvenile justice subsystems. Ideally, as previously stated, juvenile justice agencies are so interrelated that the flow of justice moves in the following sequence: law violation, police contact, judicial process, disposition, and rehabilitation. Figure 1–1 illustrates this flow of justice.

In reality, cooperation and communication are typically so lacking among the subsystems that the entire system becomes disjointed and fragmented. In fact, the fragmentation is so great that both the juvenile and adult justice systems are frequently referred to as nonsystems.

Juvenile justice is actually more fragmented than adult corrections because juvenile offenders are dealt with in quite different ways in different communities. An offender may be referred to social worker agencies in one jurisdiction, processed as an adult in another, and be dealt with by the juvenile court in still another. In some jurisdictions, offenses are ignored in favor of dealing with youths' emotional problems; other jurisdictions use all available community resources before committing youths to juvenile institutions; others are quick to commit offenders to juvenile institutions for even minor offenses; and others place juveniles in adult facilities.[52]

This fragmentation is caused by several factors. The first is the lack of a common goal among the segments of the juvenile justice system. Each subsystem selects its own goals, which, unfortunately, change with each new police chief, juvenile judge, chief probation officer, or institutional superintendent. A second cause of fragmentation is local bias; local governments control their own affairs and set standards that are often reflections of local biases rather than of professional competence. This becomes quite apparent when the goals and standards of such commissions as the National Advisory Commission for Criminal Justice Standards and Goals of the American Correctional Association's accreditation process are compared with the actual practices in juvenile justices. Another cause of fragmentation is the extensive proliferation of agencies responsible for juvenile justice in the United States.

The consequences of such fragmentation are manifest in duplicated and soaring costs. Examples of such duplication are the establishment of identical recreation programs for the same adolescents and several different agencies seeing a family with multiple problems at the same time. The usual outcome is that the agencies work at cross-purposes.

Negative impact on juvenile offenders is another possible consequence of fragmentation. Some youths who are guilty of minor crimes are placed in training schools with youths who have committed serious crimes. Such minor offenders may not be able to protect themselves against more antisocial delinquents, and, even if they are able to protect themselves, their institutional stay will probably result in their learning more about the criminal way of life. In addition, more sophisticated offenders are able to play agencies against one another as they avoid attempts to change their behavior. This disjointed system thus results in some adolescent males and females being sentenced to inappropriate institutions or being denied needed services.

Fragmentation also creates tension among professionals working with juvenile offenders. Conflict particularly arises between the juvenile judge and the police when the police may want to see the "one-person crime wave" put away and the judge disagrees and places the youth on probation. Similarly, prosecuting attorneys are unhappy with judges who fail to waive a youth who has committed a serious offense to the adult court. Probation officers, in addition, become unhappy when judges neither read their reports nor follow their recommendations. Institutional social workers and aftercare specialists often disagree over the decision of when a youth should be released and to whom. The aftercare specialist may challenge the placement recommendation of the institutional social worker because he or she believes the youth has not had sufficient confinement.

Juvenile justice clearly can function effectively only to the degree that each segment of the system takes into account its subparts. The efficiency, accountability, and fairness of the system depend greatly on the coordination and communication among the subsystems. As long as so many jurisdictions continue to go their own ways, the juvenile justice system will remain disjointed and fragmented.

SUMMARY

The juvenile justice system has been given the mandate to correct and control youthful offenders. This challenge has created a furor of activity to bring about a more just and humane juvenile system, but the conflicting philosophies and methods of correcting juvenile offenders and the limitations of the juvenile justice system make it difficult to succeed in the mission of correcting juveniles in trouble. Crime control policies of the 1980s proposed a get tough strategy, especially with violent juveniles, as the most effective way to deal with youth crime. But the means to accomplish this goal have not proved satisfactory in the past and are probably no more likely to be successful in the future.

These differing philosophies and methods will continue to pose problems well into the new millennium. Those who believe in crime control are unlikely to attack the root causes of crime. Those who believe that families, neighborhoods, and jobs must be improved in order to prevent the spread of delinquency will lack the power and finances to effect change. Debate over and research into the issues on which fragmentation is greatest must continue so that either the reconciliation of opposing viewpoints or new directions for juvenile justice can result.

WEB SITES OF INTEREST

To find information and resources on general areas of interest about juvenile justice and delinquency, go to the OJJDP home page at

http://ojjdp.ncjrs.org/

Information on the Office of Juvenile Justice Programs and its mission can be found at

http://www.ojp.usdoj.gov/home.htm

CRITICAL THINKING QUESTIONS

1. The juvenile justice system has devised four ways to deal with youth crime: the treatment model, the justice model, the crime control model, and the balanced and restorative model. Which do you think works the best? Why?
2. Why is justice so important to the juvenile justice system? How can the juvenile justice system become more just, fair, and effective?
3. What do you believe can be done about racial disparity in the juvenile justice system?

NOTES

1. Jerome G. Miller, *Last One Over the Wall: The Massachusetts Experience in Closing Reform Schools* (Columbus: the Ohio State University Press, 1991), 3. Miller has also frequently been critical of the juvenile and adult justice system for their discriminatory treatment of minorities; see Jerome G. Miller, *Search and Destroy: African-American Males in the Criminal Justice System* (New York: Cambridge, 1996).
2. Ibid.
3. Statement made in 1990.
4. Charles E. Springer, *Justice for Juveniles* (Rockville, MD: National Institute for Juvenile Justice and Delinquency Prevention, 1987).
5. The section on the early history of juvenile justice is based on William Wakefield and J. David Hirschel, "England," in *International Handbook on Juvenile Justice,* edited by Donald J. Shoemaker (Westport, CT: Greenwood Press, 1996), 91.
6. Leon Radzinowicz, *A History of English Criminal Law and Its Administration from 1750–1833* (London: Stevens and Sons, 1948), 14.
7. David Rothman, *The Discovery of the Asylum* (Boston: Little, Brown, 1971), 46–53.
8. For further discussion of the problems of the family, see Chapters 14 and 16.
9. Barry Krisberg and James Austin, *The Children of Ishmael: Critical Perspectives on Juvenile Justice* (Palo Alto, CA: Mayfield, 1978), 569.
10. Thomas J. Bernard, *The Cycle of Juvenile Justice* (New York: Oxford University Press, 1992), 3.
11. Ibid., 4.
12. S. I. Singer, *Recriminalizing Delinquency: Violent Juvenile Crimes and Juvenile Justice Reform* (New York: Cambridge University Press, 1996).
13. R. B. Coates, A. D. Miller, and L. E. Ohlin, *Diversity in a Youth Correctional System: Handling Delinquents in Massachusetts* (Cambridge, MA: Ballinger, 1978), 190.

14. Barry Krisberg et al., "The Watershed of Juvenile Justice Reform," *Crime and Delinquency* 32 (January 1986), 40.
15. National Crime Justice Association, *Juvenile Justice Reform Initiatives in the States 1994–1996* (Washington, DC: Office of Juvenile Justice and Delinquency Prevention, 1997), 9.
16. David Matza, *Delinquency and Drift* (New York: John Wiley & Sons, 1964); Edwin M. Schur, Radical Non-Intervention: Rethinking the Delinquency Problem (Upper Saddle River, NJ: Prentice Hall, 1973).
17. Schur, *Radical Non-Intervention.*
18. Rothman, *Discovery of the Asylum,* 78.
19. Anthony M. Platt, *The Child Savers* (Chicago: University of Chicago Press, 1969).
20. Elijah Anderson, *Street Wise: Race, Class, and Change in an Urban Community* (Chicago: University of Chicago Press, 1990), 163–164.
21. Rothman, *Discovery of the Asylum,* 78.
22. Ibid.
23. Ysabel Rennie, *The Search for Criminal Man* (Lexington, MA: Lexington Books, 1978), 273.
24. See Kathleen Maguire and Ann L. Pastore, *Sourcebook of Criminal Justice Statistics—1994* (Washington, DC: Government Printing Office, 1995).
25. Roscoe Pound, "The Juvenile Court and the Law," *National Probation and Parole Association Yearbook* 1 (1944), 145.
26. Warren H. Dunham, "The Juvenile Court: Contradictory Orientation in Processing Offenders," *Law and Contemporary Problems* 23 (Summer 1958).
27. Anthony M. Platt, *The Child Savers,* 2d ed. (Chicago: University of Chicago Press, 1977).
28. Charles Shireman, "The Juvenile Justice System: Structure, Problems and Prospects," in *Justice as Fairness,* edited by David Fogel and Joe Hudson (Cincinnati: W. H. Anderson, 1981), 136–41.
29. David Fogel, " . . . *We Are the Living Proof . . .": The Justice Model for Corrections* (Cincinnati, OH: W. H. Anderson, 1975).
30. Fogel, "Preface," in *Justice as Fairness,* viii.
31. Springer, *Justice for Juveniles,* 82–83.
32. Adapted from Shireman, "The Juvenile Justice System."
33. A shortened version of the standards developed by the Institute of Judicial Administration and the American Bar Association Joint Commission on Juvenile Justice Standards is listed in the juvenile court chapters and was published in 1977 by Ballinger Press; Twentieth-Century Task Force on Sentencing Policy on Young Offenders, *Confronting Youth Crime: Report of the Twentieth-Century Force on Sentencing Policy on Young Offenders* (New York: Holmes and Meier, 1978).

34. Personal correspondence was received from Ms. Hamparian in February 1978 and is used with permission.
35. Adapted from D. Maloney, D. Romig, and T. Armstrong, "Juvenile Probation: The Balanced Approach," *Juvenile and Family Court Journal* 39 (1988); and G. Bazemore, "On Mission Statements and Reform in Juvenile Justice: The Case for the Balanced Approach," *Federal Probation* 56 (1992); G. Bazemore, "What's 'New' about the Balanced Approach?" *Juvenile and Family Count Judge* (1997), 2, 3.
36. Loc. cit.
37. Ibid.
38. Carl E. Pope and William H. Feyerherm, "Minority Status and Juvenile Justice Processing: An Assessment of the Research Literature," *Criminal Justice Abstract* (June 1990), 333–34. For another review of this literature, see Donna Bishop and Charles E. Frazier, "The Influence of Race in Juvenile Justice Processing," *Journal of Research in Crime and Delinquency* 25 (August 1988), 242.
39. Pope and Feyerherm, "Minority Status and Juvenile Justice Processing."
40. Donna Hamparian and Michael J. Leiber, *Disproportionate Confinement of Minority Juveniles in Secure Facilities: 1996 National Report* (Champaign, IL: Community Research Associates, 1997), 1.
41. Ibid.
42. R. E. DeComo, *Juveniles Taken into Custody Research Program: Estimating the Prevalence of Juvenile Custody by Race and Gender* (San Francisco: National Council on Crime and Delinquency, 1993).
43. Melissa Sickmund, Howard N. Snyder, and Eileen Poe-Yamagata, *Juvenile Offenders and Victims* (Washington, DC: U.S. Department of Justice, Office of Juvenile Justice and Delinquency Prevention, 1997).
44. Ibid.
45. Meda Chesney-Lind and Randall G. Sheldon, *Girls: Delinquency and Juvenile Justice* (Pacific Grove, CA: Brooks/Cole, 1992).
46. Ibid.
47. These statements summarize Meda Chesney-Lind's feminist theory of delinquency. For a more expansive development of this theory, see Clemens Bartollas, *Juvenile Delinquency,* 5th ed. (Needham Heights, MA: Allyn & Bacon, 2000).
48. Christine Adler, "Gender Bias in Juvenile Diversion," *Crime and Delinquency* (1984), 400–414. See also Clarice Feinman, "Criminal Codes, Criminal Justice and Female Offenders: New Jersey as a Case Study," in *The Changing Role of Women in the Criminal Justice System,* edited by Imogene L. Moyer (Prospect Heights, IL: Waveland, 1985).
49. Chesney-Lind, *Girls,* 116.

50. Charles E. Frazier and Donna M. Bishop, "Gender Bias in Juvenile Justice Processing: Implications of the JJDP." Paper presented at the annual meeting of the Academy of Criminal Justice Sciences, Denver (March 1990).
51. Ibid.
52. For another discussion on the fragmentation of the juvenile justice system, see Mark D. Jacobs, *Screwing the System and Making It Work: Juvenile Justice in the No-Fault Society* (Chicago: University of Chicago Press, 1990).

2

THE MEASUREMENT OF JUVENILE CRIME AND VICTIMIZATION

OBJECTIVES

1. To examine the extent of official juvenile lawbreaking
2. To reveal the findings of unofficial studies of juvenile lawbreaking
3. To compare official and unofficial findings of juvenile lawbreaking
4. To explore the extent to which juveniles are the victims of crime

KEY TERMS

age of onset
bullying
chronic offenders
cohort studies
desistance from crime
escalation of offenses
Juvenile Court Statistics
National Crime Victimization Survey
official statistics
school safety
self-report studies
specialization of offenses
transition to adult crime
Uniform Crime Reports

> *What countless human tragedies, what immeasurable sorrow are concealed upon a page of statistics? Often the very size of the numbers acts to immunize us from the pain; for how can we identify with the broken lives, the periods of repeated confinement, the furtive and violent struggles against authority, the hardened acts of victimization against fellow men, of men whose namelessness is turned into figures and percentages on one page and table after another? A single person, called John or James or David or whatever, a name created to conceal the identity, emerges when his story is revealed. We feel his pain no matter how strongly we feel the pain of those who have been his victims, we cry out against some cosmic injustice that has brought him to his wretched status, and whether some of us feel responsible for him because we are our brother's keeper, or issue words of condemnation motivated by the need for personal and social defense, he emerges in all his pathetic dimensions: the violent criminal among us. But multiply him by hundreds, or by some 1,500 in this instance, remove the fictional name and the details of his own case history, make no mention of an intoxicated father who beat a child or an unemployed youth filled with rage. Instead, dehumanize the individual, place him with hundreds under some social microscope, tell us whether the time between the first and second arrest, was greater if the first arrest was for this crime or that one, and what have you? With scores of meticulously constructed tables, with tests of significance that tape the most sophisticated techniques, we have the stuff out of which social science is built, but it shall be a human and humane science only if we bring the fore that each number on the page, each column in the table, is a coalescence behind which are found these human beings, the forces that shaped them, and the people into whose lives they introduced great harm.*
>
> —Edward Sagarin[1]

This quote from one of the Dangerous Offender Project's publications illustrates well how statistics can dehumanize the offenders and victims of crime. It is a reminder that all statistical measurements of crime must retain the individuals behind the statistics if we are to be part of a humane science. Another equally vexing problem is the difficulty of obtaining accurate information about crime. A simple enumeration of the data is interesting and sometimes illuminating, but it is often notable for the information *not* conveyed. A responsible researcher must make use of many different sources of data to understand fully the crime problem. Nowhere is this more true than with respect to juvenile crime. Debates persist over what juvenile crime is and should be, where the causes of crime can be found, and what special issues concern juveniles, such as gangs, drugs, guns, and schools. The result is that many different sources of information are available today to provide us with insights into juvenile misbehaviors. All sources must be studied, their strengths and weaknesses analyzed, and their contributions to understanding stated clearly.

This chapter examines those youths who for one reason or another pursue law-violating behaviors. The purpose of such study is to unmask the amount, the nature, and the extent of official and unofficial juvenile lawbreaking in the United States. *Juvenile lawbreaking*, in official terms, is a violation of the legal or social norms of society that evokes official response from one or more elements of the juvenile justice system. Youthful misbehavior, then, does not officially occur until officials respond.

The various studies on officially undetected delinquency have found that adolescents should not be divided into offenders and nonoffenders, because the majority of youths occasionally commit minor offenses.[2] The evidence, in fact, suggests that the youth who never violates the law is a rarity. Some are minor offenders, some break the law regularly, a few commit violent or predatory crimes, and a few support themselves through crime and are committed to crime as a way of life.[3] Studies also demonstrate that the victims of crime frequently are juveniles. Whether minority or white, male or female, infant or adolescent, the very young are harmed more by crime than are their older counterparts.

In this chapter, we identify the main tools used to measure juvenile crime, we report official and unofficial statistics concerning juvenile crime, and we discuss the problems of these statistical approaches. Finally, we examine juvenile victims and address the most important questions related to the future of juvenile crime.

WHAT ARE OFFICIAL MEASUREMENTS OF JUVENILE CRIME?

The ***Uniform Crime Reports,*** juvenile court statistics, and national victimization studies are the three main sources of **official statistics.** The *Uniform Crime Reports* and juvenile court statistics are based on the tabulation of data collected from the police and juvenile courts. National victimization surveys ask respondents to tell about the crimes committed against them.

UNIFORM CRIME REPORTS

The *Uniform Crime Reports,* or UCRs, have been our major source of information on the amount of crime in society since 1930. Then, in an effort to better understand the nature and extent of the crime problem, the International Association of the Chiefs of Police recommended that national crime statistics be collected and reported. The Federal Bureau of Investigation (FBI) was chosen as the clearinghouse for these data, and police departments across the United States were requested to report all arrests to the FBI. This information is published by the FBI on both a quarterly and a yearly basis and is probably the most popular of all the crime statistics. Reports of offenses are not always sent from the local police directly to the FBI. Some states have state reporting agencies; the locals report to the state agency, and it, in turn, reports to the FBI.

The UCRs classify crimes into Part I and Part II offenses. This classification is used to differentiate very serious from less serious crimes for the purpose of national statistics. Part I offenses include murder, rape, aggravated assault, robbery, burglary, larceny, auto theft, and arson. Part II offenses include all crimes not listed as Part I, such as simple assaults; buying, receiving, and possessing stolen property; carrying and possessing weapons; fraud; forgery; and counterfeiting. All states classify these behaviors as crimes and call for their prosecution.

In addition to reporting arrest data, the UCRs provide data on the age, sex, and race of offenders as well as on the amount of crime they commit. Information also is available on whether the total amount of crime is increasing or decreasing, as well as on the amount of crime by size of city and by the sex and race of the offenders. In addition to the Federal Bureau of Investigation, the Office of Juvenile Justice and Delinquency Prevention (OJJDP) also uses these data in its analysis of juvenile crime.

Crime Rates by Age Group

The UCRs reveal that in 2001 juveniles (individuals under age eighteen) were arrested for 1.4 million crimes. This age group constituted about 26 percent of the population and accounted for 16.7 percent of all persons arrested nationally in 2001. These youths accounted for 28 percent of all index crimes; more specifically, youths were responsible for 15.4 percent of the violent crimes and 39 percent of the index property crimes.[4] Table 2–1 shows that juvenile arrests were highest for larceny-theft, other assaults, drug abuse, curfew violations, disorderly conduct, liquor law violations, and vandalism. Juveniles constituted 31 percent of burglary arrests, 24 percent of robbery arrests, 23 percent of weapons arrests, 10 percent of murder arrests, and 14 percent of aggravated assault arrests in 2001. Juvenile arrests for murder declined 54.9 percent between 1996 and 2000, when they reached their lowest level since 1987.[5] These numbers continue to decrease. See Focus on Research 2–1 for why juvenile homicides are declining.

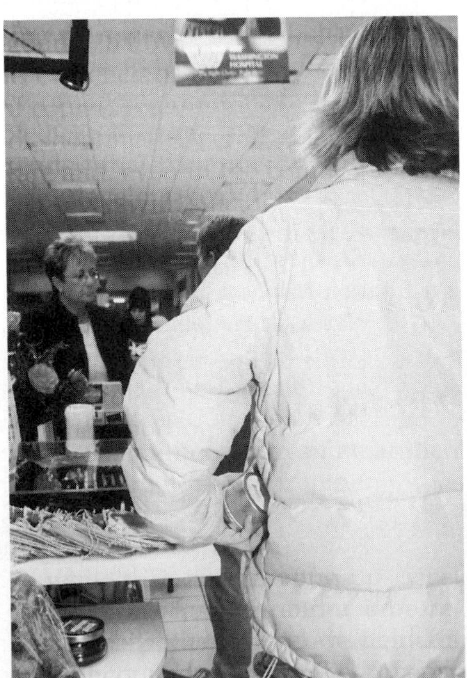

Veteran female shoplifter distracts sales clerk while her accomplice pockets an item. (Photo by Kathryn Miller.)

Table 2–1 *Arrests of Juveniles by Age, 2001 [9,511 Agencies; 2001 Estimated Population 192,580,262]*

Offense Charged	*Total All Ages*	*Ages Under 15*	*Ages Under 18*	*Ages 18 and Over*	*Under 10*	*10–12*	*13–14*	*15*	*16*	*17*
Total	**9,324,953**	**498,986**	**1,558,496**	**7,766,457**	**22,966**	**119,245**	**356,775**	**300,890**	**365,291**	**393,329**
Percent distribution[a]	**100.0**	**5.4**	**16.7**	**83.3**	**0.2**	**1.3**	**3.8**	**3.2**	**3.9**	**4.2**
Murder and nonnegligent manslaughter	9,426	114	957	8,469	6	9	99	134	254	455
Forcible rape	18,576	1,180	3,119	15,457	34	323	823	509	662	768
Robbery	76,667	4,354	18,111	58,556	95	920	3,339	3,515	4,746	5,496
Aggravated assault	329,722	16,498	44,815	284,907	878	4,524	11,096	8,215	9,646	10,456
Burglary	198,883	23,287	61,623	137,260	1,390	6,344	15,553	11,631	13,066	13,639
Larceny-theft	806,093	92,317	238,605	567,488	3,859	25,384	63,074	44,914	50,469	50,905
Motor vehicle theft	102,607	8,425	33,563	69,044	68	1,036	7,321	8,007	8,892	8,239
Arson	12,763	4,048	6,313	6,450	677	1,439	1,932	905	757	603
Violent crime[b]	434,391	22,146	67,002	367,389	1,013	5,776	15,357	12,373	15,308	17,175
Percent distribution[a]	100.0	5.1	15.4	84.6	0.2	1.3	3.5	2.8	3.5	4.0
Property crime[c]	1,120,346	128,077	340,104	780,242	5,994	34,203	87,880	65,457	73,184	73,386
Percent distribution[a]	100.0	11.4	30.4	69.6	0.5	3.1	7.8	5.8	6.5	6.6
Crime Index total[d]	1,554,737	150,223	407,106	1,147,631	7,007	39,979	103,237	77,830	88,492	90,561
Percent distribution[a]	100.0	9.7	26.2	73.8	0.5	2.6	6.6	5.0	5.7	5.8
Other assaults	898,298	70,642	163,142	735,156	3,348	20,436	46,858	30,260	31,942	30,298
Forgery and counterfeiting	77,692	422	3,975	73,717	22	81	319	525	1,117	1,911
Fraud	211,177	958	5,830	205,347	54	173	731	880	1,558	2,434
Embezzlement	13,836	83	1,258	12,578	1	16	66	86	380	709
Stolen property; buying, receiving, possessing	84,047	4,982	18,467	65,580	135	1,008	3,839	3,630	4,637	5,218

(continued)

Table 2–1 *(Continued)*

Offense Charged	*Total All Ages*	*Ages Under 15*	*Ages Under 18*	*Ages 18 and Over*	*Under 10*	*10–12*	*13–14*	*15*	*16*	*17*
Vandalism	184,972	31,597	71,962	113,010	2,921	9,608	19,068	12,391	14,202	13,772
Weapons; carrying possessing, etc.	114,325	8,691	25,861	88,464	479	2,203	6,009	4,721	5,763	6,686
Prostitution and commercialized vice	58,638	155	1,034	57,604	4	16	135	152	263	464
Sex offenses (except forcible rape and prostitution)	62,997	6,625	12,381	50,616	428	2,010	4,187	2,016	1,833	1,907
Drug abuse violations	1,091,240	24,061	139,238	952,002	297	2,976	20,788	24,956	38,401	51,820
Gambling	7,769	129	1,000	6,769	2	11	116	191	266	414
Offenses against the family and children	93,909	2,296	6,286	87,623	253	592	1,451	1,245	1,443	1,302
Driving under the influence	946,694	629	13,397	933,297	381	28	220	613	3,425	8,730
Liquor laws	408,203	8,879	92,326	315,877	174	643	8,062	14,209	27,162	42,076
Drunkenness	423,561	1,805	13,971	409,590	128	152	1,525	2,081	3,493	6,592
Disorderly conduct	425,751	47,043	117,635	308,116	1,463	12,240	33,340	23,932	23,891	22,769
Vagrancy	19,509	394	1,607	17,902	9	81	304	307	424	482
All other offenses (except traffic)	2,453,100	76,546	269,317	2,183,783	4,083	16,011	56,452	53,524	65,657	73,590
Suspicion	2,629	277	834	1,795	20	51	206	194	215	148
Curfew and loitering law violations	100,701	28,245	100,701	—	570	5,020	22,655	22,910	28,394	21,152
Runaways	91,168	34,304	91,168	—	1,187	5,910	27,207	24,237	22,333	10,294

[a] Because of rounding, the percentages may not add to total.
[b] Violent crimes are offenses of murder, forcible rape, robbery, and aggravated assault.
[c] Property crimes are offenses of burglary, larceny-theft, motor vehicle theft, and arson.
[d] Includes arson.

Source: Crime in the United States 2001 (Washington, DC: Government Printing Office, 2002), Table 38, p. 44.

FOCUS ON RESEARCH 2–1

JUVENILE HOMICIDES ARE DECLINING

Blumstein contends that the crime rate of juveniles changed dramatically in 1985 with the introduction of crack cocaine, especially in urban areas. This "gave rise to a large demand for crack, and the recruitment of lots of people, particularly young people, into the market to sell crack." Young people soon began carrying guns, adds Blumstein,

> to protect themselves because they were carrying lots of valuable stuff; they were in no position to call the police if somebody set upon them. The more kids started carrying guns, the more the incentive for the other kids to start carrying.
>
> This gave rise to an escalating arms race out in the streets among the kids. Kids are not very good at resolving disputes verbally, as most middle-class folks are. When you look in school yards, we're always seeing pushing and shoving. When the guns are around, that pushing and shoving and fighting escalate into shooting. That's really contributed to what has been the most dramatic growth of homicide by young people of young people.

Blumstein is arguing that a long-term decline in the rates of homicide by young people depends on both getting the guns out of the hands of the young and addressing the issue that we will have an increasing number of youths who are being socialized in high-risk settings.

James Alan Fox also sees a grim picture in the future concerning increased juvenile violence. He states that "there are now 39 million children in the country who are under the age of ten, more children than we've had for decades." The critical problem, according to Fox, is that millions of these children are at high risk, live in poverty, and lack full-time supervision at home and that "by the year 2005, the number of teens, ages 14-17 year-olds who will commit murder, should increase to nearly 5,000 annually because of changing demographics."

William Bennett, John DiIulio Jr., and John Walters further argue that a new generation of juvenile criminals is emerging that is far worse than those in the past. In referring to this new generation of juvenile criminals as "superpredators," they state that "today's bad boys are far worse than yesteryear's, and tomorrow's will be even worse than today's." The result is that "America is now home to thicker ranks of juvenile's 'superpredators'—radically impulsive, brutally remorseless youngsters, including even more preteenage boys who murder, assault, rob, burglarize, deal deadly drugs, join gun-toting gangs, and create serious communal disorders." The underlying cause of the super-predator phenomenon, they assert is "moral poverty—children growing up without love, care, and guidance from responsible adults."

In the midst of this support for a violent juvenile crime wave, Franklin E. Zimring as well as Philip J. Cook and John Laub represent dissenting voices as to whether this violent juvenile crime wave will materialize. Zimring argues that "using demographic statistics to project how many kids are going to commit homicide [has] extremely limited utility." He adds that "... the overall incidence of homicide, which is variable and cyclical, is still a much better predictor of future violence than assumptions based on demographic shifts."

Cook and Laub's explanation for why the epidemic of youth gun violence peaked in 1993 and has rapidly declined since then represents another dissenting voice. Their analysis suggests that a change in context rather than the "moral poverty" explanation makes far more sense of the reduced juvenile homicides between 1993 and 1997. This changing context, especially in terms of limiting the availability of guns, according to Cook and Laub, will continue to depress rather than to escalate youth homicide in the immediate future.

In a 1998 publication, Blumstein and Richard Rosenfeld abandoned somewhat their earlier prophecy of gloom about the prospects of a juvenile crime wave. They agree that the reductions in arrests of juveniles for homicides can be attributed in a large part to the reduced use of handguns by young people. But Blumstein and his colleague warn that "no one can be certain when the next upturn in homicide [with juveniles] will occur, but the present reductions cannot continue indefinitely."

In sum, the early support for a violent juvenile crime wave, especially from such recognized scholars as Blumstein, Fox, and DiIulio, has given way to the realization that youth homicide rates have been declining since 1994 and that the reduced use of handguns by minority young people in large cities has been a chief contributor to this decline. There is no reason to believe that this downturn will change in the immediate future, even with an upsurge over the next decade or so in the numbers of young people in the United States.

Sources:

Marie Simonetti Rosen, "A LEN Interview with Professor Alfred Blumstein," *Law Enforcement News*, John Jay College of Criminal Justice, New York City, 21 (April 30, 1995), 10.

James Alan Fox, *Trends in Juvenile Violence: A Report to the United States Attorney General on Current and Future Rates of Juvenile Offending.* Prepared for the Bureau of Justice Statistics (March 1996), executive summary, 19.

William J. Bennett, John J. DiIulio, and John P. Walters, *Body Count: Moral Poverty and How to Win America's War against Crime and Drugs* (New York: Simon & Schuster, 1996).

Franklin E. Zimring, Presentation at National Criminal Justice Association Annual Meeting (May 30, 1996).

Franklin E. Zimring, "Crying Wolf Over Teen Demons," L.A. Times, August 19, 1996, A17.

Philip J. Cook and John Laub, "The Unprecedented Epidemic in Youth Violence," in Crime and Justice, edited by Mark H. Moore and Michael Tonry (Chicago: University of Chicago Press, 1998), 101–138.

Alfred Blumstein and Richard Rosenfeld, "Assessing the Recent Ups and Downs in U.S. Homicide Rates," National Institute of Justice Journal, Issue No. 237 (October 1998), 10–11.

Critical Thinking Questions:

Can you think of any other reason why the rate of homicides committed by juveniles are going down? Does the decline of homicide rates mean at the same time that juveniles are becoming less violent in their behaviors?

Crime Rates by Sex

National data for juveniles and adults *combined* show that males account for 73.3 percent of violent crimes and 70 percent of property crimes. Females were most frequently arrested for larceny-theft, which accounted for 70.1 percent of all female index offenses, with 26 percent of these arrests of women under eighteen years of age.[6] These data indicate further that males under the age of fifteen were arrested for approximately 344,000 offenses, whereas females under the age of fifteen were arrested for 155,000 offenses. Males under age eighteen had a total of about 1,116,000 arrests; females under age eighteen accounted for 442,000 arrests.[7]

Focusing on juvenile violence, the UCR's report that the violent crime index arrests for females under eighteen decreased 20 percent between 1997 and 2001, whereas that for males decreased 31.2 percent. Overall, however, female arrest rates tended either to increase slightly compared to males or not to decline as much as males over this time period. Females increased their share of robbery and aggravated assault arrests proportionate to that of males; the one offense for which youthful females are arrested more often than males is for running away.[8] Although juvenile arrests decreased 19.6 percent between

1997 and 2001, the rate decreased 4.1 percent between 2000 and 2001; male and female crime rates for adults and juveniles began to drop in most crime categories in 1994 and continue to decrease today.[9]

Crime Rates by Race

Whites constitute roughly 78 percent and African Americans constitute about 13 percent of the population. Examining juveniles under eighteen years of age, Whites experienced 1,102,875 arrests for 71 percent of all juvenile arrests in 2001, compared to 410,668 or 26.4 percent for African Americans; 18,580 or 1.2 percent for Native Americans; and 23,228 or 1.5 percent for Asian Americans. Breaking down these data further, Whites accounted for 55.2 percent of the violent offenses; African Americans, 43 percent; Native Americans, 0.9 percent; and Asian Americans, 1.4 percent. The figures for property crimes were Whites 69 percent, African Americans 28 percent, Native Americans 1.3 percent, and Asian Americans 1.8 percent.[10] This arrest pattern of juveniles parallels that of adults; minority members of the U.S. population clearly are arrested in disproportionately high numbers.[11]

Trends in Juvenile Arrest Rates

Some major trends noted by the UCRs are as follows:

1. Juvenile arrest rates climbed throughout most of the 1990s but have dropped 15.3 percent overall since 1996. The drop was 4.8 percent from 1999 to 2000.
2. The juvenile violent crime arrest rate decreased 23.1 percent between 1996 and 2000.
3. Female arrest rates increased relative to that of males between 1996 and 2000 in most arrest categories; just as with males, female violent crime arrest rates now appear to be dropping.
4. Illicit drug use among juveniles as measured by arrests increased for six consecutive years beginning in 1992 but dropped somewhat in 1998. From 1996 until 2000, the overall decrease in drug use was 3.6 percent. Currently, drug usage appears to be increasing slightly.
5. The number of arrests for homicide dropped 55 percent between 1996 and 2000.[12]
6. Preliminary reports for late 2002 and early 2003 indicate that homicide rates today may be increasing.

Several reasons exist for challenging the validity of the UCRs' findings. For example, the police can make arrests only when crimes come to their attention (which results in an underestimation of the actual amount of youth crime in this nation). The police also arrest only those offenders who commit serious crimes and ignore many lesser offenses committed by juveniles. Furthermore, youth crime rates are inflated because youthful offenders are easier to detect in the act of committing a crime. Finally, juveniles frequently commit offenses in groups, and the reporting of all the groups' members may actually overestimate the amount of youth crime. Even so, new reporting procedures and computerization make the reporting and recording of offenses easier than ever before, resulting in the improved accuracy of the UCRs' data.

JUVENILE COURT STATISTICS

Juvenile Court Statistics was first published in 1929. Its purpose was threefold:

- To furnish an index of the nature and extent of the problems brought before courts with juvenile jurisdiction
- To show the nature and extent of the services given by these courts in such a way that significant trends could be identified
- To show the extent to which service given by courts has been effective in correcting social problems[13]

These data were collected by the Children's Bureau in the Department of the Census, and from the very beginning, the report included such information as the age, sex, and race of the offender, as well as the reasons for referral, the child's living arrangements, the source of the referral, where the child was detained while awaiting adjudication, how the case was being handled, and the case's disposition. In addition, information was recorded on each delinquency, status offense, and dependency case that came before the courts.

In 1974, the stage was set for the current system of data collection. After the Juvenile Justice and Delinquency Prevention Act of 1974 was passed, the Department of Justice took over the *Juvenile Court Statistics* series, which was by now in the Department of Health, Education and Welfare. The National Center for Juvenile Justice requested that state agencies complete the juvenile justice statistics form and send the information to the Center. Most state agencies not only did this but also indicated that they would send case-level information they had collected for their own purposes. These new data permitted the National Center for Juvenile Justice to reach the original goals set forth in 1923. Let us look at some of the types of information released for 1997.[14]

Status Offenses

Status offenses are behaviors for which juveniles, but not adults, may be arrested. Data summarized for 1997 in Table 2–2 reveals that the largest number

Table 2–2 *Percent Change in Petitioned Status Offenses Cases and Case Rates, 1988–1997*

				Percent Change	
Most Serious Offense	*1988*	*1993*	*1997*	*1988–1997*	*1993–1997*
Number of Cases					
Status Offense	79,000	112,300	158,500	101%	41%
Runaway	12,400	19,900	24,000	93	21
Truancy	20,600	33,700	40,500	96	20
Ungovernable	12,900	14,900	21,300	65	43
Liquor	26,200	27,800	40,700	56	46
Miscellaneous	6,900	16,000	32,100	367	100
Case Rates					
Status Offense	3.1	4.1	5.5	78%	34%
Runaway	0.5	0.7	0.8	71	14
Truancy	0.8	1.2	1.4	74	14
Ungovernable	0.5	0.5	0.7	46	35
Liquor	1.0	1.0	1.4	38	39
Miscellaneous	0.3	0.6	1.1	313	90

Case Rate = Cases per 1,000 juveniles.

Note: Detail may not add to totals because of rounding. Percent change calculations are based on unrounded numbers.

Source: Charles Puzzanchera, Anne L. Stahl, Terrence Finnegan, Howard N. Snyder, Rowen S. Poole, and Nancy Tierney, *Juvenile Court Statistics 1997* (Washington, DC: Office of Juvenile Justice and Delinquency Prevention, 2000), p. 37.

of status offenses were liquor law violations, followed by truancy, runaway, and ungovernable. Miscellaneous offenses include such behaviors as curfew violations and sexual misbehavior. Table 2–2 also shows the increase of status offense cases that came before the juvenile courts between 1988 and 1997 and between 1993 and 1997.

Figure 2–1 shows how the courts handled these offenders. Of the 158,500 offenses before the courts, 52 percent were adjudicated and 48 percent were nonadjudicated. Of those offenders who were adjudicated, the majority, 61 percent, were placed on probation, with 14 percent taken out of their homes and placed in either secure or nonsecure facilities. The 23 percent in the "other" category were required to pay fines or restitution, participate in some type of community service or treatment program; only 3 percent were released after adjudication.

Juvenile court data also are broken down by age, sex, and race. Data from the mid 90s show that the rate per thousand brought before the courts increased by age of offender for status offenses; that is, as youths get older, they are processed at higher rates. Other data indicate that the rate for males is higher than that for females; that Whites are processed proportionately to

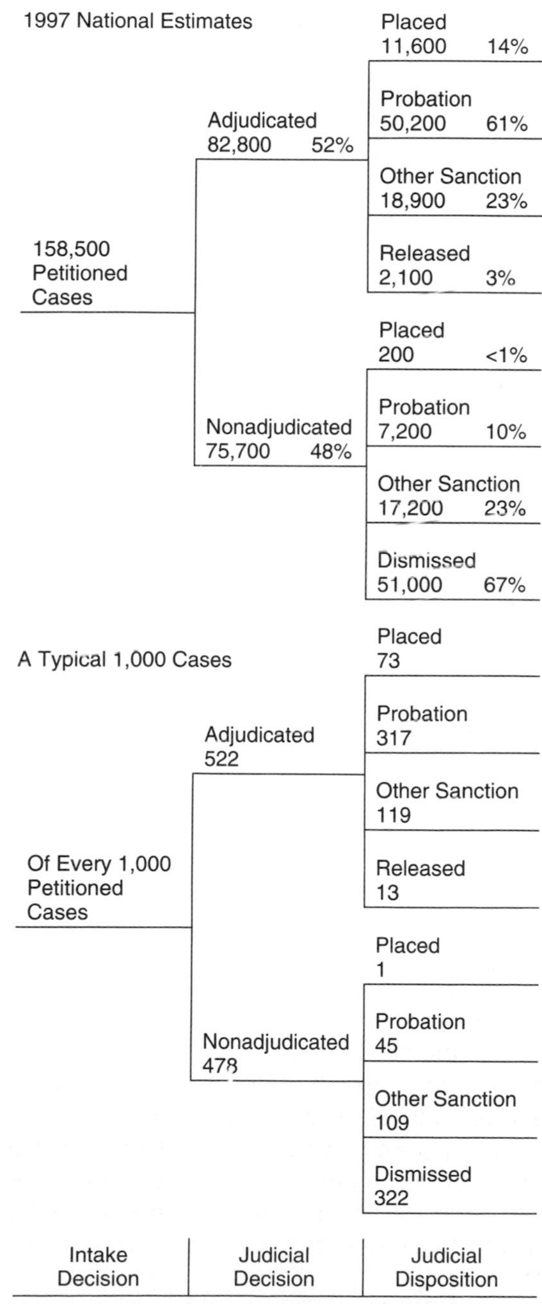

Figure 2–1 *Juvenile Court Processing of Petitioned Status Offense Cases, 1997*

Source: Charles, Puzzanchera, Anne L. Stahl, Terrence Finnegan, Howard N. Synder, Rowen S. Poole, and Nancy Tierney, *Juvenile Court Statistics 1997* (Washington, DC: Office of Juvenile Justice and Delinquency Prevention, May 2000), p. 39.

their numbers in the population; and that minority group members are processed at rates higher than their numbers in the population would warrant. With the exception of liquor law violations, for which Whites experienced a significantly greater number of referrals to the juvenile court than did African Americans, status offense data are comparable to data from the Uniform Crime Reports.[15]

Of some interest is a comparison between males and females by offense categories. An examination of the *Juvenile Court Statistics 1997* status offenses shows that 68 percent of the liquor law violators were males and that 60 percent of the runaways were females; males and females were about equally involved in ungovernability and truancy cases. The data also show that females were processed through the courts at relatively higher rates than males for runaway and truancy but that males were processed at higher rates for liquor and miscellaneous offenses.[16] In an examination of the difference between petitioned African Americans and Whites by offense categories shows that Whites were responsible for 90 percent of the liquor law violations—as opposed to only 6 percent for African Americans—but in proportionate numbers for most other status offenses; Blacks were overrepresented in arrests for other status offenses.[17]

Delinquency Cases. In 1999, juvenile courts in the United States disposed of almost 1.7 million delinquency cases.[18] An analysis of Table 2–3 indicates that 42 percent of these cases were property offenses, 23 percent, person offenses; 23 percent, public order offenses; and 11 percent, drug offenses. Of the person offenses, the largest percentage consisted of simple assaults, followed by aggravated assaults and then robberies; larceny-theft made up the largest number of property offenses, followed by burglary and vandalism. Obstruction of justice and weapons offenses comprised the largest percentages of the public order offenses. Table 2–3 also reveals the percent change in the number of delinquency cases before the juvenile courts between the periods 1990 and 1999, 1995 and 1999, and 1998 and 1999.

Juvenile Court Statistics 1997 depicts well what happens to the cases brought into the system. Figure 2–2 demonstrates, for example, that 57 percent of the delinquency cases were petitioned; that is, the youths came into the juvenile court as a result of the filing of a petition, complaint, or other legal instrument requesting the court to declare the child a delinquent or a dependent, or to transfer the child to an adult court.[19]

Nonpetitioned cases, 43 percent of the total, are informally handled cases in which duly authorized court personnel screen a case prior to the filing of a formal petition. Figure 2–2 shows how juvenile courts across the country disposed of the nonpetitioned cases coming before them. Of interest is that 43 percent of the cases were nonadjudicated, that is, determined insufficiently delinquent for further court action, but were dealt with by the courts in some manner. Of the nonpetitioned delinquency cases, 44 percent were dismissed.

Table 2–3 *Juvenile Court Disposition of Delinquency Cases, by Most Serious Offense, 1999*

Most Serious Offense	*Number of Cases*	*Percentage Change* 1990–1999	1995–1999	1998–1999
Total Delinquency	**1,683,500**	**28%**	**−5%**	**−4%**
Person Offenses	**389,200**	**56%**	**1%**	**−4%**
Criminal homicide	1,900	−21	−34	−4
Forcible rape	4,200	−17	−37	−28
Robbery	25,200	−9	−37	−14
Aggravated assault	56,300	−4	−35	−15
Simple assault	256,900	95	18	−2
Other violent sex offenses	11,700	53	13	11
Other person offenses	33,000	97	56	19
Property Offenses	**710,600**	**−8%**	**−20%**	**−11%**
Burglary	115,200	−21	−19	−10
Larceny−theft	323,200	−5	−24	−12
Motor vehicle theft	38,700	−45	−28	−11
Arson	8,600	29	−19	4
Vandalism	112,100	13	−12	−5
Trespassing	59,000	13	−11	−7
Stolen property offenses	26,700	−10	−23	−21
Other property offenses	27,300	−2	−9	−14
Drug Law Violations	**192,700**	**171**	**16**	**0**
Public Order Offenses	**391,000**	**75**	**20**	**9**
Obstruction of justice	172,500	116	42	15
Disorderly conduct	91,100	68	1	0
Weapons offenses	40,000	32	−14	0
Liquor law violations	20,200	23	22	3
Nonviolent sex offenses	13,700	10	36	26
Other public order offenses	53,400	77	31	12
Violent Crime Index[a]	**87,600**	**−6%**	**−36%**	**−15%**
Property Crime Index[b]	**485,700**	**−14%**	**−23%**	**−12%**

[a] Includes criminal homicide, forcible rape, robbery, and aggravated assault.
[b] Includes burglary, larceny-theft, motor vehicle theft, and arson.

Note: Detail may not add to totals because of rounding. Percent-change calculations are based on unrounded numbers.

- Delinquency offenses are acts committed by juveniles that would be crimes if committed by adults.
- The overall juvenile court delinquency caseload was less in 1999 than in 1998 but 28 percent greater than the 1990 caseload.

Sources: Adapted from C. Puzzanchera, A. Stahl, T. Finnegan, H. Snyder, R. Poole, and N. Tierney, *Juvenile Court Statistics 1999* (Forthcoming). Washington, DC: Office of Juvenile Justice and Delinquency Prevention, 2002.

Data Source: A. Stahl, T. Finnegan, and W. Kang, *Easy Access to Juvenile Court Statistics: 1990–1999* [data analysis and presentation package]. Pittsburgh, PA: National Center for Juvenile Justice [producer]. Washington, DC: Office of Juvenile Justice and Delinquency Prevention [distributor], 2002.

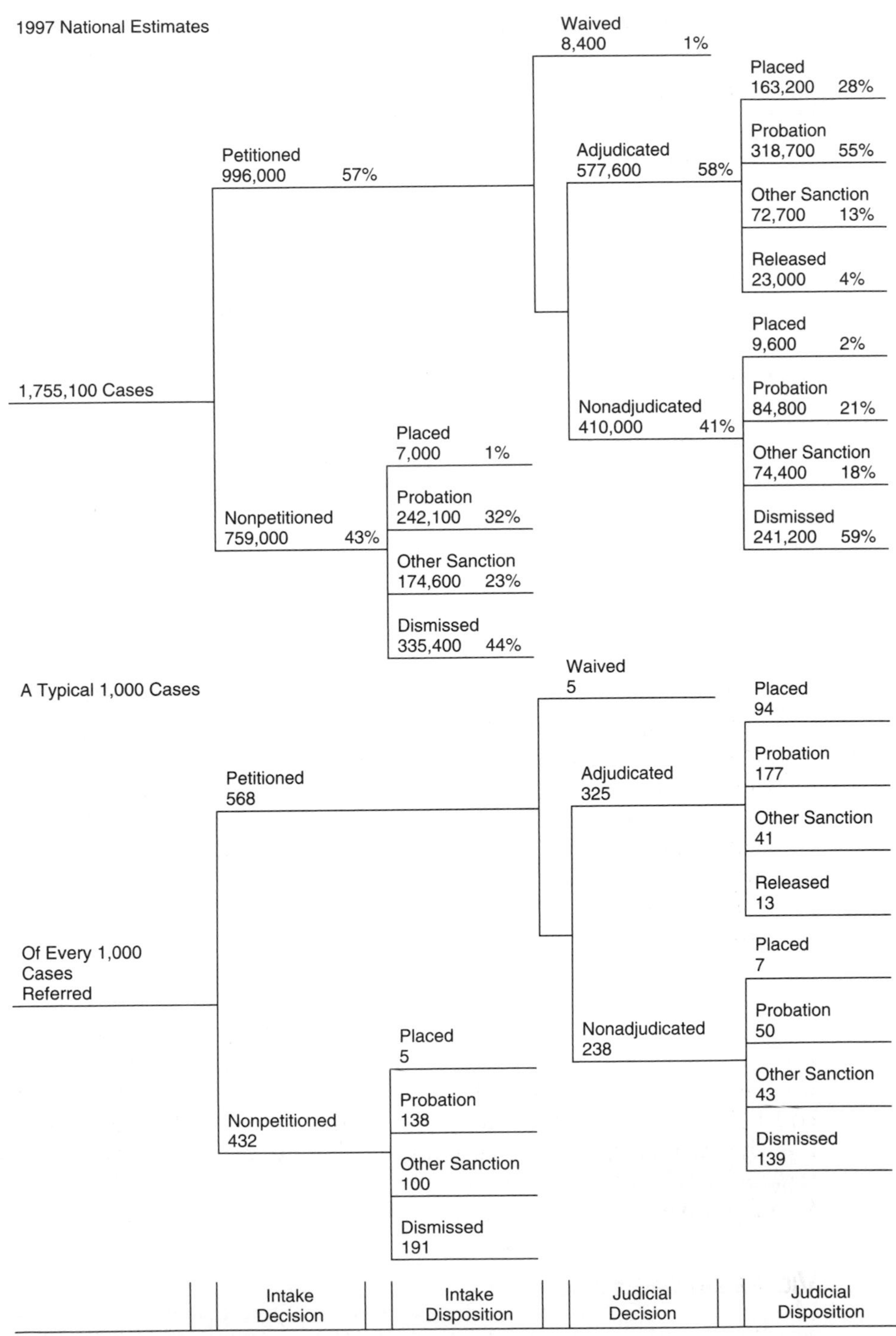

Note: Detail may not add to 100 because of rounding.

Figure 2–2 *Juvenile Court Processing of Delinquency Cases, 1997*

Source: Charles Puzzanchera, Anne L. Stahl, Terrence Finnegan, Howard N. Synder, Rowen S. Poole, and Nancy Tierney (2000). *Juvenile Court Statistics 1997.* Washington, DC: Office of Juvenile Justice and Delinquency Prevention, p. 9.

The chief findings of juvenile court statistics are as follows:

1. The number of cases appearing before the juvenile court increased until the mid-1970s, leveled out until the late 1980s, rose dramatically from the late 1980s to the mid-1990s, and then began to show signs of stabilizing.
2. Of status offenses, truancy and ungovernability rates peak at age fifteen, runaway cases peak at age sixteen, and liquor law violations increase continuously with age.
3. Males are more frequently referred to the juvenile court than are females.
4. Females are likely to be referred to juvenile court for status offenses at about the same rate as males.
5. White males are referred to the juvenile court roughly in proportion to their numbers in the population; black males are referred to juvenile court at rates highly disproportionate to their numbers in the population.

The findings of juvenile court statistics parallel those of the *Uniform Crime Reports.* The advantage of the court statistics, however, is that they reveal not only who the offenders are but also what types of dispositions are handed down. The juvenile court statistics are further able to track the number of offenders coming to the courts over specific periods of time as well as to follow trends in the changing characteristics of offenders and the dispositions handed down. These latter data are helpful in determining the success of suggested and mandated social policy changes in who should come to court and what should happen to them.

Juvenile court statistics do have serious limitations. The usual time lag in the publication of the statistics lessens their usefulness, and, in addition, these cases make up only a small percentage of the total number of juvenile offenses. Moreover, the data collected by the National Institute of Juvenile Justice and Delinquency Prevention represent only an estimate of the total number of juvenile crimes that come to the attention of the juvenile court. Finally, juvenile court statistics provide limited information about juvenile court transactions and the characteristics of referred juveniles. Yet these statistics still provide a means by which researchers can examine some characteristics of youths referred to juvenile courts.

Victimization Surveys

In 1972, the U.S. Bureau of the Census began victimization studies to determine as accurately as possible the extent of crime in the United States. Some changes have been made in the study design in the past five years. The ***National Crime***

Victimization Survey of 2001 selected a random sample of approximately 79,950 residents in 44,000 households across the United States.[20] Data from these individuals are used to measure all crimes—whether or not reported to the police—in the previous six-month period. To collect the data, representatives of the Bureau of the Census interview all household residents 12 years of age or older in the selected sample.

The *National Crime Victimization Survey* reports that in 2001, persons twelve years or older in this nation experienced nearly 24.2 million crimes, of which 18.3 million were property crimes, 5.7 million were violent crimes, and approximately 484,000 were personal thefts.[21] Overall, the number of offenses reported to the police was much lower than the total number of offenses uncovered by the victimization surveys.

Juveniles, as might be expected, were highly overrepresented compared to other age groups in the population. In 2001, juveniles between the ages of sixteen and nineteen experienced the highest victimization rate per one thousand population of any age group for all violent crimes. Youths between twelve and fifteen had the next highest rate, with rates then dropping with the increasing age of the victim. (See Table 2–4 for the rates of victimization by age and type of violent offense.) Within the adolescent population itself, older adolescents (ages sixteen to nineteen) had higher overall violent-crime victimization rates than did younger ones (ages twelve to fifteen).[22] Data also show that adolescents were more likely than adults to commit violent crimes against peers and to report knowing their assailants. Crimes against adolescents also were less likely to be reported to the police than crimes against adults.[23]

Victimization surveys have not been as widely used in analyzing youth crime as have the other means of the measurement of youth crime, but they do add to what is known about crime in the United States. Some of the principal findings of victimization surveys are as follows:

1. Much more crime is committed than is recorded.
2. The discrepancy between the number of people who say they have been victimized and the number of crimes known to the police varies with the type of offense.
3. The probability of being victimized varies with the type of crime and one's place of residence. The centers of U.S. cities are the more probable sites of violent crimes.
4. Juveniles are more likely to be victimized than any other age group.
5. Victimization studies do have limitations. Information on status offenses is not included; victims may forget the victimization they have experienced; or victims may state that a specific crime took place within the research year when it took place before or after that period.

Table 2–4 *Victimization Rates for Persons Age Twelve and Over, by Type of Crime and Age of Victims*

Type of Crime	Rate per 1,000 Persons in Each Age Group						
	12–15	16–19	20–24	25–34	35–49	50–64	65 and over
All personal crimes	**55.6**	**58.8**	**46.5**	**30.3**	**23.2**	**9.9**	**3.8**
Crimes of violence	55.1	55.8	44.7	29.3	22.9	9.5	3.2
Completed violence	17.4	18.9	17.8	10.0	6.1	2.1	1.2
Attempted/threatened violence	37.7	36.9	26.9	19.3	16.8	7.4	2.0
Rape/Sexual assault	1.7*	3.4	2.4	1.1	1.0	0.2*	0.1*
Rape/Attempted rape	0.8*	2.6	1.3*	0.6	0.6	0.1*	0.1*
Rape	0.5*	1.5*	1.0*	0.4	0.2*	0.1*	0.0*
Attempted rape[a]	0.3*	1.1*	0.3*	0.2	0.3*	0.1*	0.1*
Sexual assault[b]	0.9*	0.8*	1.1*	0.5	0.5	0.1*	0.1*
Robbery	5.2	6.4	4.2	3.6	2.1	1.2	1.3
Completed/property taken	2.8	4.5	2.7	2.6	1.4	0.8	1.0
With injury	1.0*	1.3*	0.6*	1.0	0.7	0.4*	0.7*
Without injury	1.8	3.2	2.1	1.5	0.7	0.4*	0.3*
Attempted to take property	2.4	1.9	1.5*	1.1	0.6	0.4*	0.3*
With injury	1.1*	0.9*	0.5*	0.4	0.1*	0.1*	0.1*
Without injury	1.3*	1.0*	1.0*	0.7	0.6	0.3*	0.2*
Assault	48.3	46.1	38.1	24.6	19.7	8.2	1.8
Aggravated	8.7	12.3	10.7	6.5	5.2	2.0	0.4*
With injury	3.3	4.8	4.3	1.7	1.5	0.4*	0.0*
Threatened with weapon	5.4	7.5	6.5	4.8	3.7	1.6	0.4*
Simple	39.6	33.8	27.4	18.1	14.5	6.2	1.4
With minor injury	9.9	7.6	8.8	4.9	2.7	0.8	0.1*
Without injury	29.6	26.2	18.6	13.2	11.9	5.4	1.3
Purse snatching/pocket picking	0.5*	3.0	1.8	1.0	0.4*	0.3*	0.7*
Population in each age group	16,277,310	16,125,600	18,957,780	37,555,740	65,211,500	42,217,420	32,869,960

Note: Detail may not add to total shown because of rounding.
*Estimate is based on about 10 or fewer sample cases.
[a]Includes verbal threats of rape.
[b] Includes threats.

Source: Adapted from Cathy Maston and Patsy Klaus, *National Crime Victimization Survey 2001*, accessed at BJS Web site, February 10, 2003, Washington, D.C.: U.S. Department of Justice Statistics. Criminal Victimization in the United States, N.P. see Table 3.

WHAT ARE THE UNOFFICIAL MEASUREMENTS OF JUVENILE CRIME?

Self-report and cohort studies are the main sources of unofficial accounts of delinquent behavior. **Self-report studies** ask juveniles to tell about offenses they have committed in a previous period of time. **Cohort studies** usually utilize raw police files along with a variety of official and unofficial data.

SELF-REPORT STUDIES

Self-report studies have been used since the 1940s to measure hidden youth crime. The reason for their use is to obtain a fuller and more accurate picture of the amount of crime than can be obtained through the UCRs. The UCRs, for example, generally show that lower-class youths commit more crime than do middle- or upper-class youths. Researchers can test this finding by going to different classes of youths and asking them about the number and type of offenses they have committed. Researchers also can obtain considerable information on offender characteristics such as age, sex, and race, as well as on the amount of gang delinquency and the extent of drug and alcohol abuse. In this section, we look at self-reporting and offenders' demographic characteristics.

One of the most significant findings of all the self-report studies is that the amount of youth crime is much greater than that indicated by the UCRs. Indeed, practically every youth commits some type of crime. Very few, however, ever come to the attention of the authorities.[24] This means that little reason exists for dividing youths into offenders and nonoffenders as many students of the juvenile justice system are prone to do. The self-report studies contradict or expand on the UCRs in other ways as well.

Self-Report Studies and Race

Official statistics tend to show that the differences between African Americans and Whites are greater than self-report studies indicate. In looking at race, for example, David Huizinga and Delbert S. Elliott's examination of the National Youth Survey concluded that "there are few if any substantial and consistent differences between the delinquency involvement of different racial groups."[25] The *Monitoring the Future Project* for 1994 also found that differences in the amount of crime between African Americans and Whites were not as great as suggested by the UCRs. In examining African-American and White responses to sixteen questions, for example, the two groups of subjects were within eight percentage points of each other in fourteen of the sixteen questions.[26] Two other national studies reported involvement in seventeen delinquent behaviors with similar frequencies, but further analysis of the data revealed that the seriousness of self-reported delinquency was slightly greater for African-American males than for white males.[27] Delbert Elliott and Suzanne Ageton's study revealed that the offense rate was greater for African Americans because they were more likely to be involved in serious property crime and because they were more likely to be chronic or repeat offenders.[28]

Sex and Self-Report

Similar discrepancies appear between official data and self-report studies when examining the sex of youthful offenders. Self-report studies show that female delinquency is higher than reported in official data.[29] Steven Cernkovich and Peggy Giordano's self-report study of Midwestern youths found that the ratio of male to female arrests was about one-half as large as the 4:1 ratio found in the *Uniform Crime Reports.*[30] Self-report studies do show that females are less likely to be involved in serious crime. For example, the findings of *Monitoring the Future 1994* revealed that female high school students reported being involved in fewer fights in school, being involved in fewer fights between groups, hurting someone badly less frequently, and using a weapon less frequently.[31]

Social Class and Delinquency

The finding that unlawful behavior is unrelated or only slightly related to a juvenile's social class is one of the most significant findings of self-report studies.[32] Travis Hirschi's survey of four thousand junior and senior high-school students in Richmond, California, found little association between self-reported delinquencies and income, education, and occupation.[33] Richard E. Johnson, in redefining social class as underclass and earning class, added: "The data provide no firm evidence that social class, no matter how it is measured, is a salient factor in generating delinquent involvement."[34]

Elliott and Ageton's national study, however, found a different pattern when youths were asked how many times they had violated that law during the previous year. The average number of delinquent acts reported by lower-class juveniles, according to these researchers, exceeded that reported by working-class or middle-class youths. Indeed, the average number of crimes against persons reported by lower-class youths was one and one-half times greater than that reported by working- or middle-class youths.

Evaluation of Self-Report Studies

The realization that official statistics on juvenile delinquency have serious limitations led to a growing reliance on the use of self-report studies. These studies have revealed the following conclusions:

1. There is a significant amount of undetected delinquency in the United States.
2. Middle-class juveniles are involved in a considerable number of juvenile offenses.
3. Hidden delinquency also includes a large number of serious crimes each year that elude detection by the police.
4. The differences between the offenses of African Americans and those of Whites are less in self-report than in official statistics.
5. Girls commit more delinquent acts than official statistics indicate, but boys commit more delinquent acts and commit more serious youth crimes than girls do.

Cohort Studies

Cohort studies are another valuable tool of researchers. These research designs do not start by counting offenses or by asking who has been victimized. Rather, these studies identify every juvenile born in a certain time frame in a particular city and then follow the juveniles for many years. Depending on the goals of the study, police files, school records, and/or socioeconomic data are collected and then scrutinized for all the juveniles. These data and any evidence that the youths have gotten into trouble are collected by the researchers for their study. The result is a wealth of information not attainable through the use of official statistics.[35] Three of the most important older cohort studies involve data collected on cohorts of youths in Philadelphia; Columbus, Ohio; and Racine, Wisconsin.[36] For more recent cohort studies, see Focus on Research 2–2.

Delinquency in the Philadelphia Cohort. Marvin Wolfgang and colleagues conducted two important **cohort studies.** The first study consisted of all males born in 1945 who resided in the city of Philadelphia from their tenth through their eighteenth birthdays. The second study consisted of all males and females born in 1958 in Philadelphia who resided in the city from their tenth through their eighteenth birthdays.[37]

> *Cohort I.* Of the nearly ten thousand cohort subjects, Wolfgang and colleagues found that 35 percent had at least one contact with the police at some time during the span of their juvenile court age. Significantly, 6.3 percent of the total cohort were responsible for 51 percent of the total number of delinquent acts. **Chronic offenders,** as these recidivists were called, were responsible for 71 percent of the homicides, 73 percent of the rapes, 82 percent of the robberies, and 69 percent of the aggravated assaults.
>
> *Cohort II.* Of the 13,160 male subjects, 33 percent had at least one police contact before reaching their eighteenth birthday. Of the 14,000 females in the cohort, about 14 percent had at least one police contact before age 18. The 1958 cohort contained 982 male chronic offenders, or 7.5 percent of the males, and 147 female chronic delinquents, or 7.5 percent of the females.
>
> In sum, Wolfgang and colleagues found that a few youths committed at least half of all juvenile offenses and an even higher percentage of the violent juvenile offenses in Philadelphia. Overall, youthful offenders in Cohort II committed much more serious and more frequent offenses than those in Cohort I, and in both cohorts, males committed more frequent and more serious offenses than females did. Finally, both studies found that if an individual had been arrested before the age of nineteen, he was three times more likely to be arrested as an adult.

FOCUS ON RESEARCH 2–2

HIGHLIGHTS FROM DENVER, PITTSBURGH, AND ROCHESTER YOUTH SURVEYS

Denver

The Denver study follows 1,527 boys and girls from high-risk neighborhoods in Denver who were seven, nine, eleven, thirteen, and fifteen years old in 1987. In exploring the changes in the nature of delinquency and drug use from the 1970s to the 1990s, the Denver study's finding are as follows:

- Overall, there was little change in the prevalence rates of delinquency, including serious delinquency and serious violence. However, the prevalence rate of gang fights among males doubled (from 8 percent to 16 percent).
- The level of injury from violence offenses increased substantially.
- The prevalence of drug use decreased substantially: alcohol, from 80 percent to 50 percent; marijuana, from 41 percent to 18 percent; and other drug use, from 19 percent to 4 percent.
- The relationships between drug use and delinquency have changed in that a smaller percentage (from 48 percent to 17 percent) of serious delinquents are using hard drugs other than marijuana, and a greater percentage (from 27 percent to 48 percent) of hard drug users are serious offenders.
- More than half (53 percent) of the youth in the study ages eleven through fifteen in 1987 were arrested over the next five years.

Pittsburgh

The Pittsburgh study, a longitudinal study of 1,517 inner-city boys, followed three samples of boys for more than a decade to advance knowledge about how and why boys become involved in delinquency and other problem behaviors. Its chief findings are as follows:

- There were no differences between African-American and White boys at age six, but differences gradually developed, the prevalence of serious delinquency at age sixteen reaching 27 percent for African-American boys and 19 percent for White boys.
- As prevalence increased, so did the average frequency of serious offending, which rose more rapidly for African-American boys than for White boys.

- The onset of offending among the boys involved in serious delinquency occurred by age fifteen, when 51 percent of African-American boys and 28 percent of White boys had committed serious delinquent acts.
- The boys generally developed disruptive and delinquent behavior in an orderly, progressive fashion, with less serious problem behaviors preceding more serious problem behaviors.
- Three groups of developmental pathways were identified that displayed progressively more serious problem behaviors:

  Authority Conflict: Youths on this pathway exhibit stubbornness prior to age twelve, then move on to defiance and avoidance of authority.

  Covert: This pathway includes minor acts, such as lying, followed by property damage and moderately serious delinquency.

  Overt: This pathway includes minor aggression followed by fighting and violence.

Rochester

The Rochester study, a longitudinal study of one thousand urban adolescents, investigates the causes and consequences of adolescent delinquency and drug use by following a sample of high-risk urban adolescents from their early teenage years through their early adult years. Its chief findings are as follows:

- Attachment and involvement were both significantly related to delinquency. Children who were more attached to and involved with their parents were less involved in delinquency.
- The relationship between family process factors and delinquency was bidirectional—poor parenting increased the probability of delinquent behavior and delinquent behavior further weakened the relationship between parent and child.
- The impact of family variables appeared to fade as adolescents became older and more independent from their parents. Weak school commitment and poor school performance were associated with increased involvement in delinquency and drug use.
- Associating with delinquent peers was strongly and consistently related to delinquency, in part because peers provide positive reinforcements for delinquency. There is a strong relationship between gang membership and delinquent behavior, particularly serious and violent delinquency.

Sources: Katharine Browning, Terence P. Thornberry, and Pamela K. Porter, "Highlights of Findings from the Rochester Youth Development Study," *OJJDP Fact Sheet* (Washington, D.C.: Office of Juvenile Justice and Delinquency Prevention, 1999); Katharine Browning and Rolf Loeber, "Highlights from the Pittsburgh Youth Study," *OJJDP Fact Sheet* (Washington, DC: Office of Juvenile Justice and Delinquency Prevention, 1999); and Katharine Browning and David Huizinga, "Highlights from the Denver Youth Study," *OJJDP Fact Sheet* (Washington, DC: Office of Juvenile Justice and Delinquency Prevention, 1999).

Critical Thinking Questions

What do the findings of these three studies have in common? How do they differ? What would you say are the most important ways the findings overall?

Evaluation of Cohort Studies

Cohort studies conducted in Columbus, Ohio, and Racine, Wisconsin, generally agree with the following conclusions of the two Philadelphia cohort studies:

1. A few youths commit at least half of all juvenile offenses and an even higher percentage of the violent juvenile offenses.
2. African-American urban youths as a group commit more frequent and more serious delinquent offenses than do Whites.
3. Females typically have fewer contacts and less serious involvements with the police than do males.
4. The more frequent and the more serious the police contacts are that a juvenile has, the more likely it is that that youth will continue on to adult crime.
5. Interventions by the justice system appear to raise the likelihood of frequency and seriousness of unlawful behavior in the future.

Cohort studies, like other forms of crime statistics, do have two major problems. First, their findings cannot be generalized confidently beyond those persons in the cohort. Second, cohort studies are extremely expensive and time consuming to conduct. Indeed, keeping track of a sample of individuals even up to age thirty-five is next to impossible because names and addresses change, some people die, and others simply drop out of sight. Still, even with these drawbacks, cohort studies remain a useful addition to other official and unofficial measurements of crime.

HOW MUCH DRUG USE IS THERE AMONG JUVENILES?

In addition to the general types of studies noted previously, researchers today are studying specific problem areas of societal concern. Gangs, drugs, guns, and schools are all at the forefront of public attention, and as a result,

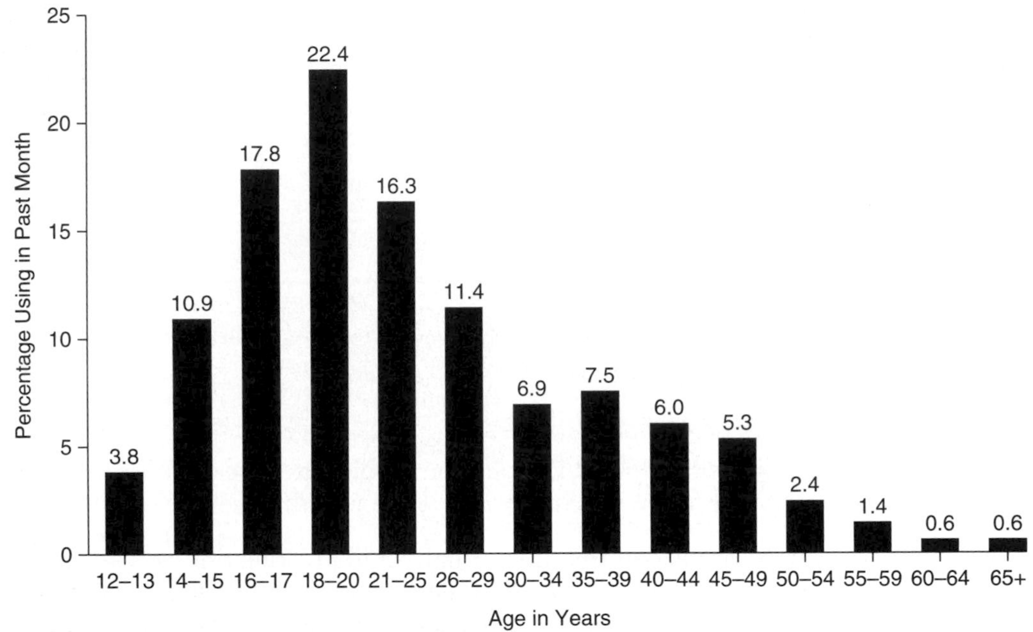

Figure 2–3 *Past Month Illicit Drug Use, by Age: 2001*

Source: National Clearing House for Alcohol and Drug Information. (2002). Results from the 2001 National Household Survey on Drug Abuse: Vol. 1. Summary of National Findings (Office of Applied Studies, NHSDA Series H-17, DHHS Publication No. SMA 02-3758). Rockville, MD, p. 4.

both official and unofficial data are being collected to shed light on the depth and breadth of the problems. Some of the data are collected systematically by federal and state agencies, and others are the result of often less than rigorous studies by journalists and interest groups. Drugs and schools will receive attention in this chapter, and gangs and guns will be considered in other chapters.

The abuse of alcohol and the abuse of drugs are identified, along with juvenile unlawful behavior, as two of the most serious problems of adolescents. Figure 2–3 shows for a one-month period the illicit use of drugs of any kind for a national household sample of 24,505 juveniles and adults. Young people are clearly the leaders in illicit drug use in the United States. After age eighteen, drug use tends to drop off, with only 1 percent of persons over age fifty using illicit drugs of any kind. Our attention here, of course, is focused on the use of alcohol and other drugs by juveniles.

One of the most important subjects studied by the *Monitoring the Future Project* is drug use by school students. Data for 2001 indicate that an upturn in drug use that started in the early 1980s has reversed modestly and stabilized in recent years. For example, the proportion of eighth-graders taking any illicit drug increased some between 1994 and 1996 from 25.7 percent to

31.2 percent. By 2001, the proportion of eighth-graders who had used any illicit drugs in the previous year dropped to 19.5 percent, while drug use by tenth graders and that of twelfth graders had stabilized. Nevertheless, lifetime prevalence for using any drug by tenth- and twelfth-graders was at 45.6 and 53.9 percent, respectively. Alcohol and marijuana remain the drugs of choice for school students, but the use of even these is decreasing slightly. By 2001, only a very slight, if any, drop was registered among students. Time will tell whether the decrease will continue, remain stable, or rise into this century.[38]

Even with this recent drop, rates of drug use are higher than anyone would like. Table 2–5 shows the percentage of alcohol and other drug use by juveniles in the eighth, tenth, and twelfth grades in 2000 on a lifetime, annual, monthly, and daily basis. It is somewhat sobering that approximately 54 percent of all high school seniors have tried illicit drugs at some time in their lives, followed by 46 percent of tenth graders and 27 percent of eighth graders. Examination of the tabular data from left to right shows an expected drop-off as longer time periods correlate with reduced illicit drug use. Of some interest, a significant proportion of these students used marijuana only, but the data also indicate that many students used other more potent drugs as well. In addition to alcohol and marijuana, rather large percentages of youths over their lifetimes used inhalants, hallucinogens, stimulants, and sedatives. Disconcerting is the extent to which youths experimented with cocaine, heroin, and other opiates.

WHAT ARE THE DIMENSIONS OF LAW-VIOLATING BEHAVIORS?

The age of onset, escalation of numbers of offenses, specialization of offenses, desistance from crime, and transition to adult crime are important dimensions of juveniles' law-violating behavior.

Age of Onset

Several studies have found that the earlier juveniles began law-violating behaviors (their **age of onset**), the more likely they were to continue such behaviors. Marvin E. Wolfgang, Terence P. Thornberry, and Robert M. Figlio followed a 10 percent sample of Cohort I (of the Philadelphia cohort study) to the age of thirty and found that the average number of offenses tended to decline nearly uniformly as their age of onset increased.[39] Alfred Blumstein, David P. Farrington, and Soumyo Moitra also showed that one of the factors predicting those who became chronic offenders was offending at an early age.[40] Farrington further found that those who were first convicted at the earliest age (ten to twelve) offended consistently at a higher rate and for a longer time period than did those who were first convicted at later ages.[41]

Table 2–5 *Prevalence of Use of Various Drugs for Eighth-, Tenth-, and Twelfth-Graders, 2001*

	Lifetime			*Annual*			*30-Day*			*Daily*		
Grade:	*8th*	*10th*	*12th*	*8th*	*10th*	*12th*	*8th*	*10th*	*12th*	*8th*	*10th*	*12th*
Approx. N =	*16,200*	*14,000*	*12,800*	*16,200*	*14,000*	*12,800*	*16,200*	*14,000*	*12,800*	*16,200*	*14,000*	*12,800*
Any illicit drug[a]	26.8	45.6	53.9	19.5	37.2	41.4	11.7	22.7	25.7	—	—	—
Any illicit drug other than marijuana[a,b,c]	14.8	23.4	28.5	9.9	16.8	19.8	5.5	8.7	10.8	—	—	—
Any illicit drug including inhalants[a,c]	34.5	48.8	56.0	23.9	38.7	42.6	14.0	23.6	26.5	—	—	—
Marijuana/hashish	20.4	40.1	49.0	15.4	32.7	37.0	9.2	19.8	22.4	1.3	4.5	5.8
Inhalants[c]	17.1	15.2	13.0	9.1	6.6	4.5	4.0	2.4	1.7	—	—	0.1
Inhalants, adjusted[c,d]	—	—	13.8	—	—	4.9	—	—	2.1	—	—	0.1
Amyl/butyl nitrites[e]	—	—	1.9	—	—	0.6	—	—	0.5	—	—	0.1
Hallucinogens[b,c]	4.0	7.8	12.8	2.5	5.2	8.4	1.2	2.1	3.2	—	—	0.2
Hallucinogens, adjusted[c,d]	—	—	13.4	—	—	9.0	—	—	3.4	—	—	0.3
LSD	3.4	6.3	10.9	2.2	4.1	6.6	1.0	1.5	2.3	—	—	0.2
Hallucinogens Other than LSD[b,c]	1.8	4.0	7.0	1.1	2.8	4.4	0.6	1.1	1.8	—	—	0.1
PCP[e]	—	—	3.5	—	—	1.8	—	—	0.5	—	—	0.1
MDMA (Ecstasy)[e,f]	5.2	8.0	11.7	3.5	6.2	9.2	1.8	2.6	2.8	—	—	0.2
Cocaine	4.3	5.7	8.2	2.5	3.6	4.8	1.2	1.3	2.1	—	—	0.1
Crack	3.0	3.1	3.7	1.7	1.8	2.1	0.8	0.7	1.1	—	—	0.1
Other cocaine[g]	3.3	5.0	7.4	1.9	3.0	4.4	0.9	1.2	1.8	—	—	0.1
Heroin												
Any use	1.7	1.7	1.8	1.0	0.9	0.9	0.6	0.3	0.4	—	—	0.1
With a needle[c]	1.2	0.8	0.7	0.7	0.4	0.3	0.4	0.2	0.2	—	—	*
Without a needle[c]	1.1	1.3	1.5	0.6	0.7	0.8	0.4	0.2	0.3	—	—	*
Other narcotics[h]	—	—	9.9	—	—	6.7	—	—	3.0	—	—	0.2
Amphetamines[h]	10.2	16.0	16.2	6.7	11.7	10.9	3.2	5.6	5.6	—	—	0.5
Methamphetamine[i, j]	4.4	6.4	6.9	2.8	3.7	3.9	1.3	1.5	1.5	—	—	0.1
Crystal meth. (ice)[j]	—	—	4.1	—	—	2.5	—	—	1.1	—	—	0.2
Sedatives[h,k]	—	—	8.9	—	—	5.9	—	—	3.0	—	—	0.1
Barbiturates[h]	—	—	8.7	—	—	5.7	—	—	2.8	—	—	0.1
Methaqualone[e,h]	—	—	1.1	—	—	0.8	—	—	0.5	—	—	0.0

(continued)

Table 2–5 *(Continued)*

Tranquilizers[b,c,h]	4.7	8.1	9.2	3.0	5.9	6.5	1.6	2.9	3.0	—	—	*
Rohypnol[e,f]	1.1	1.5	1.7	0.7	1.0	0.9	0.4	0.2	0.3	—	—	*
GHB[e,i]	—	—	—	1.1	1.0	1.6	—	—	—	—	—	—
Ketamine[e,i]	—	—	—	1.3	2.1	2.5	—	—	—	—	—	—
Alcohol												
Any use	50.5	70.1	79.7	41.9	63.5	73.3	21.5	39.0	49.8	0.9	1.9	3.6
Been drunk[j]	23.4	48.2	63.9	16.6	39.9	53.2	7.7	21.9	32.7	0.2	0.6	1.4
5+ Drinks in a row in last 2 weeks	—	—	—	—	—	—	—	—	—	13.2	24.9	29.7
Cigarettes												
Any use	36.6	52.8	61.0	—	—	—	12.2	21.3	29.5	5.5	12.2	19.0
1/2 Pack+/day	—	—	—	—	—	—	—	—	—	2.3	5.5	10.3
Bidis[i,j]	—	—	—	2.7	4.9	7.0	—	—	—	—	—	—
Kreteks[i,j]	—	—	—	2.6	6.0	10.1	—	—	—	—	—	—
Smokeless tobacco[b,e]	11.7	19.5	19.7	—	—	—	4.0	6.9	7.8	1.2	2.2	2.8
Steroids[j]	2.8	3.5	3.7	1.6	2.1	2.4	0.7	0.9	1.3	—	—	0.2

Notes: '—' indicates data not available. '*' indicates less than .05 percent but greater than 0 percent.

Source: The Monitoring the Future Study, the University of Michigan.

[a] For 12th-graders only: Use of "any illicit drugs" includes any use of marijuana, LSD, other hallucinogens, crack, other cocaine, or heroin, *or* any use of other narcotics, amphetamines, barbiturates, or tranquilizers not under a doctor's orders. For 8th- and 10th-graders only: The use of other narcotics and barbiturates has been excluded, because these younger respondents appear to overreport use (perhaps because they include the use of nonprescription drugs in their answers).
[b] For 8th- and 10th-graders only: Data based on two of four forms; *N* is one-half of *N* indicated.
[c] For 12th-graders only: Data based on three of six forms; *N* is one-half of *N* indicated.
[d] For 12th-graders only: Adjusted for underreporting of certain drugs. See text for details.
[e] For 12th-graders only: Data based on one of six forms; *N* is one-sixth of *N* indicated.
[f] For 8th- and 10th-graders only: Data based on two of four forms; *N* is one-third of *N* indicated due to changes in the questionnaire forms.
[g] For 12th-graders only: Data based on four of six forms; *N* is four-sixths of *N* indicated.
[h] Only drug use which was not under a doctor's orders is included here.
[i] For 8th- and 10th-graders only: Data based on one of four forms; *N* is one-third of *N* indicated.
[j] For 12th-graders only: Data based on two of six forms; *N* is two-sixths of *N* indicated.
[k] For 12th-graders only: Data based on six forms adjusted by one form data.

Source: Adapted from Lloyd D. Johnston, Patrick M. O'Malley, and Jerald G. Bachman, *Monitoring The Future National Survey Results on Drug Use 1975–2001.* Volume 1, Secondary School Students (NIH Publication No. 02 5106) Bethesda, MD National Institute on Drug Abuse, 81.

Escalation of Offenses

The findings on **escalation of offenses** (an increase in the number of crimes committed by an individual) are less consistent than those on age of onset. Official studies have typically found that the incidence of arrest accelerates at age thirteen and peaks at about age seventeen, but this pattern is less evident in self-report studies. For example, Ageton and Elliott found that the incidence of some offenses, such as assault and robbery, increased with age, whereas that of others peaked between ages thirteen and fifteen.[42]

Specialization of Offenses

The findings on **specialization of offenses** (the tendency to repeat one type of crime) are more consistent than those on escalation. The cohort studies, especially, revealed little or no specialization of offenses among delinquents.[43] Some evidence exists, however, that specialization was much more typical of status offenders. Susan K. Datesman and Michael Aickin's examination of a sample of status offenders found that the majority, regardless of sex and race, were referred to court within the same offense category 50 to 70 percent of the time. Females, especially white females, specialized in official offense behavior to a greater extent than did males; 35 percent of the white females were referred to court for the same offenses, a sizable proportion of them for running away.[44]

Desistance from Crime

Desistance from crime, or the age of termination of delinquency, seems to be strongly related to the maturation process as juveniles become aware of either the desirability of pursuing a conventional lifestyle or the undesirability of continuing unlawful activities. Some of the stronger motivations to desist from further involvement with unlawful behavior are the following:

- They realize that they are going nowhere and that it is necessary to make changes in their lives if they are going to be successful as adults.[45]
- A conventional lifestyle, marked by marriage, military service, or education, becomes more attractive than the relatively minor gains from a life of crime.[46]
- They fear jail or imprisonment that would result if they were apprehended as adults.[47]
- They have spent enough time in the justice system.[48]
- They have brought enough embarrassment to their families.[49]

Transition to Adult Crime

Studies have identified three groups of criminal offenders. One group offends only during their juvenile years; a second group offends only during their adult

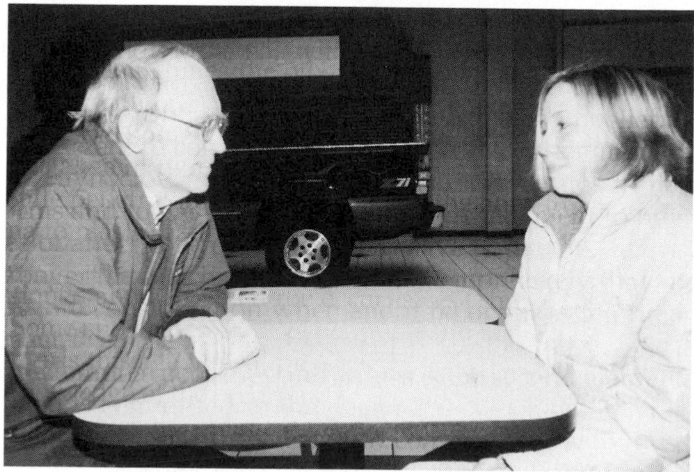

Lured to a mall after several months of contact on the internet, this young girl's life could well be in extreme danger. (Photo by Kathryn Miller.)

years; and a third group persistently offends during both periods.[50] Some scholars argue that juvenile offenders' **transition to adult crime** is due to their prior participation in unlawful activities. This prior participation, according to this position, reduces the inhibitions against engaging in future unlawful behavior. Other scholars contend that some individuals have a higher propensity to delinquency than do others and that this higher propensity is persistent over time. This higher propensity is related to such factors as poor parental supervision, parental rejection, parental criminality, delinquent siblings, and low IQ.[51]

WHAT ABOUT JUVENILE VICTIMS?

As the victimization surveys indicate, children too frequently are the targets of crime. In many countries throughout the world, in fact, attention to the plight of children is increasing the focus on the victimization of youths in dysfunctional families, in schools, in their neighborhoods, and by authorities. Emotionally damaged as a result of neglect and abuse, children often are unable to relate to adults and peers, to perform in school, and to make realistic plans for the future. It is no wonder that many of these juveniles become involved in law-violating behaviors.

THE MALTREATMENT OF CHILDREN

Reports by child protective agencies indicate that the maltreatment of children increased 155 percent between 1980 and 1993.[52] According to the National Center on Child Abuse and Family Violence, the amount of childhood victimization stabilized through 1994, and began dropping through 1999 only to rise slightly in 2000.[53] In spite of the decrease, the magnitude of child abuse and neglect remains unacceptably high, with almost three million investigations of alleged victims in 2000. Citizens, doctors, and hospitals continue to report offenses as states now mandate the reporting of abuse when discovered.

The problem of parental maltreatment of children can be divided into several different categories. The Childrens' Bureau reports that in 2000, roughly 63 percent of reported maltreatment stemmed from neglect, with 19 percent from physical abuse, 10 percent from sexual abuse, and 8 percent from emotional maltreatment; 16 percent fell into an "other" category that included such factors as medical neglect, abandonment, and "congenital drug addiction."[54]

Homicide is the most serious victimization of children. The *Uniform Crime Reports* indicate that 1,402 people under the age of eighteen were murdered in 2001, a total of 10 percent of all murders in the United States in that year. This breaks down to almost three juveniles murdered each day.[55] Other estimates suggest that between two thousand and five thousand children are killed each year.[56] The discrepancies among these different estimates stem from the fact that the deaths of many young children and infants may be attributed to SIDS or other accidental causes instead of being labeled as deliberate maltreatment by parents or others. An analysis of the UCRs for 2001 indicates that 51 percent of the murdered children were under the age of twelve and that 28 percent were between the ages of thirteen and sixteen.[57] For ages seventeen and older, the number of youths murdered each year increases dramatically.

In 1997, twenty-two percent of all child murder victims were killed by their parents, 5 percent by other family members, 36 percent by acquaintances, 11 percent by strangers, and 25 percent by unknown assailants.[58] Females were twice as likely as males to be killed by family members; in addition, children under age eight were more likely to die as a result of neglect or repeated abuse, whereas children over age eight more frequently died as a result of physical or sexual abuse. Younger children generally died at the hands of family members, whereas older children were more likely murdered by non-family members.

Overwhelmingly, youths are killed by members of their own race, with the majority of older juveniles being killed by firearms. For example, 73 percent of youths between the ages of thirteen and sixteen and 82 percent of youths between seventeen and nineteen years of age died in this manner.[59] Although African Americans make up only 13 percent of the population, the number of African Americans killed is greater than the number of White juveniles killed. Finally, males and females are murdered at about the same rate until they become teenagers, at which time the rate for males soars.[60]

The consequences for the *survivors* of child abuse and neglect can be severe. Although some victims of abuse appear to survive their victimization with only minor damage, evidence is mounting that the majority suffer serious problems of negative self-concepts, an inability to form normal relationships with other people, and symptoms of depression, anxiety, and self-destructive behavior. Furthermore, evidence is emerging that the victims of violence and neglect are arrested more frequently than are individuals who escaped maltreatment in their early childhoods.[61]

Cathy Spatz Widom's study of 908 victims of childhood abuse demonstrates clearly that any type of maltreatment of children puts them at a greater risk for arrest—both as juveniles and as adults. Widom found that 16.8 percent of a control group of 667 children who had experienced no abuse of any kind were arrested as juveniles. In contrast, 28.4 percent of neglected youths experienced arrest, as did 19.9 percent of physically abused children and 22.2 percent of sexually abused children. Similarly, as adults, 21 percent of the control group was arrested, along with 30.7 percent who had experienced neglect, 27.4 percent of the physically abused, and 20.3 percent of the sexually abused.[62]

Victimized at School

In the past, the major problems teachers and administrators in the nation's school systems faced were those of juveniles running the halls, leaving class without permission, writing graffiti on the walls, and occasionally fighting. Today's students, however, are likely to experience the same problems in the schools as on the streets. Drugs, alcohol, suicide, rape, robbery, assault, arson, and bomb threats combine with knives and guns to change the atmosphere of schools and to generate fear on the part of parents who worry about their children's safety.

In addition, as suggested by George Knox and others, schools in the 1990s became fertile soil for the violence of youth gangs.[63] Gangs perpetrate school violence in a number of ways. First, gang members frequently bring concealed weapons to school.[64] Second, gangs are always recruiting new members, and non-gang members may be assaulted if they refuse to join. Third, conflict takes place on a regular basis if more than one group is present in a school. Warring gang members may start a mass riot, in which stabbings and shootings take place. Finally, conflicts among rival gangs in different schools commonly lead to drive-by shootings.[65] It is little wonder schools no longer are perceived as havens of safety and learning for juveniles.

All of these events do happen, yet we must ask just how dangerous our schools really are. Are children likely to be murdered or assaulted when out of parents' sight and behind school walls? Part of the problem modern society faces today is separating fact from fiction. The reality is that the media contribute to a frenzy of fear by publicizing the slightest incident as well as the most tragic event. (See Chapter 12 and Table 12–1, for further commentary and data on schools.) The national scope of reporting means that a parent in northern Maine hears about events in southern California. Students too hear about these events and fear for their safety.

A 2002 report by the National Center for Education Statistics (NCES) documents the extent of student victimization. This survey, which was undertaken on a sample of students twelve through eighteen years old, focused on the nature of student victimization over time.[66]

A visual inspection of the totals column from 1995 to 2001 in Table 2–6 indicates a general drop in school victimization over that five year period. The trends over these years demonstrate that males experienced higher rates of victimization than females; blacks were victimized more than Hispanics and whites; ninth- and tenth-graders were victims more frequently than youths in

***Table 2–6** Percentage of Students Ages Twelve Through Eighteen Who Reported Criminal Victimization at School During the Previous Six Months, by Type of Victimization and Selected Student Characteristics: 1995, 1999, and 2001*

Student Characteristics	*1995*				*1999*				*2001*			
	Total[a]	*Theft*	*Violent*[b]	*Serious Violent*[c]	*Total*[a]	*Theft*	*Violent*[b]	*Serious Violent*[c]	*Total*[a]	*Theft*	*Violent*[b]	*Serious Violent*[c]
Total	9.5	7.1	3.0	0.7	7.6	5.7	2.3	0.5	5.5	4.2	1.8	0.4
Gender												
Male	10.0	7.1	3.5	0.9	7.8	5.7	2.5	0.6	6.1	4.5	2.1	0.5
Female	9.0	7.1	2.4	0.4	7.3	5.7	2.0	0.5	4.9	3.8	1.5	0.4
Race/ethnicity												
White, non-Hispanic	9.8	7.4	3.0	0.6	7.5	5.8	2.1	0.4	5.8	4.2	2.0	0.4
Black, non-Hispanic	10.2	7.1	3.4	1.0	9.9	7.4	3.5	1.2	6.1	5.0	1.3	0.5
Hispanic	7.6	5.8	2.7	0.9	5.7	3.9	1.9	0.6	4.6	3.7	1.5	0.8
Other, non-Hispanic	8.8	6.5	2.5	0.5	6.4	4.4	2.2	—[d]	3.1	2.9	0.4	—[d]
Grade												
6th	9.6	5.4	5.1	1.5	8.0	5.2	3.8	1.3	5.9	4.0	2.6	0.1
7th	11.2	8.1	3.8	0.9	8.2	6.0	2.6	0.9	5.8	3.4	2.6	0.6
8th	10.5	7.9	3.1	0.8	7.6	5.9	2.4	0.5	4.3	3.3	1.3	0.3
9th	11.9	9.1	3.4	0.7	8.9	6.5	3.2	0.6	7.9	6.2	2.4	0.8
10th	9.1	7.7	2.1	0.4	8.0	6.5	1.7	0.5	6.5	5.7	1.2	0.4
11th	7.3	5.5	1.9	0.4	7.2	5.5	1.8	0.1	4.8	3.8	1.6	0.3
12th	6.1	4.6	1.9	0.4	4.8	4.0	0.8	0.3	2.9	2.3	0.9	0.3
Urbanicity												
Urban	9.3	6.6	3.3	1.3	8.4	6.9	2.3	0.7	5.9	4.5	1.7	0.5
Suburban	10.3	7.6	3.5	0.6	7.6	5.4	2.4	0.5	5.7	4.3	1.7	0.4
Rural	8.3	6.8	1.8	0.3	6.4	5.0	1.9	0.4	4.7	3.4	2.0	0.5
Control												
Public	9.8	7.3	3.1	0.7	7.9	5.9	2.5	0.6	5.7	4.4	1.9	0.5
Private	6.6	5.2	1.7	0.1	4.5	4.3	0.3	—[d]	3.4	2.5	1.0	—[d]

[a] Total victimization is a combination of violent victimization and theft. If the student reported an incident in either, he or she is counted as having experienced "total" victimization. If the student reported having experienced both, he or she is counted once under "total" victimization.
[b] Violent crimes include rape, sexual assault, robbery, aggravated assault, and simple assault.
[c] Serious violent crimes include rape, sexual assault, robbery, and aggravated assault. Serious violent crimes are also included in violent crimes.
[d] No cases are reported in this cell, although the event defined by this cell could have been reported by some students with these characteristics, had a different sample been drawn.

Note: "At school" includes inside the school building, on school property, or on the way to or from school. Because of rounding or missing data, detail may not add to totals.

Source: U.S. Department of Justice, Bureau of Justice Statistics, School Crime Supplement to the National Crime Victimization Survey, January–June 1995, 1999, and 2001; See also, J. F. DeVoe, K. Peter, P. Kaufman, S. A. Ruddy, A. K. Miller, M. Planty, T. D. Snyder, D. T. Duhart, and M. R. Rand, *Indicators of School Crime and Safety: 2002* U.S. Departments of Education and Justice. NCES 2003-009/NCJ 196753. Washington DC 2002, p. 61.

the earlier or later grades; students from urban areas were more highly victimized than those in suburban and rural schools; and public school children were victimized more than those in private schools. Hidden within these statistics is a current public concern over bullying. Roughly 9 percent of students avoided one or more areas in their schools because of concern for their own safety.[67]

An examination of reports on schools further clarifies the risk to students. *Indicators of School Crime and Safety, 1998* reveals that in 1996–1997, ten percent of all public schools reported to the police at least one serious violent crime, including murder, rape, sexual battery, suicide, physical attack or a fight with a weapon, or robbery. Another 47 percent reported a less serious or nonviolent crime such as a physical attack or a fight without a weapon, theft-larceny, or vandalism; the remaining 43 percent of the schools reported neither serious nor less serious violent or nonviolent crimes.[68]

Whether victimization occurred was related to the size and location of the schools. Urban schools were more likely to experience serious violent crimes than were suburban or rural schools. Furthermore, serious violent crime is concentrated in only a small fraction of the nation's schools. During the 1996–1997 school year, only 12 percent of middle schools and 13 percent of high schools reported to police at least one attack or fight involving a weapon. Only 5 percent of middle schools and 8 percent of high schools reported at least one incident of robbery, rape, or sexual battery. Larger percentages of schools—55 percent of middle schools and 51 percent of high schools—did report incidents of unarmed assaults or fighting; 55 percent of middle schools and 44 percent of high schools reported thefts.[69] Vandalism occurred in both types of schools at about the same rates as unarmed assaults or fighting.

Bullying

Bullying has burst on the scene in the past few years because of its apparent connection with school shootings by bullying victims. Basically, bullying is when a stronger, more aggressive child induces fear, distress or harm in a weaker child through physical, verbal or psychological intimidation.[70] Not only is physical harm done by bullies, but their threats and violence result in their victims being distressed and fearful to the point targets are afraid to attend classes, traverse the halls, play during recess or walk home after school; their entire lives and the school atmosphere suffer as a result.

Figure 2–4 graphically portrays the grades in which youths are most likely to be bullied. Roughly 5.1 percent of all students experience bullying during any given year. Although data are not available for Grades 1 through 5, recent research suggests that bullying may well begin in the first grade and continue to rise until the sixth grade; the extent of bullying in the sixth grade is clearly higher than that for succeeding years. From the sixth grade on, the evidence of bullying drops off steadily through the twelfth grade.

School environment is related to reports of bullying. The presence of street gangs in schools results in higher rates of bullying, as does the presence of students who are afraid of becoming the victims of attacks either at or on

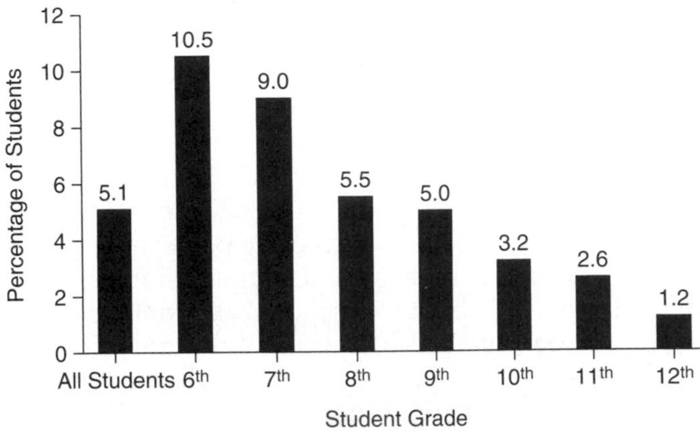

Figure 2–4 *Percentage of Students Ages Twelve Through Eighteen Who Reported Being Bullied at School, by Grade: 1999*

Source: Presented in U.S. Department of Education, National Center for Education Statistics. *Are America's Schools Safe? Students Speak Out:* 1999 School Crime Supplement (NCES 2002-331), by Lynn A. Addington, Sally A. Ruddy, Amanda K. Miller, and Jill F. DeVoe. Project Officer: Kathryn A. Chandler. Washington, DC: 2002, p. 57.

the way to school. Other important factors include those students who carry guns to school and students who avoid school classes and activities are also likely to be bullied, although whether these factors are causes or effects of bullying behavior are unclear. Somewhat surprising is the finding that increased security, such as the presence of security guards, hallway monitors and metal detectors apparently are unrelated to the evidence of bullying.[71] The most dramatic outcome of this mix of factors, of course, is shootings in the schools:

Just how bad is the problem of school shootings? Overall, the chances of students dying in school are exceedingly rare and, even in the communities in which they occur, are atypical events. Murder (even with suicide added), which occupies center stage in the minds of most parents, has less than one chance in a million of occurring in school.[72] In fact, juveniles are murdered at a rate forty times greater out of school than in school. Even the numbers of murdered students are overstated. The counts of the number of deaths, depending on the source, sometimes include suicides, youths murdered on the way to school, students who are on school grounds, and adults murdered by other adults. These distinctions sometimes are not made clear by the reporting media.

SUMMARY

The vast majority of all youths misbehave while they are growing up. Most end up being ignored or reprimanded lightly by their families and communities. Some find themselves in the custody of the police, some are held for juvenile court, and a few are remanded to adult courts.

Official statistics have contributed important findings about youth crime in American society: (1) Juveniles commit a disproportionate number of property and violent offenses. (2) Lower-class youths are involved in more frequent and more serious offenses than are middle-class youths; indeed, youth crime is primarily focused among lower-class youths. (3) African-American youths commit more frequent and more serious offenses than do White youths. (4) Urban youths commit more frequent and more serious offenses than do suburban or rural youths. (5) A small group of youthful offenders, primarily lower-class minority youths, commits at least half of the serious offenses in urban areas. (6) The interventions by the juvenile justice system frequently make youths worse rather than better.

Self-report studies have revealed that most youths are involved in delinquent behavior and that upward of 90 percent of delinquent acts are undetected or ignored. Self-report studies also indicate that girls commit more delinquent acts than are recorded in official accounts of delinquency, but boys still appear to commit more serious crimes than girls do. Victimization surveys reveal nearly four times as many victims each year as the statistics show in the Uniform Crime Reports. These surveys also reveal that juveniles are more likely to become victims than are adults. Together, these unofficial measurements of delinquency add to what is known officially about juvenile crime in the United States. As we continue to seek out the parameters of youth crime, important data are well developed in the area of drug use, and comprehensive data are beginning to emerge on school violence and bullying.

WEB SITES OF INTEREST

The student interested in examining statistics and research findings on juvenile crime, new data from the Bureau of Justice Statistics, or information on drugs and crime facts should go to the Bureau of Justice Statistics at http://www.ojp.usdoj.gov/bjs/ and click on the subject link of interest; for example, for new data click on the link titled "What's new."

CRITICAL THINKING QUESTIONS

1. What do the Uniform Crime Reports generally show about youth crime in the United States?
2. What do juvenile court statistics show about youth crime in the United States?
3. What can self-report studies tell us that official accounts of youth crime cannot?
4. What do you believe the connection is between the maltreatment of children in their homes and on the streets and their involvement in crime and delinquency?

NOTES

1. Edward Sagarin, "Foreword," in *Careers of the Violent: The Dangerous Offender and Criminal Justice,* Stuart J. Miller, Simon Dinitz, and John P. Conrad (Lexington, MA: Lexington Books, 1982), ix.
2. LaMar T. Empey, *Studies in Delinquency: Alternatives to Incarceration* (Washington, DC: U.S. Department of Health, Education and Welfare, Office of Juvenile Delinquency and Youth Development, 1967), 27–32; Maynard L. Erickson and LaMar T. Empey, "Court Records, Undetected Delinquency and Decision-Making," *Journal of Criminal Law, Criminology and Police Science* 54 (December 1963), 456–469.
3. William T. Pink and Mervin F. White, "Delinquency Prevention: The State of the Art," in *The Juvenile Justice System,* edited by Malcolm W. Klein (Beverly Hills, CA: Sage Publications, 1976), 9.
4. Howard N. Snyder, *Juvenile Arrests 1998* (Washington DC: Office of Juvenile Justice and Delinquency Prevention, 1999), pp. 1–2; Federal Bureau of Investigation, *Crime in the United States: Uniform Crime Reports 2001* (Washington, DC: Government Printing Office, 2002), 242.
5. Federal Bureau of Investigation, Uniform Crime Reports 2000, Oct. 28, 2001, Table 39, 222–226, 228–231, 246.
6. Federal Bureau of Investigation, Uniform Crime Reports 2001, 216, 250, 251.
7. *Uniform Crime Reports 2001 Tables 39, 40,* 246, 248.
8. Federal Bureau of Investigation, Uniform Crime Reports 2001, p. 241; and from Charles Puzzanchera, Anne L. Stahl, Terrence A. Finnegan, Howard N. Snyder, Rowen S. Poole, and Nancy Tierney. (2000). *Juvenile Court Statistics 1999.* Washington, DC: Office of Juvenile Justice and Delinquency Prevention, 2002, 39.
9. Federal Bureau of Investigation, Uniform Crime Reports 2001, Table 36, 242.
10. Federal Bureau of Investigation, Uniform Crime Reports 2001, Table 43, 253.
11. Uniform Crime Reports 2001, Table 43, 253.
12. Federal Bureau of Investigation, *Crime in the United States 2000* (Washington, DC: Uniform Crime Reports, U.S. Department of Justice, Oct. 22, 2001), 222–226, 228–231.
13. Howard N. Snyder et al., *Juvenile Court Statistics, 1984* (Washington, DC: Office of Juvenile Justice and Delinquency Prevention, 1987).
14. The data noted below are for 1997, the last year for which these data are published. See Charles Puzzanchera, Anne L. Stahl, Terrence A. Finnegan, Howard N. Snyder, Rowen S. Poole and Nancy Tierney, *Juvenile Court Statistics 1997*. Washington, DC: Office of Juvenile Justice and Delinquency Preventions, 2000, 7.
15. Ibid., 46–47.
16. Ibid., 15.
17. Ibid., 46–47.

18. And from Charles Puzzanchera, Anne L. Stahl, Terrence A. Finnegan, Howard N. Snyder, Rowen S. Poole, and Nancy Tierney, *Juvenile Court Statistics 1999*. Washington, DC: Office of Juvenile Justice and Delinquency Prevention, 2002, 39.
19. Ibid., 8–9.
20. Cathy Maston and Patsy Klaus, *National Crime Victimization Survey 2001*. Accessed at BJS Web site, February 10, 2003 (Washington, DC: U.S. Department of Justice, Bureau of Justice Statistics), Criminal Victimization in the United States. N.P. listed. See table numbers.
21. U.S. Department of Justice, Bureau of Justice Statistics, *Criminal Victimization*, Summary Findings (Washington, DC: U.S. Department of Justice), nd, http://www.ojp.usdoj.gov/bjs/, 2/11/03.ncj143288, 1.
22. Ibid., Table 3.
23. For an excellent review of the reporting of crimes against juveniles, see David Finkelhor and Richard Ormrod, "Reporting Crimes Against Juveniles" (Washington, DC: Office of Juvenile Justice and Delinquency Prevention, 1999).
24. Austin L. Porterfield, "Delinquency and Its Outcome in Court and College," *American Journal of Sociology* 49 (November 1947), 199–208; James F. Short, Jr., "A Report on the Incidence of Criminal Behavior, Arrests, and Convictions in Selected Groups," *Research Studies of the State College of Washington* 22 (June 1954), 110–118; James F. Short Jr. and F. Ivan Nye, "Extent of Unrecorded Juvenile Delinquency: Tentative Conclusions," *Journal of Criminal Law, Criminology, and Police Science* 49 (November–December 1958), 207–13); James F. Short Jr., and F. Ivan Nye, "Reported Behavior as a Criterion of Deviant Behavior," *Social Problems* 5 (Winter 1957–1958), 207–13; LaMar T. Empey, *Studies in Delinquency: Alternatives to Incarceration* (Washington, DC: Government Printing Office, 1967), 27–32; Maynard L. Erickson and LaMar T. Empey, "Court Records, Undetected Delinquency, and Decision Making," *Journal of Criminal Law, Criminology, and Police Science* 54 (December 1963), 456–469.
25. David Huizinga and Delbert S. Elliott, "Juvenile Offenders: Prevalence, Offender Incidence, and Arrest Rates by Race," *Crime and Delinquency* 33 (April 1987), 208, 210; Franklin W. Dunford and Delbert S. Elliott, "Identifying Career Offenders Using Self-Report Data," *Journal of Research in Crime and Delinquency* 21 (February 1984), 57–82, 215.
26. Jerald G. Bachman, Lloyd D. Johnston, and Patrick M. O'Malley, *Monitoring the Future 1994* (Ann Arbor: Institute for Social Research, University of Michigan, 1994). Prepublication data received from the project staff of *Monitoring the Future 1995* just prior to the publication of the 2d edition of this book indicate that the trends for 1995 were, for the most part, within two percentage points of those noted in 1994.
27. J. R. Williams and Martin Gold, "From Delinquent Behavior to Official Delinquency," *Social Problems* 20 (1972), 202–229; Martin Gold and David J.

Reimer, *Changing Patterns of Delinquent Behavior Among Americans 13 to 16 Years Old* (Ann Arbor: Institute for Social Research, University of Michigan, 1974).

28. Delbert S. Elliott and Suzanne S. Ageton, "Reconciling Race and Class Differences in Self-Reported and Official Estimates of Delinquency," *American Sociological Review* 45 (February 1980), 103.
29. Gary Jensen and Raymond Eve, "Sex Differences in Delinquency: An Examination of Popular Sociological Explanations," *Criminology* 13 (1976), 427–488; Michael Hindelang, "Age, Sex, and the Versatility of Delinquent Involvements," *Social Problems* 18 (1979), 522–535; James Short and F. Ivan Nye, "Reported Behavior as a Criterion of Deviant Behavior," *Social Problems* 5 (1958), 207–213.
30. Steven Cernkovich and Peggy Giordano, "A Comparative Analysis of Male and Female Delinquency," *Sociological Quarterly* 20 (1979), 136–137.
31. Bachman et al., *Monitoring the Future 1994.*
32. Short and Nye, "Reported Behavior as a Criterion of Deviant Behavior," 207–213; F. Ivan Nye, James Short, and Virgil Olsen, "Socio-Economic Status and Delinquent Behavior," *American Journal of Sociology* 63 (1958), 381–89; Robert Dentler and Lawrence Monroe, "Social Correlates of Early Adolescent Theft," *American Sociological Review* 26 (1961), 381–89.
33. Travis Hirschi, *Causes of Delinquency* (Berkeley: University of California Press, 1969).
34. Richard E. Johnson, "Social Class and Delinquent Behavior: A New Test," *Criminology* 18 (May 1980), 91.
35. For a more complete examination of cohort studies, see Clemens Bartollas, *Juvenile Delinquency* (Boston: Allyn & Bacon, 1997), 37–43.
36. Marvin E. Wolfgang, Robert M. Figlio, and Thorsten Sellin, *Delinquency in a Birth Cohort* (Chicago: University of Chicago Press, 1972); Donna Martin Hamparian et al., *The Violent Few: A Study of Dangerous Juvenile Offenders* (Lexington, MA: Lexington Books, 1980); Lyle W. Shannon, *Assessing the Relationships of Adult Criminal Careers to Juvenile Careers: A Summary* (Washington, DC: Government Printing Office, 1982).
37. See Paul E. Tracy, Marvin E. Wolfgang, and Robert M. Figlio, *Delinquency in Two Birth Cohorts: Executive Summary* (Washington, DC: Government Printing Office, 1985).
38. Lloyd D. Johnston, Patrick M. O'Malley, and Jerald G. Bachman, *Monitoring the Future National Survey Results on Drug Use 1975–2001.* Volume 1: Secondary School Students (NIH Publication No. 02-5106). Bethesda, MD: National Institute on Drug Use, 9, 36–40.
39. Marvin E. Wolfgang, Terence P. Thornberry, and Robert M. Figlio, eds., *From Boy to Man, from Delinquency to Crime* (Chicago: University of Chicago Press, 1987), 37, 39.
40. Alfred Blumstein, David P. Farrington, and Soumyo Moitra, "Delinquency Careers: Innocents, Amateurs, and Persisters," in *Crime and Justice: An*

Annual Review, 6th ed., edited by Michael Tonry and Norval Morris (Chicago: University of Chicago Press, 1985), 187–220.

41. D. P. Farrington, "Offending from 10 to 25 Years of Age," in *Prospective Studies of Crime and Delinquency*, edited by K. T. Van Dusen and S. A. Mednick (Boston: Kluwer-Nijhoff, 1983).
42. Suzanne S. Ageton and Delbert S. Elliott, *The Incidence of Delinquent Behavior in a National Probability Sample of Adolescents* (Boulder, CO: Behavioral Research Institute, 1978).
43. See Wolfgang et al., *Delinquency in a Birth Cohort*, and Hamparian et al., *The Violent Few.*
44. Susan K. Datesman and Michael Aickin, "Offense Specialization and Escalation Among Status Offenders," *Journal of Criminal Law and Criminology* 75 (1984), 1260–1273.
45. Edward Mulvey and John LaRosa, "Delinquency Cessation and Adolescent Development: Preliminary Data," *American Journal of Orthopsychiatry* 56 (1986), 212–214.
46. Alicia Rand, "Transitional Life Events and Desistance from Delinquency and Crime," in *From Boy to Man*, edited by Wolfgang et al., 134–163.
47. Barry Glassner, Margaret Ksander, and Bruce Berg, "A Note on the Deterrent Effect of Juvenile vs. Adult Jurisdiction," *Social Problems* 31 (December 1983), 221.
48. Clemens Bartollas, Stuart J. Miller, and Simon Dinitz, *Juvenile Victimization: The Institutional Paradox* (New York: Halsted Press, 1976).
49. Ibid.
50. See Wolfgang et al., *From Boy to Man*, 21.
51. Daniel S. Nagin and Raymond Paternoster, "On the Relationship of Past to Future Participation in Delinquency," *Criminology* 29 (May 1991), 163, 165.
52. Snyder et al., *Juvenile Offenders and Victims*, 8.
53. Childrens Bureau, *Victims: Child Maltreatment 2000* (Washington, DC: U.S. Department of Health and Human Services). Go to http://www.acf.dhhs.gov/programs/cb/publications/cm98/ and then scroll down to Child Maltreatment.
54. Ibid.
55. Federal Bureau of Investigation, *Crime in the U.S. 2001: Uniform Crime Reports* (Washington, DC: U.S. Department of Justice), 23.
56. See "Child Fatalities Fact Sheet," National Center on Child Abuse and Neglect, downloaded on Jan. 7, 2000, from http://www.calib.com/nccanch
57. FBI, *Crime in the United States*, 2001, 23.
58. Howard N. Snyder, *Juvenile Offenders and Victims: 1999 National Report* (Washington, DC: National Center for Juvenile Justice, 1999) 18.
59. Calculated from FBI, *Crime in the United States*, 18, Table 2–11.
60. *Ibid.*, 16, Table 2–6.

61. Cathy Spatz Widom and Michael Mansfield, *The Cycle of Violence Revisited* (Washington, DC: National Institute of Justice, 1996).
62. Cathy Spatz Widom, "Victims of Childhood Sexual Abuse—Later Criminal Consequences," *Research Brief* (Washington, DC: National Institute of Justice, Office of Justice Programs, 1995), 4–5.
63. George G. Knox, *An Introduction to Gangs* (Berrien Springs, MI: Vande Verde, 1993).
64. G. Knox, D. Laske, and E. Tromanhauser, "Chicago Schools Revisited," *Bulletin of the Illinois Public Education Association* 16 (Spring 1992).
65. For more information on drive-by shootings, see William B. Sanders, *Gangbangs and Drive-By: Grounded Culture and Juvenile Gang Violence* (New York: Aldine De Gruyter, 1994).
66. U.S. Department of Education, National Center for Education Statistics. *Are America's Schools Safe? Students Speak Out: 1999* School Crime Supplement (NCES 2002-2003) by Lynn Addington, Sally A. Ruddy, Amanda K. Miller, and Jill F. DeVoe, Project Officer: Kathryn A. Chandler. Washington, DC: 2002, iii, 30–39.
67. Phillip Kaufman, Xianglei Chen, Susan P. Choy, Kathryn A. Chandler, Christopher D. Chapman, Michael R. Rand, and Cheryl Ringel, *Executive Summary: Indicators of School Crime and Safety 1998* (Washington, DC: U.S. Department of Education, U.S. Department of Justice, October 1998), 5, 6.
68. Phillip Kaufman et al., *Executive Summary,* 6.
69. Howard N. Snyder, *Juvenile Offenders and Victims: 1999 National Report,* 32, 33.
70. D. P. Farrington (1993). "Understanding and Preventing Bullying," in Tonry, M. (ed.). "Crime and Justice: A Review of Research (vol. 17). (Chicago, IL: University of Chicago Press, 381–458), cited in U.S. Department of Education, National Center for Education Statistics. *Are America's Schools Safe? Students Speak Out: 1999 School Crime Supplement* (NCES 2002–331), by Lynn A. Addington, Sally A. Ruddy, Amanda K. Miller, and Jill F. DeVoe. Project Officer: Kathryn A. Chandler. Washington, DC: 2002), 55.
71. Ibid.
72. Elizabeth Donohue, Vincent Schiraldi, and Jason Ziedenberg, "Schoolhouse Hype: School Shootings and the Real Risks Kids Face in America," accessed July 1999, http://www.cjcj.org/jpi/schoolhouse.html

3

CAUSES OF JUVENILE CRIME

OBJECTIVES

1. To understand the role free will has in the classical school's understanding of delinquent behavior
2. To be able to discuss the main forms of positivism
3. To examine how each form of positivism explains juvenile law breaking
4. To be able to determine what types of juvenile offenders are more responsible for their actions
5. To understand how rational choice theory differs from positivism

KEY TERMS

autonomy
biological positivism
containment theory
criminal opportunity theory
cultural deviance theory
deterministic view
differential association theory
excitement
fate
felicific calculus
free will
labeling perspective
Marxist perspective
positivism
psychoanalysis
rational choice theory
reinforcement theory
routine activity approach
smartness
social control theory
social disorganization theory
sociobiologists
sociopath
strain theory
trouble
toughness

I made up my mind the last time I was released from Fairfield that I was going to stay out of trouble. I went home and told my friends that I was going to stay clean. Then, my mother got sick, needed an operation, and couldn't work, I am older than my brothers and sisters and someone had to put food on the table. Instead of telling my friends to stay out of my face, I agreed to pull an armed robbery with them. We got caught and here I am.

—Nineteen-year-old institutionalized male

I got to the point that I was drug dependent. I went from pot to pills. Crystal (meth) is what really hooked me. To get money for drugs, I sold drugs, robbed houses, and did everything but sell my body. When you are drug dependent, you are willing to do anything to get your drugs. Even when I was arrested and sat in jail at 18 for a drug bust, I didn't know if I could walk away from drugs. But I knew if I didn't, the next step was the penitentiary.

—Twenty-two-year-old female college senior

We robbed the liquor store because we knew we wouldn't get caught. The owner of this store was half blind and old. He didn't move too good. He had a gun, but we knew there was no way he could hit us. If he went for his gun, we would have blown him away. Man, robbing that place was like taking candy from a baby.

—Seventeen-year-old male on aftercare[1]

These three juvenile offenders had some understanding of why they were violating the law. The first suggested that he committed the armed robbery because his mother became sick, and, as the oldest sibling, he felt responsible for putting food on the table. The second offender was aware that she committed crimes to support her drug dependency. With the assistance of another youth, the third offender committed the armed robbery because it made sense to rob a store in which the owner had poor sight and was old.

More typically, juvenile offenders do not know why they broke the law. An institutional social worker confronted Leo, a repetitive juvenile offender, "How could you rape that woman who had been so good to you? You told me she had given you cookies and milk on your way home from school for years. She was a good friend of your family and she was in her mid-70s. Why in the world did you rape her?" The youth responded, "I don't know." "And in my mind," the social worker added, "it is even more disturbing to me that you brag about it." "I don't brag about it," the youth interrupted. The social worker, shaking his head and dropping his voice, retorted, "I heard you talking with your peers yesterday about it. You were joking and lauging about what you had done." The youth said nothing.[2]

Even adult offenders are frequently unable to explain why they broke the law. Richard Speck, the murderer of seven student nurses in Chicago during the mid-1960s, reported to one of the authors: "I don't remember the crime. I don't remember killing those girls. I was stoned and drunk at the time. People think I'm some kind of monster. I don't know why I did it."[3]

Four explanations have been widely used to explain why juveniles commit youth crime. First, some hold that juveniles commit unlawful behavior because they have free will and rationally choose to do so. Second, biological and psychological causes have long had support for those seeking explanations for youth crime. This position supports the view that juvenile offenders either are biologically different from other youth or have experienced emotional damage in their early years. Third, social structural explanations argue that youths are out of step with the norms of society because they are inadequately socialized, have been influenced by antisocial peers, or are poor and have no stake in the system. Finally, multidimensional explanations are needed to understand why juveniles violate the law. Integrated explanations of delinquent behavior imply the combination of two or more existing theories on the basis of their perceived commonalities.

However, whether talking about youth crime arising from free will, biological or psychological inferiority, social causes, or integrated explanations (two or more existing theories), it is clear that any particular theory only accounts for part of the reasons for juvenile offenses. Some explanations are more powerful than others in explaining youth crime, but even the most powerful amounts to only a small piece in the larger puzzle of why juveniles commit youth crime.

WHAT IS THE RELATIONSHIP BETWEEN THEORY AND RESEARCH?

Throughout history, civilizations have developed many techniques for seeking truth. Magic and superstition; the divine right of kings; the guidance of prophets, priests, and philosophers; intuition; and common sense have all been called on to provide the answers to the great questions. The failure of these methods to provide reliable and valid knowledge has led thinkers to search for other, better sources of truth. The contemporary solution is called science, the proponents of which contend it provides more accurate answers than any other method yet discovered.

The two basic tools of science are theory and research, which are inextricably bound. Each helps to guide and direct the other. Research finds methods to collect data, helps to identify variables to be studied, tests variables for their worth, analyzes related variables, and suggests new directions for theory. Theory points the way to new research, helps derive new variables, builds interconnections among variables, interprets new and old ideas, builds systems of thoughts, and leads the way to new social and theoretical conclusions. Research collects and theory analyzes; research discovers and theory explains; research disproves and theory reorders. The process is never ending. Without it, we would be likely to wallow in ignorance, personal prejudice, and inaccurate information. We would also be doomed to repeat harmful and even dangerous practices.

Thus, the main task of a theory is to explain the events in the world. A theory attempts to explain the cause of past events and predicts when, where, and how future events will occur.[4] A theory is a basic building block indispensable for the advancement of human knowledge, but because social science theories can rarely be proven or rejected with the same finality as theory in the natural sciences, there exist several competing theories.

One of the most critical theoretical debates in the study of crime is over that of determinism versus free will. The basic issue is whether humans freely choose or whether other factors determine their choices. The concept of free will is based on the notion that we choose how to act. Crime or delinquency is viewed as purposeful activity resulting from rational decisions in which the pros and cons are weighed and the acts that promise the greatest potential gains are performed. Because juveniles and adults possess free will, make choices, and know what they are doing, those who commit crime are presumed to deserve punishment rather than treatment.

In contrast, the **deterministic view** holds that individuals cannot help committing criminal or delinquent acts because they are controlled either by internal factors (biological or psychological imbalances) or by external factors (poverty, learning crime from others, strain, or societal labeling). To put it another way, offenders are objects that react like billiard balls in response to different forces.[5] They, then, are presumed to need treatment rather than punishment because they are driven into crime. Our interpretation of this free will debate determines how we explain why individuals commit crime and what can be done about crime. Focus on Causation 3–1 examines the life of Lee Malvo, one of the snipers who terrorized the southeastern part of the nation during the fall of 2002.

FOCUS ON CAUSATION 3–1

THE MAKING OF A SNIPER: IS ANYONE TO BLAME?

Lee Boyd Malvo was born February 18, 1985, on the island of Jamaica. Malvo was raised in a single-parent home by his mother Una James, because his father, Leslie Samuel Malvo had abandoned him at an age when a son really needed his father. While trying to make money, Una James would leave her son alone on many occasions, sometimes for months at a time. One can only imagine the desperation, heartache, and feelings of not being wanted that a young boy would experience. Watching gangster rap on TV was one of the only hobbies Lee had in those early days, and he began to act out his aggressions at the age of fourteen; he reportedly smashed large holes in the walls of where he was living after the landlord shut off the electricity because of unpaid rent.

John Muhammad had his own problems. He had survived the Gulf War but apparently experienced many problems, including being a loner, unemployed, homeless, friendless, and, very likely, feelings of powerlessness and alienation; he also was divorced and, according to news reports, likely to lose contact with his children. Muhammad apparently felt a need for someone to control or, as some have argued, manipulated Malvo so that Muhammed's ex-wife could be a sniper victim.

Local media reports said that Malvo and John Muhammad might have met one another in Antigua where his mother left Malvo when he was younger. Malvo and Muhammad became very close in a short period of time and it wasn't long before Malvo was referring to Muhammad as "Dad." Getting rid of his Jamaican accent to sound more like Muhammad, Lee did whatever he could to make this new friend, who was now a dominant father figure in his life, happy. Becoming intrigued by Muhammad's books, Malvo started to read the Qu'ran instead of the Bible. We can only speculate at this time what Muhammad told, taught, or convinced Malvo into thinking and doing.

Malvo and Muhammad moved to Washington State and lived in a homeless shelter. Learning how to shoot a gun and working out every day, Lee became very strong and very good with a rifle. Muhammad nick-named Malvo "Sniper" and introduced him as such to friends; their shooting spree across the United States began shortly thereafter.

Arrested on October 24, 2002, Lee Malvo and John Muhammad were accused in at least twenty shootings, including thirteen deaths. At the time of the incidents, Malvo was seventeen years of age. After turning eighteen in 2003, Malvo was transferred to adult court in Virginia where he was found guilty of the charges and sentenced to life in prison without parole. Malvo may now be tried in Maryland and Louisiana. Muhammad was sentenced to death in Virginia.

Source: Alanna Santee and Stuart Miller prepared the above materials especially for this volume from the following sources, as well as materials in the public domain.

Newsweek "Father, Where Are Thou?", Fox News Channel, Associated Press, Bio: Lee Malvo, abc News "Brainwashed? Accused Sniper's Former Guardian Believes Malvo Was Influenced," www.abcnews.com, and from NewsMax.com, "Sniper Malvo's Double Life Revealed" PRNewsire.

Critical Thinking Questions:

Think through the theories of this chapter. Why did Malvo join with Muhammad to commit their murders? Did he have free will? Or was he programmed to commit his crimes because of the lack of a father, poor nurturing from his mother, or brainwashing by a substitute father? What do you think?

IS JUVENILE CRIME RATIONAL BEHAVIOR?

The association between criminal behavior and the rationality of crime has roots in the eighteenth-century classical school of criminology. More recently, there have been a number of approaches to the rationality of crime, especially rational choice theory.

CLASSICAL SCHOOL OF CRIMINOLOGY

Cesare Beccaria and Jeremy Bentham were the founders of the classical school of criminology. These scholars viewed humans as rational creatures who were willing to surrender enough liberty to the state so that society could establish rules and sanctions for the preservation of the social order.

In 1763, Cesare Bonesana Beccaria, Marquis of Beccaria, then only twenty-six and just out of law school, published *On Crimes and Punishment*. This essay was read avidly and translated into the languages of Europe.[6] Beccaria based the legitimacy of criminal sanctions on the social contract. The authority of making laws rested with the legislator, who should have only one view in sight: "the greatest happiness of the greatest number." Beccaria also saw punishment as a necessary evil and suggested that "it should be public, immediate, and necessary: the least possible in the case given; proportioned to the crime; and determined by the laws."[7] He then defined the purpose and consequences of punishment as being "to deter persons from the commission of crime and not to provide social revenge. Not severity, but certainty and swiftness in punishment best secure this result."[8]

In 1780, the Englishman Jeremy Bentham published *An Introduction to the Principles of Morals and Legislation*, which further developed the philosophy of the classical school.

Believing that a rational person would do what was necessary to achieve the most pleasure and the least pain, Bentham contended that punishment would deter criminal behavior, provided it was made appropriate to the crime. He stated that punishment has four objectives: (1) to prevent all offenses if possible, (2) to persuade a person who has decided to commit an offense to commit a less rather than a more serious one, (3) "to dispose [a person who has resolved upon a particular offense] to do no more mischief than is necessary to his purpose," and (4) to prevent the crime at as cheap a cost to society as possible.[9]

The basic theoretical constructs of the classical school of criminology were developed from the writings of Beccaria and Bentham: First, human beings were all looked on as rational creatures who, being free to choose their actions, could be held responsible for their behavior. This doctrine of **free will** was substituted for the widely accepted concept of theological determinism, which saw humans as predestined to certain actions. Second, punishment was justified because of its practical usefulness, or utilitarianism. No longer was punishment acceptable on the grounds of vengeful retaliation or as expiation on the basis of superstitious theories of guilt and repayment. The aim of punishment was the protection of society, and its dominant theme was deterrence. Third, the human being was presumed to be a creature governed by a **felicific calculus** oriented toward obtaining a favorable balance of pleasure and pain. Fourth, a rational scale of punishment was proposed that should be painful enough to deter the criminal from further offenses and to prevent others from following his or her example of crime. Fifth, sanctions should be proclaimed in advance of their use; these sanctions should be proportionate to the offense and should outweigh the rewards of crime. Sixth, equal justice should be offered to everyone. Finally, proponents of the classical school urged that individuals should be judged by the law solely for their acts, not for their beliefs.

According to the principles of the classical school, then, juveniles who commit serious crimes or continue to break the law are presumed to deserve punishment rather than treatment, because they possess free will and know what they are doing. Their delinquencies are viewed as purposeful activity resulting from rational decisions in which the pros and cons are weighed and the acts that promise the greatest potential gains are performed.[10]

Rational Choice Theory

Rational choice theory, largely borrowed primarily from the utility model in economics, is one of the hottest present-day topics in criminology. In its pure form, rational choice theory can be seen, at least in part, as an extension of the deterrence doctrine found in the classical school to include incentives as well as deterrence and to focus on the rational calculation of payoffs and costs before delinquent and criminal acts are committed.[11]

Philip J. Cook has developed what he calls **criminal opportunity theory.** He claims that "criminals tend to be somewhat selective in choosing a crime target and are most attracted to targets that appear to offer a high payoff with little effort or risk of legal consequence."[12] He sees the interaction between potential offenders who respond to the net payoff to crime and potential victims who take actions to modify the payoff to crime as akin to the interaction between buyers and sellers in a marketplace. Thus, in using the market perspective to examine the interaction between potential victims and offenders, criminal opportunity theory emphasizes individual choice guided by the perceived costs and benefits of criminal activity.[13]

Lawrence E. Cohen and Marcus Felson are guided by ecological concepts and the presumed rationality of offenders in developing a **routine activity approach** for analyzing crime rate trends and cycles. This approach links the dramatic increase in crime rates since 1960 to changes in the routine activity structure of U.S. society and to a corresponding increase in target suitability and decrease in the presence of "guardians," such as neighbors, friends, and family. The decline of the daytime presence of adult caretakers in homes and neighborhoods is partly the result of a trend toward increased female participation in the labor force.

Cohen and Felson believe that the volume and distribution of predatory crime are related to the interaction of three variables relating to the routine activities of U.S. life: the availability of suitable targets, the absence of capable guardians, and the presence of motivated offenders.[14]

Steven F. Messner and Kenneth Tardiff used the routine activities approach to help interpret patterns of homicides in Manhattan (New York City) and found that the routine activities approach does indeed provide a useful framework for interpreting the social ecology involved in urban homicides. They found that people's lifestyles affected their chances of being victimized. People who were victimized by strangers tended to go out more often, whereas those who preferred to stay at home were more likely to be killed by someone they knew.[15]

Ronald L. Akers's examination of rational choice theory led him to conclude that a key issue is whether or not the rational choice perspective proposes a purely "rational man" theory of criminal behavior. He questions: Does it argue for a direct resurrection of classical criminology in which each person approaches the commission or noncommission of a crime with a highly rational calculus? Is rational choice theory essentially free of all constraining elements? Does it propose that each individual chooses, with full free will and knowledge, to commit or not to commit a crime, taking into account a carefully reasoned set of costs and benefits?[16]

Akers answers these questions by saying that current rational choice models emphasize "limitations and constraints on rationality through lack of information, structural constraints, values, and other 'non-rational' influences?" "Indeed," Akers adds, "the rational choice models in the literature . . . paint a picture of partial rationality with all kinds of situational and cognitive constraints and all kinds of positivistic and deterministic notions of causes."[17]

Derek B. Cornish and Ronald V. Clarke's *The Reasoning Criminal* is probably the most frequently cited source on rational choice and crime. Yet in both the preface and the introductory essay, Cornish and Clarke say that the starting assumption of their model is that

> offenders seek to benefit themselves by their criminal behavior; that this involves the making of decisions and choices, however rudimentary on occasion, these processes might be; and that these processes exhibit a measure of rationality, albeit constrained by limits of time and ability and the availability of relevant information.[18]

They perceive offenders as "reasoning decision makers" based on the assumption that criminals or delinquents "exercise some degree of planning and foresight."[19]

In sum, rational choice theory in criminology has recently moved away from the strictly rational, reasoning model of behavior to a more limited and constrained role for rational thought. Rational choice theory does not even assume that all or even most delinquent or criminal acts result from clear, planned, well-informed, and calculated choices.[20] It can still be argued, of course, that the rational choice model places more emphasis on rationality and free will than do other theories of delinquent behavior and that this degree of rationality is not present in most juvenile crimes.[21]

HOW HAS DETERMINISM INFLUENCED THE DEVELOPMENT OF THE POSITIVE SCHOOL?

Beginning with a brief introduction to the theoretical constructs of the positive school, the biological, psychological, and sociological explanations of delinquency and crime are examined in this section.

Development of Positivism

According to **positivism,** human behavior is but one more facet of a universe that is part of a natural order, but human beings can study behavior and discover how natural laws operate. Two positions diverge at this point of natural law. One view states that, because a natural order with its own laws exists, to change human behavior is impossible. The other view is that, just as laws operate in the medical, biological, and physical sciences, laws govern human behavior, and these laws can be understood and used. The causes of human behavior, once discovered, can be modified to eliminate or ameliorate many of society's problems. This second position is the one most scientists accept. The concept, as it applies to juvenile justice, is called positivism.

Positivism became the dominant philosophical perspective of juvenile justice at the time the juvenile court was established at the beginning of the twentieth century. During the Progressive Era (the period from about 1890 to 1920), the wave of optimism that swept through U.S. society led to the acceptance of positivism. The doctrines of the emerging social sciences assured reformers that through positivism their problems could be solved. The initial step was to gather all the facts of the case. Equipped with these data, reformers were then expected to analyze the issues in scientific fashion and discover the right solution.[22]

Armed with these principles, reformers set out to deal with the problem of delinquency, confident that they knew how to find its cause. Progressives looked first to environmental factors, pinpointing poverty as the major cause of delinquency. Some Progressives were attracted also to the doctrine of eugenics and believed that the biological limitations of youthful offenders drove them to delinquency. But eventually the psychological origins of delinquency came to be more widely accepted than either the environmental or the biological origins.[23]

Positivism has three basic assumptions.[24] First, the character and personal backgrounds of individuals explain delinquent behavior. Positivism, relegating the law and its administration to a secondary role, looks for the cause of deviancy in the actor.

Second, the existence of scientific determinism is a critical assumption of positivism. Delinquency, like any other phenomenon, is seen as determined by prior causes; it does not just happen. Because of this deterministic position, positivism rejects the view that the individual exercises freedom, possesses reason, and is capable of choice.

Third, the delinquent is seen as fundamentally different from the nondelinquent. The task then is to identify the factors that have made the delinquent a different kind of person. In attempting to explain this difference, positivism has concluded that wayward youths are driven into crime by something in their physical makeup, by aberrant psychological impulses, or by the meanness and harshness of their social environment.[25]

Biological Positivism

Positivism was first applied to the study of crime with the writings of Cesare Lombroso, who is frequently acknowledged as the father of criminology. Lombroso insisted that all criminals were "born" criminal or atavistic, a reversion to an earlier evolutionary level; that is, the characteristics of primitive human beings periodically reappeared in certain individuals. He identified these characteristics as enormous jaws, high cheek bones, prominent superciliary arches, solitary lines in the palms, extreme size of the orbits, handle-shaped or sensile ears, insensibility to pain, extreme acute sight, tattooing, excessive idleness, love of orgies, and the irresistible craving for evil for its own sake.[26]

Early **biological positivism,** like Lombroso's theory of the born criminal, was quickly dismissed. The physical signs that Lombroso claimed identified the born criminal have been pointed out as a result of social environment and poor nutrition rather than as part of an individual's constitutional makeup. Charles Goring studied three thousand English convicts, with students and sailors serving as controls, and his results did not confirm Lombroso's assertion concerning the atavistic (or born) criminal.[27]

In the second half of the twentieth century, **sociobiologists** began to link genetic and environmental factors; they claimed that criminal behavior, like other behaviors, has both biological and social aspects. These sociobiologists have investigated the relationship between antisocial behavior and biological factors and environment through studies of twins and adoption, chromosomal abnormalities, electrodermal activity and pyschopathy, minimal functioning, intelligence, physique, and chemical imbalances in the body.

In the twenty-first century, the two areas of sociobiology that are receiving the most attention are neuropsychological factors and delinquency and the relationship between temperament and negative behavior.

Terrie E. Moffitt's work is highly regarded in terms of neuropsychological factors and delinquency. Moffitt and colleagues' examination of the neuropsychological status of several hundred New Zealand males between the ages of thirteen and eighteen found that poor neuropsychological scores "were associated with early onset of delinquency" but were "unrelated to delinquency that began in adolescence."[28] Moffitt's developmental theory views delinquent behavior as proceeding along two developmental paths. On one path, children develop a lifelong path of delinquency at an age as early as three. They may begin to hit and bite at age four, shoplift and be truant at age ten, sell cars and steal cars at age sixteen, rob and rape at age twenty-two, and commit fraud and child abuse at age thirty. [29] According to Moffitt, these "life-course-persistent" (LCP) delinquents continue their illegal acts throughout the conditions and situations they face. During childhood, they may also exhibit such neuropsychological problems as deficit disorders or hyperactivity and learning problems in schools. On the other path, the majority of delinquents begin offending during the adolescent years and desist from delinquent behaviors around the eighteenth birthday. Moffitt refers to these youthful offenders as "adolescent-limited" (AL) delinquents.[30]

Activity and emotionality are two behaviors that identify a child's temperament. Activity refers to motor movements, such as the movement of arms and legs, crawling, or walking. Children who exhibit an inordinate amount of movement compared with peers are often labeled "hyperactive" or as having an attention deficit disorder (generally referred to as attention deficit hyperactivity disorder or ADHD). Emotionality ranges from very little reaction to intense emotional reactions that are out of control.

The hyperactive child remains a temperamental mystery. This child's three behaviors are impulsivity (shifts quickly from one activity to another), inattention (is easily distracted and does not want to listen), and excessive motor activity (cannot sit still, runs about, is talkative, and noisy). Educators note that ADHD children have difficulty staying on task, sustaining academic achievement in the school setting, maintaining control over their behavior, and remaining cognitively organized.[31]

In sum, early biological positivism was replaced by sociobiology and has more support in the criminological community. However, criminologists generally are reluctant to place much credence in biological explanations of delinquent behaviors because they generally omit social explanations.

Psychological Positivism

Psychological factors have always been more popular in the United States in explaining juvenile offending than have biological or sociobiological

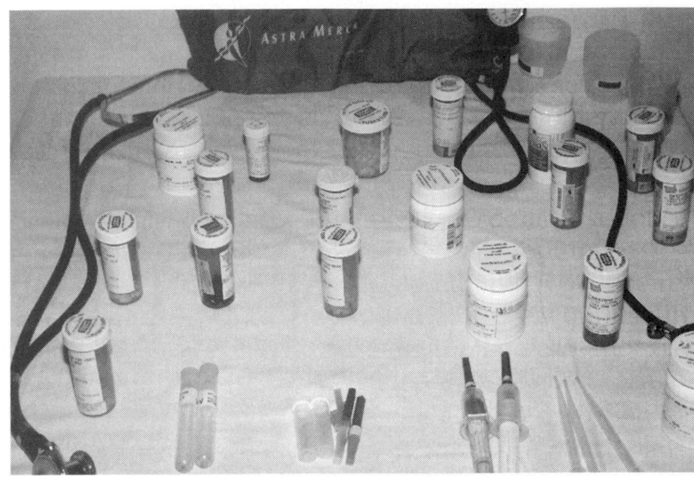

Modern biological and medical research is changing our conceptions of what causes delinquency and thus, how to treat it. (Photo by Kathryn Miller.)

factors. An early psychological explanation of juvenile offending was the psychoanalytic explanation. More recently, psychopathic factors, sensation seeking and delinquency, and reinforcement theory have received considerable attention.

Psychoanalytic Explanations

Sigmund Freud, in developing **psychoanalysis,** contributed three insights that have shaped the handling of juvenile delinquents: (1) the personality is made up of three components; (2) all normal children pass through three psychosexual stages of development; and (3) a person's personality traits are developed in early childhood.

Freud's theory of the personality involves the id, the ego, and the superego. The id has to do with the person's raw instincts and primitive drives; it wants immediate gratification of its needs and therefore tends to be primitive and savage. The ego and superego, the other two components, have the express purpose of controlling the primitive drives of the id. The ego mediates between the id and the superego and is important in the socialization of the child. The superego, or the conscience, internalizes the rules of society. Thus, as a child develops, he or she learns to distinguish socially acceptable behavior from socially unacceptable behavior.[32]

Freud identified the oral, anal, and phallic stages as the life stages that shape personality development. The first stage, the oral one, is experienced by the newborn infant. In this stage, pleasure is realized through eating, sucking, and chewing. In the anal stage, normally occurring between one and three years of age, urinary and bowel movements replace sucking as the basic source of pleasure for the child. During the phallic stage, which normally takes place between the ages of three and six, the child receives pleasure from the genitals. Each stage brings increased social demands on the child and affects the way in which he or she deals with basic, innate drives. The sexual and aggressive drives, in particular, create tensions that a child must learn to resolve in socially acceptable ways.[33]

Freud also contended that by age five, all of the essential ingredients of a child's adult personality are determined. Consequently, what a child has experienced emotionally by the age of five will affect that child the rest of his or her life. If emotional traumas are experienced in childhood, they are likely to cause lifelong psychological problems.[34] Offending across the life course, according to this position, is continually affected by what a person has experienced as a young child.

Freud's followers have identified four ways in which emotional problems developed in childhood might lead to delinquent behavior.[35] First, delinquent behavior is related to neurotic development in the personality. Freud established a relationship between desire and behavior; that is, youths may feel guilty about a socially unacceptable desire, and, as a result, seek out situations in which to be punished and then follow their punishments up with inappropriate and self-defeating behaviors.

Second, Freudians attribute delinquent behavior to a defective superego. The failure to develop a normally functioning superego can result in the inability to feel guilt, to learn from experience, or to feel affection toward others.[36] Such individuals, sometimes called sociopathic or psychopathic, may express aggressive and antisocial behavior toward others.

Third, violent delinquent behavior is sometimes explained by the tendency of children with an overly developed superego to repress all negative emotional feelings throughout childhood to the degree that these repressed feelings explode in a violent act in adolescence. So-called model adolescents occasionally become involved in violent crimes toward parents and neighbors, sometimes horribly mutilating their victims.[37] (See Focus on Causation 3–2.)

Fourth, unlawful activities can be related to a search for compensatory gratification. According to Freud, individuals who were deprived at an early age of development will later seek the gratification they missed. The Freudian interpretation is that an adolescent may become an alcoholic to satisfy an oral craving or may become sadistic because of poor toilet training received during the anal period.

Sensation Seeking and Delinquency

Sensation seeking can be defined "as an individual's need for varied, novel and complex sensations and experiences and the willingness to take physical and social risks for the sake of such experience."[38] Derived from optimal arousal theory, this construct assumes that organisms are driven or motivated to obtain an optimal level of arousal.[39]

Recently, the relationship between sensation seeking and crime has received frequent attention. M. J. Hindelang found that delinquents are more pleasure seeking than are nondelinquents.[40] Helene Raskin White, Erich W.

FOCUS ON CAUSATION 3–2

KEEPING THE LID ON THE ID

The authors have worked with and are familiar with a number of youths whose behavior appears to be explained by Freudian theory. The theory, it may be remembered, argues that the internal forces of the id constantly are seeking expression in society. Some of these forces are instinctual in nature, with some being destructive and some pleasure seeking. All of us, in other words, come into society ready and desiring to be destructive on the one hand and to seek pleasure on the other. Society, however, cannot permit these types of behavior and still survive, so society and its agents—the family, religion, education, and other institutions—attempt to shape our desires in socially acceptable directions. The results can sometimes be disastrous.

A fairly common scenario therapists experience is that of youths who, for seemingly unexplained reasons, suddenly break out into violent and uncontrollable behaviors. One youth the authors worked with was an Eagle Scout, straight "A" student, Sunday school teacher, and all-around good kid.

One day, however, he took a rifle and shot his mother through the kitchen window and went back to the family's garage and killed his father. Upon examination, therapists found that his parents, who were rigidly fundamentalist, always demanded perfection from him and never permitted him to express his own feelings and desires. Freud would argue that his feelings were totally suppressed by his ego and superego. As time went on, his rage built until his ego and superego could no longer contain it. The rage finally broke through his defenses and the result was the killing of his parents.

Labouvie, and Marsha E. Bates found that both male and female delinquents have higher rates of sensation seeking and lower rates of inhibited behavior than nondelinquents.[41]

Jack Katz's controversial book, *Seduction of Crime,* conjectures that when individuals commit a crime, they become involved in "an emotional process—seductions and compulsions that have special dynamics." It is this "magical" and "transformative" experience that makes crime "sensible," even sensually "compelling." For example, he states that for many adolescents, shoplifting and vandalism offer an exciting experience, not because of the act, but because if adults see them do it and the youths still can get away with it, the youths will feel they have proved their competence in society.[42]

Katz is arguing that instead of approaching criminal or delinquent behavior from the traditional focus on background factors, what needs more consideration are the foreground or situational factors that directly precipitate antisocial acts and reflect crimes' sensuality. According to Katz, offenders' immediate social environment and experiences encourage them to conceive of crimes as sensually compelling.[43]

The Psychopath

The psychopath (also known as the **sociopath,** antisocial personality, person with a conduct disorder, and a host of other names) is acknowledged as the personality of the hard-core juvenile offender. The claim is made that these are chiefly the unwanted, rejected children, who grow up but remain undomesticated "children" and never develop trust in or loyalty to other adults.[44] Hervey Cleckley gave the most complete clinical description of this type of personality. He indicated that the psychopath is charming and of good intelligence; is not delusional or irrational; is unreliable; is insecure and cannot be trusted; lacks shame and remorse; will commit all kinds of misdeeds for astonishingly small stakes; and sometimes, for no reason at all; has poor judgment, never learns from experience, and will repeat over and over again patterns of self-defeating behavior; has no real capacity for love; lacks insight; does not respond to consideration, kindness, or trust; and shows a consistent inability to make or follow any sort of life plan.[45]

The continuity between childhood symptoms of emotional problems and adult behavior emerged in L. N. Robins' thirty-year follow-up of 526 white childhood patients in a St. Louis, Missouri, guidance clinic in the 1920s. Robins was looking for clues of the adult "antisocial personality," or "sociopathy."[46] Excluding cases involving organic brain damage, schizophrenia, mental retardation, or symptoms that appeared only after heavy drug or alcohol use, she found that the adult sociopath is almost invariably an antisocial child grown up. Indeed, she found no case of adult sociopathy without antisocial behavior before the age of eighteen. Over 50 percent of the sociopathic males showed an onset of symptoms before the age of eight.[47]

Linda Mealey argues that there are two kinds of sociopaths: primary sociopaths and secondary sociopaths. Primary sociopaths have inherited traits that predispose them to illegal behavior; that is, they have a genotype that predisposes them to antisocial behavior. Secondary sociopaths, in contrast, are constitutionally normal but are influenced by such environmental factors as poor parenting. Thus, she argues that one type of sociopathic behavior has a genetic basis and the other is environmentally induced.[48]

Reinforcement Theory

James Q. Wilson and Richard Herrnstein's *Crime and Human Nature* combines biosocial factors and psychological research with rational choice theory to redevelop reinforcement theory.[49] Wilson and Herrnstein consider potential causes of crime and of noncrime within the context of **reinforcement theory,** that is, the theory that behavior is governed by its consequent rewards and punishments, as reflected in the history of the individual.

The rewards of crime, according to Wilson and Herrnstein, are found in the form of material gain, revenge against an enemy, peer approval, and sexual gratification. The consequences of crime take place with pains of conscience, disapproval of peers, revenge of the victim and, most importantly, the possibility of punishment. The rewards of crime tend to be more immediate, whereas the rewards of noncrime generally are realized in the future. The authors are quick to dismiss evidence that is inconsistent with their theoretical framework, but, as few have done in the field of criminology, they are able to show how gender, age, intelligence, families, schools, communities, labor markets, mass media, drugs, as well as variations across time, culture, and race greatly influence the propensity to commit criminal behavior, especially violent offenses.[50]

Wilson and Herrnstein's theory does have serious flaws. Most important, their theory consistently shows a disdain for the social context in which crime occurs. What Wilson and Herrnstein do, in effect, is to factor society out of their considerations of crime. Instead of examining criminal behavior as part of complex social mechanisms and attempting to understand the connection, they typically conclude that no conclusion is possible from the available data, and therefore no programs for reducing criminality among groups perceived as major sources of crime are worth their costs.[51] In Focus on the Offender 3–3, some of the emotional problems that contributed to unlawful behaviors are documented.

Sociological Positivism

Social structure, social process, and conflict theories are the three main divisions of the sociological explanations of crime and delinquency. The basic flaw of explanations based on the individual, according to these sociological theories, is that such interpretations fail to come to grips with the underlying social and cultural conditions giving rise to youthful offending. These sociological theories add that the overall crime picture reflects conditions requiring collective social solutions and that therefore social reform, rather than individual counseling, must be given the highest priory in efforts to reduce crime problems.

Social Structural Theories

Using official statistics as their guide, social structure theorists claim that such forces as social disorganization, cultural deviance, and status frustration are so powerful that they induce lower-class individuals to become involved in criminal and delinquent behaviors.

1. *Social disorganization theory.* Clifford R. Shaw and Henry D. McKay's **social disorganization theory** views crime as resulting from the breakdown of social control by the traditional primary groups, such as the family and the neighborhood, because of the social disorganization of the community.

FOCUS ON THE OFFENDER 3–3

EMOTIONAL PROBLEMS OF DELINQUENTS

We've the kids that mental health has called untreatable. We've the severe type of kids who have been involved in some heavy acts. They've pulled knives on people and are physically aggressive.

—Alternative school teacher

A lot of our kids realize that they really can't cope like the other kids their age and that they've inadequacies. They don't feel very good about themselves and have poor self-concepts. Their façade is a means of overcompensation for some of their inadequacies.

—Alternative school teacher

They've real problems dealing with authority. You've got to relate with them differently. You don't want to diminish your authority in any way, but yet you can't come across as being rigid and unyielding. You have to maintain the view that you'll call the shots. It's also important for you to communicate that you want to work with them and that their opinion is important.

—Alternative school teacher

I had a 15-year-old boy on my caseload who committed a lot of burglaries and then eventually killed his father. He had been terribly abused all his life.

—Probation officer

Gang kids were like other kids the first time you met them, but then as you got to know them you realized that they really had a lot of emotional problems. The way they looked at life was a negative sort of way. Their basic theme was to rip off everyone you can because they would rip you off if you gave them a chance.

—Probation officer

Source: Interviewed between 1985 and 1988 in a Midwestern state.

Critical Thinking Questions:

Do these individuals who work with these youths make the point that their emotional problems caused their behaviors? What would it take (degree of emotional problems) so that adolescents would no longer be considered responsible for their negative behaviors?

Shaw and McKay's studies revealed that high–delinquency areas are found in disorganized communities characterized by physically deteriorated and condemned buildings, economic dependence, population mobility, heterogeneous populations, high rates of school truancy, infant morality, and tuberculosis.[52]

2. *Cultural deviance theory.* Walter B. Miller contends that the lower class has its own cultural history and that the motivation to become involved in criminal activities is intrinsic to lower-class culture. Miller's **cultural deviance theory** argues that the lower-class culture is characterized by a set of focal concerns, or values, that command widespread attention and a high degree of emotional involvement. The focal concerns consist of trouble, toughness, smartness, excitement, fate and autonomy.[53]

Trouble: Getting into and out of trouble represents a major preoccupation of the lower class, and fighting, drinking, and sexual adventures are basic causes of trouble for the lower class.

Toughness: The "tough guy" who is hard, fearless, undemonstrative, and a good fighter is the ideal personality in the eyes of lower-class males.

Smartness: This value among the lower class involves the desire to outsmart, outfox, con, and dupe others.

Excitement: The quest for excitement leads to the widespread use of alcohol and drugs by other sexes and to extensive gambling.

Fate: Lower-class individuals feel that their lives are subject to a set of forces over which they have little control.

Autonomy: Desire for personal independence is an important concern for lower-class persons because they feel controlled so much of the time.[54]

Marvin Wolfgang and Franco Ferracuti also agree that a subculture of violence exists among males in the lower class that legitimizes the use of violence in various social situations. The subculture's norms, according to Wolfgang and Ferracuti, are separated from the larger societal value system. An always-present theme of violence influences lifestyles, the socialization process, and interpersonal relationships. It is anticipated that violence will be used to solve social conflicts and dilemmas. Indeed, those who fail to turn to violence, especially when they are threatened or insulted, will encounter rejection by their peer group.[55]

3. *Status frustration theory.* In an early version of **strain theory,** Robert K. Merton theorized that cultural goals and the means to achieving these goals must be reasonably well integrated if a culture is to be stable and smooth-running. If individuals feel that a particular goal is important, they should have legitimate means of attaining it. The cultural goal of American society, according to Merton, is success, but the inequality of life in this nation produces structural pressures toward deviation in criminal behavior. In Table 3–1,

Table 3–1 *Merton's Theory of Anomie*

1. Conformity	+	+
2. Innovation	+	−
3. Ritualism	−	+
4. Retreatism	−	−
5. Rebellion	±	±

Source: This material appears in Robert K. Merton, "Social Structure and Anomie," *American Sociological Review* 3 (1938), p. 676.

types of individual adaptation are listed: a plus (+) signifies acceptance, a minus (−) signifies rejection, and a plus-and-minus (±) signifies a rejection of the prevailing values and a substitution of new ones.

Richard A. Cloward and Lloyd E. Ohlin added that lower-class cultures are asked to orient their behavior toward the prospect of accumulating wealth, while they are largely denied the means of doing so legitimately. Thus, delinquent subcultures developed as collective social adjustments to the strains of blocked opportunity.[56] Albert K. Cohen's status frustration (or strain) theory suggests that the destructive and malicious behavior of lower-class delinquent subcultures is a reaction to their failure to achieve middle-class norms and values.[57]

Social Process Theories

Social process theories examine the interactions between people and their environment that influence individuals to become involved in criminal or delinquent behaviors. These sociopsychological theories became popular in the 1960s because they provided a theoretical mechanism for understanding how environmental factors influence individual decision making. Differential association, containment, social control, and labeling theories are the social process theories that have been the most widely received.

1. *Differential association theory.* According to Edwin H. Sutherland's **differential association theory,** criminals and youthful offenders learn crime from others. Thus, crime, like any other form of behavior, is a product of social interaction. Sutherland began with the notion that criminal behavior is to be expected of those individuals who have internalized a preponderance of definitions favorable to law violations. That is, individuals are taught their basic values, norms, skills, and perceptions of self from others, and, therefore, it only makes sense that they also learn crime from "significant others."[58]

The life of Jack Henry Abbott aptly shows how individuals learn crime from others. While in prison, Abbott wrote In the Belly of the Beast, a convincing narration and a penetrating insight into the brutality of prison life. His book gained him a reputation as a skilled author and a rehabilitated inmate. Praised in the high circles of New York's literary elite, he was soon granted an early parole by state officials. Shortly after his release, Abbott became engaged in a verbal dispute with a New York City waiter. Abbott wanted to use the restaurant's restroom, but the waiter informed him that there was none available. Although accounts differ about what happened next, the result was that Abbott fatally knifed the waiter in the alley. When he was apprehended and charged with the murder, Abbott claimed that he acted as he did because he had learned to act that way. He had spent most of his life in juvenile and adult correctional institutions, and it was this experience that taught him to act the way he did.[59]

2. *Containment theory.* Walter C. Reckless developed **containment theory** in order to explain why individuals do not commit crime and delinquent acts. He argued that individuals are affected by a variety of forces, some driving them toward—and others restraining them from—crime. As a control theory, which can explain both conforming behavior and deviance, containment theory has two elements: an inner control system and an outer control system. Internal containment is made up of self-control, positive self-concept, ego strength, a well-developed superego, high frustration tolerance, and a high sense of responsibility. External containment represents the buffers in the person's immediate environment that are able to hold him or her within socially acceptable bounds. The assumption is that strong internal containment and reinforcing external containment provide insulation against delinquent or criminal behavior.[60]

Containment theory involves both outer and inner containment, but inner containment, or self-concept, has received far more attention than has outer containment. Walter C. Reckless, Simon Dinitz, and their students spent over a decade investigating the effects of self-concept on delinquent behavior. The subjects for this study were sixth-grade boys living in the area of Columbus, Ohio, that had the highest white delinquency rate. Teachers were asked to nominate those boys who, in their point of view, were insulated against delinquency. In the second phase of the study, teachers in the same-area schools were asked to nominate sixth-grade boys who appeared to be heading toward delinquency. Both the "good boy" group and the "bad boy" group were given the same battery of psychological tests; the mothers of members of both groups too were interviewed.[61]

Reckless and Dinitz concluded from these studies that one of the preconditions of law-abiding conduct is a good self-concept. This "insulation" against delinquency may be viewed as an ongoing process reflecting an internalization of nondelinquent values and conformity to the expectations of significant others—parents, teachers, and peers. Thus, a good self-concept, the product of favorable socialization, steers youths away from delinquency by acting as an inner buffer or containment against delinquency.

3. *Social control theory.* Travis Hirschi developed another version of control theory that examines the individual's ties to conventional society. In *Causes of*

Delinquency, Hirschi outlined **social control theory** in which he linked delinquent behavior to the bond an individual has with conventional social groups, such as the family and the school. The social bond, according to Hirschi, is made up of four main elements: attachment, commitment, involvement, and belief.[62]

An individual's attachment to conventional others is the first element of the social bond. The sensitivity toward others, argues Hirschi, relates to the ability to internalize norms and to develop a conscience.[63] Attachment to others also includes the ties of affect and respect children have to parents, teachers, and friends. The stronger the attachment to others, the more likely that an individual will take this into consideration when and if he or she is tempted to commit a delinquent act.[64]

Commitment to conventional activities and values is the second element of the bond. An individual is committed to the degree that he or she is willing to invest time, energy, and himself or herself in conventional activities, such as educational goals, property, or reputation. When a committed individual considers the cost of delinquent behavior, he or she uses common sense and thinks of the risk of losing the investment already made in conventional behavior.[65]

Involvement also protects an individual from delinquent behavior. Because time and energy are limited, involvement in conventional activities leaves no time for delinquent behavior. "The person involved in conventional activities is tied to appointments, deadlines, working hours, plans, and the like," reasoned Hirschi, "so the opportunity to commit deviant acts rarely arises. To the extent that he is engrossed in conventional activities, he cannot even think about deviant acts, let alone act out his inclinations."[66]

The fourth element is belief. Delinquency arises from the absence of effective beliefs that forbid socially unacceptable behavior. Respect for the law and for the social norms of society are important components of belief. This respect for the values of the law and legal system is derived from intimate relations with other people, especially parents.[67]

4. *Labeling perspective.* Labeling theory contends that society creates the deviant by labeling those who are apprehended as "different" from others, when in reality they are different only because they have been "tagged" with a criminal label. Edwin Lemert and Howard Becker are the chief proponents of the view that formal and informal societal reactions to criminal behavior can influence the subsequent attitudes and behaviors of criminals and delinquents.[68]

Lemert focused attention on the interaction between social control agents and rule violators and the way certain behavior came to be labeled "criminal" or "deviant." His concept of primary and secondary deviation is regarded as one of the most important insights of this **labeling perspective.** According to Lemert, primary deviation refers to the behavior of the individual, and secondary deviation is society's response to that behavior. Lemert contended that society's reaction to the deviant forces a change in the status or role of the individual and, in effect, causes the person to pursue deviant or criminal behavior.[69]

Thus, the social reaction to the criminal is crucial in understanding the progressive commitment of a person to a criminal way of life.

Becker adds that once a person is caught and labeled, that person becomes an outsider and gains a new social status, with consequences for both one's self-image and one's public identity. The person is regarded as a different kind of person, and he or she finds it difficult to regain social acceptance. Hence, society's labeling ultimately forces a juvenile or an adult into a deviant career.[70]

Conflict Theory

A great deal of variation exists among conflict theories. Some theories emphasize the importance of socioeconomic class, some focus primarily on power and authority, and others emphasize group and cultural conflict.

1. *Socioeconomic class and marxist criminology.* Karl Marx, who wrote very little on the subject of crime as the term is defined today, inspired a new school of criminology that is variously defined as "Marxist," "radical," "critical," "left-wing," "socialist," or "new." The **Marxist perspective** views the state and the law itself as ultimately tools of the economic interests of the ownership class. It is capitalism, rather than human nature, that produces, egocentric, greedy, and predatory human beings. The ownership class is guilty of the crime of the brutal exploitation of the working class. Conventional crime, according to this perspective, is caused by extreme poverty and economic alienation, products of the dehumanizing and demoralizing capitalist system.

2. *Power and authority relationships.* Ralf Dahrendorf and Austin T. Turk have emphasized the relationships between authorities and their subjects. Dahrendorf contends that power is the critical variable explaining crime. He argues that although Marx built his theory on only one form of power (property ownership), a more useful perspective could be constructed by incorporating broader concepts of power.[71]

3. *Group and cultural conflict.* Another dimension of the conflict perspective focuses on group and cultural conflict. Thorsten Sellin and George Vold advocated this approach to the study of crime. Sellin argued that to understand the cause of crime, it is necessary to understand the concept of conduct norms. This concept refers to the rules of a group concerning how its members should act under particular conditions. The violation of these rules guiding behavior arouses a group reaction.[72]

George Vold views society "as a congeries [an aggregation] of groups held together in a shifting, but dynamic equilibrium of opposing group interests and efforts."[73] He formulated a theory of group conflict that contends that "the whole political process of law making, law breaking, and law enforcement directly reflects deep-seated and fundamental conflicts between interest groups and the more general struggles for the control of the police power of the state."[74] See Table 3–2 for a comparison of the biological, psychological, and sociological theories.

Table 3–2 Comparison of Biological, Psychological, and Sociological Theories

Theory	*Proponents*	*Causes of Crime Identified*
Atavistic, or born criminal	Lombroso	The atavistic criminal is a reversion to an earlier evolutionary form.
Developmental	Moffitt	Delinquent behavior proceeds along two developmental paths: On one path, early-age delinquents develop a lifelong pattern of delinquency; on the other, the adolescent develops a limited path and desists from delinquency around eighteen years of age.
Psychoanalytic	Freud	Unconscious motivations resulting from early childhood experiences
Emotional process and situational factors	Katz	Delinquency becomes an emotional process that is seductive and sensually compelling.
Psychopathic personality	Cleckley	Inner emptiness as well as biological limitations
Reinforcement	Wilson and Herrnstein	Several key constitutional and psychological factors
Social disorganization	Shaw and McKay	Delinquent behavior becomes an alternative mode of socialization through which youths who are part of disorganized communities are attracted to delinquent values and traditions.
Cultural deviance	Miller	Lower class culture has a distinctive culture of its own, and its local concerns, or values, make lower class boys more likely to become involved in delinquent behavior.
Strain	Merton	Social structure exerts pressure on those individuals who cannot attain the cultural goal of success to engage in nonconforming behavior.
Delinquency opportunity	Cloward and Ohlin	Lower class boys seek out illegitimate means to attain middle-class success goals if they are unable to attain them through legitimate means.
Status frustration	Cohen	Lower class boys are unable to attain the goals of middle-class culture, and therefore they become involved in nonutilitarian, malicious, and negative behavior.
Differential association	Sutherland	Criminal behavior is expected of those individuals who have internalized a preponderance of definitions favorable to law violations.
Containment	Reckless	Strong and inner and reinforcing external containment provides an insulation against delinquent behavior.

(continued)

Table 3–2 (Continued)

Theory	*Proponents*	*Causes of Crime Identified*
Social control	Hirschi	Delinquent acts result when individuals' bond to society is weak or broken.
Labeling	Lemert and Becker	Society creates the deviant by labeling those who are apprehended as different from other juveniles, when in reality, they are different only because they have been given a deviant label.
Marxist perspective	Marx	Conventional delinquency and crime are caused by extreme poverty and economic alienation.
General theory of crime	Gottfredson and Hirschi	Lack of self-control is the common factor underlying problem behaviors.
Integrated social process theory	Elliott and colleagues	Integrates the strongest elements of stain, social control, and social contol, and social learning perspectives into a single paradigm that accounts for delinquent behavior and drug use
Interactional theory	Thornberry	Associations with delinquent peers and delinquent values make up the social delinquency; especially prolonged serious delinquency is learned and reinforced.

In sum, when social structural, social process, and social conflict theories are considered separately, a piece of the puzzle of how the environment influences a youth to become involved in crime is missing. Together, they provide a more satisfactory explanation than do biological or psychological explanations, for why juveniles become involved in delinquency.

HOW DOES INTEGRATED THEORY EXPLAIN JUVENILE CRIME?

The theoretical development of integrated explanations of juvenile crime has been one of the most highly praised concepts in criminology. Theory integration generally implies the combination of two or more already existing theories on the basis of their perceived commonalities. The overarching purpose of theoretical integration is the development of a new theory that improves on the constituent theories from which the reformulated theory is derived. The ultimate goal of theory integration, then, is the advancement of our understanding of crime and delinquency.[75]

Travis Hirschi has identified three types or forms that theoretical integration may take: side-by-side or parallel integration, end-to-end or sequential integration, and up-and-down or deductive integration. Side-by-side refers to the dividing of the subject matter into constituent types or forms; the most common expression of side-by-side integration is offender topologies.

End-to-end integration, perhaps the most widely used today, refers to placing causal variables in a temporal order so that the independent variables of some theories are used to become the dependent variables of the integrated theory. The process of integrating macrolevel causes with microlevel causes is another common use of the end-to-end approach. Up-and-down integration refers to the process of consolidating into one formulation the ideas of two or more theories by identifying a more abstract or general perspective from which at least parts of the theories can be deducted. This strategy is not frequently used because of the difficulty in compromising different assumptions.[76]

Several integrated theories for delinquent behavior have been developed. Three of the most important are Michael Gottfredson and Travis Hirschi's general theory of crime, Delbert Elliott's integrated social process theory, and Terence P. Thornberry's interactional theory.[77]

Gottredson and Hirschi's General Theory of Crime

In their 1990 publication, *A General Theory of Crime,* Gottfredson and Hirschi define lack of self-control as the common factor underlying problem behaviors.[78]

> People who lack self-control will tend to be impulsive, insensitive, physical (as opposed to mental), risk-taking, short-sighted, and nonverbal, and they will tend, therefore, to engage in criminal and analogous acts [which include smoking, drinking, using drugs, gambling, having children out of wedlock, and engaging in illicit sex]. Since these traits can be identified prior to the age of responsibility for crime, since there is considerable tendency for these traits to come together in the same people, and since the traits tend to persist through life, it seems reasonable to consider them as comprising a stable construct useful in the explanation of crime.[79]

Thus, self-control is the degree to which an individual is "vulnerable to the temptations of the moment."[80] The other pivotal construct in this theory of crime is crime opportunity, which is a function of the structural or situational circumstances encountered by the individual. In combination, these two constructs are intended to capture the simultaneous influence of external and internal restraints on behavior.[81]

More than two dozen studies have been conducted on general theory, and the vast majority have been largely favorable.[82] It has been found that self-control is related to self-reported crime among college students, juveniles, and adults; tends to predict future criminal convictions and self-reported delinquency; and is related to social consequences other than crime.

Gottfredson and Hirschi's theory of self-control is part of a trend that pushes the causes of crime and delinquency further back in the life course into the family. In some respects it is a return to the emphasis found in the works of the Gluecks and also resembles the important themes in Wilson and

Herrnstein's reinforcement theory. This emphasis on early childhood socialization as the cause of crime, of course, departs from the emphasis on more proximate causes of crime found in rational choice theory and in most sociological theories.[83] Gottfredson and Hirschi's focus on a unidimensional trait also departs from the movement toward multidimensional and integrated theories of crime.[84]

Criticisms of general theory have focused largely on its lack of conceptual clarity.[85] It is argued that key elements of the theory remain to be tested,[86] that the theory does not have the power to explain all forms of delinquency and crime,[87] and that "questions remain regarding the ubiquity of self-concept."[88] Nevertheless, in spite of these criticisms, general theory will likely continue to spark continued interest and research.

Elliott and Colleagues' Integrated Social Process Theory

Delbert Elliott and colleagues offer "an explanatory model that expands and synthesizes traditional strain, social control, and social learning perspectives into a single paradigm that accounts for delinquent behavior and drug use."[89] They argued that all three theories are flawed in explaining delinquent behavior. Strain theory is able to account for some initial delinquent acts but does not adequately explain why some juveniles enter into delinquent careers whereas others avoid them. Control theory is unable to explain prolonged involvement in delinquent behavior in light of there being no reward for this behavior, and learning theories portray the delinquent as passive and susceptible to influence when they are confronted with delinquency-producing reinforcements.

Integrating the strongest features of these theories into a single theoretical model, Elliott and colleagues contended that the experience of living in socially disorganized areas lead youths to develop weak bonds with conventional groups, activities, and norms. High levels of strain, as well as weak bonds with conventional groups, lead some youth to seek out delinquent peer groups. These antisocial peer groups provide both positive reinforcement for delinquent behavior and role models for this behavior. Consequently, Elliott and colleagues theorize, there is a high probability of involvement in delinquent behavior when bonding to delinquent groups is combined with weak bonding to conventional groups.[90]

This theory represents a pure type of integrated theory. It can be argued that both general theory and interactional theory are not fully integrated theories but are rather elaborations of established theories. In contrast, there is no question that integrated social process theory is an integrated theory.

Examinations of this theory have generally been positive. Yet some question has been raised about its application to various types of delinquent behaviors. Questions have even been raised about its power and utility with different types of drug activity. For example, integrated social process theory explained 59 percent of the variation in marijuana use but only 29 to 34 percent of the distribution of hard drug use.[91]

Thornberry's Interactional Theory

In Thornberry's interactional theory of delinquency the initial impetus toward delinquency comes from a weakening of the person's bond to conventional society, represented by attachment to parents, commitment to school, and belief in conventional values. Associations with delinquent peers and delinquent values make up the social setting in which delinquency, especially prolonged serious delinquency, is learned and reinforced. These two variables, along with delinquent behavior itself, form a mutually reinforcing causal loop that leads toward increasing delinquency involvement over time.[92]

Moreover, this interactive process develops over the person's life cycle. During early adolescence the family is the most influential factor in bonding the youngster to conventional society and reducing delinquency. But as the youth matures and moves through middle adolescence, the world of friends, school, and youth culture becomes the dominant influence over behavior. Finally, as the person enters adulthood, commitment to conventional activities and to family, especially, offer new avenues to reshape the person's bond to society and involvement with delinquent behavior.[93]

Finally, interactional theory holds that these process variables are systematically related to the youngster's position in the social structure. Class, minority-group status, and the social disorganization of the community all affect the initial values of the interactive variables as well as the behavioral trajectories. It is argued that youths from the most socially disadvantaged backgrounds begin the process least bonded to conventional society and most exposed to the world of delinquency. The nature of the process increases the chances that they will continue on to a career of serious criminal involvement; on the other hand, youths from middle-class families enter a trajectory that is oriented toward conformity and away from delinquency.

Thornberry's theory essentially views delinquency as the result of events occurring in a developmental fashion. Delinquency is not viewed as the end product; instead, it leads to the formation of delinquent values, which then contribute to disconnections in social bonds, more attachments to antisocial peers, and additional involvement in delinquent behavior. As found in other developmental theories, some variables affect unlawful behavior at certain ages and other factors at other ages.[94]

Interactinal theory has several positive features which should assure its continued examination. It seems to make sense of much of the literature on explanations of delinquent behavior. In addition, studies that use an interactional framework are not only more commonly used among delinquency researchers, but also being increasingly used in interdisciplinary research. Furthermore, interactional approaches are consistent with the social settings in which individuals live and interact with others.[95]

Interactional theory has several shortcomings. Most significantly, interactional theory fails to address the presence of middle-class delinquency and basically ignores racial and gender issues. Its viewpoint that delinquency will persist throughout adolescence and into adulthood, with which Hirschi and Gottfredson would find agreement, leaves little room for short-term discontinued or permanent termination of illegal behavior patterns.[96]

SUMMARY

This chapter has described four different explanations for why juveniles become involved in unlawful acts. These explanations range from delinquency as a rational act stemming from free will to the juvenile's behavior arising from biological, psychological, and sociological causes. The behavior, then, was determined, which would remove or reduce the juvenile's responsibility for what he or she had done. The fourth explanation was found in integrated theories which provided more multidimensional explanations for understanding why juveniles violate the law.

In addition to addressing these basic explanations for crime causation, other social factors exist that cannot be dismissed. The nurturing that takes place or does not take place in a family setting is an important factor. So is the degree of success that a juvenile has in the school setting. Those who do poorly in school are more likely to become involved in delinquency than those who do well. Those juveniles who become involved in drug use or a gang are also more likely to become involved in delinquent behavior. These social factors will be considered later in this book.

WEB SITES OF INTEREST

Check this Crime Theory Web site to learn more about the classical school of criminology.

http://www.crimetheory.com

Read about Opportunity and Strain Theory in greater detail from the Hewett School of Norwich, Norfolk, UK.

http://www.hewett.norfolk.sch.uk

Learn more about Social Control Theory from the University of Washington site. **Go to Web site and click search and type in social control theory**.

Learn more about Labeling theory on the University of Missouri, St. Louis site.

CRITICAL THINKING QUESTIONS

1. What is the labeling perspective's definition of why adolescents become delinquent? Do you agree with this interpretation?

2. Which of the three integrated theories make the most sense to you? What are the advantages of integrated theory? What are its disadvantages?
3. Should poverty exclude an adolescent from responsibility for delinquent behavior? Why or why not?
4. Why have the juvenile courts been so quick to apply the concept of free will and rationality to violent juvenile criminals?
5. To what extent do you believe juveniles are rational in their behavior? What are the implications of your answer for the justice system?

NOTES

1. Interviewed in three Midwestern states in the 1990s.
2. Incident that took place when one of the authors was an institutional social worker.
3. Interviewed in 1981 at Stateville Correctional Center, Joliet, Illinois.
4. Jonathan H. Turner, *The Structure of Sociological Theory* (Homewood, IL: Dorsey, 1974), 2.
5. Michael Phillipson, *Understanding Crime and Delinquency* (Chicago: Aldine Publishing Co., 1974), 18.
6. Cesare Bonesana Beccaria, *On Crimes and Punishment*, translated by H. Paolucci (1764); reprinted ed., Indianapolis, IN: Bobbs-Merrill, 1963).
7. Ysabel Rennie, *The Search for Criminal Man: A Conceptual History of the Dangerous Offender* (Lexington, MA: Lexington Books, 1978), 15.
8. Beccaria, *On Crimes and Punishment*, 179.
9. Rennie, *The Search for Criminal Man*, 22.
10. Edward Cimler and Lee Roy Bearch, "Factors Involved in Juvenile Decisions about Crime," *Criminal Justice and Behavior* 8 (September 1981), 275–286.
11. Ronald L. Akers, "Deterrence, Rational Choice, and Social Learning Theory: The Path Not Taken." Paper presented to the Annual Meeting of the American Society of Criminology, Reno, NV (November 1989), 2–3.
12. Phillip J. Cook, "The Demand and Supply of Criminal Opportunities," in *Crime and Justice* 7, edited by Michael Tonry and Norval Morris (Chicago: University of Chicago Press, 1986), 2.
13. Ibid., 2–3.
14. Lawrence E. Cohen and Marcus Felson, "Social Change and Crime Rate Trends: A Routine Activity Approach," *American Sociological Review* (August 1979), 588–609.
15. Steven E. Messner and Kenneth Tardiff, "The Social Ecology of Urban Homicides: An Application of the 'Routine Activities' Approach," *Criminology* 23 (1985), 241–67.
16. Akers, "Deterrence, Rational Choice, and Social Learning Theory," 8.

17. Ibid., 8–9.
18. Derek B. Cornish and Ronald V. Clarke, eds., *The Reasoning Criminal: Rational Choice Perspectives on Offending* (New York: Springer, 1986), 1–2.
19. Ibid., 13.
20. Akers, "Deterrence, Rational Choice, and Social Learning Theory," 12.
21. Akers, however, questions this in his paper, "Deterrence, Rational Choice, and Social Learning Theory," 11.
22. See David J. Rothman, *Conscience and Convenience: The Asylum and its Alternatives in Progressive America* (Boston: Little, Brown, 1980), 32.
23. Ibid., 43–60.
24. David Matza, *Delinquency and Drift* (New York: Wiley, 1964), 5.
25. Donald C. Gibbons, "Differential Treatment of Delinquents and Interpersonal Maturity Level: A Critique," *Social Services Review* 44 (1970), 68.
26. Cesare Lombroso, Introduction to C. Lombroso-Ferrero, *Criminal Man According to the Classification of Cesare Lombroso* (New York: Putnam, 1911), xiv.
27. Charles Goring, *The Criminal Convict: A Statistical Study* (Montclair, NJ: Patterson Smith, 1972).
28. Terrie E. Moffitt, Donald R. Lynam, and Phil A. Silva, "Neuropsychological Tests Predicted Persistent Male Delinquency," *Criminology* 32 (May 1994), 277.
29. Terrie E. Moffitt, "Adolescent-Limited and Life-Course-Persistent Antisocial Behavior: A Developmental Taxonomy, *Psychological Review* (1993), 277.
30. Terrie E. Moffitt, "The Neuropsychology of Conduct Disorder," *Development and Psychopathology* 5 (1993).
31. Curt R. Bartol and Anne M. Bartol, *Delinquency and Justice: A Psychosocial Approach*, 2d ed. (Upper Saddle River, NJ: Prentice-Hall, 1998), 89.
32. Sigmund Freud, *An Outline of Psychoanalysis*, translated by James Strachey (1940 reprint, New York: W. W. Norton, 1963).
33. Ibid.
34. Ibid.
35. *LaMar T. Empey, American Delinquency: Its Meaning and Construction* (Homewood, IL: Dorsey Press, 1982), 172–73.
36. Herbert Cleckley, *The Mask of Sanity*, 3d ed. (St. Louis, MO: Mosby, 1935), 382–417.
37. See Kathleen M. Heide, "Parents Who Get Killed and the Children Who Kill Them," *Journal of Interpersonal Violence* 8 (December 1993), 531–44.
38. Marvin Zuckerman, *Sensation Seeking Beyond the Optimal Level of Arousal* (Hillsdale, NJ: Lawrence Erlbaum, 1979), 10.
39. Ibid.
40. M. J. Hindelang, "The Relationship of Self-Reported Delinquency to Scales of the CPI and MMPI," *Journal of Criminal Law, Criminology and Police Science* (1972), 75–81.

41. Helene Raskin White, Erich W. Labouvie, and Marsha E. Bales, "The Relationship between Sensation Seeking and Delinquency: A Longitudinal Analysis," *Journal of Research in Crime and Delinquency* 22 (August 1985), 195–211.
42. Jack Katz, *Seductions of Crime: Moral and Sensual Attractions in Doing Evil* (New York: Basic Books, 1988).
43. Ibid.
44. Richard L. Jenkins, "Delinquency and a Treatment Philosophy," in *Crime, Law and Corrections*, edited by Ralph Slovenko (Springfield, IL: Charles C Thomas, 1966), 135–36.
45. Cleckley, *The Mask of Sanity*, 132–137.
46. L. N. Robins, *Deviant Children Grown Up: A Sociological and Psychiatric Study of Sociopathic Personality* (Baltimore, MD: Williams & Wilkins, 1966), 256.
47. L. N. Robins, et al., "The Adult Psychiatric Status of Black Schoolboys," *Archives of General Psychiatry* 24 (1971), 338–45.
48. Linda Mealey, "The Sociobiology of Sociopathy: An Integrated Evolutionary Model," *Behavioral and Brain Sciences* 18 (1995), 523–40.
49. James Q. Wilson and Richard J. Herrnstein, *Crime and Human Nature* (New York: Simon & Schuster, 1985).
50. Ibid.
51. Edgar Z. Friedenberg, "Solving Crime," *Readings: A Journal of Reviews* (March 1986), 21.
52. Clifford R. Shaw and Henry D. McKay, *Juvenile Delinquency and Urban Areas* (Chicago: University of Chicago Press, 1942).
53. Walter B. Miller, "Lower-Class Culture as a Generating Milieu of Gang Delinquency," *Journal of Social Issues* 14 (1958), 9–10.
54. Ibid.
55. Marvin Wolfgang and Franco Ferracuti, *Subculture of Violence* (London: Tavistock, 1957).
56. Richard A. Cloward and Lloyd E. Ohlin, *Delinquency and Opportunity: A Theory of Delinquency* (New York: Free Press, 1960).
57. Albert K. Cohen, *Delinquent Boys: The Culture of the Gang* (New York: Free Press, 1955).
58. Edwin H. Sutherland, *Principles of Criminology* (Philadelphia: J. B. Lippincott Company, 1947).
59. Jack Henry Abbott, *In the Belly of the Beast: Letters from Prison* (New York: Vintage, 1981).
60. The principles of containment theory are described in Walter C. Reckless, "A New Theory of Delinquency and Crime," *Federal Probation* 24 (December 1952), 133–38.
61. Simon Dinitz and Betty A. Pfau-Vicent, "Self-Concept and Juvenile Delinquency: An Update," *Youth and Society* 14 (December 1982), 133–38.

62. Travis Hirschi, *Causes of Delinquency* (Berkeley, CA: University of California Press, 1969).
63. Ibid., 18.
64. Ibid., 83.
65. Ibid., 20.
66. Ibid., 22.
67. Ibid., 198.
68. Edwin L. Lemert, *Social Pathology* (New York: McGraw-Hill Book Company, 1951); and Howard S. Becker, *Outsiders* (New York: Free Press, 1958).
69. Lemert, *Social Pathology.*
70. Becker, *Outsiders.*
71. Ralf Dahrendorf and A. T. Turk, *Class and Class Conflict in Industrial Society* (Palo Alto, CA: Stanford University Press, 1959).
72. Thorsten Sellin, *Culture, Conflict, and Crime* (New York: Social Science Research Council, 1938), 28.
73. George B. Vold, *Theoretical Criminology*, 2d ed., prepared by Thomas J. Bernard (New York: Oxford University Press, 1979), 283.
74. Ibid., 288.
75. Margaret Farnworth, "Theory Integration Versus Model Building," in *Theoretical Integration in the Study of Deviance and Crime: Problems and Prospects* (Albany: State University of New York at Albany Press, 1989), 93.
76. Cited in Thomas J. Bernard and Jeffrey B. Snipes, "Theoretical Integration in Criminology," in *Crime and Justice: A Review of Research*, Volume 20, edited by Michael Tonry (Chicago and London: the University of Chicago Press, 1994), 307.
77. Michael G. Gottfredson and Travis Hirschi, *A General Theory of Crime* (Stanford, CA: Stanford University Press, 1990); Elliott et al., *Explaining Delinquency and Drug Use*; Delbert S. Elliott, Suzanne S. Ageton, and Rachelle J. Canter, "An Integrated Theoretical Perspective on Delinquent Behavior," *Journal of Research in Crime and Delinquency* 16 (1979), 3–27; Terence P. Thornberry, "Toward an Interactional Theory of Delinquency," *Criminology* 25 (1987), 862–91; and Terence P. Thornberry, Alan J. Lizotte, Marvin D. Krohn, Margaret Farnworth, and Sung Joon Jang, "Testing Interactional Theory: An Examination of Reciprocal Causal Relationships among Family, School and Delinquency," *Journal of Criminal Law and Criminology* 82 (1991), 3–35.
78. Gottfredson and Hirschi, *A General Theory of Crime.*
79. Ibid., 90–91.
80. Ibid., 87.
81. Ibid., 87.
82. For a review of these studies, see T. David Evans, Francis T. Cullen, Velmer S. Burton, Jr., R. Gregory Dunaway, and Michael L. Benson, "The Social

Consequences of Self-Control: Testing the General Theory of Crime," *Criminology* (1997), 476–77.

83. Harold G. Grasmick, Charles R. Tittle, Robert J. Bursik, Jr., and Bruce J. Arneklev, "Testing the Core Empirical Implications of Gottfredson and Hirschi's General Theory of Crime, *Journal of Research in Crime and Delinquency* 30 (February 1993), 5.
84. See Ronald L. Akers, "Self-Control as a General Theory of Crime, *Journal of Quantitative Criminology* 7 (1991), 191–211.
85. Shoemaker, *Theories of Delinquency*, 252.
86. Dennis M. Giever, Dana C. Lynskey, and Danette S. Monnet, "Gottfredson and Hirschi's General Theory of Crime and Youth Gangs: An Empirical Test on a Sample of Middle-School Students." Unpublished paper sent to authors, 1998.
87. Michael Polakowski, "Linking Self- and Social Control with Deviance: Illuminating the Structure Underlying a General Theory of Crime and Its Relation to Deviant Activity," *Journal of Quantitative Criminology* 10 (1994), 41–77.
88. Ibid., 41.
89. Elliott, et al., "An Integrated Theoretical Perspective on Delinquent Behavior," 11.
90. Ibid.
91. Cynthia Chien, "Testing the Effect of the Key Theoretical Variable of Theories of Strain, Social Control and Social Learning on Types of Delinquency." Paper presented to the Annual Meeting of the American Society of Criminology, Baltimore, Maryland (November 1990).
92. Thornberry, "Toward an Interactional Theory of Delinquency," 886.
93. Ibid.
94. Shoemaker, *Theories of Delinquency,* 161–63.
95. Ibid., 262–63.
96. Ibid., 262.

4

THE POLICE

OBJECTIVES

1. To examine juveniles' attitudes toward the police
2. To discuss police intervention with the various types of juvenile offenders
3. To examine the legal rights of arrested juveniles
4. To portray the various ways that police departments handle juvenile crime

KEY TERMS

discretion
fingerprinting
gang detail
gang unit
interrogation
lineup
photographs
problem-oriented policing
school searches
search and seizure
Youth Service Program

How does one explain the raw excitement of being a cop? This is an excitement so powerful that it consumes and changes the officer's personality. For the officer all five senses are involved, especially in dangerous situations. They are stirred in a soup of emotions and adrenaline and provide an adrenaline rush that surpasses anything felt before. You are stronger and more agile; your mind functions on a higher level of quickness and alertness. Afterwards, the grass seems greener; the air fresher; food tastes better; and the spouse and children are even more precious. It is an addictive feeling that makes the runner's high in comparison feel like a hangover. Police work gets into the blood and possesses the spirit. You become the job and the job becomes you, until the day you die.

—Veteran police officer[1]

This veteran police officer makes a passionate statement about the joys of becoming a police officer. He clearly sees policing more as a calling than as a job or a set of bureaucratically defined duties. He believes that policing is worthy of demanding the very best that a person has to offer. Once it gets into your blood, he warns, it will change your identity and self-image and will stay with you for the rest of your life.

This officer, despite his positive attitude about a police career, has little interest in working with juveniles. With him, as well as with many officers, there are a number of problems in policing juveniles. Juvenile crimes are viewed as minor, and the arrest of a juvenile is not considered a "real" arrest. The due process rights recently accorded juveniles also make the police feel that their crime-fighting hands are tied. Furthermore, police officers are distrusted by many juveniles, some of whom view the police as the "enemy." The police must deal then with juveniles' hostile attitudes, which can become explosive and violent at a moment's notice. Finally, the nature of juvenile crime is changing; the spread of malls, the explosion of drugs, and the proliferation of gangs have complicated the lives of police officers all across the country.

Police officers are faced with juveniles whose behaviors range from drinking in parks to murder. At one end of the spectrum are status offenders who have conflicts with their parents, schools, and community, but who are not true criminals in either behavior or intent. At the other end are the violent, repetitive offenders. These youths commit murder, aggravated assault, rape, and grand theft; some are in organized crime, and some deal in drugs. Between these extremes are varieties of runaways and mentally ill, dependent, neglected, abused, victimized, and delinquent youths.

The history of the police in the United States is reviewed in this chapter, followed by juveniles' attitudes toward the police, factors that influence discretion, the informal and formal dispositions of juvenile offenders, the changing legal rights of juveniles. The final sections of this chapter consider police organizations and functions as they relate to juveniles, as well as the special challenges that juveniles' drug use, gang involvement, and gun possession bring to community-based policing.

WHAT IS THE HISTORY OF POLICE–JUVENILE RELATIONS?

The earliest Puritan communities in the United States used informal methods of controlling juveniles. Probably the most effective of these informal methods was *socialization,* by which youths were taught the rules of society from the time they were born until the rules became internalized. If a youth violated a law, the family, church, and community stepped in to bring the youth back into line. The family was expected to punish the youth, and, if the family failed, church and community elders turned to other punishments.

The industrialization and urbanization that began in the late 1700s reduced the effectiveness of informal social controls. As the population increased and cities grew, the traditional tight-knit family and community structures became disorganized and street crime increased. Religious, ethnic, and political violence also increased, leading the society to look for other methods of social control.[2] Police forces were created to help solve the problem.

In the 1830s and 1840s, full-time police forces were established in larger cities, such as Boston, New York, and Philadelphia; by the 1870s, all the major cities had full-time forces, and many of the smaller cities had part-time forces. Social control had moved from the family to police officers walking the beat. The police emerged as a coercive force employed to keep youthful criminals, gangs, ethnic minorities, and immigrants in line.

Police officers had the power to arrest juveniles, but they still used many informal techniques of social control. Some officers undoubtedly were effective in striking up friendships with juveniles and convincing them to mend their ways. In other cases, police reprimanded juveniles verbally or turned them over to their parents or parish priests. Unfortunately, the power of police officers at this time was virtually unlimited; some officers talked abusively to children, roughed them up, or beat them in alleys. Added to the corruption found in many police departments, the result was that considerable tension existed between police officers and the communities they patrolled. Few, if any, efforts to remedy this problem occurred before the 1900s.

In the first three decades of the twentieth century, the Portland, Oregon; New York City; and Washington, DC, police departments started to address the problem of juvenile crime. Police chiefs began to think in terms of prevention instead of merely in terms of control. Policewomen were hired to work with delinquents and runaway and truant children by patrolling amusement parks, dance halls, and other places where juveniles might be corrupted. The job of these officers was to dissuade the youths from engaging in a life of crime.[3]

The idea of prevention was so popular that 90 percent of the nation's largest cities had instituted some type of juvenile program by 1924.[4] The Police Athletic League was launched in the 1920s, and, by the 1930s, most large departments had either assigned welfare officers to difficult districts, initiated employment bureaus for youthful males, assigned officers to juvenile courts, or set up special squads to deal with juvenile crime.[5] Other innovations included instituting relief programs, giving poor children gifts at Christmas, and developing programs whereby police spoke to various groups of youths, such as Boy Scouts and Campfire Girls.[6]

A major development occurred in the mid-1920s. Until this time, departments had not effectively organized their juvenile crime prevention efforts. Chief August Vollmer of the Berkeley, California, Police Department is credited with being the first chief to bring together the various segments of a police force to form a youth bureau.[7] The concept spread to other urban areas, and soon youth bureaus, often called youth aid bureaus, juvenile bureaus, juvenile control bureaus, juvenile divisions, or crime prevention bureaus, were found throughout major cities in the United States. The police in these bureaus were the forerunners of the modern juvenile officer.

Two developments formalized the increasingly important role of the juvenile officer in the United States. In 1955, the Central States Juvenile Officer's Association was formed, followed soon after by the International Juvenile Officers Association in 1957. Meetings were held by these and similar groups at regional, national, and international levels. For the first time, the responsibilities, standards, and procedures necessary in juvenile work were being developed. In addition, the increase in social science research on youths highlighted the necessity of training juvenile officers better, as these officers were expected to help, rather than punish, youthful offenders.

Preventive police work with juveniles continued through the 1960s. Programs were developed to reduce delinquency and to improve how youths viewed the police. Police officers volunteered to speak to elementary, junior high, and high school students, and some departments developed special programs for these purposes. The Police Athletic League expanded its athletic programs and set up courses in leadership and moral training for youths. Furthermore, some police agencies helped youths find jobs and worked with schools to reduce truancy. Programs to fight drugs and alcohol and to show the consequences of drinking and driving were also developed.

In the 1970s, 1980s, and 1990s, severe budgetary restrictions forced many police departments to reduce their emphasis on juvenile programs. Some dropped their juvenile divisions altogether, whereas others limited their activity to dependent, neglected, and abused children, which had commenced in response to the increasingly recognized problems of domestic violence.

HAVE JUVENILES' ATTITUDES TOWARD THE POLICE CHANGED?

Researchers began studying the public's attitudes toward the police more than forty years ago.[8] Numerous charges of police corruption, police brutality, violation of citizens' rights, and rising crime rates generated much discussion over the role of the police in modern society. In addition, public administrators were well aware of a "we versus they" mentality that shaped relations between the police and the public and inhibited their cooperation. Administrators wanted to reduce this split and to increase the public's willingness to report victimization and cooperate with the police in preventing as well as more effectively combating crime and delinquency. Since then, numerous surveys of the public and of juveniles have been conducted. Juveniles are of particular concern because they are disproportionately involved in crime and because they will eventually be adults whose cooperation would be greatly appreciated by the police.

One of the most important early studies was conducted by Robert Portune on one thousand junior high school students in Cincinnati. Portune concluded that hostility toward the law and police increased from grades seven through nine; that Whites had much more favorable attitudes than did African Americans; that girls had more favorable attitudes than did boys; that better students had more favorable attitudes than did poorer students; and that the higher the occupational status of the father, the more favorable was the child's attitude toward the police.[9]

In a more detailed study, Donald Bouma and his associates administered ten thousand questionnaires to Michigan school children in ten cities. These students, most of whom were in grades seven through nine, were asked about their attitudes, their parents' attitudes, and their friends' attitudes toward the police. This study, which agreed with all the major findings of Portune's research, additionally established the following:

1. Even though hositility toward the police significantly increased as students moved through their junior high years, the majority of students would still cooperate with the police if they saw someone other than a friend commit a crime.
2. Most youths perceived friends to be more antagonistic toward the police than they were, and they perceived attitudes of parents toward the police to be quite similar to their own.
3. A majority of students believed that the police were "pretty nice guys." In fact, more than half of all students believed that the police were criticized too often.
4. One-third of the White and two-thirds of the African-American youths believed that the police accused students of things they did not do.
5. Although two out of every three students believed that the city would be better off with more police officers, only 8 percent reported that they would like to be police officers.[10]

L. Thomas Winfree Jr. and Curt T. Griffiths's 1977 study of students in seventeen high schools found that, to a considerable degree, juveniles' attitudes toward the police were shaped by contacts with police officers. Juvenile attitudes were influenced more by negative contacts than by sex, race, socioeconomic status, or residence, and the negative contacts were twice as important as positive contacts in determining juvenile attitudes toward police officers.[11]

William T. Rusinko and colleagues' 1978 examination of twelve hundred ninth-grade students in three junior high schools in Lansing, Michigan, explored the importance of police contact in formulating juveniles' attitudes toward the police. They found that positive police contact with the White youths in their study neutralized negative encounters. But positive police contact did not reduce the tendency for African-American youths to be less positive in their opinions of police. These findings agree with those of several other studies that show the development of a culturally accepted view of police among African Americans independent of their arrest experience.[12]

Scott H. Decker, in a 1980s review of literature on attitudes toward the police, concluded that youths had more negative attitudes toward the police than did older citizens; and that race, the quality of police services, and previous experiences with the police also affected citizens' attitudes.[13] James R. Davis found in a very small sample of New Yorkers younger than twenty years of age, however, that attitudes toward the police were not statistically related to age.[14]

Komanduri S. Murty, Julian B. Roebuck, and Joann D. Smith found in an Atlanta study that "older, married, white-collar, highly educated, and employed respondents reported a more positive image of the police than did their counterparts—younger, single, blue-collar, low-educated, unemployed/underemployed respondents."[15] Murty and colleagues offered support for previous findings that younger African-American males are particularly hostile toward the police. These researchers demonstrated that the chances that respondents will have negative attitudes toward the police also vary, in descending order, with residence in high-crime census tracts, single marital status, negative contacts with the police, and blue-collar occupations.[16]

Michael J. Leiber, Mahesh K. Nalla, and Margaret Farnworth challenged the traditional argument that juveniles' interactions with the police are the primary determinant of their attitudes toward law enforcement officers. Instead, they saw juveniles' attitudes toward authority and social control developing in a larger sociocultural context. In their sample of Iowa youths who were accused of delinquency and adjudicated as delinquents, they found that social background variables (particularly minority status) and subcultural preferences (particularly commitment to delinquent norms) affected juveniles' attitudes toward the police both directly and indirectly (through police–juvenile interactions).[17]

The *Monitoring the Future Project,* conducted by researchers at the University of Michigan, has surveyed nationwide samples of high school seniors on their views of law enforcement officers since the late 1970s.[18] Students were asked, "How good or how bad a job is being done for the country as a whole by . . . the police and other law enforcement agencies?" Available responses included "very poor," "poor, " "fair," "good," and "very good." The sample was analyzed by sex, race, region of the country, educational plans, and type of illicit drugs used by respondents during their lifetimes.

A summary of data from the late 1980s through the mid 1990s indicates that high school seniors' attitudes toward the police became more negative during those decades across all subsets of the sample. For example, the percentage of youths responding "good" and "very good" tended to decline throughout the 1980s and into the early 1990s across the categories of sex, race, and region of the country. These general downward trends, however, showed some improvement in later years.[19]

The *Monitoring the Future Project* data for 2001 are fairly representative of the one hundred most recent years (see Table 4–1).[20] Some 33.2 percent of high school seniors responded either "good" or "very good" in response to a question asking about their attitudes toward the police and law enforcement agencies. If the 33.7 percent of "fair" responses were added to the "good" and "very good" categories, roughly 67 percent of high school seniors could be considered to have a positive attitude toward the police.

Table 4–1 *High School Seniors' Attitudes Toward the Performance of the Police and Other Law Enforcement Agencies, 2001*

	Percentage Responding, by Category						
	Very Poor	*Poor*	*Fair*	*Good*	*Very Good*	*No Opinion*	N*(Wtd)*
Total	7.6	13.8	33.7	26.0	7.2	11.6	2170
Sex							
Male	10.5	13.7	32.8	26.0	7.8	9.3	1006
Female	4.5	13.1	35.4	26.6	6.9	13.6	1061
Race							
White	6.0	11.9	33.7	29.4	7.8	11.2	1370
Black	13.9	20.0	38.3	14.0	6.0	9.8	251
Region							
Northeast	7.4	10.3	31.5	26.7	9.1	15.0	410
North central	7.7	12.9	32.9	28.8	6.9	10.8	620
South	8.1	15.8	34.3	25.0	7.9	8.9	699
West	7.1	15.3	35.9	23.1	4.6	13.9	441
4-Year College Plans							
Yes	6.9	13.6	34.2	27.5	7.4	10.4	1617
No	8.8	13.2	35.8	20.9	8.1	13.3	407
Illicit drug use: Lifetime							
None	4.2	11.0	36.7	29.0	8.1	11.0	942
Marijuana only	8.8	17.6	30.3	24.0	8.0	11.3	476
Few pills	4.4	15.3	33.8	28.3	5.9	12.3	279
More pills	13.7	15.0	33.2	21.6	5.2	11.3	376
Heroin	24.5	7.4	20.5	21.7	8.8	17.0	45

Source: Adapted from Lloyd D. Johnston, Jerald G. Bachman, and Patrick M. O'Malley, *Monitoring the Future, 2001* (Ann Arbor: Institute for Social Research, University of Michigan, 2002). Reprinted by permission.

Breaking the seniors down demographically and combining the same ranking categories as above, females, at 68.9 percent, were only slightly more positive than males who totaled 66.6 percent. Combining male scores for the "very poor" and "poor" categories, 24.2 percent of males as opposed to 17.6 percent of females were very negative. Significantly, Whites were considerably more positive than Blacks in their attitudes toward the police; thirty-four percent of Blacks, for example, rated police and other law enforcement agencies as "very poor" or "poor" as opposed to 18 percent of Whites. Some variation existed by region of the country and whether students intended to go to college. Students who had not engaged in illicit drug use were slightly more positive toward the police than those who had taken illicit drugs. Strikingly, 24.5 percent of those who had used heroin rated the police and other law enforcement agencies as "very poor."[21]

In sum, research demonstrates that younger juveniles tend to be more positive than older ones, White juveniles more positive than African Americans, and female juveniles more positive than males. A positive attitude also seems to be influenced by social class, for middle-class youths tend to be more positive than lower-class youths. Generally, juveniles who have not had contact with the police are more positive than those who have had police contact. The most hostile attitudes are typically those who have extensive histories of law-violating activities or those who are involved in youth gangs.

HOW DO THE POLICE RESPOND TO YOUTHFUL LAWBREAKERS?

Two major aspects of police response to youthful lawbreakers are the factors that influence police processing of juveniles and the ways in which the police handle juvenile offenders.

FACTORS THAT INFLUENCE POLICE DISCRETION

Police **discretion** can be defined as "the choice between two or more possible means of handling a situation confronting the police officer."[22] By exercising discretion, the police officer can use various methods to detour juveniles from the juvenile justice system or to involve them in it. Although it is sometimes argued that the police abuse their broad powers of discretion with juveniles, studies generally estimate that only 10 to 20 percent of police–juvenile encounters become official contacts.[23]

The police officer's disposition of the juvenile is largely determined by nine factors: the nature of the offense; citizen complainants; the juvenile's sex, race, socioeconomic status, and other individual characteristics; the nature of the interaction between the police officer and the juvenile; departmental policy; and external pressures in the community.

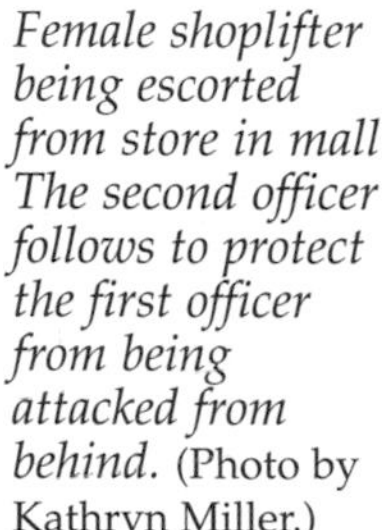

Female shoplifter being escorted from store in mall. The second officer follows to protect the first officer from being attacked from behind. (Photo by Kathryn Miller.)

The nature of the offense. The most important factor that influences the disposition of the youthful offender is the seriousness of the offense. Research has consistently documented that the probability of arrest increases with the legal severity of the alleged offense.[24]

Citizen complainants. Another important factor influencing the disposition of the youth is a citizen's presence or filing of a complaint against a youth.[25] If a citizen initiates a complaint, remains present, and wishes the arrest of a juvenile, the likelihood increases that the juvenile will be arrested and processed.[26]

Sex. Police officers generally are less likely to arrest a young female than a young male if she has committed an offense, but they are more likely to arrest a female if she violates traditional role expectations for females, such as failing to obey parents, being sexually promiscuous, or running away from home.[27]

Race. Studies differ in their findings on the importance of race in determining juvenile dispositions.[28] One of the problems in appraising the importance of race is that African Americans and members of other minorities appear to be involved in more serious crimes more often than Whites are. Nevertheless, it does seem that racial bias makes minority juveniles the special targets of the police.[29]

Socioeconomic status. What makes it difficult to establish the effect of class on the disposition of cases involving juveniles is that most studies examine race and socioeconomic status together. Nevertheless, some evidence supports the long-standing conclusion that lower-class juveniles receive different justice than do middle- or upper-class juveniles. Lower-class youths, then, are dragged into the net of the system for the same offense for which middle- and upper-class juveniles are often sent home.

Individual characteristics. Prior arrest record, previous offenses, prior police contacts, age, peer relationships, family situation, and conduct of parents also may influence how the police officer handles a juvenile offender.[30] The juvenile most likely to be arrested is older, has a serious record, and fits the image of a delinquent and dangerous person.[31]

Nature of police–juvenile interaction. Those juveniles who defer to a police officer reduce the likelihood of a formal disposition.[32] But those juveniles who are hostile increase the likelihood that they will be referred to the juvenile court.[33] One study found that in encounters in which no evidence linked a juvenile to an offense, the demeanor of the juvenile was the most important determinant of whether formal action was taken.[34]

Departmental policy. Departmental policy also may influence police handling of juveniles.[35] Some evidence suggests that the more professional departments had higher numbers of juveniles referred to the juvenile court because they used discretion less often than did the departments that were not as professional.[36]

External pressures in the community. The status of the complainant or victim, the attitudes of the press and the public, and the philosophy and available resources of referral agencies also may influence the disposition of the law-violating youth.

In sum, this empirical portrait of police–juvenile contacts in the community reveals that the seriousness of the offense and complaints by citizens appear to be the most important factors influencing the disposition of juveniles. Other less influential factors are the individual characteristics of the juvenile, departmental policy, and external pressures in the community. The sex, race, and socioeconomic status of the offender do not appear to be as influential as they were in the past.

Informal and Formal Dispositions of Juvenile Offenders

When investigating a complaint or arriving at a scene of criminal activity, a juvenile or patrol officer has at least five options. The first option is to question and then release the juvenile to the community. This informal encounter can be brief or can involve an interview at the police station. The law enforcement officer is likely to give the juvenile an informal reprimand.

The second option is to release the youth and make a referral to a youth service bureau, a mental health agency, or some type of social agency, such as Child Welfare, Big Brothers/Big Sisters, the Boys and Girls Clubs, or the YMCA. With this option, the police officer chooses to divert the youth from the juvenile justice system.

The third option is to take the misbehaving youngster to the police station, have the contact recorded, issue an official reprimand, and then release him/her to the community; this is sometimes called a " station adjustment." If the police officer deems it necessary and policy permits, the juvenile can be placed under police supervision; that is, the youth remains under the supervision of the police department until released from the police-imposed probation.

A fourth option is to issue a citation and refer the youth to the juvenile court. It is commonly agreed that this type of referral should be made when the offense is serious, when a youth has a history of repeated delinquent behavior, when diversionary programming has failed, or when the officer believes that the youth or his family are in need of assistance.

The fifth and final option is to issue a citation, refer the youth to the juvenile court, and take him or her to the detention facility. In communities that do not have such a facility, youths must be taken to the county jail or the police lock-up. Obviously, taking children out of their homes and placing them in a detention facility is used as a last resort.

WHAT LEGAL RIGHTS DO JUVENILES HAVE WITH THE POLICE?

Juveniles were at the mercy of the police for much of the twentieth century. Few or no laws protected juveniles in trouble because of the rehabilitative ideal in juvenile justice. Police officers, whose primary mission was to maintain law and order, used whatever tactics seemed appropriate to restore the peace. Friendliness, persuasion, threats, coercion, and force were all used to gain the compliance of juveniles. If these tactics failed, juveniles were taken into juvenile court or, depending on the laws of the states and the seriousness of the crimes, to the adult court for prosecution. Few protections were granted juveniles in the areas of search and seizure, interrogation, fingerprinting, lineups, or other procedures.

In the 1960s, the U.S. Supreme Court's decisions began to change this relationship between the police and juveniles. Although not all police departments have endorsed or practiced the guidelines laid down by the courts, most departments have made a conscientious effort to abide by the standards of justice and fairness implied by these decisions.[37]

SEARCH AND SEIZURE

The Fourth Amendment to the Constitution of the United States protects citizens from unauthorized **search and seizure.** In 1961, the Supreme Court Decision in *Mapp v. Ohio* affirmed Fourth Amendment rights for adults. This decision stated that evidence gathered in an unreasonable search and seizure—that is, evidence seized without probable cause and without a proper search warrant—was inadmissible in court.[38]

In the 1967 *State v. Lowery* case, the Supreme Court applied the Fourth Amendment ban against unreasonable searches and seizures to juveniles:

> Is it not more outrageous for the police to treat children more harshly than adult offenders, especially when such is violative of due process and fair treatment? Can a court countenance a system, where, as here, an adult may suppress evidence with the usual effect of having the charges dropped for lack of proof, and, on the other hand, a juvenile can be institutionalized—lose the most sacred possession a human being has, his freedom—for "rehabilitative" purposes because the Fourth Amendment right is unavailable to him?[39]

Juveniles, therefore, are protected from unreasonable searches and seizures. Juveniles must be presented with a valid search warrant unless they have either waived that right, have consented to having their person or property searched, or have been caught in the act. If these conditions have not been met, courts have overturned rulings against the juveniles. For example, evidence was dismissed in one case when police entered a juvenile's apartment at 5:00 AM without a warrant to arrest him.[40] In another case, Houston police discovered marijuana on a youth five hours after he had been stopped for driving a car without lights and a driver's license. Confined to a Texas training school for this drug offense, the youth was ordered released by an appellate court because the search took place too late to be related to the arrest.[41]

Juveniles' use of weapons and drugs is changing the nature of police–student relations in school. The police are called on in increasing numbers of communities across the nation to enforce drug-free school zone laws. The drug-free zones generally are defined as the school property and the area within a one thousand-foot radius of the property's boundaries. The police are also called on to enforce the 1990 federal Gun-Free School Zones Act.

The use of dogs to sniff for drugs; the administration of breathalyzers; the installation of hidden video cameras; and the routine searches of students' purses, pockets, school lockers, desks, and vehicles on school grounds are increasing as school officials struggle to regain control. In some cases, school officials conduct their own searches, and in other cases, the police are brought in to conduct the searches.[42]

In the *New Jersey v. T. L. O.* decision (1985), the U.S. Supreme Court examined whether Fourth Amendment rights against unreasonable searches and seizures apply to the school setting.[43] The facts behind this case are the following: A teacher at Piscataway High School in Middlesex County, New Jersey, discovered on March 7, 1980, that two girls were smoking in a bathroom. He reported this violation of school rules to the principal's office, and the two students were summoned to meet with the assistant vice principal. T. L. O., one of the two, claimed that she had done no wrong, and the assistant principal demanded to see her purse. His examination discovered a pack of cigarettes and cigarette rolling papers, some marijuana, a pipe, a considerable amount of money, a list of students who owed T. L. O. money, and letters implicating her in marijuana dealing. T. L. O. confessed later at the police station to dealing drugs on school grounds.[44]

The juvenile court found T. L. O. delinquent and sentenced her to probation for one year. She then appealed her case to the New Jersey Supreme Court on the grounds that the search of her purse was not justified in the circumstances of the case. When the New Jersey Supreme Court upheld her appeal, the state appealed to the U.S. Supreme Court, which ruled that school personnel have the right to search lockers, desks, and students as long as they believe that the law or the school rules have been violated. The importance of this case is that the Court defined that the legality of **school searches** need not be based on obtaining a warrant or on having probable cause that a crime has taken place. Instead, the legality of the search depends on its reasonableness, considering the scope of the search, the student's gender and age, and the student's behavior at the time.[45] See Focus on Law, 4–1.

School officials' searches of students suspected of violating school rules, especially regarding drugs and guns, have continued to be upheld by the courts since the *T. L. O.* decision. Indeed, of the eighteen cases decided since 1985, state appellate decisions applied the *T. L. O.* decisions in fifteen of the cases.[46]

FOCUS ON LAW 4–1

The Wisconsin Department of Justice has summarized Fourth Amendment requirements for search and seizure rules as applicable to Wisconsin schools.* These rules are as follows:

School Officials

- The Fourth Amendment restricts public school officials, but to a lesser degree than are the police. The Fourth Amendment does not apply to private or parochial school officials.
- School officials may search students and their belongings with "reasonable suspicion."
- The police may also search with "reasonable suspicion" (as opposed to their usual "probable cause" standard) if they are working at the request of, and in conjunction with, school officials.

Consent Searches

- In order for consent to be valid, the consent must be voluntary and the person giving consent must have the authority to do so.

- Consent does not have to be in writing but it is preferable that it be so.
- A refusal to consent does not give a school official reasonable suspicion to believe the student is hiding something.
- It is recommended that the student be advised as to what a school official is searching for prior to asking for consent to search.
- Consent to search a generalized area is a consent to search any items found in that area.

Nonconsensual Searches of the Student's Person and Personal Belongings

- A school official may search a student or his or her belongings if they have a reasonable suspicion that the area being searched contains contraband or evidence of a violation.
- School officials should balance the intrusion of the search with the severity of the violation involved.
- A school official of the same gender as the student should do any physical touching of a student.
- School officials may not strip search students.

Locker Searches

- School officials may make random searches of lockers if the school has a written policy as to this practice and the policy is widely disseminated to the student body.
- The Legislature recently passed Wis. Stats. Sec. 118.325. which codifies the school's right to random searches of lockers.

Vehicle Searches

- School officials may search a vehicle parked on school premises if they have a reasonable suspicion that the vehicle contains contraband or evidence of a violation.
- School officials may also search a vehicle with the consent of the student.

Drug-Detection Canines

- Random canine searches on school property are permissible, as they do not constitute a search within the meaning of the Fourth Amendment.
- If a properly trained canine alerts to any piece of property, this constitutes probable cause upon which to justify a search of the alerted to area.

Point of Entry/Exit Inspections

- Random inspection of student items at specific locations are permissive if the school has a clear policy as to this practice, clearly marks the area involved, and performs these inspections in a fair and even-handed way.

Metal Detectors

- Metal detectors are considered minor intrusions and thus can be justified without reasonable suspicion of consent.
- The use of the "wand" metal detector is more intrusive than a stationary unit and should be limited to those occasions where the school official has an articulable suspicion.

Surveillance Technology and Search Issues

- School officials may use visual surveillance in any area where a student does not have a reasonable expectation of privacy.
- School officials should refrain from visual surveillance in areas where it is likely that students could be observed in a partially nude state.
- Audio surveillance is a Fourth Amendment intrusion and schools should not engage in monitoring telephone conversations without the consent of one of the participants in the conversation.

* Some of these requirements will vary by state.

Source: For the complete Search and Seizure statement by the Department of Justice for the State of Wisconsin.See http://www.doj.state.wi.us

Critical Thinking Questions:
What is your evaluation of these search and seizure requirements?

Interrogation and Confession

The Fourteenth Amendment of the Constitution states that standards of fairness and due process must be used in obtaining confessions. The totality of the circumstances in extracting confessions must also be taken into consideration in determining the appropriateness of a confession.

The Supreme Court ruled in *Brown v. Mississippi* (1936) that force may not be used to obtain confessions.[47] In this case, police used physical force in extracting an admission of guilt from a suspect. Other confessions have been ruled invalid because the accused was too tired; was questioned too long; or was not permitted to talk to his wife, friends, or lawyer either while being interrogated or until he confessed.[48]

The *Haley v. Ohio* case (1948) is an early example of police interrogation excesses.[49] Haley, a fifteen-year-old juvenile, was arrested five days after a robbery and shooting of a store owner. The youth confessed after five hours of **interrogation** (i.e., formal questioning) by five or six police officers with neither parents nor lawyer present. During the questioning, the officers showed him alleged confessions of two other youths. The Supreme Court responded by stating:

> The age of the petitioner, the hours when he was grilled, the duration of his quizzing, the fact that he had no friend or counsel to advise him, the callous attitude of the police toward his rights combine to convince us that this was a confession wrung from a child by means which the law should not sanction. Neither man nor child can be allowed to stand condemned by methods which flout constitutional requirements of due process of law.[50]

Juveniles who are taken into custody are also entitled to the rights stated in the 1966 *Miranda v. Arizona* decision. This U.S. Supreme Court decision prohibits the use of a confession in court unless the individual was advised of his or her rights before interrogation, especially of the right to remain silent, the right to have an attorney present during questioning, and the right to be assigned an attorney by the state if he or she cannot afford one.[51] The *In re Gault* (1967) decision, which is discussed in Chapter 5, made the right against self-incrimination and the right to counsel applicable to juveniles.[52] Yet the *Gault* decision failed to clarify if a youth could waive the protection of the *Miranda* rules. It further failed to specify what is necessary for a juvenile to waive his or her *Miranda* rights intelligently and knowingly. At what age does a juvenile become capable of intellectually understanding the importance of the rights? Are juveniles under the influence of drugs or alcohol capable of legally waiving their rights? Should mentally ill or retarded youths be able to waive their rights? What about youths who do not understand English well?

These issues have been coming before the various state courts for a number of years. In one case, the state of California upheld the confessions of two Spanish-speaking youths, one of whom had a mental age of slightly over ten years.[53] A North Carolina court upheld the confession of a twelve-year-old.[54] In another case, a Maryland appeals court upheld the confession of a sixteen-year-old high school dropout with an eighth-grade education.[55]

The questions raised by these court decisions require careful consideration. A study by T. Grisso found that almost all the juveniles questioned by St. Louis police in 1981 had waived their *Miranda* rights. Yet Grisso questioned whether these juveniles were able to understand the significance of the *Miranda* warnings. Grisso also concluded, after conducting a survey of juveniles, that almost all fourteen-year-olds and one-half of fifteen and sixteen-year-olds were too young to understand the importance of their Miranda rights.[56]

The *Fare v. Michael C.* decision (1979) applies the "totality of the circumstances" approach to juveniles' interrogations. In this case, sixteen-year-old

Michael C. was implicated in a murder that took place during a robbery. The police arrested the youth and brought him to the station. After he was advised of his *Miranda* rights, he requested to see his probation officer. When this request was denied, he proceeded to talk with the police officer, implicating himself in the murder. The Supreme Court ruled that Michael seemed to understand his rights, and even when his request to talk with his probation officer was denied, he still was willing to waive his rights and continue the interrogation.[57]

The states have passed statutes to force the police and the courts to comply with the standards of a constitutional interrogation of juveniles. Among these requirements are that parents or attorneys must be notified and present during questioning and that questioning should take place in areas other than police stations. In *Commonwealth v. Guyton* (1989), the Massachusetts court held that no other minor, not even a relative, can act as an interested adult.[58] Some states require that questioning occur at a juvenile detention facility, at the juvenile court, or at some other neutral place where the juvenile will not be intimidated by the surroundings. For an example of a very complicated police interrogation with juveniles, see Focus on Practice 4–2.

FOCUS ON PRACTICE 4–2

INTERROGATION AND VICTIMIZATION

On November 15, 1996, we traveled to a residence to investigate a theft case. The house was a known party house for juveniles and a hideout for juvenile runaways. Living in the house were four female children ages four, six, eight, and ten; two adult parents; and one male juvenile age seventeen, who was a ward of the young girls' parents.

After knocking on the rear door, the door was opened and the smell of burning marijuana could be detected. Marijuana was in plain view on the kitchen table near the door. After getting consent to search the residence, more drug paraphernalia was discovered.

Only the electric stove in the kitchen was heating the house. The house was in deplorable condition and unfit for adult habitation let alone for children. The children's rooms contained four-inch-square unplugged holes in the walls where a porch roof used to be attached. The children's beds were next to these holes. The plumbing in the bathroom was inoperable. Garbage was piled up inside and outside the house. Children and Youth Services (CYS) was called to take custody of the four girls. The children were put into the care of their paternal grandparents by CYS.

Once in the custody of the grandparents, the children began talking to the grandmother about people at their home beating them, taping their mouths shut, and having sex with them.

The grandmother reported this to CYS. CYS notified the North Franklin Township Police Department, which set up interviews with the children. CYS also sent out notices to the suspects to tell them of the accusations.

The police and CYS jointly interviewed all four girls on several occasions. It was discovered that all of the girls had been victims of sexual assault on multiple occasions, sometimes by multiple assailants. The girls reported assaults by four individuals (an adult in his forties, an eighteen-year-old youth, a sixteen-year-old juvenile, and another seventeen-year-old juvenile who was the chief offender). Both agencies tape-recorded the interviews. (The D.A.'s office later set up a protocol that forbid the tape-recording of child interviews.) Then the children were interviewed again. Some of the girls were interviewed before each hearing. Additional information was developed during these interviews.

The assistance of CYS workers at the initial interviews was invaluable. They are excellent at creating rapport with small children and testing the truthfulness of a child in identifying body parts. Such interviews are especially difficult. Besides the need to create rapport so that children will speak to strangers about such incidents, the integrity of the child's memory must be maintained. The children were given counseling to lessen the impact of their experiences. Such counseling might dull their memories, which would be counter to the objective of a criminal prosecution, in which accurate memories are needed.

Unfortunately, CYS also sent out notices to suspects. This works against police interviewers, who prefer to catch the suspects "cold," providing a different dynamic to the interview.

The investigators found that the home was a flophouse for drunks and drug abusers. The forty-year-old adult offender was a homeless person who came there to party; the eighteen-year-old stayed there off and on to get away from his own home; the sixteen-year-old came to party; the seventeen-year-old lived there as a ward of the victims' parents. Often the parents would throw parties attended mostly by juveniles who were given alcohol, marijuana, and cocaine. Sexual encounters between consenting juveniles were frequent. The young girls' parents would go out a few nights a week to drink and play dart ball, leaving the seventeen-year-old to baby-sit the children, and the pedophile orgies would begin. Quite often the participants would be drinking or smoking marijuana. The children would be called in the ward's bedroom where they would be forced, at times with their mouths taped shut, to watch the babysitter having sex with one of the sisters. They would then get their turn in bed. Sometimes the other offenders would join in and have various types of sex with one of the girls. Some involved sexual touching or rubbing of genitals and some involved penetration. The girls all reported nude pictures being taken of two of the sisters.

The sex ranged from penile penetration of the vagina and the anus to placing fingers in the vagina to masturbation of the victims. No oral intercourse was reported.

The suspects were questioned and all denied the occurrences. The victims were medically examined. Some showed signs of penetration and some did not. It is not uncommon for girls this age to heal physically after violation.

The parents denied any knowledge of the occurrences. The mother denied having knowledge of the photos, which the girls said they found and gave to the mother. The girls said that their mother beat the ward with a frying pan upon seeing the photos recovered from his room. She denied seeing the photos and said that she herself had been molested by her father and no one believed her.

A break came when the eighteen-year-old suspect confessed to having had sexual contact with one of the girls.

Four assailants were charged and the juveniles jailed or put into juvenile detention. The parents were charged with neglect and corruption-related charges. Charts were created for each offender to show who molested whom, and in what manner. The chart on the next page is an example.

Two other juvenile boys were implicated when the girls recounted times when the ward would take them on walks in the woods with their male cousins and have them engage in mock sex acts. These boys were noted but not charged because investigators believed that their arrest would only serve to further complicate the case and their charges would be relatively minor compared to those of the other suspects. The girls could also avoid additional court appearances. Since each defendant was entitled to a hearing in which the victims would be required to testify, the four girls had to testify at least four times about their experiences.

The investigators took a statement from a juvenile in detention with the ward, who had been bragging to him about having sex with the little girls.

The two juvenile defendants were certified adult by the juvenile judge and were put into the county jail adult facility. After doing a year awaiting trial, the eighteen-year-old and the sixteen-year-old gave statements against the other assailants.

About one year after their removal from their parents' home, the young girls went to visit their maternal grandparents. While there, a neighbor of the grandparents molested two of the youngest. This fellow was arrested and the girls testified at his trial. He was found guilty and jailed. This heightened our concern about facts from one case "bleeding into the other."

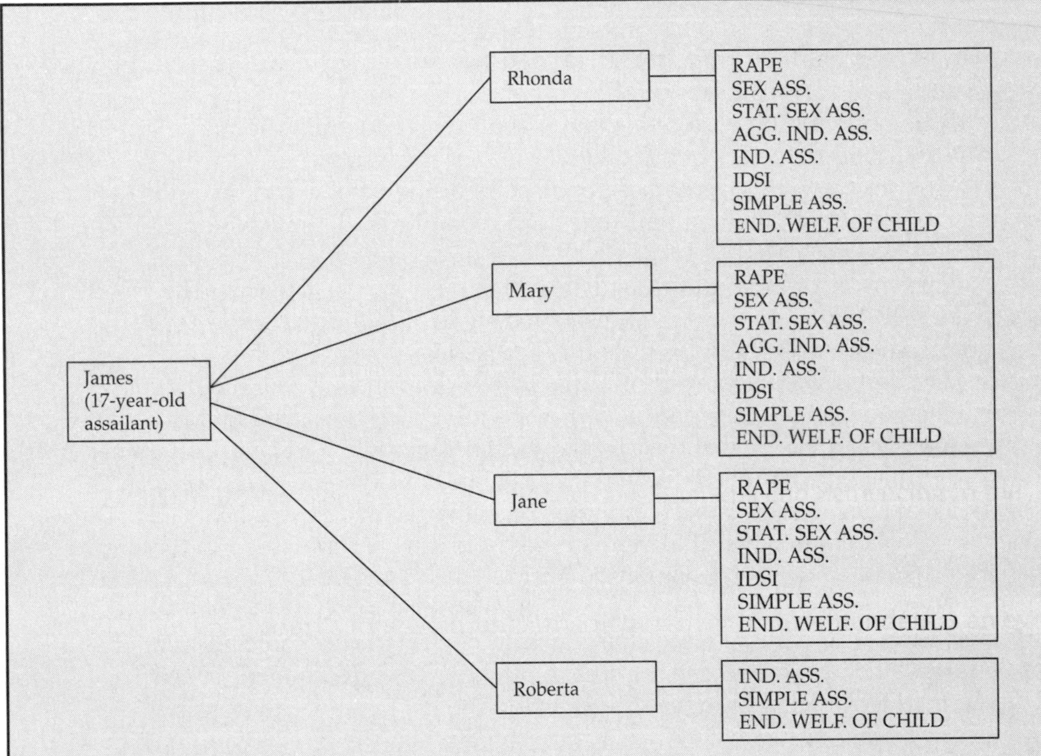

Numerous problems were encountered in this case. First, the children had to be able to articulate what happened to them. Second, rapport had to be developed between them and the investigators. Third, CYS notified the suspects of the allegations prior to police contact; this destroyed the "surprise" effect used in typical investigations. Fourth, with so many actors and victims, "score" cards had to be created to keep track of who did what with whom and how it was done. Additionally, several other juveniles had to be located and questioned. These were youths who attended parties, or who the children saw having sex. Of course, most of these people did not remember anything about the alleged incidents. Even though some juvenile girls reported their girlfriends telling them they were raped there while drunk or drugged, these victims would not confirm the reports.

Also, the victims were undergoing counseling. This counseling involved therapy, which can blur their memories. Although this is good for the girls, it is bad for the purposes of testimony.

Added to this mix was an another molestation in different jurisdiction. This led to the blending of stories, which made it even harder for the very young girls to distinguish the separate occurrences. Nevertheless, all offenders were found guilty.

The case took more than two years to complete. All four victims underwent counseling and appear to be doing well. Now, seven years later, the officers in charge of the original case still run into the two youngest children. These two appear to be well-adjusted and happy children. They are playing softball in a summer league and are now living with their parents who also appear to have pulled their lives together and are involved closely with their children.

Needless to say, everyone who came in contact with the case found it emotionally draining. The secretary typing the statements would become upset just listening to the statements while typing them. The investigators had to be more compassionate with these children, who quite often required hugs and reassurance. This was not typical cop behavior in dealing with victims.

Postnote: Rumors on the street indicate that one of the seventeen-year-olds found guilty was placed in a maximum-security adult prison where he was viciously gang-raped; he had to have a colostomy because of the rape.

Source: Information supplied by former Police Chief Roger Cuccaro, Lt. Kirk Hessler, and Sgt. Richard Horner of the North Franklin Police Department and unnamed sources. Updated July 7, 2003.

Critical Thinking Questions:

What is your reaction to the police interrogation in this incident? What particular difficulties would you have if you were a police detective dealing with the molestation found in this case?

FINGERPRINTING

The **fingerprinting** of juveniles is a controversial practice. The basic concern of critics is that the juveniles' records will not be destroyed when youths no longer fall under juvenile court jurisdiction. Labeled as criminals early in life, it is feared that juveniles will not be able to escape such labels as they mature.

Some states have passed statutes that prohibit the fingerprinting of juveniles without a judge's permission. Many of these states also require that judges control who has access to the fingerprints and further require that the fingerprints be destroyed after the juvenile becomes an adult.[59] In other states, the police control fingerprinting policy. Some police departments follow the courts' suggested guidelines, whereas other departments routinely fingerprint every juvenile taken into custody.

The most important fingerprinting case to reach the courts to date is *Davis v. Mississippi.*[60] In that case, the Supreme Court ruled, among other things, that fingerprints taken by the police could not be used as evidence. The youth in question was detained by the police without authorization by a judicial officer, was interrogated at the time he was first fingerprinted, and then was fingerprinted again at a later date. The court ruled that the police should not have detained the youth without authorization by a judicial officer, that the youth was unnecessarily fingerprinted a second time, and that the youth should not have been interrogated at the first detention when he was fingerprinted.[61]

Lineups and Photographs

A **lineup** consists of the police placing a number of suspects in front of witnesses or victims who try to identify the person who committed the crime against them. If no one can be identified, the suspects are released to the community. If one of the persons is identified as the perpetrator, the police then proceed with their prosecution. The courts have been careful to set standards for the police to follow, because innocent youths could end up labeled as delinquents and confined in an institution.

One important standard is that the offender must have an attorney at the initial identification lineup. This is to ensure that the identification of the offender is not tainted. For example, if a single suspect is shown to a victim with the suggestion by the police that they think "they got the offender," a victim might be pressured to identify the person even though the victim had never seen the accused before. Another concern is the possibility that simply showing a single suspect is "unnecessarily suggestive" and might bias the victim or witness.[62]

In *United States v. Wade* (1967), the Supreme Court ruled that the accused has the right to have counsel present at postindictment lineup procedures.[63] In *Kirby v. Illinois* (1972), the Court went on to say that the defendant's right to counsel at postindictment lineup procedures goes into effect as soon as the complaint or the indictment has been issued.[64] In *In re Holley* (1970), a youth who was accused of rape had his conviction reversed by the appellate court because of the lack of counsel during the lineup identification procedure.[65]

Photographs also can play an important part in the identification of offenders. For example, in one case, a rape victim was shown a photograph of one suspect only. She could not identify the offender from the photograph but then later identified her attacker in a probation office. A California appellate court noted that permitting the identification of offenders on the basis of only one photograph was inappropriate because it could prejudice the victim.[66]

Another problem with photographs is their permanency and potential stigmatizing effect on youths in the community. A youth taken in for questioning who has his or her photograph taken is easily identified. Because photographs are filed and frequently reviewed by police officers, the police examine these photographs whenever something happens in the community. Innocent youths may never be able to escape the stigma of such labeling. For these reasons, some states require that judges give the police written consent to take photographs, that the photographs not be published in the media, and that the photographs be destroyed when the youths become adults.

HOW DOES THE POLICE ORGANIZATION FUNCTION?

Police departments are organized much like the military in that the men and women are ranked in a hierarchy composed of captains (at the top), lieutenants, sergeants, detectives, and officers. Those at the top draw up the rules and make the decisions, and those at the bottom are expected to follow the rules. The officers and detectives at the bottom of this structure are responsible for the detection, investigation, and processing of juvenile offenders through the juvenile justice system. These officers also are responsible for any specialized programs that are set up to fight delinquency and other juvenile problems.

The major goal of police in most communities is simply to maintain order and keep the peace, thereby keeping the streets free from crime and the residents of the community safe. When major crimes occur, the police do vigorously attempt to solve them. These latter types of crime are relatively few in number compared to the many peacekeeping details of running drunks, addicts, and prostitutes off the streets; supervising school crossings; appearing in court; working on traffic patrol; and chasing juveniles off street corners.

The police function is divided into two major roles. One role is to prevent crime—that is, the *proactive role.* The other role is to solve crimes after an offense occurs—that is, the *reactive role.* Police deal with juveniles in both ways. On the one hand, police officers try to prevent crime by giving talks and demonstrations in the schools and participating in antidelinquency programs. On the other hand, police officers respond to crimes by investigating offenses, taking offenders into custody, and processing offenders through the justice system.

The nature of the police organization determines how juvenile problems are solved. In the following section we look at police departments without specialized juvenile officers or units as well as those with specialized personnel or units.

DEPARTMENTS WITHOUT SPECIALIZED UNITS OF PERSONNEL

Smaller departments usually do not have specialized individuals or units to deal with juvenile crime, and juvenile offenses are dealt with as a routine part of police work. Officers walking beats or assigned to traffic control, surveillance, detective work, vice squads, or other police activities come into contact with juveniles in the course of everyday work.

Officers whose major concern is adult crime often resist having to work on juvenile crime. These officers consider runaways, dependent/neglected youths, victimized/abused children, and status offenders to be nuisances. In addition, few if any of these patrol officers and detectives have had any specialized training in working with juveniles, and they are uncertain as to how to recognize or approach juveniles in difficulty. Some treat all juveniles the same way and, in some cases, in a rude, forceful, insensitive, and coercive manner in order to intimidate the youths. Police critics charge that these approaches are all too likely to antagonize or alienate the youths and the public. Furthermore, some officers tend to view juvenile crime as "kiddie crime" and resent this "low-status" juvenile work. These officers are far more interested in making arrests for serious offenses that will earn them promotions and the reputation for being a good cop.

Police officers approach serious juvenile crimes in the same way as they do serious adult crime. Because the age of an offender rarely is known at the time an offense is detected, officers and detectives often do not know whether the offender is an adult or a juvenile; nevertheless, officers may still be disappointed if the offender turns out to be a juvenile. Other officers and even prosecutors do not always view juvenile arrests to be as important as those of adults.

Departments With Specialized Units of Personnel

Departments with specialized services for juveniles usually have trained juvenile officers, juvenile units, or gang control units.

Juvenile Officers

The size of the juvenile crime problem has led many police executives to assign individual officers to work solely with juvenile crime. These men and women are pulled from the ranks of patrol officers, and, in smaller departments, they may be the only officers given this special assignment. Unfortunately, many of these men and women lack the specialized training that is believed necessary to work with juveniles. Unless they receive training, these officers will, in many cases, continue to deal with juveniles in much the same way as they deal with the adult offenders with whom they come into contact.

Larger departments often hire juvenile specialists. These officers may have backgrounds in the social sciences and have specialized training in social work, sociology, psychology, public administration, and the administration of justice. They also may understand child development, the nature of juvenile–parent relationships, the problems of adolescence, identity formation, alcoholism and other addictions, and the consequences of living under poverty-stricken conditions. But unless a special department is set up to work with juvenile problems, these officers must operate alone in their departments and endure the low status that accompanies working with juveniles.

Juvenile Units

Juvenile units are found in many larger cities. These units have the normal crime-fighting tasks of detecting, investigating, and prosecuting offenders for everything from bicycle thefts to serious felonies. The units have the responsibility to investigate any crimes believed to have been committed by juveniles, to investigate complaints that children have been abused or victimized or are dependent or neglected, and to search for runaway youths. Juvenile unit members also refer juveniles to appropriate social service agencies in the community, counsel with parents and children, supervise youth activities in the community, keep an eye on high-risk crime areas for juveniles, and develop and run antidelinquency programs.[67] The intensive nature of these efforts requires that the juvenile officers in these units be highly trained, but even these officers cannot escape the low status that comes from dealing with juveniles.

Gang Control Units

The number of street gangs has increased dramatically since the late 1980s. A survey of police departments in the seventy-nine largest cities in the United States indicated that the presence of gangs and ganglike problems was widespread. In this survey, 91.1 percent of the departments reported the presence of gangs involving juveniles. Three departments (Baltimore, Maryland; Raleigh, North Carolina; and Washington, DC) reported no gang problems, but they did indicate the presence of groups of juveniles who were involved in criminal activity. Only four departments (Memphis, Tennessee; Newark, New Jersey; Pittsburgh, Pennsylvania; and Richmond, Virginia) reported no gang or ganglike problems.[68] In the first decade of the twenty-first century, few officials in these cities still deny they have gang problems.

The characteristics of these gangs vary widely by city and by area of the country. Some of the gangs are simply groups of adolescents who hang around together and who seldom get into any serious trouble. Other gangs engage in extensive drug activity, and some have engaged in violent shootouts with one another and with the police and, in some instances, have killed innocent bystanders. Police departments have responded to the presence of these gangs by setting up, typically, one of three types of units.[69]

The first type of unit is called the **Youth Service Program.** Although members of these gang programs may be regular officers pulled from any police unit, the members most frequently are from the Youth Service Bureaus. This unit is formed to deal with a specific gang problem and is not a permanent unit within the police force. Officers continue to perform their regular duties and are not exclusively concerned with gang problems. Once a particular problem has been solved, the police officers involved return to their regular assignments. The **gang detail** is the second type of unit. The officers in the gang details generally are part of a traditional police unit assigned to gang problems. These officers do not routinely assist other members of their units on other types of problems. The **gang unit** is the third type of unit. These units are established to work solely on gang problems, and many will develop extensive intelligence networks with gang members in the community.[70]

Police departments that work with gangs engage in four types of activities.

1. Regardless of whether one officer or a whole unit is involved, intelligence must be gathered concerning gang personnel and activities.

2. Most police departments engage in delinquency prevention activities and various types of gang programs whenever resources permit.
3. When crimes are reported to the police, police are responsible for investigating the offenses and attempting to identify the offender(s).
4. Police then must either take the offender into custody or dispose of the case in some other way.[71]

WHAT ARE THE SPECIAL CHALLENGES FACING THE POLICE IN THE COMMUNITY?

Community policing, according to Vincent J. Webb and Nanette Graham, is "contemporary American police policy."[72] In a 1992 survey of the twenty-five largest police departments in the United States, 78 percent reported practicing community policing, 13 percent planned to adopt a community policing program in the near future, and only 9 percent had no plans for a community policing program.[73]

Community policing is particularly useful in juvenile justice for a number of reasons:

1. It moves police officers from anonymity in the patrol car to *direct* engagement with a community that gives them more immediate information about neighborhood problems and insights into their solutions.
2. It frees officers from an emergency response system and permits them to engage more directly in *proactive crime prevention.*
3. It makes police operations more visible to the public, *increasing police accountability to the public.*
4. It *decentralizes* operations, allowing officers greater familiarity with the workings and needs of various neighborhoods.
5. It encourages officers to view *citizens as partners*, improving relations between the public and the police.
6. It moves decision making and discretion to police officers on the streets and therefore places more authority in the hands of those who best know the community's problems and experiences.[74]

To implement community policing in the first decade of the twenty-first century, many police forces are pursuing problem-oriented policing; preventing, or at least discouraging, drug use by school-age children; getting guns out of the hands of juveniles; and participating in community-based gang prevention and control strategies.

Pursuing Problem-Oriented Policing

This approach may well be the wave of the future for the police. Traditionally, police have responded to crimes as isolated events, interviewed victims and witnesses, processed offenders through the system, and evaluated their performance using aggregate police statistics.[75] But police departments are currently turning to **problem-oriented policing,** which means that police respond to the circumstances that create juvenile problems rather than to the incidents that result from the causes.

Police who use the approach of problem-oriented policing first go through their statistics and group all similar incidents together. They then determine whether the offenses share any common underlying features. Knowing that large numbers of robberies or burglaries occur in a specific area shortly after school is dismissed, for example, suggests to the police that students are responsible for the offenses. Second, the police then analyze the problem, collecting information from a variety of public and private sources, such as schools, transportation services, private police, businesses, and citizens. Using these data, police officers analyze the basic character of the problem, try to determine its causes, and develop a range of possible solutions. Third, the police officers work with all involved parties to come up with a plan of action. Schools, businesses, service agencies, and citizens are approached to develop a workable plan to solve the problem. Finally, police officers evaluate their results to determine whether the plan actually worked.[76]

One example of problem-oriented policing is the Serious Habitual Offender Drug Involved (SHODI) program that has been devised for intensive concentration on chronic youthful offenders in Ventura, California; Colorado Springs; and Jacksonville, Florida. A key to these programs is to give police access to full data on delinquents' arrest records so that they can be checked by computer any time a youth is stopped for questioning. Once a juvenile offender is identified, based on such guidelines as four arrests for serious crimes within a year, police officers keep a closer watch on that youth.[77] Focus on Practice 4–3 provides another example of problem-oriented policing to solve a juvenile problem.

Preventing Drug Use by School-Age Children

In the 1990s, the need for substance-abuse prevention programs demanded creativity and engagement on the part of the police. Project DARE (Drug Abuse Resistance Education) is an innovative drug prevention program that rapidly expanded across the United States. Developed in 1983 as a cooperative effort by the Los Angeles Police Department and the Los Angeles Unified School District, this program uses uniformed police officers to teach a formal curriculum to fifth- and sixth-grade students in a classroom.[78]

In this program, the police officer teaches kids in school to say "no" to drugs before the youths begin to experiment with them. The officer helps

FOCUS ON PRACTICE 4–3

PROBLEM-ORIENTED POLICING IN THE MALL

Prior to 1987, Franklin Mall, a regional shopping mall in southwestern Pennsylvania that serves a population base of approximately fifty thousand people from Pennsylvania, West Virginia, and Ohio, had a low number of criminal incidents. But as the rates of retail theft, auto theft, disorderly conduct, and criminal mischief increased dramatically, mall management and security forces, merchants, and the elderly all became concerned. The elderly, particularly, became fearful that predatory juveniles would victimize them.

Mall management and local law enforcement officers were not prepared to deal with the problem. Traditional police methods of rapid response and incident-oriented policing simply did not work. Accordingly, the chief of police set out to develop a plan of action using problem-oriented policing.

Officer Richard Horner was taught the basic concepts of problem-oriented policing and was assigned to the mall. His first task was to uncover the causes or factors behind the problem. Specifically, he looked at the nature of the surrounding community; the attitudes of mall management; the practices and personnel of mall security; the attitudes and concerns of retail establishment managers; mall design; attitudes and concerns of mall patrons; and the problems of area schools.

The officer found that the elderly feared victimization because of the mere presence of juveniles. Specifically, the elderly feared "juvenile grouping," that is, large numbers of juveniles standing around and talking. The elderly did not understand that juvenile grouping is a normal social behavior of young people. The youths were perceived as more unruly and dangerous than they in fact were. Mall management and security perceived the youths similarly, and both responded inappropriately to misbehavior by verbally harassing and intimidating the youths and by treating them roughly. In addition, various security personnel were responsible for generating needless confrontations with the youths and making the problem worse.

The analysis of the juvenile arrests that had been made at the mall was another phase of the study. A profile of the juveniles indicated that eleven- to sixteen-year-old youths often drank alcohol, which led to general disorderly conduct and nuisance types of complaints. Seventeen- to nineteen-year-old youths also used alcohol and/or drugs but were engaging in the more serious and violent types of incidents.

The area schools were approached next. School personnel were experiencing the same types of problems as the malls in that the schools also were faced with increased alcohol abuse and motor vehicle violations. The alcohol

These weapons were confiscated by mall security officers and police from Neo-Nazi gang members in the Washington, Pennsylvania, area. (Photo by Stuart Miller.)

was, in addition, associated with fighting between so-called "preppy" and "vo-tech" student groups on school grounds and at the malls.

Once all the factors were understood, the police department developed a plan of action that included both traditional and innovative responses to the problem. These responses included some of the following:

1. The most violent crimes were identified as the first priority.
2. The police worked with mall management to decrease motor vehicle violations within the parking area.
3. Mall security personnel were trained to deal more appropriately with juveniles. Those unable to conform were removed from the mall security force.
4. The police initiated a campaign to reduce alcohol use. First of all, 118 juveniles were arrested in the first thirty days of the campaign, and their parents were brought in and told what the kids were doing,

what they were saying at the time of their arrest, and the types of statements the youths were making during questioning.

5. The officer assigned to the mall traveled to the local school district to heighten student awareness of the alcohol problem, drinking and driving, domestic violence, problems at the mall, the law, and citizenship. The officer solicited students' help in changing the mall environment.
6. The mall management scheduled social activities at the mall that included different juvenile age groups. This gave the juveniles positive reinforcement that they were an important part of the mall community.

The initiation of problem-solving policing produced a dramatic reduction in crime and relative peace at the mall and surrounding area for the next three to four years. During this time, police continued to teach mall security officers how to spot potential problems and how to handle groups creating problems, and they encouraged mall security to report incidents to a police officer assigned as a liaison to the mall.

The number of juveniles frequenting the mall remained at around eighty to one hundred and police problems remained stable until the mall undertook a rebuilding program in 2000 to 2001. As a result of the expansion, the mall once again became a meeting place for juveniles.

The mall was renamed, and was totally remodeled and expanded, with a fourteen-screen theater added. Now, on Friday evenings, police encounter as many as eight hundred to one thousand juveniles spending their evening at the mall or theater. A change from the past is that juveniles are not just from the town of Washington, Pennsylvania: they are coming from all across Southwestern Pennsylvania. Mall security was increased by two and township police were placed at the mall on Friday nights.

Because of the numbers, the problems associated with juveniles increased. Older people still fear the young and some occasional incidents with kids on drugs and alcohol still occur as do fights.

One interesting twist is that of juveniles who offer cocaine or marijuana for sale in the parking lots. The "contraband" is sold to buyers, but on examination, the bags are found to contain fake marijuana or cocaine; in other words, some juveniles have set up their own "scams" against their peers; this occasionally generates fights.

In addition, mall security again has a problem with the kids standing and talking and blocking the common passageways. They attempt to keep the juveniles moving, which eases the congestion. When the mall closes at either 2100 or 2200 hours, the juveniles move to the pad area in front of the theaters and gather. With the increase in size, police particularly see an increase in disorderly conducts and assaults in the area in front of the theaters where the juveniles gather.

One incident was an alleged black-on-white strong-arm robbery. About six to eight months after this incident, officers began to notice the presence of a small group of Skin Heads. One of the members was a juvenile who had been assaulted by a group of black juveniles. At this time, the North Franklin Police along with Mall and other law enforcement agencies began identifying and tracking the members of this group.

Source: Information supplied by former North Franklin Police Chief Roger Cuccaro, current chief Mark Kravakich, Lt. Kirk Hessler, Sgt. Richard Horner, and Mall Security Chief Richard Keys.

Critical Thinking Questions:

How much of a problem are juvenile related crimes in shopping malls?

What is your evaluation of how the problem was handled in this mall?

youths build their self-esteem and develop ways of saying "no." Youths are taught, for example, that real friends will not push them to use drugs and alcohol, that most of their friends do not use these substances, that being adult means they can make positive and responsible decisions, and that they are able to resist peer pressure. The lectures presented in the classrooms also help kids protect themselves, reduce stress, seek out alternatives to drug use, and, generally, take a stand against drugs.[79]

An initial evaluation of the program suggested that the self-reported behavior of seventh-grade students who had received DARE instruction in the sixth grade indicated significantly lower rates of substance abuse since graduation from sixth grade than seventh-graders who had not received DARE instruction. Furthermore, this evaluation indicated that DARE students were also more likely to use effective refusal strategies than were non-DARE students when pressured by peers to use drugs or alcohol.[80]

A 1994 analysis by the Research Triangle Institute in North Carolina was more critical of the program. This analysis showed that the DARE program was effective in increasing students' knowledge about substance abuse and enhancing their social skills, but less effective in developing negative attitudes toward drugs and improving self-esteem. The evaluation further found that DARE's short-term effects on deterring substance abuse by fifth- and sixth-graders were limited.[81] The institute recommended that DARE revise its curriculum, using more interactive strategies and participatory learning and emphasizing social and general competencies. This recommendation was launched nationwide in the fall of 1994.[82]

Getting Guns Out of the Hands of Juveniles

The control of gun-related violence in the youth population is one of the most serious problems facing the police in deterring youth crime. As discussed in Chapter 2, Alfred Blumstein believes that the increased use of guns by juveniles is one of the most serious problems that confront the juvenile justice system.[83] This problem would increase in magnitude if predictions are accurate that there will be 20 percent more juveniles in the crime-committing ages by 2010 than there were in 1995.[84]

This issue of gun control as it relates to juveniles will be no easier to manage than it has been in adult justice. Some of the possible strategies to improve gun control with juveniles are more intensive traffic enforcement in gun-crime hot spots; more raiding of drug, or crack, houses; more targeting of drug-trafficking gang members on the street and building probable cause for a search; more surveillance around gang-controlled junior and senior high schools; and more community support.[85]

Participating in Gang Prevention and Control Strategies

In the late 1980s and early 1990s, police departments across the nation were facing the problem of how to handle the emergence of drug-trafficking gangs in their communities. Encouraged by public officials, both the chiefs of police and the school administrators typically denied the existence of a gang problem. Then, a widely publicized gang-related incident would take place in the community. If the event were serious enough, such as the killing of an elderly person or a nongang youth, it would trigger a process of public recognition of a gang problem. As the public became increasingly concerned about public safety, the police and juvenile justice system would be given the mandate to deal with the problem. The police typically would be allocated new resources to hire additional officers or to develop a gang unit. Unfortunately, this effort to repress drug-trafficking youth gangs has been notoriously unsuccessful.

The problem facing law enforcement officials, especially in communities with an emerging gang problem, is that the police are not prepared to deal with the problems generated by such groups. Yet, even with an adequately trained gang unit of sufficient size, the repression of drug-trafficking youth gangs seems to worsen rather than reduce the problem.

In the next few years, police departments must decide whether to do "more of the same" with gang youths—that is, to use harassment and arrests as means of making it difficult for gangs to thrive in school and community settings. Or, as some departments have done, the police can work with concerned citizens and community agencies to develop grassroots prevention and intervention models. In these departments, the police, of course, must continue to arrest law-violating youth, but they must also commit considerable resources to help high-risk youth find more socially acceptable modes of behavior.

SUMMARY

The family and local community were able to control wayward juveniles until the end of the 1700s. The increased urbanization and industrialization of the emerging society, however, called for a different response to juvenile crime. The public believed the police were the answer to the problem during the first third of the 1800s. Social control moved from the community and the family into formal departments of police, courts, and correctional agencies.

In spite of some initial efforts by the police to set up delinquency prevention programs in the early 1900s, reformers complained that the police were too often brutal, corrupt, and uncaring. The police exercised almost unlimited discretion with juveniles until the 1960s. At that time, court decisions began to limit police powers. Police were required to follow both court and statutory guidelines in the areas of search and seizure, detention, interrogation, confession, fingerprinting, photographing, and lineup.

Police organization was undoubtedly part of the problem. Police departments were organized bureaucratically, and few had specialized units to deal with juveniles. Today, some police departments are quite effective in police-juvenile relations and have organized effective antidrug, shoplifting, and gang programs. Police also have begun to distinguish more carefully among the wide range of juveniles with whom they come into contact.

WEB SITES OF INTEREST

Information and links about the police and juvenile court processes can be found at

http://www.wiu.edu/library/govpubs/guides/p&cjuven.htm

Various links about the police and their interaction/role with juveniles can be found at

http://www.criminology.fsu.edu/jjclearinghouse/jj21.html

To see how the Oregon County Chiefs of Police are working with the community to help curb juvenile justice go to

http://www.policechief.org/magazine/spring99/juvenilejustice.html

CRITICAL THINKING QUESTIONS

1. Summarize juveniles' attitudes toward the police.
2. How do departments without specialized personnel handle juvenile offenders?
3. How do departments with specialized personnel handle juvenile offenders?
4. Summarize the legal rights of juveniles taken into custody.

NOTES

1. Interview conducted in 1997 and published in Clemens Bartollas and Larry D. Hahn, *Policing in America* (Boston: Allyn & Bacon, 1999), 53.
2. David R. Johnson, *Policing the Urban Underworld: The Impact of Crime on the Development of the American Police, 1800–1887* (Philadelphia: Temple University Press, 1979), 78–89.
3. Robert M. Fogelson, *Big-City Police* (Cambridge, MA: Harvard University Press, 1977), 86–87.
4. Ibid.
5. Ibid.
6. Ibid.
7. Ibid.
8. Larry W. Fultz, *Public Relations and the Police: A Survey of Public Opinion* (Houston, TX: University of Houston, 1959).
9. Robert Portune, *Changing Adolescent Attitudes Toward Police* (Cincinnati: W. H. Anderson, 1971).
10. Donald H. Bouma, *Kids and Cops* (Grand Rapids, MI: William B. Eerdmans, 1969), 69–79. Other studies that examine juveniles' attitudes toward the police include Peggy Giordano, "The Sense of Injustice: An Analysis of Juveniles' Reactions to the Justice System," *Criminology* 14 (May 1976), 40; L. Thomas Winfree Jr. and Curt T. Griffiths, "Adolescents' Attitudes Toward the Police: A Survey of High School Students," in *Juvenile Delinquency: Little Brother Grows Up,* edited by Theodore N. Ferdinand (Beverly Hills, CA: Sage Publications, 1977), 79–99; William T. Rusinko, W. Johnson Knowlton, and Carlton A. Hornung, "The Importance of Police Contact in the Formulation of Youths' Attitudes Toward Police," *Journal of Criminal Justice* 6 (Spring 1978), 65; J. P. Clark and E. P. Wenninger, "The Attitudes of Juveniles Toward the Legal Institution," *Journal of Criminal Law, Criminology and Police Science* 55 (1964), 482–89; V. I. Cizanckas and C. W. Pruviance, "Changing Attitudes of Black Youths," *Police Chief* 40 (1973), 42.
11. Winfree and Griffiths, "Adolescents' Attitudes Toward the Police," 79–99.
12. Rusinko et al., "The Importance of Police Contact in the Formulation of Youths' Attitudes Toward Police," 65.
13. Scott H. Decker, "Citizen Attitudes Toward the Police: A Review of Past Findings and Suggestions for Future Policy," *Journal of Police Science and Administration* 9 (1981), 80–87.
14. James R. Davis, "A Comparison of Attitudes Toward the New York City Police," *Journal of Police Science and Administration* 17 (1990), 233–42.
15. Komanduri S. Murty, Julian B. Roebuck, and Joann D. Smith, "The Image of Police in Black Atlanta Communities," *Journal of Police Science and Administration,* 17 (1990), 250–57.
16. Ibid., 256.

17. Michael J. Leiber, Mahesh K. Nalla, and Margaret Farnworth, "Explaining Juveniles' Attitudes Toward the Police," *Justice Quarterly* 15 (March 1998), 151–171.
18. These findings are taken from Kathleen Maguire and Ann Pastore, eds., *Sourcebook of Criminal Justice Statistics, 1994* (Washington, DC: U.S. Bureau of Justice Statistics, 1995), 206. Table in *Sourcebook* compiled from data provided by Lloyd D. Johnston, Jerald G. Bachman, and Patrick M. O'Malley, *Monitoring the Future Project* (Ann Arbor: Institute for Social Research, University of Michigan, 1982–1992).
19. Maguire and Pastore, eds., *Sourcebook of Criminal Justice Statistics, 1994*, 206.
20. Data for 2001 were provided by Lloyd D. Johnston, Jerald G. Bachman, and Patrick M. O'Malley, *Monitoring the Future Project* (Ann Arbor: Institute for Social Research, Survey Research Center, University of Michigan).
21. Ibid.
22. Richard W. Kobetz and Betty B. Bosarge, *Juvenile Justice Administration* (Gaithersburg, MD: International Association of Chiefs of Police, 1973).
23. James Q. Wilson, "Dilemmas of Police Administration, "*Public Administration Review* 28 (September–October 1968).
24. See Donald J. Black and Albert J. Reiss Jr., "Police Control of Juveniles," *American Sociological Review* 35 (February 1979), 63–77.
25. Robert M. Terry, "Discrimination in the Handling of Juvenile Offenders by Social Control Agencies," *Journal of Research in Crime and Delinquency* 4 (July 1967), 218–30; Nathan Goldman, *The Differential Selection of Juvenile Offenders for Court Appearances* (New York: National Council on Crime and Delinquency, 1963), pp. 35–47; Black and Reiss, "Police Control of Juveniles," 63–77; Irving Piliavin and Scott Briar, "Police Encounters with Juveniles," *American Journal of Sociology* 70 (September 1964), 206–14.
26. Terry, "Discrimination in the Handling of Juvenile Offenders by Social Control Agencies"; Black and Weiss, "Police Control of Juveniles."
27. Gail Armstrong, "Females Under the Law—Protected but Unequal," *Crime and Delinquency* 23 (April 1977), 109–20; Meda Chesney-Lind, "Girls and Status Offenses: Is Juvenile Justice Still Sexist?" *Criminal Justice Abstract* (March 1988), 144–65; and Meda Chesney-Lind and Randall G. Shelden, *Girls: Delinquency and Juvenile Justice* (Pacific Grove, CA: Brooks/Cole, 1992).
28. Studies that have found a police bias in arresting juveniles include Theodore N. Ferdinand and Elmer C. Luchtenhand, "Inner-City Youths, the Police, the Juvenile Court and Justice," *Social Problems* 17 (Spring 1970), 510–27; Goldman, *The Differential Selection of Juvenile Offenders for Court Appearances;* Piliavin and Briar, "Police Encounters with Juveniles"; and Marvin E. Wolfgang, Robert M. Figlio, and Thorstein Sellin, *Delinquency in a Birth Cohort* (Chicago: University of Chicago Press, 1972), 252.
29. Philip W. Harris, "Race and Juvenile Justice: Examining the Impact of Structural and Policy Changes on Racial Disproportionality." Paper presented at

the annual meeting of the American Society of Criminology, Montreal, Canada (November 13, 1987).

30. James T. Carey et al., *The Handling of Juveniles from Offense to Disposition* (Washington, DC: Government Printing Office, 1976), 1976; A. W. McEachern and Riva Bauzer, "Factors Related to Disposition in Juvenile-Police Contacts," in *Juvenile Gangs in Context,* edited by Malcolm W. Klein (Upper Saddle River, NJ: Prentice Hall, 1967); Ferdinand and Luchterhand, "Inner-City Youths, the Police, the Juvenile Court and Justice," 510–27; Miriam D. Sealock and Sally S. Simpson, "Unraveling Bias in Arrest Decisions: The Role of Juvenile Offender Type-Scripts," *Justice Quarterly* 15 (September 1998), 427–57.
31. Merry Morash, "Establishment of Juvenile Police Record," *Criminology* 22 (February 1984), 97–111.
32. Piliavin and Briar, "Police Encounters with Juveniles," 206–14.
33. Carl Werthman and Irving Piliavin, "Gang Members and the Police" in *The Police,* edited by David J. Bordua (New York: John Wiley, 1967), 56–98.
34. Richard J. Lundman, Richard E. Sykes, and John P. Clark, "Police Control of Juveniles: A Replication," in *Police Behavior: A Sociological Perspective,* edited by Richard J. Lundman (New York: Oxford University Press, 1980), 147–48.
35. Malcolm W. Klein, "Police Processing of Juvenile Offenders: Toward the Development of Juvenile System Rates," in Los Angeles County Sub-Regional Board, California Council on Juvenile Justice, Part III.
36. Wilson, "Dilemmas of Police Administration," 19.
37. For a discussion of the Constitution and Supreme Court decisions relevant to the schools, see Reed B. Day, *Legal Issues Surrounding Safe Schools* (Topeka, KS: National Organization on Legal Problems of Education, 1994).
38. *Mapp v. Ohio,* 367 U.S. 643 (1961); Reed B. Day, *Legal Issues Surrounding Safe Schools,* 25–38.
39. *State v. Lowery,* 230 A. 2d 907 (1967).
40. *In re Two Brothers and a Case of Liquor,* Juvenile Court of the District of Columbia, 1966, reported in *Washington Law Reporter* 95 (1967), 113.
41. *Ciulla v. State,* 434 S.W. 2d 948 (Tex. Civ. App. 1968).
42. For an extensive discussion of the relevant issues and court decisions related to police in the schools, see Samuel M. Davis, *Rights of Juveniles* 2d ed. (New York: Clark Boardman Company, 1986), Sections 3–19 to 3–34.3.
43. *New Jersey v. T. L. O.,* 469 U.S. (1985).
44. Ibid.
45. Ibid.
46. J.M. Sanchez, "Expelling the Fourth Amendment from American Schools: Students' Rights Six Years After T. L. O.," *Education Journal* 21 (1992), 381–413; Reed B. Day, *Legal Issues Surrounding Safe Schools,* 9–24.
47. *Brown v. Mississippi,* 297 U.S. 278 (1936).
48. Davis, *Rights of Juveniles,* Section 3–45.

49. *Haley v. Ohio,* 332 U.S. 596 (1948).
50. Ibid.
51. *Miranda v. Arizona,* 384 U.S. 436 (1966).
52. *In re Gault,* 387 U.S. (1967).
53. *People v. Lara,* 62 Cal. Reporter, 586 (1967), cert. denied 392 U.S. 945 (1968).
54. *In re Mellot,* 217 S. E. 2d 745 (C.A.N. Calif., 1975).
55. *In re Dennis P. Fletcher,* 248 A. 2d 364 (Md., 1968), cert. denied 396 U.S. 852 (1969).
56. T. Grisso, *Juveniles' Waiver of Rights: Legal and Psychological Competence* (New York: Plenum Press, 1981).
57. *Fare v. Michael C.,* 442 U.S. 23, 99 S. Ct. 2560 (1979).
58. *Commonwealth v. Guyton,* 405 Mass. 497 (1989).
59. Elyce Z. Ferster and Thomas F. Courtless, "The Beginning of Juvenile Justice, Police Practices, and the Juvenile Offender," *Vanderbilt Law Review* 22 (April 1969), 598–601.
60. *Davis v. Mississippi,* 394 U.S. 721 (1969).
61. Ibid.
62. See Davis, *Rights of Juveniles,* Section 3–67.
63. *United States v. Wade,* 338 U.S. 218, 87 S. Ct. 1926 (1967).
64. *Kirby v. Illinois,* 406 U.S. 682, 92 S. Ct. 1877 (1972).
65. *In re Holley,* 107 R. I. 615, 268 A. 2d 723 (1970).
66. *In re Carl T.,* 81 Cal. Reporter 655 (2d C.A., 1969).
67. Robert W. Winslow, *Juvenile Delinquency in a Free Society* (Monterey, CA: Brooks/Cole, 1977).
68. G. David Curry et al., *National Assessment of Law Enforcement Anti-Gang Information Resources* (Washington, DC: National Institute of Justice, 1992), 1. Interestingly, gangs now appear to be present in at least two of these cities: Pittsburgh and Richmond.
69. Jerome A. Needle and Wm. Vaughn Stapleton, "Police Handling of Youth Gangs," *Reports of the National Juvenile Justice Assessment Centers* (Washington, DC: U.S. Department of Justice, September, 1983).
70. Ibid.
71. Needle and Stapleton, "Police Handling of Youth Gangs," xii.
72. Vincent J. Webb and Nanette Graham, "Citizen Ratings of the Importance of Selected Police Duties." Paper presented at the annual meeting of the American Society of Criminology, Miami, Florida (November 1994).
73. Peter C. Kratcoski and Duane Dukes, *Issues in Community Policing* (Cincinnati: W. H. Anderson, 1994), 38.
74. U.S. Department of Justice, "Community Policing," *National Institute of Justice* 225 (1992), 1–32.

75. William Spelman and John E. Eck, *Problem-Oriented Policing,* National Institute of Justice (Washington, DC: U.S. Department of Justice, 1987).
76. Ibid.
77. NBC News Special, "Crime, Punishment, and Kids," July 26, 1987.
78. See William DeJong, "Project DARE: Teaching Kids to Say 'No' to Drugs," *NIJ Reports* (Washington, DC: U.S. Department of Justice, March 1986), 2–5.
79. Ibid.
80. Bureau of Justice Assistance, *Program Brief Book I, An Invitation to Project DARE: Drug Abuse Resistance Education* (Washington, DC: U.S. Department of Justice, n.d.).
81. National Institute of Justice, *The DARE Program: A Review of Prevalence, User Satisfaction, and Effectiveness* (Washington, DC: U.S. Department of Justice, 1994), 1–2.
82. Ibid.
83. Marie Simonetti Rosen, "Professor Alfred Blumstein of Carnegie Mellon University," *Law Enforcement News* 21 (April 30, 1995), 10–13.
84. Ibid.
85. The first two of these are contained in Lawrence W. Sherman, "The Police," in *Crime,* edited by James Q. Wilson and Joan Petersilia (San Francisco, CA: Institute for Contemporary Studies, 1995), 339–41.

5

THE JUVENILE COURT

OBJECTIVES

1. To present the development and legal norms of the juvenile court
2. To explore the main U.S. Supreme Court decisions that incorporated the due process movement into juvenile court proceedings
3. To discuss the intake stages of the juvenile court's proceedings
4. To examine social control of the status offender

KEY TERMS

bail
Breed v. Jones
constitutionalists
decriminalized status offenses
deinstitutionalization of status offenders
detention hearing
ex parte Crouse
In re Gault
In re Winship
intake process
Kent v. United States
Juvenile Justice and Delinquency Prevention Act
McKeiver v. Pennsylvania
parens patriae
plea bargain
preventive detention
transfer process
waiver hearing

> *To save a child from becoming a criminal, or from continuing in a career of crime, to end in maturer years in public punishment and disgrace, the legislature surely may provide for the salvation of such a child, if its parents or guardian be unable or unwilling to do so, by bringing it into one of the courts of the state without any process at all, for the purpose of subjecting it to the state's guardianship and protection.*
>
> *The action is not for the trial of a child charged with a crime, but is mercifully to save it from such an ordeal, with the prison or penitentiary in its wake, if the child's own good and the best interests of the state justify such salvation. Whether the child deserves to be saved by the state is no more a question for a jury than whether the father, if able to save it, ought to save it. The act is but an exercise by the state of its supreme power over the welfare of its children, a power over which it can take a child from its father, and let it go where it will, without committing it to any guardianship or any institution, if the welfare of the child, taking its age into consideration, can be thus best promoted.*
>
> *The design is not punishment, nor the restraint imprisonment, any more than is the wholesome restraint a parent exercises over his child. The severity in either case must necessarily be tempered to meet the necessities of the particular situation. There is no probability, in the proper administration of the law, of the child's liberty being unduly involved. Every statute which is designed to give protection, care, and training to children, as a needed substitute for parental authority, and performance of parental duty, is but a recognition of the duty of the state, as the legitimate guardian and protector of children where other guardianship fails. No constitutional right is violated.*
>
> —Julian W. Mack[1]

The purpose of the court, as expressed in the above quoted *Commonwealth v. Fisher* decision in 1905, "is not for the punishment of offenders but for the salvation of children . . . whose salvation may become the duty of the state."[2] It is this type of statement that resulted in the juvenile court receiving fanatical support from its followers. Ever since the turn of the century, supporters have argued that the informal setting of the juvenile court, coupled with the fatherly demeanor of the juvenile judge, enables children to be treated, rather than punished, for their problems.[3] The state, the argument goes, rescues these youths from a life of trouble on the streets, rehabilitates them, protects them from placement with adult criminals in correctional facilities, and saves them from a life of crime. According to Judge Leonard P. Edwards, what is implicit in this position is that "children are different from adults, that they have developmental needs which they cannot satisfy without assistance and that care and supervision are critical to their upbringing." He then argues that "if children were no different from adults, the juvenile court would be unnecessary."[4]

Critics of the juvenile court sharply challenge these idealistic claims. They argue that the juvenile court has not succeeded in rehabilitating juvenile offenders, in reducing or even stemming the rise of youth crime, or in bringing justice and compassion to youthful offenders.[5] The juvenile court, they argue, acts in an arbitrary and whimsical fashion. It selects whom it "saves" on the basis of their sex and race, not on the basis of justice. The court harms children by processing them through its system, offering them inadequate programs, and labeling them as they return to the community.[6]

This chapter, the first of two on the juvenile court, presents the juvenile court's historical development, its changing legal norms, the pretrial procedures of its proceedings, and the social control of status offenders.

WHAT IS THE TRADITION BEHIND THE JUVENILE COURT?

The roots of the American juvenile court stretch back to Puritan colonial days. Early English common law recognized that children, particularly those under the age of seven, should not be subject to the same punishments as adults. The reasoning behind the practice was that children were not assumed capable of understanding the consequences of their actions; subsequently, young children rarely were punished with the same vigor as adults. As children got older, however, the likelihood increased that they would be dealt with more harshly by colonial law. The state, even in those early days, clearly was committed to raising its children correctly and making them follow society's rules. Indeed, this early practice appears to have been incorporated into the early Massachusetts Puritan code, which was a model for the United States Constitution of 1787.[7]

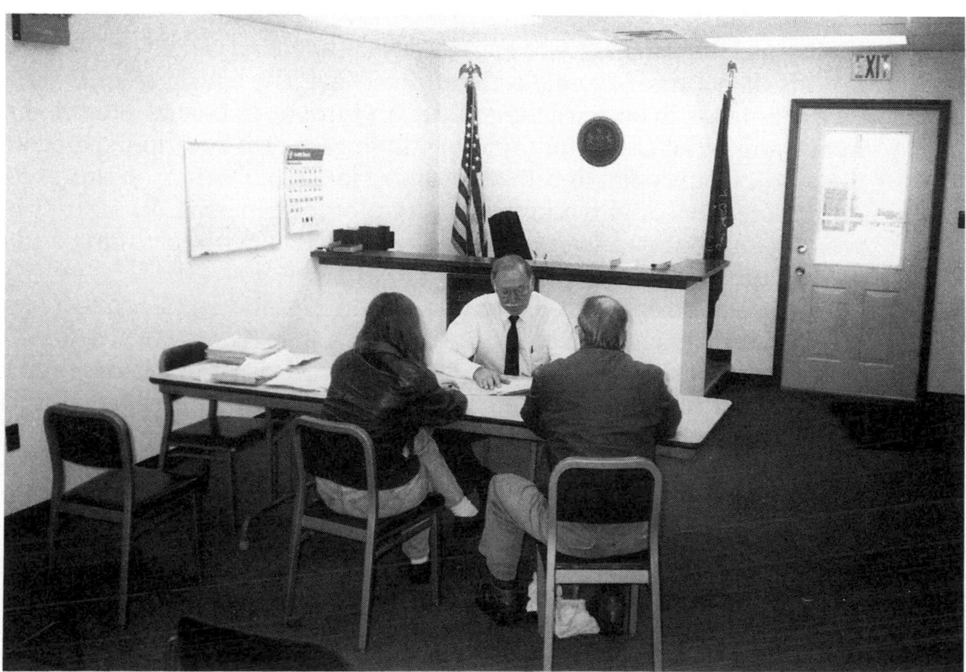

The informality with which juvenile court cases are tried varies widely. Here, a Pennsylvania magistrate hears the case of an underage teenager caught drinking. (Photo by Stuart Miller.)

The state became even more concerned about the welfare of its children in the 1800s. Increased urbanization, industrialization, and bureaucratization were changing the face of America. In the cities, particularly, increasing numbers of youths were seemingly out of control. Reformers searched for ways to teach them traditional values, and the asylum and the training school were developed to help the state maintain its control.

The courts were by now heavily involved with the juvenile problem. The concept of ***parens patriae*** (in the role of the parent) was formalized by ***ex parte Crouse*** in 1838 and gave the courts a legal basis for intervening in the lives of children. The Bill of Rights, the court ruled, did not apply to minors, and the state could legitimately confine minors who, according to the ruling, did not have the right to counsel or trial by jury, and who could be confined even in the absence of criminal behavior.

By the end of the 1800s, much of the U.S. population lived in urban areas and worked in factories. Cities were large and growing, and waves of immigration were inundating the nation's shores with millions of people destined to remain poor. Conditions in the cities were shocking; there was much poverty, crime, disease, mental illness, and dilapidation.[8] The cities' children were viewed as unfortunate victims of the urban scene.

HOW DID THE JUVENILE COURT DEVELOP?

Anthony Platt, in *The Child Savers,* adds greatly to our understanding of the origins of the first juvenile court in Chicago. The Chicago court was created, he argues, partly because the middle and upper classes wanted to control the increasing numbers of immigrants and the poor. In addition, the conditions of the Cook County Jail and the Chicago House of Correction, into which children were placed with adults, were deplorable. Increased numbers of youths were being confined with hardened adult felons who corrupted and exposed them to debauchery, crime, and sin.[9]

These reformers were primarily middle- and upper-class women who had achieved a certain amount of power and freedom. Women such as Jane Addams, Louise Bowen, and Julia Lathrop were committed to rescuing the urban American family and its youth by restoring rural values to them. They wanted to reaffirm parental authority, restore the role of the woman in the home, ensure the proper training of youths, and, most important, save youths from the sins they were exposed to on the streets.[10]

The reformers were aided in their quest by a new emerging philosophy. In the past, the classical school of criminology had argued that laws were violated because people willfully chose to violate them. People were presumed to operate on the basis of free will, having total control over their actions; punishment was required to get them to follow the law. The emerging positive school, in contrast, contended that people were pushed into crime by forces beyond their control. It argued that the causes of crime could be discovered through the use of the scientific method and that the biological, psychological, social, economic, political, and other environmental causes of crime could be discovered through rigorous and precise measurement. Once the causes of crime were discovered, this school argued, experts could then step in and cure the offender of his or her problem. Proponents of this philosophy believed that the juvenile court should use these assumptions in attacking the problems of youth.

Everything was in place. The *parens patriae* doctrine had been accepted by the courts for more than a half century. Social conditions had generated an underclass of people who appeared unable to help themselves. Conservative, humanitarian, and religious philosophies had justified the need and had provided the power necessary for change. Jails and prisons clearly were no places for children. And finally, the positivist philosophy held out the promise that if the right mechanism could be developed, the wayward children could be saved.

The Cook County Juvenile Court was founded in 1899. Its premises were that the *parens patriae* doctrine permitted it to take charge of children in need, that the causes of the children's problems could be discovered and treated, and that the court had to develop a different set of procedures and terminology from those of the adult courts to achieve these goals.

Accordingly, the Illinois court was set up to operate on an informal basis. First, this meant that traditional courtrooms were not used; all that was actually required were a table and chairs where the judge, the child and his or her parents, and probation officers could sit together and discuss the case. Second, children could be brought before the court on the basis of complaints of citizens, parents, police, school officials, or others. Third, the children's hearings were not public and their records were kept confidential because children coming before the court were not considered criminal. Fourth, proof of the child's criminality was not required for the child to be considered in need of the court's services. Fifth, the court had great discretion in determining what kind of services the child required and had wide latitude in determining a disposition. Sixth, lawyers were not required because the hearings were not adversarial. Finally, the standards and procedures long in use in adult courts were missing in the juvenile courts; the standard of proof beyond a reasonable doubt was not required, and hearsay was permitted.

The attractiveness of the juvenile court philosophy resulted in almost all states setting up juvenile courts. In fact, by 1928, only two of thirty-one states had not passed a juvenile court statute.[11] Those that did closely followed the wording and intent of the Chicago statute and its amendments. These were civil courts, usually a family court, and their purpose was rehabilitation, not punishment. The neglected, the dependent, the misbehaving youngster, the status offender, and the delinquent were all subject to the courts' dictates. But the public was assured that programs would be developed to solve the problems of wayward youth so that they would be released to the community as respectable citizens.

Juvenile courts attempted to live up to their mandate for the next sixty years. For about the first twenty years, the court was aided by religiously motivated volunteers who brought strong moral commitments to their work with juveniles. Confidence in the juvenile court began to erode in 1911 and 1912, with exposés detailing the court's deplorable conditions and practices.[12] Another negative influence on the juvenile court following World War I was the general disenchantment with the idea that society was improving.

Immediately following World War I, volunteers were replaced with paid social work professionals called "social adjusters." The social work orientation of these professionals enabled them to help redefine the juvenile court as a social agency and to lobby successfully for more paid social workers. In the 1920s, the field of social work adopted Freudian psychoanalysis, which focused on the client's inner emotional feelings. Thus, instead of attempting to deal with social environmental problems as the cause of delinquency as did earlier reformers, social workers began to focus on the inner mental workings of the child.

HOW HAVE LEGAL NORMS CHANGED?

A group known as the **constitutionalists** argued that the juvenile court was unconstitutional because under its auspices the principles of a fair trial and individual rights were denied. This group primarily was concerned that children appearing before the juvenile court were denied their procedural rights as well as the rights to shelter, protection, and guardianship. The constitutionalists proposed that the procedures of the juvenile court be modified in three ways: (1) by the adoption of separate procedures for dealing with dependent and neglected children and those who are accused of criminal behavior; (2) by the use of informal adjustments to avoid official court actions as frequently as possible; and (3) by the provision of rigorous procedural safeguards and rights for children appearing before the court at the adjudicatory stage.[13]

A series of decisions by the U.S. Supreme Court in the 1960s and early 1970s rapidly accelerated the influence of the constitutionalists on the juvenile court. The five most important cases were *Kent v. United States* (1966), *In re Gault* (1967), *In re Winship* (1970), *McKeiver v. Pennsylvania* (1971), and *Breed v. Jones* (1975).

KENT V. UNITED STATES

The first major case was **Kent v. United States.**[14] In this 1961 case, the juvenile court had disregarded all Kent's due process rights in transferring the case to the adult court. The judge of the juvenile court did not rule on Kent's lawyer's motions. The judge also did not discuss the case with either Kent or Kent's parents, did not present any findings, did not offer any reason for waiving Kent to the adult court, and, in fact, made no reference to the motions filed by Kent's attorney. The judge also apparently ignored reports from juvenile court staff and the Juvenile Probation Section that indicated that Kent's mental condition was deteriorating. Rather, the judge entered an order waiving Kent to the adult court for trial. There, Kent was indicted by a grand jury on eight counts of housebreaking, robbery, and rape and was sentenced to a total of thirty to ninety years in prison. Focus on Law 5–1 describes the facts of this case.

Kent's counsel initiated a series of appeals that led to review of the case by the U.S. Supreme Court. The counsel argued throughout these appeals that Kent's parents had not been notified in time, that Kent's interrogation and

FOCUS ON LAW 5–1

KENT V. UNITED STATES

Morris A. Kent Jr., a sixteen-year-old living in Washington, DC, was on juvenile probation, when he broke into a house and raped and robbed a woman on September 2, 1961. His fingerprints were found in the woman's apartment, and he was taken into custody by the police on September 5, 1961. He was charged with three counts each of house-breaking and robbery and two counts of rape. Kent apparently admitted not only the offense for which he was taken into custody, but other housebreaking, robbery, and rape offenses as well. He was interrogated by the police into the evening, was taken to the Receiving Home for Juveniles late that evening, and was returned to the police the next day for more questioning. No record exists as to when Kent's mother found out about his detention, but she retained counsel on the second day of Kent's detainment.

The social service director of the Juvenile Court discussed with Kent's counsel the possibility that Kent's case might be waived to adult court; Kent's counsel opposed the waiver and also arranged for Kent to undergo psychiatric evaluation. Kent's lawyer then filed a motion for a waiver hearing on the Juvenile Court's jurisdiction and provided a psychiatrist's affidavit certifying that Kent was "a victim of severe psychopathology" and recommending that he be hospitalized for psychiatric observation. The affidavit concluded that Kent could be rehabilitated if provided adequate treatment. Kent's counsel also requested a copy of Kent's social service file for use in his defense.

Source: Kent v. United States, 383 U.S. 541, 86 S.Ct. 1045, 16 L.Ed. 2d 84 (1966).

detention were illegal because neither his parents nor his counsel were present, that probable cause for Kent's detention had not been established, that he had not been told of his right to remain silent or of his right to counsel, and that he was fingerprinted illegally.

The Supreme Court agreed that the procedures followed by the juvenile court were inadequate. In addition, the Court ruled that Kent had the right to a transfer hearing in which evidence was presented, that Kent had the right to be present at a waiver hearing, that Kent's attorney had the right to see the social service reports, and that the judge had to state the reasons for the transfer.[15] In this decision, Judge Abe Fortas stated:

> There is evidence, in fact, that there may be grounds for concern that the child receives the worst of both worlds; that he gets neither the protection accorded to adults nor the solicitous care and regenerative treatment postulated for children.[16]

Critical Thinking Questions:

What did Supreme Court Justice Fortas mean when he said "that there may be grounds for concern that the child receives the worst of both worlds?" Do you agree with his criticism of the juvenile court?

In re Gault

In May 1967, the U.S. Supreme Court reversed the conviction of a minor in the case of ***In re Gault.***[17] This has been one of the most influential and far-reaching decisions to affect the juvenile court. In this case, the Court overruled the Arizona Supreme Court for its dismissal of a writ of habeas corpus. This writ had sought the release of Gerald Gault, who had been adjudicated to the state industrial school by the Juvenile Court of Gila County, Arizona. Focus on Law 5–2 presents the facts of this case.

In reviewing the decision of the Arizona Supreme Court, which upheld the confinement of Gault, the U.S. Supreme Court considered which of the following rights should apply to juveniles:

1. Right to receive notice of the charges
2. Right to be represented by counsel
3. Right to confront and cross-examine witnesses
4. Right to avoid self-incrimination
5. Right to receive a transcript of the proceedings
6. Right to request appellate review[18]

Justice Fortas, in delivering the Court's opinion, recalled other cases that had provided juveniles with due process of law. In both *Haley v. Ohio* (1948) and *Gallegos v. Colorado* (1962), the U.S. Supreme Court had prohibited the use of confessions coerced from juveniles; in *Kent v. United States*, the Court had given the juvenile the right to be represented by counsel.[19] Justice Fortas

FOCUS ON LAW 5–2

IN RE GAULT

Gerald Gault, a fifteen-year-old Arizona boy, and a friend, Ronald Lewis, were taken into custody on June 8, 1964, on a verbal complaint made by a neighbor. The neighbor had accused the boys of making lewd and indecent remarks to her over the phone. Gault's parents were not notified that he was taken into custody; he was not advised of his right to counsel; he was not advised that he could remain silent; and no notice of charges was made to either Gerald or his parents. Additionally, the complainant was not present at either of the hearings. In spite of considerable confusion about whether or not Gerald had made the alleged phone call, what he had said over the phone, and what he had said to the judge during the course of the two hearings, Judge McGhee committed him to the State Industrial School until he reached the age of twenty-one or until he was discharged by the law.

Source: In re Gault, 387 U.S. 1, 18, 1, 18 L. Ed. 2d 527, 87 S. Ct. 1428 (1967).

Critical Thinking Questions:
What due process rights did this case grant juveniles? What due process rights did juveniles still lack after the decision?

concluded this review of legal precedent with the sweeping statement that juveniles have those fundamental rights incorporated in the due process clause of the Fourteenth Amendment of the Constitution.

The *In Re Gault* decision answered in the affirmative the question of whether a juvenile has the right to due process safeguards during confinement. But the Supreme Court did not rule that juveniles have the right to a transcript of the proceedings or the right to appellate review.

In rejecting the latter two rights, the Court clearly did not want to make the informal juvenile hearing into an adversarial trial. The cautiousness of this decision was expressed in a footnote that indicated the decision did not apply to preadjudication or postadjudication treatment of juveniles. Several other important issues were also left unanswered, such as the following:

1. May a judge consider hearsay in juvenile court?
2. Does the exclusionary evidence principle derived from the Fourth Amendment apply?
3. What is the constitutionally required burden of proof necessary to support a finding of delinquency?

4. Is a jury trial required?
5. Does the requirement of a "speedy and public trial" apply in juvenile court?[20]

In re Winship

The Supreme Court ruled in the ***In re Winship*** case (1970) that juveniles are entitled to proof "beyond a reasonable doubt."[21] The *Winship* case involved a New York boy who was sent to a state training school at the age of twelve for taking $112 from a woman's purse. The commitment was based on a New York statute that permitted juvenile court decisions on the basis of a "preponderance of evidence." The Court reasoned that "preponderance of evidence," a standard much less strict than "beyond a reasonable doubt," is not a sufficient basis for a decision when youths are charged with acts that would be criminal if committed by adults.

The findings in the *Winship* case not only expanded the implications of *In re Gault* but also reflected other concerns of the U.S. Supreme Court. The Court desired both to protect juveniles at adjudicatory hearings and to maintain the confidentiality, informality, flexibility, and speed of the juvenile process in the prejudicial and postadjudicative states. The Court obviously did not want to bring too much rigidity and impersonality to the juvenile hearing.

McKeiver v. Pennsylvania, In re Terry, and In re Barbara Burrus

The Supreme Court heard three cases together (*McKeiver v. Pennsylvania, In re Terry,* and *In re Barbara Burrus*) to determine whether the due process clause of the Fourteenth Amendment (guaranteeing the right to a jury trial) applied to juveniles.[22] The decision, which was issued in *McKeiver v. Pennsylvania* (1971), denied the right of juveniles to have jury trials. Focus on Law 5–3 reveals the facts of these three cases.

The Supreme Court explained its ruling that juveniles do not have the right to a jury trial as follows:

1. Not all rights that are constitutionally assured for adults are to be given to juveniles.
2. If a jury trial is required for juveniles, the juvenile proceedings may become a fully adversarial process, putting an end to what has been the idealistic prospect of an intimate, informal, protective proceeding.
3. A jury trial is not necessarily a part of every criminal process that is fair and equitable.
4. If the jury trial is injected into the juvenile court system, it could bring with it the traditional delays, the formality, and the clamor of the adversarial system.

FOCUS ON LAW 5–3

RIGHT OF A JURY TRIAL FOR JUVENILES

McKeiver v. Pennsylvania

Joseph McKeiver, who was sixteen years of age, was charged with robbery, larceny, and receiving stolen goods, all of which were felonies under Pennsylvania law. Found delinquent at an adjudication hearing, the youth was placed on probation after his request for a jury trial was denied.

In re Terry

Edward Terry, who was fifteen years of age, was charged with assault and battery on a police officer, which were misdemeanors under Pennsylvania law. His counsel requested a jury trial, which was denied, and he was adjudicated a delinquent on the charges.

In re Barbara Burrus

Barbara Burrus and approximately forty-five other youths, ranging in age from eleven to fifteen years, received juvenile court summonses in Hyde County, North Carolina. The charges arose out of a series of demonstrations in the county in late 1968 by African-American adults and children who were protesting school assignments and a school construction plan. The youths were charged with willfully impeding traffic. The several cases were consolidated into groups for hearing before the district judge, sitting as a juvenile court. A request for a jury trial in each case was denied. Each youth was found delinquent and placed on probation.

Source: McKeiver v. Pennsylvania, 403 U.S. 528, 535 (1971); *In re Terry,* 438 Pa., 339, 265A.2d 350 (1970); and *In re Barbara Burrus,* 275 N.C. 517, 169 Sk. E. 2d 879 (1969k).

Critical Thinking Questions:
What is the actual difference between "preponderance of the evidence" and proof beyond a reasonable doubt? What was the importance of this difference in this case?

5. There is nothing to prevent an individual juvenile judge from using an advisory jury when he or she feels the need. For that matter, there is nothing to prevent individual states from adopting jury trials.[23]

Although a number of states do permit jury trials for juveniles, most states adhere to this constitutional standard set by the Supreme Court. What is significant about this decision is that the Court indicated an unwillingness to apply further procedural safeguards to juvenile proceedings. This especially appears to be true concerning the preadjudicatory and postadjudicatory treatment of juveniles.

Breed v. Jones

The *Breed v. Jones* (1975) case was slightly different from the *Kent* case. Jones was taken into custody for committing a robbery and was detained for a hearing in juvenile court. At the juvenile court hearing, the allegations against Jones were found to be true. At the disposition hearing, the court determined that Jones could not be helped by the services of the juvenile court; Jones was waived to adult court, where he was found guilty of robbery.

Jones's lawyer appealed the case, arguing that Jones had been subjected to double jeopardy; that is, this decision had violated the standard used in adult courts that prevents adults from being tried twice for the same crime. The Supreme Court concurred, stating that Jones's hearing in the juvenile court was an adjudicatory hearing and that his trial in adult court constituted double jeopardy.[24] For waiver to adult court to occur legally according to the Supreme Court, juvenile courts must transfer youths to the adult court jurisdiction before any adjudicatory hearings are held on their cases.

In sum, the *In re Gault* and the *In re Winship* decisions have unquestionably effected profound changes in the legal status of the juvenile justice system. The *McKeiver v. Pennsylvania* decision and the more conservative stance of the Supreme Court since 1971, however, have raised some question about whether or not this ultimate appellate court will be willing to change legal norms much more. These court decisions have of course received varying endorsements from juvenile courts across the United States. Some juvenile courts gave procedural rights to juveniles even before the Supreme Court decisions, but others have lagged far behind in implementing these decisions.

HOW IS THE STATUS OFFENDER CONTROLLED?

Youths can be charged with at least three different categories of offenses. First, they can be charged with a felony or misdemeanor by federal, state, and local statutes. Second, they are subject to relatively specific statutes applying exclusively to juvenile behavior: truancy, consumption of alcoholic beverages, and running away from home are examples. Third, juveniles can be prosecuted under general omnibus statutes that include such offenses as acting beyond control of parents, engaging in immoral conduct, and being ungovernable and incorrigible. Offenses under both the second and the third categories are status offenses. The status offense statutes pertaining to behavior for which an adult could not be prosecuted have drawn increasing attention in recent years. Status offenders can be processed through the juvenile justice system along with youths who have committed criminal offenses, or they can be handled separately from felons and misdemeanants. States that pursue the latter course usually refer to status offenders as MINS (minors in need of supervision), CINS (children in need of supervision), PINS (persons in need of supervision), FINS (families in need of supervision), or JINS (juveniles in need of supervision). Some jurisdictions handle these youths in a different court; others will not place them in detention with delinquents nor send them to a juvenile correctional institution.

The handling of status offenders, one of the most controversial issues in juvenile justice, has focused on two questions: should status offenders be placed with delinquents in correctional settings, and should the juvenile court retain jurisdiction over status offenders?

Deinstitutionalization of Status Offenders

There have been four positions expressed about the **deinstitutionalization of status offenders** (to no longer confine status offenders in secure detention facilities or secure correctional facilities with delinquents). First, researchers have raised real doubt about the policy of confining status offenders with delinquents. One study found that before their dispositional hearing, status offenders were more likely to be detained or treated more harshly than delinquents.[25] Examinations of juvenile institutionalization also revealed that status offenders stayed longer in training school than did delinquents, were vulnerable to victimization in these settings, and found institutionalization with delinquents to be a destructive experience.[26]

Second, other researchers have questioned whether status offenders are innocent youths who are that much different from delinquents. That is, they have found that status offenders are more than incorrigible youths with family problems. Charles W. Thomas found that status offenders not only differ very little in offense behavior but also tend to progress from status to delinquent offenses.[27] P. Erickson also found that most adolescents who are brought to court for status offense behavior are mixed offenders who have, at one time or another, been involved in misdemeanors and felonies as well as status offenses.[28] Solomon Kobrin, Frank R. Hellum, and John W. Peterson's national study of status offenders found three groups of such offenders: The "heavies" committed serious offenses as well as some incidental status offenses; the "lightweights" committed misdemeanors as well as status offenses; and "conforming youths" were basically law abiding but occasionally committed a status offense. Conforming youths would normally not be considered a problem by the courts, but the fact that the lightweights committed misdemeanors as well as status offenses suggests that it might be a mistake to keep them out of institutions.[29]

Third, juvenile judges have resisted this deinstitutionalization movement in some states, and they have found a way to continue the institutionalization of status offenders with delinquents (even in states that strongly support deinstitutionalization). What these juvenile judges do is redefine status offenders as delinquents.[30] A truant may be charged with a minor delinquent offense and be institutionalized for that reason; similarly, school attendance may be required as a condition of probation, and further truancy is then defined as a delinquent offense.[31]

Fourth, what served as the real impetus for a nationwide deinstitutionalization of status offenders was the passage of the 1974 **Juvenile Justice and Delinquency Prevention** (JJDP) **Act** and its various modifications.[32] In order for states to continue receiving federal funding for juvenile justice programs, the JJDP Act required that status offenders be kept separate from delinquents in secure detention and institutionalization. The act also limited the placement of juveniles in adult jail facilities. The effectiveness of this federal mandate could be seen in the dramatic decrease in the number of status offenders being held in secure facilities over several decades. For example, in 1975, an estimated 143,000 status offense cases involved detention; in 1992, the figure was 24,300.[33]

Jurisdiction Over Status Offenders

The juvenile court's long-standing jurisdiction over status offenders is an even more volatile issue. There are at least four distinct arguments for the removal of status offenders from the jurisdiction of the juvenile court. The legal argument states that the lack of clarity of the status offender statutes makes them unconstitutionally vague in their construction; that they often are blatantly discriminatory, especially in regard to sex; and that government bodies have no legitimate interest in many of these proscribed behaviors. Second, although status offenders have not committed a criminal act, they frequently are confined with chronic or hard-core offenders. Third, in keeping with the *parens patriae* philosophy of the juvenile court, the procedure of processing and confining the status offender is not in his or her best interests. Some theorists argue that the formal intervention of the juvenile court promotes rather than inhibits unlawful behavior. Fourth, many charge that status offenders are a special class of youth who must be treated differently from delinquents.[34]

Juvenile court judges, not surprisingly, challenge the movement to strip the court of jurisdiction over status offenders. They charge that status offenders will have no one to provide for them or to protect them if they are removed from the court's jurisdiction. The essence of this position is that other agencies will have to take over if the court relinquishes jurisdiction over these offenders and that few options are presently available for providing status offenders a nurturing environment in lieu of the home.

Maine, New York, and Washington are states that have **decriminalized status offenses,** thus removing from the juvenile court's jurisdiction youthful behavior that would not be a chargeable offense if committed by an adult.[35] The most broad-based movement to strip the juvenile court of jurisdiction over status offenders has taken place in New York State, heralded by the passage of the 1985 PINS Adjustment Services Act. A central purpose of this legislation was to displace the family court as the institution of first choice for minor family-related matters. The PINS legislation also has constructed an innovative system of its own that operates as formally as the juvenile court. Children whose families are receptive are referred to the Designated Assessment Service, which in turn refers these youths to a community-based agency for long-term services. The legal proceedings are suspended, as long as youths are responsive to the rehabilitative programs designed for them.[36]

It would appear unlikely that many more states will remove status offenders from the juvenile court's jurisdiction in the near future. In fact, between 1988 and 1992, the juvenile court's status offense caseload grew 18 percent.[37] The widespread resistance comes mainly from those who feel that status offenders need the control of the juvenile court over their lives or they will become involved in increasingly destructive behaviors. The juvenile court and its supporters also resist because they fear that loss of jurisdiction over serious offenders as well as status offenders may signal the beginning of the juvenile court's demise.

WHAT ARE THE PRETRIAL PROCEDURES OF THE JUVENILE COURT?

The jurisdiction of the juvenile court, despite variations among and even within states, generally includes delinquency, neglect, and dependency cases. Children's courts may also deal with cases concerning adoption, termination of parental rights, appointment of guardians for minors, custody, contributing to delinquency or neglect, and nonsupport. The proceedings of the juvenile court can be divided into pretrial procedures and adjudicatory and dispositional hearings. This chapter considers pretrial procedures, and Chapter 6 examines the adjudicatory and dispositional stages of the court's proceedings.

The pretrial procedures consist of the detention hearing, the intake process, and the transfer procedure, which are discussed later. Eighty-six percent of delinquency cases are brought before the courts by law enforcement authorities, but there are variations across offense categories. Ninety-four percent of drug law violation cases, as well as 91 percent of property cases and 86 percent of person offense cases, are referred by law enforcement agencies. The remaining cases result from complaints by parents, citizens, probation officers, victims, school officials, and others.[38]

The reasons for referring youths to the courts vary. Of the delinquency offenses, police officers brought youths to the juvenile court for property and drug offenses more than any other category. Of the status offenses, liquor law and curfew violation headed the list for law enforcement officers. Conversely, sources other than law enforcement officers were most likely to refer youths for public order offenses and for status offenses, such as truancy, curfew

Table 5–1 Age Profile of Detained Delinquency Cases, 1988, 1993, and 1997

Age at Referral	*1986*	*1993*	*1997*
10 or Younger	1%	1%	1%
11	1	1	1
12	3	4	4
13	8	10	8
14	16	18	16
15	24	24	24
16	27	25	26
17 or Older	20	18	20
Total	100%	100%	100%

Note: Detail may not total 100% because of rounding.

Source: Adapted from Charles Puzzanchera, Anne L. Stahl, Melissa Sickmund, Terrence A. Finnegan, Howard N. Snyder, Rowen S. Poole, and Nancy Tierney, *Juvenile Court Statistics 1997* (Washington , DC: Office of Juvenile Justice and Delinquency Prevention, 2000).

violations, and ungovernability; the referral of runaways was about equally divided between law enforcement and other sources.

Older youths are more likely to be referred than are younger ones (see Table 5–1). Youths below the age of sixteen accounted for 53 percent of the cases that involved detention in 1996; those below the age of fourteen accounted for 15 percent. Person and property offenses case rates peaked at the sixteen-year-old age group, whereas drug law violations and public order offenses increased continuously with age. For example, the case rate for drug offenses among seventeen-year-olds was nearly 300 percent greater than the corresponding case rate for thirteen-year-olds.[39]

Detention Hearing

The use of detention has been a problem ever since the founding of the juvenile court. The original purpose of detention was to hold children securely until intake personnel reviewed the case and made a decision. The **detention hearing,** at which the decision to detain is made, must be held within a short period of time, generally forty-eight to seventy-two hours, excluding weekends and holidays. Those urban courts having intake units on duty twenty-four hours a day for detention hearings frequently act within a few hours.[40]

Detention hearings may occur at three points: (1) when the youth is taken in by the police, (2) during and after the time intake personnel review the case to decide whether to refer the case to juvenile court, and (3) after the adjudicatory hearing.

Police, as noted previously, make the first detention decision. Frequently, they must place the youth in a police lockup or local jail while they notify parents and decide what to do with the youth. The police usually exercise the option of simply releasing the youth to his or her parents. If police believe conditions warrant, as they often do with serious offenders and sometimes do with status offenders, they may hold these youths for their protection or for the protection of society. In other words, the police base their decision partly on how they classify the youth.[41]

The second point at which detention may occur is after the police take the youth to the intake personnel of the juvenile court. Intake personnel then review the case to determine whether the youth should be referred to the juvenile court. They, too, often make the decision to release the youth to his or her parents, but the intake personnel may decide that the youth needs to be detained either for his or her own protection or while awaiting the adjudicatory hearing.

The third point at which a detention hearing may be held is after the adjudicatory hearing. If the youth is adjudicated delinquent, the court may in some circumstances sentence the youth to a detention center, shelter care, or in-home detention for a period of time for punishment. More commonly, the court sentences the youth to a private or public training school or some other secure facility.

Youths who are held in detention are assigned to one of four types of placement. The detention home is the most physically restrictive. Shelter care is physically nonrestrictive and is available for those who lack home placements or who require juvenile court intervention. The jail or police lockup is juveniles' most undesirable detention placement. The final option available in many jurisdictions is in-home detention, which restricts a juvenile to his or her home, usually under the supervision of a paraprofessional staff member.

Five states have legislated a hearing on probable cause for detained youths, and appellate cases in other states have moved in the direction of mandating a probable-cause hearing to justify further detention. Georgia and Alaska courts have ruled that a juvenile is entitled to counsel at a detention hearing and to free counsel if indigent. The supreme courts in California and Alaska, as well as a Pennsylvania appellate court, have overturned cases in which no reason or an inadequate reason was stated for continuing detention. Furthermore, courts in the District of Columbia, Maryland, and Nevada have ruled that a youth in detention is entitled to humane care.

Bail for Children

Bail is *not* a form of punishment. Rather, its purpose is to ensure that the defendant will show up at his or her adjudicatory hearing. The court usually determines the amount of bail required at an early intake hearing, which reviews such factors as the youth's behavior, past history, and relationship with parents and school authorities. Once bail is set, the defendants and their families then have to come up with a percentage (usually 10 percent) of the required amount.

The controversies over bail are similar in adult and juvenile justice. The Eighth Amendment to the U.S. Constitution states that bail shall not be excessive, but determining what is excessive is difficult. In addition, the U.S. Supreme Court in *ex parte Crouse* stated that the Bill of Rights did not apply to children. This ruling therefore implied that the states and their courts may do as they please in setting bail. The result is that few can agree whether juveniles may be released on bail, and states and courts vary widely in their practices.

For example, some states prohibit bail altogether; Hawaii, Kentucky, Oregon, and Utah fall into this category. Other states allow bail, but not for juveniles. This practice is based on the assumption that normal juvenile court procedures and due process guarantees are sufficient to protect juveniles and allow their early release. In some of these states, it should be noted, judges occasionally require a juvenile to post bond. For the most part, however, requirements that juveniles are to be released to their parents as soon as possible are believed to be sufficient protection for juveniles.

Bail for juveniles is permitted in nine states: Arkansas, Colorado, Connecticut, Georgia, Massachusetts, Nebraska, Oklahoma, South Dakota, and West Virginia. Even though few juveniles are released on bail, most juvenile court statutes do limit the time that accused juveniles may be held in custody before their hearings.[42]

Alida V. Merlo and William D. Bennett's study of bail in Massachusetts indicated that bail was a factor in 72 percent of juvenile cases statewide in 1988. The trend for higher bail in Massachusetts is reflected in the detention admissions receiving from \$101 to \$500 bail (up 16 percent), \$501 to \$1,000 bail (up 70 percent), and more than \$1,000 bail (up 48 percent). They conclude that these statewide trends indicate that juvenile judges may be starting to use bail as a means of ensuring the youth's detention and that judges, without actually using the term, may be engaging in the practice of **preventive detention** (confinement that is proactive, not punitive for a specific offense).[43]

The possibility of judges setting excessive bail has led some states to require higher courts to review the bail set by lower courts. In addition, some experts suggest releasing more youths on their own recognizance or under the supervision of third parties. Some recommend that states utilize citation programs; that is, police officers simply issue youths a "ticket," or summons, that requires the youth to appear in court on a certain date. Others suggest that police should require youths to report to the station house for a consultation with officers or members of the police youth bureau.

Preventive Detention

The 1984 *Schall v. Martin* decision of the U.S. Supreme Court represents a fundamental change that appears to be taking place in detention practices.[44] The plaintiffs originally filed a lawsuit in federal district court claiming that the New York Family Court Act was unconstitutional because it allowed for the preventive detention of juveniles:

> The District Court struck down the statute as permitting detention without due process and ordered the release of all class members. The Court of Appeals affirmed, holding . . . the statute is administered not for preventive purposes, but to impose punishment for unadjudicated criminal acts, and that therefore the statute is unconstitutional.[45]

In reversing the decision of the appeals court, Justice William Rehnquist declared that the "preventive detention under the statute serves the legitimate state objective held in common with every state, of protecting both the juvenile and the society from the hazards of pretrial crime"[46] Although the ultimate impact of this decision remains to be felt, there is reason to believe that the Court's ruling may encourage a significant expansion of preventive or secure detention for juveniles.

Preventive detention raises several controversial questions. First, laws are not supposed to be enforced against people unless some sort of overt act has occurred that violates the juvenile or criminal code. To put a youth in preventive detention under the assumption that he or she might commit an offense runs counter to the intent and, supposedly, the practice of the law. Second, preventive detention is experienced by the detainee as *punitive* confinement, regardless of the stated purpose of the practice. Finally, the propriety of incarceration before the determination of guilt and the procedural safeguards that must accompany such a practice is a major issue to be considered. Indeed, evaluations of the detention process indicate that the majority of juveniles who are preventively detained are not charged with serious offenses.[47]

Intake Process

The **intake process** has several purposes: First, it screens cases to determine whether children need the help of the juvenile court. Second, it controls the use of detention, which is discussed later. Third, it reduces the courts' overwhelming caseloads. Fourth, it keeps inappropriate cases (e.g., minor cases) out of the juvenile court. Finally, it directs children to appropriate community agencies.[48]

Intake units, despite the similarity of their functions, do not all operate the same way. Juvenile court organization and available resources vary widely among the states. In addition, few states have attempted to spell out the criteria intake personnel should use to make their decisions. The result is that intake personnel exercise a great amount of discretion in deciding what to do with youths.

The first decision intake personnel must make is whether the case comes under its jurisdiction; for example, staff must determine whether the child or the child's offense falls under the appropriate age or offense category. If not, then the second decision of the staff will be either to dismiss the case or to refer it to an appropriate social agency or the adult court. Third, staff must decide whether the youth before them requires secure detention. Other options are to divert the case to a nonjudicial agency through an informal adjustment, put the youth on informal probation, issue a consent decree, or file a petition.

Case Dismissal

An intake officer reviews the cases of all youths brought to the court's attention. Often this review takes place with the police officer, the youths' parents, and perhaps, the prosecutor and the youths' lawyers present. If the particular behavior in question is not an offense under the state's code, the charge will be dismissed. The case also will likely be dismissed if the case is too weak to bring before the court, if it is the youth's first offense, if the youth appears genuinely contrite, and if the parents appear concerned about the youth's behavior and promise to get the youth help. Youths whose cases are dismissed are sent home with their parents.

Informal Adjustment

This alternative, sometimes called nonjudicial adjustment, often is used for status and other minor offenders. One option of the intake official is simply to warn the child and to release him or her to parents. A more stringent option is to require the youth to pay restitution to the victim. A third option is to refer the youth to local diversion programs, which include youth service bureaus or other social agencies that are qualified to work with the problems of youth. The agencies to which the youth is referred are then responsible for supervising the youth and reporting back to the court.

Informal Probation

Informal probation means that the youth is released back to the community but must accept certain conditions that are spelled out by the court. The youth is usually supervised for a specified period of time by either a volunteer or a probation officer. If the youth is able to stay out of trouble in the community, a report is then sent back to the court, and the case is discontinued at that time. If the youth has difficulty, a petition may be filed with the court, and the youth may be held for further adjudication.

Consent Decree

Consent decrees are intermediate steps between informal handling and probation, and they are used to place the child under the jurisdiction of the court without a finding that the child is delinquent. Generally, a consent decree requires the child to agree to fulfill certain conditions in spite of the fact that he or she has not been found guilty. For informal sanctions, see Focus on Law 5–4.

FOCUS ON LAW 5–4

INFORMAL SANCTIONS

Informal processing usually is considered when the decision makers (such as the police, intake workers, probation officers, prosecutors, or other screening officers) believe that accountability and rehabilitation can be achieved without intervention from formal courts.

Informal sanctions are voluntary and, therefore, a juvenile cannot be forced to comply with an informal disposition. If a court decides to handle a matter informally (in lieu of formal prosecution), a youthful offender at that time has to agree to comply with one or more sanctions. These sanctions could include voluntary probation supervision, community service, and victim restitution. In some jurisdictions, the youth not only had to agree to sanctions but also has to agree that they committed the alleged act.

A case that is informally handled is usually held open pending the successful completion of the informal disposition. After the agreement on sanctions and the completion of this disposition, the charges against the offenders are dismissed. But if the offender does not fulfill the court's conditions for informal handling, the case is likely to be reopened and formally prosecuted.

Informal handling has become less common but still occurs in a large number of cases. According to Juvenile Court Statistics 1996, 44 percent of delinquency cases disposed in 1996 were handled informally, compared with more than half in 1987.

Source: Howard N. Snyder and Melissa Sickmund, *Juvenile Offenders and Victims: A National Report* (Washington, DC: Office of Juvenile Justice and Delinquency Prevention, 1995), 159.

Critical Thinking Questions:
What is your evaluation of informal sanctions? What do you see as their strengths and weaknesses?

The intake officer can choose to file a petition if none of these options is satisfactory. There is some evidence that the broad discretionary power given to intake workers is sometimes abused. For example, Duran Bell Jr. and Kevin Lang's study of intake in Los Angeles found that some extralegal factors, especially cooperative behavior, are important in reducing the length of detention.[49]

THE TRANSFER PROCEDURE

Some critics contend that the juvenile court should only work with youths who fall into the dependent/neglected and victimized/abused categories, not with those who violate the criminal code. These latter offenders, some critics believe, should be dealt with by adult courts.[50] They argue that the juvenile court not only has failed in its rehabilitative mission, but is relatively powerless to effect change in more seasoned and hard-core youthful offenders. Thus, the critics insist that offenders who commit felonious behaviors should be subject to the same punishments as adults. The popularity of this position led to an increase in the number of youths transferred to adult court in the past decade (see Chapter 7 for an expanded discussion and evaluation of transfer to adult court).

Since *Kent* and *Jones,* most states now require that waiver hearings be held before transferring juveniles to adult court. These hearings are not required in all states, however, as some permit prosecutors to make the waiver decision. In addition, states that provide for mandatory legislative waiver are not required to have such hearings. Where juvenile courts are responsible for making the waiver decision, the Supreme Court stated, in *Kent,* that they must use the following criteria:

1. The seriousness of the alleged offense to the community and whether the protection of the community requires waiver
2. Whether the alleged offense was committed in an aggressive, violent, premeditated, or willful manner
3. Whether the alleged offense was against persons or against property, greater weight being given to offenses against persons, especially if personal injury resulted
4. The prosecutive merit of the complaint, that is, whether there is evidence on which a grand jury may be expected to return an indictment
5. The desirability of trial and disposition of the entire offense in one court when the juvenile's associates in the alleged offense are adults who will be charged with a crime in the [criminal court]
6. The sophistication and maturity of the juvenile as determined by consideration of his home, environment, emotional attitude, and pattern of living
7. The record and previous history of the juvenile
8. The prospects for adequate protection of the public and the likelihood of reasonable rehabilitation of the juvenile (if he is found to have committed the alleged offense) by the use of procedures, services, and facilities currently available to the juvenile court[51]

Plea Bargaining

The issue of plea bargaining is increasingly emerging as an important one in juvenile justice. One juvenile probation officer noted, "When I was a juvenile probation officer in a mid-sized urban county in Pennsylvania, many, if not most, of the cases were plea bargained."[52] Although little is known about how often or when it occurs, the increased trend toward "criminalization" of the juvenile court makes it likely that plea bargaining will come under increased scrutiny.[53]

A **plea bargain** is a deal made between the prosecutor and the defense attorney. The defense attorney, after consultation with his or her client, agrees that the client will admit to committing a lesser offense if the prosecutor will drop the more serious charges. The client receives a lighter sentence, and the necessity of having an adjudicatory hearing is avoided. The caseload of the court is thereby reduced.[54]

Critics of plea bargaining are concerned with its fairness. Their fear is that juveniles who are innocent of any wrongdoing may plead guilty to a lesser offense for fear they will receive a harsh sentence if tried and found guilty of the more serious offense. This obviously is unfair to the innocent; even guilty youths may be subjected to inappropriate community referrals or placements if care is not taken to place them wisely. In addition, truly violent and dangerous youths may be able to negotiate a release back into the community when they should in all probability be placed in secure institutions. The problem at this time is that few guidelines exist to help direct prosecutors and defense attorneys in plea bargaining.

SUMMARY

The juvenile court's roots extend back to English Common Law. Puritans in colonial days accepted the long-standing English practice that children under the age of seven should not receive the same punishments as adults. Puritans also evaluated whether children between the ages of seven and fourteen should be subject to harsh punishments.

These concerns were reflected in early state codes and, eventually, in the Constitution of the United States. They remained in the public's attention throughout the 1800s as the nation transformed from a rural, agriculturally based country into an urbanized and industrialized nation. The number of youths needing help increased, and the country developed several mechanisms to help control them, including schools, mental hospitals, and, in 1899, the juvenile court.

The philosophy of the juvenile court was to help all youths in need. The early reformers believed firmly that putting youths in facilities with adults was inappropriate and harmful. They also believed that because youths were young and needed help, the juvenile court could not be modeled after the adult criminal courts. Their response was to staff the juvenile court with helping personnel and to develop procedures that protected youths from the more stigmatizing, and thus harmful, effects of adult trials and commitments to maximum security facilities. The procedures that were developed were made informal, court staff were given much discretion in how they handled cases, and any youth who came before the court was treated for his or her problems.

Nevertheless, the juvenile court was strongly criticized over the years. Many critics believed the court was overstepping its mission by attempting to address all youth crime. Critics also disparaged the informal procedures and discretion afforded court personnel and deplored the quality of the services offered by the court. Other critics simply contended that the juvenile court was ineffective and could not deal with increasing numbers of hardened juvenile offenders.

Two trends have resulted. The first trend has been to formalize the procedures of the juvenile court. This guarantees juveniles more due process rights in an effort to keep them from being unfairly and unjustly processed through the system. The second trend, as discussed in Chapter 7, has been to waive more and more juveniles to adult court through various legislative and judicial waiver provisions and through giving adult and juvenile courts concurrent jurisdiction. This trend is supported by those who want to subject juveniles to the same punishments as adults. The idea is to deter offenders from committing more crimes and to set an example for those who have not yet violated the law. The goal is to reduce the interventions of the juvenile court with minor offenders and perhaps with status offenders. Thus, while some today would prefer that the juvenile court retain its original mission, the juvenile court is in the midst of conflict and change. The resolutions of the current debate will have long-term repercussions in juvenile justice in the United States. It is hoped that the juvenile court will survive; the eternal optimism found in this nation that we can make a difference in the lives of children must remain a vital force in juvenile justice.[55]

WEB SITES OF INTEREST

Information and links on the juvenile court process and related subjects can be found at

http://www.wiu.edu/library/govpubs/guides/p&cjuven.htm

To find general information as well as an overview of the juvenile court go to

http://www.superiorcourt.maricopa.gov/juvenile/court/court.htm

CRITICAL THINKING QUESTIONS

1. Trace the development of the juvenile court.
2. What is preventive detention? What is your evaluation of this movement in juvenile justice?
3. What role does plea bargaining play in juvenile court proceedings? What is your evaluation of plea bargaining?
4. Do you think the juvenile court should be changed? Why? How?

NOTES

1. Quoted in Julian W. Mack, "The Juvenile Court," in *Readings in Juvenile Justice Administration,* edited by Barry C. Feld (New York: Oxford University Press, 1999), 15–16.
2. G. Larry Mays, "Transferring Juveniles to Adult Courts: Legal Guidelines and Constraints." Paper presented at the annual meeting of the American Society of Criminology, Reno, Nevada (November 1989), 1.
3. *Commonwealth v. Fisher,* 213 P. 48, 62 A, 198–200.
4. Leonard P. Edwards, "The Juvenile Court and the Role of the Juvenile Court Judge," *National Council of Juvenile and Family Court Judges* 43 (1992), 4.
5. Barry Krisberg, *The Juvenile Court: Reclaiming the Vision* (San Francisco, CA: National Council on Crime and Delinquency, 1988); Arnold Binder, "The Juvenile Court: The U.S. Constitution, and When the Twain Shall Meet," *Journal of Criminal Justice* 12 (1982), 355–66; and Charles E. Springer, *Justice for Children* (Washington, DC: U.S. Department of Justice, 1986).
6. Barry C. Feld, "The Transformation of the Juvenile Court," *Minnesota Law Review* 75 (February 1991), 711; Barry C. Feld, "The Juvenile Court Meets the Principle of the Offense: Legislative Changes in Juvenile Waiver Statutes," *Journal of Criminal Law and Criminology* 78 (1987), 571–73; and Barry C. Feld, "*In re Gault* Revisited: The Right to Counsel in the Juvenile Court." Paper presented at the annual meeting of the American Society of Criminology, Montreal, Canada (November 1988).
7. Edwin Powers, *Crime and Punishment in Early Massachusetts, 1620–1692,* (Boston: Beacon Press, 1966), 94, 529.
8. Frederick L. Faust and Paul J. Brantingham, eds., *Juvenile Justice Philosophy* (St. Paul, MN: West Publishing Company, 1974), 569–75.
9. Anthony M. Platt, *The Child Savers* (Chicago: University of Chicago Press, 1969), 121–36.
10. Ibid., 98.
11. Sanford J. Fox, "Juvenile Justice Reform: An Historical Perspective," *Stanford Law Review* 22, no. 6 (June 1970), 1187–1239.
12. Ellen Ryerson, *The Best Laid Plans: America's Juvenile Court Experiment* (New York: Hill and Wang, 1978), 78.
13. Ibid., 574–75.
14. *Kent v. United States,* 383 U.S. 541, 86 S. Ct. 1045, 16 L. Ed. 2d 84 (1986).
15. Ibid.
16. Ibid.
17. *In re Gault,* 387 U.S. 1, 18 L. Ed. 527, 87 S. Ctg. 1428 (1967).
18. Ibid.
19. *Haley v. Ohio,* 332 U.S. 596 (1948); *Gallegos v. Colorado,* 370 U.S. 49, 82, S. Ct. 1209 (1962); and *Kent v. United States.*

20. Noah Weinstein, *Supreme Court Decisions and Juvenile Justice* (Reno: National Council of Juvenile Court Judges, 1973).
21. *In re Winship,* 397 U.S. 358, 90 S. Ct. 1968, 25 L. Ed. 2d 368 (1970).
22. *McKeiver v. Pennsylvania,* 403 U.S. 528, 535 (1971). *In re Barbara Burrus,* 275 N.C. 517, 169 S.E. 2d 879 (1969).
23. Ibid.
24. 421 U.S. 519, 95 S. Ct. 1779 (1975).
25. See Chris E. Marshall, Ineke Haen Marshall, and Charles W. Thomas, "The Implementation of Formal Procedures in Juvenile Court Processing of Status Offenders," *Journal of Criminal Justice* 11 (1983), 195–211.
26. See Clemens Bartollas, Stuart J. Miller, and Simon Dinitz, *Juvenile Victimization: The Institutional Paradox* (New York: Halsted Press, 1976).
27. Charles W. Thomas, "Are Status Offenders Really So Different: A Comparative and Longitudinal Assessment," *Crime and Delinquency* 22 (October 1976), 440–42.
28. P. Erickson, "Some Empirical Questions Concerning the Current Revolution in Juvenile Justice," in *The Future of Childhood and Juvenile Justice,* edited by LeMar Empey (Charlottesville: University of Virginia Press, 1979).
29. Solomon Kobrin, Frank R. Hellum, and John W. Peterson, "Offense Patterns of Status Offenders," in *Critical Issues in Juvenile Delinquency,* edited by David Shichor and Delos H. Kelley (Lexington, MA: D. C. Heath, 1980), 211.
30. Thomas C. Castellano, "The Justice Model in the Juvenile Justice System: Washington State's Experience," *Law and Policy* (October 1986), 479–506.
31. Thomas J. Bernard, *The Cycle of Juvenile Justice* (New York: Oxford University Press, 1992), 28.
32. U.S. Congress, Senate Committee on the Judiciary, Subcommittee to Investigate Juvenile Delinquency, 1973, *The Juvenile Justice and Delinquency Prevention Act,* S.3148 and S.821. 92d Cong. 2d. sess.; 93d Cong., 1st sess.
33. National Council on Juvenile Justice, *National Juvenile Court Case Records 1975–1992* (Pittsburgh, PA: National Center for Juvenile Justice, 1994).
34. Thomas, "Are Status Offenders Really So Different" 440–42.
35. Martin Rouse, "The Diversion of Status Offenders, Criminalization, and the New York Family Court." Paper presented at the annual meeting of the American Society of Criminology, Reno, Nevada (November 1989), 1, 2, 10–11.
36. Ibid.
37. Howard N. Snyder and Melissa Sickmund, *Juvenile Offenders and Victims: A National Report* (Pittsburgh, PA: National Center for Juvenile Justice, 1995), 138.
38. Charles Puzzanchera, Anne L. Stahl, Melissa Sickmund, Terrence A. Finnegan, Howard N. Snyder, Rowen S. Poole, and Nancy Tierney, *Juvenile Court*

Statistics, (Pittsburgh, PA: National Center for Juvenile Justice, 2000), 6; NCIRS. org/html/ojjp/p/jcs/1997/detention htm

39. Ibid.
40. Brenda R. McCarthy, "An Analysis of Detention," *Juvenile and Family Court Journal* 36 (1985), 49–50. For other discussions of detention, see Lydia Rosner, "Juvenile Secure Detention," *Journal of Offender Counseling, Services, and Rehabilitation* 12 (1988), 77–93; and Charles E. Frazier and Donna M. Bishop, "The Pretrial Detention of Juveniles and Its Impact on Case Dispositions," *Journal of Criminal Law and Criminology* 76 (1985), 1132–52.
41. Charles P. Smith, T. Edwin Black, and Fred R. Campbell, *A National Assessment of Case Disposition and Classification in the Juvenile Justice System: Inconsistent Labeling,* Vol. III, Reports of the National Juvenile Justice Assessment Centers (Washington, DC: Government Printing Office, April 1980), 97.
42. For a discussion of the use of bail for juveniles in Massachusetts, see Alida V. Merlo and William D. Bennett, "Criteria for Juvenile Detention: Who Gets Detained?" Paper presented at the annual meeting of the American Society of Criminology, Reno, Nevada (November 1989).
43. Ibid.
44. *Schall v. Martin* (1984), United States Law Review 52 (47), 4681–96.
45. Ibid., 4681.
46. Ibid.
47. Barry C. Feld, "Criminalizing Juvenile Justice: Rules of Procedure for Juvenile Court," *Minnesota Law Review* 69 (1984), 191, 199. See also Deborah A. Lee, "The Constitutionality of Juvenile Preventive Detention: *Schall v. Martin:* Who Is Preventive Detention Protecting?" *New England Law Review* 38 (1987), 13–19.
48. Duran Bell Jr. and Kevin Lang, "The Intake Dispositions of Juvenile Offenders," *Journal of Research on Crime and Delinquency* 22 (1985), 309–28. See also Randall G. Sheldon and John A. Horvath, "Intake Processing in a Juvenile Court: A Comparison of Legal and Nonlegal Variables," *Juvenile and Family Court Journal* 38 (1987), 13–19.
49. Bell and Lang, "The Intake Dispositions of Juvenile Offenders," 309–28. See also Randall G. Sheldon and John A. Horvath, "Intake Processing in a Juvenile Court: A Comparison of Legal and Nonlegal Variables," *Juvenile and Family Court Journal* 38 (1987), 13–19.
50. Samuel M. Davis, *Rights of Juveniles: The Juvenile Justice System* (New York: Clark Boardman Company, 1984, Reprinted with Permission of West, a Thompson Business, (St. Paul, MN, Updated March 2003), 4–26, 4–27. See also Barry C. Feld, "The Transformation of the Juvenile Court" *Minnesota Law Review* 75 (February 1991), 711; Barry C. Feld, "The Juvenile Court Meets the Principle of the Offense: Legislative Changes in

Juvenile Waiver Statutes," *Journal of Criminal Law and Criminology* 78 (1987), 571–73.

51. Davis, *Rights of Juveniles*, 566–67.
52. Conversation with this officer in 1990.
53. For an excellent discussion of the "criminalization" of the juvenile court, see Feld, "Criminalizing Juvenile Justice," 141–276.
54. Joyce Dougherty, "Negotiating Justice in the Juvenile Justice System: A Comparison of Adult Plea Bargaining and Juvenile Intake," *Federal Probation* 52 (1988), 72–80.
55. Charles M. McGee, "Measured Steps Toward Clarity and Balance in the Juvenile Justice System," *Juvenile and Family Court Journal* 40 (1989), 13.

6

JUVENILE TRIAL AND DISPOSITION

OBJECTIVES

1. To discuss the various stages of juvenile court proceedings
2. To consider judicial alternatives in the dispositional stage and the right to appeal
3. To evaluate the various sentencing structures for juveniles
4. To examine the feasibility of maintaining a separate court for juveniles

KEY TERMS

adjudicatory hearing
disposition hearing
guardian *ad litem*
Missouri Plan
National Council of Juvenile and Family Court Judges

As the juvenile court approaches its 100th birthday . . . its future is less secure than at any point in its history. Recent increases in juvenile violent crime, including historic increases in juvenile homicides, have led politicians to "reform" the court by passing laws which minimize the court's jurisdiction, including a new wave of laws that transfer more juveniles, at younger ages, into the adult criminal court system. In most cases, these youthful offenders, once transferred, are treated no differently from adults. In fact, "reforms" in the sentencing of adult offenders, like mandatory minimum sentencing and "truth-in-sentencing," have made it increasingly common for youthful offenders to receive long incarcerative sentences in adult correctional facilities. In this rush to punish and incapacitate youthful offenders, policy makers have given less and less weight to the developmental perspective that led to the creation of separate courts and treatment interventions for juveniles and adults.[1]

Thomas F. Geraghty and Steven A. Drizin, in this introduction to a symposium on the future of the juvenile court, suggest that the future of the juvenile court "is less secure than at any point in its history." They state that part of the problem relates to the perceived seriousness of juvenile crime, and part of the problem is found in a "get tough" attitude that is affecting the handling of juvenile as well as adult crime. In Donna Martin Hamparian and colleagues' study of dangerous juvenile offenders, they contend that another aspect of the problem is the need for an overhaul of the juvenile justice system:

> Troubled young people are responding to the troubles of our times. The overloaded juvenile justice system has responded erratically to them, mixing hostility with understanding, callous harshness with unreasoned lenience, and obsolete notions about human behavior with the insights of the latest research. In the most literal sense of the cliché, the juvenile justice system is much more a part of the problem than a part of the solution. The need for an overhaul is sensed everywhere, but prescriptions for change have not emerged from the incessant discussion of the issues.[2]

WHO ARE THE JUVENILE COURTROOM PLAYERS?

The structure of the juvenile court varies from jurisdiction to jurisdiction. Special and separate juvenile courts in certain urban areas devote their total effort to the legal problems of children. Juveniles in smaller cities and rural areas are often tried by judges of the adult courts. A separate statewide court exists in several states, and only juvenile judges sit on cases in the various districts of those states. In other parts of the country, juvenile offenders are handled exclusively by family court judges who hear both juvenile and domestic relations cases.

More typically, juvenile courts are part of a circuit, district, county, superior, common pleas, probate, or municipal court. This broad-based trial court may be either the highest court of general trial jurisdiction or the lower trial court in which lesser criminal and limited-claim civil matters are heard.

Nationally, juvenile courts today are affected by a movement toward a single trial court, inclusive of all courts in which initial trials take place. For example, in a massive court reorganization in Cook County, Illinois, 208 courts became the circuit court for Cook County. The juvenile court of the District of Columbia was absorbed into the new single trial court for the District.

A variety of personnel serve the juvenile court. These include the judge, who heads up the court; the defense attorney and the prosecutor, who, respectively, defends the client and tries the case; referees, who are assistants to the judge; probation officers, who investigate and supervise cases; and the nonjudicial support personnel, who do everything from providing client services to keeping the court running smoothly. The numbers and qualifications of these persons vary widely from court to court.[3]

The Judge

Juvenile court judges have an enormously important and difficult job. The most traditional role of the juvenile court judge is to decide the legal issues that appear before the court. The judge must make a determination, according to Leonard P. Edwards, "whether certain facts are true, whether a child should be removed from a parent, what types of services should be offered to the family and whether the child should be returned to the family and the community or placed permanently in another setting."[4]

The juvenile court judge also has the following responsibilities:

1. To set juvenile justice standards within the community and within the criminal and juvenile justice systems
2. To make certain that juveniles appearing before the court receive the legal and constitutional rights to which they are entitled
3. To ensure that the systems that detect, investigate, resolve, and bring cases to court are working fairly and efficiently
4. To make certain that there are an adequate number of attorneys of satisfactory quality to represent juveniles in court
5. To know how cases that do not reach the juvenile court are being resolved
6. To monitor the progress of the child, the family, and the supervisory agency to make certain that each complies with the terms of the court's orders
7. To be an advocate within the community on behalf of children and their families
8. In some communities, to oversee the juvenile probation department and court staff[5]

Juvenile judges are chosen by a variety of methods. In some states the governor appoints candidates chosen by a screening board. In some states judges are chosen through partisan elections, and in other states judges run for office without party affiliation. The legislature appoints judges in a few states. A dozen states have adopted the **Missouri Plan,** which involves (1) a commission being appointed to nominate candidates for judge vacancies; (2) an elected official, generally the governor, making judicial appointments from the list submitted by the commission; and (3) nonpartisan and uncontested election being held (usually every three years) to give incumbent judges an opportunity to run on their records.[6]

Juvenile judges wield considerable power, and, not surprisingly, a few do abuse their power as they become despots or dictators in "their courts." But many juvenile judges rise to the challenge and do remarkable jobs. They scrupulously observe procedural safeguards and due process rights for juveniles. They are always seeking better means of detention and reserve the use of training schools as a last resort. They are extremely committed to the work of the juvenile court and sometimes even pass up promotions to more highly paid judgeships with greater prestige. The end result is that these judges change the quality of juvenile justice in their jurisdictions.

The **National Council of Juvenile and Family Court Judges,** located in Reno, Nevada, has done much to upgrade the juvenile court judiciary. This organization has sponsored research and continuing legal education efforts. It also conducts a research facility, the National Center for Juvenile Justice in Pittsburgh, Pennsylvania. The council publishes quarterly the *Juvenile and Family Journal;* monthly, the *Juvenile and Family Law Digest;* and eight times per year, the *Juvenile and Family Court Newsletter.*

The Referee

Juvenile courts frequently employ the services of a referee, who may or may not be a member of the bar. In the state of Washington, a referee is called a commissioner; in Maryland, a master. California uses both referees and commissioners. Although a number of states use only judges in the juvenile court, other states use referees, masters, and commissioners as the primary hearing officers. All perform similar functions for the courts.

Referees generally have a fundamental grasp of juvenile law, some basic understanding of psychology and sociology, and even some experience or training in social work. In some courts, referees hear cases at the fact-finding and detention hearings and may even adjudicate cases at the discretion of the judge. If a judicial disposition is necessary, it usually is left to the juvenile judge. The use of referees appears to be on the increase in some urban areas where the caseload pressures are great.

The Defense Attorney

Defense attorneys, or *respondents,* have been part of the juvenile court structure ever since the *Gault* decision stated that juveniles have the right to be represented by an attorney. Whether they are public defenders, court-appointed attorneys, or privately retained attorneys, defense attorneys presently play an increasingly important role in juvenile trials.[7] Yet Barry C. Feld found that nearly half the juveniles who appeared before the juvenile courts for delinquency and status-offense referrals in Minnesota, Nebraska, and North Dakota were not represented by counsel. Equally serious, he found that many of the juveniles who were placed out of their homes in these states also did not have counsel.[8]

Defense attorneys typically have at least three roles from which to choose: (1) an adversarial advocate for the child, (2) a surrogate guardian or parent to the child, or (3) an assistant to the court with responsibilities to the children.[9] Defense attorneys from public defenders' offices tend to do a better job of representing the rights of youth than do private and court-appointed counsel, primarily because public defenders appear in juvenile court day after day, thereby gaining valuable experience, whereas private attorneys appear only occasionally.

Some evidence suggests that juveniles who had counsel received more severe dispositions than those who did not have counsel.[10] For example, juveniles with counsel seem more likely to receive an institutional disposition than do those without counsel.[11] Such a pattern could result if juvenile judges punished youths who chose to be represented by counsel. Other studies have not found juveniles to be penalized or to fare worse in juvenile courts because they were represented by counsel.[12]

Joseph B. Sanborn Jr.'s 1994 study of juvenile courts found that "judges never encouraged defendants to waive their right to counsel nor appointed any particular type of defense lawyer to represent children." He further found that there were a number of obstacles to fairness in the juvenile court. Representation by counsel was not always complete in the suburban and rural courts, and some counsel was not vigorous, effective, and competent. Sanborn determined that these obstacles to fairness were also found in adult courts in the counties studied. Finally, as with adult courts, these juvenile courts were pressured to hear a heavy volume of cases.[13]

A **guardian *ad litem*** is usually a lawyer who is appointed by the court to take care of youths who need help, especially in neglect, dependency, and abuse cases, but also occasionally in delinquency cases. In delinquency cases, a guardian *ad litem* may be appointed if there is a question of a need for a particular treatment intervention, such as placement in a mental health center, and the offender and her or his attorney are resisting placement.[14]

The Prosecutor

The prosecutor, or *petitioner,* is expected to protect society and, at the same time, to ensure that children appearing before the court are provided with their basic constitutional rights. In urban courts, prosecutors typically are involved in every stage of the proceedings, from intake and detention through disposition. Prosecutors are particularly involved before the adjudication stage because witnesses must be interviewed, police investigations must be checked out, and court rules and case decisions must be researched. Prosecutors also play a role in detention decisions and represent the local or state government in all pretrial motions, probable cause hearings, and consent decrees. Prosecutors are especially involved in deciding whether juveniles should be waived to the adult court or kept in the juvenile court. In states in which certain offenses are excluded from juvenile court jurisdiction, prosecutors play the role of sending juveniles who commit those offenses to the adult court. Prosecutors further represent the county or state at the adjudication hearing and at the disposition of the case. In some urban courts, prosecutors may be involved in plea bargaining with the defense counsel. Prosecutors in some states are permitted to initiate appeals for the limited purpose of clarifying a given law or procedure. Moreover, prosecutors represent the state or county on appeals and in habeas corpus proceedings. Some critics contend that the prosecutor in some juvenile courts has come to dominate juvenile court proceedings.[15]

The Nonjudicial Support Personnel

Nonjudicial support personnel include volunteers, staff from agencies providing services to the court, and paid workers who perform routine administrative functions. Personnel from social service agencies also frequent the court as they make contact with youths and their families, but they have the job of writing reports to the courts summarizing the characteristics of youths as well as the progress youths are making. Finally, the court employs secretaries, clerks, bailiffs, legal researchers, and court administrators to perform the routine but necessary tasks of processing youths through the system.

WHAT ARE OTHER STAGES OF JUVENILE COURT PROCEEDINGS?

After the pretrial procedures (discussed in Chapter 5), the adjudicatory hearing, or the fact-finding stage, and the disposition hearing are the two remaining stages of the juvenile proceedings.

Adjudicatory Hearing

The **adjudicatory hearing** for juveniles is equivalent to the trial in adult court. It is the point at which the judge reviews the charges as described in the petition, hears testimony from the parties involved, and decides whether the youth committed the offense.

Adjudicatory hearings today are a blend of the old and the new. First, the hearings are still somewhat less formal than the adult trial. Second, the hearings are closed in order to protect the juvenile's name and reputation in the community. Third, some juvenile courts, because they disagree strongly with the recent Supreme Court decisions, tend to ignore the new standards and operate much as in the past. Little change has occurred in these courts.

On the other side of the ledger, most states now spell out their procedural requirements very carefully. For example, all juveniles now have the right to a hearing, which is likely to be much more formal than in the past. Written petitions are required, and these may be amended if necessary. Hearsay is prohibited, and the case must be proved beyond a reasonable doubt. Youths have the right to protect themselves against self-incrimination, and they may cross-examine witnesses and victims. Attorneys and prosecutors are likely to be present. Finally, some state codes call for a separation of the adjudication and disposition hearings.

In most juvenile courts, prosecutors begin the proceedings by presenting the case of the state. The arresting officer and witnesses at the scene of the crime testify, and other evidence bearing on the case is introduced. The defense attorney, who is present in the majority of juvenile courts today, then cross-examines the witnesses. Defense counsel also has the opportunity at this time to introduce evidence favorable to the accused, and the juvenile may testify in his or her own behalf. The prosecutor then cross-examines the defense witnesses. The prosecution and the defense present summaries of the case to the judge, who reaches a finding or a verdict.

In some jurisdictions, it is possible for juveniles to receive a jury trial. Twelve states presently mandate a jury trial for juveniles who request one during their adjudicatory hearings and who face the possibility of institutional confinement. But twenty-three states deny juveniles the right to a jury trial. South Dakota is the only state of the remaining ones that specifies whether juveniles are entitled to jury trial. In that state, a juvenile court order is required for a jury trial to be conducted in juvenile court.[16]

Disposition Hearing

Disposition hearings, which are equivalent to sentencing in adult courts, are of two basic types. The first type, which is used less and less frequently in the United States, occurs at the same time as the adjudicatory hearing. The judge, after hearing the case and discussing it with the youth, the youth's parents, the prosecutor, and the defense attorney, then reviews the social service report submitted by a probation officer and decides what disposition would be most effective for the youth.

The second type of disposition hearing occurs at a considerably later date than the adjudicatory hearing. This bifurcated system, as it is sometimes called, has different evidentiary rules than are used in the single adjudicatory hearing.[17] In the adjudicatory hearing, for example, the standard of "proof beyond a reasonable doubt" requires stringent rules and a limiting of the kinds of information that may be introduced. The dispositional hearing, however, calls for the judge to have as wide a range of information as possible concerning the

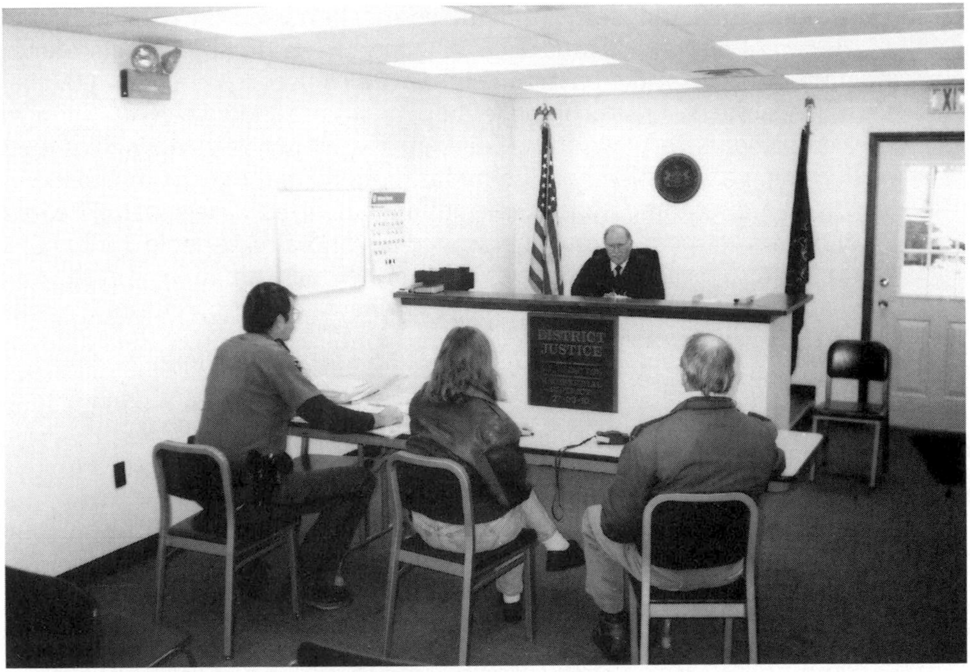

In this more formal courtroom setting, courtroom, the judge is hearing testimony from a police officer and an offender who is accompanied by her parent. (Photo by Stuart Miller.)

youth; this often involves information that would be inadmissable or inappropriate in the adjudicatory hearing.

The reason for separating the two hearings is to prevent judges from learning information that is prejudicial to the defendant. In a combined hearing the judge may discover information that is not relevant to the case but nevertheless biases his or her findings of guilt or innocence. If the judge does not receive this extraneous information until after the finding of guilt, the defendant is protected from being found guilty on the basis of information unrelated to the specific allegation.

Another advantage of the bifurcated system is that it gives the probation department time to make a more comprehensive study of the youth's needs and background than is possible when presentencing reports are given at the time of the adjudicatory hearing. This, too, increases the amount of information available to the judge in making a disposition decision.

Predisposition reports are essential to defendants, defense attorneys, prosecutors, probation departments, and judges. California and Maryland Supreme Courts, in fact, have overturned lower court decisions because judges have not held dispositional hearings to consider relevant sentencing information.[18] This information is crucial because the reports contain background information on defendants that helps judges make individualized decisions.

The social work perspective has helped shape the way caseworkers and probation officers develop the predisposition reports. Since the 1920s, for example, the court has used psychiatric and psychological information obtained from existing school, social agency, and medical records.[19] If such information is not available, but believed necessary, probation officers may refer juveniles for appropriate medical, psychological, or psychiatric evaluations to determine whether the child is mentally ill or restricted. Other information is collected from law enforcement agencies, social service agencies that have dealt with the juvenile previously, the juvenile, and the juvenile's family, friends, and neighbors. The object is to collect any and all information that might be relevant to the case.

The written report, then, contains a description of the referral incident as well as the youth's past conduct, prior contacts with the police and courts, and family environment and relationships. Information on the youth's employment history, school records, interests, and activities is also collected. If police officers have information on special problems of the youth or if special needs of the youth are discovered, these, too, are included in the report.

Once the fact-finding is completed, probation officers recommend a course of action to the court. The predisposition report draws up a plan for what the youth needs and how he or she can best be helped. The report is submitted to the judge, who reviews the report for the dispositional hearing and usually follows the advice given in the report. The juvenile has the right to be present at this hearing.

Both formal and informal factors influence decision making at the dispositional stage. The most important formal factors are the recommendation of the probation officer and the information contained in the social study investigation, or predisposition report; the seriousness of the delinquent offense; the juvenile's previous contact with the court; and the available options. Although the recommendation of the probation officer is usually followed by the juvenile judge, the seriousness of the delinquent behavior and the previous contacts with the court probably have the greatest impact on judicial decision making at this stage.[20] M. A. Bortner found from his examination of disposition decision making in a large midwestern county that age, prior referrals, and the detention decision were the most important influences.[21]

The informal factors that sometimes influence judicial decision making include the values and philosophy of the judge, the social and racial background of the youth, the youth's demeanor, the presence or absence of defense counsel, and political repercussions of the alleged delinquent acts. The most disturbing of these informal factors relate to the social and racial background of the youth. Ruth D. Peterson found that racial, ethnic, gender, and age disparities affected the disposition of older adolescents in New York State courts. Although race and ethnicity did not significantly influence disposition decisions in New York City, minority juveniles tended to be stereotyped and to receive harsh treatment outside the city.[22]

Judicial Alternatives

Dispositions vary according to whether children are adjudicated delinquent, in need of supervision, abandoned/neglected, runaway, or abused/victimized. Some cases are dismissed. This may occur either as the adjudicatory hearing is beginning or as late as after the child has been found guilty of the charge. The judge may decide that the child's family environment, special circumstances, or other factors are such that the child may be sent home with his or her parents.

In other cases the child is assessed a fine or ordered to pay restitution to the victim. Parents, of course, usually end up paying the fine or restitution, but juveniles frequently are required to work for the victim or do community service in order to pay back the community.

Youths who are mentally restricted or mentally ill are sometimes required to undergo special training or therapy. Some larger courts in urban areas have their own clinics, but youths commonly are sent to community clinics, to private psychologists or psychiatrists, or to family services programs. Status offenders, minor delinquents, runaways, or youths who have been physically or sexually abused may be referred to these programs. Middle-class offenders appear to have greater access to these programs than do lower-class youths. One reason for this is the belief that middle-class offenders have more support at home. In this regard, the greater availability of programs to middle-class youths shows the biases of the system against lower-class youths.

Probation is used when youths are found guilty of an offense and in need of supervision, but not secure confinement. The youths are released back to their parents and community under conditions stipulated by the court and are supervised by probation officers or court volunteers. A violation of the conditions laid down by the court may result in the youth being held in contempt of court and placed in a secure facility. For the most part, however, the courts direct the youths to any of a wide variety of community agencies for needed treatment. What is problematic about this approach is that communities vary widely in the quality and availability of services. For high-risk youths, some communities have intensive probation programs, in-house detention, and even electronic monitoring devices.

A much more severe disposition is to remove youths from their natural homes. This most often occurs when parents neglect or abuse their children or are in some other way unable to provide the youths with adequate care. These youngsters are placed in foster homes for short or extended periods of time, depending on their problems. A less extreme variation is to put the youths in day treatment programs. Youths are required to attend a structured program during the day but are allowed to return home in the evening.

Youths are removed from their homes in community-based correctional programs as well. These range from minimum-security facilities such as group homes and halfway houses to more secure homelike facilities. Whereas some of these homes are used simply for feeding and housing kids who need shelter, other homes offer specialized services for drug addicts, alcoholics, and mentally ill or mentally disturbed youths. Not surprisingly, people who live near such facilities often resist the placement of these homes in their local communities; they are afraid that the youths who are in them will get into trouble and be a bad influence on their own children.

Judges occasionally use mental hospitals for placements. Some youths are confined in mental hospitals at the time of intake for evaluation, but these stays are fairly short, ranging from several to ninety days. After adjudication, youths may be confined until they either are ready for community living or, if necessary, reach the age of maturity.

Another kind of facility found in some parts of the country are county or city institutions. These are often fairly new facilities constructed because of the inadequacy of older county jails and detention centers. Youths who do not need placement in state training schools may be placed in these institutions for short periods of time.

The most secure juvenile facilities used by judges are state training schools. These range from minimum-security forestry camps and ranches to maximum-security training schools. In jurisdictions where juvenile judges have the authority to commit a youth to an institution rather than to the state correctional agency, judges will usually place the less serious of these offenders in medium- or minimum-security forestry camps and ranches. Maximum-security institutions are especially foreboding: They are often surrounded by high fences and barbed wire; steel bars and doors and heavy screens govern exits and entrances, and staff are extremely security conscious. The youths in these institutions typically have committed serious, repetitive, or violent offenses, but status and minor offenders also are occasionally placed in them.

Finally, some states permit juvenile judges to place youths in adult institutions. This practice has been used when youths presented a danger to themselves, other residents, or the staff, or were serious escape risks. But this practice has basically ceased for two reasons. First, the "mutual compact theory of *parens patriae*" argues that juveniles give up due process rights in exchange for treatment by the juvenile court.[23] On this basis, the Vermont Supreme Court ruled in *In re Rich* that the state has to treat juveniles rather than transfer them to an adult facility because to do otherwise would subvert the mission of the juvenile court.[24]

Second, the Vermont Supreme Court also pointed out in *In re Rich* that transfer is unconstitutional if the juvenile has not received all of his or her due process rights at a legal hearing.[25] Thus, to the extent that juveniles today are not given all the rights accorded adults, their transfer to an adult institution would undoubtedly be ruled unconstitutional by the reviewing courts.

WHAT RIGHT DOES THE CHILD HAVE TO APPEAL?

Juveniles do not yet have a constitutional right to appeal. Nevertheless, practically all states grant them the right to appeal by statute for some of the following reasons. The states are following the lead of the U.S. Supreme Court. The Court pointed out in *Gault* that juveniles should have the same absolute right as adults have to appeal under the "equal protection" clause of the Constitution. Since that ruling, most state legislatures have passed laws granting juveniles the right to appeal. In addition, state courts have ruled that statutes granting the right to appeal for juveniles must be applied uniformly to all juveniles; this decision effectively undermines the tradition in some courts of giving judges the discretion to determine which juvenile cases could be appealed. The common practice today is to give juveniles the same rights to appeal as adults are given.[26]

The right to appeal is for the most part limited to juveniles and their parents. States may appeal in some circumstances, but this right is seldom exercised, and few such cases have come before the courts. Some variation exists in the type of orders that may be appealed. States generally permit the appeal of "final" orders, although what is "final" varies from state to state. For example, some states authorize juvenile courts to order juveniles to be confined in secure facilities for a period of time. That is a "final" order. Nevertheless, certain states permit the youth or his or her parents to appeal that "final" order. States also vary in how they handle appeals. Most state statutes call for the case to be appealed to an appellate court, but a few states call for a completely new trial. Other common statutory rights of juveniles at appeal are the right to a transcript of the case and the right to counsel.[27]

WHAT IS THE JUVENILE SENTENCING STRUCTURE?

Determinate sentencing is a new form of sentencing in juvenile justice and is replacing in some jurisdictions the traditional form of indeterminate sentencing. In addition, increasing numbers of juvenile courts are using a "blended" form of sentencing.

Criticism of the decision making of the juvenile court has increased in the past twenty years. Early on, the criticism focused on the arbitrary nature of the decision making that violated the due process rights of juveniles; more recently, this criticism has been based on the belief that the juvenile court is too "soft" on crime. This latter criticism, especially, has led to a number of procedures that change sentencing and other juvenile procedures.

One of the first efforts at reform was the Juvenile Justice Standards Project, jointly sponsored by the Institute of Judicial Administration and the American Bar Association. Officially launched in 1971 by a national planning committee under the chairmanship of Judge Irving R. Kaufman, comprehensive guidelines for juvenile offenders were designed that would base sentences on the seriousness of the crime rather than on the needs of the youth. The proposed guidelines represented radical philosophical changes and still are used by proponents to attempt to standardize the handling of juvenile lawbreakers.

The belief that disparity in juvenile sentencing must end was one of the fundamental thrusts of the recommended standards. To accomplish this goal, the commission attempted to limit the discretion of juvenile judges and to make them accountable for their decisions, which would then be subject to judicial review. Also important in the standards was the provision that certain court procedures would be open to the public, although the names of juveniles still would remain confidential.

At the beginning of the twenty-first century, juvenile court judges remain quite concerned about these proposed standards. Their basic concern is that these standards attack the underlying philosophy and structure of the juvenile court. Judges also are concerned about how these standards would limit their authority. They see the influence of the hardliners behind this movement toward standardization and feel that the needs of children will be neglected in the long run. They also challenge the idea that it is possible, much less feasible, to treat all children alike.

Nevertheless, the adoption of the standards has been taking place across the nation. New York State was the first to act on them through the Juvenile Justice Reform Act of 1976, which went into effect on February 1, 1977. The act orders a determinate sentence of five years for Class A felonies, which include murder, first-degree kidnapping, and first-degree arson. The initial term can be extended by at least one year. The juvenile, according to the act, should be placed in a residential facility after the first year. Then, if approved by the director of the division, the confined youth can be placed in a nonresidential program for the remainder of the five-year term. But the youth must remain under intensive supervision for the entire five-year term.

In 1977, the state of Washington also created a determinate sentencing system for juveniles in line with the recommendations of the Juvenile Justice Standards Project. Moreover, in the 1980s, a number of states stiffened juvenile court penalties for serious juvenile offenders, either by mandating minimum terms of incarceration (Colorado, Kentucky, and Idaho) or by enacting a comprehensive system of sentencing guidelines (Arizona, Georgia, and Minnesota).[28]

In 1995, the Texas Legislature introduced such get tough changes in the juvenile justice system as lowering the age at which waiver could occur to fourteen-year-olds for capital, first-degree, and aggravated controlled-substance felony offenses and greatly expanding the determinate sentence statute that was first enacted in 1987. Under determinate sentences, any juvenile, regardless of age, can be sentenced for up to forty years in the Texas Youth Commission, with possible transfer to the Texas Department of Corrections. Finally, prosecutors can choose to pursue determinate sentence proceedings rather than delinquency proceedings, but they first must obtain grand jury approval.[29]

Daniel P. Mears and Samuel F. Field's examination of the determinate sentencing statute for Texas found that increased proceduralization and criminalization of juvenile courts did not eliminate consideration of age, gender, or race/ethnicity in sentencing decisions.[30]

In the 1990s, nearly every state enacted mandatory sentences for violent and repetitive juvenile offenders. The development of graduated, or accountability-based, sanctions was another means in the 1990s that states used to ensure that juveniles who are adjudicated delinquent receive an appropriate disposition by the juvenile court. Several states have created a blended sentencing structure for cases involving repeat and serious juvenile offenders. Blended sentences are a mechanism for holding those juveniles accountable for their offenses. This expanded sentencing authority allows criminal and juvenile courts to impose either juvenile or adult sentences, or at times both, in cases involving juveniles.[31]

Critical Thinking Question:
Which sentencing standards could best be required for all states?

WHAT WOULD JUSTICE FOR JUVENILES LOOK LIKE?

The rationale for handling most delinquents within the juvenile court is that there is no evidence that the adult system works any better with these youths than does the juvenile system. But to make a persuasive case for maintaining a separate juvenile justice system, children must receive fairness and justice in the juvenile court.

Thomas F. Geraghty's article "Justice for Children: How Do We Get There?" makes a powerful case for the retention of the juvenile court.[32] He contributes two basic arguments for retaining and strengthening juvenile courts rather than abolishing them. First, "criminal courts will never adapt themselves to the distinct challenges of doing justice for children." Second, "procedural protections (including the right to jury trial) could be provided in 're-tooled' juvenile courts without destroying the distinctive mission of juvenile courts."[33]

In turning to the reasons why reliance on criminal courts to try children would be an exercise in futility, he makes the following points:

- **a.** The operations of criminal courts, especially in urban areas, fall short.
- **b.** Children will be second-class citizens in criminal court.
- **c.** Children will be subjected to the influence of adults charged with crimes tried in criminal court.

d. Jury trials conducted in criminal courts will be incomprehensible and intimidating to children.
e. Jury trials held in juvenile court need not be frightening and incomprehensible.
f. The legal culture of criminal courts will damage children.
g. Plea bargaining in adult court will be unfair to children.
h. Sentences in adult court will be too harsh, and the focus on the development of youth-oriented correctional systems will be abandoned.
i. Adult court judges, prosecutors, and defenders will not be child specialists.[34]

Geraghty's general suggestion for reinvigorating juvenile courts is that they "must preserve individualized decision making with respect to the culpability and developmental needs of children, while insisting on appropriate imposition of responsibility."[35] His specific suggestions include more dedicated and "concerted efforts to create and support excellent juvenile courts," increased attention "to accurate fact-finding during adjudication hearings," less reliance on plea bargaining, and improvement in "the quality of judging, lawyering, and social work in juvenile courts."[36] What Geraghty is proposing is a court with a child-centered focus that, at the same time, provides "fair, impartial, and informed adjudications and dispositions of cases."[37]

Other suggestions that seem to be in order for juveniles to receive justice in the juvenile court are the following:

1. The juvenile court should no longer have jurisdiction over status offenders.
2. Policymakers must implement monitoring procedures to ensure that the nonjudicial agencies designated for status offenders are providing adequate care.
3. Juveniles accused of crimes should have the same due process rights and procedural safeguards accorded to adults, with the exception that juveniles should have a nonwaivable right to counsel.[38]
4. The quality of representation in juvenile court hearings must be raised.
5. Plea bargaining must be avoided if at all possible. Urban courts will have difficulty operating without plea bargaining, but too many opportunities for abuse are present in this practice.
6. The control of prosecutors over juvenile court must be minimized.
7. A youthful offender system between the juvenile and adult justice system should be implemented, and the juvenile court should retain supervision over youths placed in this system.
8. Mandatory sentences of hard-core juveniles must replace indeterminate sentencing. The process of institutional release in indeterminate

sentencing results in decision making that is too frequently unfair to the juvenile.

9. The lengths of mandatory sentences are to be designed by the National Council of Juvenile Court Judges rather than by state legislatures.

SUMMARY

A significant portion of the juvenile justice system consists of the adjudicatory hearing, or trial, and the disposition. The courtroom actors are in charge of these procedures. The quality of these actors and the norms of the juvenile courts tend to vary from one jurisdiction to another. Juvenile courts have improved, especially in ensuring constitutional rights to juveniles, but there are many who believe that their improvements have been too slow and too limited. Critics also find fault with the dispositions of the juvenile court, because they claim that the dispositions are too soft and too much based on the needs of juveniles. Instead, the courts ought to be concerned with justice for society, and this involves juveniles being punished appropriately for the seriousness of their offenses. The changing juvenile sentencing structures reflect the changing mood of the times, with the individualized sentencing structure of the juvenile court giving way to mandatory and determinate sentencing structures. A number of measures have been suggested that would ensure justice for juveniles, but these have not yet been consistently adopted.

WEB SITES OF INTEREST

To find information on court officials in the Snake River Basin Adjudication as well as other links, see

http://www.srba.state.id.us/

For publications of the National Center for Juvenile Justice, including *Juvenile Court Statistics,* see

http://www.ncjrs.org

CRITICAL THINKING QUESTIONS

1. Who are the judges of the juvenile court and what are their roles?
2. Discuss the adjudicatory hearing and the procedures followed in it.
3. Describe the disposition hearing and the role of the disposition report in that hearing.
4. Discuss the range of dispositions available to judges in the disposition hearings.
5. What are the basic arguments in favor of and in opposition to the retention of the juvenile court?

NOTES

1. Thomas F. Geraghty and Steven A. Drizin, "The Debate over the Future of Juvenile Courts: Can We Reach *Consensus*?" *Journal of Criminal Law and Criminology* 88 (1998), 2–3.
2. Donna Martin Hamparian, Richard Schuster, Simon Dinitz, and John P. Conrad, *The Violent Few: A Study of Dangerous Juvenile Offenders* (Lexington, MA: Lexington Books, 1978), 1.
3. For a more expansive examination of juvenile court personnel, especially the juvenile court judge, see Ted. H. Rubin, *Behind the Black Robes: Juvenile Court Judges and the Court* (Beverly Hills, CA: Sage Publications, 1985); Ted. H. Rubin, "The Juvenile Court Landscape," in *Juvenile Justice: Policies, Programs, and Services,* edited by Albert R. Roberts (Chicago, IL: Dorsey Press, 1989); and Leonard P. Edwards, "The Juvenile Court and the Role of the Juvenile Court Judge," *National Council of Juvenile and Family Court Judges* 43 (1992).
4. Edwards, "The Juvenile Court and the Role of the Juvenile Court Judge," 25.
5. Ibid., 25–28.
6. Larry J. Siegel and Joseph J. Senna, *Juvenile Delinquency: Theory, Practice, and Law,* 7th ed. (Belmont, CA: Wadsworth, 2000), 559.
7. See Floyd Feeney, "Defense Counsel for Delinquents: Does Quality Matter?" Paper presented at the annual meeting of the American Society of Criminology, Montreal, Canada (November 1987).
8. Barry Feld, "Criminalizing Juvenile Justice: Rules of Procedure for Juvenile Court," *Minnesota Law Review* 69 (1984), 191, 199.
9. Ted H. Rubin, *Juvenile Justice: Policy, Practice, and the Law* (Santa Monica, CA: Goodyear Publishing, 1979), 194.
10. See Charles Thomas and Ineke Marshall, "The Effect of Legal Representation on Juvenile Court Disposition." Paper presented at the annual meeting of the Southern Sociological Society, Louisville, Kentucky, (1981); and S. H. Clarke and G. G. Koch, "Juvenile Court: Therapy or Crime Control and Do Lawyers Make a Difference?," *Law and Society Review* 14 (1980), 263–308.
11. Ibid.
12. Joseph B. Sanborn Jr., *Crime and Delinquency* 40, 4 ("Remnants of *Parens Patriae* in the Adjudication Hearing—Is a Fair Trial Possible in Juvenile Court?," 1994), 599–615.
13. Ibid., 157.
14. Siegel and Senna, *Juvenile Delinquency,* 561.
15. For other examinations of the prosecutor's role in the juvenile court, see John H. Laub and Bruce K. MacMurray, "Increasing the Prosecutor's Role in Juvenile Court: Expectation and Realities," *Justice System Journal* 12 (1987), 196–209; and Charles W. Thomas and Shay Bilchik, "Prosecuting Juveniles in Criminal Courts: Legal and Empirical Analysis," *Journal of Criminal Law and Criminology* 76 (1985), 438–79.

16. Kathleen Maguire and Ann L. Pastore, *Bureau of Justice Statistics: Sourcebook of Criminal Justice Statistics—1994* (Washington, DC: Government Printing Office, 1995).
17. Samuel M. Davis, *Rights of Juveniles: The Juvenile Justice System,* 2d ed. (New York: Clark Boardman Company, 1986), Sections 6.1–6.2.
18. Ibid.
19. Ibid.
20. Terence P. Thornberry, "Sentencing Disparities in the Juvenile Justice System," *Journal of Criminal Law and Criminology* 70 (Summer 1979); M. A. Bortner, *Inside a Juvenile Court: The Tarnished Idea of Individualized Justice* (New York: New York University Press, 1982); Lawrence Cohen, "Delinquency Dispositions: An Empirical Analysis of Processing Decisions in Three Juvenile Courts, *Analytic Report* 9 (Washington, DC: Government Printing Office, 1975), 51.
21. Bortner, *Inside a Juvenile Court.*
22. Ruth D. Peterson, "Youthful Offender Designations and Sentencing in the New York Criminal Courts," *Social Problems* 35 (April 1988), 125–26.
23. Davis, *Rights of Juveniles,* 6–7–6–8.
24. Ibid., 6–29.
25. Ibid., see 125 Vt. 373, 216 A.2d 266 (1966).
26. Ibid.
27. Ibid., 6–34–6–37. See 408 U.S. 471 (1972) and 411 U.S. 778 (1973).
28. Martin L. Forst, Bruce A. Fisher, and Robert B. Coates, "Indeterminate and Determinate Sentencing of Juvenile Delinquents: A National Survey of Approaches to Commitment and Release Decision-Making," *Juvenile and Family Court Journal* 36 (Summer 1985), 1.
29. Daniel P. Mears and Samuel H. Field, "Theorizing Sanctioning in a Criminalized Juvenile Court," *Criminology* 38 (November 2000), 985–86.
30. Ibid., 983.
31. Barry C. Feld, "Violent Youth and Public Policy: Minnesota Juvenile Justice Task Force and 1994 Legislative Reform." Paper presented at the annual meeting of the American Society of Criminology, Miami (1994), 4. See also Feld, "Violent Youth and Public Policy: A Case Study of Juvenile Justice Law Reform," *Minnesota Law Review* 79 (May 1995), 965–1128.
32. Thomas F. Geraghty, "Justice for Children: How Do We Get There?" *Journal of Criminal Law and Criminology* 88 (1998), 190–241.
33. Ibid., 217.
34. Ibid., 217–28.
35. Ibid., 229.
36. Ibid., 230–33.
37. Ibid., 238.
38. Schwartz, *(In)justice for Juveniles,* 171.

7

JUVENILES IN ADULT COURT

OBJECTIVES

1. To consider the differences in maturity between juveniles and adults
2. To describe and evaluate the policy of transferring juveniles to the adult court
3. To examine the possibility of the development of an intermediate correctional system for juveniles
4. To examine the quality of life for a juvenile sentenced to an adult prison
5. To discuss the death penalty for juveniles
6. To evaluate the proposed adult court for juveniles

KEY TERMS

concurrent jurisdiction
judicial waiver
life without parole sentence
prosecutorial discretion
statutorial exclusion
youthful offender system

We have a saying for young dudes in here. They have three choices and one don't count. They can either fight, fuck, or climb a tree. There are no trees in here. Young guys have it so hard. There are bootie bandits waiting for them as soon as they get off the van. The smaller you are the worse it is. Everytime I have went to bat for a young dude I have gotten egg in my face. If a dude will fight or use a knife he will have no problems after he draws blood. But is it right? No! But we live in a different world, we are governed by the same set of laws, but they mean little. White, young inmates have it the hardest. Different cons play on them, white and black bandits. They look out for the dude, run game on them and then say, you owe me, or if you liked me you would take care of me.

—Interviewed adult inmate[1]

The mission of the juvenile court, as previously discussed, is hotly debated today. Proponents contend that its original mission was to deal with all juvenile misbehavior, from minor misbehaviors to assault, robbery, and murder. The increase in violent youth crime over the past decade, however, has increased the public's fear of juvenile crime. In addition, the emergence of a "hard line" since the late 1970s has increased the willingness of others to question the juvenile court's original mission. The result of this get tough policy, is that numerous proposals are being made that increase the chances that juveniles, even very young ones, will be punished with the same severity as their adult counterparts.

This chapter examines some of the issues involved in ensuring justice for both juveniles and society. Beginning with the issue of immaturity and responsibility, this chapter considers the transfer to adult court, the sentence of a juvenile to a youthful offender system or to an adult prison, the decision by the majority of state legislatures that juveniles may be sentenced to death and executed for their offenses, and the proposed adult court for juveniles.

CHILDREN OR ADULTS?

The point at which children become adults has varied from one period to another. An examination of the history of childhood suggests that in the Middle Ages, children became adults around the age of seven—when they could work in fields and begin to learn a trade. During the Renaissance, the children of the poor still became adults at the age of seven, but the children of the aristocracy became adults only after schooling that prepared them to help rule society.[2] One result of the industrial revolution was a demand for even more schooling for youths; society determined that childhood would not end, nor would adulthood begin, until children were out of school. Whether children were adults or not, in other words, depended partly on the socioeconomic conditions under which they lived and whether they had learned enough in school to hold down an adult job.

The age at which a juvenile becomes an adult is defined in much the same way even today. Youths are not adults until they graduate from high school or college or are able to hold down a job considered appropriate for an adult. Confusion is evident even here, for youths who reach these milestones may be of widely different ages. When one considers further that theaters consider youths as adults at age twelve, the State Bureau of Transportation at age sixteen, the military and the voting commission at age eighteen, and the State Liquor Control Board at age twenty-one, it is clear why the criminal justice system has such a difficult time determining the age of responsibility.

In terms of wrongdoing, the elusive concept of responsibility has its roots in the notions that juveniles know right from wrong, have developed a social conscience, feel guilty or remorseful over their actions, are mentally sharp enough to know the rules, do not have any disease that reduces their ability to get along in society, fully understand that their actions are harming others, and are emotionally mature. None of these criteria are measurable, yet, for almost a century, the assumption of the juvenile court has been that juveniles are deficient in one or more of these conditions. Proponents of the juvenile court also assume that it should have jurisdiction over the youths until their deficiencies are corrected and until they have developed the mental and emotional maturity of adults. What fuels the controversy over waiver to adult court is the disagreement over when youths reach this stage.

Stephen J. Morse has this to say about when individuals reach a state of minimal rationality in which they can be held responsible for their behavior:

> Law, unlike mechanistic explanation or the conflicted stance of the social sciences, views human action as almost entirely reason-governed. The law's concept of a person is a practical reasoning, rule-following being, most of whose legally relevant movements must be understood in terms of beliefs, desires and intentions. As a system of rules to guide and govern human interaction, the law presupposes that people use legal rules as premises in the practical syllogisms that guide much human action. No "instinct" governs how fast a person drives on the open highway. But among the various explanatory variables, the posted speed limit and the belief in the probability of paying the consequences for exceeding it surely play a large role in the driver's choice of speed. For the law, then, a person is a practical reasoner. The legal view of the person is not that all people behave consistently rationally according to some preordained, normative notion of rationality. It is simply that people are creatures who act for and consistently with their reasons for action and who are generally capable of minimal rationality according to most conventional, socially constructed standards.[3]

In examining the extent to which young people should be held responsible for their criminal activity, Morse contends that a "robust" theory of responsibility would result in most youths (in mid-to-late adolescence) being held responsible for their actions. He claims that there is empirical research to substantiate the position that it is often difficult to distinguish between the moral responsibility of children and young adults. Thus, he reasons, the responsibility of a juvenile should be no less than that of a similarly situated young adult. He does not believe that juveniles' susceptibility to peer pressure justifies differential allocation of responsibility.[4]

Elizabeth Scott and Thomas Grisso, in evaluating the differences between adults and youth, conclude that substantial differences exist between very young juveniles and adults in "moral, cognitive, and social development."[5] The differences between juvenile and adult decision making are more subtle as youths approach mid-adolescence, however. As Scott and Grisso express it: "A categorical presumption of adolescent nonresponsibility, such as that which was endorsed by the traditional juvenile justice system, is hard to defend on the grounds of immaturity alone."[6]

Scott and Grisso's developmental evidence does "support the argument of the post-Gault reformers of the 1970s and 1980s that a presumptive diminished responsibility standard be applied to juveniles."[7] They believe that this presumptive diminished responsibility is best applied in juvenile court systems, and they question whether the criminal justice system is able to respond to this developmental reality: "The ability or inclination of the criminal justice system to tailor its response to juvenile crime so as to utilize the lessons of developmental psychology is questionable. The evidence suggests that political pressure functions as a one-way ratchet, in the direction of ever stiffer penalties."[8]

They further question the assumption proposed by Morse and others that most juvenile offenders, even those in mid-adolescence, are as cognitively competent as adults are in decision-making capacity. They claim that the cognitive decision-making abilities of adolescents and adults are similar only when nondelinquent juveniles from middle-class backgrounds of above-average intelligence are compared with adults. But when children involved in the justice system, many of whom have emotional problems and learning disabilities that hinder their capacity for understanding, are compared with adults, there is real reason to question the cognitive competence of these youths.[9]

The fact of the matter is that some youths do commit brutal crimes, and the viciousness of their acts causes one to question the justice of their remaining in the juvenile system. Indeed, the media testify nearly daily to violent youth crime as they describe senseless killings and rapes committed by juveniles. Violent youth crime has contributed to the perception that something is seriously wrong with this society. Those who have been victims of youthful thugs feel especially vulnerable and call for stronger measures to deal with youthful predators.

One of the most vivid expressions of predatory and violent youth crime is found in the April 1989 assault of a jogger in Central Park in New York City. In that incident, the public was shocked by the viciousness of the attack. The 1999 shooting at Columbine High School in Littleton, Colorado, which is described elsewhere, is a much more recent example of the viciousness of youth crime.

HOW DOES TRANSFER TO ADULT COURT TAKE PLACE?

The waiver of juveniles, as suggested in Chapter 5, is taking place more frequently than it has in the past. Indeed, only ten states permitted juveniles to be tried in adult court before the 1920s; since then, the numbers slowly have increased. Today, all state legislatures have passed laws permitting juveniles to be transferred to adult court. Of course, states vary widely in the criteria they use in making the waiver decision. Some states focus on the age of the offender, and others consider both age and offense. Table 7–1 summarizes the broad age and offense provisions related to the transfer of juvenile offenders. Vermont (age ten), Montana (age twelve), Georgia, Illinois, and Mississippi (age thirteen), transfer children at a very young age. More states transfer

The formal setting of the adult court differs dramatically from the informal setting of the juvenile court. (Photo by Kathryn Miller.)

Table 7–1 *Age and Offense Provisions for Judicial Waiver*

In most states, juvenile court judges can waive juvenile court jurisdiction over certain cases and transfer them to criminal court

		Judicial Waiver Offense and Minimum Age Criteria, 1997							
State	*Minimum Age for Judicial Waiver*	*Any Criminal Offense*	*Certain Felonies*	*Capital Crimes*	*Murder*	*Certain Person Offenses*	*Certain Property Offenses*	*Certain Drug Offenses*	*Certain Weapon Offenses*
Alabama	14	14							
Alaska	NS	NS				NS			
Arizona	NS		NS						
Arkansas	14		14	14	14	14			14
California	14	16	16		14	14	14	14	
Colorado	12		12		12	12			
Connecticut	14		14	14	14				
Delaware	NS	NS	15[a]		NS	NS	16[b]	16[b]	
Dist. of Columbia	NS	15	15		15	15	15		NS
Florida	14	14							
Georgia	13	15		13	14[c]	14[c]	15[b]		
Hawaii	NS		14		NS	NS			
Idaho	NS	14	NS		NS	NS	NS	NS	
Illinois	13	13	15						
Indiana	NS	14	NS[b]		10			16	
Iowa	14	14	15						
Kansas	10	10	14			14		14	
Kentucky	14		14	14					
Louisiana	14				14	14			
Maine	NS		NS		NS				
Maryland	NS	15		NS					
Michigan	14	14							
Minnesota	14		14						
Mississippi	13	13							
Missouri	12		12						
Montana	NS	NS							
Nevada	14	14	14			14			
New Hampshire	13		15		13	13		15	
New Jersey	14	14[b]			14	14	14	14	14

Table 7–1 *(Continued)*

State	Minimum Age for Judicial Waiver	*Judicial Waiver Offense and Minimum Age Criteria, 1997* Any Criminal Offense	Certain Felonies	Capital Crimes	Murder	Certain Person Offenses	Certain Property Offenses	Certain Drug Offenses	Certain Weapon Offenses
North Carolina	13		13	13					
North Dakota	14	16	14[b]		14	14		14	
Ohio	14		14		14	14	16		
Oklahoma	NS		NS						
Oregon	NS		15		NS	NS	15		
Pennsylvania	14		14		15	15			
Rhode Island	NS		16	NS	17	17			
South Carolina	NS	16	14		NS	NS		14	14
South Dakota	NS		NS						
Tennessee	NS	16			NS	NS			
Texas	14		14	14				14	
Utah	14		14			16	16		16
Vermont	10				10	10	10		
Virginia	14		14		14	14			
Washington	NS	NS							
West Virginia	NS		NS		NS	NS	NS	NS	
Wisconsin	14	15	14		14	14	14	14	
Wyoming	13	13							

Examples: Alabama allows waiver for any delinquency (criminal) offense involving a juvenile age 14 or older. Arizona allows waiver for any juvenile charged with a felony. New Jersey allows waiver for juveniles age 14 or older who are charged with murder or certain person, property, drug, or weapon offenses. In New Jersey, juveniles age 14 or older who have prior adjudications or convictions for certain offenses can be waived regardless of the current offense.

Note: Ages in minimum age column may not apply to all offense restrictions, but represent the youngest possible age at which a juvenile may be judicially waived to criminal court. "NS" indicates that in at least one of the offense restrictions indicated, no minimum age is specified.

[a]Only if committed while escaping from specified juvenile facilities.

[b]Requires prior adjudication(s) or conviction(s), which may be required to have been for the same or a more serious offense type.

[c]Only if committed while in custody.

Sources: Author's adaptation of Griffin et al.'s *Trying Juveniles as Adults in Criminal Court: An Analysis of State Transfer Provisions;* adapted from Melissa Sickmund, Howard N. Snyder, and Eileen Poe-Yamagata, *Juvenile Offenders and Victims: 1997 Update on Violence.* (Washington, DC: Office of Juvenile Justice and Delinquency Prevention, 1999 National Report), 104.

juveniles at fourteen than at any other age; seven states transfer juveniles at either fifteen or sixteen years of age.

The offenses juveniles commit are also important in the waiver decision. Some states permit waiver for any criminal offense, whereas others waive only those offenses specifically mentioned in the state's statutes. Many states permit waiver to the adult court if the juvenile previously has been adjudicated delinquent or has a prior criminal conviction. Depending on the state, three major mechanisms are used to waive juveniles: judicial waiver, prosecutorial discretion, and statutorial exclusion.

Judicial Waiver

Except where state laws mandate that a youth be tried in adult court, someone has to make the decision to waive a youth. **Judicial waiver,** the most widely used transfer mechanism, involves the actual decision-making process that begins when the juvenile is brought to intake. Predictably, the mechanisms used vary by state. In some states, intake personnel, juvenile prosecutors or judges make the decision based, in part, on the age or offense criteria spelled out in Table 7–1. In other states, a court other than the juvenile court makes the decision. For example, the prosecutor or judge in the adult court may decide where a juvenile is to be tried.[10] The decision is determined by the requirements of the state and the way the intake officer, prosecutor, or judge interprets the youth's background. Typically, the criteria used include the age and maturity of the child; the child's relationship with parents, school, and community; whether the child is considered dangerous; and whether court officials believe that the child may be helped by juvenile court services.

Prosecutorial Discretion

Prosecutorial discretion occurs in states with **concurrent jurisdiction** statutes. These laws give prosecutors the authority to decide whether to try juveniles in either juvenile or adult courts. Table 7–2 illustrates which states utilize concurrent jurisdiction statutes and the statutory conditions that prosecutors must use in making their decisions. Table 7–2 demonstrates that age is one factor taken into consideration by the states in setting up these statutes. It also indicates that three states, Nevada, Vermont, and Wyoming, permit charges to be filed in either juvenile or adult court for any criminal offense, but most states specifically mention in their juvenile codes precisely which offenses may be tried in either court.

Statutorial Exclusion

Some states have a **statutorial exclusion** of certain offenses from juvenile court, thereby automatically transferring perpetrators of those offenses to adult court. Table 7–3 shows that the states that exclude offenses from juvenile court primarily focus on "safety" crimes such as murder and other offenses

Table 7–2 States That Permit Prosecutorial Discretion

In states with concurrent jurisdiction, the prosecutor has discretion to file certain cases, generally involving juveniles charged with serious offenses, in either criminal court or juvenile court

State	Minimum Age for Concurrent Jurisdiction	Concurrent Jurisdiction Offense and Minimum Age Criteria, 1997							
		Any Criminal Offense	Certain Felonies	Capital Crimes	Murder	Certain Person Offenses	Certain Property Offenses	Certain Drug Offenses	Certain Weapon Offenses
Arizona	14		14						
Arkansas	14		14	14	14	14			14
Colorado	14		14		14	14	14		14
Dist. of Columbia	16				16	16	16		
Florida	NS	16[a]	16	NS[b]	14	14	14		14
Georgia	NS			NS					
Louisiana	15				15	15	15	15	
Massachusetts	14		14			14			14
Michigan	14		14		14	14	14	14	
Montana	12				12	12	16	16	16
Nebraska	NS	16[c]	NS						
Oklahoma	15				15	15	15	16	15
Vermont	16	16							
Virginia	14				14	14			
Wyoming	14	17	14						

Examples: In Arizona, prosecutors have discretion to file directly in criminal court those cases involving juveniles age 14 or older charged with certain felonies (defined in state statutes). In Florida, prosecutors may "direct file" cases involving juveniles age 16 or older charged with a misdemeanor (if they have a prior adjudication) or a felony offense, as well as those age 14 or older charged with murder or certain person, property, or weapon offenses; no minimum age is specified for cases in which a grand jury indicts a juvenile for a capital offense.

Note: Ages in minimum age column may not apply to all offense restrictions, but represent the youngest possible age at which a juvenile may be filed directly in criminal court. "NS" indicates that in at least one of the offense restrictions indicated, no minimum age is specified.

[a]Applies to misdemeanors and requires prior adjudication(s), which may be required to have been for the same or a more serious offense type.

[b]Requires grand jury indictment.

[c]Applies to misdemeanors.

Source: Authors' adaptation of Griffin et al.'s *Trying Juveniles as Adults in Criminal Court: An Analysis of State Transfer Provisions.* Adapted from Melissa Sickmund, Howard N. Snyder, and Eileen Poe-Yamagata, *Juvenile Offenders and Victims: 1997 Update on Violence* (Washington, DC: Office of Juvenile Justice and Delinquency Prevention, 1999 National Report), 105.

against a person. The statutes also, however, spell out the minimum age that youths must reach before they may be transferred to adult court.

Other variations on waiver also exist, some very subtle. One such variation is a state legislature lowering the age over which the juvenile court has jurisdiction. For example, if a state's age of juvenile court jurisdiction is eighteen, the legislature may lower the age to sixteen. This approach focuses entirely on the age of the juvenile but ignores the offenses committed.

Table 7–3 *States With Statutorial Exclusion*

In states with statutory exclusion provisions, certain cases involving juveniles originate in criminal court rather than juvenile court

		Staturory Exclusion Offense and Minimum Age Criteria, 1997							
State	*Minimum Age for Statutory Exclusion*	*Any Criminal Offense*	*Certain Felonies*	*Capital Crimes*	*Murder*	*Certain Person Offenses*	*Certain Property Offenses*	*Certain Drug Offenses*	*Certain Weapon Offenses*
Alabama	16		16	16				16	
Alaska	16					16	16		
Arizona	15		15[a]		15	15			
Delaware	15		15						
Florida	NS	NS[a]				NS			
Georgia	13				13	13			
Idaho	14				14	14	14	14	
Illinois	13		15[b]		13	15		15	15
Indiana	16		16		16	16		16	16
Iowa	16		16					16	16
Louisiana	15				15	15			
Maryland	14			14	16	16			16
Massachusetts	14				14				
Minnesota	16				16				
Mississippi	13		13	13					
Montana	17				17	17	17	17	17
Nevada	NS	NS[a]			NS	16[a]			
New Mexico	15				15[c]				
New York	13				13	14	14		
Oklahoma	13				13				
Oregon	15				15	15			
Pennsylvania	NS				NS	15			
South Carolina	16		16						
South Dakota	16		16						
Utah	16		16[d]		16				
Vermont	14				14	14	14		
Washington	16				16	16	16		
Wisconsin	NS				10	NS[e]			

Examples: In Delaware, juveniles age 15 or older charged with certain felonies must be tried as adults. In Arizona, juveniles age 15 or older must be tried as adults if they are charged with murder or certain person offenses or they have prior felony adjudications and are changed with a felony.

Note: Ages in minimum age column may not apply to all offense restrictions, but represent the youngest possible age at which a juvenile may be excluded from juvenile court. "NS" indicates that in at least one of the offense restrictions indicated, no minimum age is specified.

[a]Requires prior adjudication(s) or conviction(s), which may be required to have been for the same or a more serious offense type.
[b]Only escape or bail violation while subject to prosecution in criminal court.
[c]Requires grand jury indictment.
[d]Requires prior commitment in a secure facility.
[e]Only if charged while confined or on probation or parole.

Source: Authors' adaptation of Griffin et al.'s *Trying Juveniles as Adults in Criminal Court: An Analysis of State Transfer Provisions.* Adapted from Melissa Sickmund, Howard N. Snyder, and Eileen Poe-Yamagata, *Juvenile Offenders and Victims: 1997 Update on Violence* (Washington, DC: Office of Juvenile Justice and Delinquency Prevention, 1999 National Report), 107.

Yet other state legislatures have specified that juveniles of specific ages who commit specific crimes are to be tried by adult court. For example, until recently, Indiana statutes stated that any child age ten or older who committed murder would be tried as an adult. This method of legislative waiver focuses as much on the offense as it does on the age of the offender.

Another method of waiver is one in which the statutes simply state that anyone who commits a specific crime may be tried in adult court. No reference is made to the age of the offender. This approach is attractive to those who believe that any youth who violates the law should receive an appropriate punishment.

Finally, many state laws permit youths who are over the maximum age of jurisdiction to be sent back to the juvenile court if the adult court believes the case is appropriate for juvenile court jurisdiction.[11]

Changing Criteria for Waiver

It is clear from the previous discussion that state statutes provide the courts with the basis for waiver. Those making the decision to transfer a youth still have a great deal of discretion, however. In the past, youths were waived to adult court without hearings, without sufficient fact-finding on the part of the court, without reasons being given for the waiver, and without the youth having the benefit of an attorney.

Critics fought these procedures. Their essential argument was that the decision to waive juveniles to adult court was a serious matter and that youths should be entitled to due process rights. Upon reviewing two cases in particular, *Kent v. United States* and *Breed v. Jones* (see Chapter 5), the United States Supreme Court ruled that traditional juvenile court procedures for waiver were inadequate and that juveniles were guaranteed many of the same due process rights as adults.

Since *Kent* and *Jones,* most states now require that waiver hearings be held before transferring juveniles to adult court. Yet, these hearings are not required in all states, as some permit prosecutors to make the waiver decision. In addition, states that provide for mandatory legislative waiver do not have to hold such hearings.

Evaluation of Waiver

Four conclusions can be drawn about the process of waiving juveniles to the adult court. First, although waivers are still relatively infrequent, composing only 5 percent of juvenile court delinquency dispositions, the number of waivers appears to be increasing all the time.[12] M. A. Bortner found that since 1979 the rate of transfers has tripled in various jurisdictions.[13] Dean J. Champion's study of waiver in Georgia, Mississippi, Tennessee, and Virginia found that between 1980 and 1988 the number of juvenile waiver hearings in these states rose from 228 to 446, an increase of almost 100 percent. The percentage of hearings resulting in successful waiver also increased from 71.5 to 86.2 percent during these years.[14]

Second, juveniles waived to adult court are not always the more serious and violent offenders. Bortner, for example, found that juveniles who were waived were neither particularly violent nor intractable, nor were they serious threats to public safety.[15] Howard N. Snyder and colleagues' study of 1,917 cases waived to criminal court in ten states in 1985 found that 65 percent were charged with property offenses, primarily burglary, and with nonindex delinquency offenses. [16] Donna Bishop and colleagues' examination of 583 prosecutorial waivers of sixteen- and seventeen-year-old youths in Florida from 1981 to 1984 revealed that most transferred juveniles were property and low-risk offenders.[17] A study by Donna Hamparian and others, which covered four variations of waiver—judicial waiver, concurrent jurisdiction, excluded offense, and the lower age of jurisdiction—supported those of Bortner and others who found that many minor and nonthreatening offenders are remanded to adult court. Hamparian and colleagues discovered that many states make it a regular practice to send public order cases on to adult court as well as cases that involve the violation of traffic and fish and game violations.[18]

Several explanations have been given for why so many property and nonserious juvenile offenders are being transferred to the adult court. Ted Rubin's analysis revealed that in many jurisdictions, transfers are used for cosmetic purposes to create the impression or illusion that the juvenile court is enforcing a get tough policy against hardcore offenders.[19] Bortner's study revealed that organizational and political factors accounted for the high rate of remand.[20] Several studies have found that juvenile courts regularly use transfer to get rid of "troublesome cases."[21]

Third, the seriousness of offenses is not the only concern of researchers interested in waiver criteria. Marcy R. Podkopacz and Barry C. Feld recently examined eight variables, including court services recommendations, differential rates of waiver by different judges, age at present offense, prior program placements, number of present offense charges, present offense characteristics, felony versus property offenses, and race. With the exception of the last two variables, felony versus property offenses and race, all the preceding variables were found to be significantly related to the waiver decision.[22] These findings make it clear that little consensus exists today on which criteria should be used in making the waiver decision.

Fourth, although some remanded youth are receiving severe penalties, including the death penalty, waiver generally does not result in more severe penalities for juvenile offenders than they would have received in juvenile court. In one of the few studies that challenges this conclusion, Carl Rudman and others found that whether juveniles were sent to adult or juvenile court made little difference in the severity of their sentence because youths are adjudicated at high rates in both courts. Yet, youths remanded to adult court received even more severe sentences than the maximum juvenile court sentences of juveniles considered for transfer.[23]

In contrast, several studies have found a high degree of leniency in dealing with those transferred to the adult court. David Ream's examination of 346 transfers in the period between 1975 and 1981 revealed that 66 percent either were dropped, led to acquittals, or were plea-bargained.[24] Simon Singer found from his investigation of transfer in New York State that probation and shorter incarceration sentences were widely used for youths transferred to adult court.[25] Hamparian and others found that states vary rather dramatically in the sentences that juveniles receive in adult courts. For example, some judicial waiver states sentenced almost all youths to adult correctional facilities or juvenile institutions and seldom used fines and probation, whereas other judicial waiver states primarily used fines and probation.[26]

Several states have attempted to develop a process that would identify those juveniles unfit for retention in juvenile court. For example, using such criteria as age, offense, and prior record, Minnesota has codified the transfer procedures to be followed by judges and prosecutors. But Lee Ann Osburn and Peter A. Rose's evaluation concluded that Minnesota's procedures were inadequate for making acceptable transfer decisions.[27]

Even more problematic is whether waiver, even if done in a consistent and standardized manner, achieves the goals of punishing offenders and reducing crime. Bishop and colleagues studied a matched sample of 2,887 youths to compare recidivism rates of youths handled within the juvenile court as opposed to those who were waived to adult court. Their findings were, very simply, that "transfer actually aggravated short-term recidivism."[28]

In sum, although waiver to the adult court spares the juvenile court from contending with its most difficult cases, we are unsure exactly what the waiver criteria are, because not all juveniles transferred to the adult court have committed serious crimes. Once transfer is accomplished, other problems appear. With adult courts' massive caseload and their limited judicial experience with sentencing youths, little evidence exists that adult judges know what to do with juveniles appearing before them. Indeed, variations in practices among jurisdictions and judges sometimes result in juveniles being treated more leniently than adults are. Finally, even when waiver does occur, initial findings indicate that waiver may have the effect, not of deterring crime by juveniles, but of increasing it.

HOW DOES A YOUTHFUL OFFENDER SYSTEM WORK?

Juveniles sentenced in adult courts are subject to the same range of dispositions as are adults. Cases may be dismissed or offenders may be found guilty. If found guilty, youths may be released to the care of their parents, placed on probation, fined, ordered to pay restitution, or referred to a social agency qualified to deal with their problem. But a very controversial disposition is the placement of youths in adult correctional facilities.

The crowding, violence, and exploitative relationships found in adult prisons make this disposition extremely questionable. Furthermore, although some states have attempted to develop special institutions for juveniles, even these would appear to have the same characteristics as adult prisons. Youths who are placed in them can no better protect themselves here than they can in adult facilities. Given the young age of even the most violent of these offenders, society has the task of deciding whether any type of adult institutional placement is appropriate for these youths.

At the time of the Hamparian study, only two states, Delaware and Kentucky, prohibited the placement of juveniles in state correctional institutions.[29] Some variations on the practice of confining a juvenile in an adult institution do exist among the states. In some jurisdictions, states have no alternative but to place juveniles in adult institutions if the courts require incarceration. Some states can, under special circumstances, place youths in either juvenile or adult institutions, yet other states can refer juveniles back to juvenile court for their disposition. In some instances, very young juveniles are sent to juvenile facilities but then are transferred to adult institutions when they become of age. Recognizing the dangers and inadequacies of placing juveniles with adults, some jurisdictions have developed special institutions for these younger adult offenders.

Hamparian and colleagues propose that a **youthful offender system** be developed for young adults (sixteen to nineteen years of age). In these institutions, programs would emphasize work readiness, job training, and work experience. They would also attempt to establish close ties to the community to which the youth would return; employ flexible staff who would act as positive role models; enforce the rules strictly; provide opportunities for decision making, with consequences clearly and fully related to the choices made; provide opportunities to enhance self esteem; create a continuity of care between the program or treatment sequence and integration into the community to which the youth is returning; and offer supportive services in the community after completion of the program or treatment sequence as long as the youth needs them.[30]

The California Youth Authority has long extended its jurisdiction over youthful offenders to those up to twenty-three years of age. North Carolina was one of the first states to develop Youthful Offender Camps for sixteen- to eighteen-year-old males. In the 1990s, Colorado, New Mexico, and Minnesota also developed transitional, or intermediate, systems between the juvenile and adult systems. The Minnesota Juvenile Justice Task Force recommended the following:

> a more graduated juvenile justice system that establishes a new *transitional component between the juvenile and adult systems*. . . . [T]his new [Serious Youthful Offender] category will create viable new dispositional options for juvenile court judges facing juveniles who have committed serious or repeat offenses. It will give the juvenile *one last chance* at success in the juvenile system, with the threat of adult sanctions as an incentive not to re-offend.[31]

In 1994, the Minnesota legislature adopted the task force's recommendation but relabeled the category "Extended Jurisdiction Juvenile" (EJJ) to make the label less attractive to delinquent "wannabes." For juveniles who are designated as EJJs, final legislation extended the juvenile court's jurisdiction until age twenty-one. The Department of Corrections was also required to license and regulate regional secure treatment facilities for EJJs.[32]

Intermediate sentencing for youthful offenders that bridges the juvenile and adult systems certainly appears to be a positive means to keep some juveniles out of adult correctional facilities. It is hoped that the 1994 legislation in Minnesota, as well as the youthful offender systems in Colorado and New Mexico, might encourage the development of such legislation in more states.

The current get tough mood of society does not seem to be a time in which the development of youthful offender systems will be viewed as an attractive option to policymakers in many states. Yet, if the juvenile population explosion occurs in the next two decades as predicted by some experts and increasing numbers of juveniles are referred to the adult systems, perhaps there will be a greater receptivity toward an intermediate correctional system for youthful offenders.

WHAT IS LIFE LIKE FOR A JUVENILE SENT TO PRISON?

Adult prisons are a world apart from most training schools. Prisons are much larger, sometimes containing several thousand inmates and covering many acres of ground. Life on the inside is generally austere, crowded, and dangerous. As suggested in the opening quote of this chapter, institutionalized juveniles are especially subject to sexual victimization and sexual assault. Richard E. Redding concluded from his review of the programming that juveniles receive in adult correctional facilities: "Once incarcerated in adult facilities, juveniles typically receive fewer age-appropriate rehabilitative, medical, mental health and educational services, and are at greater risk of physical and sexual abuse and suicide."[33]

A 1990 national survey found that 5,212 juveniles were admitted that year to state and federal adult correctional facilities. The states imprisoning the most juveniles were Florida (1,212), North Carolina (760), Texas (572), New York (558), Michigan (288), Illinois (257), South Carolina (227), and California (133). The states imprisoning the fewest juveniles were Utah (2), Oregon (7), Iowa (16), Washington (17), Minnesota (18), and Colorado (19).[34] The number of juveniles who were sentenced to adult prison was on the rise during the 1990s, and by 1996 more than 13,000 juveniles were held as adults.[35]

In some states, judges opt for the **life without parole sentence** to incarcerate juveniles for the rest of their natural lives.[36] See Focus on Law 7–1 for a Iowa case in which a fifteen-year-old received a life without parole sentence.

FOCUS ON LAW 7–1

YOU WILL SPEND THE REMAINDER OF YOUR NATURAL LIFE IN PRISON

In 1994, four Midwestern teenagers decided to take a Ford Bronco belonging to one of their parents and run away to Canada. The Bronco broke down in a neighboring state, and they realized that they would need to steal another car. They stopped a woman, who thought that the Bronco with lights on top was a police vehicle. One of the teenagers approached the woman and pretended to be a police officer. She demanded to see identification. He returned to the Bronco and instructed one of his companions to take the .22 rifle they had brought along and shoot her. The fifteen-year-old youth, who had committed no more serious acts than vandalism, complied. He shot her once, broke the window of her vehicle on the driver's side when she locked the door, and stabbed her thirty-one times.

The four youths called their parents after they left the crime scene. Later that night one of their parents arrived and took them home. Within a couple days, all four were arrested and charged with this crime. Tried in the jurisdiction where the crime was committed, the four juveniles were quickly transferred to the adult court.

During the trial of the youth who had committed the stabbing, his defense attorney attempted to explain the youth's ruthless behavior: The jury was informed that he came from a totally inadequate family background. He had been sexually abused by his natural father at the age of two and had been physically assaulted by an adopted father at the age of fifteen. His mother had been married eight times, and she failed to supply his emotional needs in a number of ways. He also did poorly in school and had failed twice. He had been charged with using marijuana on a couple of occasions but had not been involved in any serious personal or property offenses. He was particularly fearful of the youth who had instructed him to shoot the woman. In summary, the defense attorney claimed that what had taken place that night emerged from the totality of the youth's experiences, frustrations, inadequacies, and unmet needs. The child deserved punishment, the attorney admitted, but not to the extent of spending the rest of his life in prison.

Upon being sentenced to prison, the youth admitted that he was fearful of being sexually assaulted. As a small, white youth, his fears were not unreasonable. He said that he had made up his mind to be placed in population [with other inmates]. He did not want to be locked up twenty-four hours a day for the rest of his life. Whatever it took, he vowed, he would keep the other inmates off him. He was briefly placed in a diagnostic facility, and then when he was transferred to an adult reformatory, it did not take him long to attack a pressuring inmate with a shank. He was charged with attempted murder and placed in administrative segregation.

Source: One of the authors was involved with this defense as an expert witness.

Critical Thinking Questions:
How long do you believe this offender should spend in prison for a crime he committed when he was fifteen? If you were this inmate, would you want to be locked up in protective custody or try to make it in the prison population? If you chose the prison population, what would you be willing to do to protect yourself?

Providing for the care and special needs of juvenile offenders in adult facilities is proving to be a real problem. The youthful offender may be as young as thirteen and feel overwhelmed by older and more aggressive offenders. Indeed, most juvenile offenders placed in adult prisons are not violent offenders. A gang culture may be present in the prison, in which gang members pressure youthful offenders to become part of their gang, usually to exploit them. Furthermore, with their need to be part of something, youthful offenders tend to be highly impressionable and easily used or manipulated.[37]

The state of Washington has attempted to manage more effectively imprisoned youthful offenders. In 1997, the state of Washington enacted Senate bill 3900 defining the jurisdiction, custody, and management requirements for juvenile offenders. This new legislation requires juvenile offenders to be placed in adult prisons for serious offenses such as aggravated murder. In addition, this new law dictates the housing and educational requirements for youthful offenders within the Department of Corrections (DOC) as follows:

- An offender under the age of eighteen who is convicted in adult criminal court and sentenced to the DOC must be placed in a housing unit, or a portion of a housing unit, separated from adult inmates;
- The offender may be housed in an intensive management unit or administrative segregation unit, if necessary, for the safety or security of the offender or the staff; and
- The DOC must provide an educational program to an offender under the age of eighteen who is incarcerated at a DOC facility. The program must enable the offender to obtain a high school diploma or general equivalency diploma (GED).[38]

Female youthful offenders are placed at the Washington Corrections Center for Women (WCCW), and males are confined at the Clallam Bay Corrections Center. A multidisciplinary team was formed in September 1997 in order to meet the challenge of accommodating juveniles in adult prisons. This team has been concerned with meeting the objectives of providing a safe and secure environment, of providing an environment distant from adult offenders' contact and influences, of providing programs and services similar to those available to the general population, and of providing an educational program offering credit for a high school diploma or GED.[39]

SHOULD JUVENILES BE PUT TO DEATH?

The most severe sentence is, of course, the death penalty. Much debate has centered on this issue, and in June 1989, the United States Supreme Court ruled that sixteen- and seventeen-year-old juveniles may be executed for their crimes.[40]

This decision generated an outburst of debate. The decision was applauded by conservatives, who contend that society needs the death penalty for its retributive and deterrent effects on violent crime. Conservatives also believe that juveniles are "molly-coddled" by the juvenile court and that juveniles who break the law deserve the same punishments as adults. Liberals, however, decried the decision. Their objections reflect, in part, the disdain that many have for the appropriateness of the death penalty in a "civilized" society. These modern progressives also believe that youthful offenders should be rehabilitated because they are young and still in the formative years of their lives.

Victor L. Strieb traces the development of the current debate.[41] The constitutionality of the death penalty was decided in *Gregg v. Georgia* in 1976.[42] In that decision, the U.S. Supreme Court ruled that the death penalty did not violate the Eighth Amendment's prohibition against cruel and unusual punishment. The Court did stipulate that before lower courts could hand down the death penalty, the special characteristics of the offender, such as his or her age, as well as the circumstances of the crime, had to be considered by the court.[43] In later decisions considering statutes in Ohio and other states, the Court ruled that mitigating circumstances had to be considered in any death penalty case.[44] Accordingly, states that have handed down the death penalty without considering mitigating circumstances have had their cases overturned.[45] States that permit the death penalty today, in other words, must statutorily require that mitigating circumstances be considered.

In some ways the debate over the death penalty for juveniles is a curious one. Strieb points out that historically, few juveniles have ever been executed for their crimes. Indeed, even when juveniles have been sentenced to death, few if any executions have been carried out.[46] In the United States, for example, youths under the age of eighteen were executed at the rate of twenty- to twenty-seven per decade, or about 1.6 to 2.3 percent of all executions from the 1880s to the 1920s.[47] The highest peak in the United States was in the 1940s, when fifty-three, or 4.1 percent of all those executed, were juveniles.[48]

Table 7–4 Executions of Juvenile Offenders, January 1, 1973, through June 30, 2003

Name	Date of Execution	Place of Execution	Race and Sex of Offender/Victim	Age at Crime	Age at Execution
Charles Rumbaugh	9-11-1985	Texas	WM/WM	17	28
J. Terry Roach	1-10-1986	South Carolina	WM/WM, WF	17	25
Jay Pinkerton	5-15-1986	Texas	WM/WF, WF	17	24
Dalton Prejean	5-18-1990	Louisiana	BM/WM	17	30
Johnny Garrett	2-11-1992	Texas	WM/WF	17	28
Curtis Harris	7-1-1993	Texas	BM/WM	17	31
Frederick Lashley	7-28-1993	Missouri	BM/BF	17	29
Ruben Cantu	8-24-1993	Texas	LM/LM	17	26
Chris Burger	12-7-1993	Georgia	WM/WM	17	33
Joseph John Cannon	4-22-1998	Texas	WM/WF	17	38
Robert A. Carter	5-18-1998	Texas	BM/LF	17	34
Dwight A. Wright	10-14-1998	Virginia	BM/BF	17	26
Sean R. Sellers	2-4-1999	Oklahoma	WM/WM, WM, WF	16	29
Christopher Thomas	1-10-2000	Virginia	WM/WF	17	26
Steve E. Roach	1-19-2000	Virginia	WM/WF	17	23
Glen C. McGinnis	1-25-2000	Texas	BM/WF	17	27
Gary L. Graham	6-22-2000	Texas	BM/WM	17	36
Gerald L. Mitchell	10-22-2001	Texas	BM/WM	17	33
Napoleon Beazley	5-28-2002	Texas	BM/WM	17	25
T. J. Jones	8-8-2002	Texas	BM/WM	17	25
Toronto Patterson	8-28-2002	Texas	BM/BF	17	24
Scott A. Hain	4-3-2003	Oklahoma	WM/WM, WF	17	32

- All but one of these executed juvenile offenders were age 17 at the time of their crimes, with only Sean Sellers (Oklahoma) being age 16.
- Only 45% of executed juvenile offenders have been White, whereas 57% of executed adult offenders have been White. (NAACP-LDF, DEATH ROW U.S.A. at 7 [Winter 2003]).
- Race of victim is exactly the same for executed juvenile offenders (81% White victims) and for executed adult offenders (81%). However, the overrepresentation of female victims is even more apparent in juvenile offender executions (59% female victims) as compared to adult offender executions (49% female victims). (NAACP-LDF, DEATH ROW U.S.A. at 7 [Winter 2003]).
- The periods on death row awaiting execution for these executed juvenile offenders ranged from 6 years to over 20 years, resulting in the age at execution ranging from 23 to 38.
- The dominance of juvenile executions in Oklahoma, Texas, and Virginia is apparent, and no other state has executed a juvenile offender in the last 10 years.

Sources: Victor L. Streib, "Moratorium on the Death Penalty for Juveniles," *Law and Contemporary Problems,* 19. Reprinted by permission of the author. Updated June 2003, from Death Penalty Information Centre at Victor+Streib&oq=&url=http.

Fourteen states have never executed juveniles, but Georgia leads all states with forty-one juvenile executions, followed by North Carolina and Ohio, with nineteen each. Table 7–4 lists the executions of juvenile offenders from January 1, 1973, through June 1, 1998.

Table 7–5 *Minimum Death Penalty Ages by Jurisdiction as of June 30, 2003*

Age 18	*Age 17*	*Age 16*
California[a]	Florida[b]	Alabama[a]
Colorado[a]	Georgia[a]	Arizona[c]
Connecticut[a]	New Hampshire[a]	Arkansas[c]
Illinois[a]	North Carolina[a]	Delaware[c]
Indiana[a]	Texas[a]	Idaho[c]
Kansas[a]		Kentucky[a]
Maryland[a]	5 states	Louisiana[c]
Montana[a]		Mississippi[c]
Nebraska[a]		Missouri[a]
New Jersey[a]		Nevada[a]
New Mexico[a]		Oklahoma[c]
New York[a]		Pennsylvania[c]
Ohio[a]		South Carolina[c]
Oregon[a]		South Dakota[c]
Tennessee[a]		Utah[c]
Washington[a]		Virginia[a]
Federal Civilian[a]		Wyoming[a]
Federal Military[a]		
		17 states
16 states and 2 federal jurisdictions		

[a]Express minimum age in statute.
[b]Minimum age required by Florida Constitution per Florida Supreme Court in *Brennan v. State*, 754 So.2d 1 (FL 1999).
[c]Minimum age required by U.S. Constitution per U.S. Supreme Court in *Thompson v. Oklahoma*, 487 U.S. 815 (1998).

Source: This chart is found at http://www.law.onu.edu/faculty/streib/juvdeath.htm

Of the thirty-eight states that permit capital punishment, twenty-four allow it for individuals who were under the age of eighteen when they committed the crime (see Table 7–5). In 1982, in the case of *Eddings v. Oklahoma*, the Supreme Court was able to avoid directly addressing the constitutionality of the juvenile death penalty by ruling that "the chronological age of a minor is itself a relevant mitigating factor of great weight."[49] Monty Lee Eddings was sixteen when he shot and killed an Oklahoma State Highway Patrol officer, but his execution sentence was reversed in 1982 because of his age.[50]

In 1988, the Supreme Court heard the case of *Thompson v. Oklahoma*.[51] Wayne Thompson was fifteen when he was arrested along with his twenty-seven-year-old half-brother and two other older men for the shooting and stabbing death of Charles Keene, Thompson's former brother-in-law. The Court ruled by a five to three vote that "the Eighth and Fourteenth Amendment[s] prohibit the execution of a person who was under sixteen years of age at the time of his or her offense."[52]

The Supreme Court upheld the constitutionality of the death penalty for juveniles in two 1989 cases. In the case of *Stanford v. Kentucky,* Kevin Stanford, a seventeen-year-old African-American youth, repeatedly raped and sodomized his victim during a robbery.[53] He then drove her to a secluded area, where he shot her point-blank in the face and in the back of the head. A jury convicted Stanford of first-degree murder, first-degree sodomy, first-degree robbery, and receiving stolen property. Stanford was sentenced to death on September 28, 1989, and was transferred to death row, where he awaits execution.[54]

In *Wilkins v. Missouri,* sixteen-year-old Heath A. Wilkins of Missouri stabbed Nancy Allen Moore to death on July 27, 1985, as she worked behind the counter of a convenience store. The jury found him guilty of first-degree murder, armed criminal action, and carrying a concealed weapon. During the sentencing hearing, both the prosecution and Wilkins himself urged the court to apply the death penalty. The aggravating circumstances within the case led the court to the decision that the death penalty was appropriate and sentenced Wilkins to die. The Missouri Supreme Court later upheld this decision.[55]

Individuals who were given capital sentences for crimes committed while they were juveniles are continuing to be executed. For example, on February 1, 1999, Sean Sellers was executed in Oklahoma for a murder committed when he was sixteen years old. Nevertheless, the juvenile death penalty has many vocal opponents. The human rights organization Amnesty International and the United Nations General Assembly have expressed their disapproval of the juvenile death penalty. Because many juvenile death penalty sentences were reversed in the 1990s, in the United States there is reason to believe that the executions of individuals who committed capital crimes when they were juveniles will take place less frequently in the future than they have in the past several decades. Nevertheless, the United States is delaying signing the convention on the Rights of the Child, drawn up November 20, 1986 (See Focus on Law 7–2).

A PROPOSED ADULT COURT FOR JUVENILES

Whereas Thomas Geraghty and others advocate retaining the juvenile court (see Chapter 6), Barry C. Feld recommends abolishing it altogether. In one of the most highly respected articles on juvenile justice, Feld's "Criminalizing the American Juvenile Court" argues that youthful offenders should be tried in criminal court:

> If the child is a criminal and the primary purpose of formal intervention is social control, then young offenders could be tried in criminal courts alongside their adult counterparts. Before returning young offenders to criminal courts, however, there are preliminary issues of substance and procedure that a legislature should address. Issues of substantive justice include developing a rationale for sentencing young offenders differently, and more

FOCUS ON LAW 7–2

RATIFICATION OF CHILDRENS' RIGHTS DOCUMENT

Status of Ratification

Convention on the Rights of the Child

- Ratified by 192 countries
- Only 2 countries have not ratified: the United States and Somalia, which have signaled their intention to ratify by formally signing the Convention.

Source: http://www.unicef.org/crc/crc.htm. Accessed January 19, 2004.

Critical Thinking Questions:
Why do you believe the United States refuses to sign the document on the Rights of the Child? Should it? To what extent should the United States be influenced by International Law in cases such as this?

FOCUS ON LAW 7–3

A KID ON DEATH ROW

When you were little, what did you dream of becoming when you got older? Would it be a doctor, teacher, singer, or sports star? Seventeen-year-old Mark Young's dreams were to marry, have children, and become a microbiologist. Unfortunately, his dreams will never become reality. He's now on death row.

December 6, 2002, Young raped and then murdered a fourteen-year-old when he thought that she would report the rape to police. One night is costing Young his life. He is now on death row awaiting his execution.

The year 1642 marked the first execution of a juvenile on this continent and at least 366 more juvenile offenders have been executed since then. Twenty-two of these executions have occurred between 1973 and 2003.

International rights treaties such as the United Nations' Economic and Social Council Safeguards Guaranteeing Protection of the Rights of Those Facing the Death Penalty and The United Nations Convention on the Rights of the Child prohibit the imposition of the death penalty on anyone under eighteen years of age. The United States and Somalia are the only two countries that have not ratified the latter of these, the Convention on the Rights of the Child, which also prohibits the execution of juveniles under the age of eighteen at the time the crime was committed.

Since 1990, Iran, Pakistan, Saudi Arabia, Yemen, and the United States are the only countries known to have executed juvenile offenders.

Once a person is sentenced to death, like Mark Young, the execution can be delayed for years while the inmate makes appeals to the court; Mark has, perhaps, eight years to wait. While the prisoner waits, he stays in a part of a state or federal prison called death row.

After a prisoner's appeals are exhausted, an execution order is given and his execution date is set. Unlike most people, an inmate on death row knows his time of death. Each prisoner handles this knowledge of death differently. Some become hysterical and others remain calm. During the inmate's last twenty-four hours he can be visited by anyone, including family, friends, and spiritual advisors. The final few hours before the execution involves a last meal, visitation of the warden, chaplain, and witnesses, and the inmate makes his final preparations. These may include showering and putting on clothes such as pants and shirt for the males, and a dress for the females. A heart monitor is connected which will monitor when the heart stops and death is assumed to have occurred.

After dressing, the prisoner waits in the death-watch cell with a spiritual advisor until the warden calls for the inmate to be brought to the execution chamber.

Once arriving at the execution chamber, the inmate is secured to a gurney with lined ankle and wrist restraints. A sheet may or may not be placed over the inmate. Following placement of the restraints, two intravenous tubes are inserted, one tube in each arm. The tubes are connected through an opening in the wall that leads to the anteroom where the execution team is located. As soon as the IV tubes are inserted, the witness is allowed to make a final statement, either written or verbal.

At the warden's signal, unless a call is received from state officials to stay the execution, the execution team begins to inject the two or three lethal drugs into the IVs. The first drug administered is an anesthetic—sodium thiopental, which puts the prisoner into a deep sleep. Saline solution then flushes the intravenous line. Pancuronium bromide, a paralyzing agent that paralyzes the diaphragm to stop breathing is then injected. Again, saline solution flushes out the intravenous line. Then a toxic agent, potassium chloride, is given in order to interrupt the electrical signaling essential to heart functions. Death of the inmate usually occurs from five to eighteen minutes after the execution order is given. The body is then taken to a medical examiner who may or may not perform an autopsy.

Mark Young is scheduled for execution on March 16, 2010.

Alanna Santee prepared the previous materials especially for this volume from the following sources, Victor Streib's *Moratorium on the Death Penalty for Juveniles,* http://www.law.duke.edu/journals/lcp/articles/lcp61dAutumn1998p55.htm, © Amnesty International Publications. http://web.amnesty.org/library/index/ENGAMR510101998, *United States of America The Death Penalty in Texas: Lethal Injustice,* and Kevin Bonsor's *How Lethal Injection Works,* http://people.howstuffworks.com/lethal-injectionl.htm.

Critical Thinking Questions:

Do you agree that this young man should be executed? Would you personally be able to start the dripping of the lethal injection drugs? What form other than execution should be used if you don't agree with the death penalty?

> leniently, than older defendants. Issues of procedural justice include affording youths alternative safeguards *in addition* to full procedural parity with adult defendants. Taken in combination, legislation can avoid the worst of both worlds, provide more than the protections accorded to adults, and do justice in sentencing.[56]

Feld is quick to admit that "juveniles deserve less severe punishment than adults for comparable crimes."[57] Reasons for this, he adds, are that "juveniles are less able to understand the consequences of their acts" and that a juvenile's "removal from home is a more severe punishment than it would be for adults."[58]

The basis of Feld's argument for the handling of juveniles in the adult system is that "shorter sentences for reduced responsibility is a more modest rationale for treating young people differently than [are] the rehabilitative justifications advanced by the Progressive child savers."[59] He acknowledges that adult courts would be able to "impose shorter sentences for reduced culpability on a discretionary basis," but he thinks it would make more sense for legislatures "to provide youths with categorical fractional reductions of adult sentences. This could take the form of a formal "youth discount of adult sentences."[60] For example, he suggests that "a fourteen-year-old might receive 33 percent of the adult penalty, a sixteen-year-old 66 percent, and an eighteen-year-old the full penalty."[61]

He goes on to state that this "graduated age/culpability sentencing scheme" in adult court provides more justice than is typically found in juvenile waiver proceedings, such as assuring similar consequences to similar youthful offenders, and that it saves considerable resources, especially eliminating the need for transfer hearings. It also assures that juvenile offenders receive the same due process protections as are accorded adult offenders. Indeed, he says that "differentials in age and competency suggest that youths should receive more protection than adults, rather than less."[62]

In a number of other articles, Feld renews his previous call for the abolition of the juvenile court and, at the same time, recognizes youthfulness as a mitigating factor in sentencing juveniles in criminal court.[63] He charges that the abolition of the juvenile court is necessary because changes in this court's jurisdiction, purpose, and procedures since its inception have transformed the court from its "original model as a social service agency into a deficient second-rate criminal court that provides people with neither positive treatment nor criminal procedural justice."[64]

Feld's solution is an integrated criminal court that has a separate sentencing policy for younger offenders, or a "youth discount." This discount is only fair because juveniles are more likely, due to their age, impulsiveness, and grandiosity, to be greater risk-takers than adults are. They also have limited ability to think about the long-term consequences of what they do and are more susceptible than adults are to negative peer influences. Feld also suggests that "[s]tates should maintain separate age-segregated youth correctional facilities to protect both younger offenders and older inmates."[65]

Feld is mindful of dangers to his approach. He states:

> [A]lthough abolition of the juvenile court, enhanced procedural protections and a "youth discount" constitute essential components of a youth sentencing policy, nothing can prevent legislators from selectively choosing only those elements that serve their "get tough" agenda, even though doing so unravels the threads that make coherent a proposal for an integrated court.[66]

Irene Merker Rosenberg concurs with Feld's fear that legislatures' get tough agendas will corrupt this proposal for an integrated court. She charges that this proposal has two other serious flaws. First, she questions whether "the disparity in procedural and constitutional protection between the adult and juvenile courts [is] significant enough to justify opting out of the juvenile justice system."[67] She does not believe that these differences are as substantial as Feld and others claim. Second, she questions: "If children are tried in the criminal courts, will their immaturity and vulnerability be taken into account adequately in assessing culpability and determining sentencing?"[68] She argues that states are likely to conclude that "bringing children within the criminal jurisdiction is an assertion by the state that minors do not deserve specialized treatment."[69] Rosenberg then adds what perhaps is the fatal flaw of abolishing the juvenile court:

> Initially, perhaps there would be a burst of concern for the kiddie defendants. But once the glow wore off, and that would not take long, it would be back to business as usual: treadmill processing for adults both over and under the age of eighteen. Let us face it: As bad as the juvenile courts are, the adult criminal courts are worse. Adding a new class of defendants to an already overburdened system can only exacerbate the situation, all to the detriment of children.[70]

SUMMARY

Justice for juveniles takes place within the context of society grappling with ways to solve the juvenile crime problem. Defining just when childhood ends and adulthood begins is a worrisome problem facing society, but, unfortunately, no objective tests are available to help society draw the line. The result is much confusion from state to state over the ways in which youths and adults are defined.

Concern about status offenders persists, but the real debate focuses on the handling of serious juvenile crime. One trend is toward harsher treatment of younger violent and repetitive offenders. Punishments are being called for with increasing stridency, and state legislatures have developed mechanisms to ensure that punishment occurs. One such mechanism is to transfer juveniles to adult court through various types of waiver. Proponents of this practice believe that if juveniles are processed by adult courts, punishment is ensured, and society will become safer as a result.

The most serious consequence for juveniles is the possibility of being sentenced to the death penalty. Although a miniscule proportion of youths receive this sentence and are executed, the practice is now permissible according to recent Supreme Court rulings. The death penalty for juveniles is one of the most hotly debated issues in juvenile justice today.

WEB SITES OF INTEREST

Various links about juveniles and the death penalty can be found at

http//www.abanet.org/crimjust/juvjus/links.html#death

For specific information and sources on the United States and foreign countries' handling of juveniles and the death penalty, see

http://infoseek.go.com/?win=_search&sv=M6&qt=Victor+Streib&oq=&url=http

CRITICAL THINKING QUESTIONS

1. Define the main types of waiver to the adult court.
2. Why is waiver such a controversial matter in juvenile justice?
3. Take a stand on the death penalty for juveniles. Defend your position.
4. When is treatment in the juvenile system no longer desirable for a juvenile?

NOTES

1. An inmate in an eastern U.S. prison who was interviewed in 1991.
2. John P. Conrad, "Crime and the Child," in Donna Hamparian et al., *Major Issues in Juvenile Justice Information and Training* (Columbus, OH: Academy for Contemporary Problems, 1981), 179–82.

3. Stephen J. Morse, "Immaturity and Responsibility," *Journal of Criminal Law and Criminology* 88 (1998), 19–20.
4. Thomas F. Geraghty and Steven A. Drizin, "Foreword—The Debate over the Future of Juvenile Courts: Can We Reach Consensus?" *Journal of Criminal Law and Criminology* 88 (1998), 6.
5. Elizabeth S. Scott and Thomas Grisso, "The Evolution of Adolescence: A Developmental Perspective on Juvenile Justice Reform," *Journal of Criminology and Criminal Justice* 88 (1998), 137, 174.
6. Ibid.
7. Ibid., 174–75.
8. Ibid., 189.
9. Ibid., 174–75.
10. Samuel M. Davis, *Rights of Juveniles: The Juvenile Justice System*, 2d ed. (New York: Clark Boardman Company, 1986), Section 4-2; see also Melissa Sickmund, *How Juveniles Get to Juvenile Court* (Washington, DC: Juvenile Justice Bulletin, 1994).
11. Davis, *Rights of Juveniles*, 24–26.
12. Juvenile Justice Bulletin, *The Juvenile Court's Response to Violent Crime* (Washington, DC: U.S. Department of Justice, 1989); Howard N. Snyder, "A National Portrait of Juvenile Court Caseloads: A Summary of Delinquency in the United States, 1983," *Juvenile and Family Court Journal* 31 (1984), 46.
13. M. A. Bortner, "Traditional Rhetoric, Organizational Realities: Remand of Juveniles to Adult Court," *Crime and Delinquency* (January 1986), 53–73.
14. Dean J. Champion, "Teenage Felons and Waiver Hearings: Some Recent Trends, 1980–1988," *Crime and Delinquency* 35 (October 1989), 578.
15. Bortner, "Traditional Rhetoric, Organizational Realities," 53–73.
16. Howard N. Snyder et al., *Juvenile Court Statistics* (Pittsburgh, PA: National Center for Juvenile Justice, 1989). See also Ellen H. Nimick, Linda Szymanski, and Howard Snyder, *Juvenile Court Waiver: A Study of Juvenile Court Cases Transferred to Criminal Court* (Pittsburgh, PA: National Center for Juvenile Justice, 1986).
17. Donna Bishop, Charles E. Frazier, and John C. Henretta, "Prosecutorial Waiver: Case Study of a Questionable Reform," *Crime and Delinquency* 35 (1989), 179–201.
18. Donna M. Hamparian et al., "Youth in Adult Court: Between Two Worlds, " *Major Issues in Juvenile Justice Information and Training* (Columbus, OH: Academy for Contemporary Problems, 1981), 104–40.
19. Ted Rubin, *Behind the Black Robes: Juvenile Court Judges and the Court* (Beverly Hills, CA: Sage Publications, 1985).
20. Bortner, "Traditional Rhetoric, Organizational Realities."
21. Rubin, *Behind the Black Robes;* Nimick et al., *Juvenile Court Waiver*; Thomas Grisso, Alan Tomkins, and Pamela Casey, "Psychosocial Concepts in Juvenile Law," *Law and Human Behavior* 12 (1988), 403–38.

22. Marcy R. Podkopacz and Barry C. Feld, "The End of the Line: An Empirical Study of Judicial Waiver," *Journal of Criminal Law and Criminology* 86 (1996), 449–92.
23. Carl Rudman et al., "Violent Youth in Adult Court: Process and Punishment," *Crime and Delinquency* (January 1986), 53–73. Other studies also have found that juveniles transferred to adult court will be institutionalized for longer periods of time. See J. Fagan, Martin Forst, and T. Scott Vivona, *Separating the Men from the Boys: The Criminalization of Youth Violence Through Judicial Waiver* (New York: City Justice Agency, 1987); and Peter W. Greenwood et al., *Youth Crime and Juvenile Justice in California: A Report to the Legislature* (Santa Monica, CA: Rand, 1983).
24. David Ream, *Needed: Serious Solutions for Serious Juvenile Crime* (Chicago, IL: Chicago Law Enforcement Study Group, 1983).
25. Simon Singer, *Relocating Juvenile Crime: The Shift from Juvenile to Criminal Justice* (Albany, NY: Nelson A. Rockefeller Institute of Government, 1985).
26. Hamparian et al., "Youth in Adult Court."
27. Lee Ann Osburn and Peter A. Rose, "Prosecuting Juveniles as Adults: The Quest for 'Objective' Decisions," *Criminology* 22 (1984), 187–202.
28. Donna M. Bishop, Charles E. Frazier, Lonn Lanza-Kaduce, and Lawrence Winner, "The Transfer of Juveniles to Criminal Court: Does It Makes a Difference?" *Crime and Delinquency* 42 (1996), 171–91.
29. Hamparian et al., "Youth in Adult Court."
30. Donna Martin Hamparian et al., *The Violent Few: A Study of Dangerous Juvenile Offenders* (Lexington, MA: Lexington Books, 1980), 33–34
31. Quoted in Barry C. Feld, "Violent Youth and Public Policy: Minnesota Juvenile Justice Task Force and 1994 Legislative Reform." Paper presented at the annual meeting of the American Society of Criminology, Miami (1994), 9.
32. Ibid. See also Barry C. Feld, "Violent Youth and Public Policy: A Case Study of Juvenile Justice Law Reform," *Minnesota Law Review* 79 (May 1995), 965–1128.
33. Richard E. Redding, "Juvenile Offenders in Criminal Court and Adult Prison: Legal, Psychological, and Behavioral Outcomes," *Juvenile and Family Court Journal* 50 (1999), 1–20.
34. James Austin, Barry Krisberg, Robert DeComo, Sonya Rudenstine, and Dominic DelRosario, *Juveniles Taken into Custody: Fiscal Year 1993* (Washington, DC: Office of Juvenile Justice and Delinquency Prevention, 1995), 79.
35. Gary Fleming and Gerald Winkler, "Sending Them to Prison: Washington State Learns to Accommodate Female Youthful Offenders in Prison," *Corrections Today* 61 (April 1999), 132.
36. Twenty-three states report having a life-without-parole sentence. See E. Herricks, "Number of Lifers in U.S. Jumps 9 Percent in Four Years," *Corrections Compendium* 13 (April 1989), 9–11.

37. Salvador A. Godinez, "Managing Juveniles in Adult Facilities," *Corrections Today* 61 (April 1999), 86–87.
38. Fleming and Winkler, "Sending Them to Prison," 132–33.
39. Ibid., 133.
40. The decision was rendered in two cases. One was *Stanford v. Kentucky,* No. 87-5765. See Linda Greenhouse, "Death Sentences Against Retarded and Young Upheld," *New York Times,* June 27, 1989, A1, A18.
41. Much of the current section on the development of the death penalty comes from Victor L. Strieb, *Death Penalty for Juveniles* (Bloomington, IN: Indiana University Press, 1987), 21–40.
42. *Gregg v. Georgia,* 48 U.S. 153 (1976).
43. Ibid., 197.
44. Lockett v. Ohio, 438 U.S. 536 (1978).
45. Strieb, *Death Penalty for Juveniles,* 22.
46. Ibid., 24–25.
47. Ibid.
48. Ibid.
49. *Eddings v. Oklahoma,* 102 S. Ct. (1982).
50. Ibid.
51. *Thompson v. Oklahoma,* 102 S. Ct. (1988).
52. Ibid.
53. *Stanford v. Kentucky,* 492 U.S. 361 (1989).
54. "Capital Punishment for Minors," *Journal of Juvenile Law* (1994), 150–67.
55. *Stanford v. Kentucky; Wilkins v. Missouri,* 109 S. Ct. 2969 (1989).
56. Barry C. Feld, "Criminalizing the American Juvenile Court," in *Readings in Juvenile Justice Administration,* edited by Barry C. Feld (New York: Oxford University Press, 1999), 361.
57. Ibid., 364.
58. Ibid.
59. Ibid.
60. Ibid.
61. Ibid.
62. Ibid., 366.
63. Barry C. Feld, "The Transformation of the Juvenile Court," *Minnesota Law Review* 75 (1991), 691–725; Barry C. Feld, "Abolish the Juvenile Court: Youthfulness, Criminal Responsibility, and Sentencing Policy," *Journal of Criminal Law and Criminology* 88 (1997), 115–31.
64. Feld, "Abolish the Juvenile Court," 90.
65. Ibid., 130.

66. Ibid., 133.
67. Irene Merker Rosenberg, "Leaving Bad Enough Alone: A Response to the Juvenile Court Abolitionists," in *Readings in Juvenile Justice Administration*, 368.
68. Ibid.
69. Ibid., 370.
70. Ibid.

8

JUVENILE PROBATION

OBJECTIVES

1. To define juvenile probation and discuss its operations
2. To discuss the history of probation services
3. To reveal the problems and challenges of probation services
4. To evaluate the effectiveness of juvenile probation

KEY TERMS

balanced approach to juvenile probation
electronic monitoring
house arrest
intake
intensive supervision programs (ISP)
investigation
justice model
probation
probation subsidy programs
restitution
restorative justice model
social study report
supervision
Wisconsin system

One success story I remember is a 17-year-old black girl who had been arrested on first-degree robbery and prostitution. She had never been referred before. What it came down to was there were two juvenile girls with two adult males who were their boyfriends, and they were in a bar trying to shake down this white guy. The girls got him up to their apartment, and they were going to get it on with him. Then their boyfriends came up and were real mad because he was with their women. The white guy said, "Take anything," and they took some money he had in his car. The robbery charge was dropped, but there was a finding of fact on prostitution charge. She was placed on supervision until her 18th birthday. When I got her, the first thing we did was go out to the hospital's family practice center to have her checked and placed on birth control. But she was already pregnant. The majority of time we spent together was concentrated on job, education, getting ready for the baby, and independent living skills. It wasn't a traditional probation case. We spent a lot of time together, getting ready for her future. Her mother was dead and her father was in the Mental Health Institute. Several older sisters were already on ADC [Aid to Dependent Children], weren't married, and were not models by any means. So I felt like I'm the one she counted on. I took her to the hospital when she had her baby and was with her during delivery. It was a neat experience. She asked me to be the godmother for her baby. She's now very motivated to make something out of herself. She is now 19, has her own car, and keeps an apartment fairly well. She has either gone to school or worked since before she had the baby. With what she has had to work with, it's amazing she is doing so well.

—Probation officer[1]

Probation is a judicial disposition under which youthful offenders are subject to certain conditions imposed by the juvenile court and are permitted to remain in the community under the supervision of a probation officer. The probation officer assists offenders in their efforts to meet the conditions of the court. As expressed vividly in this chapter's opening quote, the basic goal of probation, over and above giving troublesome youths a second chance, is to provide services that will help offenders stay out of trouble with the law. Probation is the most widely used judicial disposition of the juvenile court.

In 1998, the juvenile court ordered probation in 58 percent of the more than one million cases that received a juvenile court sanction. Probation was ordered in 58 percent of the cases involving person offenses, 59 percent involving property offenses, 59 percent involving drug law violations, and 54 percent involving public order offenses.[2]

The word *probation* is used in at least four ways in the juvenile justice system. It can refer to (1) a disposition of the juvenile court in lieu of institutionalization, (2) the status of an adjudicated offender, (3) a subsystem of the juvenile justice system (the term's most common use), and (4) the activities, functions, and services that characterize this subsystem's transactions with the juvenile court, the youthful offender, and the community. The probation process includes the intake phase of the juvenile court's proceedings, preparation of the social investigation for the disposition stage, supervision of probationers, and obtaining or providing services for youths on probation.

Probation is considered a desirable alternative to institutionalization for several reasons: First, it allows offenders to retain their liberty but provides society with some protection against continued disregard for the law. Second, it promotes the rehabilitation of offenders because they can maintain normal community contacts by living at home, attending school, and participating in community activities. Third, it avoids the negative impact of institutional confinement, and furthermore, it costs less than incarceration.

HOW DID PROBATION DEVELOP?

John Augustus, a Boston cobbler, is considered to be the father of probation in this country. He spent considerable time in the courtroom and in 1841 accepted his first probation client, whose offense was "yielding to his appetite for strong drink."[3] Beginning with this "common drunkard," he was able to devote himself to the cause of probation as he became convinced that many lawbreakers needed only the interest and concern of another to be able to straighten out their lives. Augustus worked with women and children as well as with male offenders; in fact, he was willing to work with all types of offenders—drunkards, petty thieves, prostitutes, and felons—as long as he met a contrite heart. Augustus instigated such services as investigation and screening, supervision of probationers, interviewing, and arranging for relief, employment, and education—all of which are still provided today.

The state of Massachusetts, very much impressed with Augustus's work, established a visiting-probation-agent system in 1869. The philosophy of this system, which was set up to assist both youths and adults, was that first offenders who showed definite promise should be released on probation. Youths would be allowed to return to their parents and to live at home as long as they obeyed the injunction, "Go and sin no more."[4]

Probation was regulated by statute for the first time in 1878, when the mayor of Boston was authorized to appoint a paid probation officer to the police force, to serve under the police chief. In 1880, the authority to appoint probation officers was extended to all cities and towns in Massachusetts. By 1890, probation had become statewide, with the authority to appoint resting with the courts rather than with municipal authorities. Soon thereafter, Vermont, Missouri, Illinois, Minnesota, Rhode Island, and New Jersey enacted probation statutes.

Although probation was radically extended in the wake of the juvenile court movement, probation systems varied from one jurisdiction to another. Probation officers generally considered themselves servants of the juvenile court judge rather than defenders of the rights of children. Thus, they would gather relevant facts and opinions on each case to help the judge make his decision, sometimes blatantly disregarding the due process safeguards of the law. Judges, in turn, saw nothing objectionable about returning children to the care of the probation officer who had placed them at the court's mercy in the first place. Most juvenile courts relied at first on volunteer juvenile probation officers. One observer said that their work "is the chord upon which all the pearls of the Juvenile Court are strung. It is the keynote of a beautiful harmony; without it the Juvenile Court could not exist."[5] Probation volunteers, however, largely disappeared by the second decade of the twentieth century, not to return until the late 1950s.

The spread of probation was marked by the founding in 1907 of the National Association of Probation Officers (renamed the National Probation Association in 1911). Homer Folks, one of the early advocates of probation, summarized the perception of probation in the early part of this century: "Probation provides a new kind of reformatory, without walls and without much coercion."[6] Nevertheless, the idea of coercion lurked close to the surface, and force was used without hesitation if the delinquent continued to disobey the law. "When sterner treatment was demanded," said one officer, "the friendly advisor became the official representative of the court with the demand that certain conditions be observed or that the probationer be returned to the court."[7]

After World War I, there was an ever-increasing demand for trained social workers to serve as probation officers. These social workers, trained under the medical model, began to treat juvenile probationers as disturbed children who needed psychiatric therapy. The philosophy and administration of probation thus retained the older concern with helping children adjust to their environment as it added a new concern with helping them resolve their emotional problems.

In addition to a greater concern for treating children's problems, twentieth-century probation theory also includes the idea of more responsibility for the delivery of services to probationers, a greater consciousness of standards, and a desire to upgrade the probation officer and restore the volunteer to probation services.

In the late 1970s, the numbers of juveniles placed on probation skyrocketed. Although probation remained the most widely used judicial disposition, both probation and aftercare services were charged by policymakers to enforce a hard-line policy with juvenile offenders. Probation officers, as well as other practitioners in the juvenile justice system, admitted that probation was too "soft," or permissive. A residential counselor of a youth shelter said at the time, "I'm not very impressed with probation. When a kid gets picked up for shoplifting, it's a joke. I think probation is like a slap on the hand. Many kids simply disregard it. The kids will verbalize that they know they [probation officials] are not going to do a damn thing to them. It's just an empty threat. They'll say, 'Oh, I *just* got probation.'"[8] A probation supervisor tells how this charge of permissiveness affected his agency:

> Our agency was social work oriented. We wanted to be problem solvers and help children and their families. Then, we got a new chief who had a different philosophy, and the types of kids and types of crimes are different from six or seven years ago. We've become more law oriented, shying away from the social work ethic. We're now holding kids accountable for their actions.[9]

In the 1990s, a new mission in probation services was defined, articulating five major themes. First, risk control and crime reduction efforts, especially intensive probation supervision, have gained acceptance as the means by which high-risk probationers can be left in the community without endangering society. Second, as part of this short-term behavior control emphasis, community restitution programs and work orders have become an almost inevitable condition of probation status. Third, the increased number of adolescent substance abusers in the United States, as well as public concern about alcohol, substance abuse, and guns, has resulted in increased supervision of probationers with histories of drug abuse. Fourth, probation departments are increasingly contracting community-based programs from privately operated programs. Finally, bureaucratic efficiency and accountability are now demanded of probation departments across the nation.

HOW IS PROBATION ADMINISTERED?

In fifteen states and the District of Columbia, probation is under the control of the juvenile court and is funded by city or county government as shown in Table 8–1. In the other thirty-five states, a variety of means to organize and administer juvenile probation are found. The most effective strategy is probably placing juvenile probation under the control of the juvenile court and funding it through local government agencies. This is particularly true in states that provide revenue support of staff to local systems that meet state standards. Private contractors are increasingly being used in juvenile probation, especially in providing intensive probation and aftercare services.

Private contractors are increasingly being used in juvenile probation, especially in providing intensive probation and aftercare services. To encourage the expansion of privatization in juvenile probation, the Office of Juvenile Justice and Delinquency Prevention funded a $1.7 million three-year project, the Private Sector Probation Initiative. The selected experimental sites were the Third Judicial District of Utah (Salt Lake City); Cuyahoga County (Cleveland), Ohio; Kenosha County, Wisconsin; Oklahoma County (Oklahoma City), Oklahoma; and the city and county of San Francisco.[10]

In order to bring about greater uniformity in administration of local probation, several states offer rewards of either revenue support or manpower to local systems if they comply with state standards. Michigan, for example,

Table 8–1 National Summary of the Organization and Administration of Juvenile Probation

Organizational and Administration of Probation	*Number of States*	*States*
Local/judicial	15	Alabama, Arizona, Arkansas, Colorado, District of Columbia, Illinois, Indiana, Kansas, Michigan, Missouri, Montana, Nevada, New Jersey, Pennsylvania, Texas
State/judicial	10	Connecticut, Hawaii, Maine, Maryland, New Hampshire, New Mexico, North Carolina, Rhode Island, South Carolina, Vermont
State/executive	11	Alaska, Delaware, Florida, Maine, Maryland, New Hampshire, New Mexico, North Carolina, Rhode Island, South Carolina, Vermont
Local/executive	3	Idaho, New York, Oregon
Combination	4	California, Kentucky, Washington, Wisconsin

Source: National Center for Juvenile Justice 2000. "National Overviews." State Juvenile Justice Profiles (Pittsburgh, PA: NCJJ). Online: http://www.ncjj.org/stateprofiles/.

assigns state-paid probation officers to work with local probation officers. Usually, though, states make direct payments to local governments to defray part of the costs of probation services. In New York State, for example, a local community that is willing to meet state staffing patterns is reimbursed for up to 50 percent of its operating costs for probation services.

Other states, such as California, Nevada, Oregon, and Washington, have developed **probation subsidy programs** that encourage a decreased rate of commitment of offenders by counties to state institutions. The money saved by the state is returned to the counties. California initiated this program after a study indicated that many offenders committed to state correctional institutions could safely remain in the community under good probation supervision.

The California Probation Subsidy Program was set up in 1966 by the state's youth authority, which was authorized to pay up to $4,000 to each county for every adult and juvenile offender not committed to a state correctional institution. In turn, the counties were required to improve probation services by employing additional probation officers and reducing caseloads. Additionally, it was required that each county demonstrate innovative approaches to probation, such as intensive supervision of hard-core adult offenders and certain types of juvenile offenders.

Washington's juvenile probation subsidy is modeled on the one in California. It has been instrumental in reducing commitment rates to juvenile institutions and in improving the quality of probation services because 90 percent of Washington's thirty-nine counties participate in the program.

WHAT ARE THE FUNCTIONS OF PROBATION SERVICES?

The three basic functions of juvenile probation are intake, investigation, and supervision. At the intake stage of the court proceedings, the probation officer decides whether or not to file a petition on a child referred to the court. Investigation involves compiling a social history or study of a child judged delinquent to assist the judge in making the wisest disposition. Supervision, initiated when the judge places a youth on probation, focuses primarily on risk control and crime reduction.

INTAKE

During the intake stage of the court proceedings (which was discussed in Chapter 5), the probation officer carefully screens the referrals to the court. Both the statutes of the state and the office of the state's prosecutor are helpful in determining whether or not any case referred to the court actually falls under its jurisdiction. At **intake,** the probation officer also conducts a preliminary investigation, which includes an interview during which the youth is advised of his or her legal rights. If parents or guardians have not already been contacted, the probation department gets in touch with them to discuss the status of the child and to advise them of their right to have an attorney. The intake probation officer may need to interview the family, witnesses, victims, arresting officers, peers, or neighbors to obtain sufficient information with which to make a sound determination on the necessity of filing a court petition for detention of the child. The probation officer also may need to contact the school and other agencies that have worked with the child. If the youth has been in court before or is already on probation, the intake officer must also familiarize himself with the previous reports.

INVESTIGATION

If a juvenile court uses the bifurcated hearing (separation of adjudicatory and disposition stages), a **social study report** is ordered by the judge when a youth is found delinquent at the fact-finding stage of the court proceedings. Probation officers usually are given up to sixty days to make their **investigation,** but if the court combines the adjudicatory and disposition stages, the social study must be completed before a youth appears in front of the judge. The judge is not supposed to read this social study *until* the child is found to be delinquent.

The social study report details the minor's personal background, family, educational program, present offense, previous violations of the law, and employment. Also included are a description of the offender's neighborhood; the family's ability to pay court and institutionalization costs; the minor's physical and mental health; the attitude of the family, the police, the neighbors, and the community toward the minor; and the attitude of the minor toward the offense in question and toward himself or herself. The social study concludes with the probation officer's diagnosis and treatment plan for the youth. An important part of this treatment plan is the probation officer's recommended course of action. In this report the officer determines whether the youth should remain in the community; if so, the conditions of probation are stated. For a social study report, see Focus on Practice 8–1.

Supervision

The length of time a juvenile must spend on probation varies among states. The maximum length in some states is until the juvenile reaches the age of majority, which is usually age sixteen or seventeen. Other states limit juvenile probation to a specific duration. In Illinois, it is limited to five years; in New York, two years; in Washington, DC, one year; and in California, six months.

Once a youth has been placed on probation, the probation officer is required to provide the best possible **supervision,** which includes surveillance, casework services, and counseling or guidance. Surveillance involves careful monitoring of the minor's adjustment to the community. To accomplish this, the officer must establish personal contact with the minor and must learn whether the youth is attending school or is working each day, whether adequate guidance is being received from parents, and whether the child is obeying the terms of probation. At the same time, the probation officer must determine if the youth is continuing to break the law.

In 1973, the job responsibilities of the probation officer changed when the National Advisory Commission on Criminal Justice Standards and Goals recommended that a community resource manager could meet the goals of probation and parole more effectively than could a caseworker. Fulfilling the community resource manager, or broker, role required probation officers to refer clients to the community resources needed for their rehabilitation. This role requires the probation officer to mesh a probationer's identified needs with the range of available services. In helping probationers to obtain needed services, the probation officer must assess the situation, contact the appropriate available resource providers, assist the probationer in obtaining needed services, and follow up on the case. The probation officer, in this new role, should take the responsibility for ensuring that

FOCUS ON PRACTICE 8–1

JUVENILE COURT RECOMMENDATIONS

I. Juvenile Under Consideration

Name: (juvenile)
D.O.B.: 00-00-0000
Court Docket No. JVJV00—XXXXX

A. Intake Information

On mm/dd/yy, the juvenile was charged with Disorderly Conduct by the Waterloo Police Department. This incident centered around a neighborhood conflict that led to (juvenile) throwing rocks and yelling out profanities.

On mm/dd/yy, the juvenile was charged with two counts of Third Degree Burglary and Possession of Burglar Tools by the Waterloo Police Department. These charges were in reference to car burglaries that occurred in a parking ramp in downtown Waterloo.

On mm/dd/yy, a delinquency petition was filed in the Black Hawk County Juvenile Court alleging the juvenile to be a delinquent child regarding three counts of delinquency.

II. Victim Impact Information

(Juvenile) has been Court ordered to pay $417.82 as his share of restitution regarding the Third Degree Burglary charge that was dismissed.

B. Referral and Court History

The juvenile was first referred to this office on mm/dd/yy by the Waterloo Police Department in regard to the delinquent act of Criminal Mischief in the Third Degree. The juvenile was placed on an Informal Adjustment Agreement on mm/dd/yy, that he successfully completed, warranting the case to be dismissed in month 1997.

The juvenile was referred to the Department of Juvenile Court Services on mm/dd/yy, regarding the delinquent act of Theft in the Fifth Degree. The juvenile was once again placed on an Informal Adjustment Agreement; however, the family moved to Cedar Rapids, Iowa, three months after that agreement was entered into. He remained on an Informal Adjustment Agreement and the matter was closed in month 1998.

Between month, 1998, and month, 1998, the juvenile was referred to the Department of Juvenile Court Services on the delinquent acts of Third Degree Burglary, Theft Fourth Degree, and Disorderly Conduct. On mm/dd/yy, the juvenile admitted to the Third Degree Burglary charge and a formal adjudication of delinquency was withheld of Theft in the Fourth Degree and Disorderly Conduct.

On mm/dd/yy, a Pre-Trial Conference was held in the interest of Juvenile Case No. JVJV009053 in front of Associate Juvenile Court Judge. The parties were unable to come to an agreement in this matter so a contested Adjudication Hearing was scheduled.

An Adjudication Hearing was held on mm/dd/yy, in the interest of (juvenile) in front of an Associate Juvenile Court Judge. At the time of the hearing, the Court was informed that the juvenile would be admitting to the charges of Disorderly Conduct and Theft Fifth. In return for this admission, the State would agree to dismiss paragraph 3(b) alleging the delinquent act of Third Degree Burglary as long as the juvenile agreed to pay restitution. The Court accepted the plea agreement and entered formal adjudications of delinquency on the charges of Disorderly Conduct and Theft Fifth and ordered the juvenile to pay the restitution in regards to the dismissed charge of Third Degree Burglary. The juvenile was also Court ordered to complete twenty hours of community service in regards to the Disorderly Conduct charge. The matter was then scheduled for a Dispositional Hearing.

C. Personal History

(Juvenile was born mm/dd, 1986, in Chicago, Illinois. (Please see Certificate of Birth attached to this document for verification.)

a. Health History

The juvenile and his mother are unable to report any significant health concerns that would prohibit this juvenile from successfully complying with the terms of his probation.

b. Parental Concerns Regarding Juvenile's Behavior

The parent reports that the juvenile has always been respectful toward her and his grandparent. She reports that her biggest concerns regarding her son are the struggles he has academically in school and his tendency to be a follower.

c. Juvenile's Attitude toward Parents
(Juvenile) readily admits that he respects and loves his mother and that he wants to reside in her home. However, he is also quick to admit that he is somewhat confused and not real comfortable with the current situation. (Juvenile), his younger siblings, and his mother were just recently evicted from their home.

d. Juvenile's Attitude Regarding Offense
(Juvenile) claims he does not like breaking the law and wants to get off of probation as soon as possible. He understands that the acts of delinquency he did commit were wrong and that if he continues to behave in that manner he will find himself deeper and deeper into the system which is something he wants to avoid. He has agreed to comply with the Juvenile Court and up until this time he has for the most part.

D. Education

Other than attending preschool through third grade in Chicago, Illinois, and a brief portion of his sixth-grade year in Cedar Rapids, the juvenile has attended school in the Waterloo Public School System for the majority of his educational needs. He is currently a ninth-grade student at the high school. He does receive special education services through Area Educational Agency VII for mental and learning disabilities and has been involved with these services since 1993.

(Juvenile) is performing at an unacceptable level currently academically. His third-quarter grades consisted of five F's and two C's. His teachers feel that he can do better, as does (juvenile). His school progress will continue to be monitored and it is hoped that this officer can arrange for some tutorial assistance this summer through an agency like University of Northern Iowa—Center for Urban Education (UNI-CUE) in an effort to assist (juvenile) with achieving some high school credits or at least enhancing his academic ability.

III. The Family

A. Father

(Parent) is (juvenile's) biological father. (Parent) is thirty-six years of age and resides in the Chicago area. (Juvenile) has not had any significant contact with his father in almost ten years.

B. Mother

(Parent) is (juvenile's) biological mother. (Parent) was born mm/dd, 1968, in the State of Illinois. (Parent) has earned her GED since moving to Waterloo, Iowa, in 1992. She reports no criminal or military history.

(Parent) is currently unemployed. Her previous work experience includes working for a telephone company and in the housekeeping department through a local hotel.

C. Siblings

(Sibling), fifteen, is (juvenile's) half-brother. (Sibling) recently moved back to the area after living with his grandfather briefly in Cincinnati, Ohio. (Sibling) has a history with the Department of Juvenile Court Services that included his participation in day/evening treatment programming.

(Sibling), thirteen, is (juvenile's) half-sister. (Sibling) is residing at current time with her grandmother in Waterloo, and is attending school. She does have a history regarding a misdemeanor charge with this office and was supervised by a Volunteer Juvenile Court.

(Sibling), nine, is (juvenile's) half-brother. He is currently residing with his mother.

D. Child Abuse Information

There was a registered child abuse complaint regarding (parent). This involved denial of critical care due to the conditions of her home. There were services offered to the family through the Department of Human Services at that time.

IV. Conclusions

A. Recommendation to the Court

It is the recommendation of the First Judicial District Department of Juvenile Court Services that the custody of (juvenile) remain with his mother while he is placed under the formal supervision of the Department of Juvenile Court Services, and ordered to abide by the conditions of a probation contract that will be submitted to the Court the day of the hearing.

B. Reasons Supporting Recommendations

a. The juvenile has been adjudicated delinquent on the charges of Disorderly Conduct and Theft in the Fifth Degree, as well as ordered to pay restitution in the amount of $417.82 in regard to a Third Degree Burglary charge that was dismissed.
b. (Juvenile) has demonstrated some compliance with the expectations laid upon him by the Juvenile Court since the time of his Adjudication Hearing. Examples of this compliance are no unexcused absences from school and repayment of approximately $100.00 toward his restitution obligation.
c. The Juvenile Court can add some structure and guidance, as well as supervision, to this juvenile's life during this chaotic period with his family.
d. If (juvenile's) family situation does not stabilize or if he experiences further behavior problems, more restrictive dispositional alternatives may have to be considered.

Source: Provided by Juvenile Court Services, Blackhawk County (Iowa), 2001.

Critical Thinking Questions:
What were your impressions of this juvenile after reading his social study report? Why do you think he became involved in juvenile crime? Are his law-violating behaviors likely to continue?

the needed services are delivered, and then should monitor and evaluate the services.[11]

As the reintegration model came under increased attack in the mid-1970s, a number of juvenile probation departments adopted the concept of the Community Resource Management Team (CRMT). Under this approach to probation services, officers are divided into teams, and each team takes responsibility for a caseload and makes decisions on what community resources are needed by clients. New probationers are interviewed by a member of the team, and their needs are plotted on a needs-assessment scale. The members of the teams are usually specialists in "needs subsystems" dealing with such problems as drug abuse, alcoholism, mental illness, or runaway behavior, and the specialist links the probationer with the necessary services in the community.[12] A director of court services in a midwestern state indicates why she supports such a team approach:

> For probation to really be effective, the credibility of the probation officer would have to be enhanced and caseloads would have to be [limited to] 15. If we took all the resources we're putting into institutions, group homes, and psychiatric resources, we would have the necessary resources for probation.

I would go with the team approach; we need a case manager so that we could use different treatment for different kids.[13]

In the 1980s, supervision in juvenile probation was influenced by the Wisconsin system, the justice model, the balanced approach to probation, and the reduced risk and increased surveillance models.

Concerns for public safety in the 1980s persuaded many probation departments to develop classification systems or to use the Wisconsin system to place probationers under intensive, medium, or minimum supervision. Under the **Wisconsin system,** a risk/needs assessment is conducted for each probationer at regular intervals. The risk scale was derived from empirical studies that showed certain factors to be good predictors of recidivism—prior arrest record, age at first conviction, the nature of the offense for which the probationer was convicted, school or employment patterns, and so forth. The needs assessment focuses on such indicators as emotional stability, financial management, family relationships, and health. The scores derived from the risk/needs assessment are used to classify probationers by required level of supervision—intensive, medium, or minimum. Reassessment of cases takes place at regular intervals, and the level of supervision may be increased or reduced.[14]

The use of risk/needs assessments in juvenile probation, such as the Wisconsin system, raises the issue of how effective they are in predicting juveniles' behaviors. The fact of the matter is that it is very difficult to predict behavior, especially for juveniles. Thus, whatever predictive techniques, or classification systems, are used in juvenile justice, the results are far less than desirable in forecasting juvenile behavior.

The **justice model** has influenced the reduction of discretion in juvenile probation in the 1980s and early 1990s. David Fogel, in advocating the reduction of the discretionary authority of probation officers, recommended that the standard of proof for the revocation of probation be as strong as the original finding that resulted in the sentence of probation (i.e., beyond a reasonable doubt). Proponents of the justice model contend that the social study report should be regarded as a legal document, and defendants have the right to know the contents of this report. Fogel and other advocates of the justice model have recommended increasing restitution programs, because they believe it is only fair for offenders to pay for the social harm they have inflicted.[15] Not everyone would agree; for example, a female juvenile probation officer in the Midwest described this legal movement in juvenile probation: "It was a lot easier for us to get things done five years ago when the law was more flexible."[16]

Accountability models began to be formulated in the 1980s for supervising juvenile probationers. For example, Dennis Maloney, Dennis Romig, and Troy Armstrong developed what they called the **balanced approach to juvenile probation.** Its purpose is "to protect the community from delinquency, to impose accountability for offenses committed, and to equip juvenile offenders

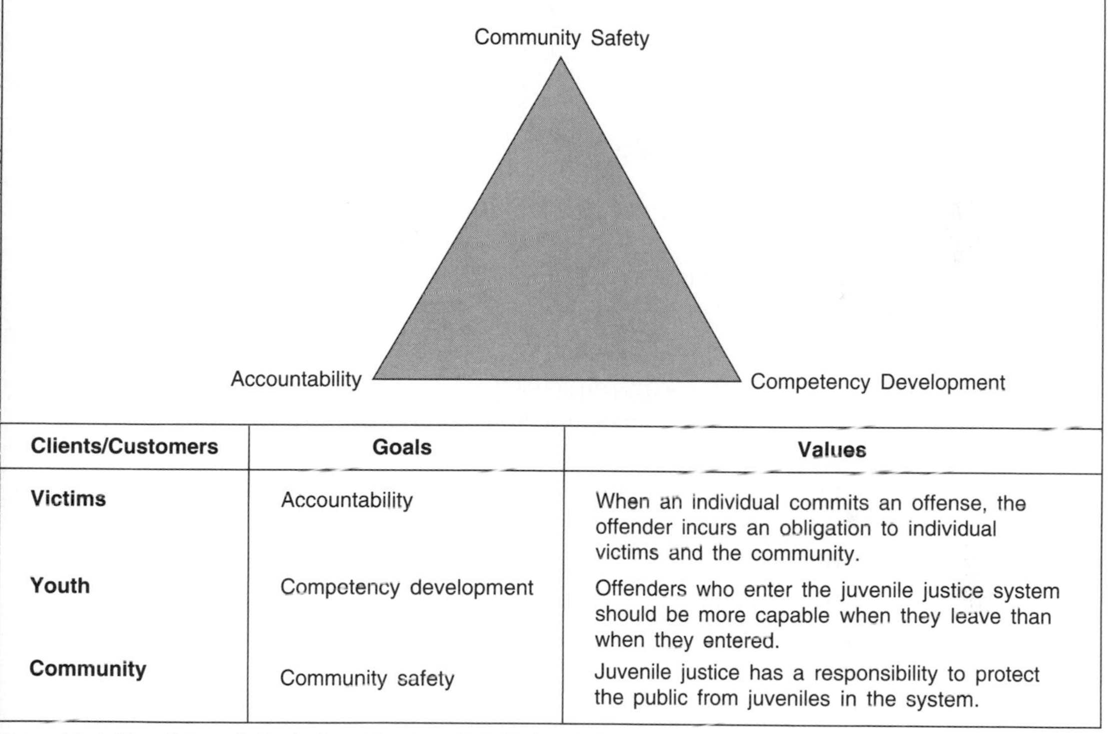

Clients/Customers	Goals	Values
Victims	Accountability	When an individual commits an offense, the offender incurs an obligation to individual victims and the community.
Youth	Competency development	Offenders who enter the juvenile justice system should be more capable when they leave than when they entered.
Community	Community safety	Juvenile justice has a responsibility to protect the public from juveniles in the system.

Source: Adapted from Maloney, D. Romig, D. and Armstrong, T. 1998: Juvenile Probation! The Balanced Approach, Reno, NV. National Council of Juvenile and Family Court Judges.

Figure 8–1 Graphic Representation of the Balanced Approach Mission.

with the required competencies to live productively and responsibly in the community."[17] One of the popular features of this balanced approach is the equal attention it gives to the community, the victim, and the juvenile offender (see Figure 8–1). Juvenile probation departments in Oregon, Texas, and Wisconsin have implemented this accountability model in supervising juvenile probationers.[18]

The formulation of the balanced approach to juvenile probation has led to the development of the **restorative justice model.** This restorative justice perspective, as suggested, in Chapter 1, gained impetus in the 1970s and 1980s from the victim's movement, from youthful offenders' experiences with reparative sanctions, and from the rise of informal neighborhood programs and dispute resolution programs in the community.[19] The purpose of this integrated balanced and restorative justice model is to reconcile "the interests of victims, offenders, and the community through common programs and supervision practices that meet mutual needs."[20] For a restorative justice yardstick, see Focus on Practice 8–2.

FOCUS ON PRACTICE 8–2

A RESTORATIVE JUSTICE YARDSTICK

1. Do victims experience justice?
    - Do victims have sufficient opportunities to tell their truth to relevant listeners?
    - Do victims receive needed compensation or restitution?
    - Is the injustice adequately acknowledged?
    - Are victims sufficiently protected against further violation?
    - Does the outcome adequately reflect the severity of the offense?
    - Do victims receive adequate information about the crime, the offender, and the legal process?
    - Do victims have a voice in the legal process?
    - Is the experience of justice adequately public?
    - Do victims receive adequate support from others?
    - Do victims' families receive adequate assistance and support?
    - Are other needs—material, psychological, and spiritual—being addressed?
2. Do offenders experience justice?
    - Are offenders encouraged to understand and take responsibility for what they have done?
    - Are misattributions challenged?
    - Are offenders given encouragement and opportunities to make things right?
    - Are offenders given opportunities to participate in the process?
    - Are offenders encouraged to change their behavior?
    - Is there a mechanism for monitoring or verifying changes?
    - Are offenders' needs being addressed?
    - Do offenders' families receive support and assistance?
3. Is the victim–offender relationship addressed?
    - Is there an opportunity for victims and offenders to meet, if appropriate?
    - Is there an opportunity for victims and offenders to exchange information about the event and about one another?

4. Are community concerns being taken into account?
   - Is the process and the outcome sufficiently public?
   - Is community protection being addressed?
   - Is there a need for restitution or a symbolic action for the community?
   - Is the community represented in some way in the legal process?
5. Is the future addressed?
   - Is there provision for solving the problems that led to this event?
   - Is there provision for solving problems caused by this event?
   - Have future intentions been addressed?
   - Are there provisions for monitoring and verifying outcomes and for problem solving?

Source: Howard Zehr, *Changing Lenses* (Scottsdale: Pennsylvania Herald Press, 1990).

Critical Thinking Questions:
What is your evaluation of this restorative justice yardstick? Do you believe that restorative justice is a good direction for juvenile justice to go? Why or why not?

HOW ABOUT RISK CONTROL AND CRIME REDUCTION?

In the 1990s, as juvenile probation continued to face the criticism that it allowed probationers to escape punishment, reduced risk and increased surveillance models received major emphasis. Restitution and intensive supervision were the most widely used of these short term behavior control models, but house arrest and electronic monitoring and shock probation also gained some attention.

Restitution

Restitution, a disposition that requires offenders to pay back their victims or the community for their crime, began to be used widely in probation during the 1970s and 1980s. Indeed, by 1985, formal programs were known to exist in more than four hundred jurisdictions; more than thirty-five states now have statutory authority to order monetary or community service restitution.[21] Part of the reason for the skyrocketing growth of restitution programs is that the Office of Juvenile Justice and Delinquency Prevention has spent some $30 million promoting the use of restitution in eighty-five juvenile courts across the nation.[22]

Table 8–2 *Major Components of Restitution Programs*

Program Component
Financial restitution
Community service
Victim–offender mediation
Victim services
Job information services
Work crews
Transportation
Job slots in private sector
Subsidies

Source: Office of Juvenile Justice and Delinquency Prevention, *National Trends in Juvenile Restitution Programming* (Washington, DC: Government Printing Office, 1989), p. 3.

Another survey of restitution programs found that 75 percent of jurisdictions provide for both financial restitution and community service within the same program. Many programs engaged in activities related to developing or implementing restitution orders. Over half the programs provided victims or job information services or sponso·ed work crews. About one-third used victim–offender mediation, arranged for job slots in the private sector, and provided transportation to work. Last, one-quarter of the programs subsidized employment for some probationers assigned restitution.[23]

Restitution programs most commonly sited the following goals:

- Holding juveniles accountable
- Providing reparation to victims
- Treating and rehabilitating juveniles
- Punishing juveniles[24]

Juvenile courts have instituted job-skills preparation classes to help juveniles with ordered restitution to find and hold jobs. The private and public sectors sometimes provide jobs in which youths required to make restitution can earn money and compensate victims. Juveniles failing to complete their restitution payments may have their probation term extended.

With community work restitution, probationers generally are required to perform a certain number of work hours at a private nonprofit or government agency. Sites where the work may be performed include public libraries, parks, nursing homes, animal shelters, community centers, day-care centers, youth agencies, YMCAs and YWCAs, and local streets. In large departments, restitution programs provide supervised work crews, in which juveniles go to a site and work under the supervision of an adult.

A juvenile probation officer tells why he supports the restitution program in his department:

> The restitution program deals with kids who damage property and harm others. The kids who go into the C.R.P. [Community Restitution Program] aren't hard-core offenders; they are less serious—simple assaults, theft in fifth-degree. Actually, they don't need supervision of a PO [probation officer]. Things at home are OK; school and peer relationships are also OK. So there's no real service we can provide. But we feel they need some kind of consequence for the action they've taken and that's why they're placed in the program. POs also use our program for those who won't comply with supervision. For example, if they have a kid who is missing appointments, they'll ask the judge to assign him so many hours to work in the C.R.P.[25]

In Hennepin County, Minnesota (Minneapolis), youthful offenders quickly discover themselves placed by the juvenile judge on a Saturday work squad for a specified amount of community service. First-time offenders usually find that they are sentenced to forty hours. Every Saturday morning, these youths are required to be at the downtown meeting place at 8:00 AM. From here, five trucks are sent out with ten youths and two staff members in each truck. The coordinator of the program, who is on the staff of the probation department, then assigns each to a specific work detail. These details include recycling bottles and cans, visiting with patients at a nursing home, doing janitorial work, cleaning bus stops, planting trees or removing barbed wire fences at a city park, and working at a park reserve.[26]

A survey performed in 1991 found that most of these juveniles were referred to these strictly juvenile programs by becoming diverted from the formal justice system. Some restitution programs accept both juveniles and adults. Community service programs are more widely employed than are financial restitution programs because many juveniles lack the means to pay financial restitution. Some probation offices have a full-time restitution officer who administers such programs, and other offices divide restitution into formal and informal programs.

Intensive Supervision

In the early 1980s, **intensive supervision programs** (ISP) began to be used in adult probation as a response to the emerging issues of prison crowding, cost escalation, and society's hard-line response to crime. It was called "intensive probation supervision" (IPS) because it was operated or administered by probation, because it involved increased contacts, and because it generally emphasized external controls and surveillance.[27]

Juvenile justice soon followed adult justice, as so frequently happens, in implementing intensive supervision programs in juvenile probation. Georgia, New Jersey, Oregon, and Pennsylvania have experimented with or have instituted statewide intensive supervision programs for juveniles.[28] Indeed, by the end of the 1980s, juvenile judges across the nation were commonly placing high-risk offenders on small caseloads and assigning them frequent contact with a probation officer.

For example, the Juvenile Court Judges' Commission in the Commonwealth of Pennsylvania developed such a project in the 1980s because of its concern with increased commitments to training schools.[29] The standards adopted for this project included a caseload size of no more than fifteen, a minimum of three contacts per week with the youth, a minimum of one contact per week with the family or guardian, and a minimum of six months and a maximum of twelve months of intensive services.[30] Thirty-two counties in Pennsylvania had established intensive supervision programs with these standards by the end of 1989.[31]

An Integrated Social Control (ISC) model of intensive supervision recently has been developed to address the major causal factors identified in delinquency theory and research. This proposed model integrates the central components of strain, control, and social learning theories. It contends that the combined forces of inadequate socialization, strains between educational and occupational aspirations and expectations, and social disorganization in the neighborhood lead to weak bonding to conventional values and to activities in the family, school, and community. Weak bonding, in turn, can lead juveniles to delinquent behavior through negative peer influence.[32]

The evaluation of adult intensive supervision programs in adult probation has received encouraging results in prevention of recidivism.[33] Two national evaluations of intensive supervision programs in juvenile probation, however, have discovered that "neither the possible effectiveness nor the possible ineffectiveness of these programs had been carefully examined. As a result, their status in this regard, including their impact on recidivism, was essentially unknown."[34]

House Arrest and Electronic Monitoring

House arrest, or home confinement, is a program of intermediate punishment whereby youths are ordered to remain confined in their own residences during evening hours after curfew and on weekends.[35] Those receiving house arrest may be allowed to leave during the day for doctors' appointments, school, employment, or approved religious services. Electronic monitoring equipment may be used to verify probationers' presence in the residence in which they are required to remain.[36]

Electronic monitoring was inspired when a New Mexico district court judge read a comic strip in which the character Spiderman was tracked by a transmitter affixed to his wrist. At the judge's request, an engineer designed an electronic bracelet to emit a signal picked up by a receiver placed in a home telephone. The design of the bracelet was such that if an offender moved more

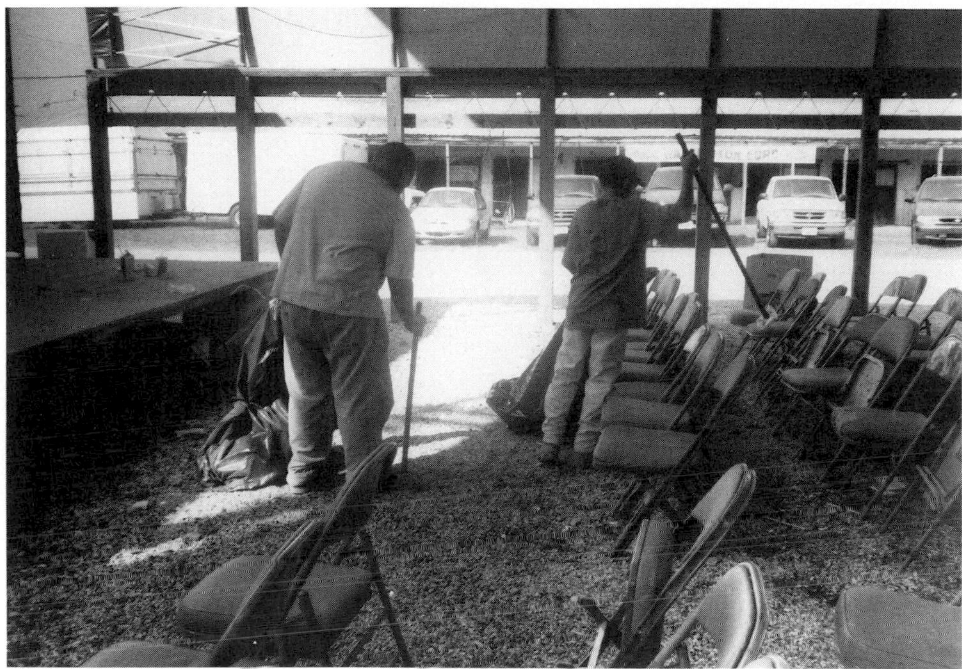

These youths on probation are working to clean up county fairgrounds as part of their restitution and community service. (Photo by Stuart Miller.)

than 150 feet from his or her home telephone, the transmission signal would be broken. Authorities then would know that the offender had left his or her residence.[37]

One survey reports that electronic monitoring devices were used in thirty-three states to supervise nearly twenty-three hundred adult offenders in 1988.[38] In contrast to the popularity of these devices in adult corrections, only eleven home-confinement programs existed in juvenile justice in 1988.[39] These programs in juvenile justice frequently used private contractors and included the following goals:

- To increase the number of juveniles safely released into existing home-confinement programs
- To reduce the number of juveniles returned to juvenile detention for violating home-confinement restrictions
- To reduce the number of field contacts required of home-confinement officers
- To provide a reasonably safe alternative for lower-risk offenders
- To provide for early reunification with the juvenile's family
- To allow the juvenile to return to school[40]

HOW DO PROBATION OFFICERS DO THEIR JOBS?

The probation officer does not have an easy job. He or she is sometimes asked to supervise youths on aftercare as well as those on probation. The officer may be given an intensive caseload, may be responsible for youths who are on house arrest and are monitored with electronic equipment, or may be charged with intake or secure detention responsibilities. In addition, the probation officer is expected to be a treatment agent as well as an agent of social control.[41]

Role Conflict

The nearly opposite roles of law enforcement and treatment create problems for the probation officer. The police and citizens of the community are constantly challenging the treatment role of probation officers, berating them for leaving dangerous and hard-core youths in the community. But, at the same time, probation officers encounter hostility from probationers because of their law enforcement role. The wide use of urinalysis to test for alcohol and drug use certainly bears testimony to this law enforcement role. Probation officers must convince the juvenile judge that they are properly filling both roles and are doling out proper portions of treatment and control.

Ann Strong has identified four different orientations, or self-perceptions, of probation officers toward their clients. First, probation officers whose orientation is the enforcer role perceive themselves as enforcement officers who are charged with regulating juvenile behavior. Second, probation officers whose orientation is the detector role attempt to identify problematic juveniles in advance on the basis of previous rule infractions. Third, probation officers whose orientation is the broker role refer juveniles to appropriate community services and programs. Finally, probation officers whose orientation is the educator, mediator, and enabler role are more likely to instruct and assist youthful offenders in dealing with the problems that impede their successful adjustment to the community.[42]

Conflicting Pressures

Probation officers not only encounter role dilemmas, but they also must satisfy three elements—the juvenile justice system, their own ego needs, and the human needs of the client. That the system comes first is a reality that probation officers face early in their careers. If the juvenile judge wants a youth's social study completed by the next Tuesday, it must be done, regardless of the needs and problems of other probationers during that week. Similarly, probation officers know that the system will not tolerate too much adverse publicity; consequently, it is wise for them to be conservative in terms of taking chances on troublesome youths.

Probation officers, too, are human. They have ego needs and want to feel important. They want approval and acceptance from the juvenile judge; from the director of probation, or court, services; from other probation officers; and from clients. Granted that interest in others brought many of them to their jobs, few probation officers can function very effectively or happily if their own needs are not met. If an adolescent female fails to respect her probation officer, she is not likely to receive much tolerance from that officer. If an adolescent male is constantly arguing with or harassing his officer, he can expect the full weight of justice if he violates his probation terms.

The client, all too often, is considered long after the needs of the system and the officer have been satisfied. If the officer's initial job enthusiasm and involvement have waned and he or she regards the job only as one that demands much, pays little, and offers slight opportunity for advancement, his or her client may indeed be shortchanged. The endless paperwork, the hours spent on the road trying to locate clients, the broken appointments, the intractable and undependable probationers, and the hostility directed toward the probation officer also make it difficult for the officer to maintain a close involvement with clients.

Communication with Clients

Probation officers who relate well and do an effective job with clients tend to have certain characteristics in common:

1. They are genuine in their relationships with probationers and do not hide behind a professional role; that is, they attempt to avoid barriers that would isolate them from their clients. Furthermore, they try to be honest with their clients and expect the juveniles to be honest in return.
2. They respond to others with respect, kindness, and compassion. Because they are caring persons, they are able to listen and reach out to others.
3. They are not gullible nor easily hoodwinked by probationers, because they know what life on the streets is like.
4. They are able to encourage others to pursue positive success experiences; they also have an uncanny knack of knowing what to say and do when others fail.
5. They have a good understanding of themselves and have a reasonable idea of their own problems, shortcomings, and needs. They know, in addition, their biases, prejudices, and pet peeves.
6. They are very committed to their jobs, for the job to them is much more than a paycheck. Moreover, their enthusiasm does not wane following the first few weeks or months as probation officers.

Probation officers who continually have problems with clients also have certain characteristics in common:

1. They do not keep their word. Either they promise more than they are capable of delivering or they simply fail to follow through on what they have said they would do.
2. They become bored with their jobs, chiefly because they see little meaning in working with youths whom they regard as losers who will always be marginal citizens.
3. They either have unreal expectations for probationers or are inflexible in interpreting the terms of probation.
4. They permit their personality problems to affect their performance on the job, which often results in a lack of warmth, a preoccupation with self, or a sharp, biting response to others. Not surprisingly, these personality traits alienate them from both probationers and other probation staff.
5. They seem to be unable to respond to lower-class youths who do not share their own middle-class values, so they become judgmental and moralistic in dealing with clients.
6. They are unwilling to pay the price of changing their own lives in order to influence or alter the lives of juvenile offenders.

A basic problem for the conscientious probation officer is disciplining the violator without alienating him or her. For example, one probation officer, in describing the problems he had working with a boy, lamented the fact that just as he began to get close to him, he would be forced to discipline him: "I can't let him go too far or you'll have to snap him back. And this destroys any kind of relationship. . . . He just clams up. . . . Underneath it all, I think he's an angry boy."[43]

But regardless of how effective and committed the probation officer may be, a number of troublesome youths will flagrantly violate their probation terms and will have to be returned to the juvenile court, which may lead to probation revocation. Before punishing a youngster who has violated the terms of his or her probation, the probation officer should make every effort to gain the compliance of the youth. An understanding of the negative impact of institutionalization should compel the probation officer to return a youth to the court only as an extreme last resort.

WHAT ARE THE RIGHTS OF PROBATIONERS?

The U.S. Supreme Court has ruled on two cases concerning probation revocation: *Mempa v. Rhay*[44] and *Gagnon v. Scarpelli*.[45] The Court held in the *Mempa* case that the Sixth Amendment's right to counsel applies to the sentencing hearing because it is an important step of criminal prosecution. The Court then extended this right to deferred sentencing and probation revocation hearings, and it reversed the decision of the lower courts because Mempa did not have counsel at his revocation hearing.

Gagnon v. Scarpelli involved an offender whose probation was revoked in Wisconsin without a hearing. Scarpelli, who had been sentenced to fifteen years of imprisonment for armed robbery, had his sentence suspended and was placed on probation for seven years. He was given permission to reside in Illinois, where he was subsequently arrested for burglary. His probation at that point was revoked without a hearing. Scarpelli appealed this revocation, claiming that the failure to receive a hearing and to have counsel violated his due process rights. Although the Supreme Court held that the right to counsel should be decided on a case-by-case basis, the Court did indicate that counsel should be provided on request when the probationer denies that he or she committed the violation or when the reasons for the violation are complex.[46]

These two adult cases have influenced what takes place during probation revocation in juvenile court, because in many jurisdictions the juvenile probationer has the same basic rights as an adult has. The juvenile has the right to a hearing, the right of a five-day notification of the probation revocation hearing, the right of being represented by an attorney, the right of confrontation, and the right to see the reports citing his or her violations.

"Reasonable efforts" is the standard that most juvenile judges adhere to at the probation revocation hearing. According to this standard, the probation officer must show that "reasonable efforts" have been made to provide different services and programs to the probationer. It, therefore, provides clear and convincing evidence that the youth's refusal or inability to profit from these services and programs show that he or she cannot be kept in the community.[47]

WHAT IS THE ROLE OF VOLUNTEERS IN PROBATION?

As mentioned earlier, throughout the second half of the nineteenth century, volunteers were used widely to provide probation services, but they largely disappeared at the beginning of the twentieth century and did not reappear until the late 1950s. Indeed, only four courts were using volunteers in 1961; but today more than two thousand court-sponsored volunteer programs are in operation in this country. The use of volunteers has become one of the most valuable ways to help offenders adjust to community life.

The National Information Center on Volunteers in Court has identified several areas in which volunteers can work effectively with juvenile offenders. A volunteer can provide a one-to-one support relationship for the youth with a trustworthy adult; can function as a child advocate with teachers, employers, and the police; can be a good role model; can set limits and teach prosocial values; can teach skills or academic subjects; and can help the youth to develop a realistic response to the environment.

In addition to these areas of direct contact, volunteers can assist in administrative work. They can help recruit, train, and supervise other volunteers; can serve as consultants to the regular staff; can become advisers to the court, especially in the policymaking area; can develop good public relations with the community; and can contribute money, materials, or facilities.

Volunteers can improve the morale of the regular probation staff, because they are usually positive and enthusiastic about the services they provide. Because many volunteers are professionals (physicians, psychiatrists, psychologists, and dentists), they can provide services that the probation department may not have the financial resources to obtain. Finally, their contributions can reduce the caseload of the regular staff.

Several criticisms have been leveled at volunteer programs: The programs tend to attract a high ratio of middle-class persons, and they often create more work than they return in service. Volunteers cannot handle serious problems and sometimes in fact can harm their clients. Parents may resist the volunteer as an untrained worker. Although inappropriate volunteers clearly can do a great deal of damage, proper screening, training, and supervision can do much to ensure high quality of probation services from volunteers. See Focus on Practice 8–3 for a list of guidelines for working with juveniles.

FOCUS ON PRACTICE 8–3

CONSIDERATIONS WHEN WORKING WITH JUVENILES

1. Keep in contact with the child. We recommend one visit a week as a minimum.
2. Patience. Don't expect overnight success. When things have been going wrong for years, they don't get corrected in a few weeks, or months, or even years.
3. Be ready for setbacks. Although we all like to achieve success with a child, remember he or she does not owe it to us; the youth owes it only to himself or herself.
4. Give attention and affection. The child you are working with may never have known really sustained attention and affection and (at least at first) may not know how to handle it in a normal way.
5. Be prepared to listen and to understand what your child says. Too much talking on your part is more likely to break communication than enhance it.

6. Be a discerning listener. But listening does not mean you have to believe everything you hear.
7. Don't prejudge. Avoid forming fixed and premature opinions, until you have gathered all the background information you can.
8. Know your youngster. Get all the information you can on him or her.
9. Respect confidentiality, utterly and completely. Whatever you know about a youngster is under no circumstances to be divulged to or discussed with anyone but a person fully authorized by the court to receive this information.
10. Report violations. Confidentiality does not include keeping known violations a secret from the probation officer in charge of the youngster.
11. Be supportive, encouraging, friendly, but also firm. Although you have to report infractions, you can still be supportive, encouraging, and friendly, to the limit possible.
12. Present your ideas clearly, firmly, and simply. Always mean what you say, be consistent, and keep your promises.
13. Be a good role model. Before accepting court volunteer work, you must decide to live up to this special condition.
14. Avoid being caught in the middle. Be careful not to get caught between the child and his or her parents, the child and his or her teachers, or the child and the court.
15. Be yourself and care sincerely about the child. The more you are yourself, the easier it will be to communicate with the child.

Source: "Manual for Volunteer Probation Officer Aides" (Waterloo, IA: Black Hawk County Juvenile Court Services, 1981), pp. 35–39.

Critical Thinking Questions:

Is this a good list of considerations for working with juveniles? Would you like to be a volunteer probation officer? Which of these considerations would be most difficult for you to follow?

IS PROBATION EFFECTIVE?

The evaluative studies of probation in the 1960s and 1970s indicated that probation was more effective than any other method for rehabilitating youthful offenders. For example, Douglas Lipton and colleagues' work reviewed the studies of adult and juvenile probation and arrived at the following conclusions: (1) evidence exists that a large proportion of offenders now incarcerated could be placed on probation instead without any change in the recidivism rates; (2) probationers have a significantly lower violation rate than do parolees; and (3) intensive probation supervision (fifteen-ward caseload) is associated with lower recidivism rates for youths under age eighteen.[48]

But a major problem in evaluating the effectiveness of probation today is that probation has changed so much since these early evaluation studies. The risk-reduction programs, such as restitution, intensive supervision, and house arrest, are still in the early stages of evaluation. Evidence suggests that restitution and intensive supervision studies are experiencing some positive results, but it is much too early to draw any conclusions about the present effectiveness of juvenile probation from these studies.

SUMMARY

Juvenile probation continues to have more supporters than does any other disposition within the justice system. Traditionally, it alone can point to a positive impact on youthful and adult offenders. Yet juvenile probation has experienced a major change in focus during the past two decades—from rehabilitation to crime control—and these new methods of crime control are currently being evaluated.

Juvenile probation continues to be plagued by the problems of the past, as well as by new challenges. Probation is primarily under the control of the juvenile court and too frequently is poorly funded by local government agencies. Probation officers often feel overworked and underpaid; they sometimes are young, inexperienced, and inadequately trained. Some states and many localities have underdeveloped probation services, and probationers tend to perceive the law enforcement role of probation more than its counseling or supportive role. Difficult challenges for probation services include the continuing get tough mood of society and the increased use of drugs and guns by juvenile offenders. The ability of probation to become an even more effective vehicle of juvenile justice depends on whether it can resolve creatively these problems and challenges.

WEB SITES OF INTEREST

To view a report on juvenile probation by the OJP, go to

http://www.ojp.usdoj.gov/probation/rethink.pdf

The Probation Model Report by the OJJDP can be found at

http://www.ncjrs.org/txtfiles/d0010.txt

To see how one juvenile probation department is set up, go to the Superior Court of Arizona web site:

http://www.maricopa.gov/juvenile/Default.htm

CRITICAL THINKING QUESTIONS

1. What do you feel is the most effective way to administer probation?
2. Do you believe that probation and parole should be administered together?
3. How can probation officers establish better relations with probationers?
4. Would you like to be a probation officer? Why or why not? What major problems would you face? How would you attempt to solve them?

NOTES

1. Probation officer interviewed in 1985 in the Midwest.
2. Meghan C. Black, *Juvenile Delinquent Probation Caseload, 1989–1998* (Washington, DC: Office of Juvenile Justice and Delinquency Prevention, 2001), 2.
3. *John Augustus, First Probation Officer* (Montclair, NJ: Patterson-Smith Company, 1972), 4–5.
4. Board of State Charities of Massachusetts, *Sixth Annual Report, 1869,* 269.
5. Robert M. Mennel, *Thorns and Thistles* (Hanover: University of New Hampshire Press, 1973), 140.
6. Homer Folks, "Juvenile Probation," *NCCD Proceedings, 1906,* 117–22.
7. Mennel, *Thorns and Thistles,* 142.
8. Interviewed in 1979.
9. Interviewed in 1985.
10. "Privatizing Juvenile Probation Services: Five Local Experiments," *OJJDP Update on Programs* (Washington, DC: Office of Juvenile Justice and Delinquency Prevention, 1989), 1.
11. National Advisory Commission on Criminal Justice Standards and Goals, *Corrections* (Washington, DC: U.S. Government Printing Office, 1973), 313–16.
12. Rob Wilson, "Probation/Parole Officers as 'Resource Brokers,'" *Corrections Magazine* 5 (June 1978), 48.
13. Interviewed in July 1984.
14. Joan Petersilia, *The Influence of Criminal Justice Research* (Santa Monica, CA: Rand, 1987), 72.
15. For Fogel's thoughts on probation, see the interview in Clemens Bartollas, *Correctional Treatment: Theory and Practice* (Englewood Cliffs, NJ: Prentice Hall, 1985), 45–46.
16. Interviewed in April 1983.
17. See Dennis Maloney, Dennis Romig, and Troy Armstrong, "The Balanced Approach to Juvenile Probation," *Juvenile and Family Court Journal* 39 (1989), 1–49.

18. Ibid., 10. See also Gordon Bazemore and Mark S. Umbreit, *Balanced and Restorative Justice: Program Summary* (Washington, DC: Office of Juvenile Justice and Delinquency Prevention, 1994).
19. Bazemore and Umbreit, *Balanced and Restorative Justice,* 5.
20. Ibid., 7.
21. Anne L. Schneider, "Restitution and Recidivism Rates of Juvenile Offenders: Results from Four Experimental Studies," *Criminology* 24 (1986), 533.
22. William G. Staples, "Restitution as a Sanction in Juvenile Court," *Crime and Delinquency* 32 (April 1986), 177.
23. Office of Juvenile Justice and Delinquency Prevention, *National Trends in Juvenile Restitution Programming* (Washington, DC: Government Printing Office, 1989), 3.
24. Anne L. Schneider, *Guide to Juvenile Restitution* Washington, DC: U.S. Department of Justice, 1985), 1.
25. Interviewed in August 1985.
26. Information gained during an on-site visit and updated in a phone call to a staff member in September 2001.
27. Ted Palmer, *The Re-Emergence of Correctional Intervention* (Newbury Park, CA: Sage, 1992), 80.
28. Emily Walker, "The Community Intensive Treatment for Youth Program: A Specialized Community-Based Program for High-Risk Youth in Alabama," *Law and Psychiatry Review* 13 (1989), 175–99.
29. Cecil Marshall and Keith Snyder, "Intensive and Aftercare Probation Services in Pennsylvania." Paper presented at the annual meeting of the American Society of Criminology, Baltimore, Maryland (November 7, 1990), 3.
30. Bernadette Jones, "Intensive Probation, Philadelphia County, November 1986–February 1989." Paper presented at the annual meeting of the American Society of Criminology, Baltimore, Maryland (November 1990), p. 1 of Appendix.
31. Marshall and Snyder, "Intensive and Aftercare Probation Services in Pennsylvania," 3.
32. Barry Krisberg et al., *Juvenile Intensive Supervision: Planning Guide* (Washington, DC: Office of Juvenile Justice and Delinquency Prevention, 1994), 7.
33. For a review of these studies in intensive supervision programs for adults, see Clemens Bartollas and John P. Conrad, *Introduction to Corrections,* 2d ed. (New York: HarperCollins, 1992).
34. Palmer, *The Re-Emergence of Correctional Intervention,* 82.
35. J. Robert Lilly and Richard A. Ball, "A Brief History of House Arrest and Electronic Monitoring," *Northern Kentucky Law Review* 13 (1987), 343–74.
36. Joan Petersilia, *Expanding Options for Criminal Sentencing* (Santa Monica, CA: Rand, 1987), 32.

37. Richard A. Ball, Ronald Huff, and Robert Lilly, *House Arrest and Correctional Policy: Doing Time at Home* (Newbury Park, CA: Sage Publications, 1988), 35–36.
38. Annesley K. Schmidt, "Electronic Monitoring of Offenders Increases," in *Research in Action* (Washington, DC: U.S. Department of Justice, 1989), 3.
39. Joseph B. Vaughn, "A Survey of Juvenile Electronic Monitoring and Home Confinement Program," *Juvenile and Family Court Journal* 40 (1989), 4, 22. For a description of another program, see Michael T. Charles, "The Development of a Juvenile Electronic Monitoring Program," *Federal Probation* 53 (1989), 3–12.
40. Vaughn, "A Survey of Juvenile Electronic Monitoring and Home Confinement Program."
41. See Lori L. Colley, Robert C. Culbertson, and Edward J. Latessa, "Juvenile Probation Officers: A Job Analysis," *Juvenile and Family Court Journal* 38 (1987), 1–12.
42. Ann Strong, *Case Classification Manual, Module One: Technical Aspects of Interviewing* (Austin: Texas Adult Probation Commission, 1981).
43. Robert Emerson, *Judging Delinquents: Context and Process in the Juvenile Court* (Chicago: Aldine Publishing Company, 1969), 253.
44. *Mempa v. Rhay,* 339 U.S. 128 Cir. 3023 (1968).
45. *Gagnon v. Scarpelli,* 411 U.S. 778 (1973).
46. Ibid.
47. Information gained from a September 1992 interview with a juvenile probation officer in Iowa.
48. Lipton et al., *The Effectiveness of Correctional Treatment: A Survey of Evaluation Studies* (New York: Praeger Publishers, 1975), 59–61.

9

COMMUNITY-BASED PROGRAMS

OBJECTIVES

1. To examine the history of deinstitutionalization in juvenile justice
2. To discuss the operations of the main types of community-based programs
3. To evaluate the effectiveness of these programs
4. To examine the main issues in community-based programming

KEY TERMS

community corrections acts
day treatment programs
deinstitutionalization
delinquency prevention
diversion programs
group home
reintegration philosophy
wilderness programs

I was a real terror as a kid. I was into gangs, violence, and drugs and was in and out of training school. I was also in and out of a number of foster placements. Then I met Mr. Sullivan, and he turned my life around. I gave him a run for his money, but he wouldn't give up on me. If it wouldn't have been for Mr. Sullivan, I don't know what would have become of me, but I can tell you this, that I wouldn't be talking with you today.

—Director of Court Services[1]

In the opening quote, a director of court services in a midwestern state tells of the impact a foster parent had on him. An impressive array of programs for juvenile offenders exists in the community. These programs include delinquency prevention, runaway facilities, foster care, diversion, day treatment, group homes, and wilderness learning experiences. The ongoing search for a panacea to the problem of youth crime, the popularity of deinstitutionalization in juvenile justice, and the emphasis in the 1980s and 1990s on short-term behavior control probably best explain why there are so many programs for juvenile offenders. These community-based programs range from those focusing on prevention and diversion from the juvenile justice system to those designed for short-term residential care.

HOW HAVE COMMUNITY-BASED PROGRAMS EVOLVED?

Community-based programs are part of a larger movement to keep juveniles who are in trouble out of training schools. Most of these programs had their origins in the success of several guided-group-interaction, short-term institutional programs initiated in the 1950s and 1960s, among them the Highfields, Southfields, Essexfields, and Pinehills projects. The Highfields project, known officially as the New Jersey Experimental Project for the Treatment of Youthful Offenders, is the most famous of these short-term programs. Established in 1950 on an estate that is the former home of Colonel and Mrs. Charles Lindbergh, the program involved twenty delinquent boys who worked during the day at the nearby New Jersey Neuro-Psychiatric Institute and met in two guided-group-interaction units five evenings per week. In these groups, which were established at the Highfields facility, youths were molded into close-knit groups responsible for controlling the behavior of their members. In addition, residents accompanied by staff members were permitted to go shopping and to attend movies in town. This project—short-term, small, and informally structured—became a real alternative to the typical training school.

The New York Division for Youth established several similar centers in the 1960s and called them START (short-term adolescent residential treatment) centers. Youths living at these START centers also worked at nearby state hospitals. Southfields, another residential group center of the Highfields type, was set up in Jefferson County near Louisville in Kentucky. Pinehills, established in 1959 in Provo, Utah, adopted the Highfields philosophy but abandoned the residential aspect (boys returned to their homes in the evenings and on weekends). Essexfields, founded in the early 1960s in Newark, New Jersey, was another nonresidential facility based on the Highfields philosophy.

The most dramatic advance in this trend toward **deinstitutionalization,** that is, the removal of youths from secure confinement and the placement of all qualified youths in community programs, rather than in institutions, occurred when the state of Massachusetts announced that it was closing all of its training schools. This rather startling move resulted from a number of factors. First, the dynamic leadership of Jerome Miller focused public attention on the negative impact of these institutions. Miller traveled throughout the state, giving speeches on what institutionalization does to juveniles. He often took with him a juvenile offender who informed the audience how it feels to be institutionalized.[2] Another factor contributing to institutional closings was a series of scandals in and disclosures about Massachusetts juvenile training schools that had begun in 1965. Institutional staff, in particular, were widely attacked by the media for their brutality. The refusal of the training schools to cooperate with the central office also prevented the Massachusetts Department of Youth Services from improving the quality of institutional services in that area. This resistance of staff members throughout the system made the central authority realize that it had little influence in setting up new programs. Also of importance in the dissolution of the training schools was the leadership of Governor Francis Sargent, who believed that major reform in Massachusetts was imperative:

> I had been to some of the state and county [training schools], and God, I was repulsed—to think that we were paying something like $10,000 a year just to keep a kid in a cage without any type of rehabilitation. It was just really horrible. And I figured that if I didn't do any other damn thing while I was governor, I was going to [change] that system.[3]

Bridgewater was closed first. Then, in early 1972, Miller closed Shirley and Lyman. When Shirley was closed, the press featured stories and pictures of Miller, members of the legislature, staff, and youths hammering down the bars and locks of the segregation cells of Cottage #9. The closing of Lyman created even more fanfare because a caravan of cars took youths from the institution to the University of Massachusetts to stay for a month while placements were arranged for them. Lancaster and two detention centers were also closed at this time, and their residents, too, were taken to the University of Massachusetts. Oakdale, the last training school to remain open, was finally closed in late 1972. Jerome Miller had accomplished the remarkable feat of closing all the training schools in Massachusetts, and except for a few girls remaining in the Shirley Training School and a few youths sent to private training schools in other states, Massachusetts had succeeded in placing all its adjudicated juvenile offenders in community-based programs.

The idea of deinstitutionalization soon became popular in other states. The trend was so firmly entrenched by 1973 that the National Advisory Commission on Criminal Justice Standards and Goals recommended that the states not build any more juvenile training institutions and that any existing institutions be phased out over a five-year period.[4]

It was not long before community-based corrections seemed to be the primary topic for discussion. The case appeared to be closed. The empiricist had established the futility of treatment, the reformer had documented the essential inhumanity of training schools, and the cost-benefit analyst had determined that alternatives to incarceration were effective at far less expense to the taxpayer. Many students of penology thought that the millennium was at hand. Commitment to training schools was declining, and training schools were closing down.

The talk continued and some action followed. Kansas, Maryland, Minnesota, North Dakota, Oregon, South Dakota, and Utah soon were assigning as many youths to community-based facilities as they were confining in correctional institutions. Yet, because of the adverse publicity about youth crime and the substantial number of youthful offenders whose predatory activities represented a danger to their communities, few policymakers advocated closing all state juvenile institutions.

In the 1980s, community-based programs encountered several challenges. First, the hard-liners continued to alarm the general public about the extent and dangers of youth crime. The shift in public opinion put community-based programs in a defensive and retreating position. Second, the end of Law Enforcement Education Assistance (LEAA) funding in the late 1970s left many community programs unable to find sufficient funding to keep doors open. Third, many of the high-impact community-based programs for juveniles are led by charismatic and dedicated leaders and are strongly dependent on the continued tenure of these leaders. Thus, unless bureaucratic agencies are capable of projecting the personal qualities of such leaders, many effective community-based programs for juveniles will disappear. Fourth, community-based programs for juveniles must develop a more elaborate network of services. Research in Massachusetts has indicated that communities with networks of services are more likely to have effective programs for juveniles than are communities without such networks.[5]

In the 1990s, increasing evidence suggested that the retrenchment found only a few years earlier throughout the nation had been replaced by a new spirit of deinstitutionalization. This new wave of reform is found in such diverse states as Minnesota, Utah, Vermont, and West Virginia. In other states, the spirit of deinstitutionalization was spurred by overcrowded training schools and the cost of long-term institutional care.

WHAT HAS BEEN THE COMMUNITY'S ACCEPTANCE OF COMMUNITY-BASED PROGRAMS?

Community-based programs rest on a **reintegration philosophy** that assumes that both the offender and the receiving community must be changed. The community is as important as the client and plays a vital role in facilitating the reabsorption of offenders into its life. The task of corrections, according to this philosophy, involves the reconstruction, or construction, of ties between offenders and the community through maintenance of family bonds, employment and education, and placement in the mainstream of social life. Youths should be directed to community resources, and the community should be acquainted with the skills and needs of youthful lawbreakers.

Critics of community-based programs challenge several assumptions of reintegrative philosophy. They hold that the community deserves protection from predatory youths who intimidate and hurt the young, rape women of all ages, and victimize the elderly. They further contend that youths sent to juvenile institutions are those who have failed to benefit from a number of community placements. It is also argued that keeping youths in the community only reinforces their antisocial behavior; institutional confinement provides the punishment they deserve.

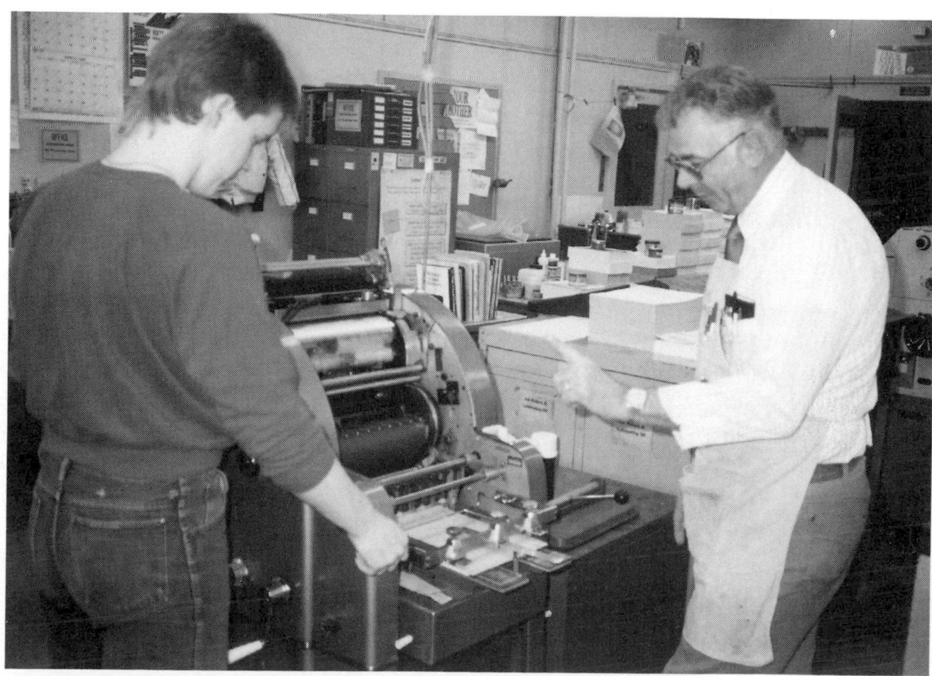

On-the-job training is one way youths are reintegrated into their local communities. (Photo courtesy of Ohio Department of Youth Services.)

Communities often have resisted the charge that they must assume responsibility for the problems they generate. It is much easier (and more comforting) for the community to blame the crime problem on the failure of training schools, the inefficiency of the juvenile justice system, or the personalities of offenders themselves than to accept responsibility for its social problems. Instead of coordination between the justice system and the community, all too frequently an adversarial we-they relationship exists. Citizens often believe that the youth commission is trying to foist a group home or a day treatment facility on their community; correctional administrators, in turn, often tend to perceive negativism or outright hostility on the part of many citizens.

HOW ARE COMMUNITY-BASED PROGRAMS ADMINISTERED?

Comprehensive state-sponsored, locally sponsored, and privately administrated programs are the three basic types of organizational structures in community-based programs.

In California, Indiana, Kansas, Michigan, Minnesota, and Oregon, the state sponsors residential and day treatment programs under **community corrections acts.** The Minnesota Community Corrections Act, which has become a model for other community corrections acts, provides a state subsidy to any county or group of counties that chooses to develop its own community corrections system. The costs for juvenile offenders who are adjudicated to a training school are charged back to the county, and these costs are subtracted from the county's subsidy. Counties in Minnesota have been understandably reluctant to commit youths to a training school because of the prohibitive costs and therefore have established and encouraged a wide variety of residential and day treatment programs.

The deinstitutionalization movement in Maryland, Massachusetts, North Dakota, South Dakota, and Utah also has led to the development of a wide network of residential and day treatment programs for youths. In Massachusetts, the Department of Youth Services administers some of these programs, but more often the juvenile court sponsors these programs, or state or local agencies contract services for those youths from private vendors in the community. Whoever administers these community programs, the most innovative and effective ones attempt to provide a continuum of care for youthful offenders.

Private delivery of correctional services to youthful offenders originated in the early days of juvenile justice in this nation. Most of these programs were religious or business backed. In 1972, the private sector reentered the field of juvenile corrections in unprecedented manner. Privatization, or placing control of facilities in the hands of the private sector, has expanded significantly in the past few decades. Privately run programs are emerging as a result of budget problems that prevent local or state agencies from supplying the services in an efficient manner. Privatization has become big business and has sparked the interests of investors from all walks of life. Those operating in the private sector receive payment for their programs through federal, state, or local funding, from insurance plans, or from the juvenile's parents.[6]

Federal grants are the basis of the funding of many community programs. SafeFutures is a new program funded by the Office of Juvenile Justice and Delinquency Prevention that appears to be a model worth replicating in communities across the nation. SafeFutures urban sites are Boston, Massachusetts; Contra Costa County, California; Seattle, Washington; and St. Louis, Missouri. The other two sites are Imperial County, California (rural), and Fort Belknap Indian Community, Harlem, Montana (tribal government). SafeFutures seeks to improve the service delivery system by creating a continuum of care responsive to the needs of youths and their families at any point along the path toward juvenile offending. This coordinated approach of prevention, intervention, and treatment is designed both to serve the juveniles of a community and to encompass the human service and the juvenile justice systems. A national evaluation is being conducted to determine the success of the continuum of services in all six sites.[7]

Project CRAFT (community restitution and apprenticeship focused training program), a vocational training program for high-risk youths, is sponsored by the Home Builders Institute (HBI), the educational arm of the National Association of Home Builders (NAHB). Project CRAFT offers preapprenticeship training and job training for adjudicated juveniles who are referred to the program. It was started in 1994 by HBI in Bismarck, North Dakota; Nashville, Tennessee; and Sabillasville, Maryland. It has been replicated in five sites in Florida (Avon Park, Daytona Beach, Fort Lauderdale, Lantana, and Orlando) and in Texas. This program works in partnership with private facilities, juvenile judges, juvenile justice system personnel, educational agencies, and other human service agencies.[8]

WHAT IS THE ROLE OF DELINQUENCY PREVENTION?

Delinquency prevention is defined as any attempt to thwart youths' illegal behavior before it occurs. The Juvenile Justice and Delinquency Prevention Act of 1974 and the Juvenile Justice Amendments of 1977, 1980, and 1984 established the prevention of delinquency as a national priority.[9] Anne Newton has identified three levels of delinquency prevention:

Primary prevention is directed at modifying conditions in the physical and social environment at large.

Secondary prevention is directed at early identification and intervention in the lives of individuals or groups in criminogenic circumstances.

Tertiary prevention is directed at the prevention of recidivism (after delinquent acts have been committed and detected).[10]

Numerous cities across the United States support programs to help youths before they get into difficulty. (Photo by Allison Bartosh.)

An example of primary prevention is the Mobilization for Youth program, which took place in a 67-block area of Manhattan's Lower East Side in New York City. This project was designed to improve educational and work opportunities for area youth, to make a variety of services available to individuals and families, and to provide assistance in community organization.[11] DARE, a drug prevention program conducted by the police for elementary school students, is an expression of secondary prevention. Tertiary prevention is aptly illustrated by "Scared Straight," a label derived from the title of an award-winning documentary film about the Juvenile Awareness Project at New Jersey's Rahway State Prison. The "Scared Straight" programs conducted at Rahway and other prisons across the nation used the horrors of prison life, as well as intensive confrontation sessions between adult prisoners and juveniles, to deter youths from committing any or additional delinquent acts (see Focus on Programs 9–1 for background information on the Straight Life program, an example of a recent "Scared Straight"-type program).[12]

An impressive number of primary and secondary prevention programs have been conducted since the beginning of the twentieth century, using neighborhood groups, the family and school environment, youth gangs, and social and mental health agencies as points of intervention.[13] Unfortunately, the results of most of these programs have been disappointing.[14] The Chicago

FOCUS ON PROGRAMS 9–1

TEENS TASTE PRISON

Inmates Help Turn Young Lives Around

TRACY [CALIF.]—Angel couldn't stop the tears from clouding his 14-year-old eyes as he faced, then embraced, the smiling man clad in prison blue.

They hugged, saying nothing, the convict and the boy he helped save.

A few months before, Angel had been running with the wrong crowd, a Hispanic gang based in southern San Joaquin County. Drinking, drugs, crime, F-riddled report cards—it was a way of life, one Angel knew was wrong but couldn't escape.

"I felt no reason to live anymore," he said.

Enter a school counselor who convinced him, and some of his home boys, to attend the Straight Life youth-diversion program run by inmates at Deuel Vocational Institution.

Sessions are right in the prison, where youths get a feel for what life is like when they don't play by society's rules.

Inmates, almost all of them sentenced to life terms, confronted the young toughs in Angel's group. One handed him a pen, explained how to use it as a weapon, then ordered him to kill another prisoner.

"I just stood there," Angel recalled. "It freaked the hell out of me."

"When they brought me here, I decided this was where I did not want to be," Angel said.

Except for last week, when he returned one more time for the seventh annual Straight Life banquet, it was a chance to say thanks to men he credits with changing his life, men who were buoyed by the obvious turnaround in the boy.

"Through this program, our lives' worth increases," inmate Tony Young said.

Straight Life, which has brought nearly 3,000 at-risk youth from Sacramento to Fresno to within the walls of Deuel, is the best program inmate Michael de Vries has ever been involved in, he said. For the youths, and for the convicts.

"It makes us look at what got us here," said de Vries, convicted of murder in Berkeley in 1984. "If this were happening everywhere, we might not have the problems we're having."

Source: Garth Stapley, "Teens Taste Prison," *Modesto Bee*, Summer 1996, A1, A10.

Critical Thinking Questions:

What is your evaluation of this program? How does this program appear to be different from the critically evaluated Scared Straight program?

Area Projects, Perry Preschool, School Development Program, Program Development and Parent Training are programs that have shown some measure of success. In addition, there has been a recent attempt to apply delinquency prevention to the violent juvenile.

Chicago Area Projects

Clifford Shaw and Henry McKay, the founders in 1934 of the Chicago Area Projects (CAP), were committed to creating a community consciousness directed at solving social problems on the local level. The first projects were initiated in three areas: South Chicago, the Near West Side, and the Near North Side. Shaw and his colleagues recruited local leaders to promote youth welfare because they had lost confidence in official agencies. These local leaders supported indigenous community organizations and made a special effort to involve those who played important formal and informal roles in community life. Shaw was also able to get men with criminal records to agree to work in the program because he made no moral judgment about what they had done previously. He regarded youth crime as a normal response to the situation of the inner city, believing that individuals did what they had to do to survive, but that this illegal behavior was no indication of an offender's true beliefs and commitments.[15]

Each project area has a committee that operates as an independent unit under the guidance of a board of directors chosen by the local community residents. The Chicago Area Projects have also received support from the state of Illinois—at first, from the Illinois Department of Welfare through the Institute of Juvenile Research, then from the Illinois Youth Commission, and most recently from the Department of Corrections. Twenty such projects are now functioning in Chicago, and others have formed throughout the state. In addition, other groups in Illinois have taken the projects as the model for their own delinquency control programs.[16]

The projects have three basic goals: First, they provide a forum for local residents to become acquainted with new scientific perspectives on child rearing, child welfare, and juvenile delinquency. Second, they initiate new channels of communication between local residents and the institutional representatives of the larger community, those influencing the life chances of local youth. Third, they bring adults into contact with local youths, especially with those having difficulties with the law.

The philosophy of the Chicago Area Projects is based on the belief that instead of throwing youth so quickly to the justice system, the community should deal with its own problems and intervene on behalf of its youth. Citizens of the community show up in juvenile court to speak on behalf of the youths; they organize social and recreational programs so that youths have constructive activities in which to participate. The leaders of the local groups, often individuals who were once in CAP programs, know how to relate to and deal with youths who are having problems at school or with the law.

The Chicago Area Projects have several noteworthy strengths: they have had far-reaching impacts on youths who have participated in their activities; they have encouraged communities to deal with their own social problems; and, depending primarily on volunteers, they have been excellent sources of leadership development within local communities.[17] Steven Schlossman's fifty-year assessment of the CAP concluded: "All of our data consistently suggest that the CAP has long been effective in organizing local communities and reducing juvenile delinquency."[18]

Yet critics contend that the CAP have been ineffective in dealing with youth crime in its most serious forms in the areas of the city with the highest crime rates.[19] Jon Snodgrass adds that the Chicago Area Projects' neglect of the realities of politics and economics made CAP a basically conservative response to the radical changes needed in disorganized communities.[20]

More than fifty years ago, Saul Alinsky made the statement, "It's impossible to overemphasize the enormous importance of people doing things for themselves."[21] What is ultimately significant about the Chicago Area Projects is that this philosophy was its basic approach to delinquency prevention. The CAP advocated grassroots leadership, neighborhood revitalization, the community's role in policing itself, and the importance of community dispute-resolution. These same emphases also have been incorporated into most community crime prevention strategies in the late 1990s.[22]

Perry Preschool

Operated by the High Scope foundation in Ypsilanti, Michigan, the Perry Preschool's early-childhood demonstration program has received national recognition for its impact on pregnancy, education, and delinquency.[23] Directed by David Weikart, the program involved a small random sample of disadvantaged African-American children who attended a high-quality, two-year preschool program and received weekly home visits from program personnel. Compared to controls at age twenty-seven, according to official police records and an excellent research design, the children who had attended this enrichment program were less likely to become habitual offenders and had only half the number of arrests compared to members of the control group. Self-reported behavior at age twenty-seven, consistent with police and court data, revealed that preschool attendees reported less fighting and involvement with the police than did control group members.

Analysis of data from this early childhood program revealed that the arrest data were influenced by two variables: educational attainment and rating of social behavior by teachers through elementary school. This study demonstrates the well-established link between childhood experience and later social behavior. Power enhancement, education, and skill development strategies were in effect in this program, as those with preschool intervention improved in their later classroom behavior and intellectual performance throughout the elementary grades. This, in turn, ultimately affected the amount of education the students completed and indirectly acted to reduce delinquency rates.[24]

One of the most consistent findings of delinquency research is that the earlier any kind of behavior problem begins, the greater are the consequences and the lasting effects. The Perry Preschool program was the only preschool or Head Start program identified as being designed toward preventing later delinquency, but its results indicated that early positive intervention can have later positive results.[25]

School Development Program

Developed by James Comer and colleagues at the Yale Child Study Center, the School Development Program has been implemented in more than one hundred elementary and middle schools in the United States. The model uses the following three team components to improve school and community integration: (1) a planning and management team (consisting of the principal, teachers, parents, counselors, and support staff), (2) a mental health team (composed of a psychologist, the principal, teachers, a nurse, social workers, and counselors), and (3) a parents' group (e.g., the PTA).[26]

The School Development model requires extensive parental outreach and involvement as parents are involved in both the management team and the PTA. They also participate in workshops that are designed to improve their children's skills and are encouraged to participate in any activities that support their children's academic and social development. This program emphasizes problem solving, collaboration, and consensus. Toward this end, both teachers and school administrators arrange their schedules to allow for the schedules of working parents.[27]

Although there is much excitement surrounding this model's ability to enhance power and education and skill development strategies, there also has been critique. This critique centers around the costly implementation of the program, the heavy support of the principal which requires both his or her understanding and commitment to the process, and the need to engage a considerable number of participants to facilitate the process.[28] This model also requires several years to implement and is now in the process of nationwide evaluation.

Program Development Evaluation

Gary and Denise Gottfredson developed a prevention model, in connection with the Center for Social Organization of Schools at Johns Hopkins University, that is designed to improve youths' attachment to school, increase the school's responsiveness to the range of student needs, and improve the school's relationship with the community.[29]

Program Development Evaluation (PDE) has been implemented across all grade levels and throughout the school districts in many states, including

California, Illinois, Maryland, Michigan, New York, and South Carolina.[30] The PDE model is a school management strategy that is designed to identify problems with schools and to develop a program to manage these problems. A school improvement team—consisting of district-level staff, school administrators, teachers, and parents—follow predetermined steps in order to identify school problems, establish objectives and goals, develop programs, and monitor the implementation process. As the model is guided by a trained coordinator, the process is continually evaluated and adjusted to changing needs.[31]

This education and skill development strategy model has shown positive results after extensive evaluations. A Baltimore school's implementation study has revealed the significant improvement in teacher morale and innovation as well as a decrease in negative attitudes and rebellious behaviors among students. An evaluation of PDE in Charleston, South Carolina, found that this prevention strategy resulted in improved classroom organization and the clarity of rules.[32]

Parent Training

The Oregon Social Learning Center provides parental training in techniques that are designed to monitor and change the behavior of children. G. R. Patterson and his colleagues at this center discovered that the parents of socially aggressive children did not identify with the role of the parent and were not attached to their children. In response to these findings, the researchers designed a therapy program that focused on teaching parents how to interact with, and change their behavior toward, their children.[33]

The program begins by having the parents read a programmed text, *Living with Children*, and subsequently identifying a specific behavior of their child they want to work on with trained therapists. The process is to teach parents to record their child's behavior and to administer punishments and rewards in a consistent and appropriate manner. Families are contacted via telephone calls and home visits by staff members, and parents are encouraged to participate in structured parent-training groups.[34]

The most frequent criticism of this program is its applicability to high-crime areas. Eugene, Oregon, where Patterson researched and designed the program, is a university community that is not typical of high-crime areas. Attempts to apply it to high-risk populations have demonstrated that the program is ineffective with dysfunctional families, with disinterested or apathetic parents, and with parents who are unable to master the educational materials.[35]

J. David Hawkins and colleagues have also developed a parent-training program, in Seattle, as part of their larger emphasis on the social development approach to preventing delinquent behavior. This elementary school program, entitled "Catch 'Em Being Good," has seven sessions for parents of first- and second-graders. The goal of these sessions is to teach parents what to expect from their children and how to establish a reward and punishment system. It also provides four sessions for later grades, entitled "How to Help Your Child

Succeed in School," which focuses on parent–child communication and homework help.[36]

Initial evaluations of this program have shown that participating parents report improved parenting skills and reduced rates of aggressiveness among their children. Although a special effort has been made to involve the parents of high-risk children, this program has had the same lack of participation from parents of high-risk children, especially high-risk minority children, found in the Oregon program.[37]

The Violent Juvenile and Delinquency Prevention

Funded and spearheaded by the Office of Juvenile Justice and Delinquency Prevention, the belief emerged in the 1990s that the most effective strategy for juvenile corrections is to place the thrust of the prevention and diversion emphases on high-risk juveniles who commit violent acts. These juveniles are the ones that commit the more serious and most frequent delinquent acts and are the ones that officials are quick to place into the adult system. At the same time that the seriousness of their behaviors have effected changes in juvenile codes across the country, research is beginning to find that these high-risk youths can be impacted by well-equipped and well-implemented prevention and treatment programs.[38]

These programs are based on the assumption that the juvenile justice system does not see most serious offenders until it is too late to effectively intervene.[39] It also presumes that in order to reduce the overall level of violence in American society, it is necessary to successfully intervene in the lives of high-risk youth offenders, who commit about 75 percent of all violent juvenile offenses.[40]

The general characteristics of these programs is that they: (1) address key areas of risk in youths' lives, (2) seek to strengthen the personal and institutional factors that contribute to the development of a healthy adolescent, (3) provide adequate supervision and support, and (4) offer youths a long-term stage in the community.[41] It is emphasized that these prevention programs must be integrated with local police, child welfare, social services, school, and family-preservation programs. Comprehensive approaches to delinquency prevention and intervention require a strong collaborative effort between the juvenile justice system and other service provision systems, such as health, mental health, child welfare, and education. An important component of a community's comprehensive plan is to develop mechanisms that effectively link these service providers at the program level.[42]

The comprehensive, or multisystemic, aspects of these programs are designed to deal simultaneously with many aspects of youths' lives. The intent is that they are intensive, often involving multiple contacts weekly, or possibly daily, with at-risk youth. They build on the strength of these youths, rather than dwell on their deficiencies. These programs operate mostly, although not exclusively, outside of the formal justice system, under a variety of public, nonprofit, or university auspices. Finally, they combine accountability and sanctions with increasingly intensive treatment and rehabilitation services which is achieved through a system of graduated sanctions, in which an integrated approach is employed to stop the penetration of youthful offenders into the system.[43]

In 1996, three communities, Lee and Duval Counties in Florida and San Diego County in California, collaborated with the Office of Juvenile Justice and Delinquency Prevention to apply the processes and principles that were described in *Comprehensive Strategy*. Initial evaluations of the three pilot projects found that each of the sites has benefited significantly from the comprehensive planning process. Although it was deemed premature to assess any long-term impact on juvenile delinquency, there are several short-term indicators of success.[44] The following are among the pilot programs' accomplishments:

- Enhanced community-wide understanding of prevention services and sanctions options for juveniles
- Expanded networking capacity and better coordination among agencies and service providers
- Institution of performance measurement systems
- Hiring of staff to spearhead the ongoing Comprehensive Strategy planning and implementation efforts
- Development of comprehensive five-year strategic action plans[45]

WHAT IS THE ROLE OF DIVERSION?

In the late 1960s and early 1970s, **diversion programs** sprouted across the nation. Diversion, which refers to keeping juveniles outside the formal justice system, can be attempted either through the police and the courts or through agencies outside the juvenile justice system. The main characteristic of diversion initiated by the courts or police is that the justice subsystems retain control over youthful offenders. A youth who fails to respond to such a program usually will be returned to the juvenile court for continued processing within the system.

In the 1970s, youth service bureaus (YSBs) and runaway centers were the most widely used diversion programs outside the juvenile justice system. More recently, family counseling, substance abuse, teen courts, juvenile drug court movement, and juvenile mediation programs have been used by juvenile courts and probation departments to divert juveniles from the formal justice system. Gang intervention programs have been implemented in some communities across the nation to divert gang youths from the justice system.

The Youth Service Bureau

The major impetus to YSBs came in 1967 when the President's Commission on Law Enforcement and Administration of Justice recommended that such agencies be established to work with youths outside the juvenile justice system. Although Youth Service Bureau is the name most frequently used, other names used include Youth Resource Bureau, Youth Assistance Program, the Listening Post, or the Focus on Youth.

Sherwood Norman, who was highly influential in the development of youth service bureaus, identified the basic objectives of this diversion agency:

> The Youth Service Bureau is a noncoercive, independent, public [some are private] agency established to divert children and youth from the justice system by (1) mobilizing community resources to solve youth problems, (2) strengthening existing youth resources and developing new ones, and (3) promoting positive programs to remedy delinquency-breeding conditions.[46]

From 1967 to 1973, one hundred fifty YSBs were established throughout the nation. More YSBs were created in California than in any other state; Illinois had the second largest number. But the decline of federal funding in the late 1970s and early 1980s reduced the number of YSBs in this nation. In 1981, the director of a YSB in Illinois noted, "There are now 54 YSBs in Illinois; there were 78 two years ago."[47] Before the end of the 1980s, nearly all of the YSBs across the nation had closed their doors.

At the peak of their popularity, youth service bureaus offered a variety of programs. Drop-in centers, hot lines, truancy and school outreach programs, and twenty-four-hour crisis programs were common services. Some large YSBs also arrange temporary care for runaways, conducted programs for pregnant teenagers, and provided school dropouts with employment, for which they were paid a minimum wage.

Runaway Centers

An estimated one million youths run away from home each year. Some of these have been thrown out of their homes, but the majority choose to leave because of child abuse, unmanageable conflicts with parents, the influence of peers, or the thrill of being on their own. Youths who are absent from home for a period of time must deal with survival, and about 50 percent of these runaways become involved in delinquent acts such as stealing, prostitution, and drug abuse.[48] Although the 1983 Missing Persons Act allows parents to list missing children with the FBI, runaway centers remain one of the few services that exist for runaway youths.

Under the Runaway and Homeless Youth Act, Title III of the 1974 Juvenile Justice and Delinquency Prevention Act, assistance was given to states, localities, and nonprofit private agencies in order to operate temporary shelters for runaway youths, resulting in the creation of such centers throughout the nation. A staff member of Covenant House, a twenty-four-hour drop-in crisis center located near Times Square in New York City, explains why these programs are needed:

> Thousands of runaway and nomadic adolescents are drawn to the Times Square area each year. These young people survive by panhandling, stealing, by exploiting and being exploited. Many, perhaps most, must touch at least temporarily the life of prostitution. . . . There is a total lack of service available to them in the Times Square area. There are no public or private agencies meeting the immediate and urgent needs of the runaway and delinquency-prone youth, hundreds of whom can be seen in Times Square at literally any hour of the day and night, drifting and wandering.[49]

The Door—A Center of Alternatives, also in New York City, was cited as a model program by the Department of Health, Education, and Welfare (now Health and Human Services) and is frequently mentioned at national conferences. The heart of this program is the S.O.S. Service, which provides emergency shelter, food, and clothing for desperate youths. It is one of the largest runaway programs in the United States, and four hundred or more youths are involved at any one time in such activities as drug-abuse counseling, job advising, prenatal counseling, dance or theater workshops, and martial arts classes. A number of other New York City programs have been established. Group-Live-In Experience (GLIE), located in the Bronx, has expanded from a storefront location to an operation including three temporary care shelters, where thirty homeless youths can stay from three to eight months; two crash pads are found where nineteen youths can stay up to two weeks; and a reentry program, called Last Stop, is present in which fourteen youngsters can prepare for as much as a year for independent living. Hot Line Cares, located in Spanish Harlem, operates a telephone crisis line and referral agency; after screening callers carefully, hot line workers place them in seven temporary safe houses, where youths can stay for seven weeks.[50]

A number of safe houses in St. Paul and Minneapolis, Minnesota, provide temporary placement for runaway youths with no place to go. The high rate of female and male prostitution in the Twin Cities, which are known as a national pipeline of prostitution, was a factor in the establishment of these houses. In addition to food and shelter, these programs also provide group and individual counseling.

Runaway centers contribute a great deal to youths who are receptive to these temporary placements. The centers provide runaways with food and shelter. Staff members furnish support and crisis counseling, and the larger runaway centers offer many helpful programs. Nevertheless, the impact of such centers on runaway youths is still minimal because they are considered undesirable places by most runaways and because the few centers in existence generally are located in large urban areas. To lessen the involvement of runaways in crime, increased family and community services are clearly needed for them.

ÉLAN

Élan, a therapeutic community for juveniles in Poland Springs, Maine, is a treatment program for substance abusers and predelinquents between the ages of twelve and twenty. Started in 1971 by Dr. Gerald Davidson, a psychiatrist, and Joe Ricci, a former drug addict, Élan has grown into a finely tuned million-dollar operation with twenty-five therapeutic staff members, seventeen educational staff members, forty support staff members, five houses, an accredited school, and one hundred forty residents.[51]

The program involves self-responsibility, intense peer pressure, self-disclosure, and hard physical and emotional work. This two-year program costs $38,765 for twelve months. Sixty members of its population in September 1995 were funded by parents and third-party insurance, fifty-five by school districts, and the remaining twenty-five by state agencies. About 60 to 70 percent of those who are admitted to this two-year program graduate or receive "diplomas." Of this number, an in-house evaluation found that about 80 percent have stayed out of trouble.[52]

Although there is little evidence that the majority of substance abuse programs for juveniles are any more successful than those for adults, it is clear that Élan is several notches above the average. Other noteworthy youth substance abuse programs are Rocky Mountain in Colorado; Provo Canyon in Utah; and Cascade, Cedu, and Hilltop in California.[53]

Yet critics regard these programs' confrontative environments with intense pressure from peers and staff members as coercive and brutal.[54] Other shortcomings are that few individuals can afford the cost of such programs and that they do not have the necessary beds available for the juveniles who need such a therapeutic experience.

TEEN COURTS

Teen courts, also known as youth courts, have become a widely used form of intervention for young, and usually first-time, offenders. An evaluation of teen courts, with 335 teen courts responding, which is more than 70 percent of the programs contacted, was performed in 1998.[55] See Figure 9–1 for a graph of the rise of teen courts across the nation.

More than two-thirds of the court programs that were surveyed indicated that they had existed for less than five years. Twenty percent had been operating for less than one year. Most of the courts had a small caseload with 48 percent indicating that they received fewer than one hundred referrals per year. Survey findings also revealed that United States teen courts handled about sixty-five thousand cases in 1998.[56]

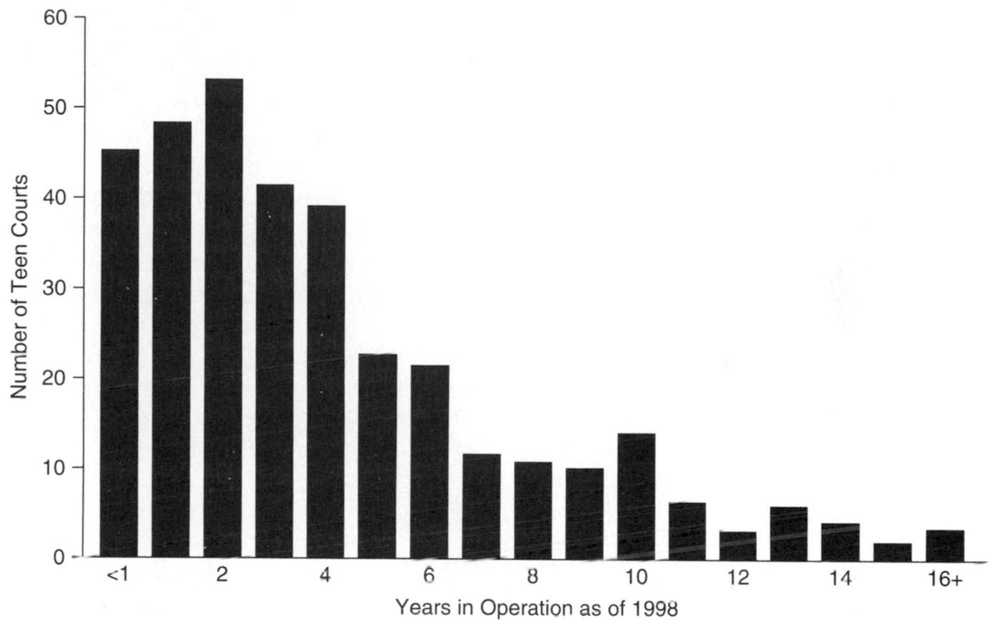

Figure 9–1 *Most Teen Courts Are Less Than Five Years Old.*

Source: Jeffrey Butts, Dean Hoffman, and Janeen Buck "Teen Courts in the United States: A Profile of Current Programs," *OJJDP Fact Sheet* (Washington, DC: Office of Juvenile Justice and Delinquency Prevention, 1999), p. 1.

Four possible case-processing models are used by these courts:

- *Adult judge.* An adult serves as judge and rules on legal terminology and courtroom procedures. Youth serve as attorneys, jurors, clerks, bailiffs, and so forth.
- *Youth judge.* This is similar to the adult judge model, except a youth serves as the judge.
- *Tribunal.* Youth attorneys present the case to a panel of three youth judges, who decide the appropriate disposition for the defendant. A jury is not used.
- *Peer jury.* This model does not use youth attorneys: the case is presented to a youth jury by a youth or adult. The youth jury then questions the defendant directly.[57]

Most courts surveyed indicated that they used only one of these case-processing models. Forty-seven percent used the adult judge model, 12 percent used the peer jury model, 10 percent used the tribunal model, and 9 percent used the youth judge model. The remaining 22 percent used more than one case-processing model.[58]

FOCUS ON OUTCOME 9–1

Early research on the effectiveness of teen courts suggests that they might well be more effective than traditional juvenile courts, at least in the short-term. The graph in Figure 9–2 shows that juveniles who go before teen courts have a recidivism rate of less than half that of youths who are processed traditionally. Only further longitudinal research will demonstrate whether the effects of teen courts are long-term.

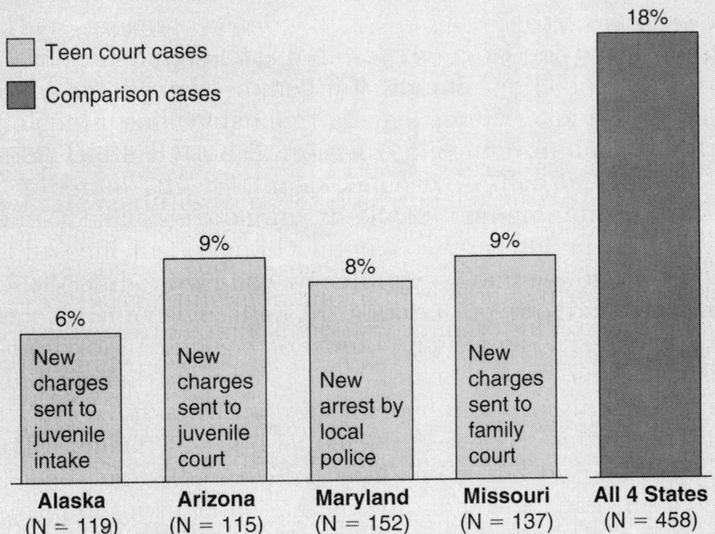

Figure 9–2 *What Happened to Youth Six Months Later?*

Source: Jeffrey A. Butts, Janeen Buck and Mark B. Coggeshall, "The Impact of Teen Court on Young Offenders," *Research Report*, The Urban Institute Justice Policy Center (Washington, DC: OJJDP, April 2002), Front Matter, Online under Teen Courts.

Teen courts usually handle first-time offenders who are charged with offenses such as theft, misdemeanor assault, disorderly conduct, and possession of alcohol. The majority of these teen courts (87 percent) reported that they rarely or never accepted any juveniles with prior arrest records. The most common disposition used by these courts is community service. Following this disposition in level of use are victim apology letters (86 percent), apology essays (79 percent), teen court jury duty (75 percent), drug/alcohol classes (59 percent), and monetary restitution (34 percent).[59] See Figure 9–2 for the offenses handled in teen court in 2000. See Focus on Outcome 9–1 for the results of some teen court programs.

The Juvenile Drug Court Movement

Currently, there are more than 244 drug court programs that are either underway or are being planned. Twenty-five of these programs are dedicated to juveniles. This juvenile court movement is part of the adult drug court movement that has been stimulated by Title V of the Violent Crime Control and Law Enforcement Act of 1994, an act that authorizes the Attorney General to make grants to various agencies to establish drug courts. These agencies include states, state and local courts, units of local government, and Indian tribal governments.[60]

A number of strategies are common to juvenile drug courts compared with traditional juvenile courts:

- Much earlier and much more comprehensive intake assessments
- Much greater focus on the functioning of the juvenile and the family throughout the juvenile court system
- Much closer integration of the information obtained during the assessment process as it relates to the juvenile and the family
- Much greater coordination among the court, the treatment community, the school system, and other community agencies in responding to the needs of the juvenile and the court
- Much more active and continuous judicial supervision of the juvenile's case and treatment process
- Increased use of immediate sanctions for noncompliance and incentives for progress for both the juvenile and the family[61]

Currently there are six states that operate juvenile drug courts, with the greatest activity in California (two programs) and Florida (four programs). For example, the Escambia County Juvenile Drug Court in Pensacola, Florida, began operating in April 1996. It is a twelve-month, three-phase approach to treating substance use and abuse. Phase I lasts about two months, Phase II lasts four months, and Phase III lasts six months. The drug court judge supervises treatment of up to forty offenders by reviewing reports from treatment personnel to determine the need for either positive or negative incentives to encourage participation and involvement.[62]

Juvenile Mediation Program

The purpose of these programs is for all involved parties to join together to resolve differences without court involvement. The Juvenile Mediation Program began in Brooke County and then spread to Hancock, Marshall, Ohio, Tyler, and Wetzel counties in West Virginia. The program works with school-age children and adolescents, ages six to eighteen, and their families or guardians.[63]

Status and nonviolent offenders from the aforementioned five counties are eligible to participate in this program. There is a mediator whose responsibilities include determining the sincerity of remorse from the accused juvenile, deciding a fair and just penalty for his or her wrongdoing, and concluding whether any services are necessary. Before proceeding into the mediation hearing the juvenile has admitted that he or she is guilty of a crime and sign a waiver of rights. This waiver relinquishes the rights of having witnesses or lawyers present.[64]

The program is designed to last no more than ninety days and is terminated under one of the following conditions: (1) successful: juveniles completed the required contractual agreement in ninety days; (2) unsuccessful: juveniles failed to meet the required agreement and are referred to the probation department for formal proceedings; and (3) dismissal: the mediator recommends dismissal prior to disposition. As of September 30, 2000, the rate of successful contract resolutions was 93 percent, or 625 of the first 670 participants. As of July 1, 2001, all 625 juveniles have remained delinquent and status offense-free.[65]

Gang Intervention Programs

Communities have a tendency to deny that they have gangs even when gang youths are causing considerable problems at school and in the neighborhood.[66] But when a dramatic incident takes place, such as the killing of an innocent victim or a drive-by shooting, this initial denial may give way to a process of using all available means to repress gangs.

Some communities across the nation have attempted a variety of means to divert gang youth from the juvenile and adult justice systems. For example, Paramount, California, developed the highly regarded Alternative to Gang Membership Program. In six years, only fifteen of the three thousand youths who participated in the antigang curriculum in school joined gangs. Moreover, more than 250 neighborhood meetings on gang awareness attracted twenty-five hundred parents. The city is proud of the fact that the $75,000 cost of the program is much *less* than putting one patrol car on the streets. Twelve other California communities have also adopted the Paramount plan.[67]

The fact of the matter is that although such approaches are promising, only an integrated, multidimensional, community-organized model is likely to have any long-term effect in preventing and diverting gang participation in the United States.

In sum, excited by the original vision of diversion, reformers promised that it would bring far-reaching changes in juvenile justice. But by the end of the 1970s, it became clear that the lack of funding, the hard-line mood toward crime, and the problems with implementation of the programs would make it difficult for diversion to survive, much less thrive. Although diversion has made some comeback in recent years, inadequate funding plagues diversion efforts; the political mood of the nation is still not overly receptive to diversion, and implementation problems have not been resolved.[68]

HOW DO DAY TREATMENT PROGRAMS OPERATE?

Day treatment programs, in which youngsters spend each day in the program and return home in the evenings, have been widely used in community-based juvenile corrections. These court-mandated programs are popular because they are more economical than residential placements—they do not need to provide living and sleeping quarters; they make parental participation easier; they require fewer staff members; and they are less coercive and punishment-oriented.

Nonresidential programs generally serve male juveniles, although California has operated two programs for girls and several coeducational ones. Nonresidential programs have been used widely by the California Treatment Project, the New York Division for Youth, and the Florida Division of Youth Services. Nonresidential programs in New York, which are called STAY, are similar to many other nonresidential programs in that they expose youths to a guided-group interaction experience.

Day treatment programs, similar to diversion programs, were used less in the 1980s and early 1990s than they were in the 1970s, but two of the most promising programs—the Associated Marine Institute (AMI) and Project New Pride—continue to thrive.

Camp counselors for the Washington, PA Leader Program prepare to take their youths on a rafting trip as part of their day treatment assignment. (Photo by Tony Hood.)

Associated Marine Institute

The Associated Marine Institute is a privately operated program funded jointly by state and private donations. The AMI tailors its programs to the geographical strengths of each community, using the ocean, wilderness, rivers, and lakes to stimulate productive behavior in youths referred by the courts or by the Division of Youth Services. Of the forty schools and institutes of the AMI, twenty-five are nonresidential. The fourteen- to eighteen-year-old male and female trainees in the nonresidential programs live at home or in foster homes.[69]

The marine institutes, which constitute most of the schools, set individual goals for the training period in a dozen categories, including diving, ship-handling skills, ocean science, lifesaving, first aid, and such electives as photography and marine maintenance. The most popular incentive for the youths is to earn official certification as a scuba diver. Other incentives designed to maintain enthusiasm are certificates awarded for short-term achievement in first aid, ship-handling skills, and diving; trophies for trainees of the month; and field trips to the Bahamas or the Florida Keys.[70]

The AMI has three main ingredients. First, it has a strong commitment to meaningful work. Regarding work as one of the most beneficial forms of therapy, it teaches that nothing worthwhile is achieved without hard work. Second, academic success is emphasized. The intent of the AMI programs is to motivate students and to give them the right tools and opportunities to succeed in school. Students are encouraged to take their GED exam and then attend vocational school, community college, or a four-year college. Third, modeling is emphasized throughout this experience because it is believed that what staff do is more important than what they say. An apt expression of the AMI's philosophy on modeling is this: Tell me, I'll forget. Show me, I may remember. Involve me, I'll be committed.[71] Focus on Practice 9–2 communicates the basic values of the AMI.

In September 1993, Attorney General Janet Reno and President Bill Clinton visited the Pinellas Marine Institute in St. Petersburg, Florida. In a nationally broadcast television program in which he announced his crime bill, the president said, "These [AMI] programs are giving young people a chance to take their future back, a chance to understand that there is good inside them."[72]

Clearly, the AMI programs provide interesting activities and teach worthwhile skills to youths. For those who can qualify, these programs certainly are more preferable than placements in residential settings in the community or in long-term juvenile correctional institutions. Yet such programs are expensive, tend to be limited to certain parts of the country, and appear to be more suited to minor than serious offenders.

Project New Pride

A community program that offers services to youths who have committed serious offenses is Project New Pride in Denver, Colorado. Most of the young-

FOCUS ON PRACTICE 9–2

AMI VALUES

Integrity: Doing what we say, when we said we would do it, or notifying the other party in advance.

Safety: Creation of the environment where staff and students can function free from hazard and injury.

Honesty: Dealing with everyone who comes in contact with us in an upright and truthful fashion.

Enthusiasm: Operating with a strong inspirational display of excitement and commitment to the mission and goals of AMI.

Leadership: Using others in pursuit of common goals.

"Kids First": All key decisions are made on the basis of what's best for the students in the program. All other priorities relate to this value.

Excellence: Our goal is to be the best. Our promise is to pursue any strategy that might improve service.

Loyalty: Our company is operated in such a way that no one should be asked to compromise on ethical issues. On all other issues, each employee has two obligations: (1) to make every effort to communicate pertinent facts and opinions, and (2) to implement the final decision with enthusiasm and commitment.

Dedication: A commitment to making all decisions in the best interest of the youths we serve.

Creativity: Each employee strives to create an environment which fosters new ideas and champions them to make those ideas reality, with the goal of providing the safest, most effective service possible.

Family: Creation of an environment that provides warmth, discipline and empowerment for student and staff.

Goal Orientation: We are a result-oriented organization that believes in setting goals and pursuing the most direct and effective paths to achieving those goals.

Source: Memo circulated throughout the schools and institutes of the AMI and revised July 19, 1995.

Critical Thinking Questions:
What is your evaluation of these goals? How difficult would it be to actually obtain these goals?

sters involved in the project, which has been designated as an exemplary project by LEAA, are African Americans or Mexican Americans. Each youth receives intensive services in the program for the first three months and then continues treatment geared to individual needs and interests for a nine-month follow-up period. Academic education, counseling, employment, and cultural education are the four main areas of service provided in Project New Pride. For education, youths are assigned to classes in either the New Pride Alternative School or the Learning Disabilities Center. The goal of the counseling, which tries to match specific counselors and clients, is to enhance a youth's self-image and to help him or her cope with the environment. Job preparation is heavily emphasized; youths attend a job-skills workshop and then receive on-the-job training. The purpose of cultural education is to expose youths to a range of experiences and activities in the Denver area.[73]

Project New Pride has established four primary goals in working with its difficult clientele: (1) reduction of recidivism, (2) job placement, (3) school reintegration, and (4) remediation of academic and learning disabilities. The project has had some success in achieving the first three of these goals, but less success on educational remediation. The success of this project also has been demonstrated by its replication in Boston; Chicago; Fresno, California; Haddonfield, New Jersey; Kansas City, Missouri; Los Angeles; San Francisco; Pensacola, Florida; Providence, Rhode Island, and Washington, DC.[74]

The New Pride Replication Program, which examined the recidivism of the ten replication programs, was conducted from 1980 to 1984. It began with a six-month intensive phase involving daily or nearly daily contacts with each program participant, followed by six months of decreasing involvements. The study found that "essentially no significant recidivism differences (e.g., new petitions and readjudications) existed between New Pride youths and their fairly well-matched site-by-site comparisons, after an average of 2.6 years follow-up from program entry."[75]

In sum, although there is no question that nonresidential programs play a much smaller role in community-based corrections than they did a decade or two ago, these programs appear to be a preferred way of handling minor youthful offenders. They are more economical, more humane (as they permit the juvenile to live at home), and less coercive and punishment oriented than are residential facilities. But the conflicting findings on their success with hard-core offenders make them a somewhat questionable placement for the serious juvenile delinquent. Some juvenile recidivists seem to require more secure placements to gain control over themselves and their antisocial behaviors.

HOW DO GROUP HOMES OPERATE?

The group home, the group residence, and the group foster home are all used in juvenile corrections in this country. The term **group home** generally refers to a single dwelling owned or rented by an organization or agency for the purpose of housing offenders. Although it is not part of an institutional campus, this facility provides care for a group of about four to twelve children, and staff are viewed as houseparents or counselors rather than as foster parents. The administrative, supervisory, and service responsibility for the group home rests with the parent agency or organization. Usually indistinguishable from nearby homes or apartments, the group home reaches out to the community for resources and service.

The terms *group residence* or *halfway house* are used in some parts of the country to identify a small facility serving about thirteen to thirty-five youths. It usually houses two or more groups of youths, each with its own child-care staff. This residence tends to use agency rather than community services, and its architecture and large size differentiate it from nearby homes and apartments.

Group homes fulfill several purposes in juvenile corrections. First, they provide an alternative to institutionalization. Dependent, neglected, and other noncriminal youths, especially, are referred to them. Second, group homes may be used as short-term residences. The communities in which they are located provide the youths with the resources to deal with such problems as family conflict, school difficulties, and peer interactions. Third, group homes can be used either as a "halfway in" setting for offenders who are having difficulty keeping to the conditions of probation or as a "halfway out" setting for juvenile offenders who are returning to the community but do not have adequate home placement.

Group home programs tend to vary from home to home because they have been developed to meet varying needs for different populations and communities and standard guidelines do not exist. Consequently, group homes often reflect the personal philosophies of their founders or directors. Intake criteria, length of stay, treatment goals, target population serviced, quantity and quality of staffing, services offered, physical facilities, location in relation to the rest of the city, and house rules are extremely diverse in group homes in this country. This diversity need not be a problem, however, if additional support services are available. One of the most important studies in juvenile justice found a significant reduction in recidivisim in Massachusetts when community-based programs had an integrated network of services.[76]

Many group homes are treatment oriented. Group therapy often is used as a treatment modality. These group sessions are largely supportive; they do not probe very deeply, and discussion usually is limited to problems as they arise. Guided Group Interaction (GGI) is probably the most popular treatment method; the members of the group are expected to support, confront, and be honest with one another so that they may be helped in dealing with their own problems. The role of the therapist in GGI is to help the members develop a more positive and prosocial group culture. Some group homes deliberately avoid a comfortable climate, and staff may even try to arouse anxiety. The treatment philosophy behind this is that without a relaxed atmosphere, youths are more likely to become unsettled and thereby more receptive to personality change.

The teaching-family group home concept was developed in 1967 with the establishment of the Achievement Place group home in Lawrence, Kansas. In the 1970s, the teaching-family model was used in more than forty homes in twelve states.[77] Group foster homes also shelter youthful offenders. These homes sometimes are effective for youngsters who are unable to tolerate a close one-on-one relationship with foster parents. Group-care foster homes have become increasingly popular in the Midwest, chiefly in Iowa, Michigan, Minnesota, Ohio, and Wisconsin.

Florida has developed a fairly extensive network of group homes. Of the seventeen community-based treatment centers serving four hundred youngsters, nine are halfway houses, or group homes, developed on the Criswell House model. The first Criswell House in Florida was established in 1958; it housed twenty-five youths on probation and parole and used guided group interaction.[78] In addition to these larger halfway houses, Florida has three START centers—small group homes located in rural settings with their own schools on the grounds—and five group homes for emotionally disturbed children, administered by husband-and-wife teams.

The Dynamic Action Residence Enterprise (DARE) program in Massachusetts is another widely used group home model. Established in 1964, this program currently has ten specialized programs and nine group homes, four foster home programs, two residential schools, shelter care programs, and an intensive-care high-security facility.[79]

Yet the innovative programs still are not typical of group homes across the nation. In too many group homes, vacancies are hard to find and there may even be a long waiting list. Staff are notoriously underpaid, believe that they have not been properly trained, and have high rates of turnover.[80] See Focus on Careers 9–3 for a staff member's perspective on working in a group home. Residents also typically have longer stays than they would have in training schools, and this raises real questions about whether group homes are a less punitive placement than juvenile institutions are. The evaluations of residential programs further make it difficult to support the conclusion that residential programs in the community result in lower rates of recidivism than do institutional programs. Nevertheless, a convincing case can be made that residential programs are at least as successful as training schools, at far less trauma to youths and usually at less cost to the state.

WHAT ARE WILDERNESS PROGRAMS?

Outward Bound and VisionQuest are the two best known wilderness, or survival, programs. All of these outdoor **wilderness programs,** whether they take place in the mountains, the canoe country, the forest, the sea, or the desert, conclude that the "overcoming of a seemingly impossible task" is one of the best means to gain self-reliance, to prove one's worth, and to define oneself as a person.

OUTWARD BOUND

Outward Bound programs were first used in England during World War II. The first Outward Bound school in the United States was the Colorado Outward

FOCUS ON CAREERS 9–3

A STAFF MEMBER'S PERSPECTIVE ON A GROUP HOME

It seems to me that the two most important considerations of the child care worker's job are to work effectively with residents and to develop a good relationship with staff.

There are a number of characteristics that we must possess as effective child care workers. First, we must have the respect of residents. We earn residents' respect by demonstrating confidence in our ability to handle the situations we face every day. We earn residents' respect by refusing to be intimidated and by not allowing them to give us verbal abuse. We earn their respect by being wise to the games they play and not permitting them to manipulate us. We earn their respect when we are fair and consistent in dealing with them. Finally, we earn their respect when holding them accountable for their behavior.

Second, in order to be an effective child care worker, you must have your own "stuff" together. What this means is that we cannot be on the job to fulfill our own needs; we must be there to help residents fulfill their needs and become responsible in their behaviors. Workers who are insecure, who have too great a need to be liked, or who have to rescue residents, will not last.

Third, the best child care workers are perceptive, sensitive, patient, and compassionate. They have the ability to read the residents and to see through the "fronting" or putting on an act. They seem to operate on a gut feeling level and are continually able to sense what is really going on with residents. They are patient with the struggles of residents. They know that it has taken 16 years or so for residents to develop their problems, and they are not likely to change overnight. They are caring individuals and are able to communicate this caring to their charges.

Another part of being an effective child care worker is developing a good relationship with other staff. A good relationship is based on respect. You earn the respect of other staff members the same way that you earn the respect of residents. Workers despise weak coworkers as much as, if not more than, residents despise weak staff. It is necessary to pick up the "slack" caused by weak coworkers as well as to deal with the frequent problems they create.

A good relationship with other staff is harmed when a staff member does not follow through with enforcing the rules or confronting residents' behaviors. This is particularly seen with those who have the need to be rescuers. Rescuers typically minimize behaviors and allow excuses for behaviors. They turn their backs on rule violations and don't follow through on consequences given by others. If there is a rescuer in the chain of workers, the residents will use this weak link to their advantage.

It is also hard to work with those who are inconsistent, especially when it is intentional. Staff members sometimes have a secret agenda, which refers to a coworker attempting to obtain goals other than those developed by the team or agency. This can also occur when a coworker attempts to reach established goals in a different manner than what was developed by the team.

Another problem with coworkers results from a staff member who is able to function only when things are black and white and is unable to deal with grey areas. If these coworkers are confronted with a problem for which there is no specific rule, they are lost and do not know what to do. When you remember that a great deal of the problems we face lie in the grey areas where there are no specific rules, it becomes clear why such staff members create the problems they do.

A final coworker problem is caused by supervisors who either are out of touch with the residents or do not accept the input of child care workers who are in direct contact with residents and know them the best. These supervisors then make poor policy and treatment decisions. This creates alienation, lowers morale, and simply makes the job so much harder.

Source: Robert A. Quirk supplied this statement for this volume. For several years, he was a staff member in a large group home for status offenders and delinquents operated by a private agency.

Critical Thinking Questions:

Based on Robert Quirk's statements, what do you think he likes about his job? What do you think is most frustrating for him? Does a job in a juvenile residential program sound attractive to you as a career option?

Bound School, which was established in 1962 and accepted its first delinquents in 1964. This program, situated in the Rocky Mountains at the altitude of eighty-eight hundred feet, consists of mountain walking, backpacking, high-altitude camping, solo survival, rappelling, and rock climbing. Other Outward Bound programs soon followed in Maine, Minnesota, North Carolina, Oregon, and Texas. A similar program, a Homeward Bound school, was opened in 1970 in Massachusetts. Several community-based wilderness programs that begin and end in the community but include sessions in a nearby wilderness area are also in operation.[81]

Outward Bound schools and other adventure-centered programs have used the challenge of wilderness training to develop a successful experience. This wilderness experience, lasting approximately three weeks, has four phases: training in basic skills, a long expedition, solo, and a final testing period. The skills necessary to survive and travel in a wilderness environment are taught in basic training. Today, more than one thousand Outward Bound programs or their variations are found throughout the United States.[82]

The most important staff member in Outward Bound is the person who works directly with youths. These counselors literally have the lives of youths in their hands; several youths, in fact, have lost their lives in Outward Bound programs. Enrollees may be experts on how to survive in the streets, but they are usually experiencing a new and frightening world in the wilderness. Participants must be motivated to give their best, supported while they are struggling with the difficulty and fear of the tasks, and responded to with praise and reinforcement when they successfully complete each experience. The job of the counselor is to make certain that the program is a successful experience for as many as possible. He or she has to be a master psychologist, knowing how to push and when to quit. He or she must be able to encourage those who are ready to drop out and to alert those whose carelessness may cost them their own lives or the lives of others.

John Calhoun, former commissioner of youth services in Massachusetts, is positive about this wilderness experience, which is called Homeward Bound in his state:

> That's done well; we love it. It probably is the single most consistently effective program we have. The problem is a kid comes back on his twenty-seventh day on a high, having battered the elements for his last solo. Then, he hits the hard streets. It's a magnificent temporary program, but where we have failed in that program is in the aftercare. These kids feel they're world beaters when they [get] back to the grim reality of the projects. What we have to figure out is how to support that wondrous high.[83]

Francis J. Kelly and Daniel J. Baer presented the results of a two-year demonstration project conducted by the Massachusetts Department of Youth Services that involved sixty boys who attended Outward Bound schools and sixty boys who were treated routinely by juvenile corrections authorities. Effectiveness was measured primarily by comparing the recidivism rates between the two matched groups twelve months after parole. Recidivism among the experimental group was much lower after the first year: 42 percent of the control group had failed, compared to 20 percent of the experimental group. But the differences between the two groups had nearly disappeared after five years.[84]

Kelly and Baer's evaluation of the Homeward Bound program, along with Calhoun's statement, appears to evaluate accurately the effectiveness of wilderness survival programs; the programs have an initial positive impact on youths, which wears off as youths return to their home environments. Effective aftercare services for those youths who have participated in Outward Bound programs are clearly needed.

VisionQuest

VisionQuest, another survival program, is much more controversial than is Outward or Homeward Bound. Started by Robert Ledger Burton in 1973 in Tucson, Arizona, this program presently has 250 staff members and 250 youngsters enrolled from ten states. The wide variety of programs includes wilderness training, a mule and horse wagon train, alternative school, nine group homes, and a home-based counseling program. This rigorous twelve-to-eighteen-month program requires that a youth complete two "high-impact" activities, such as wilderness training, a sea survival experience, or the mule and horse wagon train. The wagon train, which travels from coast to coast, has been featured in a CBS television documentary, a *Life* magazine pictorial article, and countless newspaper articles across the nation.[85]

Peter W. Greenwood and Susan Turner's examination of the effectiveness of VisionQuest on youths assigned to it by the San Diego Juvenile Court found that the probation department strongly opposed placement to this program. Among the probation department's criticisms were that VisionQuest placed youths in potentially dangerous activities; that it resisted interference by probation staff; that it insisted on determining when youths would be released from the program; and that it handled youths in abusive ways. Indeed, probation staff filed child abuse charges, none of which led to further legal action.[86]

ARE COMMUNITY-BASED PROGRAMS EFFECTIVE?

It would appear that improving the effectiveness of community-based corrections ultimately requires some positive gains in breaking down community resistance, in obtaining greater citizen involvement in community-based programs, and in developing a broader continuum of services in the community for juveniles who need such services.

First, to break down community resistance and to obtain greater citizen involvement in community-based programs, departments of juvenile corrections must develop and implement a certain plan of action. This plan needs to include a well-developed plan for the establishment of programs and for deciding who will be placed in community facilities. Unfortunately, no agreement has been reached on how to implement either of these strategies.

Careful planning is obviously necessary to gain greater public support for community-based programs. A department should mount a massive public education effort through the communications media, should seek support for the project from the various subcommunities of the community—ethnic, racial, and special interest groups—and should develop a sophisticated understanding of the decision-making processes in society. But should this be done before or after a program has been initiated in the community?

Advocates of keeping the community informed as soon as a site for a program is chosen, claim that to do otherwise is dishonest. Opponents of this approach argue that advance information will permit the community to mobilize resistance against the proposed community program. They claim that the community is more likely to accept an already established and successful program than one that exists only on the drawing board.

Widespread controversy also exists over the selection of youths to be placed in community-based programs. One approach is conservative: If the wrong youth is put in the wrong place at the wrong time and commits a serious or violent crime, such as rape or murder, the adverse publicity may destroy the best planned and implemented program. Therefore, to preserve the viability of community-based programs, only juveniles most likely to be helped should be kept in the community. The opposite approach argues that all but the hard-core recidivist should be retained in the community, for it is there that the youth's problems began in the first place. Advocates of this position believe that institutionalization will only make more serious criminals out of confined youths. Some of these supporters even propose leaving many of the hard-core or difficult-to-handle youths in the community.

Second, improving the continuum of services for juveniles in a community usually requires a strong deinstitutionalization emphasis. The programs that have this integration of services are more likely to have positive effects on youthful offenders assigned to them. Another advantage of these continuum-of-service programs is that they are not as likely to experience fragmentation and duplication of services that is found so frequently in other programs in the juvenile justice system.

SUMMARY

Advocated by national commissions, supported by reintegrative philosophy, and funded largely by federal grants, community programs for juveniles expanded to include an impressive variety of situations during the 1970s and 1980s. Some proponents of community-based programs for juveniles even advocated dealing with all youthful offenders within the community and closing all training schools.

The evidence of the effectiveness of these programs is conflicting. Even in studies that have found lower recidivism rates for youths left in the community, the criticism is often made that juveniles who were more likely to succeed were selected for the experimental group and the authorities altered the results by giving the experimentals more chances than controls before returning them to the juvenile court. Thus, it is very difficult to substantiate the widespread conclusion that community-based programs lower the recidivism rate. But a very good case can be made for the assumption that community-based corrections programs are at least as successful as institutional confinement is, with far less trauma to youngsters and less cost to the state. If three weeks in a wilderness program, for example, is as effective as months or even years of confinement in training schools, then it would make sense for society to place a major emphasis on community-based corrections when establishing social policy and planning.

Community-based programs continue to face several challenges, especially those posed by the demise of federal funding and the public's preference for getting tough on youth crime. Yet the cost effectiveness of these programs as opposed to the prohibitive expense of long-term institutions should lead to an increased use of alternative programs.

WEB SITES OF INTEREST

To find many links on various kinds of prevention programs, go to
http://www.criminology.fsu.edu/jjclearinghouse/jj19.html

Links to community-based programs can be found at
http://www.criminology.fsu.edu/jjclearinghouse/jj27.html

Vision Quest 2002: http://www.vqconference.com/

Outward Bound: http://www.outwardbound.org/

Associated Marine Institutes: www.amikids.org/

CRITICAL THINKING QUESTIONS

1. Why have delinquency prevention programs generally been so ineffective?
2. Why is the net widening criticism of many of these programs a serious indictment?
3. Of the programs discussed in this chapter, which do you feel is the most ideal for helping offenders reintegrate into the community?
4. What specific strategies can departments of juvenile corrections pursue to enlist greater support from the community for community programs?
5. What are the main types of residential and nonresidential programs for juvenile delinquents?
6. How effective are community-based corrections? What is the essential link in increasing the effectiveness of community-based corrections?

NOTES

1. Interview with a director of court services in 1978.
2. See Jerome G. Miller, *Last One over the Wall: The Massachusetts Experiment in Closing Reform Schools* (Columbus: Ohio State University Press, 1991).
3. Statement by Governor Sargent, quoted in *Corrections Magazine* 2 (November–December 1975), 30–31.
4. National Advisory Commission on Criminal Justice Standards and Goals, *Corrections* (Washington, DC: Government Printing Office, 1973), 360.
5. Barry Krisberg, James Austin, and Patricia A. Steele, *Unlocking Juvenile Corrections: Evaluating the Massachusetts Department of Youth Services* (San Francisco: National Council on Crime and Delinquency, 1989).
6. Willie T. Barney contributed this material on privatization to this volume. He is a high school guidance counselor who has worked in the private sector with youthful offenders.
7. Kristgen Krackle, *SafeFutures: Partnership to Reduce Youth Violence and Delinquency* (Washington, DC: Office of Juvenile Justice and Delinquency Prevention, 1996), 1.

8. Robin Hamilton and Kay McKinney, "Job Training for Juveniles: Project CRAFT," *OJJDP Fact Sheet* (Washington DC.: Office of Juvenile Justice and Delinquency Prevention, 1999), 1.
9. For an expanded treatment of delinquency prevention, see Clemens Bartollas, *Juvenile Delinquency,* 4th ed. (Boston: Allyn & Bacon, 1997), 524–51.
10. Anne M. Newton, "Prevention of Crime and Delinquency," *Criminal Justice Abstracts* (June 1978), 4.
11. Marylyn Bibb, "Gang-Related Services of Mobilization for Youth," in *Juvenile Gangs in Context: Theory, Research, and Action,* edited by Malcolm W. Klein (Upper Saddle River, NJ: Prentice Hall, 1967), 175–182.
12. For a description and evaluation of "Scared Straight," see James O. Finckenauer, *Scared Straight! and the Panacea Phenomenon* (Upper Saddle River NJ: Prentice Hall, 1982).
13. For a description of the various prevention programs, see Clemens Bartollas, *Juvenile Delinquency,* 4th ed. (Boston: Allyn & Bacon, 1997), 521–51.
14. For a review of these studies examining the effectiveness of prevention programs, see Ibid., 524.
15. The following description of the Chicago Area Projects is largely derived from Harold Finestone, *Victims of Change: Juvenile Delinquents in American Society* (Westport, CT: Greenwood Press, 1976), 125–130. For more recent evaluations of the Chicago Area Projects, see Steven Schlossman and Michael Sedlak, "The Chicago Area Projects Revisited," *Crime and Delinquency* (July 1983), 398–460; and Steven Schlossman, Gail Zellman, and Richard Shavelson, *Delinquency Prevention in South Chicago: A Fifty-Year Assessment of the Chicago Area Project* (Santa Monica, CA: Rand, 1984).
16. A book describing the organization and goals of the Chicago Area Projects on the Near West Side by one of these local leaders is Anthony Sorrentino's *Organizing Against Crime* (New York: Human Sciences Press, 1977).
17. For the best evaluation of the Chicago Area Projects, see Solomon Kobrin, "The Chicago Area Projects—A Twenty-Five-Year Assessment," *Annals of the American Academy of Political and Social Sciences* 322 (March 1959), 20–29.
18. Schlossman et al., *Delinquency Prevention in South Chicago,* v.
19. Kobrin, "The Chicago Area Projects—A Twenty-Five-Year Assessment," 23.
20. Jon Snodgrass, "Clifford Shaw and Henry D. McKay," in *Delinquency, Crime, and Society,* edited by James F. Short Jr. (Chicago: University of Chicago Press, 1976), 16. See also Jon Snodgrass, *The American Criminological Tradition: Portraits of the Men and Ideology in a Discipline.* Ph.D. dissertation, University of Pennsylvania, 1972.
21. Cited in Jeremy Travis, "Communities and Criminal Justice: A Powerful Alignment," *National Institute of Justice Journal* (August 1996), 2.
22. For these same emphases, see the table of contents of Ibid.

23. Greg Parks, "The High/Scope Perry Preschool Project." *Juvenile Justice Bulletin* (Washington, DC: Office of Juvenile Justice and Delinquency Prevention, 2000), 1–2.
24. Ibid.
25. Ibid.
26. Catherine H. Conley, *Street Gangs: Current Knowledge and Strategies* (Washington, DC: U.S. Department of Justice, 1993), 37–38.
27. Ibid., 60.
28. Susan Hlesciak Hall and Anne Henderson, "The Comer Process: Bonding to Family and School," *Community Education Journal* (Fall 1990), 22.
29. Conley, *Street Gangs*, 37.
30. Ibid., 38.
31. See Gary D. Gottfredson, *A Workbook for Your School Improvement Program* (Baltimore: Johns Hopkins University Press, 1988).
32. Results reported in "School Development and Management," Chapter 5 *Communities that Care: Action for Drug Abuse Prevention. A Guide for Community Leaders* (March 5, 1991), 101.
33. G. R. Patterson, "Children Who Steal," in *Understanding Crime: Current Theory and Research*, edited by Travis Hirschi and Michael Gottfredson (Beverly Hills, CA: Sage, 1980), 114.
34. J. G. Dryfoos, *Adolescents at Risk: Prevalence and Prevention* (1990), 133.
35. Ibid., 133.
36. D. Hawkins, R. Catalano, G. Jones, and D. Fine, "Delinquency Prevention through Parent Training: Results and Issues from Work in Progress," *In Children to Citizens: Families, Schools, and Deliquency Prevention*, Vol. 3, edited by J. Wilson and G. Loury (New York: Springer-Verlag, 1987), 186–204.
37. Ibid., 2.
38. James C. Howell, ed., *Guide for Implementing the Comprehensive Strategy for Serious, Violent, and Chronic Juvenile Offenders* (Washington, DC: Office of Juvenile Justice and Delinquency Prevention, 1995), 10.
39. Ibid., 3.
40. Ibid., 5.
41. Ibid.
42. Ibid., 9–10.
43. Ibid., 11.
44. Kathleen Collbaugh and Cynthia J. Hansel, "The Comprehensive Strategy: Lessons Learned From the Pilot Sites," *Juvenile Justice Bulletin* 2000, 1.
45. Ibid., 10.
46. Sherwood Norman, *Youth Service Bureau: A Key to Prevention* (Paramus, NJ: National Council on Crime and Delinquency, 1972), 12–13.
47. Interviewed in October 1981.

48. Tim Brennan, David Huizinga, and Delbert S. Elliott, *The Social Psychology of Runaways* (Lexington, MA: D. C. Heath, 1978).
49. U.S. Senate Subcommittee on the Constitution of the Committee on the Judiciary, *Homeless Youth: The Saga of "Pushouts" and "Throwaways" in America,* 96th Cong., 1980, 36.
50. Ibid., 35–44.
51. For the early history of Élan, see Philip B. Taft Jr., "Élan: Does Its Bizaare Regimen Transform Troubled Youth or Abuse Them?" *Corrections Magazine* 5 (March 1979), 18–28. The recent materials on Élan were contributed by Deanna Atkinson, an administrator in the Élan program, in a September 1995 phone conversation with one of the authors.
52. Atkinson's phone conversation.
53. Ibid.
54. See Taft, "Élan: Does Its Bizarre Regimen Transform Troubled Youth or Abuse Them?"
55. Survey results are found in Jeffrey Butts, Dean Hoffman, and Jancen Buck "Teen Courts in the United States: A Profile of Current Programs," *OJJDP Fact Sheet* (Washington, DC: Office of Juvenile Justice and Delinquency Prevention, 1999).
56. Ibid., 1.
57. T. M. Godwin, *Peer Justice and Youth Empowerment: An Implementation Guide for Teen Court Programs* (Lexington, KY: American Probation and Parole Association, 1998).
58. Butts, Hoffman, and Buck, "Teen Courts in the United States," 1.
59. Ibid., 2.
60. Marilyn Roberts, Jennifer Brophy, and Caroline Cooper, *The Juvenile Drug Court Movement* (Washington, DC: Office of the Juvenile Justice and Delinquency Prevention, 1997), 1.
61. Ibid., 1–2.
62. Ibid., 2.
63. Robert R. Smith and Victor S. Lombardo, "Evaluation Report of the Juvenile Mediation Program *Corrections and Comprendium* (Laurel, MD: American Correctional Association, 2001), 1.
64. Ibid., 2.
65. Ibid., 21.
66. See C. Ronald Huff, "Youth Gangs and Public Policy," *Crime and Delinquency* 35 (October 1989), 524–537.
67. Elaine S. Knapp, *Embattled Youth: Kids, Gangs, and Drugs* (Chicago: Council of State Governments, 1988), 14.
68. Stanley Cohen, *Vision of Social Control: Crime, Punishment and Classification* (Cambridge, England: Policy Press, 1985), 93.

69. Information on the Associated Marine Institute was supplied in a 1995 phone conversation with Magie Valdés.
70. Ibid. See also Ronald H. Bailey, "Can Delinquents Be Saved by the Sea?" *Corrections Magazine* 1 (September 1974), 77–84.
71. "The Programs of the Associated Marine Institute." Mimeographed, n.d.
72. Unpublished mimeographed statement circulated by AMI, n.d.
73. S. E. Lawrence and B. R. West, *National Evaluation of the New Pride Replication Program: Final Report,* Vol. 1 (Lafayette, CA: Pacific Institute for Research and Evaluation, 1985).
74. Ibid.
75. Ted Palmer, *The Re-Emergence of Correctional Intervention* (Newbury Park, CA: Sage Publications, 1992), 84.
76. Krisberg, Austin, and Steele, *Unlocking Juvenile Corrections.*
77. D. L. Fixsen, E. L. Phillips, and M. M. Wolf, "The Teaching Family Model of Group Home Treatment," in *Closing Correctional Institutions,* edited by Yitzhak Bakal (Lexington, MA: D. C. Heath, 1973).
78. For the early history of Criswell House, see Ronald H. Bailey, "Florida," *Corrections Magazine* 1 (September 1974), 66.
79. Information from Dynamic Action Residence Enterprise (DARE), Jamaica Plain, MA, n.d.
80. One of the authors has had a number of former students who were employed in group homes, and they consistently make these criticisms.
81. Joshua L. Miner and Joe Boldt, *Outward Bound USA: Learning Through Experience* (New York: Morrow, 1981).
82. For recent examinations of Outward Bound–type programs, see Steven Flagg Scott, "Outward Bound: An Adjunct to the Treatment of Juvenile Delinquents: Florida's STEP Program," *New Engand Journal on Criminal and Civil Confinement* 11 (1985), 420–36; and Thomas C. Castellano and Irina R. Solderstrom, "Wilderness Challenges and Recidivism: A Program Evaluation." Paper presented at the annual meeting of the American Society of Criminology, Baltimore, Maryland (November 1990).
83. Interviewed in June 1978.
84. Cited in Joseph Nold and Mary Wilpers, "Wilderness Training as an Alternative to Incarceration," in *A Nation Without Prisons,* edited by Calvert R. Dodge (Lexington, MA: D. C. Heath, 1975), 157–58.
85. Paul Sweeney, "VisionQuest's Rites of Passage," *Corrections Magazine* 8 (February 1982), 22–32.
86. Peter W. Greenwood and Susan Turner, *The VisionQuest Program: An Evaluation* (Santa Monica, CA: Rand, 1987).

10

JUVENILE AFTERCARE

OBJECTIVES

1. To define juvenile aftercare and explain how it works
2. To examine why so many youths fail on aftercare
3. To discuss the role of the aftercare officer
4. To suggest means by which aftercare can be improved

KEY TERMS

aftercare
determinate parole
intensive supervision programs
interstate compact
parole
predictor items
presumptive minimum
reentry programs

An institution isn't a real life situation. Youths become dependent upon someone making decisions for them and caring for them. They become really dependent upon institutions. A lot of these kids have been to each of the local institutions. The system doesn't know what to do with them. They push them from institution to institution until they're eighteen. Then, they're on their own after having people always telling them what to do. This means that they've to make their own decisions. That's tough!

—Juvenile Probation Officer[1]

Release is the prime goal of a confined youth. The days, weeks, months, and sometimes years spent in confinement are occupied by thoughts and fantasies of release or even escape. For many youths, these thoughts and desires become all-consuming passions and govern every action. Youths who have been intractable become compliant, the weak feign strength, the ill pretend health, and the worst become the best. Every action becomes a show for the benefit of those who can expedite release—the staff, social workers, teachers, chaplains, and others. In the opening quote, a Midwestern juvenile probation officer, who also supervises youth on aftercare, gives her version of why the failure rate is high on aftercare.

The entire juvenile justice system is focused on release. Staff are responsible for guiding residents throughout their confinement. Punishment, educational and vocational training, and rehabilitative techniques are used in an effort to guarantee that a resident's return to the community will be permanent and positive. Understandably, too, staff may become emotionally involved with a particular youth, and they are concerned about what will happen once he or she "hits the streets." Administrators, too, are concerned because they know that they and their decision-making processes will come under fire if the youth turns to any type of crime after he or she is released. The parole officer or aftercare specialist is also concerned about whether or not this youth will create problems or will embarrass him. Needless to say, members of a youth's home community are also concerned, for they want a guarantee that the juvenile who is returning will be a law-abiding citizen. But, paradoxically, in spite of the tremendous concern exhibited by all those affected by parole and by aftercare personnel, little has been done in the corrections field to guarantee the desired outcome.

This chapter, then, considers juvenile aftercare, the final episode in the correctional endeavor. Beginning with a definition and a discussion of the release process and considering it from the perspectives of resident, staff, and society, the chapter reviews the problems and opportunities facing the youth on aftercare status, the aftercare officer, and society once a youth is released. General operational problems are considered, and, finally, the issue of improving aftercare is discussed.

WHAT IS THE DEFINITION AND SCOPE OF JUVENILE AFTERCARE?

Juvenile aftercare is concerned with the release and the supervision of a juvenile who has been committed to a public or private training school. Ideally, many factors contribute to a successful adjustment to the community. These are examined later, but first, the history of juvenile aftercare is discussed briefly.

HISTORY OF AFTERCARE

Juvenile aftercare is as old as the juvenile institution. Superintendents of the early houses of refuge had the authority to release youths when they saw fit. Some youths were returned directly to their families; others were placed in the community as indentured servants and apprentices. After such service, they were released from their obligations and reentered the community as free citizens. For some, placement amounted to little more than slavery. They were sent to stores, factories, or farms that needed cheap labor. For others, the situation was more favorable, and some youths in trouble benefited from placement with caring and responsible families. Nevertheless, the system was not at all formalized; only in the 1840s did states begin to set up inspection procedures to keep watch on those with whom youths were placed.[2]

Parole, the period of time after institutional release when offenders are still under the control of the courts or state, continued to be used throughout the 1800s and into the 1900s. With the formation of the juvenile court, parole generally was called **aftercare.** Professionally trained individuals were added to the juvenile court to deal with released juveniles in the early 1900s. In addition, aftercare officers generally mirrored probation officers in trying to utilize current popular treatment modalities. Aftercare officers' caseloads were generally extremely high, and few resources were available to them. Even today, aftercare officers in many jurisdictions have the task of monitoring extremely large caseloads.

The development of aftercare programs was far from rapid, and the system remains underdeveloped even today.[3] Citizens and professionals perhaps thought that institutionalization was sufficient for youth, or they may have been more concerned about adults, whom they feared and mistrusted more. Whatever the reason, not until fairly recently have innovative efforts been undertaken to improve juvenile aftercare systems.

AFTERCARE OBJECTIVES

A major concern in juvenile justice in the past forty years has been the development of a workable philosophy and concept of aftercare. To achieve this end, the Task Force on Corrections of the President's Commission on Law

Enforcement and Administration of Justice proposed these objectives for juvenile aftercare or parole:

1. Release from confinement at the most favorable time, with appropriate consideration of the requirements of justice, the expected subsequent behavior, and the cost
2. The largest possible number of successful aftercare completions
3. Reduction of crimes committed by released juveniles
4. Reduction of violent acts committed by released offenders
5. An increase in community confidence in parole[4]

More recently, aftercare, or parole, has added the objectives of alleviating overcrowding of training schools, of monitoring youthful offenders so that they refrain from abusing or trafficking drugs, and of discouraging the return to street gangs. The achievement of these objectives requires extensive planning and research. For example, to determine the most favorable time for release requires far more knowledge than is presently available. Many new and innovative research designs must be developed before the needed techniques for prediction can be achieved, and research must enable releasing authorities to compare the costs of leaving juveniles in institutions with the possible harm to society if they are released.

Planning must clearly take place in each institution. Such planning is necessary if the functions of the various community agencies are to be articulated with institutional services. Evaluation procedures must be developed to assist institutions and agencies to determine their success. Realistic goals and objectives must be spelled out. Then the necessary guidelines for achieving a more effective aftercare policy can be implemented, and arbitrary, whimsical, and idiosyncratic aftercare revocation by individual aftercare officers will be diminished.

HOW DOES JUVENILE AFTERCARE OPERATE?

States vary in their standards for determining when a youth should be released from institutional care. The indeterminate sentencing structure of most states means that this decision must be made during the process of a youth's confinement. In 1994, thirty-six state agencies reported that 57,359 juveniles were released from institutional care. The average length of stay for juveniles released was 9.8 months. The recidivism rates for eighteen agencies averaged 36.5 percent (the follow-up periods used to estimate recidivism for eighteen of these nineteen agencies averaged 3.7 years).[5]

Juveniles released from training school are placed on aftercare or parole status. The bases on which they are released from these schools vary, and so do those individuals responsible for making the release decision. In forty-four states the authority for making this decision for juveniles rests with the executive branch of state governments. In forty-four states the decision is made by probation or parole officers, and in three states other boards and agencies make the decision.[6] In Illinois and several other states, juvenile judges have the authority to remove juveniles from training schools.

At present, some controversy exists about who should make the aftercare decision. Some believe that staff who work with residents know them best and are, therefore, the best judges of when they should be released. The staff see their charges daily, work with them in therapy, interact with them informally, and observe their interaction with peers. This twenty-four hour living experience should, according to the proponents of institutional decision making, make the institution and its staff outstanding experts on the progress and character of their youths. Such experience, it is believed, will enable institutional officials to know better than anyone the optimum time for release.

This argument has been countered by another: that institutional officials and staff are prone to overreact to residents' inability to get along in the institution. If offenders can stay out of institutional problems and can remain on the good side of the staff members, or if they reach a certain age, or if the institution becomes overcrowded, they are deemed ready for release. But if a youth has a personality conflict with a particular staff member or fights to protect himself or herself, he or she may not be able to get out. According to this view, staff members sometimes are prejudiced or opposed ideologically to what the youth believes. The accusation also is made that staff members occasionally release troublemakers just to get them out of the institution.

Many believe that the decision to release residents should be made by independent agencies and boards that are not swayed by what happens in institutions. One major advantage of setting up independent agencies and boards is that idiosyncratic and irrational decision making by staff would be eliminated. No longer would release be based on factors irrelevant to a resident's ability to get along in the community. Release would be decided impartially, regardless of whether or not a few rules were violated or a resident did talk back to staff from time to time.

Institutional staff members, however, believe that those in independent agencies and boards are too far removed from institutions to know what is going on within them. Staff members further believe that autonomous boards are unrealistic and uninformed about the problems that staff members and other officials face in working with difficult and troublesome youths. They also believe that important aspects of various cases are ignored by independent boards, resulting in inappropriate decisions at times. Moreover, staff members believe that the establishment of these boards downgrades their own professional competence and introduces an unnecessary complication.

States that use determinate or mandatory sentencing for juveniles usually have determined the time of institutional release when the youth is committed to training school. A variation of this approach is for the length of confinement to be determined within the department responsible for institutional care, using such guidelines as offense severity, previous offense history, and, perhaps, other criteria. For example, in the late 1980s, the Ohio Department of Youth Services established an Office of Release Review in order to provide a structured, centralized, objective release decision-making process. The goal of this office has been to set a length of institutional stay for each juvenile felony offender proportionate to the severity of his or her offenses and the impact on the victims. A parole hearing officer scores each youth using a specialized worksheet. In most cases, the score establishes the length of stay unless overriding conditions are present, as determined by an administrative committee with the office (see Figure 10–1 for an example of the release guideline worksheet).[7]

In Minnesota, the release of a juvenile from a training school is the responsibility of a juvenile aftercare hearing officer who uses a scale incorporating the severity of the offense and the offense history (see Figure 10–2). For example, a youthful offender who committed first-degree burglary would have a severity level of 3. If his or her delinquent history factors equaled 3, this offender would normally be paroled somewhere between the ninth and thirteenth months. This scale, consistent with other sentencing structures for juveniles in Minnesota, is based on the justice model.[8]

Early release from training school due to overcrowded conditions has complicated this decision-making process. In six states, a parole board appointed by the governor considers early release for institutionalized juveniles.[9] Michael D. Norman's study of the Utah Youth Parole Authority found that the early-release criteria were related primarily to institutional behavior, rather than to prospects for successful reintegration into the community.[10]

It would appear that this impasse on decision making for institutional release will not be easily resolved. Institutional officials and staff deserve the wide criticisms they have received. Little evidence exists that juvenile parole boards are any better than those found in adult justice, and adult parole boards have been sharply criticized in recent years. The recent movement in juvenile justice to use formalized and structured instruments to make release decisions also has its share of problems. Unless we are able to predict with some accuracy the success of those released on aftercare or parole, this approach becomes extremely questionable.

The Prediction and Reduction of Recidivism

Prediction is common in the sciences. Every field, including political science, psychology, sociology, medicine, and space science, tries to forecast the future. That some are eminently successful becomes apparent when their results are examined. Political science is becoming more and more accurate in predicting the outcomes of elections; psychology, through its testing programs, is beginning to successfully predict learning rates and vocational achievements of students; space science is accurately predicting trajectories of space vehicles; and

STATE OF OHIO
DEPARTMENT OF YOUTH SERVICES

RELEASE GUIDELINE WORKSHEET

Youth's Name JOHN SMITH
County SUMMIT
Adm. Date 03/13/90 MSED 03/12/91

DYS # 999999
Institution IRS
Region AKRON

1. This Commitment

List most serious committing offense:
Offense ORC# 2907.02 F 1 Offense RAPE

A. Score committing offense

- ☒ Class 1 = 12
- ☐ Class 2 = 10
- ☐ Class 3 = 6
- ☐ Class 4 = 4

A 12

B. Score enhancements (6 point maximum)

- ☐ Death of victim = 6
- ☐ Firearm/dangerous ordnance = 3
- ☐ Other deadly weapon = 2
- ☐ Vulnerable victim = 2
- ☒ Serious injury to victim = 2
- ☐ Multiple felony offenses or victims [#] = 2

List other felonies heard:
1. ORC#______
2. ORC#______
3. ORC#______

B 2

COMMITMENT TOTAL (A + B) = 1 14

2. Previous Offense History

Score number of prior endangering offenses

- ☐ None (0) = 1.00
- ☒ One (1) = 1.25
- ☐ Two (2) = 1.50
- ☐ Three (3) or more = 1.75

ORC #	Disposition Date
1. 2907.05	09/14/89
2.	
3.	

2 1.25

3. Determine Base Guideline Score (#1 X #2) = 3 17.50

4. Guideline Override: Add ☐ Sub ☐

(If used, provide additional written justification)

5. Total Guideline Score (#3 + #4) 5 18

6. Recommendation For Release

Early Release Eligibility: Yes ☐ Conditional ☐ No ☒

For those youth Early Release eligible, submit request by: ___/___/___

For those youth not Early Release eligible, revised sentence expiration date: 09 / 12 / 91

prepared by Edwin Heller date 03/13/90

Figure 10–1 Release Guideline Worksheet

(*Source:* State of Ohio, Department of Youth Services.)

Juvenile Commitment to the Minnesota Department of Corrections

Projected Institution Length of Stay in Months					
Severity Level	Most Serious Current Offense*	Delinquent History Factors 0	1	2	3
I	Violation of Probation Contempt of Court Prostitution Assault—4th & 5th Degree Driving Under Influence of Alcohol Negligent Fires Burglary—3rd & 4th Degree Damage to Property—$2,500 or less Forgery—$2,500 or less Possession of Controlled Substance Receiving Stolen Goods—$2,500 or less Theft—$2,500 or less Unauthorized Use of Motor Vehicle Dangerous Weapons (not including firearms) Trespass All Other Misdemeanors and Gross Misdemeanors	4–3	5–3	6–4	7–5
II	Assault—2nd & 3rd Degree Burglary—2nd Degree Damage to Property—Over $2,500 Forgery—Over $2,500 False Imprisonment Receiving Stolen Goods—$2,500 Felony Possession/Sale of Controlled Substance Theft from Person Theft—Over $2,500 Arson—3rd Degree Criminal Sexual Conduct—3rd & 4th Degree Simple Robbery Terroristic Threats Criminal Vehicular Homicide Dangerous Weapons—Firearms	6–3	7–4	8–5	9–6
III	Burglary—1st Degree Criminal Negligence Resulting in Death Aggravated Robbery Arson—1st & 2nd Degree Criminal Sexual Conduct—1st & 2nd Degree Kidnapping Manslaughter Assault—1st Degree	10–6	11–7	12–8	13–9
IV	Murder (all degrees)	**	**	**	**

* Commitment offenses not specifically listed shall be placed on the grid at the discretion of the hearing officer at the time of the initial institution review.

** Murder shall be dealt with on an individual basis.

Figure 10–2 *Projected Institution Length of Stay, in Months*

medicine, although often less spectacular in its ability to forecast the control of certain diseases, is nevertheless making tremendous strides. It is because of specialized knowledge in medicine, demography, biology, and other fields that the highly profitable insurance industry thrives. Equally efficient predictions are now, and have been, requested of the field of corrections.

Areas in criminology and corrections in which prediction is common are forecasting delinquency and predicting the outcome of aftercare. The principles used in these efforts are basically the same as those in other fields. No attempt is made to predict what an individual will do; instead, the goal is to predict what *groups* of individuals will do. The methods depend on sophisticated computer techniques and statistics; only the fundamentals of their development and use will be discussed here.

Prediction, basically, attempts to assemble accurate knowledge about offenders that will help forecast their later behavior. This information is assembled in units known as **predictor items** and is used to determine whether offenders will remain law-abiding or get into trouble after release. The same principles are used in forecasting delinquency as youths are growing up. The theory is that if these behaviors can be predicted, special programs can be formulated to help the various categories of youths adjust.

The problem lies in finding valid predictive information. It is difficult to determine which psychological test will be effective in predicting residents' behavior. The Minnesota Multiphasic Personality Inventory, the Jesness Personality Inventory, and other written tests are used. The sociological variables include family background, size of family, number of siblings, nature of family relationships, and the neighborhood from which offenders come. Criminological variables include such items as prior criminal history, prior institutional history, types and seriousness of offenses, and the length of confinement.

The research goal is to be able to show a high correlation between the test results and the after-release behavior of the youths tested. It is very probable that youths with a long history of serious offenses are more likely to get into trouble than are those without a criminal history. A serious prior criminal history is almost inevitably correlated with trouble after release. As the number and seriousness of any juvenile's criminal acts increase, so do the chances that he will get into additional trouble. Another method determines the percentages of youths whose specific characteristics tend to predispose them to either getting into or staying out of trouble. Once these characteristics are known, *prediction tables,* or, as they are sometimes called, *experience tables* or *base-expectancy tables,* can then be constructed.

Don M. Gottfredson impressively points out that prediction tables used in California distinguish between adult recidivists and no recidivists at around the 80 percent level.[11] The U.S. Parole Commission arranged for studies in the 1970s leading, it was hoped, to the creation of actuarial tables showing statistical risks of recidivism for adults or juvenile offenders as shown by experience with offenders with similar methods. A team of criminologists, composed of Don Gottfredson, Leslie T. Wilkins, and Peter B. Hoffman, was commissioned to produce such an instrument.[12] The decision was made after a year or so of experimentation that the actuarial tables would be impractical to produce and not of great use in decision making. The researchers, then, decided that guidelines should be developed using eight factors taken from offenders' personal history to predict the risk of their committing new offenses after release. The severity of the crime was the second element used for the construction of the guidelines. From the risk-severity ratings, the researchers deemed that it was possible to construct a grid on which the risk ratings of the offender was the horizontal axis and the severity rating of the crime was the vertical axis. The Parole Commission has been guided by this model since 1978 and will continue to use it until the last prisoner received before November 1, 1987, has been discharged from the system.[13]

In October 1984, Congress passed the Comprehensive Crime Control Act, which, among other things, abolished parole, effective November 1987. The U.S. Sentencing Commission was created in a companion Sentencing Reform Act of 1984. Its first function was to design a new set of guidelines to establish flat terms for all federal offenders. An elaborate sentencing structure was produced after two years of research and discussion. It is anticipated that in time it will influence sentencing structures in state criminal justice systems as well.[14]

Juvenile aftercare, long the most undeveloped subsystem in juvenile justice, has recently experienced several efforts to develop risk-assessment instruments. Christopher Baird and colleagues' review of these risk-assessment instruments found that the following variables appeared to be predictive of continued criminal involvement for youthful parolees:

- Age of first adjudication
- Prior delinquent behavior (combined measure of number and severity of priors)
- Number of prior commitments to juvenile facilities
- Drug/chemical abuse
- Alcohol abuse
- Family relationships (parental control)
- School problems
- Peer relationships[15]

It is likely, based on aftercare guidelines developed in Minnesota, Ohio, and other states, that some form of predictive instrument will increasingly guide the release procedures in juvenile justice. But the most important reason for questioning prediction tables in aftercare is that they are far from perfect. Even if 80 percent of the outcomes could be predicted for released juveniles, we do not know which 80 percent. The remaining 20 percent could commit serious crimes, and many parole-granting agencies do not want to take a chance.

These agencies would rather keep the 80 percent confined than take a chance that the remaining 20 percent would get into trouble.

The Reentry Process

The juvenile justice system gives some attention to the juvenile's preparation for return to the community. Home visits, especially in private facilities, are frequently made available to juveniles before their release. In Minnesota and other states, parole, or aftercare, officers will visit institutionalized juveniles to help them plan for their community reintegration. Home placements and usually school or job assignments must also be finalized in most jurisdictions before the juvenile will be released.

Yet, unlike adult corrections, few training schools place much emphasis on prerelease programs that attempt to prepare residents for community experiences. Those that do typically include information and instruction on such matters as job opportunities and employment aids; the importance of being on time; motor vehicle driver training; legal problems and contracts; basic financial management; personal health practices and proper diet; perspectives on family responsibilities; human relations; and the dangers of alcohol, drugs, and cigarettes.[16]

Nor are many juveniles provided the opportunity to work in the community before their release. Private facilities appear to be more concerned than public institutions about juveniles having a work experience prior to their release, but the objections to such programs include the security risks involved, the lack of staff to locate jobs and supervise residents, and the inability of residents to handle jobs constructively for more than a short period of time.[17] In juvenile facilities providing such programs, residents leave the facility in the morning, usually with lunch and enough money for transportation, and return at the end of the work day. Some residents are provided transportation to and from work; others depend on public transportation.

Furthermore, in contrast to the number of halfway-in placements for juvenile probationers, relatively few halfway-out houses exist for juvenile parolees. The negative response that juveniles frequently made to such placements in the past apparently has discouraged this movement in juvenile corrections.[18] What has taken the place of halfway-out facilities for juveniles are independent living placements. Although such placements usually are made for juveniles who lack adequate placements with families or relatives, they do not offer a gradual transition to release that halfway-out residential facilities would permit.

It can be argued that juveniles who have been confined for only a few months in a training school do not need **reentry programs** as much as do adults who may has spent years within prison walls. Some adults experience an unexpected jolt when released suddenly and without preparation. They may feel disoriented and confused by the transition from controlled living to life in free society. In contrast, this disorientation and confusion appears much less frequently with released juveniles. In addition to the much shorter period of confinement, the openness of many training schools permits juveniles to move back and forth between the institution and the community.

Yet a convincing case can be made that juveniles need more of these reentry programs than they usually experience. Confined juveniles often have distorted ideas of what awaits them in the community. They anticipate that long-standing problems with family members will no longer exist. As one aptly put it, "I'm more mature now; I can handle my mom."[19] They also believe that their school adjustment will go more smoothly than it usually does. Moreover, juveniles typically underestimate the difficulty of returning to the same community and peer relationships. Finally, nearly all juveniles entering the job market dramatically overestimate how much they will earn and what standard of living they will be able to maintain with this income.

The Length of Aftercare Supervision

José B. Ashford and Craig Winston LeCroy's national survey of aftercare identified eight types of aftercare or parole supervision.[20] Types 1 through 4 were determinate, and types 5 through 8 were indeterminate. The duration of a youth's period on supervised release or aftercare was determined by which type was used in that particular jurisdiction.

Type 1 is a **determinate parole,** in which the length of supervision is related to the period of commitment specified by the juvenile court and is proportionate to the youth's offense. The decision to discharge a juvenile involves the computation of time since the beginning of the youth's confinement. Washington was the only state that had this type of aftercare supervision. Type 2 is a form of determinate parole that is set by administrative agency, based on offense and criminal history. The aftercare release date is set as soon as a youth arrives at an institutional placement. Georgia and New Jersey were the only states that used this type. Type 3 is a **presumptive minimum,** which involves the assumption that aftercare should terminate after the youthful offender completes a specified period of supervised release. The aftercare officer cannot depart from the prescribed period without evidence of behavior dictating the extension of aftercare. Arkansas, Kansas, and Mississippi used this determinate approach to the length of aftercare supervision. Type 4 is also a presumptive minimum, in which the aftercare officer has the discretion to extend supervision for an unspecified length of time until the maximum age for termination of the juvenile court's jurisdiction. Massachusetts, Michigan, Montana, and Nevada all used this type of parole supervision.

Type 5 is a presumptive minimum with the possibility of extending supervision for an indeterminate period. The assumption involved in this approach is that aftercare supervision should terminate after a minimum period, but can be extended at the discretion of the paroling agency. Policies in Arizona, Florida, New Hampshire, New York, and Pennsylvania fit this criteria. Type 6 is an indeterminate parole specifying a maximum and a discretionary minimum period of supervision. Consistent with the Model Juvenile Court Act of 1968, this approach leaves the length of confinement and the period of supervised release to the discretion of aftercare authorities. Aftercare supervision in Alabama, Colorado, Connecticut, Delaware, Louisiana, New Mexico, North Carolina, North Dakota, Tennessee, Vermont, and Wisconsin met the criteria of a specified maximum and a discretionary minimum. Type 7 is another indeterminate form of aftercare with a legal minimum and a maximum period of supervision. According to this approach, the aftercare agency has the discretion to discharge the youthful offender from aftercare within a broad range of time. Dominant in adult corrections before the determinancy movement to sentencing, this approach was used by juvenile authorities in Alaska, California, Kentucky, Maine, Ohio, Texas, and Utah. Finally, Type 8 is a purely discretionary and indeterminate approach. Discharge decisions rely solely on the discretion of the aftercare staff, who have the authority to assess the youthful offender's readiness for discharge from supervision. Hawaii, Idaho, Illinois, Maryland, Missouri, Nebraska, Oklahoma, Oregon, Rhode Island, South Carolina, Virginia, West Virginia, and Wyoming used this form of aftercare supervision. Figure 10–3 reveals that the majority of states use some type of indeterminate aftercare supervision.

Risk Control and Crime Reduction

The current emphasis in aftercare, as in juvenile probation, is on short-term behavior control. Consequently, we can assume that even if more states adopt determinate sentencing statutes for juveniles, the likelihood is that mandatory aftercare services will continue to be provided for those released from public and private placements. Similar to juvenile probation, **intensive supervision programs** are increasingly being used, but in-house detention and electronic monitoring programs still have not received the attention that they have in

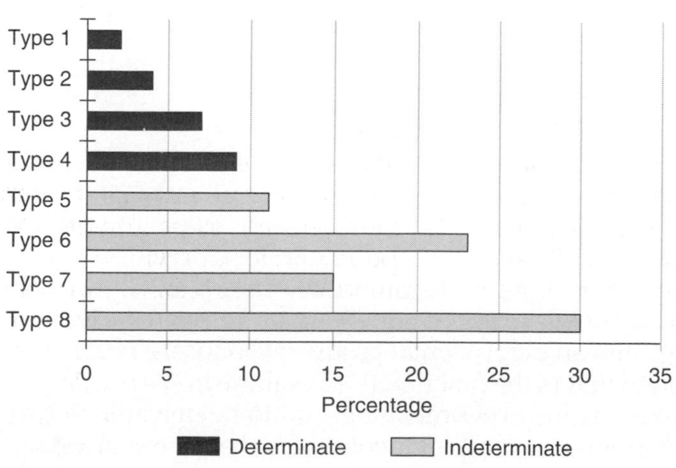

Figure 10–3 *Percentages of Parole Types Across the United States.*

Source: Jose B. Ashford and Craig Winston LeCroy, "Juvenile Parole Policy in the United States: Determinate versus Indeterminate Models," *Justice Quarterly* 10 (June 1993), p. 191. Reprinted with permission of the Academy of Criminal Justice Sciences.

juvenile probation.[21] Juvenile aftercare also emphasizes drug and alcohol urinalysis (sometimes called "drug drops") and is turning to "boot camp" programs as a means of releasing juveniles early from training school.

Intensive Aftercare Supervision (IAS)

Intensive aftercare can be conceived as operating "in the context of decision making and planning for the *early release* of juveniles from secure confinement" and as "imposing higher levels of supervision on youth[s] being released after serving a *full institutional term.*"[22] In terms of intensive aftercare supervision, three populations of juveniles can be targeted: medium-to-low-risk parolees, all parolees, and high-risk parolees.[23]

There appear to be more than eighty intensive aftercare supervision programs in the United States today.[24] The most noteworthy of these intensive programs are the ones in the thirty counties in Pennsylvania; "Lifeskills 95", the Violent Juvenile Offender Research and Development Program in Boston, Memphis, Newark, and Detroit; juvenile aftercare in a Maryland drug treatment program; the Skillman Intensive Aftercare Project; the Michigan Nokomis Challenge program; the PARJO program in New York; and the Office of Juvenile Justice and Delinquency Prevention IAP Project.

In 1988, the Juvenile Court Judges' Commission of Pennsylvania established pilot intensive aftercare supervision programs in Philadelphia and Pittsburgh for juveniles who would otherwise be classified as habitually serious and violent offenders.[25] The Philadelphia sample consisted of ninety youths who were released from the Bensalem Youth Development Center between December 1988 and January 1990. These youths were placed on a caseload of no larger than twelve and supervised by probation officers. About 50 percent of the juveniles assigned to intensive aftercare were rearrested. In contrast, 64 percent of the control subjects, with equal seriousness of new offenses for both groups, were rearrested. Encouraged by this initial evaluation, thirty Pennsylvania counties established intensive aftercare programs by the end of 1989. Further examination revealed that this intensive aftercare program was effective in reducing the frequency, although not the incidence, of criminal behavior in this group of high-risk youthful offenders during the period immediately following institutional release.[26]

Lifeskills '95 is an intensive aftercare treatment program in California that is designed to assist high-risk and chronic juvenile offenders who are released from secure confinement.[27] The basic paradigm of this intensive aftercare program uses a series of lifestyle and life-skill treatment modalities in an integrated educational approach to healthy decision making.[28] Don A. Josi and Dale K. Sechrist's 1995 study of this treatment intervention compared the parole performance of a control and an experimental group of California Youth Authority offenders. They found that in the first ninety days those in the control group were about twice as likely as the experimental group to be unemployed, to lack the resources to gain or maintain employment, and to have been arrested.[29]

The Violent Juvenile Offender Research and Development Program is a large-scale evaluation of intensive aftercare for serious or high-risk juvenile offenders. From 1981 to 1985, the Office of Juvenile Justice and Delinquency Prevention implemented this program in Boston, Memphis, Newark, and Detroit to test the feasibility and effectiveness of intensive aftercare with juveniles who had committed a violent offense or a serious felony.[30]

Program participants (Es) were first placed in small secure facilities. They were then reintegrated into community life through placement in community-based residences, and upon returning home, they received intensive supervision (frequent contacts in small caseloads). The intensive aftercare programs focused on extinguishing delinquent behavior, helping participants develop the skills needed to get along with other people, training for employment, and providing assistance with family and peer issues. Control youths (Cs), in contrast, were institutionalized for an average of eight months in "standard juvenile institutional programs," after which they were placed on standard aftercare in regular-size caseloads.[31]

The two-year follow-up after release from secure confinement had mixed findings. Es outperformed Cs on rearrest rates in one site, Cs outperformed Es in a second site, and no significant differences were found in the other two. In addition, when all four were combined, no significant differences emerged between Es and Cs. The reliability of this two-year follow-up is unclear, primarily because Es and Cs in most sites were inadequately matched on crucial variables. Still, the good news is that intensive aftercare programs could be established and maintained in the community for serious or violent juvenile offenders, without jeopardizing public safety. In the 1960s to early 1970s, this finding had been demonstrated by the California Community Treatment Project.[32]

The Maryland Department of Juvenile Justice developed an aftercare program that was intended to complement short-term residential treatment for drug-abusing or chemically addicted youthful offenders. Only youth who resided in Baltimore City were included in the program. During the intensive phase, which consisted of the first two months in the community, staff were supposed to have daily contact with program participants and hold youth support group meetings and family support sessions.[33]

M. D. Sealock, D. C. Gottfredson, and C. A. Gallagher, in their evaluation, found this aftercare program to be highly questionable. The residential treatment services were highly uneven in scope and quality; most of the residential program's intermediate goals (e.g., internal control, increased coping skills, and family communication) were not realized, and only thirty-six of the 162 juveniles beginning the program actually completed it. For those few who completed the program, the evaluators conclude, the quality and nature of the aftercare services seemed insufficient for a drug-involved population.[34]

The innovative Nokomis Challenge Program was developed by the Michigan Department of Social Services in 1989. This program combines three months of residence and outdoor challenge programming in a wilderness camp with nine months of intensive aftercare supervision. Designed for low- and medium-risk juveniles convicted of a felony offense who would otherwise be placed in a residential facility for fourteen to sixteen months, the primary focus of the program is on relapse prevention. Both the residential and the community components provide extensive family services.[35]

The Rand Corporation measured the program's effectiveness in terms of participants' social adjustment, recidivism, and family functioning. This 1996 evaluation found that only about 40 percent completed the twelve-month Nokomis program (residential and community phases), compared to an 84 percent completion rate for youths in the control group, who were assigned to a typical residential program where the length of stay averages 15.5 months. An even more alarming finding was that the total failure rate was 70 percent for youths in the experimental group receiving intensive aftercare supervision and 24 percent for youths in the control group. Those more likely to succeed in Nokomis had fewer prior arrests, were older at the onset of delinquency, and had stronger family ties. Another discouraging finding was that there appeared to be few significant differences between the experimental and control groups in terms of improved family functioning. This evaluation did suggest that the community phase of the Nokomis program needed to provide additional support for the gains made during the residential phase and that the success rate would likely be higher if a more appropriate target population for the Nokomis program were identified.[36]

New York has developed PARJO, a pilot intensive supervision program for juvenile parolees. This program was implemented for 368 participants in 1983 and 1984. Juvenile parole officers were assigned small caseloads and helped their high-risk parolees find jobs and other needed services. An evaluation of this program found it moderately successful at reducing recidivism and at increasing parolees' rate of employment.[37]

The Skillman Intensive Aftercare Project was implemented in two experimental intensive aftercare programs for chronic juvenile offenders in Detroit and Pittsburgh. The two separate private providers who developed and operated these projects were committed to the Skillman program model, which emphasized prelease contacts and planning three months before release; included intensive supervision contacts, beginning at several per day and gradually diminishing; mobilized community resources, especially in relation to education and jobs; and enlisted role-modeling, motivated caseworkers. Approximately one hundred juveniles in a two-year period completed residential placement in each city, and they were assigned to either intensive aftercare or regular supervision.[38]

P. W. Greenwood, E. P. Deschenes, and J. Adams's evaluation of these programs revealed disappointing results. The study found no difference between control and experimental groups in the self-reporting of offenses, the proportion of juveniles arrested, or drug use during a twelve-month follow-up period. Greenwood and colleagues concluded that a number of factors explained the results, including aftercare workers failing to target specific problems that were contributing to risk, aftercare workers devoting insufficient attention to programs addressing risk factors related to offending behavior, and programs lacking formal methods of assessing progress and need.[39]

One recent concern has been to develop an integrated theoretical framework for guiding intensive supervision of chronic juvenile offenders. This Intensive Aftercare Program (IAP) model is a combination of social control, strain, and social learning theories, and it focuses on the reintegrative process. Figure 10–4 shows the program elements of this model. Its basic assumptions are that serious and chronic delinquency is related to weak controls produced by social disorganization, inadequate socialization, and strain; that strain is produced by social disorganization independent of weak controls; and that peer group influences intervene as a social force between youths with weak bonds and/or strain on one hand and delinquent behaviors on the other.[40]

The IAP project has been implemented in four pilot programs: Colorado (Arapahoe and Jefferson Counties), Nevada (Clark County), New Jersey (Camden and Essex Counties), and Virginia (Norfolk County). The participation

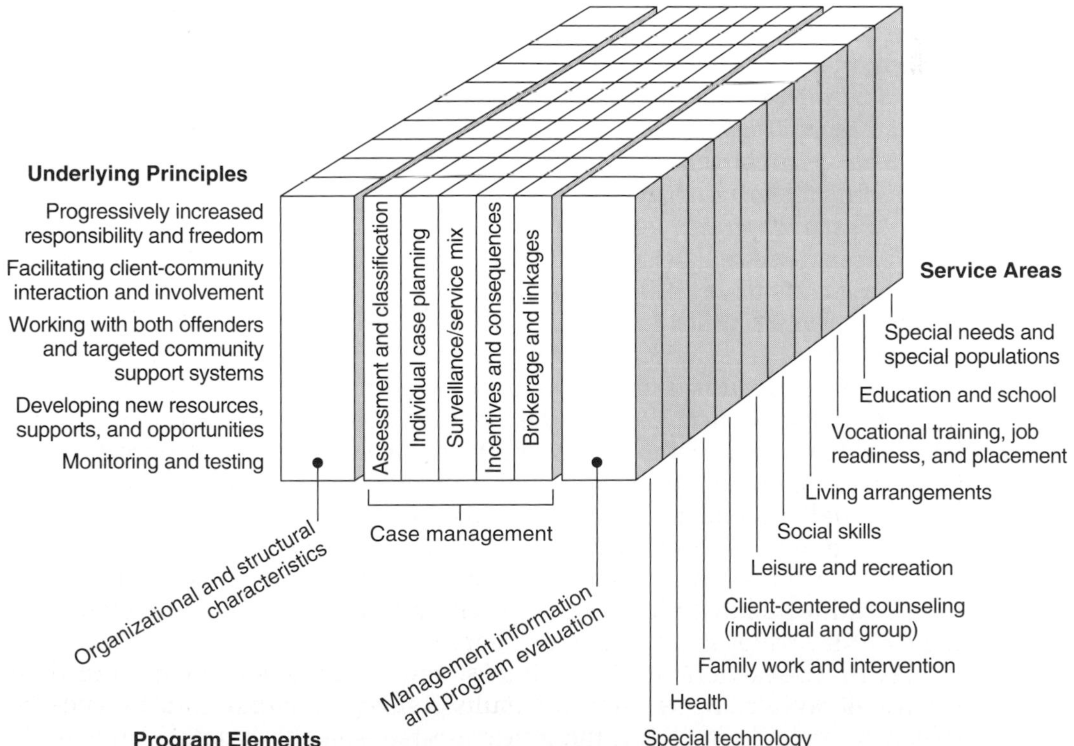

Figure 10–4 *Intervention Model for Juvenile Intensive Aftercare*

Source: David M. Altschuler and Troy L. Armstrong, *Intensive Aftercare for High-Risk Juveniles: Policies and Procedures* (Washington, DC: Office of Juvenile Justice and Delinquency Prevention, 1994), p. 3.

of the New Jersey counties ended in 1997, but the other three programs carried through on preparing high-risk offenders for progressively increased responsibility and freedom in the community. The well-developed transition components that began shortly after a youth was adjudicated to an institution and continued through the early months of community adjustments are particularly strict about these programs (see Figure 12.4 for these transition components). The results of the first five years of implementation (1995–2000) reveal a dramatically improved level of communication and coordination between institutional and aftercare staff as well as the ability to involve parolees in community services almost immediately after institutional release.[41]

Community Experience

In spite of various institutional and parole programs, many youths do get into trouble after release. Recidivism rates on aftercare, depending largely on how recidivism is measured, tend to vary from 25 to 40 percent.[39] The reasons for the failure of aftercare range from organizational factors to the lack of support in the community, and to the youths themselves. Organizational factors include the extreme fragmentation encountered in the system, the dubious and even destructive nature of institutional life, and the sometimes arbitrary decision making by aftercare officers. The lack of support systems in the community, including the inability to get a job, the stigma associated with being a "bad" person, and the lack of mentors to guide and encourage the youths, also make it easy to return to crime. Finally, personal factors include an appetite for drugs and alcohol; an inability to walk away from gang involvement; and conflict with parole officers, school authorities, and parents.

William R. Arnold examined some of the reintegration problems in a study of juveniles after their release from an institution. He found that the problem of family control of youths reasserts itself when they return from confinement. Even when both parents are in the home, they may find that the youths are still out of control. Many parents resolve to do better, so they keep their children under constant surveillance for several weeks. But usually this constant supervision eventually proves impossible, and the youths are back on the streets. Other parents admit the situation is hopeless and give up trying altogether. Most fall somewhere between the two extremes and try to at least maintain some form of curfew. But in no cases are parents particularly effective.[40]

Peer groups have the most impact. Arnold's study found that most youths went back to their old group within a day or so of their return, and none of the groups failed to accept them. If the old groups no longer existed, the youths then sought new ones. If the family had moved, the problem of influence of antisocial peers was solved by a slowly decreasing rate of interaction with the old group and the gradual establishment of new friends in the new area. The Arnold study supports the contention that youths return to the environments that originally produced their delinquencies and that expectations of peers are more important than those of the parents.

Another interesting finding was that the youths did not immediately assume a greater status as a result of the training school stay. Their own parents, obviously, were upset over them, but so were other parents who did not want their children associating with the newly released youths. Also, some of the parolees themselves indicated disapproval of the training school experience. Young women, too, tended to shy away from the male parolees. Released youths, in other words, do not necessarily become highly respected members of the peer culture.

Parolees face major, sometimes monumental, problems in returning to school and getting jobs. Parole officers look upon school attendance and jobs as signs that the youths are performing successfully. Yet many of the youths who did not do well in school before their incarceration do not find it any easier after they return. They usually were behind their classmates when they entered the training schools and are still behind when they come out. Their classmates have changed, principals are leery of accepting these labeled youths, teachers remember them unfavorably, and the training schools have failed to change their attitudes toward academic courses.

The job situation is not much better. Training school programs are often either of a make-work type or otherwise irrelevant to actual jobs available in the home community. In other cases the training schools prepare the youths for jobs that are available in the area where the training schools are located but not in the youths' home communities. The youths may be able to do odd jobs, but their immaturity, lack of desire for a job, and inexperience preclude them from looking for anything more substantial.

These factors, then, provide the matrix within which the youths must operate. What leads them to become delinquent again? For some time it has been known that younger parolees are more likely to fail than older parolees, that persons who were involved in crime for longer periods of time are more likely to fail than individuals with short records, that those who begin early are more likely to continue, that individuals more heavily involved in crime are more likely to fail than those not so heavily involved, that persons frequently confined are more likely to fail than those who have not been confined, and that crimes-against-property offenders fail more often than violent offenders. These characteristics, nevertheless, still do not *explain* the conditions that cause a youth to fail.

Arnold has attempted to formulate a theory to answer this question. He points out that delinquency and crime are on-again off-again affairs. Juveniles usually engage in crime only on occasion and in provocative situations. The risks of getting caught are weighed against gaining status in the eyes of their peers. This need for peer approval leads youths toward delinquency, even if they actually do not wish to participate in illegal activity; they assume that everyone else is going to, so they had better go along also.

So far, the general theory has been applied only to already-delinquent youths, but Arnold believes that they also hold for juveniles on parole. Certainly those on parole return to peer groups that have considerable experience with delinquency. The youths, too, have little or no contact with older persons or with others who would regard delinquent behavior as undesirable. The parolee thus moves into a social situation that affords little restraint from further delinquency. In addition, Arnold feels that youths who become recidivists experience four specific problems:

- They have more difficulty adjusting to their peers than do nonrecidivists.
- They are more likely than nonrecidivists to be in groups to which it is difficult to adjust.
- They are more likely than nonrecidivists to maintain interaction with older groups that have a history of delinquency.
- They receive less effective antidelinquent teaching than do nonrecidivists.[41]

WHAT ARE THE MAIN RESPONSIBILITIES OF AFTERCARE OFFICERS?

The youths placed on aftercare require supportive counseling, delivery of certain services, and supervision. But frequently they receive only supervision, because the caseloads tend to be high for each officer.

SUPERVISION

Aftercare officers have all the role conflicts of the probation officer described in Chapter 8, and, in fact, they are frequently probation officers with youths on aftercare on their caseloads. In addition, they are looked on even more as law enforcement figures because they can return offenders to institutional confinement. The director of court services for a large midwestern probation department compares juveniles on probation and those on aftercare:

> The main difference between the child on probation and the one on aftercare is that the child who has been further in the system and who has already received some sort of primary treatment has identified his or her sets of problems. Staff also are aware of these problems, and so we will more carefully scrutinize them. We are also a little more leery about those further in the system because they are more aware how to manage the system to their advantage. But they don't necessarily pose more danger either to the officer or to the community because those early in the system may be unaware of the impact or the consequences of their actions.[42]

According to Arnold, "The biggest difference between parolees and those who supervise them is probably in social-class position and in the subculture that goes with class difference."[43] He contends that the increasing amount of education required of aftercare officers will widen the social distance between them and their clients. Vocabularies, lifestyles, and mannerisms set the officers apart from their typically lower-class, minority-group clients. He argues that many officers aspire to the middle class and consequently may look down on or disapprove of the actions of their lower-class clients. In this situation, lower-class youths often find that even minor violations of rules lead to aftercare revocation. Fortunately, the trend toward due process for juveniles is providing them with greater protection from the capriciousness, pettiness, intolerance, and whims of some aftercare officers.

Arnold's dated study appears to overstate the importance of class differences between aftercare (or probation officers with aftercare caseloads) and their clients. This class differential is apparent throughout the justice system among practitioners and offenders, but this study does reflect the problematic nature of supervision and the resentment that is often apparent among aftercare officers and their clients. As indicated in the current research on intensive aftercare, supervision alone is not sufficient to prevent recidivism and relapse.[44]

To understand the resentment toward some aftercare officers, it is necessary to examine some of the rules to which youths are subject. A Pennsylvania county uses the rules set down in Focus on Practice 10–1, modified according to each parolee's needs. These rules are read by the juvenile, who then signs the statement, "I, the undersigned, have received a copy, read and understood the aforementioned rules and agree to abide by them." The rules are neither hard to agree to nor hard to break, for many of them are irrelevant to everything in the lifestyle of offenders. Enforcement of the rules drives youths even farther from genuine communication with officers. Lack of enforcement of a formal set of rules, however, gives juveniles the impression that they are free to do as they wish, and aftercare officers are left in a bind.

Some youths on release to the community will skip school, talk back to parents, get involved in minor traffic violations, or violate curfew. Most aftercare officers realize that many nondelinquent youths behave in the same manner, but no one would consider confining them. Revocation generally is based on the attitudes of the youths. For example, an expression of hostility toward the officers sometimes results in recommitment, even if the offenses and behavior are insignificant. The likelihood of revocation is increased as the severity of behavior increases. The commission of misdemeanors, the continuation of drug use, and a pattern of delinquency suggests that more serious offenses may follow. Aftercare officers may decide at this point that for the protection of both the youth and the community, revocation is necessary. Finally, if felonies are committed, little doubt exists in the minds of most officers that the youths should return to the institution

Officers who take a supervisory stance in relation to the youths and their behavior sometimes consider any violation of the rules as sufficient grounds for revocation. In the past, they simply picked up such offenders and took them

FOCUS ON PRACTICE 10–1

AFTERCARE RULES OF ONE PENNSYLVANIA COUNTY

PAROLE RULES FOR ____________________

DATE ____________________

PERIOD ____________________

PAROLE OFFICER ____________________

1. Obey all Federal, State and Local Laws.
2. Obey your parents or guardians at all times.
3. Maintain a satisfactory adjustment within an employment or educational/ vocational setting.
4. Be in your home by ______ PM every night unless you have special permission of your parents to be out later, and only for a specific reason and until a specified time.
5. You must not leave Washington County, Pennsylvania without the permission of your Parole Officer unless accompanied by a parent and remain while away with a parent.
6. Notify your Parole Officer of any change in address, school or employment and obtain his/her consent.
7. You must not frequent places of poor reputation or places where liquor is sold or consume alcoholic beverages.
8. You must not be in the company of repetitive delinquent or criminal offenders, or others presently on probation or individuals known to be law violators.
9. You must not own or control a motor vehicle without your Parole Officer's consent.
10. You must report to your Parole Officer as requested.
11. Do not use, sell or possess any narcotic or dangerous drug or marijuana.
12. Cooperate fully with any agency this Office may refer you to for service.
13. Obey all orders given by the Judge at the time of your hearing. The orders which are applicable to you are noted below.

    ____

    ____

14. Pay restitution in the amount of ________ by this date ________
15. You are forbidden to use or carry a firearm in your possession without the express permission of your Probation Officer.
16. Other regulations ____________________

Critical Thinking Questions:

Do you believe that these are reasonable rules for a juvenile on aftercare status? If you were an aftercare officer, would you add to these rules?

back to the paroling institutions, ignoring due process. The stepping over of an arbitrary line by the youths was sufficient to warrant taking them into custody. The line often was ill or vaguely defined, and the youths had no idea whether their behavior was within acceptable limits. In addition, since they seldom saw the officers, the youths could usually count on getting away with anything they tried, but often the parole officer would suddenly appear and the youth would be sent back to the training school. Revocation depended on chance, the attitude of the youth, and the personal whim of the aftercare officer.

Some of the problems faced by youths on aftercare status are possibly different from the problems faced by juvenile probationers. Youths who are confined face the shock of complete isolation from their communities. They are exposed to many degrading experiences, are sometimes "messed over" by staff and residents, learn behavior that allows them to survive, are not permitted to practice the decision making they would have to do in the community, and are stigmatized by their stay in the institution. The world they left is changing and perhaps so are they. Consequently, when youths are ready for release, they are not necessarily ready to reenter the community, but there is usually no transition stage from institution to community. In the past, these youths were simply redeposited back into that community. But as the concept of aftercare changes, more and more aftercare officers and training schools are increasingly giving youths prerelease counseling and are allowing home visits to ease their return to normal life. See Focus on Programs 10–2 for example of programs designed to ease the transition between training school and community.

Revocation of Aftercare

The revocation of aftercare is the early termination of a youth's aftercare program, which usually takes place for one or more program violations. Several outcomes are possible when a youthful offender's aftercare is terminated. The youth can be returned to training school. A less severe option is to shift the youth to a different outcome program. For example, a youth who is on regular supervision status can be shifted to an intensive caseload. Or an offender may be placed on home confinement, coupled with electronic monitoring.[45]

Aftercare revocation for juveniles is not as clear-cut as parole revocation for adults. Indeed, the U.S. Supreme Court has not yet ruled how juvenile aftercare revocation actions should be conducted. This sometimes has led to prejudicial, whimsical, arbitrary, and irrational actions on the part of aftercare officers. But the court decisions in *Mempa v. Rhay* (1967), *People ex rel. v. Warden Greenhaven* (1971), *Murray v. Page* (1970), *Morrissey v. Brewer* (1972), and *Gagnon v. Scarpelli* (1973) have been applied to juveniles.[46] The U.S. Supreme Court in the *Mempa* case stated that state probationers have the right to a hearing and counsel when accused of probation violations, and some courts have extended this right to parole violations. In *People v. Greenhaven,* it was stated that inmates are permitted to have counsel at revocation hearings. But the case that set the rationale for the requirement of due process was *Murray v. Page:*

FOCUS ON PROGRAMS 10–2

PROGRAMS DESIGNED TO EASE TRANSITION BETWEEN TRAINING SCHOOL AND COMMUNITY

The basic trust of the institutionally based counseling continuum program, a preparole reintegration program based at the Valley View Illinois Youth Center, was to send out institutionalized youth into the community for five or more days a week and to have them return to the institution for a day or more of intensive counseling. The institutionally based counseling continuum program was in operation from 1972 to the 1980s.

Youth who participated in the institutionally based counseling continuum (IBCC) program were referred to the program by their cottage team when the team concluded that they were nearing release. Reasons for referring residents usually were of three types: they could benefit from weekly assistance in the development and implementation of a community program; they had requested this assignment; or their families needed assistance in supporting their return to the community. If a referred youth chose not to participate, he simply remained in the regular institution program and was paroled through the normal process.

To be eligible for this program, residents also must be able to return to the institution for the weekly counseling session, must either be in school or hold a full-time job, and must have an adequate home environment. During their time away from the institution, the residents' behavior was monitored and evaluated through visits to their homes, schools, jobs, or other program placements. The results of these visits were recorded by the youths' counselors and were discussed when the youths returned to the institution on the weekend.

The purpose of the return to the institution was to hold the youth accountable for his community performance. This was accomplished through program agreements, performance contracts, and counseling sessions. Program agreements enabled the youth and his counselor to establish specific goals when he entered into the program. These long-term goals were written as program agreements for a parole hearing. They were further formalized into weekly performance contracts. Weekend counseling sessions generally were conducted on a one-to-one basis as the youth and his counselor reviewed the past week, discussed his evaluations, and established performance contracts for the coming week. Other pertinent issues relating to the reintegration of the youth into the community were also discussed.

A current program is the one that is in operation in the Hennepin County Home School in Minnesota. In this Intensive Aftercare Program, residents are offered a continuum of services to meet their full range of needs, including successful community reintegration and aftercare.

This continuum of care model reflects the Intensive Community Based Aftercare Model (IAP) developed by the Office of Juvenile Justice and Delinquency Prevention (OJJDP). The County school's IAP model includes six intertwined phases: assessment, case planning, institutional treatment, prerelease, transition, and community reintegration.

Source: Clemens Bartollas and Stuart J. Miller, *The Juvenile Offender: Control, Correction, and Treatment* (Boston: Hobrook Press, 1978), 309–10; the Web page of the Hennepin County Home School, 2002; and a 2002 interview conducted with Theresa E. Wise, Superintendent of the Hennepin County Home School.

Critical Thinking Questions:
What is your evaluation of these programs? What are their advantages? What are their disadvantages?

> Therefore, while a prisoner does not have a constitutional right to parole, once paroled he cannot be deprived of his freedom by means inconsistent with due process. The minimal right of the parolee to be informed of the charges and the nature of the evidence against him and to appear to be heard at the revocation hearing is inviolate. Statutory deprivation of this right is manifestly inconsistent with due process and is unconstitutional; nor can such right be lost by the subjective determination of the executive that the case for revocation is "clear."[47]

In the 1972 *Morrissey v. Brewer* decision, the Supreme Court first ruled on parole revocation procedures.[48] Morrissey had been paroled from the Iowa State Penitentiary. Seven months after his release, his parole was revoked for a technical violation, and he was returned to prison. In a related case, Booher was returned to prison on a technical parole violation. Both prisoners petitioned for habeas corpus on the grounds that they had been denied due process of law and returned to prison without opportunities to defend themselves at an open hearing. The two cases were consolidated for appeal and eventually reached the Supreme Court.

In his opinion, Chief Justice Warren Burger laid down the essential elements of due process for parole revocation. The first requirement was a hearing before an "uninvolved" hearing officer, who might be another parole officer or an "independent decision maker," who would determine whether there was reasonable cause to believe that a parole violation had taken place. If so, the parolee might be returned to prison, subject to a full revocation hearing before the parole board. Due process in such a proceeding was outlined as follows:

Our task is limited to deciding the minimum requirement[s] of due process. They include (a) written notice of the claimed violation of parole; (b) disclosure to the parolee of evidence against him; (c) opportunity to be heard in person and to present witnesses and documentary evidence; (d) the right to confront and cross-examine adverse witnesses (unless the hearing officer specifically finds good cause for not allowing confrontation); (e) a "neutral and detached" hearing body such as a traditional parole board, members of which need not be judicial officers or lawyers; and (f) a written statement by the fact finders as to the evidence relied on and reasons for revoking parole."[49]

Gagnon v. Scarpelli involved an offender, Scarpelli, whose probation was revoked in Wisconsin without a hearing. Scarpelli had been sentenced to fifteen years in prison for armed robbery in Wisconsin, but his sentence was suspended and he was placed on probation for seven years. He was given permission to reside in Illinois, where he was later arrested for burglary. His probation was then revoked without a hearing. This case was appealed on the grounds that probation revocation without a hearing and counsel violated Scarpelli's due process rights.

The Supreme Court held that the right to counsel should be decided on a case-by-case basis and that considerable latitude must be given the responsible agency in making the decision. The Court did indicate that counsel should be provided on request when the probationer claims that he or she did not commit the violation and when the reasons for the violation are complex or otherwise difficult to present. The significance of this case is that it equated probation with parole in terms of revocation hearing. Although the Court did not rule that all probationers and parolees have a right to be represented by counsel in revocation hearings, it did say that counsel should be provided when the probationer or parolee makes a good case for contesting the allegations.

Some evidence exists that aftercare revocation proceedings differ widely among jurisdictions. For example, Paul Knepper and Gray Cavender's examination of decision making with juveniles on aftercare in a western state found that "informal hearings" were conducted by a juvenile parole board in which juveniles were not present. Decisions about aftercare revocation were made at that time. Juveniles were then brought before the board and advised in a formal hearing why their aftercare status had been revoked.[50]

WHAT ARE INTERSTATE COMPACTS?

It becomes apparent to some juveniles with dysfunctional families that a home placement with a relative in another jurisdiction would probably increase the likelihood of their successful reintegration to society. They would then need to persuade their aftercare officers of the feasibility of such a placement. Or an institutional social worker or aftercare officer might come to this same conclusion, and if the youth agrees with such a placement, an **interstate compact,** if needed, would be initiated with the appropriate authorities in this other jurisdiction.

Basically, the compact is an agreement among the states to deal with both the mobility of youths and the need to keep them under supervision. The compact recognizes four basic areas in which the need for cooperation is evident:

> (1) cooperative supervision of delinquent juveniles on probation or parole; (2) the return, from one state to another, of delinquent juveniles who have escaped or absconded; (3) the return, from one state to another, of non-delinquent juveniles who have run away from home; and (4) additional measures for the protection of juveniles and of the public, which any or more of the party states may find desirable to undertake cooperatively.[51]

Interstate compacts are also drawn up when youths are wanted for crimes in several states at the same time. In addition, youths facing possible arrest, adjudication, sentencing, confinement, or aftercare supervision sometimes flee to another state to escape being held fully accountable for their offenses. The problems for the jurisdictions involved can become quite complicated. For example, an offender may have arrest warrants against him or her in several states at once, several states may wish to prosecute the youth at the same time, or one state may be attempting to rehabilitate him or her while other states are requesting transfer for prosecution. Through the implementation

Interstate compacts permit the placement of youths with special needs in facilities outside their home state. (Photo by Kathryn Miller.)

of this compact, parents, police, judges, probation officers, and institutional officials can, by going through the appropriate procedures, facilitate the return or supervision of wanted youths.

If a juvenile is to be sent to another state for treatment or rehabilitation, the states within the compact can enter into supplementary agreements that stipulate the rates to be paid for the care, treatment, and custody of out-of-state delinquent youths; that specify that the referring state shall at all times retain jurisdiction over these juveniles; and that ensure that the state receiving the youths into one of its institutions shall be the sole agent for the referring state.[52]

HOW CAN AFTERCARE BE IMPROVED?

Aftercare programs are either too frequently underdeveloped or nonexistent. In too many jurisdictions, the primary program is one in which probation or aftercare officers see their clients periodically but have few services to offer them. Many youths are required to do no more than send in monthly written reports to the parole officer or to report for a weekly "drug drop" (urinalysis).

The challenge to improve aftercare is even greater today because of the demise of traditional treatment approaches in so many training schools across the nation. As a result, males and females released from training schools are even less prepared for community living than they were in the past.

The desire to lower recidivism has led to a number of experiments based on the assumption either that the institutions are not doing their job or that conditions in the community prevent parolees from staying out of trouble. The most widely used program provides intensive supervision to high-risk youthful offenders, but, as previously discussed, these programs have had mixed results in terms of reducing recidivism. A serious concern with these programs, as the Rand Corporation evaluation of intensive supervision programs (ISP) in fourteen jurisdictions in nine states revealed, is that the programs were not successful at decreasing the "frequency of seriousness of new arrests but did increase the incidence of technical violations and jail terms . . . and drove up programs and court costs."[53] This evaluation recommended that new ISP programs continue to be developed, implemented, and tested.[54]

Lifeskills '95, one of the more promising aftercare programs, is geared to chronic, high-risk juvenile offenders and is designed to assist these offenders when released from secure confinement. This program begins with a thirteen-week reintegration treatment program that attempts to improve offenders' basic socialization skills, to stop their use or abuse of drugs, and to provide them with employment and/or educational opportunity. An evaluation of 125 experimentals and 125 controls released to either San Bernardino or Riverside County from a secure California youth authority facility found that Lifeskills '95 was successful in reducing recidivism rates during the period of program participation.[55]

Altschuler, Armstrong, and MacKenzie recommend the following reforms and changes to improve the effectiveness of aftercare services:

- Community-based aftercare is one part of a reintegrative corrections continuum that must be preceded by parallel services in the corrections facility and must include careful preparations for the aftercare to follow.
- Aftercare is frequently funded and staffed at levels far below what is required to provide truly intensive supervision and enhanced service delivery.
- Intensive aftercare, in contrast to "standard" aftercare, requires close attention via formal assessment procedures to determine which offenders are in need of a level of intervention that includes both highly intrusive supervision and enhanced treatment-related services.
- It is clear that a reduction in caseload size and an intensification in level of contacts are widely accepted operational principles for intensive aftercare programming.[56]

SUMMARY

Aftercare, or parole, is the least-developed segment of juvenile corrections. Fragmentation and lack of coordination pervade this relatively unknown phase of the treatment of juvenile offenders. States have neither developed comprehensive guidelines for coordinating agencies that work with released youths nor implemented a comprehensive plan for overseeing the administration of parole. Once youths are released from institutions, community forces often negate the effect of any positive programs in which the youths participated. It is reasonable to assume that if juveniles were provided with comprehensive and integrated complements to institutional programs, their chances of failure while on aftercare would be far less.

WEB SITES OF INTEREST

General information and links about juvenile aftercare can be found at
http://www.criminology.fsu.edu/jjclearinghouse/jj30.html

CRITICAL THINKING QUESTIONS

1. What are the major shocks a juvenile faces upon release to the community?
2. What is the purpose of aftercare?

3. What is prediction? How does it work? What are the drawbacks to effective prediction in aftercare today?
4. What programs appear to have the most promise for juvenile aftercare?
5. How might community factors interfere with a youth's chances of success on aftercare?
6. Using the information in this chapter, draw up a set of rules that juveniles on aftercare would consider reasonable and that would contribute to reducing recidivism.

NOTES

1. Juvenile probation officer interviewed in October 1986.
2. Frederick Howard Wines, *Punishment and Reformation: Rise of the Penitentiary System* (Boston: Thomas Y. Crowell and Company, 1985), 222.
3. Aftercare also remains one of the least studied, or researched, topics in juvenile justice. See Paul Knepper and Gray Cavender, "Decision-Making and the Typification of Juveniles on Parole." Unpublished paper presented at the annual meeting of the Academy of Criminal Justice Science, Denver, Colorado (April 1990).
4. Ibid.
5. George M. Camp and Camille Graham Camp, *The Corrections Yearbook, 1995* (South Salem, NY: Criminal Justice Institute, 1995), 16.
6. Hunter Hurst IV and Patricia McFall Torbet, *Organization and Administration of Juvenile Services: Probation, Aftercare, and State Institutions for Delinquent Youth* (Pittsburgh: National Center for Juvenile Justice, 1993).
7. Department of Youth Services, *Mission Statement, Office of Release Review* (Columbus, OH: Department of Youth Services, n.d.), 1.
8. Howard Abadinsky, *Probation and Parole: Theory and Practice,* 6th ed. (Upper Saddle River, NJ: Prentice Hall, 1997), 97.
9. Dean J. Champion, *The Juvenile Justice System: Delinquency, Processing, and the Law* (New York: Macmillan, 1992), 446.
10. Michael D. Norman, "Discretionary Justice: Decision-Making in a State Juvenile Parole Board," *Juvenile and Family Court Journal* 37 (1986), 19–25.
11. Don Gottfredson, "The Base Expectancy Approach," in *The Sociology of Punishment and Correction,* 2d ed., edited by Norman B. Johnston, Leonard Savitz, and Marvin E. Wolfgang (New York: John Wiley & Sons, 1970), 807–13.
12. Ibid., 807–13. For a more recent assessment of recidivism prediction in aftercare in Wisconsin and Arizona, see José B. Ashford and Craig W. LeCroy, "Decision-Making for Juvenile Offenders in Arizona," *Juvenile and Family Court Journal* 39 (1988), 47–53; and José B. Ashford and Lisa Bond-Maupin,

The Arizona Juvenile Aftercare Decision-Making (Phoenix: Arizona Department of Corrections, 1987).

13. For an extensive development of the guidelines, see Clemens Bartollas and John P. Conrad, *Introduction to Corrections* (New York: HarperCollins, 1992), 152–54.
14. The reader will find the details of the Comprehensive Crime Control Act in the U.S. Sentencing Commission, *Guidelines Manual* (Washington, DC: Government Printing Office, 1988).
15. Baird et al.'s research cited in David M. Altschuler and Troy L. Armstrong, "Intensive Aftercare for the High-Risk Juvenile Parolee: Issues and Approaches in Reintegration and Community Supervision," in *Intensive Interventions with High-Risk Youths: Promising Approaches in Juvenile Probation and Parole,* edited by Troy L. Armstrong (Monsey, NY: Criminal Justice Press, 1991), 55.
16. Bartollas and Conrad, *Introduction to Corrections,* 270.
17. Observations of one of the authors who worked in and has studied training schools in five states.
18. Ibid.
19. Interviewed in 1989.
20. The following discussion is adapted from José B. Ashford and Craig Winston LeCroy, "Juvenile Parole Policy in the United States: Determinate versus Indeterminate Models," *Justice Quarterly* 10 (June 1993), 187–91.
21. For an example of a house-detention component of an aftercare program, see W. Barton and J. Butts, "Viable Options: Intensive Supervision Programs for Juvenile Delinquents," *Crime and Delinquency* 36 (1990), 238–56. For the use of electronic monitoring with gang youth, see Elaine B. Duxbury, "Correctional Interventions," in *The Gang Intervention Handbook,* edited by Arnold Goldstein and C. Ronald Huff (Champaign, IL: Research Press, 1993), 435–36.
22. Altschuler and Armstrong, "Intensive Aftercare for the High-Risk Juvenile Parolee, 49–50.
23. Ibid., 50.
24. Ted Palmer, *The Re-Emergence of Correctional Intervention* (Newbury Park, CA: Sage Publications, 1992), 86.
25. Henry Sontheimer, Lynne Goodstein, and Michael Kovacevic, *Philadelphia Intensive Aftercare Probation Evaluation Project* (Pittsburgh: Center for Juvenile Justice Training and Research, 1990), 3.
26. Cecil Marshall and Keith Snyder, "Intensive and Aftercare Probation Services in Pennsylvania." Paper presented at the annual meeting of the American Society of Criminology, Baltimore, Maryland (November 7, 1990), 3. See also Henry Sontheimer and Lynne Goodstein, "An Evaluation of Juvenile Intensive Aftercare Probation: Aftercare versus System Response Effects," *Justice Quarterly* 10 (June 1993), 197–227; and Lynne Goodstein and

Henry Sontheimer, "The Implementation of an Intensive Aftercare Program for Serious Juvenile Offenders: A Case Study," *Criminal Justice and Behavior* (September 1997), 332–59.

27. Don A. Josi and Dale K. Sechrest, "A Pragmatic Approach to Parole Aftercare Evaluation of a Community Reintegration Program for High-Risk Youthful Offenders," *Justice Quarterly* 16 (March 1995), 66.
28. William Deganan, *Lifeskills Post-Parole Treatment Program* (Sanger, CA: Operation, New Hope, 1994).
29. Josi and Sechrest, "A Pragmatic Approach to Parole Aftercare Evaluation of a Community Reintegration Program for High-Risk Youthful Offenders," 66.
30. Palmer, *The Re-Emergence of Correctional Intervention*, 87.
31. J. Fagan, M. Forst, and T. Vivona, *Treatment and Reintegration of Violent Juvenile Offenders: Experimental Results* (San Francisco: URSA Institute, 1988), 14–15.
32. Palmer, *The Re-Emergence of Correctional Intervention*, 85–86.
33. David M. Altschuler, Troy L. Armstrong, and Doris Layton MacKenzie, "Reintegration, Supervised Release, and Intensive Aftercare," *OJJDP: Juvenile Justice Bulletin* (Washington, DC: Office of Juvenile Justice and Delinquency Prevention, 1999), 6.
34. M. D. Sealock, D. C. Gottfredson, and C. A. Gallagher, "Drug Treatment for Juvenile Offenders: Some Good and Bad News," *Journal of Research in Crime and Delinquency* 34 (1997), 210–36.
35. Elizabeth Piper Deschenes, Peter W. Greenwood, and Grant Marshall, *The Nokomis Challenge Program Evaluation* (Santa Monica, CA: Rand, 1996), ii.
36. Ibid., 121, 125, 127.
37. New York State Division of Parole, Evaluation, and Planning, *PARJO III: Final Evaluation of the PARJO Pilot Supervision Program* (Albany: New York State Division of Parole, Evaluation, and Planning, 1985).
38. Altschuler et al., "Reintegration, Supervised Release, and Intensive Aftercare, 7.
39. P. W. Greenwood, E. P. Deschenes, and J. Adams, *Chronic Juvenile Offenders: Final Results From the Skillman Aftercare Experiment* (Santa Monica, CA: Rand, 1993).
40. David M. Altschuler and Troy L. Armstrong, *Intensive Aftercare for High-Risk Juveniles: Policies and Procedures* (Washington, DC: Office of Juvenile Justice and Delinquency Prevention, 1994), 3.
41. Richard G. Wiebush, Betsie McNulty, and Thalo Le, *Implementation of the Intensive Community-Based Aftercare Program* (Washington, DC: Office of Juvenile Justice and Delinquency Prevention, 2000).
42. Altschuler et al., "Reintegration, Supervised Release, and Intensive Aftercare," 8–9.
43. Champion, *The Juvenile Justice System*, 447. See also Ted Palmer and Robert Wedge, "California's Juvenile Probation Camps: Findings and Implications,"

Crime and Delinquency 35 (1989), 234–53; and Mark R. Wiederanders, *Success on Parole: The Influence of Self-Reported Attitudes, Experiences, and Background Characteristics on the Parole Behaviors of Youthful Offenders—Final Report* (Sacramento, CA: Department of Youth Authority, 1983).

44. William R. Arnold, *Juveniles on Parole: A Sociological Perspective* (New York: Random House, 1970). The following section summarizes Arnold's theory of parole found on pages 94–131.
45. Ibid.
46. Interviewed in September 1992.
47. Arnold, *Juveniles on Parole,* 24.
48. Peter W. Greenwood, "Juvenile Crime and Juvenile Justice," in *Crime,* edited by James Q. Wilson and Joan Petersilia (San Francisco: ICS Press, 1994), 91–117.
49. Champion, *The Juvenile Justice System,* 446.
50. *Mempa v. Rhay,* 389 U.S. 128 (1967); *People ex rel. v. Warden Greenhaven,* 318 N.Y.S. 2d 449 (1971); *Murray v. Page,* 429 F.2d 1359 (10th Cir. 1970); *Morrissey v. Brewer,* 408 U.S. 1971, 928 (1972); *Gagnon v. Scarpelli,* 411 U.S. 778 (1973).
51. *Murray v. Page,* 429 F.2d 1359 (10th Cir. 1970).
52. *Morrissey v. Brewer,* 408 U.S. 1971, 928 (1972).
53. Ibid.
54. Knepper and Cavender, "Decision-Making and the Typification of Juveniles on Parole."
55. *Purdons, Pennsylvania Statutes Annotated* 62 PS. Paragraph 731, 1968, 82.
56. Joan Petersilia and Susan Turner, "Intensive Probation and Parole," in *Crime and Justice: A Review of Research* 16, edited by Michael Tonry (Chicago: University of Chicago Press, 1993), 281.
57. Ibid.
58. Don A. Josi and Dale K. Sechrest, "A Pragmatic Approach to Parole Aftercare: Evaluation of a Community Reintegration Program for High-Risk Youthful Offenders," *Justice Quarterly* 16 (March 1999), 51–80.
59. Altschuler et al., "Reintegration, Supervised Release, and Intensive Aftercare," 11, 15.

11

JUVENILE INSTITUTIONALIZATION

OBJECTIVES

1. To trace the development of juvenile institutionalization throughout the history of the United States
2. To examine the rhetoric and reality of juvenile institutionalization
3. To evaluate the quality of juvenile institutionalization
4. To portray how juveniles respond to institutionalization
5. To reveal the rights that juveniles have in juvenile institutions

KEY TERMS

attention homes
cottage system
detention centers
forestry camps
house of refuge
jails
medicalization of deviance
mental health placements
ranches
social roles
training schools
victimization

The staff here do not emphasize enough what is going on in a student's life and how the student can better himself. Students come in with one mentality, and they leave with the same mentality.

On the outs, I had a driver's license, used to drive around, had all the girls liking me, and used to deal drugs. I come in here and see people who I knew out there. It's just like a family reunion, or a party, or a vacation. You go back out there with the same mentality, only you're worse because you know better ways. You've used your experience from being locked up, from talking to other people who've been caught. You find better ways to do what you've done before.

The staff don't make you go to school or show you that schooling is important. They're more concerned with keeping you controlled, keeping your aggression on tap. They don't offer programs that will help you control your anger. They don't attempt to persuade you to go to AA or NA [Alcoholics Anonymous or Narcotics Anonymous] groups. So, if I like to sit in the cottage and do nothing, staff are happy. That keeps me quiet. I am an aggressive person, and they're happy so long as I'm not bothering nobody. They want me to make their job easy. All they are concerned about is putting in their eight hours.

—Institutionalized Youth[1]

The confined youth speaking in the opening quote makes three devastating critiques of juvenile institutionalization. First, he charges that institutional staff do not care. Second, he claims that the needed programs are not available to residents of training schools. Third, he views training schools as schools of crime, in which youths learn more about a life of crime than they knew when they were first confined. As part of this negative impact of juvenile institutionalization, this training school resident believes that confinement increases the will to commit crime in the future. One of the purposes of this chapter is to evaluate the charges made by this Ohio youth.

The juvenile justice system often is accused of being too lenient, yet youths who are believed to be dangerous or who show little sign of mending their ways frequently find themselves locked up behind walls. The facilities in which these youths are placed are divided into two general categories: temporary care facilities and correctional facilities. Detention homes, shelters, reception centers, and jails are temporary care facilities; boot camps, ranches, forestry camps, and training schools are long-term correctional facilities. The primary differences between these two categories of facilities are the absence of correctional programs and the shorter length of stay in temporary care facilities. Temporary care facilities frequently house both males and females in the same general location, whereas correctional facilities often separate them. Juveniles to the adult court can also be sentenced to adult prisons, or they can be transferred to mental health placements. This chapter focuses on the training school because of the length of time it holds youths and because of the special role it has played in juvenile justice.

WHAT IS THE HISTORY OF JUVENILE CONFINEMENT?

At the time of the American Revolution, the penal system in the colonies was modeled after that in England. The larger urban jails, county jails, and prisons contained men, women, and juveniles, whether they were felons or misdemeanants, insane or sane—sometimes all mixed together. Smaller rural counties, however, had less need for larger jails and prisons and temporarily housed their wayward citizens in small rural jails.

In neither city nor county, however, were youths expected to get into trouble. If they did, they were subject to the same punishments as adults. Beyond that, normal community processes were thought to be sufficient to keep them in line. Community norms were enforced through gossip, ridicule, and other informal social pressures, and little formal social control was needed. Local enforcers consisted of watchmen, magistrates, and sheriffs. All those who were caught, including youths, received fines, beatings, and floggings; were put in stocks; were driven through town in carts to be ridiculed by the citizenry; and in extreme cases were hanged, burned, mutilated, or banished from the community. After punishment, some youths were apprenticed to local craftsmen; until the mid-1800s others were sent on extended whaling voyages; and still others were placed with relatives or farm families.[2]

In the late 1700s and early 1800s, the United States was in a period of transition. The rural way of life was threatened, and the changes were having an irreversible effect on the structure of society. Concern about what to do with the growing numbers of juveniles who were abandoned, were runaways, or had run afoul of community norms increased and placed the young nation in a dilemma. On the one hand, thinkers reasoned that the natural depravity of humans made attempts at rehabilitation useless and that banishing the guilty was simpler than either punishment or rehabilitation. On the other hand, some hoped to find specific causes for deviancy, and the family was believed to be the primary source of the problem. Common sense and the examination of case histories indicated that older offenders usually had been problem children. The idea emerged that if institutions could be used for the poor, perhaps similar institutions could be set up for children using the well-adjusted family as the model.[3]

Regardless of the source of the problem, the situation demanded a solution. The growing number of delinquents and other children running in the streets of larger cities, the increasing population, and the changing character of U.S. society were all putting greater pressure on existing facilities. Conditions in the jails and prisons were deplorable. Youths were sentenced for fixed periods of time and were confined with the worst society had to offer. Some youths died of disease, and morals were corrupted as children ten to eighteen years old were confined with adult felons.

The House of Refuge

When citizens and reformers became concerned about these inhumane conditions, their solution was the **house of refuge.** This facility was for all children, not just delinquents. Benevolence and compassion, along with concern over the degrading conditions in the jails and prisons, motivated the reformers to establish the houses of refuge.

New York City started the first school for males in 1825, followed by Boston in 1826 and Philadelphia in 1828. Other cities, including Bangor, Richmond, Mobile, Cincinnati, and Chicago, followed suit over the years. Twenty-three houses of refuge were built in the 1830s and thirty more in the 1840s. Of these, the vast majority were for males, with an occasional institution reserved for females. Their capacity ranged from ninety at Lancaster, Massachusetts, to one thousand at the New York House of Refuge, with a median number of 210. The promise of these institutions seemed so great that youths with every type of problem were placed in them. The New York House of Refuge accepted children adjudicated guilty of committing crimes as well as those who simply were in danger of getting into trouble. The poor, destitute, incorrigible, and orphaned were all confined. Admissions policies were obviously quite flexible, and little concern was shown for due process; some youths simply were kidnapped off the streets. Not until later did these institutions begin to limit their rosters to those who had committed crimes.

The children generally were confined for periods ranging from less than six weeks to about twenty-four months, although some stayed longer. In some institutions the youths were taught trades, such as manufacturing shoes, brushes, and chairs, or were readied for apprenticeships to local craftsmen. Sentences were indeterminate, and superintendents of the institutions made the decision as to whether the apprenticed youths would be released or returned to the institution.

The first of the houses of refuge set aside for females was chartered in New York in 1824. Some schools were biracial, but many, especially those in the southern states, were segregated. Even in the North, African Americans often were sent to the state prisons and county jails rather than to the new houses of refuge.

These juvenile institutions accepted the family model whole-heartedly, for reformers desired to implant the order, discipline, and care of the family into institutional life. The institution, in effect, would become the home, peers would become the family, and staff would become the parents. Orphanages and houses of refuge substituted a rigorous system of control and discipline for the disordered life of the community.

Discipline was severe when the rules were disobeyed, but the reformers believed that once the authority of the superintendents was established, they would be looked on admiringly and as friends. Belief in these principles was so great that parents for the first time had to surrender their authority to superintendents and could not participate in the upbringing of their unruly children.

The first houses of refuge did not differ greatly from the existing state prisons and county jails. Built to hold inmates securely, some were surrounded by walls, and their interiors were designed to implant the notions of order and rationality in their charges:

> The buildings were usually four stories high, with two long hallways running along either side of a row of cells. The rooms, following one after another, were all five by eight feet wide, seven feet high, windowless, with an iron-lattice slab for a door and flues for ventilation near the ceiling. Each group of eleven cells could be locked or unlocked simultaneously with one master key; every aperture within an inmate's reach was guarded by iron. On the first floor of each wing was a huge tub for bathing, sizeable enough to hold fifteen to twenty boys; on the fourth floor were ten special punishment cells.[4]

These institutions were based on the congregate system, with large numbers of clients sharing a single room or cell. Some later facilities, especially those built after 1850, were based on the cottage system, which is discussed later in this chapter.

Treatment of the youths paralleled the routine nature of the facility's physical plant. When the youths entered, they were dressed in institutional clothing and given identical haircuts. Troublemakers were punished. Placing offenders on a diet of bread and water or depriving them of meals altogether were milder forms of discipline, but they were coupled with solitary confinement if a severe punishment was deemed necessary. Corporal punishments, used alone or in combination with other corrections, consisted of whipping with a cat-o'-nine-tails or manacling with a ball and chain. The worst offenders were shipped off to sea.

The school, the workshop, and the church were all brought into the house of refuge to teach order, obedience, and discipline. Routines were established, schedules were organized, and the institutions began to resemble military organizations rather than families. Youths were awakened by bells, and their days were partitioned by the ringing of bells. They awoke at sunrise, marched to washrooms, paraded in ranks for inspections, marched to chapel, attended school for an hour, and went to breakfast when the bells rang again at seven o'clock. From seven-thirty until noon the boys worked in the shops, making nails and other needed items of the day, and the girls sewed, did laundry, cooked, and cleaned. The lunch hour was from noon until one o'clock, and then work was continued until five o'clock. A half-hour was allotted for washing and eating, following which there were two-and-a-half hours of evening classes. After the evening prayer, youths were marched back to their cells, were locked in, and were expected to be quiet for the night until the routine began again.[5]

The specific order of daily events varied from institution to institution, but all followed the same basic schedule and routine. In some, youths were counted frequently to make sure that none had escaped, and in many facilities silence was maintained at all times, even during the recreation and exercise periods. Eating at times other than regularly scheduled meals was forbidden, and youths who wanted extra food had to raise their hands. In school everyone recited in unison.

Reformers were enthusiastic about the house of refuge, but the residents apparently did not share the same positive feelings. Hutchins Hapgood, sent to the New York House of Refuge in the nineteenth century, viewed this setting as a "school for crime," in which "unspeakably bad habits were contracted there. The older boys wrecked the younger ones," and children who were orphans had an especially hard time. The residents, he added, were overworked making overalls and were beaten frequently. He bluntly concluded, "I say without hesitation that lads sent to an institution like the House of Refuge, the Catholic Protectory, or the Juvenile Asylum might better be taken out and shot."[6]

The Reformatory or Training School

Reformatories, also called training schools or industrial schools, developed in the mid-nineteenth century. The new reformatories were essentially a continuation of the houses of refuge, although they did stress a longer period of schooling, usually half a day. Another change is that the contracting of inmates' labor became more exploitative, as manufacturers often inflicted cruelty and violence against juveniles during working hours. The cat-o'nine-tails, for example, would be used on youths who slacked off on their work in the reformatory shops.

In spite of the questionable nature of these institutions, states continued to build reformatories or training schools. In 1847 Massachusetts opened the first state-operated training school, the Lyman School for Boys, and in 1856 established the State Industrial School for Girls at Lancaster. New York built an industrial school in 1849, and by 1870 Connecticut, Indiana, Maryland, Nevada, New Hampshire, New Jersey, Ohio, and Vermont had opened training schools for delinquents. By 1890 nearly every state outside of the South had established a training school.[7]

The Cottage System

Introduced in 1854, the **cottage system** spread throughout the country. Reformers had succeeded in placing the industrial schools outside cities, their rationale being that youths on farms would be reformed when exposed to the rural virtues, the simple way of life, and the bounty of Mother Nature. With the new cottage system, the process of individual reform could be furthered, as residents were housed in separate buildings, usually no more than twenty to forty per cottage. The training schools were no longer supposed to be fortresslike either in physical design or in the relationships among residents and staff. The first cottages were log cabins; later ones were of brick or

Todays cottage system often reflects the past with rustic décors. This cottage is on the Mel Blount Youth Homegrounds. (Photo by Stuart Miller.)

stone. This form of organization was widely accepted and is the basic design for many juvenile facilities even today.

Three major changes began to affect juvenile institutions in the closing decades of the nineteenth century—the increasing size of institutional populations, a decrease in funding from state legislatures, and the admission of more dangerous offenders. As a result, the industrial school became custodial, and superintendents had to accept custodianship as an adequate goal.[8] Yet faith in the industrial school continued into the twentieth century.

WHAT ARE TWENTIETH-CENTURY CHANGES IN JUVENILE CONFINEMENT?

The most important change in the way society dealt with institutionalized juveniles in the twentieth century was the evolution of treatment. Although case histories had been used since the founding of the very first houses of refuge, they became a fundamental element of juvenile corrections by the 1920s. Juvenile corrections also moved toward the scientific handling of clients, as they were classified into many different gradations in many facilities. An emphasis began to be placed on individualized diagnosis and treatment; reality therapy, transactional analysis (TA), guided group interaction, and positive peer culture, in particular, became popular therapies (see Chapter 12 for an explanation of these treatment modalities).

Juveniles were able to graduate from state-accredited high school programs while confined in training schools. Some youths were permitted home furloughs, and some were allowed to work in the community during the day. Recreational programs became more diverse, as did vocational programs, with printing, barbering, welding, and painting among the courses offered in well-equipped training schools.

Finally, the structure of juvenile institutions changed somewhat during the twentieth century. The types of institutions expanded to include ranches and forestry camps, educational and vocational training schools, and end-of-the-line or maximum-security training schools. Some of the larger training schools abandoned the cottage system and returned to incorporating the entire facility under one roof. Cottage parents were replaced in many institutions by staff members who worked eight-hour shifts.

Brutal Treatment and Critical Response

Institutional brutality has a long history in training schools of this nation. For example, a report on the St. Charles School for Boys by the Illinois Crime Commission in 1928 notes:

> All whippings were administered by a disciplinary officer who went . . . to each cottage each evening after supper and whipped any boys who had been reported earlier by the house father, or for whom the house father requested punishment at that time. Some boys were punished by being locked up in the "hole" for up to thirty-two days with no shoes and no mattress. They slept on wooden boards nailed to the concrete floor. Some were handcuffed to iron pipes and kept manacled day and night.[9]

Institutional brutality, however, escaped public attention until the late 1960s and early 1970s. Jerome Miller, director of the Division of Youth Services (DYS) in Massachusetts, was appalled in the early 1970s at what he termed the "sadistic discipline" found in the training schools of that state. Residents at Shirley Training School informed him that they had to drink from toilets or kneel for hours on the stone floor with a pencil under their knees.[10]

Miller then received one day from an anonymous staff member of Shirley Training School a file containing summaries for male residents in Cottage Nine, the disciplinary cottage. It included the following, shocking information:

> Donald, 16, beaten on the soles of his bare feet with straps. Walter, 16, handcuffed for 22 days and nights when returned from escape. Charles, 17, padlocked to water pipe, given a cold shower for six minutes.[11]

Miller also discovered that one resident of this cottage had his feet strapped to a bed frame and was beaten on the bare soles with wooden paddles or the wooden back of floor brushes. If all this was not enough, the

DYS commissioner was informed why the escape rate at Shirley was so low, for after a runaway was returned to the institution, "the escapee's ring finger was bent back across the top of his left hand until the finger broke."[12]

One of the authors recalls well the brutal treatment of residents that he observed while working in a maximum-security training school from 1969 to 1973. "Instant therapy," a popular treatment approach with disciplinary staff, involved a hard punch to the face or body of a recalcitrant youth. Then there was the "goon squad," whose primary responsibility was to "work over" runaways who had been returned to the institution. The mop squad, reserved for youths with disciplinary write-ups, was designed to break a resident's spirits; each participant had to work double-time with a mop handle one-third the size of a regular mop handle for several hours without a break.[13]

Institutional Reforms

It is no wonder that reformers accused training schools of being violent, inhumane, and criminogenic. Fortunately, this widespread criticism of training schools in the early and mid-1970s led to several positive reforms.

The process of removing status offenders from public training schools took place soon after the Juvenile Justice and Delinquency Prevention Act of 1974 was passed into law. The reduction of staff brutality became a major concern in states across the nation—so much so that by the end of the 1970s, striking a youth would lead to dismissal in the majority of state institutions in this nation. Staff training programs, especially for line staff, were developed and required in many states. Institutional staff frequently were trained at states' correctional training academies. Grievance procedures for residents, initiated in California in the 1970s, gained acceptance and wide use across the nation. In addition, the policy of converting single-sex institutions into coeducational facilities (sometimes called "cocorrections") was experimented with in the 1970s in several states. For example, North Carolina converted all its juvenile institutions into coeducational facilities in the 1970s. Furthermore, the American Correctional Association accreditation process that was widely accepted in adult corrections became increasingly accepted as a model for improving juvenile correctional institutions. Finally, the intervention of the federal courts in the 1970s and 1980s led to the reform of several of this nation's most shocking and harmful training schools.

In sum, as we examine short- and long-term juvenile confinement, it can be argued that the majority are not what they should be, but there is no question that they are much better than they were only a few decades ago.

WHAT ARE THE SHORT-TERM CONFINEMENTS OF JUVENILES?

Juvenile offenders are placed in jails, detention centers, and shelter care facilities for short-term confinement.

Jails

The degrading conditions of nineteenth-century jails, as previously suggested, were one of the reasons motivating reformers to establish houses of refuge. It was commonly agreed that the **jails** were no place for a juvenile. Overcrowded conditions and idleness fostered a lawless society, one in which the juvenile was frequently a sexual victim. Juveniles also had alarming rates of suicide in jail.[14]

Still, partly because so few alternatives were available, large numbers of juveniles continued to be confined in county jails and police lockups. Estimates varied, but between five hundred thousand and one million youths each year were locked up in jails during the 1970s.[15]

The numbers appeared to decline in the 1980s and 1990s, chiefly because of the Juvenile Justice and Delinquency Prevention Act (JJDPA) of 1974. This act provided restrictive criteria governing the confinement of juveniles in adult facilities. Congress amended the JJDPA in 1980, requiring participating states to remove all juveniles from adult jails and lockups by the end of 1985 if they wanted to receive federal funding for juvenile justice. The 1985 deadline was extended to 1988 and then again was amended in 1989, because so few states had achieved full compliance.[16]

According to the data published in April 2000, the 1999 average daily population of juveniles in jails was 9,485, an increase of 8.5 percent over the previous twelve months. Of these, 8,631 were being held as adults and 854 were being held as juveniles.[17] But it can be argued that these figures are not accurate, because youths held in jail for only a few hours are not generally included in these figures.

Several reasons exist why jail removal of juveniles continues to remain a distant goal. First, juveniles who are transferred to adult court and are waiting for criminal trials make up an increasingly large category of youths confined in jail. Second, at least forty states continue to resist full compliance with the JJDPA jail-removal mandate. The claim is frequently made that the states lack the necessary resources and alternatives to implement the jail-removal mandate.[18] Third, the belief is widely held that separating juveniles from adult inmates is sufficient to protect the juveniles against the harmful effects of jail confinement.

What is hopeful is that a number of states have taken a strong stand against the jailing of juveniles. California and Utah have made it unlawful to jail a youthful offender.[19] Illinois, Missouri, North Carolina, Tennessee, and Virginia have enacted legislation either prohibiting the jailing of minors or restricting the number of admissions.[20]

Detention Centers

Established at the end of the nineteenth century as an alternative to jail for juveniles, **detention centers,** also called juvenile halls, are intended to be temporary holding centers. According to a 1991 study, 335 public and 28 private detention centers existed. The 569,902 youths admitted to these centers in 1990 had an average length of stay of fifteen days and were most typically sixteen-year-old males who were charged with serious property offenses.[21] The court administers the majority of juvenile detention centers, although state agencies, city or county governments, welfare departments, and juvenile courts also manage these facilities. The state governments of Connecticut, Delaware, Vermont, and Puerto Rico assume responsibility for administering juvenile detention centers. Georgia, Maryland, Massachusetts, New Hampshire, and Rhode Island operate regional detention facilities.

The traditional detention center has sparked many horror stories, and, on more than one occasion, former residents have described to the authors what a toxic environment these facilities were. Fortunately, detention in the United States has experienced marked improvement in the past two decades. A nationwide movement to develop standards for detention and more innovative detention programs have provided the impetus to improve detention practices in the United States.

Attention homes were initiated in Boulder, Colorado, and have spread to other jurisdictions. Their stated purpose is to give juveniles *attention* rather than *detention*. These facilities have no fences, locked doors, or other physical restraints. They also provide more extensive programming and involvement between residents and staff. Home detention, as previously discussed, is a nonresidential approach to confinement. It was first used in St. Louis, Newport News, Norfolk, and Washington, DC, and is now being used throughout the nation.

A detention home is often the first stop for youths who have committed serious offenses or are in need of protection. (Photo by Kathryn Miller.)

In spite of their overall improvement, detention practices still exhibit many disturbing features in the United States. The most serious concern is that according to a 1991 survey of detention centers, 62 percent of these facilities offered no treatment programs.[22] As an indication of how youths need support and intervention at what may be a very turbulent time, there were more acts of suicide or attempted suicide in detention facilities in 1990 (4.59 per 100 juveniles) than in reception centers (2.02), training schools (1.48), and ranches (1.10).[23]

Another serious concern is that increasing numbers of detention centers have turned to mechanical restraints and isolation to control their populations. In 1991, 97 percent of surveyed facilities used handcuffs, 55 percent used anklets, 18 percent used security belts, 13 percent used four-point ties, and 2 percent used straitjackets. This survey also found that detention centers have higher short-term and long-term isolation rates than do training schools.[24]

Shelter Care Facilities

Shelter care facilities were developed in the early 1970s to provide short-term care for status offenders and for dependent or neglected children. Although only 23 public shelters existed in 1975, they quickly increased in number because of the funding mandate of the Juvenile Justice and Delinquency Prevention Act, which requires that noncriminal youths be placed in such facilities. In 1991, there were 309 private and 439 public shelters in operation.[25]

The length of stay in these nonsecure facilities with no locked doors varies from overnight to a few days. Occasionally, a juvenile must stay several weeks because of difficulty in scheduling court-required family therapy sessions or because of hearing delays in the juvenile court. Delinquent youths may be placed in shelter care facilities if the county has no detention center and the juvenile judge is reluctant to detain the youth in the county jail or if a judge decides to reward a delinquent youth's positive behavior in detention by transferring him or her to the more open shelter care.

Shelter care facilities do permit residents to enjoy home visits on weekends and field trips into the community during the week. However, as an associate director of a midwestern shelter care facility clearly communicates, these facilities do not offer treatment programs:

> There is no other place that will take all the kids we do. We're not here to punish kids; nor are we here to treat them. We're like a bus stop. You get into serious problems when you try to offer treatment programs. Referral sources, such as social workers and probation officers, want to have a place that is safe for children, and they want them here when they're ready to go to whatever placement they're going.[26]

The openness of these settings, not surprisingly, creates problems with runaways and makes it difficult to control contraband drugs among residents.

Another problem for staff is that these facilities have their share of disciplinary problems among residents, who often have difficulty controlling their attitudes and actions.

WHAT ARE THE LONG-TERM CONFINEMENTS OF JUVENILES?

Boot camps, reception and diagnostic centers, ranches and forestry camps, and training schools are the main forms of long-term juvenile correctional institutions. Juveniles also may be transferred to mental health placements or sentenced to youthful offender facilities and adult prisons.

BOOT CAMPS

Boot camps are receiving increased attention in juvenile justice. Emphasizing military discipline, physical training, and regimented activity for periods that typically range from 30 to 120 days, the intent of these programs is to shock youthful offenders to prevent them from committing further crimes. Boot camp programs are generally designed for offenders who have failed with lesser sanctions such as probation. The Orleans Parish program accepts anyone who is sentenced by the juvenile judge, but most programs generally exclude sex offenders, armed robbers, and violent offenders.[27]

The rationale for juvenile boot camps is consistent with the juvenile justice system's historical emphasis on rehabilitation, usually incorporating explicit assumptions about the needs of delinquent youths and providing remedial, counseling, and aftercare programs necessary to address these needs.[28] All the programs employ military customs and courtesies, including uniformed drill instructors, a platoon structure, and summary punishment of participants, including group punishment under some circumstances. Although there are differences in emphasis, with Denver creating the most militaristic environment, juvenile boot camp programs have generally discovered that they must tailor their environment to participants' maturity levels.[29]

Boot camps for juveniles are generally reserved for midrange offenders: those who have failed with lesser sanctions such as probation but who are not yet hardened delinquents. The shock aspect of the boot camp experience includes incarceration as the environment within which the program takes place.[30] These programs typically focus on youths in the mid- to late teens and exclude sex offenders, armed robbers, and violent offenders. Only a few programs limit themselves to youths who are nonviolent, have committed their first serious offense, or are being confined for the first time. In contrast, the Orleans Parish program accepts anyone who is sentenced by the juvenile judge.[31]

As of 1999, ten states had implemented about fifty boot camps, which housed about forty five hundred juvenile offenders nationwide. The oldest program was established in Orleans Parish, Louisiana, in 1985. Three of the newer programs—located in Cleveland, Denver, and Mobile—are funded through the OJJDP, which launched a three-site study of boot camps for youthful offenders in 1991.

The program guidelines of these three experimental programs identified six key components to maximize their effectiveness: education and job training and placement, community service, substance abuse counseling and treatment, health and mental health care, individualized and continuous case management, and intensive aftercare services. The 1994 evaluation of the three sites found that the sites were unable to implement the program guidelines fully. Each program "experienced considerable instability and staff turnover" and was unable to "implement and sustain stable, well-developed aftercare services."[32]

Boot camps for juveniles included some type of work detail; most allocate more than half the day to educational and counseling activities and most include some form of drug and alcohol counseling. In addition, most of the boot camp programs assign graduates to a period of intensive community supervision.[33]

A fair assessment may be that the quality of boot camps depends largely on how much they tailor their programs to participants' maturity levels and how effective they are in implementing and sustaining effective aftercare services. Doris McKenzie and colleagues recently completed a study of twenty-six juvenile boot camps, comparing them with traditional facilities (the experiences of 2,668 juveniles in twenty-six boot camps were compared to 1,848 juveniles in twenty-two traditional facilities).[34] They found that overall, juveniles in boot camps perceived their environments as more positive or therapeutic, less hostile or dangerous, and more structured than juveniles in traditional facilities perceived their environments. Moreover, this study revealed that, over time, youths in boot camps became less antisocial and less depressed than did youths in traditional facilities.[35]

Other follow-ups on juvenile boot camps have almost all found recidivism rates of boot camps to be slightly higher or about the same as those of traditional juvenile facilities.[36] Charges of abuse in boot camps have taken place in Arizona, Maryland, South Dakota, and Georgia. In the summer of 1999, a fourteen-year-old girl in South Dakota died from dehydration during a long-distance run.[37] In July 1, 2001, Anthony Haynes, a fourteen-year-old boy from Arizona, died at a boot camp, where troubled juveniles were allegedly kicked and forced to eat mud. In this camp, the regimen includes forced marches, in-your-face discipline, and a daily diet of an apple, a carrot, and a bowl of beans.[38]

The combined disappointing recidivism results, as well as the charges of abuse, have prompted Georgia, Maryland, Arizona, and South Dakota to shut down or reevaluate the get tough with juveniles approach popularized in the early 1990s. Arizona removed fifty juveniles from the boot camp in which

Haynes died. Maryland shut down one boot camp and suspended the military regimens at its other two facilities after reports of systematic assaults. In Maryland, the charges of abuse led to the ouster of the state's top five juvenile justice officials.[39]

Panaceas die hard in juvenile corrections, and this highly acclaimed approach of the past two decades will continue to be used across the nation. Its recent criticisms and disappointing recidivism data probably will result in fewer new programs being established and more scrutiny of the existing programs.

Critical Thinking Question.

On the basis of everything you have read and heard about boot camps, would you continue their use? Why or why not?

Reception and Diagnostic Centers

The purpose of **reception and diagnostic centers**—which are both publicly and privately administered—is to determine which treatment plan suits each adjudicated juvenile and which training school is the best placement. In 1990, 21,591 youths were admitted to reception centers, 86 percent of whom had committed delinquent offenses.[40]

A few of the larger states have reception and diagnostic centers, but for most states, this diagnostic process takes place in one of the training schools. Although staff are more concerned about short-term diagnosis than long-term treatment, youths frequently receive more attention during this period than at any other time during their confinement. A psychiatrist usually will evaluate the youth and will see him or her several times if the youth is confined for a violent crime. A clinical psychologist, or a person with skills in administering psychological tests, frequently will subject the youth to a battery of tests to determine intelligence, attitudes, maturity, and emotional problems. A social worker, meanwhile, completes a case study of each youth. Equipped with background material from the court, which sometimes takes a week or two to arrive at the reception center, the social case study primarily investigates the youth's family background. Academic staff identify any learning problems and determine the proper school placement. A physical and dental examination also is frequently administered. Finally, cottage or dormitory supervisors evaluate the youth's institutional adjustment and peer relationships. A case conference on each resident is held once all the reports are prepared, the needs and attitudes of the youth are summarized, and recommendations are made as to the best cottage or institutional placement.

Although staff previously have evaluated residents over a period of four to six weeks, this process has been condensed today to an average length of stay of thirty-four days.[41] The youth is then transferred to the approved institutional placement, and the diagnostic report goes with him or her. It is not uncommon for this report to receive little attention, so the youth often must repeat a similar process in the admitting institution.

Ranches and Forestry Camps

Ranches and forestry camps are minimum-security institutional placements that are normally reserved for youths who have committed minor offenses or who have been committed to the department of youth services or private corrections for the first time. Of the sixty-four **forestry camps** in the United States in 1992, sixteen were in Florida; fourteen in New York; six in South Carolina; five each in Alabama, California, Missouri, and North Carolina; and four each in Maryland and Oregon.[42]

In these camps residents typically do conservation work in a state park, cutting grass and weeds, cleaning up, and doing general maintenance. Treatment programs generally consist of individual contacts with social workers and the child-care staff, group therapy, and an occasional home visit. Residents may be taken to nearby towns on a regular, or weekly, basis to make purchases and to attend community events.

In 1990, **ranches** admitted 17,606 youths, 13 percent of all confined juveniles. The average length of stay was six and a half months (194 days), which was one month less than the average stay in training schools (seven and a half months, or 225 days). Frequently, privately administered and widely used in California and a few other states, ranches' populations tend to be predominantly White. Indeed, in 1990, 32 percent of African-American youthful offenders were confined in ranches, compared to 47 percent in training schools.[43]

The Hennepin County Home School, one of the most innovative juvenile institutions in the nation, combines features of camps and ranches. Except for a fourteen-bed security unit, it is an open facility, located in a beautiful 160-acre wooded site approximately seventeen miles from downtown Minneapolis. The 164-bed facility is coeducational and holds youths who range in age from thirteen to seventeen. with an average age of fifteen. The school receives no status offenders; instead, the population is made up of those who have committed a variety of property and personal offenses. The typical resident has had at least five prior court involvements, and well more than half the residents have been involved in some type of out-of-home placement before their commitment to the Hennepin County Home School.

The institution is divided into three Juvenile Male Offender cottages, two Juvenile Sex Offender cottages, one cottage for female offenders, and one Beta cottage for short-term restitution offenders. The residents remain in the Beta program from three to eight weeks and in other cottages as long as a year. Each resident of the Juvenile Sex Offender cottages has received an indeterminate sentence, while residents of the other cottages have received a determinate sentence. The institution's sophisticated treatment program uses such modalities as an educational program that focuses on the learning disabled, family therapy, transactional analysis, behavior modification, and reality therapy. Horseback riding and canoeing are favorite recreational activities.[44]

Residents are typically more positive about a placement at a forestry camp or ranch than about placement in a training school. They like the more relaxed security, the more frequent community contacts, the shorter stays, and the better relations with staff. Yet some youths cannot handle these settings. They may be too homesick or too victimized by peers, so they repeatedly run away until they are transferred to more secure facilities.

Training Schools

Public and private **training schools** are being used increasingly today. On October 29, 1997, 125,805 young persons were assigned beds in 1,121 public and 2,310 private facilities in the United States. Of these, 105,790 (84 percent) met the criteria for the census (under age twenty-one, assigned a bed on October 29, 1997, charged with an offense or court-adjudicated for an offense, and placed in residential placement because of that offense). Figure 11–1 lists the numbers and percentages of juveniles in public and private facilities in 1997.

California, Illinois, Michigan, New York, and Ohio have several training schools each. Smaller states have one training school for boys and another for girls, and Massachusetts and Vermont have no training schools. Although coeducational institutions gained some acceptance in the 1970s and North Carolina even converted all its training schools into coeducational institutions, that trend seems to have passed.

Organizational Goals and Security Levels

Several organizational goals exist in training schools. David Street, Robert D. Vinter, and Charles Perrow's classic study of several public and private training schools identified three basic organizational goals: obedience/conformity, reeducation/development, and treatment. They found that staff in obedience/conformity institutions kept residents under surveillance and emphasized rules. They were also punitive with residents and did not become involved with them. Although staff in reeducation/development institutions demanded conformity, hard work, and intellectual growth, they were more willing to give additional rewards for conformity to positive behavior and to develop closer relationships with residents. Staff in treatment-oriented training schools were much more involved with residents as they worked with, helped, and permitted residents to become more emotionally involved with them.[45]

The philosophy of *parens patriae* has encouraged training schools' administrators to claim rehabilitation as their official goal, but the overall objective for most training schools is to provide a safe, secure, and humane environment. The actual goal depends on the security level of the training school. States that have only one training school for boys and one for girls must enforce all security levels in the one facility, but states with several training schools have the option of developing minimum-, medium-, and maximum-security institutions.

State*	Juveniles in custody	In-State Public facilities	In-State Private facilities	Out-of-state private facilities	State*	Juveniles in custody	In-State Public facilities	In-State Private facilities	Out-of-state private facilities
U.S. total	105,790	74%	24%	2%	Missouri	1,401	81%	19%	0%
Alabama	1,685	54	46	0	Montana	302	56	14	29
Alaska	352	15	25	0	Nebraska	741	69	22	10
Arizona	1,868	86	13	1	Nevada	875	97	3	0
Arkansas	603	59	41	0	New Hampshire	186	65	30	5
California	19,899	37	8	1	New Jersey	2,251	97	3	0
Colorado	1,748	48	40	12	New Mexico	778	95	4	1
Connecticut	1,326	74	24	2	New York	4,661	56	44	1
Delaware	311	67	5	28	North Carolina	1,204	89	10	0
D. C.	265	65	32	3	North Dakota	272	36	58	6
Florida	5,975	50	48	2	Ohio	4,318	91	8	1
Georgia	3,622	85	15	0	Oklahoma	808	65	34	0
Hawaii	134	84	9	7	Oregon	1,462	80	20	0
Idaho	242	70	14	17	Pennsylvania	3,962	37	58	5
Illinois	3,425	39	5	2	Rhode Island	426	79	20	0
Indiana	2,485	66	31	2	South Carolina	1,583	88	12	0
Iowa	1,064	38	60	3	South Dakota	528	83	16	1
Kansas	1,212	67	32	0	Tennessee	2,118	57	43	0
Kentucky	1,079	75	25	0	Texas	6,898	86	13	0
Louisiana	2,776	63	36	0	Utah	768	52	42	6
Maine	318	80	16	4	Vermont	49	44	36	20
Maryland	1,498	21	48	1	Virginia	2,879	93	7	0
Massachusetts	1,065	35	64	0	Washington	2,216	94	6	0
Michigan	3,710	53	42	5	West Virginia	398	54	28	18
Minnesota	1,522	58	34	8	Wisconsin	2,013	70	0	0
Mississippi	756	99	0	1	Wyoming	340	50	49	1

Figure 11–1 *Residential Placement of Juveniles in Public and Private Facilities*

*State where the offense occurred.

Note: U.S. total includes 3,401 juveniles in private facilities for whom state of offense was not reported.

Source: Howard N. Snyder and Melissa Sickmund, *Juvenile Offenders and Victims: 1999 National Report* (Washington, DC: National Center for Juvenile Justice, 1999), p. 191.

Paint Creek Youth Center (PCYC) in southern Ohio is one of the most widely hailed minimum-security institutions in the nation. This privately operated facility has the capacity to hold thirty-three residents but generally has a population of twenty-six or twenty-seven. Juveniles who have committed serious offenses from the southern counties of the state are typically committed to PCYC. The facility features a comprehensive and integrated therapeutic approach emphasizing accountability, social learning, and positive peer culture. The PCYC treatment approach operates on three levels. A youth begins on level one and achieves level two when he or she has been problem-free for a period of time. When staff determine that a youth is ready to return to the community, this youth is granted prerelease status, or level three. Increased responsibilities and privileges are then granted to residents, contingent on positive behavior within the institution. Security is maintained by staff and peers rather than by fences and locked doors. Furthermore, PCYC has successfully implemented a family therapy program along with intensive aftercare services to those residents returning to the community.[46]

Security is a primary feature of medium- and maximum-security facilities. (Photo by Kathryn Miller.)

Peter W. Greenwood, Susan Turner, and Kathy Rosenblatt evaluated PCYC using a control group of youths who were randomly assigned to either PCYC, Training Institution Central Ohio (TICO), or another Department of Youth Services (DYS) institution. These researchers found that juveniles who had been assigned to PCYC were less likely than those from TICO to be rearrested upon their return to the community and much less likely to be recommitted to a correctional facility on new charges.[47]

The physical design of medium- and maximum-security training schools varies from fortresslike facilities with individual cells to open dormitories with little privacy to the homelike atmosphere of small cottages. Maximum-security training schools usually have one or two fairly high fences and sometimes even a wall. The interiors in maximum-security schools are characterized by bleak hallways, locked doors, and individual cells covered by heavy screens or bars; the youths' daily lives are constrained by rules (see Focus on Practice 11–1) .

Medium-security training schools usually are designed as dormitories or cottages. Similar to maximum-security institutions, medium-security training schools usually have the perimeter security of a six- or seven-foot-high fence. The atmosphere in medium-security institutions is more relaxed, and residents can move around more freely than would be true in maximum-security training schools.

Institutional security is the primary emphasis in medium- and maximum-security training schools. Administrators' jobs typically depend on their success in avoiding runaways. The account of a runaway incident from a maximum-security facility, for example, may receive statewide media coverage. If a runaway commits a violent crime, then even more "heat" is placed on institutional administrators and their staffs. Fortunately, the federal courts' recent involvement in juvenile institutions has eliminated some of the past abuses that sometimes took place to punish those who attempted to run away and those who actually did but were caught and returned.

Programs

The programs in medium- and maximum-security training schools are much more adequate than those in jails or detention homes and more varied than those in camps and ranches. Most larger training schools have a full-time nurse on duty and a physician who visits one or more days a week. Such services as the removal of tattoos are sometimes available if residents desire them.

Most medium- and maximum-security training schools provide educational programs for residents. These may be accredited by the state for granting high school diplomas, and most offer classes to prepare for a general educational development (GED) test. In addition to the regular academic courses, training schools usually offer basic skills classes consisting of a review of the necessary techniques for reading, writing, and arithmetic; some programs have laboratories and programmed instruction as well. Classes are usually small, and pupils are permitted to progress according to their

FOCUS ON PRACTICE 11–1

RULES OF YOUTH CONDUCT

1. You will not be allowed to fight with peers or staff.
2. You will follow the direct orders of staff.
3. You will treat others with courtesy by avoiding the use of profanity, disrespectful language, or physical gestures.
4. You will avoid sexually inappropriate language or gestures towards staff and other youth.
5. You will avoid horseplay, rowdy-rough play, body punching, shadow boxing, verbal taunting, running, [and] wrestling, which could lead to more serious behavior.
6. You will avoid destroying, defacing, or altering state property or the property of others.
7. You will avoid the use of and/or passing of any form of tobacco, alcohol, and drugs.
8. You will avoid the use of and/or possession of contraband.
9. You will avoid leaving trash on tables, chairs, or floors by placing it in proper receptacles.
10. You will maintain personal grooming, hygiene, and clothing at all times throughout the institution. Appropriate dress includes shirttails in pants, pants zipped and uncuffed (not pegged), belt fastened, shoes tied, and socks on.
11. You will refrain from borrowing, lending, buying, trading, betting, selling, and gambling with peers, staff, or visitors.
12. You will play radios only in acceptable areas and at acceptable times.
13. You will not enter any office or restricted areas without staff permission.
14. You will avoid interfering with staff members' duties.
15. You will report any injury or any change in a medical condition to a staff member immediately.
16. You will not steal.
17. You will adhere to all movement instructions.
18. You will not spit.
19. You will not use any phone without staff supervision.
20. You will not use the restroom without permission.

Source: Training Institution, Central Ohio, 1990.

Critical Thinking Questions:

Do you believe all these rules are necessary? What rules would you substitute? How would you feel if restricted by these rules?

own rate of learning. The Indiana Boys School is an example of one training school that focuses on the learning disabilities of residents, for Indiana correctional officials believe that learning disabilities are closely linked to delinquent behavior.

Well-equipped male training schools offer vocational training in automobile repair, printing, welding, carpentry, woodworking, barbering, machine shop skills, drafting, and food service. Training schools for girls generally are more limited, as they offer training programs in sewing, food service, secretarial skills, and beauty care. According to a 1991 survey of juvenile facilities, vocational training typically consists of such courses as auto shop/engine repair (54 percent), carpentry/building trades (67 percent), cosmetology (12 percent), computer training (39 percent), food services (55 percent), electrical trades (21 percent), secretarial trades (18 percent), retail/sales (10 percent), printing (30 percent), forestry/agriculture (33 percent), and laundry services (17 percent).[48]

As a rule, this vocational training does not help residents secure jobs after release for several reasons: They have difficulty gaining admission to the necessary labor unions; they lack the necessary credentials, such as a high school education; or they simply choose not to pursue the skills they learned. Yet some residents leave the institution and acquire excellent jobs with their acquired skills.

Recreation has always been popular in training schools. Some staff emphasize it because they believe that a tired youth is a well-behaved one, or, in the words of one recreation leader, "If we wear them out during the day, they won't fool around at night." Other staff advocate a heavy dosage of recreation because they believe that teaching residents a competitive sport builds self-respect and self-confidence. Still other staff know that juveniles like to play, and recreation is simply a good way for them to entertain themselves and to work off excessive energy. Male residents can compete in softball, volleyball, flag football, basketball, and sometimes even boxing. Cottages usually compete against one another, and the institution may even have a team that competes with other institutions or with teams in the surrounding community. Nonathletic recreational activities include movies, building model cars, painting, decorating the cottages (especially at Christmas), and playing ping-pong, pool, checkers, and chess. Female residents also have recreational possibilities such as softball, volleyball, and basketball. In addition to the nonathletic recreational activities that the boys have, girls perform in talent shows or dramatic productions, and, occasionally, they have dances with boys from nearby training schools.

Religious instruction and services are always provided in state training schools. Larger training schools usually have a full-time Protestant chaplain and a part- or full-time Roman Catholic chaplain. Smaller training schools contract services of clergy from a nearby community. Religious services generally include attending Sunday mass and morning worship, confession, baptism, instruction for church membership, choir, and the participation of community groups. Yet, few residents have much interest in organized religion, and they are usually quite resistant to compulsory attendance at these religious services.

The most widely used treatment modalities are transactional analysis, reality therapy, psychotherapy, behavior modification, guided group interaction, positive peer culture, and drug and alcohol treatment. The errors-in-thinking modality, models to deactivate gangs, and law enforcement education are new forms of treatment recently implemented in a number of private and public training schools across the nation (see Chapter 12 for an examination of these modalities).

Volunteers are an important adjunct to institutional programs, and an institution that has an active volunteer program can greatly enrich the stay of its residents. Some states have better developed volunteer programs than others and have volunteer coordinators in their major institutions. Confined offenders frequently are receptive to services rendered by unpaid volunteers who do not represent authority figures, but who can present the needs of youth and become their advocates in the community. Among the many services that volunteers provide for institutionalized youths are the following:

1. Education—tutoring and supplying books
2. Entertainment—arranging choral programs and other means of entertainment provided by community groups
3. Chaperones—escorting selected youths to community events
4. Counseling—providing one-to-one contact with offenders
5. Family service—contacting and reassuring parents on the progress of their children
6. Financial aid—providing money for youths' canteen accounts
7. Gifts—supplying Christmas and birthday remembrances
8. Job-finding—assisting youths in locating community jobs while they wait to be released or in securing permanent jobs after release
9. Letter writing—helping youths to correspond with family and friends
10. Recreation—playing basketball, softball, and other sports with residents

Finally, prerelease programs are a desired component of institutional activities. These programs typically occur more in minimum- than in medium- or maximum-security facilities. In some training schools, residents are transferred to another cottage or to another location to begin a formal program of community reintegration, including exposure to experiences designed to prepare them for a full return to the community. Techniques of interviewing for a job, instruction in reading the help-wanted section of a newspaper, and assistance in money management are important elements of these programs.

Home furloughs, afternoon trips off campus, and permission to work in the community are typical of the privileges given to residents of prerelease cottages or to those who are just a step or two away from release. Home furloughs are probably the most widely used. Some staff believe that reintegrating youths gradually to the community after a long absence of perhaps several years will help ease the shock of release. Home visits also provide opportunities for residents to interview for jobs and visit with family members. Trips off campus for several hours with parents are sometimes permitted by some training schools. This enables parents and children to spend time together away from the institution and possibly to shop for clothing or to eat in a restaurant. Community jobs generally are reserved for those youths who are only two or three months from release and who need financial resources before they return to community living. Staff members are very careful in choosing the residents who are permitted to work in the community. Prerelease programs usually have a positive impact on residents, but home visits, especially, result in a high percentage of runaways.

Social Control of Institutional Residents

Until the last ten years or so, most training schools still employed cottage parents. These individuals often were a retired couple who were attracted to this work because of their interest in young people. Cottage parents sometimes provided a strong parental model for the youth placed in their care. The cottage parents system was continued so long simply because institutional administrators felt that cottage parents created more of a homelike atmosphere for confined delinquents than did staff members who worked eight-hour shifts and lived in the nearby community. But the appearance of increasingly more difficult to handle delinquents and efforts to develop more efficient institutional management techniques resulted in the replacement of cottage parents with those staff members commonly called youth supervisors, youth leaders, cottage supervisors, group supervisors, or group-care workers. The emerging nature of this role has left a number of questions unanswered: How much of a homelike atmosphere should these supervisors establish in the cottages? How involved should they become with residents? Are they to be only custodial agents, or do they also have treatment responsibilities? What are they to do if residents refuse to cooperate? What personal fulfillment can they expect to achieve in their jobs? Although encumbered by these and other questions, the role of youth supervisor is slowly being established in juvenile correctional settings in this country.

The youth supervisors wake residents in the morning, see to it that their charges wash and dress for breakfast, supervise the serving of breakfast in the cottage or escort residents to a central dining facility, and conduct a brief room inspection. They also ensure that those youths enrolled in the academic and vocational programs go to school and that those who work on the grounds, in the kitchen, or in the community go to their jobs. In medium- and maximum—security training schools, residents are usually escorted to their particular assignments, but on many honor farms, and in conservation camps and ranches, they are permitted movement without staff supervision.[49]

Cottage parents typically remained in the cottage to prepare lunch and to take care of other cottage tasks, but youth supervisors are generally assigned duties that keep them occupied until they pick up their residents for lunch. These duties may include school patrol, inspection of the rooms of residents on restriction, and outside patrol of the recreation field.

Residents are met at the academic area and escorted back to the cottage for lunch, after which they are returned to school or to other assigned duties. The afternoon shift of supervisors picks up the youths in school and brings them back at the end of the day. If the institution has an active group program and youth supervisors are involved, they usually hold several group meetings a week after school. Guided group interaction, positive peer culture, and transactional analysis are the most popular group modalities used in these sessions. Time generally is structured after school because many administrators believe that problems arise when youths have a great deal of free time, but in some institutions the period from the end of school until the evening meal is a free one.

After the evening meal, especially during warmer weather, residents are permitted to engage in outside recreational activities. They may participate in organized activities or may choose to throw a football, shoot a basketball, pitch a softball, or talk with a friend. Staff must at this time be particularly alert, because runaways often take place during these outside activities. Following a shower and a little television, residents are usually sent to their rooms and lights are out around 10 PM.

The night shift, normally consisting of one person, takes over at 11 or 11:30 PM. This person's job basically is to make certain that youths do not escape from the cottage during the nights and to be available if a problem such as an illness or escape attempt occurs. The youth supervisor generally spends the greater part of the eight-hour shift sitting at a desk in the staff office and responding to a periodic phone check on cottage security.

As part of their daily tasks, youth supervisors also intervene in conflicts among residents, respond to emergency situations, search residents and residents' living quarters, orient new residents, advise residents concerning personal or institutional progress, and assign tasks to residents and monitor their performance.[50] For an effective youth supervisor, see Focus on Careers 11–2.

Punishment for Misbehaving Residents

Most training schools permit the isolation of misbehaving or out-of-control residents. The 1991 survey of juvenile facilities found that 20 percent of training schools do not permit isolation, 34 percent restrict isolation to twenty-four hours or less, 15 percent permit two to three days, 14 percent allow four to five days, and 6 percent allow six to ten days. Only 7 percent of training schools permit one month of isolation, and 4 percent have no limit on how long a juvenile can be isolated.[51]

Mechanical restraints are also increasingly used on misbehaving residents. According to the 1991 survey, 98 percent of training schools used handcuffs, 66 percent used anklets, 31 percent used security belts, 18 percent used

FOCUS ON CAREERS 11–2

JIM ROBERTS: PROFILE OF AN EFFECTIVE YOUTH SUPERVISOR

One of the authors of this book had the privilege of working with an individual who was a youth supervisor par excellence. Jim, a soft-spoken, middle-aged black, possessed a high school education and had no formal training in working with delinquent youth. However, it did not take long to recognize that this man was ideally suited for working with juveniles.

Jim was perceptive. He knew his "boys" and could always identify their needs and concerns. A keen listener and observer, he was able to see when a youth was hurting and knew what to do about it. It did not take a new resident long to learn that Mr. Roberts cared deeply about his charges and therefore they would flock around his office, waiting to talk with him.

Jim was trusting. He believed in adolescents. He was always willing to help residents and never seemed to burn out. When the cottage social worker objected to sending a youth on a home visit because the social worker considered him to be a poor risk, Jim quietly responded, "You've got to take a chance on kids. If we don't believe in them, how can we expect them to believe in themselves?" Of course, he had some failures, but he also had many successes.

Jim was an excellent role model. He was street-wise and could not be manipulated. He was fair, consistent, and nonprejudiced; he was mature and healthy himself and did not take his problems out on the residents. Although he was strong physically, he never struck his residents or raised his voice at them. Significantly, he had as much control over residents as any other youth supervisor in the institution.

Few residents ever left his cottage without a profound admiration for Jim Roberts. Some referred to him as "father"; others looked upon him as a big brother or a wise uncle. Youths developed such strong emotional ties with him that they did not want to let him down. They continued to write and call after they were released; many traveled across the state to visit this man who had had such a significant impact upon their lives.

Jim was a splendid teacher to all who came in contact with him. He knew what to say when a youth failed or received sad news from home. When a youth had given up and saw no more reason to go on living, Jim Roberts was usually the one person who could touch him and give him a renewed lease on life. He had a quiet but effective way of driving a painful point home to another staff member who had engaged in inappropriate behavior. He was also skillful in persuading cottage staff to reinforce youths at their three-month cottage review. Finally, he helped social worker after social worker to translate book knowledge and theory into practice.

Source: Clemens Bartollas, Stuart J. Miller, and Paul B. Wice, Participants in American Criminal Justice: The Promise and the Performance (Upper Saddle River, NJ: Prentice Hall, 1983), pp. 292–293).

Critical Thinking Questions:

Do you believe there are many like Jim Roberts working as staff members in juvenile institutions? What do you think might have motivated this remarkable youth supervisor?

four-point ties, and 5 percent used straitjackets.[52] The improper use of physical or mechanical restraints is problematic because it can result in serious physical injury or emotional trauma to a youth.

Furthermore, misbehaving residents may lose institutional privileges, may be denied home visits or off-campus trips, or may have their period of confinement prolonged. In extreme cases, such as a serious assault against another resident or a staff member, these youths may be transferred to an adult reformatory or a prison.

Differences Between Public and Private Training Schools

Public and private training schools do differ in a number of ways. First, they generally attract a somewhat different population. A youth held in a public facility in 1991 was most likely to be African-American, male, between fourteen and seventeen years of age, and held for a delinquent offense, such as a property or personal crime. In contrast, a youth held in custody in a private facility in 1991 was most likely to be White, male, fourteen to seventeen years of age, and held for a nondelinquent offense such as truancy, incorrigibility, or running away from home.[53]

David Shichor and Clemens Bartollas's examination of the patterns of public and private juvenile placements in one of the larger probation departments in southern California, however, reveals that few offense differences existed between juveniles sent to public and private facilities. Although juveniles placed in private facilities had more personal problems and those in public institutions were somewhat more delinquent, placements in private facilities included delinquents with serious offenses.[54]

Second, privately administered training schools are probably better known to the public than are state facilities because of their public solicitation of funds. Boys' Town in Nebraska and Glen Mills School in Pennsylvania (near Philadelphia) are two private institutions that are well known to the public.[55] Private training schools also have avoided most of the scathing critiques faced by public training schools during the past two decades.

Third, proponents of private training schools claim that they are more effective than public training schools because they have a limited intake policy that allows them to choose whom they want to admit, they have more professional staff, they have better staff-client ratios, they are smaller, and they are more flexible and innovative.

Gaylene Style Armstrong and Doris Layton MacKenzie examined forty-eight residential juvenile correctional facilities in nineteen states (sixteen private and thirty-two public facilities). Using both self-report surveys and data from facility records, they found that private facilities had a more extensive admission process, had a higher percentage of juvenile delinquents incarcerated for property offenses, were smaller, and held a higher percentage of males than female offenders. Yet they found that there were no significant differences between private and public juvenile facilities in terms of the quality of their environments.[56]

The advantage of private over public rehabilitation programs may have been more true in the past than in the present. The increased use of interstate commerce of children has resulted in some private schools taking as many children as they can get. Indeed, some private institutions exploit the inadequate licensing procedures of the states to warehouse youths as cheaply as possible and thereby reap good profits.[57] It is also true that private training schools are smaller than public ones, but even so, one-half of private institutions hold 100 or more children; these are still too large to effectively rehabilitate juveniles. The greater flexibility of programs is probably accurate because private institutions are relatively free from political processes and bureaucratic inertia. Yet Bartollas and Shichor's comparison of the attitudes of staff and residents at a state training school for adolescent males in the Midwest and at a private facility in the same state found that the enforcement of excessive rules in the private placement created a rigid cottage structure and living environment.[58] Moreover, Shichor and Bartollas found that private placements in southern California do not always provide the services of professional treatment personnel that they purport to provide.[59] Perhaps the old adage is true after all: The best institutions are private ones and the worst institutions are also private ones.

Mental Health Placements

A major issue in juvenile justice is the dramatic increase in the placement of children in mental health settings. For example, from 1980 to 1984, there was a more than fourfold increase in placements of juveniles in such settings (from 10,764 to 48,375).[60] Arnold Binder and Virginia L. Binder explain how this increase took place:

> Less than a third of these youths are psychotic or have other serious mental disturbances. The characteristics of youths now in mental institutions are those who experiment with drugs and/or alcohol, threaten suicide, have eating disorders, run away, have problems in school, or are generally in disagreement with their parents or other authorities. In order to receive insurance

reimbursement, many of these adolescents now receive the official psychiatric diagnoses of conduct disorder, personality disorder, or transitional disorder.[61]

Ira M. Schwartz, Marilyn Jackson-Beeck, and Roger Anderson are among those who have charged that **mental health placements** are being used excessively and unnecessarily. They stated that "gains made in removing juveniles from institutions in the justice system may have been offset by corresponding increases in the use of institutions in the child welfare and mental health systems."[62]

A study of juveniles institutionalized in the mental health and chemical dependency systems in Minnesota found "that a 'hidden' or private juvenile correctional system has rapidly evolved for disruptive or 'acting-out' youth who are no longer processed by the public juvenile justice control systems."[63] These youths, estimated to be about 60 percent females, were generally referred by their parents, and the costs were covered by third-party health care insurance plans.[64]

Several potential problems may arise with these "voluntary" mental health placements. First, this hidden system of juvenile control denies youths the due protection of the law. On entering such a program, juveniles may find themselves subject to locked quarters and denied a variety of freedoms, including home visits, in-facility visitors, and contacts with friends outside the facility. If they fail to cooperate exactly with staff requirements, they may be deprived of mail and recreation.[65]

Second, these "voluntary" commitments are sometimes pursued by parents who simply want their embarrassing children out of the way. It is not unusual for the parents to make the arrangements, place their child in the car, and take him or her to the facility as an involuntary admission. It may not even have been substantiated that this person needs mental health treatment or that the facility has qualified staff to work with the problematic behaviors.

Third, it can be argued that the return of this medicalization of deviance, especially for the children of the haves, is fueled by "the desire to make money from kids." Ira Schwartz speaks to this issue when he documents the expanding policy of committing more juveniles to inpatient psychiatric and chemical dependency units in private for profit and nonprofit hospitals. He charged that "the pressures to fill empty beds, coupled with the availability of third-party health care insurance programs with fiscal incentives that favor inpatient rather than outpatient care, are contributing to the proliferation of services that are largely inappropriate and costly."[66]

This return of the **medicalization of deviance,** which was so popular in the 1960s, has taken place because the children of the haves are having more problems in coping with life. These problems include eating disorders, drug and alcohol dependency, incorrigibility, running away from home, and sexual activity. Parents do not know how to cope with these behaviors; equipped with insurance that will pay the costs, they turn to mental health authorities. Administrators of private hospitals were quick to recognize the need and have opened up chemical dependency and psychiatric units.

Without a doubt, mental health placements must have greater controls and protections for children. It seems likely that society will increasingly turn to child psychiatry to deal with the problems faced by the children of the haves. Yet, because insurance money is available and because some people are quick to jump on the bandwagon of making money from kids, this issue will probably become more important in the years to come.

WHAT ARE THE TROUBLING ASPECTS OF JUVENILE INSTITUTIONALIZATION?

Institutionalization is a painful process for most youthful offenders, though it is clearly more painful for some than for others. The residential social system and juvenile victimization are two of the most troubling aspects of juvenile institutionalization. Together, they call into question the quality of long-term institutional care that this nation provides for juveniles in trouble.

Residential Social System

The social structure of the training school has a variety of social networks: (1) subgroups of residents based on race, age, criminal conduct, locale, or gang affiliation; (2) informal primary groupings of friends; (3) networks of instrumental relationships revolving around the production or supply of illicit goods and services; (4) social hierarchies in the living unit with expected role behavior of residents who occupy these social positions; and (5) official positions allocated by staff, such as honor unit members.[67] The more custodially oriented or coercive the training school, the more likely it is that a power-oriented social hierarchy will dominate the other social relationships.

Social Roles in Training Schools for Boys

The **social roles** in most training schools for boys are divided into aggressive, manipulative, and passive groups.[68] Youths who pursue aggressive roles are usually cottage leaders, their lieutenants, and sexual exploiters. The cottage leader is given argot names such as "wheel," "bruiser," "heavy," "El Presidente," and "duke." The leader controls physical attack, exploitation, agitation, and patronage. This leader's lieutenants may be called "vice-president," "tough," "tough boy," "all right guy," "hard rock," "thug," "bad dude," "redneck," and "wise guy." Sexual exploiters are often referred to as "daddy" and "booty bandits."

Youths who adopt manipulative roles generally do whatever is necessary to make their institutional stay easier. Residents who do whatever staff want them to do simply to reduce the length of confinement are called "slick," "cool," "con man," and "con artist." The "peddler" or "merchant" is the role occupant who trades stolen, illegal, or exploited goods from one resident to another.

Passive roles are adopted by youths who for one reason or another are uninvolved in the social structure of the cottage. Residents who are prostaff and are not embroiled in the delinquent subculture are called "straight," "straight kid," "quiet type," and "bushboy." Occupants receiving depreciation from peers are called "mess-up," "pain freak," "weak-minded," "stone-out," and "lame." Sexual victims, the social pariahs of the peer culture, are given such names as "scapegoats," "punk," "sweet boy," "girl," and "fag."

Family Social Structure

The social roles in training schools for girls are generally based on a family or **kinship social structure.** Rose Giallombardo's examination of three training schools for girls in various parts of the United States found that aggressive girls tended to adopt the male sexual roles ("butches") and put pressure on new residents to adopt the female sexual roles ("fems"). Giallombardo identified the following social types in one institution for females: "true fems," "trust-to-be-butches," "trust-to-be-fems," "jive time butches," "jive time fems," "straights," "squealers," "pimps," "foxes," "popcorns," and "cops."[69] Christopher M. Sieverdes and Bartollas's study of six southeastern coeducational training schools also revealed the presence of the family social structure in the girls' cottages. This study further divided the seven social roles found in these living units into aggressive, manipulative, and passive roles: "bruiser" and "bitch" (aggressive roles), "lady" and "bulldagger" (manipulative roles), and "child," "girlfriend," and "asskisser" (passive roles).[70] Alice Propper examined three coeducational and four girls' training schools scattered through the East, Midwest, and South, five of which were public and two of which were private Catholic facilities. In contrast to previously held assumptions, she found little overlap between pseudo-family roles and homosexual behavior; participation in homosexuality and make-believe families was just as prevalent in coeducational as in single-sex institutions, and homosexuality was as prevalent in treatment- as in custody-oriented facilities.[71]

Juvenile Victimization

Those who lack the credentials to impress peers are often forced into lowly social positions. Although they are aware that they must avoid **victimization,** these youths may not be able to protect themselves against predatory peers. Staff generally offer little help and may even inform potential victims, "If you are a man, you'll protect yourself." In institutions for older males, there may be a respected resident who is willing to protect weaker peers, but the price of protection is often steep—the protégé must become his "boy" or "sweet boy." A sexual victim finds himself on the last rung of the social hierarchy, engulfed in a social role from which escape is very difficult.

The degradation of victim status presents nearly overwhelming stress to a youth. In a revealing incident, a resident was making fun of a scapegoat one day when the scapegoat, much to the surprise of everyone, attacked the supposedly more aggressive youth. In the fight that ensued, the scapegoat clearly got the better of the other youth. Staff locked both youths in their rooms until a disciplinary meeting could be held. The youth who had had a higher position in the cottage until the fight tried to commit suicide by setting his room on fire; he clearly preferred to die rather than take on the role of the scapegoat. This youth did become the cottage scapegoat and later confessed to a staff member that he was committing oral sodomy on half of the twenty-four youths in the cottage.[72]

Bartollas and colleagues' examination of an end-of-the-line training school in Ohio concluded that 90 percent of the 150 residents were involved in an exploitation matrix and that they created an extremely brutal system. If anything, the environment of this institution was less fair, less just, less humane, and less decent than the worst aspects of the social worlds from which residents came. Brute force, manipulation, and institutional sophistication carried the day and set the standards that ultimately prevailed. In this process, many of the most dangerous and toughest delinquents in the outside community became the meek, doubly and triply stigmatized victims within the institution.[73]

Miller, Bartollas, and Simon Dinitz have reexamined the degree of victimization in this maximum-security training school. In this follow-up of the 1976 study, their preliminary findings include the following:

1. The youth culture described in the 1976 study still thrives, and the strong still victimize the weak, but mostly for food, clothing, and toiletries, rather than sex.
2. Consensual sexual behavior appears to be more widespread than in the earlier study.
3. Instead of the violent population found in the 1976 study, most of the training school's present residents are relatively minor drug dealers, addicts, and users but do include a few extremely violent and dangerous youths.
4. Gang members from the community are confined, but, unlike in some training schools in the United States, gang organization is not present nor is it providing an intimidating factor in institutional life.
5. Treatment has all but disappeared from this training school. The only treatment still existing is a drug abuse program. A social worker summed this up when he said, "We don't do anything in here for kids." A cottage staff member added, "This place is a warehouse for children."
6. Staff members are more disillusioned than they were at the time of the first study. They also are more fearful of victimization from residents.[74]

DO INSTITUTIONALIZED YOUTHS HAVE RIGHTS?

The rights of juveniles is a major issue in juvenile justice. The Children's Rights Movement, as well as proponents of due process rights of children within the juvenile justice system, challenge whether institutionalized youths have sufficient legal protection. They argue that confined juveniles ought to receive three basic rights: the right to treatment, the right not to be treated, and the right to be free from cruel and unusual punishment. The rights of confined offenders have been examined by the federal courts and the Civil Rights of Institutionalized Persons Act (CRIPA).

RIGHT TO TREATMENT

Several court rulings have found that a juvenile committed to a training school has a right to treatment. In the *White v. Reid* (1954) case, the court ruled that juveniles could not be held in institutions that did not provide for their rehabilitation.[75] The *Inmates of the Boys' Training School v. Affleck* decision also stated that juveniles have a right to treatment because rehabilitation is the true purpose of the juvenile court.[76] In *Nelson v. Heyne,* Indiana's Seventh Circuit agreed with the district court that inmates of the Indiana Boys' School have a right to rehabilitative treatment.[77]

Moreover, in the 1973 *Morales v. Turman* decision, the U.S. District Court for the Eastern District of Texas held that a number of criteria had to be followed by the state of Texas in order to assure that proper treatment would be provided to confined juveniles. These criteria included minimum standards for assessing and testing children committed to the state; minimum standards for assessing educational skills and handicaps and for providing programs aimed at advancing a child's education; minimum standards for delivering vocational education and medical and psychiatric care; and minimum standards for providing a humane institutional environment.[78] This finding was overruled by the Fifth Circuit Appeals Court on the grounds that a three-judge court should have been convened to hear the case. On *certiorari* to the U.S. Supreme Court, that Court reversed the Court of Appeals and remanded the case. What may affect future considerations of confined juveniles' right to treatment is whether the order of the District Court can withstand the assault against it.

RIGHT NOT TO BE TREATED

Advocates argue that treatment should be voluntary; should not be related to the length of institutional confinement; and should not degrade, dehumanize, punish, or humiliate residents. The standards of the Institute of Judicial Administration of the American Bar Association (IJA-ABA), for example, propose that children may voluntarily refuse services except in three cases: "services juveniles are legally obliged to accept (as school attendance), services required to prevent clear harm to physical health, and services mandated by the court as a condition to a nonresidential disposition."[79]

Right to Be Free from Cruel and Unusual Punishment

Some courts have applied the Eighth Amendment, barring cruel and unusual punishment, to juvenile institutions to forbid the use of corporal punishment in any form, the use of Thorazine and other medications for the purpose of control, and the use of extended periods of solitary confinement.[80] The *Pena v. New York State Division for Youth* decision held that the use of isolation, hand restraints, and tranquilizing drugs at Goshen Annex Center was punitive and antitherapeutic and, therefore, violated the Eighth Amendment.[81] In the case of *Inmates of the Boys' Training School v. Affleck,* the court also condemned such practices as solitary confinement and strip-cells, and it established minimum standards for youths confined at the training school.[82] In the *Morales v. Turman* decision in Texas, the court found instances of physical brutality and abuse, including staff-administered beatings and tear gassings, homosexual assaults, excessive use of solitary confinement, and the lack of clinical services.[83] In *Morgan v. Sproat,* a Mississippi case, the court found that youths were confined in padded cells with no windows or furnishings and only flush holes for toilets and were denied access to all programs or services except a Bible.[84] Finally, in *State v. Werner,* the court found that residents were locked in solitary confinement, were beaten, kicked, slapped, and sprayed with mace by staff, were required to scrub floors with a toothbrush, and were forced to stand or sit for prolonged periods without changing position.[85] In each of these cases, the courts condemned these cruel practices.

CRIPA and Juvenile Correctional Facilities

As of November 1997, the Civil Rights Division had investigated three hundred institutions under CRIPA. Of these, seventy-three institutions, or about 25 percent, were juvenile detention and correctional facilities. The Civil Rights Division is monitoring conditions in thirty-four juvenile correctional facilities through consent decrees in Kentucky, New Jersey, and Puerto Rico. The consent decree filed in Kentucky covers all thirteen juvenile facilities in the state; the decree in New Jersey is for one facility, and in Puerto Rico for twenty facilities.[86]

SUMMARY

Contemporary experts radically disagree on social policy for training schools. Some argue for an increase in the numbers of these facilities, but others claim that they all should be closed down. Some believe that with proper staff-resident ratios and improved programs, these facilities can provide well for juveniles in trouble, but others assert that these settings are violent, inhumane, and damaging to all children. Some believe that these facilities should be constructed in the community, and still others recommend isolating them in rural areas. But beyond the disagreement is the reality: more and more juveniles are being sent to these institutions.

In implementing a confinement policy, a number of factors should be taken into consideration. If at all possible, youths should be kept in their home communities. If confinement is necessary, the detention home or training school (jails should never be used for children) should be in or very near the home community. The facilities should remain small, with detention home populations not exceeding thirty and training school populations not exceeding fifty. The facilities should be pleasantly furnished and security features provided only after adequate staffing, programming, and a satisfactory, safe physical plan have been developed. If such facilities are absolutely necessary, they should be completely committed to full use of community resources and, wherever possible, should integrate residents into community programs.

CRITICAL THINKING QUESTIONS

1. Discuss the nature of the changes in American society at the time of the Revolution and immediately afterward. How did these changes affect how society handled youths in trouble?
2. How were delinquents to be improved in early institutions? What was the philosophy of the houses of refuge?
3. How would you describe the social structure of residents in training schools?
4. Why are training schools damaging to some youths?
5. How can training schools be improved in American society?

WEB SITES OF INTEREST

Information and links on the various types of boot camps can be found at
OJJDP Boot Camps for Juveniles

To view sources on Juvenile Correctional Facilities, simply type into your search engine:
Juvenile Correctional Facilities

NOTES

1. Confined youth interviewed in 1989 in an Ohio training school for boys.
2. David J. Rothman, *The Discovery of the Asylum* (Boston: Little, Brown, 1971). See also Barbara M. Brenzel, *Daughters of the State* (Cambridge, MA: MIT Press, 1983), and Alexander W. Pisciotta, "Treatment on Trial: The Rhetoric

and Reality of the New York House of Refuge, 1857–1935," *American Journal of Legal History* 29 (1985), 151–81.

3. Rothman, *The Discovery of the Asylum,* 53–54. For the origins of juvenile justice in California, see Daniel Macallair, "The San Francisco Industrial School and the Origins of Juvenile Justice in California: A Glance at the Great Reformation," *UC Davis Journal of Juvenile Law & Policy* 7 (Winter 2003), 1–60.
4. Ibid., 226.
5. Ibid., 225–27.
6. Hutchins Hapgood, *Autobiography of a Thief* (New York: Fox, Duffield, 1903), 71–72.
7. National Conference of Superintendents of Training Schools and Reformatories, *Institutional Rehabilitation of Delinquent Youth: Manual for Training School Personnel* (Albany, NY: Delman Publishers, 1962).
8. For this same tendency in the State Industrial School for Girls in Lancaster, Massachusetts, see Brenzel, *Daughters of the State.*
9. Quoted in Anthony M. Platt, *The Child Savers: The Invention of Delinquency* (Chicago: University of Chicago Press, 1969), 150.
10. Jerome G. Miller, *Last One over the Wall: The Massachusetts Experiment in Closing Reform Schools* (Columbus: Ohio State University Press, 1991), 95.
11. Contained in Ibid., 96.
12. Ibid. For other shocking accounts of staff brutality in training schools, see Ken Wooden, *Weeping in the Playtime of Others* (New York: McGraw-Hill, 1976).
13. These and other experiences are described in Clemens Bartollas, Stuart J. Miller, and Simon Dinitz, *Juvenile Victimization: The Institutional Paradox* (New York: Halsted Press, 1976).
14. The safety of juveniles in jail has become a major issue. See Dale G. Parent, Valerie Lieter, Stephen Kennedy, Lisa Livens, Daniel Wentworth, and Sarah Wilcox, *Conditions of Confinement: Juvenile Detention and Corrections Facilities* (Washington, DC: Office of Juvenile Justice and Delinquency Prevention, 1994), 102–103.
15. According to Rosemary C. Sarri, the number of youths confined in jails each year during the 1970s ranged from 90,000 (Children's Defense Fund) to 100,000 (National Council on Crime and Delinquency). See Sarri, "Gender Issues in Juvenile Justice," *Crime and Delinquency* 29 (1983), 390.
16. Howard N. Snyder and Melissa Sickmund, *Juvenile Offenders and Victims: A National Report* (Pittsburgh, PA: National Center for Juvenile Justice, 1995), 72.
17. Allen J. Beck, *Prison and Jail Inmates at Midyear 1999* (Washington, DC: Bureau of Justice Statistics, 2000).
18. Charles E. Frazier and Donna M. Bishop, "Jailing Juveniles in Florida: The Dynamics of Compliance to a Sluggish Federal Referral Initiative." Paper presented at the annual meeting of the American Society of Criminology, Baltimore, Maryland (November 1990), 4.

19. Ira M. Schwartz, Linda Harris, and Laurie Levi, "The Jailing of Juveniles in Minnesota: A Case Study," *Crime and Delinquency* 34 (1988), 146; David Steinhart, "California's Legislature Ends the Jailing of Children: The Story of a Policy Reversal," *Crime and Delinquency* 34 (1988), 169–70.
20. David Steinhart and Barry Krisberg, "Children in Jail," *State Legislature* 13 (1987), 12–16.
21. Parent et al., *Conditions of Confinement,* 29–30.
22. Ibid., 120.
23. Ibid.
24. Parent et al., *Conditions of Confinement,* 180–81. For other criticisms of detention practices, see Ira M. Schwartz and William H. Barton, eds., *Reforming Juvenile Detention: No More Hidden Closets* (Columbus: Ohio State University Press, 1994).
25. Kathleen Maguire and Ann L. Pastore, eds., *Sourcebook of Criminal Justice Statistics—1993,* (Washington, DC: Bureau of Justice Statistics, 1994), 586.
26. Interviewed in August 1996.
27. Roberta C. Cronin, *Boot Camps for Adult and Juvenile Offenders: Overview and Update,* Final Summary Report (Washington, DC: National Institute of Justice, 1994), 37. See also Mark Jones and Steven Cuvelier, "Are Boot Camp Graduates Better Probation Risks?" Paper presented at the annual meeting of the American Society of Criminology, New Orleans (November 1992); and Thomas W. Waldron, "Boot Camps Offer Second Chance to Young Felons," *Corrections Today* 52 (1990), 144–69.
28. Jean Bottcher, "Evaluating the Youth Authority's Boot Camp: The First Five Months." Paper delivered to Western Society of Criminology, Monterey, California, February 1993; Institute for Criminological Research and American Institute for Research, *Boot Camp for Juvenile Offenders: Constructive Intervention and Early Support—Implementation Evaluation Final Report* (New Brunswick, NJ: Rutgers University, 1992).
29. Roberta C. Cronin, *Boot Camps for Adults and Juvenile Offenders: Overview and Update.* A Final Summary Report Presented to the National Institute of Justice, 1994, 37.
30. Anthony W. Salerno, "Boot Camps: A Critique and a Proposed Alternative," *Journal of Offender Rehabilitation* 20 (1994), 149.
31. Ibid., 37.
32. Michael Peters, David Thomas, Christopher Zamberlan, and Caliber Associates, *Boot Camps for Juvenile Offenders: Program Summary* (Washington, DC: Office of Juvenile Justice and Delinquency Prevention, 1997), 3, 35.
33. Ibid.
34. Doris Layton MacKenzie, David B. Wilson, Gaylene Styve Armstrong, and Angela R. Glover, "The Impact of Boot Camps on Traditional Institutions of Juvenile Residents: Perceptions, Adjustment, and Change," *Journal of Research in Crime and Delinquency* 38 (August 2000), 279–313.

35. Ibid., 279.
36. Brent Zaehringer, *Koch Crime Institute White Paper Report Juvenile Boot Camps: Cost and Effectiveness vs. Residential Facilities*, http://www.kci.org/publication/whitepaper/bootcamp/introduction.htm
37. Marks, "States Fall Out of (Tough) Love with Boot Camps," 1.
38. Associated Press, "Teen Dies at Boot Camp for Troubled Teens," *Milwaukee Times*, 4 July, 2001. For an article that suggests that what takes place at boot camps may be considered cruel and unusual and gives rise to costly inmate litigation; see Faith E. Lutze and David C. Brody, "Mental Abuse as Cruel and Unusual Punishment: Do Boot Camp Prisons Violate the Eighth Amendment," *Crime and Delinquency* 45 (April 1999) 242–55.
39. Marks, "States Fall Out of (Tough) Love with Boot Camps," 1.
40. Parent et al, *Conditions of Confinement*, 22.
41. Ibid., 21.
42. *Corrections Compendium* (Lincoln, NE: CEGA, July 1992), 12–14.
43. Parent et al., *Conditions of Confinement*, 22, 23, 32.
44. A basic description of this program is included in a brochure developed by Hennepin County Home School (n.d.). This information was updated in a conversation with an official of this program in August 1996.
45. David Street, Robert D. Vinter, and Charles Perrow, *Organization for Treatment: A Comparative Study of Institutions* (New York: Free Press, 1966).
46. Peter W. Greenwood, Susan Turner, and Kathy Rosenblatt, *Evaluation of Paint Creek Youth Center: Preliminary Results* (Santa Monica, CA: Rand, 1989).
47. Ibid., 58.
48. Parent et al., *Conditions of Confinement*, 138.
49. The discussion of daily activities of youth supervisors is modified from Clemens Bartollas and Stuart J. Miller, *The Juvenile Offender: Control, Correction, and Treatment* (Boston: Holbrook Press, 1978), 268–69.
50. National Instiution of Law Enforcement and Criminal Justice, *National Manpower Survey*, 112.
51. Ibid., 182. One of the author's experiences with confined youths revealed that few can tolerate isolation for more than a couple of weeks.
52. Ibid., 185.
53. James Austin, Barry Krisberg, Robert DeComo, Sonya Rudenstine, and Dominic Del Rosario, *National Juvenile Custody Trends 1978–1989* (Washington, DC: Office of Juvenile Justice and Delinquency Prevention, 1993), 31–32.
54. David Shichor and Clemens Bartollas, "Private and Public Juvenile Placements: Is There a Difference?" *Crime and Delinquency* 36 (April 1990), 286–99.
55. Glen Mills, for example, was featured in Bill Howard, "Florida Tries to Clone Preppy Glen Mills," *Youth Today: The Newspaper on Youth Work* 5 (July/August, 1996), 1, 12, 13.

56. Gaylene Styve Armstrong and Doris Layton MacKenzie, "Private Versus Public Juvenile Correctional Facilities: Do Differences in Environmental Quality Exist," *Crime and Delinquency* 49 (October 2003), 542–63.
57. Shichor and Bartollas, "Private and Public Juvenile Placements."
58. Clemens Bartollas and David Shichor, "Juvenile Privatization: The Expected and the Unexpected." Paper presented at the annual meeting of the American Society of Criminology, Baltimore, Maryland (November 1990).
59. Shichor and Bartollas, "Private and Public Juvenile Placements," 286–99.
60. Barry Krisberg and Ira M. Schwartz, "Rethinking Juvenile Justice," *Crime and Delinquency* 29 (July 1983), 361.
61. Arnold Binder and Virginia L. Binder, "The Incarceration of Juveniles: from the Era of *Crouse* to That of Freud and Skinner," *Legal Studies Forum* 18 (July 1984), 372.
62. Ira M. Schwartz, Marilyn Jackson-Beeck, and Roger Anderson, "The 'Hidden' System of Juvenile Justice," *Crime and Delinquency* 30 (July 1984), 372.
63. Krisberg and Schwartz, "Rethinking Juvenile Justice," 361.
64. Schwartz et al., "The 'Hidden' System of Juvenile Justice," 382–83.
65. Louise Armstrong, *And They Call It Help: The Psychiatric Policing of America's Children* (Reading, MA: Addison-Wesley, 1993), 60–61.
66. Ira M. Schwartz, *(In) justice for Juveniles: Rethinking the Best Interests of the Child* (Lexington, MA: Lexington Books, 1989), 133.
67. C. A. McEwen, *Designing Correctional Organizations for Youths: Dilemmas of Subcultural Development* (Cambridge, MA: Ballinger, 1978), 151–52.
68. Clemens Bartollas, Stuart J. Miller, and Simon Dinitz, *Juvenile Victimization: The Institutional Paradox* (New York: Halsted Press, 1976); Barry Feld, *Neutralizing Inmate Violence: Juvenile Offenders in Institutions* (Cambridge, MA: Ballinger, 1977); H. W. Polsky, *Cottage Six: The Social System of Delinquent Boys in Residential Treatment* (New York: Russell Sage, 1963); Sethard Fisher, "Social Organization in a Correction Residence," *Pacific Sociological Review* 5 (Fall 1961), 89.
69. Rose Giallombardo, *The Social World of Imprisoned Girls: A Comparative Study of Institutions for Juvenile Delinquents* (New York: John Wiley, 1974).
70. Christopher M. Sieverdes and Clemens Bartollas, "Social Roles, Sex, and Racial Differences," *Deviant Behavior* 5 (1982), 203–18.
71. Alice Propper, *Prison Homosexuality: Myth and Reality* (Lexington, MA: D. C. Heath, 1981).
72. Interviewed in 1973.
73. Bartollas, Miller, and Dinitz, *Juvenile Victimization.*
74. Stuart J. Miller, Clemens Bartollas, and Simon Dinitz, *Juvenile Victimization Revisited: A Fifteen-Year Follow-Up at TICO* (unpublished manuscript).
75. *White v. Reid,* 125 F. Supp. 647 (D.D.C.) 1954.
76. *Inmates of the Boys' Training School v. Affleck,* 346 F. Supp. 1354 (D.R.I. 1972).

77. *Nelson v. Heyne,* 355 F. Supp. 451 (N.D. Ind. 1973).
78. *Morales v. Turman,* 364 F. Supp. 166 (E.D. Tex. 1973).
79. H. Swanger, "Juvenile Institutional Litigation," *Clearinghouse Review* 11 (1977), 22.
80. See *Lollis v. N.Y. State Department of Social Services* (1970) and N. N. Kittie, *The Right to Be Different: Deviance and Enforced Therapy* (Baltimore: Johns Hopkins University Press, 1971), for more information on this subject.
81. *Pena v. New York State Division for Youth,* 419 F. Supp. 203 (S.D.N.Y. 1976).
82. *Inmates of the Boys' Training School v. Affleck.*
83. *Morales v. Thurman.*
84. *Morgan v. Sproat,* 432 F. Supp. 1130 (S.D. Miss. 1977).
85. *State v. Werner,* 242 S.E.2d 907 (W. Va. 1978).
86. Patricia Puritz and Mary Ann Scali, *Beyond the Walls: Improving Conditions of Confinement for Youth in Custody Report* (Washington, DC: Office of Juvenile Justice and Delinquency Prevention, 1998), 4–7.

12

TREATMENT TECHNOLOGIES

OBJECTIVES

1. To identify different camps or positions concerning treatment in juvenile justice
2. To explain the treatment modalities that are used most frequently in juvenile justice
3. To evaluate these treatment modalities
4. To present suggestions to improve treatment in juvenile justice agencies

KEY TERMS

behavior modification
drug and alcohol abuse interventions
cognitive-behavioral interventions
family therapy
gang deactivation
guided group interaction (GGI)
Interpersonal Maturity Level (I-Level) Classification System
law-related education (LRE)
positive peer culture (PPC)
psychotherapy
Quay classification system
reality therapy
skill development
transactional analysis (TA)

We have a gym that has a basketball court and a weight room, but the cottages don't get down there very often. We are lucky if it is once a week. We are scheduled to go outside [fenced-in recreational area] every now and then, but then they usually cancel it right before it happens. All this stuff looks real good on paper, but when you come right down to it, the administration ain't really doing a lot for us back here.

They came out with this new level system. It goes from one to four—one being the lowest and four being the highest. Level fours are supposed to have a possibility of off-ground jobs, and there is a big list of things we are supposed to be able to do. But the only thing we've gotten so far is that we went off grounds once to see a movie. They run a lot of stuff down, and it looks real good for Central Office. But when you come right down to it, you are here to do your time. That's it!

We got some vocational classes, and they got their Mickey Mouse high school over there. If you don't go to school, you get a write-up and locked up. . . . We ain't even being educated to a point where we see we have a need for education. A lot of guys are illiterate. They can't even write their name or can write very little.

And these guys are taught no self-worth, except maybe a couple of staff will say something to them. There is no programs to teach them. They ain't getting a lot of help brought to them. All this place is doing is setting them for a letdown when they get back out in society. This place is setting them up for prison.

They can't get a job. They ain't even got a GED. Where are they going to get money? The first place is that they are going to go to Sam Smith's house, take his stereo, and there they go. That's really sad! There could be more help, but there is just a lot of people who don't care. It is a political game. The guys in charge don't care. It's sad that all these people are crying out for help, and there is no help for them. That's why we got to build seven new prisons in this state every year. They cry about all this money they got to spend on a prison. They should spend the money on the guys who are 16 and 17 in this institution.

—Institutionalized Male Delinquent[1]

The training school resident speaking in the opening quote claims that no positive programs are taking place in this institution for boys. Indeed, he argues that he is likely to leave in worse shape than when he was first confined by the "kindly parent, the state." In spite of the perceptions of this youth, juvenile offenders are confronted and almost overwhelmed by the various methods used to treat, save, rehabilitate, remodel, remake, or otherwise "recycle" them. Juvenile corrections, far more than adult corrections, has as its guiding premise the rehabilitation of youths before they become hardened criminals. To that end, researchers from every discipline have looked for the key that will modify the behavior of offenders.

Punishment was believed to be the answer for a long period of time. But in the 1700s, the founding fathers of our country substituted a religious orientation as the proper approach to working with wayward children. This moral and religious emphasis slowly gave way by the second half of the nineteenth century to firm discipline and rigorous work training. The study of the character and mental condition of individual lawbreakers was the accepted treatment during the first four decades of the twentieth century. Sociology began to dominate treatment efforts in the 1950s and 1960s with the use of predelinquency community programs, detached workers (social workers whose jobs are on the streets with juvenile gangs), group interaction, job training, and community reorganization. Indeed, during this period, a new idea sprang up nearly every day, each one heralded as the panacea for youth crime. In the 1970s, as discussed in the next section, correctional treatment was bombarded with criticism from all sides and still has not fully regained its former popularity.

Approaches to treatment range from individual to group methods. This chapter presents a general discussion of treatment in juvenile justice and describes and evaluates the treatment modalities that are most popular today.

WHAT IS THE TREATMENT DEBATE?

Correctional treatment came under increased criticism in the late 1960s and early 1970s. In 1966, reporting on the results of one hundred empirical evaluations of treatment, Walter C. Bailey concluded that there seemed to be little evidence that correctional treatment was effective.[2] In 1971, J. Robison and G. Smith added that "there [was] no evidence to support any program's claim to superior rehabilitative strategy."[3] Then, in 1974, the late Robert Martinson startled both correctional personnel and the public with the pronouncement that "with few and isolated exceptions, the rehabilitative efforts that have been reported so far have had no appreciable effect on recidivism."[4] The media quickly simplified Martinson's statement into the idea that "nothing works" in correctional treatment. In 1975, Douglas Lipton, Robert Martinson, and Judith Wilks published *The Effectiveness of Correctional Treatment,* which critically evaluated the effectiveness of correctional treatment programs.[5] In that same year, Martinson announced on *60 Minutes* that "there [was] no evidence that correctional rehabilitation reduces recidivism."[6] A spirited debate on the "nothing works" thesis has continued to rage since the late 1970s.

Ted Palmer, a correctional researcher in California, challenged Lipton and his colleagues' research by tabulating 82 studies mentioned in the book and showing that thirty-nine of them, or 48 percent, had positive or partly positive results on recidivism.[7] Palmer used Martinson's own words to reject the "nothing works" thesis:

> These programs seem to work best when they are new, when their subjects are amenable to treatment in the first place, and when the counselors are not only trained people, but "good people" as well.[8]

Robert R. Ross and Paul Gendreau reviewed the literature published between 1973 and 1978 and found that 86 percent of the ninety-five intervention programs studied reported success.[9] According to Gendreau and Ross, this success rate was "convincing evidence that some treatment programs, when they are applied with integrity by competent practitioners in appropriate target populations, can be effective in preventing crime or reducing recidivism."[10] In the late 1970s, Martinson conceded that "contrary to [his] previous position, some treatment programs *do* have an appreciable effect on recidivism. Some programs are indeed beneficial."[11] But, despite Martinson's recantation of his "nothing works" thesis and Palmer's and Gendreau and Ross's defense of correctional treatment, the general mood regarding offender rehabilitation in the late 1970s and early 1980s was one of pessimism and discouragement.

In the late 1980s, Gendreau and Ross reviewed the offender rehabilitation literature for the period between 1981 and 1987 and again found that the number and variety of successful reported attempts at reducing delinquent behavior dismissed the "nothing works" hypothesis.[12] Moreover, the rehabilitative evidence in the 1980s grew at a much greater rate than it did during the 1970s and suggested several strategies for developing more effective programs.[13]

Several meta-analyses have evaluated the effectiveness of correctional treatment. The statistical tool of meta-analysis has been developed to enable reviewers to combine findings from different experiments. Meta-analysis undertakes the "aggregation and side-by-side analysis of large numbers of experimental studies."[14] One of the advantages of meta-analysis is that it can "incorporate adjustments for the fact that studies vary considerably in the degree of rigour of their experimental design."[15] Focus on Programs 12–1 summarizes the findings of the most widely studied meta-analyses of correctional treatment.

Ted Palmer's 1992 publication, *The Re-Emergence of Correctional Intervention,* contends that during the 1980s, both juvenile and adult corrections struggled with institutional crowding, rising costs, and behavioral control of offenders. But interest in and commitment to rehabilitation or habilitation increased steadily through the 1980s. By the end of the decade, according to Palmer:

> Growth-centered intervention had gained still more strength in terms of focus, direction, and perceived legitimacy. This change, especially intervention's relegitimization, is a major development in American corrections, particularly considering rehabilitation's and habilitation's low status and quasi-banishment from 1975 to 1981.[16]

Intervention's new direction or emphasis, according to Palmer, resulted from the fact that many skeptics and most supporters of correctional intervention by the 1990s largely agreed on the following principles for working with serious offenders: (1) programs with multiple modalities must be used; (2) intensity of contact must be increased in most programs; and (3) greater attention must be paid to offenders' needs and characteristics so that they can be matched with particular program elements.[17]

FOCUS ON PROGRAMS 12–1

META-ANALYSIS OF CORRECTIONAL TREATMENT

- Garrett (1985) surveyed 111 papers and found a significant overall effect of treatment on a variety of outcomes, including reoffending.
- Gottschalk and colleagues (1987) examined community-based interventions and found a weaker effect.
- Lab and Whitehead (1988, 1989) reported predominantly negative findings in their meta-analyses and described only a few promising results.
- Izzo and Ross (1990) compared programs that contained a cognitive component with those that did not, and they found a marked superiority in terms of reduced recidivism among programs with a cognitive component.
- Andrews and colleagues (1990) incorporated findings from 150 research reports and included studies undertaken with adult offenders; they found overall positive effects of correctional treatment.
- Lipsey examined 397 outcome studies of offenders between the ages of twelve and twenty-one, which produced a sample in excess of forty thousand clients. A principal finding of this survey was that a total of 64.5 percent of the experiments showed positive effects of treatment in reducing recidivism.

Thus, taking all these meta-analyses together, the net effect of treatment is an average reduction in recidivism rates of between 10 and 12 percent.

Source: James McGuire and Philip Priestley, "Reviewing 'What Works': Past, Present, and Future," in *What Works: Reducing Reoffending—Guidelines from Research and Practice*, edited by James McGuire (New York: John Wiley & Sons, 1995), pp. 8–9.

Critical Thinking Questions:

Do these meta-analyses suggest that "nothing washes" in correctional treatment? What type of youthful offenders do you think would be more receptive to rehabilitative services?

HOW ARE YOUTHFUL OFFENDERS CLASSIFIED?

Throughout the twentieth century, classification was considered the first step of treatment in juvenile correction. Psychiatric evaluations and psychological workups of juvenile delinquents were conducted in child guidance clinics by the second decade of the twentieth century. A number of reception and diagnostic centers were built in the 1930s and 1940s so that delinquents could be assigned to programs compatible with their psychological, educational, and vocational needs. Classifying youths in terms of their personality dynamics, worldview, and behavior were the three most popular schemes in the 1960s and 1970s. But in the past decade, classification systems for treatment purposes in juvenile corrections have lost much of their former popularity.

Most juvenile delinquents are involved in psychiatric interviews and psychological workups on one or more occasions. Psychiatric interviews may be used to determine the psychological problems of a youth, and the therapist may use such terms as *psychoneurotic, antisocial, passive-aggressive, passive dependent, adjustment reaction to adolescence, group delinquent,* and *unsocialized* in describing the problems of a youth. Psychiatric interviews also are frequently conducted before releasing from training school a delinquent who has committed violent offenses in order to provide corrections officials with assurance that the youth is no longer dangerous. Various psychological tests, such as the Jesness Personality Inventory, categorize youthful offenders according to such concepts as social maladjustment, value orientation, immaturity, autism, alienation, manifest aggression, withdrawal-depression, social anxiety, repression, denial, and asocial index.

The **Interpersonal Maturity Level (I-Level) Classification System,** developed by J. Grant and M. Grant in the late 1950s in California, assumes that personality development follows a normal sequence and attempts to identify the developmental stage of offenders by focusing on their perception of themselves, others, and the world. A seven-point classification scheme ranges from I_1 (infantile in interpersonal maturity) to I_7 (ideal social maturity). Researchers have found that most delinquents are fixated at one of the lower levels of social maturity and, therefore, can be classified at the I_2, I_3, and I_4 levels; these levels are further divided into nine delinquent subtypes.[18] Proponents of the I-Level system contend that the impact of treatment varies from one youth to another according to his or her developmental stage; accordingly, what works with one youth may have no effect or even a negative impact on another. The I-Level system was rigorously evaluated at California's Community Treatment Project (CTP) and at the Preston Boys' School in California during the 1960s and has been widely used, especially in training schools, throughout the nation.

Herbert C. Quay developed a classification system that evaluates delinquents in terms of their behavior rather than their worldview.[19] The **Quay classification system** is based on five personality types: inadequate-immature, neurotic-conflicted, unsocialized aggressive or psychopathic, socialized or subcultural delinquent, and subcultural-immature delinquents. Inadequate-immature offenders behave childishly or irresponsibly. Neurotic-conflicted delinquents are anxious, insecure youths whose internal conflicts create problems for themselves and others. Unsocialized delinquents adhere to the values of their delinquent peer group. Offenders in the subcultural classification are usually involved in gang delinquency. Subcultural-immature delinquents are youths who violate the law but feel alienated from delinquent peer groups. The Quay classification and treatment model continues to be used but has lost much of its popularity.

WHAT ARE THE MAIN TREATMENT MODALITIES?

Various treatment modalities are widely used in community-based corrections and have been established in nearly every training school in the United States. Psychotherapy, transactional analysis, reality therapy, behavior modification, family therapy, guided group interaction, and positive peer culture are the traditional treatment modalities most widely used in juvenile justice. Drug and alcohol abuse interventions, law-related education, skill development programs, and gang deactivation groups are also increasingly used.[20]

PSYCHOTHERAPY

Various adaptations of Freudian **psychotherapy** have been used by psychiatrists, clinical psychologists, and psychiatric social workers since the early twentieth century. Either in a one-to-one relationship with a therapist or in a group context, juvenile offenders are encouraged to talk about past conflicts causing them to express emotional problems through aggressive or antisocial behavior. The insight that offenders gain from this individual or from group psychotherapy supposedly helps them resolve the conflicts and unconscious needs that drive them to crime. As a final step of psychotherapy, youthful offenders become responsible for their own behavior.

Acceptance of the therapist is a key to successful psychotherapy, for youths must discover that all adults are not like their rejecting parents. A trusting therapeutic relationship, coupled with firmness and justice on the part of the therapist, is intended to help offenders acquire a new sense of dignity and self-worth.

Within the community, psychotherapy has been used recently much more with middle- and upper-class youthful offenders than with lower-class youngsters. Middle- and upper-class youths who abuse drugs or alcohol or who have conflicts at home are likely to be referred for psychotherapy. Other than in a few private institutions, little psychotherapy takes place in institutional contexts. The few psychiatrists and clinical psychologists available in these settings spend most of their time doing intake evaluations for classification purposes and crisis intervention with acting-out youths. Crisis intervention generally consists of one interview in which the therapist recommends a treatment plan for the resident's cottage; psychiatrists may also prescribe medication to calm a youth.

One of the fundamental problems with psychotherapy is that youthful offenders usually do not see themselves as having emotional problems and, furthermore, are reluctant to share their inner thoughts with a therapist. This is particularly true of lower-class youths, most of whom can relate a bad experience with a psychiatrist or psychologist. But it is also true with middle- and upper-class youths, who frequently have authority problems and view these "treaters" as part of the establishment from which they are rebelling. It is not surprising that there is no recent evidence of the effectiveness of psychotherapy with youthful offenders.

Transactional Analysis

Transactional analysis (TA) focuses on interpreting and evaluating interpersonal relationships. This treatment modality tries to teach youthful lawbreakers to relate to others in an adult, mature way. Eric Berne, founder of TA, believes that it can overcome the typical resistance to psychotherapy:

> . . . as most kids are forced into therapy and must maintain a subservient status vis-à-vis the therapist. In TA, youths learn to interact with the therapist on an adult-to-adult basis. The youths learn the procedure of TA and are free to implement the therapy for themselves as they see fit.[21]

In applying this modality, the TA leader usually first does a script analysis, which is an attempt to understand how the "tapes" of the past are influencing the behavior of the juvenile in the present. This concept of script analysis is based on the premise that human memory acts as a three-track tape that records the events individuals experienced during their first years of life, the meaning attached to those events, and the emotions they experienced when those events occurred. Each person often replays his or her tape when similar situations are encountered later in life. The consequence of negative script replay is that many individuals become "losers," failing to attain their goals and becoming involved in self-defeating behavior. The TA leader seeks to discover the youth's script by diagnosing his or her voice, vocabulary, demeanor, gestures, and answers to questions. TA is based on the belief that persons can change their scripts, and the function of the TA leader is to help individuals make this change. For example, if a mother has told her daughter that she will never succeed at anything and if this has become a self-fulfilling prophecy, the therapist tries to communicate to the daughter that she *can* succeed in achieving her goals.

One of the hopeful outcomes of the life-script interview is that offenders are willing to negotiate a treatment contract; that is, the youths will state how they wish to change. This treatment contract normally has both short- and long-range goals, project group goals, academic goals, and social behavior goals. Once goals are set, the youth is considered to be in treatment. Throughout the treatment period, these goals and progress toward them are constantly reviewed by staff.

As soon as offenders are placed in groups, they learn that one of the first objects of TA is to make them become aware of the different kinds of social interaction they use in dealing with others. TA conceptualizes three ego states—the "Child" (relic of one's past), the "Parent" (internalization of the teaching and values of one's parental figures), and the "Adult" (the mature and responsible adult). The TA therapist then tries to help the residents recognize when they are emerging from each state so that they are able to function more often in the Adult ego state. Since the Adult can turn off the not-OK feelings of the Child tape, the TA leader tries to free the Adult state so that it can deal objectively with the other two states.

The youthful offender also is taught the four life positions that constitute the relationship perceived between the self and others:

1. I'm OK—You're OK: This is the position of the normal healthy individual who starts on the assumption that he or she and others are emotionally well adjusted to life.
2. I'm not OK—You're OK: This position reflects a neurotic, depressed outlook on life—others are emotionally healthy, but the individual is not.
3. I'm not OK—You're not OK: This position, which is that of autistic children and schizophrenics, produces severe individual problems in relating to the world and to the people in it.
4. I'm OK—You're not OK: This position, often observed in the delinquent and the sociopath, means the individual believes that he or she is justified in gratifying his or her own immediate impulses, regardless of the consequences.[22]

A further function of TA is to teach the games that group members play in their interactions. According to TA, a *game* is a series of transactions that moves toward a predictable, well-defined outcome. Berne describes game

Which approach in this chapter would you use on this skinhead? Would you use any of these? Why or why not? (Photo by Jerry Cavanaugh.)

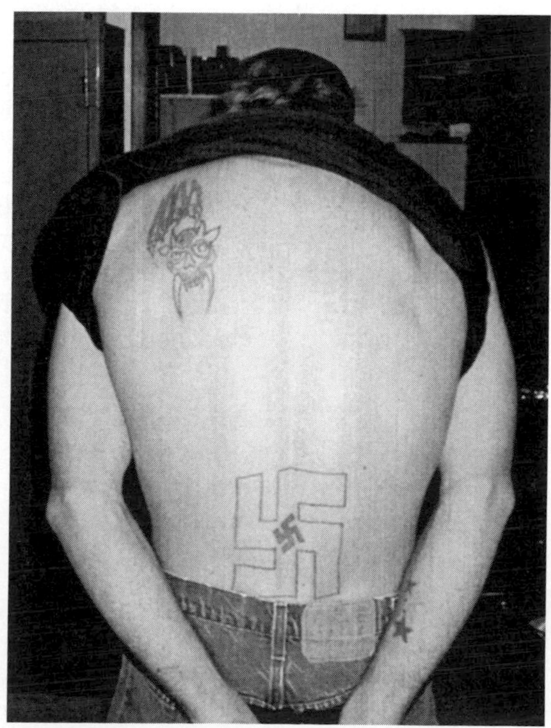

behavior as "a series of moves with a snare or 'gimmick.'"[23] Games serve to keep a person from intimacy with others, and they usually involve offenders who are "coming out" of their impulsive, immature Child states. These games are the means by which youthful offenders keep their emotional distance from staff. Such game behavior no doubt began with juveniles' feelings of powerlessness at the hands of the police and judges and continued throughout their stint in the system.

Thus, the TA leader, whether psychotherapist, psychiatric social worker, or paraprofessional, is not only a dispenser of information about the basic tenets of TA, but he or she also helps offenders become more aware of their social interactions. In addition to helping offenders individually, the TA leader observes group interactions among offenders and, when these interactions are taped on audiovisual equipment, studies in greater depth each youth's interpersonal relationships. Focus on Programs 12–2 relates the success of TA with one youthful offender.

Using TA for treating juveniles has several advantages. The first is that TA is easy to learn. Offenders, for instance, readily understand gaming behavior. One TA leader altered TA terminology further to make it even more comprehensible to offenders. The Parent ego state became "the man"; the Adult was changed to "cool head"; and the Child was altered to "the kid."[24]

Another advantage of TA, according to the only major study that examined its effectiveness, is that it appears to have positive impact on some offenders. This study of a training school in California further revealed that residents exposed to TA tend to have higher morale, develop more positive attitudes toward staff members, become more hopeful and optimistic about the future, and establish greater feelings of self-esteem and well-being. Finally, subjects paroled from this training school did significantly better during their first twelve months following release than had offenders released in prior years. The parole violation rates were also significantly lower than those of comparable age groups released from other California juvenile institutions.[25]

In spite of the popularity and success of TA, especially in the 1960s and 1970s, its most glaring limitation is the difficulty in applying the technique to youths who are evading personal change, who have gross behavior problems, and/or who are not motivated to examine their own problems. The mature are the most likely to profit; the immature and sociopathic usually withdraw, and the manipulator tries to "game" staff and the other inmates. Youthful offenders with borderline intelligence are also limited in their ability to examine their behavior through such an intellectual exercise.

Reality Therapy

Reality therapy, a very popular treatment modality, was developed by two Los Angeles psychiatrists, William Glasser and G. L. Harrington. This modality assumes that irresponsible behavior arises when a person is unable to fulfill his or her basic needs. According to this approach, the basic human needs

FOCUS ON PROGRAMS 12–2

A TA SUCCESS STORY

Bill, a sixteen-year-old African-American youth, had spent several years in juvenile institutions before he arrived at the training school. Although his home was intact, he felt a great deal of rejection from his mother. His offenses were incorrigibility at home and in school and two charges of assault and battery toward peers (fighting in school). His average to above-average intelligence was not apparent from his school performance. Psychiatric reports diagnosed him as withdrawn and as having schizoid tendencies.

His first adjustment report stated: "The prognosis is poor. Extremely depressed about his home life, especially his relationship with mother, Bill is experiencing conflict with peers and staff alike. Bill is resistant to his placement and refuses to become involved in any institutional program."

Then, Bill was persuaded by a TA leader to join a group. TA fascinated Bill, who took an active part in the group and never missed a meeting; he also read all he could find on this therapy. More important, he used the concepts of TA to change his behavior and his perception of himself. He frequently informed staff, "I changed from the Child to the Adult state on that one, didn't I?" Bill decided he would finish his last three years of high school, which he did at the institutional high school in the next year and a half. He was granted a home visit to resolve his conflict with his mother, but when she blatantly rejected him on the visit, he used TA to work through the pain of rejection. He applied to Ohio State University, was accepted, and on his release, became a college student. Four years later, the youth who had been given such a poor prognosis received his college diploma.

Source: Case study of a youth with whom one of the authors worked.

Critical Thinking Questions:
Why do you believe this youth was receptive to TA? Did rehabilitation work for him?

are relatedness and respect, and one satisfies these needs by doing what is realistic, responsible, and right.[26]

The three Rs of reality therapy are reality, responsibility, and right-and-wrong. In using this approach with older delinquent girls at the Ventura School in California, Glasser always made each adolescent face the reality of her behavior in the present; he refused to accept any reason for irresponsible behavior, and he expected the girls to maintain a satisfactory standard of behavior.

Glasser defines the major differences between conventional and reality therapy as follows:

1. Because we do not accept the concept of mental illness, the patient cannot become involved with us as a mentally ill person who has no responsibility for his behavior.
2. Working in the present and toward the future, we do not get involved with the patient's history because we can neither change what happened to him nor accept the fact that he is limited by his past.
3. We relate to patients as ourselves, not as transference figures.
4. We do not look for unconscious conflicts or the reasons for them. A patient cannot become involved with us by excusing his or her behavior on the basis of unconscious motivations.
5. We emphasize the morality of behavior. We face the issue of right and wrong which we believe solidifies the involvement, in contrast to conventional psychiatrists who do not make the distinction between right and wrong, feeling it would be detrimental to attaining the transference relationship they seek.
6. We teach patients better ways to fulfill their needs. The proper involvement will not be maintained unless the patient is helped to find more satisfactory patterns of behavior as part of therapy.[27]

Reality therapy involves three phases: first, the offender forms an honest personal relationship with the therapist; second, the therapist always accepts the youth but, at the same time, rejects the negative behavior; third, the therapist teaches offenders better ways to fulfill their needs within their social reality.

Glasser emphasizes consistent discipline and warm acceptance and believes that offenders should be given increased responsibilities:

> We firmly believe that an institutional training school, or a mental hospital, can produce better results when warm relationships along with increasing responsibilities are stressed by an undivided staff. The girl who comes to Ventura has spent her life excusing her behavior in a world where people were not consistent, where one person told her one thing, someone else told her another, and most told her different things from day to day. Every effort must be maintained to provide a unified philosophy of treatment where the staff provides both consistent discipline and warmth and affection. But warmth never supersedes discipline, nor discipline warmth.[28]

Reality therapy has not been sufficiently studied with juvenile offenders to permit any definite statements about its effectiveness. Glasser estimates that it has succeeded with about 80 percent of the girls at Ventura School. He cites as proof of his case the statistic that only 43 out of 370 girls at the school were returnees while he was a therapist there.

Using this modality with juveniles has several advantages. The first is that paraprofessionals can play a major role in working with clients because the basic tenets are easily learned. Second, paraprofessionals are much more attracted to the basic assumptions of reality therapy than to other treatment modalities. For example, they like its emphasis on responsibility, its negation of extenuating circumstances, and its focus on the present. Third, it seems to be easier to achieve consistent treatment with this modality.

Criticisms of this modality center on its oversimplification of the dynamics of the human personality. Critics believe, in this regard, that insight is helpful to certain offenders in dealing with their antisocial behavior and that an exploration of the past is sometimes necessary to deal adequately with the present. Reality therapy is further criticized for its tendency to encourage paternalistic and authoritarian attitudes in therapeutic interaction. Similarly, others suggest that this modality attracts rigid and inflexible persons who use it as a shield to hide their own authoritarian attitudes. The proponents of reality therapy are also accused of moralism and of oversimplifying the definitions of right and wrong.

Despite these criticisms, reality therapy is pervasive and influential in juvenile justice. Because so many of its assumptions are agreeable to line staff, the popularity of this modality will endure long after most of the other treatment technologies have been forgotten.

Behavior Modification

Behavior modification refers to the application of instrumental learning theory to problems of human behavior. This modality is based on the assumption that all behavior is under the control of its consequences in the external environment. If a behavior is reinforced immediately and systematically in a positive way, the frequency and rate of that behavior should increase, but if a behavior does not receive a positive reinforcement, the frequency should decrease. Attention, praise, money, food, and privileges are positive reinforcers; threats, confinement, punishment, and ridicule are negative reinforcers. Positive reinforcers produce more effective and enduring behavior changes. A wide variety of techniques are used to reinforce positive and extinguish negative behavior. They include systematic desensitization, extinction of undesirable responses, training in assertiveness, counterconditioning, conditioning against avoidance responses, and the use of tokens. Behavior modification uses environmental contingencies to alter the offender's response.[29]

Behavior modification does not employ such terms as *repressed desires, self-concept, unconscious needs,* and *superego,* because they refer unnecessarily to internal psychological characteristics. Actions, rather than self-awareness of self-knowledge, are important in behavior modification. Attending primarily to the observable stimulus and the observable response, the behavior modification therapist tries to change a person's conduct by determining the desired result, the stimuli that can control it, and the reinforcements that are contingent on the response. The behavior modification therapist attempts to reduce gradually the antisocial behavior of youthful offenders. The expectation is that each reduction will lead to greater accomplishments and that eventually the youth will be able to live within the law. Consistency is a crucial component of behavior modification therapy; therefore, each staff member must systematically provide the positive and negative reinforcers.

Behavior modification therapy also cautions against the use of punishment unless youths are dangerous to themselves or to others. When punishment is needed, swift and consistent action should follow the undesirable behavior. Instead of punishment, behavioral therapy recommends the use of brief time-out periods during which no reinforcement of any kind is available.

One of the great strengths of behavior modification therapy is that it appears to have a greater impact on the sociopathic offender than do other treatment modalities. A major reason for this is that behavior modification techniques can immediately reinforce target behaviors. A study by J. L. Bernard and R. Eisenman reported that sociopathic offenders are easier to condition than are normal subjects by either social or monetary reinforcement once the behavior therapist discovers what is rewarding for the youth who is undergoing treatment.[30] Behavior modification also appears to have a greater impact on the manipulator than do more traditional therapies. Furthermore, behavior modification is specific and often is effective in short-term intervention. Finally, behavior modification is one of the most flexible of the treatment modalities.

Opponents of behavior modification have leveled several major criticisms against it. One of the most frequent attacks states that treating only the offender's overt symptoms is too superficial to be effective. Many critics also charge that this treatment method is not lasting. Humanists believe that human beings are too unique and complicated to be treated only according to their overt behavior. It is also feared that behavior denoting even greater disturbance may take the place of the eliminated symptom. Another criticism is that the principles of behavior modification require considerable consistency and continuity, if not sophistication, which is atypical of correctional treatment. Finally, critics argue that it is very difficult to apply behavior modification to youths who do not manifest overt behavioral problems.

R. Schwitzgebel and D. A. Kolb's study of behavior modification is one of the most frequently cited. Their study involved twenty delinquent boys in Boston in a nine-month project, in which the youths were paid for talking into a tape recorder about their life experiences. The boys came to their appointments on an individual basis, two to three times a week. The measured result of the program was that attendance became more prompt. After three years, follow-up data showed significantly fewer arrests and fewer months incarcerated among those in the program than among those in a matched control group. But there was no significant difference in recidivism, as measured by those youths who went on to the reformatory or prison. The authors attributed the success that was achieved to the fact that individualized rewards were used and that the experimenters were empathetic, direct, and unorthodox in their relationships with the youths.[31]

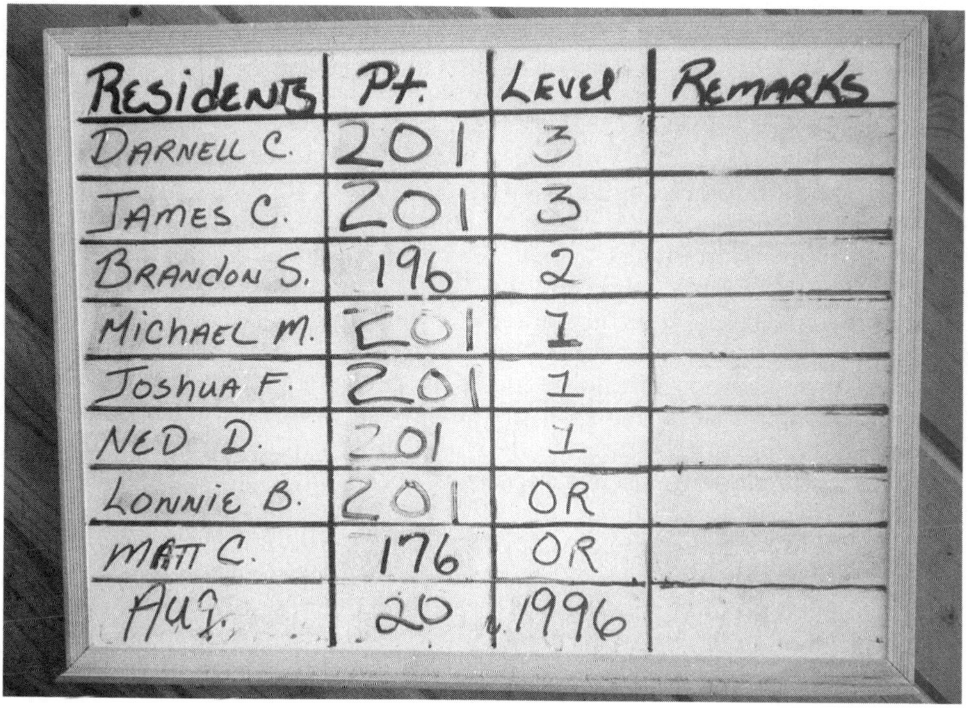

The "level system" is based on behavior modification theory. Youths receive "points" for good behavior and can move from one level to another on the basis of the number of points they receive. The higher the level, the more privileges the youth receives. (Courtesy Mel Blount Youth Homes; photo by Stuart Miller.)

Dennis A. Romig, in reviewing fourteen studies of behavior modification involving almost two thousand juvenile offenders in programs across the United States, found that behavior modification has been effective in changing certain behaviors, such as those related to school attendance, test scores, promptness, and classroom behavior. Yet it has had less impact on such global factors as delinquency or arrest rates. Romig concludes that the more the youthful offenders are involved in the process of behavior modification and the more specific and behaviorally simple the behaviors to be changed are, the more likely it is that the results will be positive.[32]

Family Therapy

Treating the entire family has become a widely used method of dealing with a youthful offender's socially unacceptable behavior. The Sacramento 601 Diversion Project is one of the most successful examples of **family therapy.** This project was designed to determine whether youths in need of supervision (status offenders) could more effectively be diverted from delinquency through short-term family crisis counseling involving the entire family than through involvement in traditional juvenile court intake procedures. The evaluation of the 601 Diversion Project indicated that it has successfully achieved its four major goals: (1) to reduce the number of cases ending in juvenile court; (2) to reduce the number of repeat offenders; (3) to decrease overnight detentions; and (4) to accomplish these goals without increasing the cost required for regular processing of cases. Romig postulates that the positive results of the 601 Diversion Project "can be attributed to the involvement of the youths' families at the crisis points and the subsequent attempts by the project staff to improve the communication patterns of the family."[33]

Romig evaluated twenty studies involving 2,180 youths and concluded that family therapy did not reduce delinquent behavior. When such therapy focused on the positive goal of improving communication among family members, however, significant decreases of youth offenses occurred. Further, crisis intervention counseling, especially when used to teach systematic problem solving, was successful.[34]

In sum, family therapy appears likely to be more effective when it is focused on teaching parents communication, problem-solving, and disciplinary skills. Accordingly, status offenders and their families are more likely than youthful offenders and their families to benefit from effective family therapy.

Guided Group Interaction

Guided group interaction (GGI) is probably the most widely used treatment modality. It has been used in at least eleven states: Florida, Georgia, Illinois, Kentucky, Maryland, Michigan, Minnesota, New Hampshire, New Jersey, South Dakota, and West Virginia. Since the 1950s, when this modality was first used, it has been based on the assumption that youths could confront their peers and force them to face the reality of their behavior more effectively than could staff.

The guided group interaction approach is characterized by a nonauthoritarian atmosphere, intensity of interaction, group homogeneity, and an emphasis on group structure. The most important characteristic is the nonauthoritarian atmosphere. Residents in many residential GGI programs, for example, are given considerable say in when a group member will be released, granted a home furlough, or approved for off-campus visits; in how a group will be punished; and in whether the outside door will be locked or left open at night.

Giving residents responsibility for decision making, of course, is a different approach to child care from that followed in most correctional settings. The adult leader constantly refers the decision making back to the group. When informed by a youth that a group member planned to run away, for example, one staff member retorted: "So what do you want me to do? He's your buddy; he's part of your group. You can talk to him if you have to; but it's up to all of you to help one another."[35]

Youthful offenders usually go through several stages in becoming involved in guided group interaction. Youths initially are guarded in their responses, but as their defenses begin to weaken, they learn to give up their games and defenses because of the encouragement received from peers and the group leader. In the second stage, the residents' interpersonal problems are brought into the open. They are encouraged to talk about themselves and to have their values scrutinized and challenged by the group. In the third stage, the offenders begin to examine the difficulties they have had with their environment. The group members, who begin to develop real trust among one another, probe the problems of institutional and street living. The fourth stage is that in which the offenders feel secure and accept reeducation. When they see that their problems are not unique and that dealing with them is possible, they feel less antagonistic toward the group and become more receptive to what is said. In the final stage, the residents set up an outline of a plan for change. Using his or her own self-evaluation, as well as that of the group, each youth makes a conscious decision about the way he or she wants to behave in the future.[36]

Guided group interaction was first used with juvenile offenders in the Highfields Project in New Jersey in the early 1950s. The success of this project led other agencies to adopt this approach to treating youthful offenders. Joseph W. Scott and Jerry B. Hissong describe the way GGI was implemented in a juvenile institution in Kentucky. In this setting, groups met five times a week for 90-minute sessions. Every attempt was made to form groups that were homogenous in sex, delinquent sophistication, and physical and emotional maturity. The group therapist checked daily with cottage parents, work supervisors, and other staff to determine the problems that were being manifested by various group members. Each meeting focused on the problems of a single youth. Residents were encouraged to disclose their problems as long as their acting out did not harm others. In return for their commitment to the prosocial values of the group process, group members had some say about when they were ready for release.[37]

A great strength of guided group interaction is its determination to circumvent the values of the delinquent-peer subculture. This modality, in urging residents to be honest and open with one another, attempts to move group participants to a more positive, prosocial stance. Another advantage is that it represents a comprehensive strategy for dealing with troubled youth. In effect, it is a total system for mitigating the impact of a delinquent subculture. A third advantage is that guided group interaction seems to have gained acceptance on the state level. Also important is the fact that guided group interaction can be led by line staff, thereby increasing staff involvement in the treatment process. A final advantage is that responsibility is given to offenders; thus, in interacting with peers, offenders become aware of their problems and are directed toward resolutions.

A major problem in using guided group interaction is the shortage of trained group leaders. Also, since this approach to group work lacks a single spokesman, a number of versions and designs of the basic principles have emerged. As a consequence, no clear and consistent philosophy guides the process of working with offenders in groups. The emphasis of GGI on peer group norms and values further tends to slight the importance of individualism. Extreme care must be taken to ensure that peer group norms established and monitored by institutional staff do not repress the youthful offenders' needs for self-identity and autonomy. Finally, peer group norms created by guided group interaction may not always be transferable to actual life situations that will be encountered upon release.

Although the research findings on guided group interaction have been mixed, the general picture that emerges is that a GGI experience in a nonresidential program is at least as effective as and much less costly than confinement in a state facility and that a GGI experience in an institutional program seems to have more positive impact on less delinquent youngsters.[38]

Positive Peer Culture

The concept of **positive peer culture (PPC)** has generated considerable excitement in juvenile corrections, especially in the 1970s. Developed by Harry Vorrath and associates as an outgrowth of guided group interaction, positive peer culture has been implemented in all of the juvenile state institutions in West Virginia, Michigan, and Missouri.[39]

Vorrath believes that PPC "is a total system for building positive youth subcultures."[40] The main philosophy of PPC is to "turn around" the negative peer culture and to mobilize the power of the peer group in a positive way. PPC does this by teaching group members to care for one another; caring is defined as wanting what is best for a person. Vorrath believes that once caring becomes "fashionable" and is accepted by the group, "hurting goes out of style."[41]

PPC involves the same stages as GGI, but it places more emphasis on positive behavior. Group members learn to speak of positive behaviors as "great," "intelligent," "independent," "improving," and "winning." In contrast, negative behavior is described as "childish," "unintelligent," "helpless," "destructive," "copping out," and "losing."

Vorrath acknowledges the pervasiveness of peer influence and feels that winning over its subculture is necessary if its influence is to be positively rechanneled. Young people, according to Vorrath, can become experts in dealing with the problems of other young people. The group meetings sponsored by PPC, however, must break through the antisocial values of young offenders if such meetings are to be positive.

Positive peer culture is developed through ninety-minute meetings five times per week. Characterized by trust and openness, PPC focuses on the direct and immediate problems of the lawbreaking youth. Believing that groups function most effectively when they are homogeneous, leaders try to include youths that are similar in age, sex, maturity, and delinquency sophistication. Coeducational groups are believed to be counterproductive.

Groups are made up of nine youths who sit in a circle; the leader is part of the circle but sits at a desk. The meeting is usually opened by each youth in turn talking about the particular problems encountered that day. Then the group decides, largely based on what has been said, who will "have" the meeting. Instead of this person being on the "hot seat," as might be the case in some encounter groups, PPC provides a context in which help is received from other group members. The group leader, a line staff member who works directly with residents, concludes the meeting with an eight- or ten-minute summary of what has taken place.

The group leader in this modality is not a therapist in the traditional sense, but instead is a special teacher or coach who instructs, guides, redirects, and motivates the group to work on problems. The leader, who must be both an effective limit setter and a sympathetic listener, also needs to have a kind of mystique. Since part of the leader's responsibility is to build a degree of anxiety into the group, group members must be prevented from understanding and predicting the leader's behavior. But the primary basis of this mystique rests in the leader's knowledge of what is taking place in the group. All interactions and the functioning of each group member must be understood. The leader can keep the group off balance by perceiving what takes place "back stage." To fulfill this demanding leadership role, the leader must be able to detect rigged meetings, read nonverbal behavior, protect weaker members from being hurt by the group process, discover each resident's basic problem, and neutralize negative or controlling leadership in the group.

The negative indigenous leader (NIL) poses a significant challenge to this group process. Usually operating with assistants, this strong peer leader generally is adept in handling staff and skilled in playing roles. Because the NIL assesses the situation, plans moves in advance, and keeps cool under stress, he or she is a real threat to a positive, caring group. To thwart this negative leader, Vorrath suggests that the most effective strategy is to undercut any foundations of peer support, which can be accomplished by capturing the lieutenants. But, according to PPC, the lieutenants must be captured outside of the group so that the negative indigenous leader cannot come to their defense. This capture can be effected by making the lieutenants responsible for both their own behavior and that of the NIL. The group leader is advised to push this a step further and to accuse the lieutenants of disloyalty to the NIL. If they really cared, the rationale states, they would want to help their leader. Once the lieutenants are captured, Vorrath recommends that new roles be given to them so that they can use their strength positively.

Vorrath also believes that the group has to be involved in decision-making processes, such as whether to give a youth a home visit or when to release a resident. Although he acknowledges that institutional staff ultimately must make these decisions, he states that the recommendations initially should come from the group members. The group, in discussing the possibility of releasing a member, concerns itself with both the member's present problems and those he or she will experience in the community.

Certain problems are implicit in the use of PPC. First, where does PPC expect to find these "ideal" leaders? The authors have met relatively few staff in juvenile corrections who come anywhere near to filling these high expectations. Also, Vorrath seems to underestimate the ingenuity and resourcefulness of peer subcultures. This modality suggests, for example, that staff must remain beyond the understanding and predictability of their charges. When it is remembered how intensively residents study staff, this presents an almost impossible obstacle to the average person. And, even if staff members could build a high enough wall around themselves to avoid disclosing "where they are coming from," this wall might be so high that their care and love could not break through. Is it possible, too, to teach caring relationships to youths who have experienced exploitation and deprivation all their lives and who, in fact, see life as a total survival experience? An additional problem is neutralizing lieutenants and, ultimately, the negative indigeneous leader, for it is not likely that this youth will give up as easily as Vorrath suggests. Finally, although Vorrath believes that the basic assumptions of these youths can be changed, few people change many of their background assumptions over the period of a lifetime—much less when they are stripped of their freedom and are in therapy.

For this modality to be properly evaluated and for these and other questions to be answered, more research is needed. But its present successes should remind both followers and critics that PPC remains one of the most promising ways to treat, change, correct, and rehabilitate juvenile offenders.

Drug and Alcohol Abuse Interventions

Drug and alcohol abuse by juveniles, as well as their drug trafficking in the community, constitutes a serious social problem today. A director of guidance in a training school acknowledged the seriousness of the problem when he said, "Rarely do we get a boy who doesn't have some history of drug or alcohol abuse in his background."[42]

Drug and alcohol abuse interventions increasingly are being developed in community-based and institutional settings to assist those who need help with such problems. These groups are being conducted in training schools in at least three ways. First, institutionalized juveniles assessed to have a problem with alcohol and/or drugs are placed in a separate cottage or in a chemical-abuse group. Specialized staff are hired to work in these cottages or lead these groups. Second, in other training schools, the social worker or another cottage staff member conducts ongoing drug and alcohol abuse groups. Third, outside groups, such as Alcoholics Anonymous (AA) or Narcotics Anonymous (NA), come into the institution and hold sessions for interested residents.

In considering the extensiveness of the problem of drug use and trafficking among juvenile offenders, there are still too few programs being offered in juvenile placements. The programs that are offered tend to be relatively unsophisticated, lacking adequate theoretical design, treatment integrity, and evaluation follow-up. Unquestionably, effective alcohol and

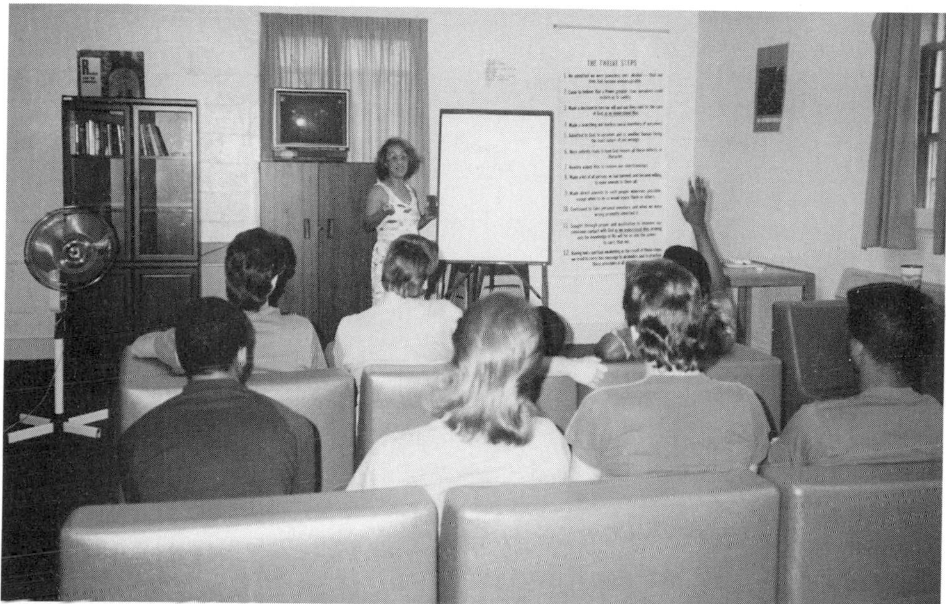

Twelve-step programs for addicted youths are popular in institutions as well as in community-based programs. (Photo courtesy of Ohio Department of Youth Services.)

drug abuse programs represent one of the most important challenges of juvenile justice today.

Cognitive-Behavioral Interventions

S. Yochelson and S. E. Samenow's research at St. Elizabeth Hospital in Washington, DC, with the criminally insane concluded that there exists a criminal personality that incorporates some fifty-two errors in thinking.[43] In the 1980s, this notion that offenders have certain personality characteristics leading to basic errors in thinking became popular as society's need to control and reform serious habitual offenders increased. During the 1980s, the Ohio Department of Youth Services used this approach in some of its institutions, and Paint Creek Youth Center also incorporated Yochelson and Samenow's principles into the facility's token economy or point system. During the 1990s, the "thinking errors," or criminal orientation, approach was widely adopted throughout the nation (see Focus on Programs 12–3 for the list of errors in thinking used by staff members of Four Oaks, Inc., an eighteen-day treatment and residential center for conduct disorder youths in Iowa).

The basic rationale of the **cognitive-behavioral interventions** is to identify the errors characteristic of a youthful offender's thinking. These errors include the blaming of others, the attempt to control or manipulate, the inability to empathize, the desire to play a victim role, the failure to accept obligations, and the

FOCUS ON PROGRAMS 12–3

DEFINITION OF THINKING ERRORS

1. Closed Channel—The criminal communicates from a closed position.
   a. When he talks, he controls what others know about him.
   b. When he listens, he lacks receptivity.
   c. When he evaluates, it is from a position of self-righteousness, faulting or blaming others.
2. Fragmentation—Fluctuation in interests, attitudes and goals . . . result in the criminal making good starts and poor finishes.
3. Uniqueness—The criminal tends to think about himself as different than others, usually superior.
4. Superoptimism—The criminal tends to think that he will be successful in all he undertakes because of his uniqueness, therefore, preparation and effort are not needed. Superoptimism is absolutely essential prior to and during criminal activity.
5. Pride—The criminal takes pride in his ability to live by his wits, to do what others are fearful of doing and [in] his "tough guy" view of himself.
6. Pretentiousness—[There is] a component of power and control whereby the criminal displays his inflated, "big shot" image in an effort to impress the world.
7. Failure to Assume Obligation—The criminal views an obligation as something that controls him. Failing to assume an obligation results in hardship for people who depend on him, i.e., child, spouse, employer.
8. Ownership—[There is] an attitude whereby the criminal assumes possession of other people's property and domination over other people.
9. Failure to Make Effort or Endure Adversity—Because of his uniqueness thinking and superoptimism thinking the criminal doesn't believe he should have to put forth effort or endure hardship to accomplish a goal.
10. Lack of Time Perspective—The criminal's time frame is mainly in the present. There is little learning from the past or using the present to prepare for the future.
11. Poor Decision Making—[This is] the outcome of poor reasoning, failure to find out facts or consider the future from a responsible perspective.

12. Lack of Trust—The criminal demands others trust him but objects to trusting others.
13. Anger—The criminal [uses] anger to control and regain control of others.
14. I Can't—the criminal [says] "I can't" when he really means "I don't want to" or "I am not going to," [which] results in rejecting responsible behavior.
15. Victimstance—The criminal uses this thinking pattern when being held accountable for wrongdoing in an attempt to avoid punishment.

Source: Materials used as part of staff training at Four Oaks, Inc., in Iowa. Used with permission.

Critical Thinking Questions:

Do you think it would be difficult to identify these thinking errors in youthful offenders? Would it be difficult for a youth to change his or her thinking errors?

attempt to lie or confuse.[44] The therapist attempts to determine the sequence of thoughts, feelings, events, and other factors that make up the "offense syndrome" and then to get the offender to "own" his or her behaviors. Once the offender takes responsibility for his or her actions, he or she is then taught how to intervene in the illegal behavior when it first starts in order to bring it under control. After a prolonged period of treatment, the offender is moved into residential aftercare, joins a support group, and is given continuing access to treatment.[45]

What is involved here is a cognitive restructuring strategy that is specifically targeted at the dysfunctional cognitive patterns of offenders. These dysfunctional cognitive patterns, or thinking errors, serve to support, excuse, and even reinforce criminal behavior. This approach presumes that the use of such errors releases inhibitions toward committing a crime, which "frees one" to behave in a criminal or delinquent manner. The job of the counselor is to correct these thinking errors, and the task of the facility is to provide an environment in which such errors can be corrected by treatment, by custody staff, and also by residents in group sessions or day-to-day institutional living.[46]

In sum, this modality is being used increasingly across the nation, largely because of the popularity of the get tough approach. Still, little evidence suggests that it has any short- or long-term benefits to juveniles who receive such a treatment intervention.

Law-Related Education

Law-related education (LRE) is an educational program designed to promote the development of characteristics that lead to healthy behavior. LRE is designed to teach students the fundamental principles and skills needed to become responsible citizens in a constitutional democracy. Programs are characterized by high-interest course material; wide use of volunteer resource persons from the justice system; field experiences (court tours, internships, and police ride-alongs); student-involved teaching methods (group discussions and poster making); and cocurricular activities (mock trials and other public performances).[47]

Law-related education has experienced remarkable growth since 1975. A 1985 national survey revealed that LRE has been added to the curriculum in more than half of the forty-six states involved in the study.[48] In 1992, fifty-six programs in training schools, diversion, detention, and community-based settings used law-related education.[49]

An instructor of LRE in a midwestern training school for boys had this to say about the program:

> Our program is based on teaching aspects of the law as it relates to everyday life. A lot of these kids haven't been habilitated in the first place, and what we try to do is to teach them such skills as problem solving and critical thinking, conflict resolution, communication skills and empathy, and avoidance of triggers or verbal and nonverbal cues that elicit negative emotions. We do this by dealing with social issues and by discussing the legal system, including the attorney's role and rights of offenders. We have had this program for the [past] eleven years and are very happy with it. Kids are interested in it, and we hope that they apply it to their own lives when they are released.[50]

One of the few studies evaluating LRE programs found that when properly conducted, these programs can reduce tendencies toward delinquent behavior and improve a range of attitudes related to responsible citizenship. Successful students, this study found, were also less likely to associate with delinquent peers and to use violence as a means of resolving conflict.[51] Although it is unreasonable to believe that such a knowledge-based course would have much impact on hard-core youthful offenders, it could very well be that LRE is a valuable delinquent prevention program.

Gang Deactivation Groups

Gangs, as noted in previous chapters, constitute one of the most serious problems facing juvenile justice today. One of the pioneer projects for working with gangs was the House of Umoja. Headed by Sister Falaka Fattah, the House of Umoja attempts to create intensive family feelings within a framework of African-inspired consciousness. Established in the early 1970s, the House of Umoja sheltered through the 1980s more than three hundred boys who had belonged to seventy-three different street gangs.[52]

A number of other community projects have been developed to work with youth gangs. The most widely known of these projects are the Youth-in-Action (Chester, Pennsylvania), El Control del Puebo (New York City), the Inner City Roundtable of Youth (New York City), the Youth Identity Program, Inc.

(New York City), the South Arsenal Neighborhood Development Corporation (Hartford, Connecticut), and SEY Yes, Inc. (Los Angeles). The basic purpose of these treatment interventions is to defuse the violence of youth gangs within urban communities and to involve gang members in more constructive activities.

In the 1990s, with the spread of gangs throughout the nation, the Maclaren Training School in Portland, Oregon; the Ethan Allen School in Wales, Wisconsin; and the School for Boys in Eldora, Iowa; found it necessary to develop specialized groups for their increasingly large numbers of gang members.[53] Usually required and perhaps even court mandated, these sessions generally consist of twelve or thirteen sessions focusing on **gang deactivation**—that is, removing youths from gang involvements. In the training school in Eldora, Iowa, which probably includes the most sophisticated model of gang deactivation, the groups were led for years by Samuel Dillon, a former gang leader in the Blackstone Rangers.

WHY IS TREATMENT EFFECTIVENESS SO DIFFICULT TO ATTAIN?

The overall quality of treatment in juvenile justice is not impressive. Enforced offender rehabilitation has sometimes resulted in making delinquents worse rather than better through treatment. The frequent criticism that offender rehabilitation is defective in theory and a disaster in practice has been true on too many occasions. Program designs have often given little consideration to what a particular program can realistically accomplish with a particular group of offenders and have frequently relied on a single cure for a variety of complex problems. In addition, programs generally have lacked integrity, because they have not delivered the services they claimed with sufficient strength to accomplish the goals of treatment. Furthermore, the research on offender rehabilitation has generally been inadequate, with many projects and reports on rehabilitation almost totally lacking in well-developed research designs.[54]

Still, enough progress has been made that the various meta-analyses and literature reviews from the 1980s indicated that treatment programs had somewhat more positive findings in reducing recidivism than earlier studies had revealed.[55] The emerging picture that has received increased support in the past decade is that "'something' apparently works though no generic method or approach, as distinct from individual programs, especially shines." Or to state this differently, several methods appear promising, but none has produced major reductions in recidivism.[56] See Focus on Careers 12–4 for the work of a sex offender therapist in juvenile corrections.

To improve the quality of institutional treatment even further, three basic steps appear to be necessary: (1) more programs must include the ingredients of effective interventions; (2) more programs must be based on better

FOCUS ON CAREERS 12–4

HOW DOES ONE BECOME A SEX OFFENDER THERAPIST?

The following interview is with Domenick A. Lombardo, former Supervisor of Psychological Services, Youth Development Center at New Castle, Pennsylvania. Mr. Lombardo is certified as an Abel Assessment Examiner and as an HARE Psychopathy Examiner.

Dr. Miller (SM): What has been your career path within the department?

Mr. Lombardo (DL): I graduated with a degree in psychology and had no experience. I started at YDC (Youth Development Center) as a houseparent in February 1976. I worked as a houseparent for probably nine months or so. Then I was promoted to a counselor in Intensive Treatment Unit (ITU) which housed all violent offenders. I worked in ITU probably nine or ten years.

SM: So you had a general degree in psychology?

DL: I had a general degree in psychology but didn't have a master's degree yet. So luckily, when I left the ITU (intensive treatment unit) I went back and I earned my master's degree at Slippery Rock University under a licensed psychologist in counseling and psychology. My idea then was to get thirty-five hundred hours of supervised experience and then sit for the licensing exam. The program at Slippery Rock was APA approved for PA psychologist licensing. I graduated in 1989, with an M.A. in counseling psychology. So to make a long story short, I continued to work at the YDC-NC* in a project for emotionally disturbed, adjudicated delinquents, known as Project Five (P-5). I worked in P-5 for approximately seven or eight years.

SM: The other people who were coming up at the same time as you were—the other counselors—did they basically have the same background?

DL: Basically the same background. There were degreed people. At that time, houseparents didn't require a college degree.

Well, simultaneously when I moved from the ITU to Project Five, a specialized program for sexual offenders was developed in the ITU. That sex offender program has been there ever since.

*Youth Development Center—New Castle

I worked several years with the emotionally disturbed, then I had a lot of post-graduate training and certifications with a number of different educational institutions including Penn State, Indiana University of Pennsylvania, University of Wisconsin, and with WPIC.[†] I then became a Psychological Services Associate II, which is similar to a staff psychologist in other agencies. I continued to work privately under the supervision of a licensed psychologist and obtained approximately twenty-eight hundred hours of experience.

SM: Did you have to finance your own education, or did the state support it?

DL: No, I basically financed my own education with the exception of partial tuition reimbursement for a course or two.

When I left Project Five, I provided services for all residents at the YDC including our satellite facility in Oakdale, PA. Once or twice a month I would go down to Oakdale and I provided psychological services. I worked with adjudicated delinquent females for nine years and I had an entire unit, Unit 7, with all females. I provided psychological services in Unit 7 as well as for our sex offenders and emotionally disturbed population.

SM: The females were general population?

DL: Yes, then it was called open. But we had a lot of mental health cases—seriously disturbed females. To conceptualize this, even though you have a fence all the way around the facility, you still have programs classified open. Even though the YDC is a secure fenced-in facility Unit 7 (dual diagnosis) and Unit 8 (emotionally disturbed and D&A) are classified as open programs. Units 5 and 6 (General Secure) and the ITV (sex offenders) are secure programs.

SM: So the next step . . .

DL: The next step—what I decided to do—was work a lot with victims. I also decided to spend more time with perpetrators.

SM: Now, did this come about as a result of working with the women as victims?

DL: It was a combination of things—you have to realize with the adjudicated delinquent in this population, physical and sexual victimization are core clinical issues, and even more so with the female residents. So I guess a combination of the girls and guys over a number of years piqued my interest—plus my interest in evaluation—my forte is clinical assessment, and that's what really interests me because forensic populations and forensic work is exciting work. So that's when I decided I was going to go down the forensic path and get what I needed to have by way of education, specialized training, and certification.

[†]Western Psychiatric Institute and Clinic.

SM: Define what you mean exactly by forensic in this case.

DL: Well, psychology and law. This is a forensic population. Our clients are adjudicated delinquents and some of which present significant mental health issues. The evaluation and treatment of sex offenders is a specialty field. I became heavily involved with the sexual offenders program in 1992, when I assumed the responsibilities of supervisor of Psychological Services at the YDC-NC.

I became more and more involved with the evaluation and treatment of sex offenders. I developed the clinical assessment part. It was a very strong part of what I wanted to do, and we were in a situation where we needed to develop our own clinical assessment protocol for sexual offenders who were committed to our facility. Some of our residents were coming to us with recommendations for antiandrogen therapy, which was not an available treatment modality at our facility. The bottom line was that we had no control over what the courts wanted. So what really moved me to get very heavily involved in the clinical assessment aspect was the need to respond to the court's increasing need for sex offender evaluation and treatment. We wanted input into how kids were treated and we felt this was the best way to proceed. Our goal was to complete a comprehensive psychological evaluation with sexual offender assessment on all new admissions to identify treatment needs internally. I devoted a considerable amount of time in literature review and consultation with experts in the field including Dr. Fred Berlin, Dr. Gene Abel, Dr. John Bradshaw, and numerous others who are well reputed in the areas of evaluation, treatment, and risk prediction.

SM: What would you recommend to a student who comes in who is interested in this field? How should they proceed with their careers?

DL: First I would recommend a degree in psychology, sociology, or social work. Psychology would be my preference. I would get my feet wet with local mental health agencies (wrap-around, mobile therapy). A lot of workers enter the system through local mental health agencies. Internships at facilities which serve sexual offenders start students in the wrap-around business. Internships at facilities which serve sexual offenders provide good experience and help individuals decide their degree of interest in this type of population. People think they might have a desire, an interest to do this kind of work but find out it might be too much.

SM: What do you mean by wrap-around?

DL: Wrap-arounds are workers who are assigned to kids and who go to their schools, and around the community with them. It is a case management kind of service. If you are really seriously interested in working with sex offenders, then you need to—depending on the level you want to go to—get your master's degree as well as postgraduate education and training certification supervision. Some people, now, are not going to be private practitioners so there are certain things that won't be required. You can work here with a four year college degree and be trained by people like me or other professionals here.

SM: But the thing that gave you the desire was the work with victims?

DL: Yes, exactly. And what I did was to make a commitment to try what I could do to stop sexual violence against children, specifically.

We would like to acknowledge Charlie Chervanik and Joan Lawer of the PA Dept. of Public Welfare; the Office of Children, Youth, and Family Services; and Bob Liggett and Elida Evans at YDC-NC for supporting and financing significant amounts of specialized education, training, and certification in sexual offender evaluation, treatment, and risk predictions.

program design, assure higher program integrity, and be evaluated by more rigorous research methods; and (3) research must provide more information on what works for whom and in what context.

Ingredients of Effective Programs

Effective programs usually have a number of ingredients in common. They usually are set up by an inspired individual or group of individuals, have developed a unified-team approach among staff, have a transmittable philosophy of life, trust offenders with decision-making responsibilities, help offenders develop needed skills, are regarded as unique and different by offenders, and provide a support network for offenders following release or graduation.[57]

The Inspired Leader Who Means Business

The inspired individual or group of individuals who has serious dedication in setting up a program has been found time after time to be one of the chief ingredients of effective programs. In Outward Bound, Kurt Hahn was able to generate enthusiasm and support among those who contacted him.[58] Sister Falaka Fattah and her husband also set up the House of Umoja in Philadelphia, committed to deal with the gang problem in that urban community.[59] The inspiration of Clifford Shaw continues to influence the Chicago Area Projects long after his death.

Unified Treatment Team

A program is more likely to have an impact on offenders if the treatment team is unified. In a unified treatment team, all staff members become treatment agents as they design the program, develop short- and long-range goals for the program, and involve themselves with offenders.

Philosophy of Life That is Transmittable

Effective programs also generate a sense of mission or purpose among offenders by transmitting a philosophy of life. Martin Groder has noted, "It's not that the guy has to adopt the philosophy of the program, but he's got to learn it well enough to integrate it with his own life experience and come out with his own version."[60] Bartollas, Miller, and Dinitz reported that having a mission or purpose in life is one characteristic of hard-core offenders who are later successful in the community.[61]

Involvement of Offenders in the Decision-Making Process

Effective programs also frequently provide decision-making responsibilities for juvenile offenders. Although many correctional interventions treat these offenders as helpless children incapable of making decisions for themselves, the more noteworthy programs encourage decision making and then make participants responsible for their choices. The more offenders are permitted to make choices concerning what happens to them, the more likely they are to be involved in a treatment program and to seek to benefit from it.

Skill Development

Effective programs include **skill development,** which helps offenders learn new tasks that prepare them for adjustment in the community. These range from educational and vocational to interpersonal and problem-solving skills. Such abilities make offenders believe that they can accomplish something or that they have acquired important insights about themselves or about life.

Uniqueness

The most distinguishing characteristic of effective interventions is sometimes their uniqueness. That is, the components of these programs that make them different from other correctional interventions are sometimes the most important factors in "grabbing" the attention of youthful offenders and in getting them involved in these interventions.

Adequate Community Support Networks

Institutional programs also require adequate community follow-up in order for offenders to sustain positive changes in their lives. Outward Bound is a prime example of a program with great initial impact that diminished over time because of the lack of community follow-up.

Strategy for Improving the Effectiveness of Correctional Programs

Improving program effectiveness requires that program designs be based on theoretical premises, that programs be implemented with integrity, and that programs be evaluated with rigorous research methods.

Program Design

The theoretical premises, or constructs, of programs must be examined in order to determine whether the theoretical constructs are appropriate for particular groups of offenders. The processes by which any set of interventions will change antisocial behavior must also be examined in order to determine whether the treatment has sufficient strength to produce the desired behavior or attitudinal change. Finally, the theoretical constructs must be meshed with the setting in which treatment takes place to ensure that programs are implemented in appropriate settings.[62]

Program Implementation

Juvenile offenders must be placed in the right program at the optimal time for them to benefit from treatment. Effective interventions must actually deliver the services they claim to deliver, with sufficient strength to accomplish the goals of treatment. In addition, program integrity requires that personnel be equipped to deliver the specified services—thus, treatment personnel must have some degree of expertise in what they are doing, must have sufficient training to do it, and must receive adequate supervision. Finally, it must be possible to modify interventions according to changing interests and needs of offenders.[63]

Program Evaluation

The Panel on Research on Rehabilitative Techniques concluded after nearly two years of examining offender rehabilitation that "the research methodology that has been brought to bear on the problem of finding ways to rehabilitate criminal offenders has been generally so inadequate that only a relatively few studies warrant any unequivocal interpretations.[64] Sample sizes must be large enough to measure subtle effects, such as changes in interactions. True randomized experiments must be conducted whenever feasible because they permit some certainty about causal relationships. Researchers need to identify the common elements of effective programs and to determine how these elements affect success with particular groups of offenders. In addition, researchers need to determine how effective programs can be replicated in other settings. Finally, more empirical work must be done on measuring the outcomes of correctional treatment.[65]

What Works for Whom and in What Context

Correctional treatment must discover what works for which offenders in what context. In other words, correctional treatment could work if amenable offenders were offered appropriate treatments by matched workers in environments conducive to producing positive effects.[66]

To match up individual offenders with the treatments most likely to benefit them will be no easy task. Only through well-planned and soundly executed research will the necessary information be gained. The Panel of Rehabilitative Techniques recommends the use of the "template-matching technique."[67] This technique creates a set of descriptors, or a "template," of the kinds of people who are most likely to benefit from a particular treatment according to the theory or basic assumptions underlying it.[68] Because of the scarcity of treatment resources, matching programs to those offenders most likely to profit from them is only sensible.

Palmer's approach is somewhat different in determining what works for which offenders in what contexts. He suggests that effective intervention for each offender must take seriously internal difficulties, skill deficits, and external pressures and disadvantages:

1. *Skill/Capacity Deficits.* Various, often major, developmental challenges—frequently including life- and social-skills deficits in such areas as educational and vocational abilities
2. *External Pressures/Disadvantages.* Major environmental pressures and/or major social disadvantages, including comparatively limited or reduced family, community, and other supports or social assistance
3. *Internal Difficulties.* Long-standing or situational feelings, attitudes, and defenses; ambivalence regarding change; particular motivations, desires, and personal and interpersonal commitments.[69]

Summary

This chapter discusses and evaluates the basic treatment technologies in juvenile justice. Another way to understand these therapies is to group them under insight (psychotherapy, transactional analysis, law-related education, and errors in thinking approach), behavior treatment (reality therapy and behavior modification), and group therapy (guided group interaction, positive peer culture, drug and alcohol interventions, and gang deactivation groups). See Table 12–1 for the relationships of these modalities to one another.

Table 12–1 *Treatment Technologies*

Type	*Treatment Goal*	*Qualifications of Therapist*	*Length of Treatment*	*Frequency of Treatment*	*Expected Offender Response*
Individual or group psychotherapy	Lead youths to insight	Psychiatrist, psychologist, psychiatric social worker	Frequently extensive or long term	Several times per week if possible	Will examine individual problems with therapist
Transactional analysis	Lead youths to insight	Psychiatrist, psychologist, trained nonprofessional staff	Usually several months	Once or more per week	Will examine individual problems in a group context and will learn a new approach to interpersonal relationships
Reality therapy	Help youths to fulfill basic needs	Psychiatrist, psychologist, trained nonprofessional staff	Short period of time	Once or more per week	To learn reality responsible behavior, and right from wrong
Behavior modification	Help youths to react positively	Anyone who can assume role of therapist	Usually long term	Continuous rather than interwoven with nontreatment	To continue their reinforced, positive behavior
Guided group interaction	Develop prosocial norms and values	Anyone trained in GGI	Several months	Four or five times per week	Will become responsible for others in the group
Positive peer culture	Develop prosocial norms and values	Anyone trained in PPC	Several months	Four or five times per week	Will genuinely care for other group members
Drug and alcohol abuse programs	Help youths to overcome addiction	Anyone who has understanding of problem	Extensive or long term	Once or more per week	Will gain skills and knowledge to overcome substance abuse
Error in thinking approach	Insight into individual behavior	Psychiatrist, psychologist, psychiatric social worker	Extensive or long term	Once or more per week	To learn responsible and prosocial behavior
Skill development programs	Personal empowerment	Anyone who can assume role of staff member	Short or long term	Daily	Will gain skills and knowledge to pursue positive behavior
Family therapy	Insight into family dynamics	Psychiatrist, psychologist, psychiatric social worker	Usually several months	Once or more per week	Will examine family problems with therapist
Law-related education	Help youths to react positively	Anyone trained in LRE	Usually long term	Once or more per week	To learn responsibility and prosocial behavior
Gang deactivation groups	Help youths to withdraw from gangs	Anyone with understanding of gangs	Several months	Once or more per week	To empower youths so they no longer need the gang

As indicated in this chapter, we may have expected too much from correctional treatment. Long-term training schools are among the least promising places for treatment to take place. But even in community-based programs, the lack of resources for overworked staff, clients' histories of failure, and drug and alcohol addictions result in far more failures than successes.

The danger, however, is to expect too little from correctional treatment. Some youthful offenders do benefit from treatment in institutional settings. The programs may simply make their present confinement more bearable, or they may provide a purpose for offenders so that they can go on to live free of crime. Thus, some programs are effective, and some treatment agents do have positive impacts on youthful offenders.

Treatment was buried in the mid-1970s with considerable fanfare, although programs continue to exist in communities and institutions. The same amount of energy should be put into reemphasizing treatment, not as a panacea for youth crime or as a condition of release, but as a viable option for those offenders who are interested in change, growth, and positive movement in their lives.

The future effectiveness of correctional treatment in juvenile justice may be contingent on three conditions: (1) funding research so that more effective technologies can be developed; (2) identifying what works for which group of offenders so that youthful offenders interested in treatment can be given the interventions most compatible with their needs and interests; and (3) creating more humane environments so that environmental conditions will not interfere with the treatment process.

Yet we suspect that this will not be enough. Ultimately, treatment is something the system tries to do to offenders. It also basically ignores the fundamental institutions that impact youths' lives. On one hand, then, treatment is viewed by offenders as coercive and thereby generates resistance, but, on the other hand, treatment will always be relevant to the growth and development of adolescents. If we pursue some of the suggestions discussed in this chapter, treatment has a chance of becoming a more effective remedy and, consequently, of helping more youthful offenders.

WEB SITES OF INTEREST

Information on criminal and juvenile justice treatment networks can be found at http://www.cjnetwork.org/

CRITICAL THINKING QUESTIONS

1. Do you agree that no treatment is effective for juvenile offenders?
2. If you were superintendent of a training school, which treatment methods would you use? Why? What treatment technologies would you use in a residential program for juvenile probationers?

3. What type of staff member would be effective in carrying out the treatment method you have chosen? Why?
4. Would you hire ex-offenders to work in your community-based or institutional facility? Why or why not?
5. Do you feel that the goals of positive peer culture are realistic?
6. How would you treat youths who do not respond to the rules of your prescribed treatment method?

NOTES

1. Interviewed in 1989.
2. Walter C. Bailey, "Correctional Outcome: An Evaluation of 100 Reports," *Journal of Criminal Law, Criminology, and Police Science* 57 (June 1957), 153–60.
3. J. Robison and G. Smith, "The Effectiveness of Correctional Programs," *Crime and Delinquency* 17 (1971), 67–70.
4. Robert Martinson, "What Works?—Questions and Answers about Prison Reform," *Public Interest* 35 (Spring 1974), 22–54.
5. Douglas Lipton, Robert Martinson, and Judith Wilks, *The Effectiveness of Correctional Treatment* (New York: Praeger, 1975).
6. CBS Television Network. Excerpted from *60 Minutes* segment, "It Doesn't Work" (August 24, 1975).
7. Ted Palmer, "Martinson Revisited," *Journal of Research in Crime and Delinquency* 12 (July 1975), 133–52.
8. Ibid., 137.
9. Paul Gendreau and Robert Ross, "Effective Correctional Treatment: Bibliotherapy for Cynics," *Crime and Delinquency* 27 (October 1979), 463–89.
10. Robert R. Ross and Paul Gendreau, eds., *Effective Correctional Treatment* (Toronto: Butterworth, 1980), viii.
11. Robert Martinson, "New Findings, New Views: A Note of Caution Regarding Sentencing Reform," *Hofstra Law Review* 7 (Winter 1979), 244.
12. Paul Gendreau and Robert R. Ross, "Revivification of Rehabilitative Evidence," *Justice Quarterly* 4 (September 1987), 349–407.
13. Ibid. For a review of the meta-analyses of correctional treatment in the 1980s, see Ted Palmer, *The Re-Emergence of Correctional Intervention* (Newbury Park, CA: Sage Publications, 1992), 50–76.
14. James McGuire and Philip Priestley, "Reviewing 'What Works': Past, Present, and Future," in *What Works: Reducing Reoffending—Guidelines from Research and Practice,* edited by James McGuire (New York: John Wiley & Sons, 1995), 7–8.
15. Ibid.

16. Palmer, *The Re-Emergence of Correctional Intervention*, xiii.
17. Ibid., 4.
18. Marguerite Q. Warren, "The Community Treatment Project: History and Prospects," in *Law Enforcement Science and Technology*, edited by S. A. Yefsky (Washington, DC: Thompson Book Company, 1972), 193–95.
19. Roy Gerard, "Institutional Innovations in Juvenile Corrections," *Federal Probation* 34 (December 1970), 38–40.
20. Rhena L. Izzo and Robert R. Ross, "Meta-Analysis of Rehabilitation Programs for Juvenile Delinquents: A Brief Report," *Criminal Justice and Behavior* 17 (March 1990), 139. See also McGuire and Priestley, "Reviewing 'What Works,'" 9–10.
21. Eric Berne, *Transactional Analysis in Psychotherapy* (New York: Grove Press), 355.
22. Thomas A. Harris, *I'm OK—You're OK* (New York: Harper and Row, 1967), 37–53.
23. Eric Berne, *Games People Play*, (New York: Grove Press, 1964), 48.
24. Lois Johnson, "TA with Juvenile Delinquents," *Transactional Analysis Bulletin* 3 (1969), 31.
25. Carl F. Jesness, "The Fricot Ranch Study: Outcomes with Small versus Large Living Groups in the Rehabilitation of Delinquents," Research Report No. 47 Processed (Sacramento: California Youth Authority, October 1965), 89, 90, 313.
26. William Glasser, *Reality Therapy* (New York: Harper and Row, 1965), xii.
27. Ibid., excerpts from 44–45.
28. Ibid., 70.
29. Jesness, "Fricot Ranch Study," 7.
30. J. L. Bernard and R. Eisenman, "Verbal Conditioning in Sociopaths with Spiral and Monetary Reinforcement," *Journal of Personality and Social Psychology* 6 (1976), 203–206.
31. R. Schwitzgebel and D. A. Kolb, "Inducing Behavior Change to Adolescent Delinquents," *Behavior Research Therapy* 1 (1964), 297–304.
32. See Dennis A. Romig, *Justice for Our Children: An Examination of Juvenile Delinquent Rehabilitation Programs* (Lexington, MA: D. C. Heath, 1978), 20–21.
33. Ibid., 87.
34. Ibid., 92–93.
35. Interview with Harry Vorrath quoted in Oliver J. Keller Jr. and Benedict S. Alper, *Halfway Houses: Community Centered Correction and Treatment* (Lexington, MA: D. C. Heath, 1970), 55.
36. Robert J. Wicks, *Correctional Psychology: Themes and Problems in Correcting the Offender* (San Francisco: Canfield Press, 1974), 50–51.
37. Joseph W. Scott and Jerry B. Hissong, "Changing the Delinquent Subculture: A Sociological Approach," in *Readings in Juvenile Delinquency*, edited by Ruth Shonle Cavan (Philadelphia: J. B. Lippincott Company, 1975), 486–88.

38. Ibid.
39. The following materials are adapted from Harry H. Vorrath and Larry K. Brendto, *Positive Peer Culture* (Chicago: Aldine Publishing Company, 1974).
40. Ibid.
41. Ibid.
42. Interviewed in 1986 in a midwestern training school.
43. S. Yochelson and S. E. Samenow, *The Criminal Personality*, 2 vols. (New York: J. Aronson, 1976, 1977).
44. David Berenson, *Ohio Department of Youth Services Sex Offender Project: Preliminary Report on a Treatment Program for Adolescent Sex Offenders* (Columbus, OH: Department of Youth Services, 1989).
45. Ibid., 6–8.
46. David Lester and Patricia Van Voorhis, "Cognitive Therapies," in *Correctional Counseling and Rehabilitation*, 3d ed., edited by Patricia Van Voorhis, Michael Braswell, and David Lester (Cincinnati: Anderson Publishing, 1997), 172.
47. Norma D. Wright, "From Risk to Resiliency: The Role of Law-Related Education." Pamphlet published by the Institute on Law and Civic Education (Des Moines, IA: June 20–21, 1995).
48. Carole L. Hahn, "The Status of the Social Studies in Public Schools of the United States: Another Look," *Social Education* 49 (March 1985), 220–23.
49. National Law-Related Education Resource Center, *Law-Related Education Programs in Juvenile Justice Settings*, September 1992.
50. Interviewed in August 1996.
51. Judith Warren Little and Frances Haley, *Implementing Effective LRE Programs* (Boulder, CO: Social Science Education Consortium, 1982).
52. For an extensive treatment of the House of Umoja, refer to Robert L. Woodson, *A Summons to Life: Mediating Structure and the Prevention of Youth Crime* (Cambridge, MA: Ballinger, 1981).
53. Catherine H. Conley, *Street Gangs: Current Knowledge and Strategies* (Washington, DC: U.S. Department of Justice, 1993), 55.
54. Lee Sechrest, Susan O. White, and Elizabeth D. Brown, eds., *The Rehabilitation of Criminal Offenders* (Washington, DC: National Academy of Sciences, 1979); and Susan Martin, Lee Sechrest, and Robin Redner, eds., *Rehabilitation of Criminal Offenders: Directions for Research* (Washington, DC: National Academy of Sciences, 1981).
55. For an examination of the various meta-analyses, see Palmer, *Re-Emergence of Intervention*, 50–76. See also Izzo and Ross, "Meta-Analyses of Rehabilitation Programs for Juvenile Delinquents," 134–42.
56. Ibid., 48.
57. These elements of effective programs are suggested by the work of Martin Groder and of Alden D. Miller, Lloyd E. Ohlin, and Robert B. Coates. See

"Dr. Martin Groder: An Angry Resignation," *Corrections Magazine* 1 (July–August 1975), 3; and Alden D. Miller, Lloyd E. Ohlin, and Robert B. Coates, *A Theory of Social Reform: Correctional Change Processes in Two States* (Cambridge, MA: Ballinger, 1977).

58. Joshua L. Miner and Joe Boldt, *Outward Bound USA: Learning Through Experience in Adventure-Based Education* (New York: William Morrow, 1981).
59. Woodson, *A Summons to Life.*
60. "Dr. Martin Groder," 33.
61. Clemens Bartollas, Stuart J. Miller, and Simon Dinitz, "Boys Who Profit: The Limits of Institutional Success," in *Reform in Corrections: Problems and Issues,* edited by Harry E. Allen and Nancy J. Beran (New York: Praeger, 1977), 18–19.
62. Sechrest, White, and Brown, eds., *The Rehabilitation of Criminal Offenders,* 35–37.
63. For the development of these various aspects of intervention, see Palmer, *The Re-Emergence of Correctional Intervention,* 151–57.
64. Sechrest, Brown, and White, eds., *The Rehabilitation of Criminal Offenders,* 3–4.
65. Martin, Sechrest, and Redner, eds., *The Rehabilitation of Criminal Offenders,* 6.
66. Sechrest, Brown, and White, eds., *The Rehabilitation of Criminal Offenders,* 45.
67. The template-matching technique was originally proposed in D. Bem and D. Funder, "Predicting More of the People More of the Time: Assessing the Personality of Situations," *Psychological Review* 85 (1978), 485–501.
68. Martin, Sechrest, and Redner, eds., *Rehabilitation of Criminal Offenders,* 82.
69. Palmer, *The Re-Emergence of Correctional Intervention,* 113.

13

JUVENILE GANGS

OBJECTIVES

1. To view how gangs have evolved in the United States
2. To examine how extensive is gang activity
3. To investigate how toxic gang activity is to communities
4. To present the seven stages of emergent gang development
5. To discuss why youths join gangs
6. To evaluate how gangs can be prevented and controlled

KEY TERMS

crack
emerging youth gangs
representing
urban gangs

The road to success is a hard one. It begins in the family unit. It is in the family that parents plant the seeds for a young person to succeed. This young person is taught morals and ethics and learns behavior patterns.

By the age of 7 or 8, this young person has learned whether he will be loved, whether his needs will be met, and how fair life is. What he thinks will have an effect on his behavior. If he feels he is on the short end of the stick, he may wake up angry as hell in the morning. He will seek elsewhere to have his needs met. He is not in a good place to compete with peer pressure.

It is not long before he is in gangs, doing drugs, and hurting people. It is also not long before he is serving time in the "joint." When he comes out, it is even harder to achieve success. It is a lot easier to go back to crime than to stay away from it.

For those of us who are determined not to go back to a life of crime, we may make it. It takes determination. It takes the opportunity to stand on your own feet. It takes support from others. It takes luck. But we are never out of the woods because it is real easy to go back.

What I am saying is that if we want to deal with youth crime, adult crime, and street gangs, we must go back to the family unit, must improve our schools, must make our neighborhoods more desirable, and must [provide] other alternatives to gangs and drugs.

—Fred "Bobby" Gore[1]

In this interview, Fred "Bobby" Gore explains why the social context is important to understanding youth crime and street gangs. Gore became one of the most influential leaders of the Conservative Vice Lords, the largest division of the Vice Lord Nation. That was thirty years ago. Today, he is the former program director for the SAFER Foundation, a community integration program for ex-offenders, and is one of the most respected former gang members in Chicago.

This chapter focuses on youth who are involved in a gang. A gang is usually identified as a group with some sense of identity and permanence and with some involvement in illegal activities.[2] Many youths, especially in urban areas, are involved in adult street gangs. Surveys of street gang samples reveal that from 14 to 30 percent of juveniles join gangs at some point.[3] Other youths form gangs or become part of gangs made up of adolescents.

Beginning in 1988 and continuing through the early 1990s, an upsurge of youth gangs suddenly appeared throughout the United States. Some of these youth gangs used names of the national urban gangs, such as the Bloods and Crips from Los Angeles or the Gangster Disciplines, Vice Lords, or Latin Kings from Chicago. Other gangs made up their own names, based on neighborhoods or images they wanted to depict to other peers and the community. By the mid-1990s, nearly every city, many suburban areas, and even some rural areas across the United States experienced the reality of youths who have banded together to form a youth gang.

The good news is that from 1996 to 1998, the estimated number of youth gangs and gang members decreased in the United States (7 and 8 percent, respectively). In 1996, it was estimated that there were 31,000 gangs and 846,000 gang members in 1996; in 1998, it was estimated that there were 28,700 gangs and 780,000 gang members.[4] The bad news is that too many juveniles, especially at-risk youths, are involved in gangs; that gang involvement is likely to lead to further involvement in delinquency and drug use; that gang involvement increases the likelihood of the carrying and use of weapons; and that gang involvement increases the probability of going on to adult crime and of spending time in prison.[5]

HOW HAVE GANGS EVOLVED IN THE UNITED STATES?

Youth gangs may have existed as early as the American Revolution.[6] Others have suggested that they first emerged in the Southwest following the Mexican Revolution in 1813.[7] In the early 1800s, youth gangs seemed to have spread in New England, with the shifts from agrarian to industrial society. Youth gangs began to flourish in Chicago, New York, and other large cities in the nineteenth century as immigration and population shifts reached record levels. Youth gangs were primarily Irish, Jewish, and Italian, but this would change in the twentieth century.

GANGS AND PLAY ACTIVITY: THE 1920S THROUGH THE 1940S

A pioneering work on youth gangs was Frederick Thrasher's *The Gang: A Study of 1,313 Gangs in Chicago*.[8] Thrasher viewed these gangs as a normal part of growing up in ethnic neighborhoods. He found that youths who went to school together and played together in the neighborhood naturally developed a strong sense of identity leading to their forming close-knit groups. Evolving from these neighborhood play groups, Thrasher found that they bonded together without any particular purpose or goal. These transitory social groups typically had fewer than thirty members. The youth gangs studied by Thrasher were usually organized in three concentric circles: a core made up of a leader and lieutenants, the rank-and-file membership, and a few youths who drifted in and out of the gang. Each gang was different, but what was universally expected was the protection of turf.[9]

WEST SIDE STORY ERA: THE 1950S

Youth gangs became established in Boston, New York, and Philadelphia from the late 1940s through the 1950s. These youth gangs spent time "hanging out" and partying together; when deemed necessary, they fought other gangs. The musical *West Side Story,* later made into a movie, presented two 1950s New York youth gangs dancing, singing, and battling over turf. It focused on the Sharks, recent immigrants from Puerto Rico, defending their neighborhood ethnic boundaries.

These **urban gangs** of the 1950s were not the lethal weapons they were in recent decades, but they were capable of violent behavior. In 1960–1961, one of the authors was hired to work with a white gang in Newark, New Jersey. This job became available because his predecessor, who had been on the job for two weeks, had a knife held to his chest, cutting his shirt, and drawing a little blood. Warned that bad things would happen if he did not quit, he chose to resign.

The 1950s gangs attracted considerable attention among researchers and policymakers. Millions of dollars in federal, state, and local money were spent on projects and programs designed to prevent and control their behaviors. One of the most widely funded efforts was the detached workers programs. This program sent professional workers into the community to work with gang youths, but this effort proved to have little or no positive effect on reducing their rates of delinquent activities. Indeed, one of the most consistent findings of these detached workers' programs was that workers' efforts ended up increasing the size of the youth gang, as well as commitment of participants.[10]

Development of the Modern Gang: The 1960s

The 1960s are known as a decade in which there was a rapidly changing social and political climate. The development of "supergangs" in Chicago and Los Angeles, the involvement of gangs in social betterment programs, and their participation in political activism were the most significant changes in youth gangs during the 1960s.

The major supergangs developed when neighborhood gangs became larger and more powerful than other gangs in surrounding neighborhoods, and they forced the small groups to become part of their gang organization. Eventually, a few gangs controlled the entire city of Chicago. During this decade, three African-American supergangs, the Vice Lords, the Blackstone Rangers, and the Disciples, either had their beginnings or developed into supergangs. In the 1960s, the Crips, an African-American supergang, began as a small clique in a section of Los Angeles.[11] It was not long before the Bloods, another African-American supergang in Los Angeles, arose to challenge the Crips. See Social World of the Offender 13–1 for the development of these supergangs.

During the late 1960s, the Vice Lords and the Blackstone Rangers, two of the Chicago supergangs, became involved in programs of community betterment. Their social action involvement began in the summer of 1967 when the Vice Lord leaders attended meetings at Western Electric and Sears and Roebuck. Operation Bootstrap, which resulted from these meetings, formed committees for education, recreation, and law, order, and justice. A grant

SOCIAL WORLD OF THE OFFENDER 13–1

ORIGINS OF THE CHICAGO "SUPERGANGS"

The Vice Lord Nation

In the late 1950s, Peppilow was a 15-year-old youth who was sent to the St. Charles reformatory for boys. He persuaded Leonard Calloway, Maurice Miller, and four others to form a new gang when they got out. They played with names. It was Calloway who thought of lords, and vice came to mind. He looked both words up in the dictionary and found vice to mean, "having a tight hold." He knew he had it. They would be called "Vice Lords."

It was not until 1964 that the name "Conservative Vice Lords" became well known. Maurice Miller was a conservative type, and he wanted conservative added to the name. They did that for him, ending up with Conservative Vice Lords.

As the Conservative Vice Lords grew in number and power, they began to take over other youth gangs in their neighborhood and in surrounding neighborhoods. One of the reasons for the success of this gang's development is that while it was annexing groups into the Conservative Vice Lords, this gang allowed other groups to retain their own identity and to became part of the Vice Lord Nation.

For example, Willie Lloyd became a member of the Vice Lords in the mid-1960s and was put in charge of the Peewees, a junior division of the Conservative Vice Lords. But when the Peewees evolved into another youth gang, Willie was not selected as an officer, nor was his suggested group name accepted. He was able to persuade two friends at that point to begin a new youth gang, which they called the "Unknown Conservative Vice Lords." This new gang, in spite of the opposition it initially received from established Vice Lord groups, eventually was accepted as a major division of the Vice Lord nation.

Alfonso Alforde became chief of the Lords in the mid-1960s. Tired of humbugging, he began to search for meaning in a world where fighting was the only honor known. Too old to go back to school and with few jobs available, Al suggested the Lords try to open a business, moving toward construction rather than destruction. The Lords just shook their heads. It just didn't sound right. They enjoyed the partying, the drinking, and the fights. But Al kept insisting that together they could make it happen. They had to try.

Between 1965 and 1967, they stopped the gang wars. They opened businesses and ran community programs for the hungry, the unemployed, the homeless, and the young with nothing to do. They reached out to show the people on the streets that there was a thing called hope. For a moment in time they made a difference, but the forces working against them do not remember the moment. They are all dead now. All but Bobby Gore, who continues to have hope and to fight for his brothers and sisters on the streets.

As the decade came to an end, the Vice Lords contained 29 branches. In addition to the Conservatives, the largest groups included the Unknown, Four Corner Hustlers, Mafia Insane, 21st Street Executioners, the Travelers, and the Maniac Vice Lords, but they were still all Lords.

Blackstone Rangers

Jeff Fort was a scrawny young man who lived in Woodlawn on the west side of Chicago. He and a few friends began to steal hubcaps and groceries, dividing the proceeds among themselves. As others were attracted to this group, they were christened the Blackstone Rangers. Fort selected 21 leaders, giving them responsibility and power. They became known as the Main 21, and their major role was to enforce the rules of the Blackstone Rangers.

The Reverend John Fry, minister of the First Presbyterian Church in Chicago, permitted this gang to hold its meetings in the gymnasium of the church. The meetings captured the emotions of a religious revival. The Blackstones filled the gym, and the Main 21 were seated in a semicircle across the stage at the end of the gym.

Jeff Fort appeared out of nowhere, going to the microphone and podium. He raised his fist, jerking it back hard, with power they all knew him to have. He yelled, "Blackstone," and together, the thunderous roar resounded back, "Blackstone."

Fort whipped the Blackstones into a frenzy. In a deep, booming voice that sent static flying across the gym, he demanded, "Stones run it!" Thousands of bodies extended their right fists like banners hammering the winds and responded, "Stones run it!" Over and over the thunder filled the gym, "Blackstones, Blackstones, Blackstones."

The Stones soon spread beyond their neighborhoods throughout Chicago. It was not long before they were known as America's most powerful gang. Some drug sales took place in the 1960s, but gang arrests were typically for crimes ranging from resisting arrest to armed robbery and murder.

The Disciples

David Barksdale was a self-directed leader who defied anyone, accustomed to reaching out and taking what he wanted. During his frequent trips as a teenager to the Illinois Youth Commission, he recruited youths from the south, west, and east sides, organizing a domain that was to extend his field of influence beyond that of just the south side. The movement spread.

He was stocky at age 15, standing about 5′ 10″ tall. He was stoic, quiet, and always serious with a charisma that instilled fear and awe at the same time. Well mannered with few words, he dressed to perfection, looking fine with processed hair. But above all else he was an excellent boxer. One of the very best.

It was Barksdale's boxing skill that led to the development of the Disciples gang. Champ Harris was the 19-year-old leader of the Devil Disciples, which had a membership of about 400 youths. Champ's girlfriend, Linda Samuels, was pursued by Barksdale, and Champ challenged the boy to a boxing match. By the time Harris hit the floor, he had lost his girlfriend and control over his gang.

Barksdale surrounded himself with leaders he could trust. They fought the Egyptian Cobras led by Charlie Adkins and the Supreme Gangsters led by Martin Givens and Larry Hoover. Barksdale looked around for the small unknown groups just coming up and recruited them easily most of the time; other times they had little choice, if any.

With Barksdale on the run a couple of years later, Robert Allen, known to most as Old Timer, assumed responsibility for the leadership of the Devil Disciples. He made the decision to offer Larry Hoover an opportunity to coexist with him as leader of this gang. They would coexist together in one land, two kings ruling one nation, each with equal power. David would be king of the Devil Disciples, and Larry would be king of the Gangster Disciples. They were allies, 6,000 strong.

In the early 1970s, David Barksdale was wounded and then died a couple of years later. His side of the kingdom was taken over by Jerome Freedman and became known as the Black Disciples. Imprisoned Larry Hoover used the magic of the name "Gangster Disciple" to become a legend and to build one of the largest gang organizations in the United States. Known as the King and Chairman of the Board, he is the head of the vast Gangster Disciples nation.

Source: Linda Dippold Bartollas researched and wrote this material. She was assisted by Nehemiah Russell and Samuel Dillon.

from the Rockefeller Foundation in February 1967 enabled the Vice Lords to found a host of economic and social ventures. The Vice Lords also worked with Jesse Jackson on Operation Breadbasket and, in the summer of 1969, joined with the Coalition for United Community Action to protest the lack of African American employees on construction sites in African-American neighborhoods.

The supergangs in Chicago became involved in political activism when they joined together to work against the reelection of Major Richard Daley's

Democratic machine. This activism brought increased strain to their relationship with the Democratic party organization. With Daley's reelection, gangs in Chicago began to experience what they perceived as harassment from the police. As soon as he began a new term, Daley announced a crackdown on gang violence, and State's Attorney Edward Hanrahan followed by appraising the gang situation as the most serious crime problem in Chicago. The courts complied with this crackdown on gangs by increasing dramatically the number of gang members sent to prison in Illinois.

Expansion, Violence, and Criminal Operations: The 1970s, 1980s, and 1990s

A number of changes took place with gangs in the past three decades. The most important of these changes were that gangs became increasingly made up of adults; that street gangs became responsible for a larger portion of crime, including violent crime; that urban gangs grew in the 1970s and expanded dramatically throughout the nation in the late 1980s and early 1990s; and that crack cocaine hit the streets in the mid-1980s.

What became evident by the late 1960s was that juveniles were not leaving the urban gangs to which they belonged when they became adults. One of the major reasons for this is that these gangs supplied certain needs that were not being met in other social groups or traditional rites of passage into adulthood. Another reason was that the increased imprisonment of gang members fostered the development of prison gangs and kept their allegiance to these gangs while and subsequent to being released from prison.

In the 1970s and 1980s, urban gangs became responsible for a major portion of muggings, robberies, extortions, and drug-trafficking operations in the United States. With leadership increasingly assumed by adults, gangs were more intent on making money from crime. With legal weapons available more so than in the past, gangs became much more violent. Walter B. Miller's research found that in the mid-1970s the rate of murder by firearms or other weapons was higher than ever before; the five cities that had the most serious gang problems averaged at least 175 gang-related killings a year between 1972 and 1974.[12]

Both youth gangs and street gangs made up largely of adults have expanded dramatically over the past thirty years. In a 1982 study, Miller expanded the original study to twenty-six localities in the United States, including twenty-four of the largest cities and two counties. According to Miller's 1982 study, 2,300 youth gangs, with 100,000 members, were found in three hundred cities.[13] An estimated 26,700 street gangs and 780,200 members were active in the United States in 1998. This was a decline from an estimated 30,500 street gangs and 816,000 gang members in 1997 and 31,000 gangs and 846,000 gang members in 1996.[14]

The mid-1980s were a turning point for many ghetto-based gangs, for crack cocaine had hit the streets. These urban street gangs competed with each other for the drug trade. Several Los Angeles gangs established direct connections to major Colombian smugglers, which ensured a continuous supply of top-quality cocaine. In some Chicago neighborhoods, heavily armed teams sold drugs openly on the street corners, using gang "pewees" (youngsters) as police lookouts.

WHAT IS IMPORTANT TO KNOW ABOUT URBAN STREET GANGS?

Important features of urban street gangs include their types, organizational features, participation in drug-trafficking, their behavior in school, and the degree of law-violating behaviors for juveniles involved in these groups. Juveniles may be in a minority in urban street gangs, but they have certain role expectations (usually drug "runners" and lookouts for crack houses) and frequently remain in the gang even after they become adults.

Types of Urban Gangs

Detroit urban gangs, according to Carl S. Taylor, can be classified as scavenger, territorial, and corporate. Scavenger gangs lack goals, purpose, and consistent leadership and prey on those who are unable to defend themselves. Territorial gangs define an area as belonging exclusively to them and attempt to defend this space from outsiders. They become the controllers of the streets and defend their territory to protect their narcotics business. Organized or corporate gangs, which Taylor views as organized crime groups, have as their main purpose the participation in illegal money-making ventures, especially trafficking **crack** cocaine. Different divisions of the gang handle sales, distribution, marketing, and enforcement.[15]

C. Ronald Huff's examination of gangs in Cleveland and Columbus, Ohio, identified informal hedonistic gangs, instrumental gangs, and predatory gangs. The basic concerns of informal hedonistic gangs were to get high (usually on alcohol, marijuana, or other drugs) and to have a good time. These gangs were more involved in property crimes than in violent personal crimes. The main focus of instrumental gangs was economic gain, and they committed a high volume of property crimes. Most of these gang members used drugs, including crack cocaine; some individual members also sold drugs, but doing so was not an organized gang activity. Predatory gangs committed robberies, street muggings, and other crimes of opportunity. Members of these gangs were likely to use crack cocaine and to sell drugs to finance the purchase of more sophisticated weapons.[16]

Jeffrey Fagan identified four types of gangs in his analysis of the crime-drug relationships in three cities. Type 1 gangs were involved in a few delinquent activities and only alcohol and marijuana use. This type of gang had low involvement in drug sales and appeared to be a social gang. Type 2 gangs were heavily involved in several kinds of drug sales, primarily to support their own drug habits. They were also heavily involved in vandalism. Type 3 gangs had the highest levels of member participation, including extensive involvements in both serious and nonserious offenses. Another feature of this type was less involvement in both drug sales and the use of such substances as cocaine, heroin, PCP, and amphetamines. Type 4 gangs were extensively involved in both serious drug use and serious and nonserious offenses and had higher rates of drug sales. This cohesive and organized type, according to Fagan, "is probably at the highest risk for becoming a more formal criminal organization."[17]

Organizational Features of Urban Gangs

Martin Sánchez Jankowski, who spent more than ten years studying thirty-seven gangs in Los Angeles, New York, and Boston, suggested that the most important organizational features of urban gangs are structure, leadership, recruitment, initiation rites, role expectations and sanctions, and migration patterns.[18] Jankowski observed three varieties of gang organizational structure:

1. The *vertical/hierarchical* structure divides leadership hierarchically into several different levels. Power and authority are related to one's position in the line of command.
2. The *horizontal/commission* structure consists of several officeholders who share about equal authority over members. The leaders share the duties as well as the power and authority.
3. The *influential* structure assigns no written duties or titles to the leadership positions. This type of system has two to four members who are regarded as the leaders of the gang. The authority of the influential leaders is derived from charisma.[19]

The most conspicious example of the vertical/hierarchical type of leadership is found in the Gangster Disciples, the Vice Lords, the Black Disciples, and the El Rukns, whose leaders have become legends.

The Bloods and the Crips, the most notorious Los Angeles gangs, are representative of the horizontal/commission type. In a real sense, they are not gangs at all but confederations among hundreds of subgroups or sets. Sets are established along neighborhood lines, and most sets have twenty to thirty members.[20]

Gangs regularly go on recruiting parties, and the recruitment of young members, or soldiers, is easy because the life of a gang member looks glamorous. The methods of initiation into some gangs include some or all of the following: (1) must be "jumped in" or fight the other members; (2) must participate in illegal acts; (3) must assist in trafficking drugs; and (4) must participate in "walk-up" or "drive-by" shootings.[21] Recently, there has been a movement away from "jumped in" initiations in urban gangs, unless there is some question about the initiate's courage.[22]

A street gang's clothing, colors, and hand signs are held sacred by gang members. Each gang has its own secret handshakes and hand signs, known as **representing.** Prayers are also rituals of many gangs; they are often said before going into battle against rivals or are chanted before wounded members die. A chief value of gangs is loyalty, and members are charged to give up everything, including their lives, to defend the gang.

A final organizational feature of urban gangs is migration. Gang migration can occur in the establishment of satellite gangs in another location, in the relocation of gang members with their families, and in the expansion of drug markets. Cheryl L. Maxson, Malcolm W. Klein, and Lea C. Cunningham surveyed law enforcement agencies in more than 1,100 cities nationwide. Of these, 713 reported some gang migration. The most frequent pattern of gang migration was the relocation of gang members with their families (39 percent); the next most common pattern was the expansion of drug markets (20 percent). But their survey failed to offer much support for gangs attempting to establish satellites in other communities across the nation.[23]

In 1994 and 1995, one of the authors asked the gang chiefs of the largest Chicago gangs whether there had been an attempt to establish satellites in other communities. These chiefs all responded that they did not have the desire or the organizational capacity to form nationwide satellite gangs. They even questioned how much control they had over gangs in other locations that use their gang name.[24]

Drug-Trafficking and Gangs

Beginning in the mid-1980s, street gangs with origins in the urban centers of Los Angeles, Chicago, New York, Miami, and Detroit became criminal entrepreneurs in supplying drugs, especially crack cocaine, to urban communities. They had begun by the late 1980s and early 1990s to develop intrastate and interstate networks to expand their illegal drug market sales.

The Crips and Bloods of Los Angeles have been the most active in drug trafficking nationwide. In a 1988 report, the Drug Enforcement Administration claimed that Los Angeles street gangs were identified with drug sales in forty-six states.[25] The Miami Boys of south Florida, the Jamaican Posses of New York and Florida, and the Vice Lords and Gangster Disciples in Chicago are also among the street gangs that have entered the field in the largest scale.[26]

The depth of gang involvement in drugs is documented in the recent *1997 National Youth Gang Survey.* Respondents to the survey estimate, on the average, that 42 percent of the drug sales across jurisdictions are conducted by gangs. Table 13–1 shows the following breakdown of drug sales by gangs: gangs are responsible for 43 percent of drug sales in suburbs, 35 percent in rural areas, 31 percent in small cities, but 49 percent in large cities.[27]

When ranking gangs according to their involvement in drug sales at low, moderate, or high levels, data indicate that more than half (53 percent) of gang

Table 13–1 *Number and Percentage of Youth Gangs Involved in Drug Distribution in 1997, by Area Type*

	Youth Gangs Involved in Drug Distribution	
Area Type	*Weighted Average*	*Unweighted Average*
Large city	458 (49%)	472 (41%)
Small city	56 (31%)	58 (26%)
Suburban county	167 (43%)	174 (42%)
Rural county	71 (35%)	77 (34%)
Total/average	752 (42%)	781 (39%)

Notes: Weighted averages account for the number of gang members reported in each jurisdiction; unweighted averages do not. The relationship between drug distribution and area type was not statistically significant at the 0.05 level. Generally, as area type becomes more urbanized, the percentage of gangs involved in drug distribution increases. However, rural counties report a higher percentage of gangs involved in street sales than do small cities.

Source: Shay Bilchik, *1997 National Youth Gang Survey* (Washington, DC: Office of Juvenile Justice and Delinquency Prevention, December 1999), 23.

members were reported to be involved at the low level of drug sales, 18 percent at the moderate level, and 29 percent at the high level.[28] The highest proportion of youth gangs involved in drug sales[63] was in large cities and the lowest was in small cities. Larger cities apparently have more opportunities for the individual entrepreneur.

Another finding of the *1996 National Youth Gang Survey* is the age of gang members who sell drugs. Data in Table 13–2 suggest that the "estimated age of gang members based on unweighted averages was as follows: 21 percent, under age 15; 45 percent, ages 15–17; 28 percent, ages 18–24; and 5 percent over the age 24."[29] Of interest here is the number of youths under the age of fifteen

Table 13–2 *Level of Gang Member Involvement in Drug Sales by Age of Gang Members*

	Age			
Level of Involvement	*Under 15*	*15–17*	*18–24*	*Over 24*
67–100% (n = 232)	20%	43%	30%	7%
34–66% (n = 217)	20	44	30	6
0–33% (n = 407)	23	47	26	4
0–100% (n = 856)	21	45	28	5

Notes: The percentages within each level of involvement may not equal 100 percent due to rounding; n = number of observations. The averages reported in this table are unweighted; that is, they do not account for the number of gang members reported in each jurisdiction.

Source: Shay Bilchik, *1996 National Youth Gang Survey* (Washington, DC: Office of Juvenile Justice and Delinquency Prevention, July 1999), 41.

who sell drugs and the relatively small number of adult gang members still left in the gangs who sell drugs; the largest number of gang members selling drugs are youths between ages fifteen and twenty-four.

Gangs in School

Urban schools have become fertile soil for the violence and drug-trafficking of juveniles who belong to gangs. C. R. Huff and K. S. Trump's examination of youth gangs in Cleveland, Ohio; Denver, Colorado; and south Florida revealed that 50 percent of their respondents reported that members of their gangs had assaulted teachers, more than 80 percent said gang members took guns and knives to school, and more than 60 percent claimed gang members sold drugs at school.[30]

Gangs perpetrate school violence in a number of ways. They are likely to bring concealed weapons into the school. They are constantly recruiting new members, and nongang youths who refuse to join may be assaulted. Also, when more than one gang is present in a school setting, conflict among these gangs takes place on a regular basis. Furthermore, conflict among rival gangs in different schools perpetrates violence.

Youths involved in gangs also are known to be disruptive in the classroom, to do poorly in their academic work, to intimidate nongang youth on the way to and from school, to frequently be absent, to be suspended or even expelled from school, and to dropout of school. When an urban high school has a large percentage of gang youths, the culture of that school tends to be chaotic, out of control, and dangerous. A visitor to a typical urban high school is likely to feel very uncomfortable.

Nehemiah Russell, a former Assistant Principal of Englewood Technical Preparatory Academy in Chicago, explains the grim situation for urban schools:

> As educators, legislators, public officials, and the concerned public approach the twenty-first century, the prevalence of students' violence and disruptive behavior in the public education system impede the academic and social performance of students. Certain public school districts spend millions of dollars to implement traditional strategies to decrease students' inappropriate behavior to no avail.[31]

See Focus on Policy 13–2 for an alternative approach to reducing the chaos and violence of urban schools. While this program was eventually disbanded, largely because of the controversy it created, it resulted in a dramatically different quality of life in an urban school dominated by two rival street gangs.[32]

Law-Violating Behaviors and Gang Activities

Despite the fluidity and diversity of gang roles and affiliation, it is commonly agreed that core members are involved in more serious delinquent acts than are situation or fringe members.

FOCUS ON POLICY 13–2

A NEW CULTURE AT THE ENGLEWOOD ACADEMY

When the Englewood community led the nation in violence in 1991, community leaders turned to gangs to help improve the neighborhood. One of the programs that was developed was the Community Liaison Program in Englewood Academy. Larry Hoover and Jerome "Shorty" Freeman, the leaders of the Gangster Disciples and the Black Disciples, joined school officials and community leaders to develop this program.

In a 1995 interview, Larry Hoover had this to say about the Englewood program:

> Other methods of decreasing negative school behavior of students have failed. This unorthodox approach to classroom management will meet resistance by certain educational authority figures, but those who adopt this approach will reap the benefits of this non-traditional program.

What is positive about this program is that it provides a constructive learning environment for students that is rarely found in an urban setting. In visiting this school on several occasions, one of the authors witnessed no drugs being sold, no conflict among gang members, no victimization of nongang members, no turmoil in the hallway or on school grounds, no disrespect of teachers. Nor did students or faculty appear to be afraid.

What is questionable about Englewood's gang deactivation program is that control that school officials permitted gangs to have. Another troubling aspect of this gang deactivation program is the corporal punishment that misbehaving gang members receive from the gangs. In a time when corporal punishment is widely forbidden in schools across the nation, a school violation at Englewood is likely to mean that a student who is a gang member will be fined or beaten, perhaps severely.

This cooperative effort with gangs certainly had its critics, and it was not long before the principal and assistant principal were terminated and the program was disbanded. Yet this program represents one of the more innovative attempts across the nation to promote a positive learning experience in an urban school. The renewal of urban education is one of the most serious challenges facing education today, and perhaps it will take such radical proposals as the one being used at Englewood to regain control of urban schools.

Source: Based on participant observation and interviews conducted by one of the authors.

Critical Thinking Questions:

What is your reaction to such a proposal? Could urban gangs who have created a problem be part of the answer to such a problem? What is the danger of such a proposal?

The follow-up of a sample of Cohort I to the age of thirty by Wolfgang and colleagues provided insights into the influence of gangs on delinquency in Philadelphia. They found that one-sixth of the Whites belonged to gangs and were responsible for one-third of the offenses committed by Whites; 44 percent of the nonwhites were gang members and were responsible for 60 percent of the offenses committed by nonwhites. Gang youths, who represented 29 percent of the total offender sample were responsible for 50 percent of the offenses.[33]

This study also found that boys who belonged to gangs persisted in delinquent behavior nearly three years longer than did those who never joined. But when racial aspects are examined, it became clear that the persistence of delinquent behavior was traceable primarily to the nonwhite gang members. Moreover, Wolfgang and colleagues found that 81 percent of the boys (90 percent of the nonwhites and 60 percent of the Whites) became delinquent after joining a gang. Another indicator of the relationship between gang membership and delinquency is that 90 percent of the Whites committed no further offenses after leaving the gang; however, for nonwhites, no clear effect of leaving the gang was evident.[34]

More recently, studies in Aurora, Colorado; Broward County, Florida; and Cleveland, Ohio, found some major differences between the behavior of gang members and that of at-risk youths.[35] Individual gang members in these studies reported that they had stolen more cars, that they had participated in more drive-by shootings, that they were far more likely to own guns, that they owned guns of larger caliber, and that they were more involved in selling drugs than were the sample of at-risk youths.[36] Of those youths selling drugs, "gang members reported doing so more frequently, having fewer customers, making more money from the sales, and relying more on out-of-state suppliers than nongang youths who sold drugs." This study added that "both gang members and at-risk youths reported that gangs do not control drug trafficking in their communities."[37]

Studies of large urban samples found that gang members are responsible for a large proportion of violent offenses. In Rochester, gang members, who made up 30 percent of the sample, self-reported committing 68 percent of all adolescent violent offenses, which was about seven times as many serious and violent acts as committed by nongang youths.[38] In Seattle, gang members, who made up 15 percent of the sample, self-reported committing 85 percent of adolescent robberies.[39] In Denver, gang members, who made up 14 percent of the sample, self-reported committing 89 percent of all serious violent adolescent offenses. Gang members committed about three times as many serious and violent offenses as did nongang youth.[40]

A further study in Columbus, Ohio, analyzed the arrest records of eighty-three gang leaders in the years 1980 to 1994. During these fifteen years, the eighty-three gang leaders accumulated 834 arrests, 37 percent of which were for violent crimes (ranging from domestic violence to murder). In this project, researchers theorized that violent crimes tended to increase as the gangs began engaging in drug activity and may have been connected to the establishment of a drug market.[41]

Gang membership appears to contribute to this pattern of violent behavior. Studies in Rochester, Denver, and Seattle showed that the influence of gang membership on levels of youth violence is greater than the influence of other delinquent peers.[42] Youths commit more serious and violent acts while they belong to a gang than they do after they leave gang membership.[43] In addition, the effects of gang membership on a propensity toward violence seems to be long lasting. In all three sites, even though gang members' offense rates dropped after leaving the gang, they still remained fairly high.[44]

The overall number of youth gang homicides declined during the 1990s, but trends varied by city. The 1996, 1997 and 1998 National Youth Gang Surveys revealed that 237 cities reported both a gang problem and a gang homicide statistic in all three years. Forty-nine percent of these cities indicated a decrease in gang homicide over the three-year period, 36 percent indicated an increase, and 15 percent indicated no change. The total number of gang homicides for these cities was 1,294 in 1996, 1,260 in 1997, and 1,061 in 1998. Los Angeles and Chicago stand out among the cities with the highest rates of gang homicides.[45]

Gang norms seem to contribute to the elevated rates of violence in youth gangs.[46] Most gangs have norms that support the expressive use of violence to settle disputes. The gang's sanctioning of violence is also dictated by a code of honor that stresses the importance of violence in demonstrating toughness and fighting ability and in establishing status in the gang. Levels of violence, as James C. Howell summarized it, do vary "from one city to another, from one community to another, from one gang to another, and even within cliques within the same gang."[47]

S. H. Decker describes a seven-step process that accounts for the peaks and valleys in the levels of gang violence.[48] The process begins with a gang that is loosely organized:

1. Loose bonds to gang
2. Collective identification of threat from a rival gang (through rumors, symbolic shows of force, cruising, and mythic violence), reinforcing the centrality of violence that expands the number of participants and increases cohesion
3. A mobilizing event, possibly, but not necessarily, violent
4. Escalation of activity
5. Violent events
6. Rapid deescalation
7. Retaliation.[49]

Juveniles' propensity for gun ownership and violence are known to be closely related. One study found that juvenile males who "own guns for protection rather than for sport are six times more likely to carry guns, eight times more likely to commit a crime with a gun, [and] four times more likely to be in a gang, and three times more likely to commit serious and violent crimes than youth who do not own guns for protection."[50] In addition, gangs are more likely to recruit youths who own firearms, and gang members are more than twice as likely as those who do not belong to a gang to own a gun for protection, more likely to have peers who own guns for protection, and more likely to carry their guns outside their home.[51]

Other researchers have also discovered a "significant connection among gang involvement, gang violence, and firearms."[52] For example, one study based on the responses of 835 institutionalized male residents of six juvenile correctional facilities in four states found that "gang membership brought increases in most forms of gun-involved conduct." Indeed, 45 percent of the respondents in this study reported that gun theft is a regular gang activity, 68 percent indicated that their gang bought and sold guns on a regular basis, and 61 percent said that "driving around shooting at people you don't like" is a regular gang activity.[53]

A final dimension of law-violating behaviors of urban street gangs is an examination of the extent to which they are becoming organized crime groups. Decker, Tim Bynum, and Deborah Weisel interviewed members of African-American and Hispanic gangs in San Diego and Chicago and found that only the Gangster Disciples (GDs) in Chicago are assuming the attributes of organized crime groups.[54] Several commentaries have spelled out the organizational features of the GDs, including a chairman of the board, two boards of directors (one for the streets and one for prisons), governors who control drug-trafficking on the streets, regents who supply the drugs, area coordinators who collect revenues from drug-selling spots, enforcers who punish those who violate the rules, and "shorties" who staff drug-selling spots and execute drug deals.[55]

It can be argued that aspects of organized crime groups are found in such drug-trafficking gangs as the Bloods and Crips in Los Angeles, the Miami Boys of south Florida, and the Jamaican Posses of New York and Florida. Beginning in the mid 1980s, these street gangs appeared to become criminal entrepreneurs in supplying illicit drugs. In a brief period of several years, many of these street gangs developed intrastate and interstate networks for the purpose of expanding their illegal drug market sales. The Crips and Bloods of Los Angeles have been the most active in drug trafficking across the United States. A study by the U.S. Congress concluded that during the latter part of the 1980s the Crips and Bloods controlled 30 percent of the crack cocaine market across the nation.[56] The Drug Enforcement Administration claimed in a 1988 report that Los Angeles street gangs were identified with drug sales in forty-six states.[57]

Racial and Ethnic Gangs

African-American gangs, such as the Bloods and Crips from Los Angeles and the Chicago supergangs, are widely recognized because they are the ones that have established drug-trafficking networks across the nation. Jamaican and

Cuban gangs also have gone into many cities to sell and supply narcotics. Hispanic street gangs are found primarily in the Southwest and Southeast. These gangs usually divide themselves into groupings called "cliques" and are distinguished by the loyalty members show to the gang. White gangs, which began on the West Coast and were known as "Stoners," frequently abuse drugs and alcohol and listen to "heavy metal" rock music. Some evidence suggests that White gangs are increasingly becoming involved in satanic cults. Asian gangs, including Chinese, Vietnamese, Filipino, Japanese, and Korean gangs, began in California and have spread to other major American cities. These gangs are often more organized and have more identifiable leadership than do other street gangs.[58]

Females in Gangs

Adolescent girls who join gangs have received more attention recently. Anne Campbell estimates that 10 percent of the members of the four hundred gangs in New York City are female. Ranging in age from fourteen to thirty some are married and many have children.[59] A CBS News report in 1986 further estimates that approximately one thousand girls participate in more than one hundred female Chicago gangs. This report claims that these gangs are not sister organizations or auxiliaries to male gangs but are independent female gangs staking out their own territory and adopting distinctive colors and insignia.[60] Lee Bowker and Malcolm W. Klein's examination of a group of African-American gang females in Los Angeles, however, found that they were an auxiliary of a male gang. The male gang never permitted them to plan a gang activity, but the female gang members were allowed to participate in drug-related gang activities and in violent crimes.[61] See Focus on Offenders 13–3. J. C. Quicker's study of Hispanic adolescent female gang members in east Los Angeles also found that these groups had connections to male gangs.[62]

What are Emergent Street Gangs?

In the late 1980s and early 1990s, gangs began to appear in most communities of this nation. In G. David Curry and colleagues' 1992 survey of law enforcement departments in the 79 largest U.S. cities, 91 percent of respondents reported the presence of gang problems. These researchers estimated that there were 4,881 gangs with 249,324 gang members. Forty cities also reported a total of 7,205 gang members. Twenty-seven cities reported that there were 83 independent female gangs. Significantly, these cities with emerging gangs reported that juveniles made up 90 percent of the gangs.[63]

Emergent gangs have been examined in Denver, Colorado; Kansas City, Missouri; Rochester, New York; and Seattle, Washington. These studies generally found that gang members were involved in levels of delinquent activity that were much greater than those of nongang members, that the

FOCUS ON OFFENDERS 13–3

FEMALE GANG INITIATION

Sandy looked at me, waiting for our answer. I wasn't afraid of a beat-down, but I figured Carmen was looking for the other answer. "I'll do something for the family," I said. Carmen cracked a smile and turned to Sandy.

"I'Il do something for the family, too."

Carmen nodded. She checked her watch. "Follow me," she said.

As she led us down the stairs and outside, Carmen briefed us on the woman who lived in the gray house next door. This bitch didn't like the family, Carmen said. She'd sit on her porch sometimes, mimicking the sign and laughing. It was time she learned the Unidad was nothing to play with. "You two will be the ones to teach her that lesson," she said.

Carmen knew the woman's schedule. She'd be passing by any minute. "Use those on her," she said, pointing to a pile of two-by-fours. "She's a big bitch. You'll need "em."

Sandy grabbed two pieces of wood and handed one to me. We crouched on either side of the gate to the front sidewalk. Carmen retreated and hid. A few minutes later, she called to us. "Okay, here she comes."

There was no way I could punk out at this point. I looked over at Sandy, crouched and ready to pounce. I watched our victim approach, focusing on her fat feet, squeezed into a pair of black sandals, "Now!" Caremen said.

"Hey!" I screamed, jumping up. The woman turned to face me. Her hair was pulled back in a ponytail. Her eyes were wide with shock. Sandy took the first swing, a loud whack to the back of the woman's head.

For a second, I just stood there, frozen. But when the woman started defending herself against Sandy, I jumped in. Raising my two-by-four above my head, I brought it down to her. She screamed. I pounded her again and again. Even after she fell to the ground, I kept hitting her.

Then everything went dark. My legs wouldn't work. It was like I was in a weird dream. "Brenda, get out of here *now*!" someone shouted. I blinked, looked around. I was slumped against the fence in front of the building, gripping a piece of two-by-four. I dropped it and ran for my life.

A few minutes later, I was in some alley, at the bottom of a flight of stairs. I was bent over, holding my stomach, gasping for air. "Bren Are you okay?" I looked up at Erika. "You did it! We're sisters now."

Brenda Medina, "Hell, and How I Got Here," in *Wally Lamb and the Women of York Correctional Institution.* (United States of America: Regan Books, 2003), pp. 164–165. Reprinted by permission.

Critical Thinking Question:

What would you do to try to break this "cycle" of gang violence if given the chance to develop a program?

Doing something for the family is often a requirement for females who want to become gang members. Here gang "wannabees" attack an 'enemy' of the gang. (Photo by Kathryn Miller.)

participation in gangs increased each year from the late 1980s to the early 1990s, and that these emerging gangs brought new levels of violence to a community.[64]

This nationwide expansion, which began in the late 1980s, appeared to occur in four different ways. First, it took place in some communities when urban gangs sent ranking gang members to persuade local youths to sell crack cocaine. Second, gang-related individuals expanded their established drug-trafficking operations among community youths. Third, youth members of urban gangs whose families had moved to these new communities were instrumental in developing local chapters of urban gangs. Fourth, youths in communities with little or no intervention from outsiders developed their own version of gangs. The first two scenarios were more likely to involve drug trafficking than were the last two.

Many communities across the nation have experienced the first form of gang expansion. Although the gangs appear to be somewhat different in each community, the degree and seriousness of gang activity in a community depends on its stage of development. Five stages of gang development could be identified by the end of 1999, with the possibility of two additional stages.

Stage 1

Gang leaders are aware of the ripe drug markets outside the major urban areas throughout the nation. They are also aware that crack cocaine in these new markets would bring a higher price than it does in the saturated urban areas. A plan is developed—which varies little from one drug-trafficking urban gang to another—for a gang member to go to a city without gangs. When he arrives, either by plane or auto, he goes to a low-income minority neighborhood and recruits several juveniles to sell crack cocaine. As part of his "sales pitch," this ghetto-based gang member assures these juveniles that the mother gang intends to develop a connection, or satellite, in their community. The recruited juveniles are promised a percentage of the money they make from the drug sales. The adult gang member agrees to return on a regular basis to supply more drugs, to pick up the money, and to check on operations. It is not long before a second and sometimes a third representative of urban-based gangs arrives to recruit youths to sell crack cocaine.

Stage 2

By stage 2, the adult gang member has informed the youths selling drugs enough about the gang that they are able to identify with it. They can wear the proper clothing, can represent the gang signs, and can come together as a group. But their basic activity remains that of selling crack cocaine. One midwestern youth claimed that he was making $40,000 a month selling crack cocaine for the Almighty Unknown Vice Lords when he was arrested and institutionalized. Competition between these youths who claim to be part of the rival street gangs inevitably results in conflict and sometimes violence. Fights are likely to break out during school functions, at athletic events, and in parks. Weapons may be discharged at this time. Police also become aware that increasing numbers of weapons are being brought into the community.

Stage 3

The organization of the gangs develops during stage 3. Gang membership increases as more youths are brought into the core group. Leadership of the gang is usually assumed by a member of the initial core group, as well as by young adult members of the community. Gang members become more visible at school and at school functions, usually by the colors or clothing they wear and by the gang signs they represent. It is not long before a sizable number of "wannabes" are considering themselves gang members. The process of initiation begins at this time, and pressure is placed especially on African-American males to join a gang. White youths also frequently are accepted as part of these developing gangs.

Stage 4

The competition between rival gangs erupts in open conflict in school, at school dances, at athletic events, and in shopping centers. Drugs also are increasingly sold in the school environment. White gangs often appear at this time, and African-American gangs are more likely to wear their colors and to demonstrate gang affiliation.

Stage 5

Drugs are openly sold in the school, on street corners, and in shopping centers. Extortion of students and victimization of both teachers and students occurs widely in the public schools. Moreover, the gangs are led by adults who remain in the community, and the organizational structure and numbers of gang members show a significant increase.

Stage 6

The gangs are clearly in control in minority neighborhoods, in the school, at school events, and in shopping centers. The criminal operations of the rival gangs also become more varied during stage 6, including robberies, burglaries, aggravated assaults, and rapes. Citizens' fear of gangs dramatically increases, and the police express the inability to control drug trafficking and violence.

Stage 7

The final stage is characterized by the deterioration of the city as a result of gang control. Citizens move out of the city, stay away from shopping centers, and keep their children home from school.

HOW IS GANG INVOLVEMENT TOXIC?

Youths involved in emergent gangs are sounding more and more like those who are members of urban gangs. They both talk about justice. Justice means that honor is revenged. "I feel that what we did that night wasn't enough. Justice, to me, would have been killing seven or eight of them. Even though only one guy shot my brother, there were three guys there."[65]

They both talk about how gang "bangin'" becomes a way of showing that a youth is "bad." "Shootin' guns and stabbin' people" is how a gang youth shows heart and courage, and killing to many gang youths "ain't nothing." The violence of this substitute family makes a youth feel powerful and connected to something worthwhile. To youths who must deal with hopelessness in so many areas of their lives, the fear of dying makes them feel alive.

They both talk about the violence of the 1990s street gangs and how this violence far exceeds that of the past:

> It's more tense now than ever before. Because back then, if you saw somebody from an enemy set, chances are you'd just fight with 'em. You know, you'd come at them from the shoulder. Whereas now—it's gunplay. Back then not as many sets were fightin' with each other. It was much simpler: Crips versus Bloods. Now, it seems as if every other Crip set is fightin' with each other, killin' each other. And everything is high-tech now. Weapons, surveillance, communications, everything. Makes you wonder what would happen if some "banger" with a hate on got his hands on a nuclear device, doesn't it?[66]

FOCUS ON THE OFFENDER 13–4

INSTITUTIONALIZED JUVENILE WHO WENT HOME AND KILLED

One of the authors was doing a research project comparing a state and private facility when he was approached by staff members who inquired whether he would like to talk to all the gang kids. It quickly got around that this coauthor knew Willie Lloyd, the leader of the Unknown Vice Lords, and so all the gang youth wanted to talk to him, especially the Vice Lords. One young man came into the office to talk when this researcher was interviewing staff youth. They were having a good talk, when suddenly the gang youth announced that he had to go home and kill the Crip who had recently killed his nephew. He would be released the next week and planned to take care of business.

The researcher tried to talk him out of it, with a variety of reasoning ploys. Nothing worked. He went home the next week, and was soon involved in the killing of a Crip on a drive-by shooting. He is presently doing life without parole for this crime (which the researcher had predicted would happen).

Critical Thinking Question:
If you were this researcher, what would you have said to this young man?

Beyond gang youths attempting to make sense of their social world is the reality that gangs are destructive to their members. First, gang youths become involved in dangerous, even deadly, games. As one former gang leader put it, "I've gone to more gang funerals than I can even count."[67] Second, although joining a gang may be a normal rite of passage for a youth, gangs minister poorly to such basic adolescent needs as preparation for marriage and employment and learning to adapt to the adult world. Third, juvenile males who join gangs for protection are exposed to dangers that most non-gang juveniles are able to avoid. Fourth, gang youth frequently are victimized by both juvenile and adult members of street gangs.[68] Adolescent females who often are exploited sexually by male gang members aptly show how gangs victimize younger members. Finally, although joining a gang may provide status and esteem in the present, it also increases the likelihood that incarceration will be forthcoming in juvenile and adult facilities.[69] See Focus on the Offender 13–4.

It is as important to note what gangs do to their own members as it is to examine what gangs do to society. When agencies were asked in the *1996 National Youth Gang Survey* about the types of crimes gang members

Table 13–3 Degree of Gang Member Criminal Activity in 1997 by Type of Offense and Area Type[a]

Degree of Offending, by Type of Offense	Area Type				
	All Areas	Large City	Small City	Suburban County	Rural County
Aggravated assault					
High	382 (28%)	256 (33%)	14 (11%)	88 (27%)	24 (15%)
Medium	520 (38%)	295 (38%)	39 (31%)	122 (38%)	64 (41%)
Low	428 (31%)	202 (26%)	64 (51%)	100 (31%)	62 (40%)
Not involved	44 (3%)	16 (2%)	8 (6%)	13 (4%)	7 (5%)
Robbery					
High	174 (13%)	116 (15%)	5 (4%)	35 (11%)	18 (12%)
Medium	400 (29%)	266 (35%)	16 (13%)	91 (28%)	27 (18%)
Low	615 (45%)	324 (42%)	59 (48%)	160 (50%)	72 (48%)
Not involved	177 (13%)	62 (8%)	44 (36%)	37 (12%)	34 (23%)
Burglary					
High	358 (26%)	175 (23%)	28 (22%)	91 (28%)	64 (41%)
Medium	538 (39%)	306 (40%)	52 (42%)	126 (39%)	54 (34%)
Low	430 (31%)	261 (34%)	38 (30%)	97 (30%)	34 (22%)
Not involved	47 (3%)	25 (3%)	7 (6%)	10 (3%)	5 (3%)
Motor vehicle theft					
High	372 (27%)	251 (33%)	16 (13%)	81 (25%)	24 (16%)
Medium	449 (33%)	256 (34%)	31 (25%)	115 (35%)	47 (30%)
Low	454 (33%)	223 (29%)	54 (43%)	111 (34%)	66 (43%)
Not involved	92 (7%)	32 (4%)	24 (19%)	18 (6%)	18 (12%)
Larceny/Theft					
High	379 (28%)	218 (28%)	38 (31%)	80 (25%)	43 (27%)
Medium	609 (44%)	356 (46%)	46 (37%)	141 (44%)	66 (42%)
Low	349 (25%)	180 (24%)	35 (28%)	92 (28%)	42 (27%)
Not involved	35 (3%)	12 (2%)	5 (4%)	11 (3%)	7 (4%)

Note: The percentages within each offense category may not equal 100 percent due to rounding.

[a]The differences in the percentages of gang member involvement by area type are statistically significant at the 0.05 level for all types of offenses except larceny/theft.

Source: Shay Bilchik, *1997 National Youth Gang Survey* (Washington, DC: Office of Juvenile Justice and Delinquency Prevention, July 1999).

committed in their area, larceny and aggravated assault were highest at 28 percent each, followed by burglary (26 percent), motor vehicle theft (27 percent) and robbery (13 percent). The types of crimes also varied by area, as juveniles in small cities and rural areas had lower participation in aggravated assault and motor vehicle theft and robbery. Burglaries were higher in suburban and rural counties, and larceny/theft offenses were highest in suburban and rural areas (see Table 13–3).

Juveniles who belong to urban street gangs or **emerging youth gangs** are involved in more serious delinquent acts than are youths who do not belong to gangs. The influence of gang participation on violent behavior has been documented by a number of studies. The studies of gangs in Rochester, New York; Denver, Colorado; and Pittsburgh, Pennsylvania; all found that gang youths committed more violent behaviors than did non-gang delinquents and that youths commit more serious and more violent acts when they are gang members than they do after leaving the gang.[70] James C. Howell's examination of youth gang homicides found that the recent growth in youth gang homicides has been driven by increased access to firearms. Yet it appears that gang-related homicides are generally not about drugs but are personal, vendetta-like, and motivated primarily by self-protection.[71]

WHAT CAN COMMUNITIES DO TO PREVENT AND CONTROL YOUTH GANGS?

Communities across the United States have had a tendency to deny that they have gangs even when gang youths are causing serious problems at schools and in the neighborhoods. When an incident takes place, such as an innocent victim is killed or a shoot-out takes place and one or more youths are killed, then communities tend to substitute repression for denial. The problem is turned over to the police with the directive to make gangs invisible. Gang units are sometimes established in police departments to focus on getting rid of the gang problem.

Irving Spergel and colleagues' 1989 survey of forty-five cities with gang problems identified five strategies of intervention: (1) community organization, including community mobilization and networking; (2) social intervention, focusing on individual behavioral and value change; (3) opportunity provision, emphasizing the improvement of basic education, training, and job opportunities for youth; (4) suppression, focusing on arrest, incarceration, monitoring, and supervision of gang members; and (5) organizational development and change, or the creation of special organizational units as well as procedures.[72]

In examining the implementation of these strategies, Spergel and colleagues found that suppression (44 percent) was most frequently used, followed by social intervention (31.5 percent), organizational development (10.9 percent), community organization (8.9 percent), and opportunity provision (4.8 percent).[73] Community organization was more likely to be used with gang programs in emerging gang cities, whereas social intervention and opportunity provision tended to be primarily strategies of programs in cities with chronic gang problems. But in only seventeen of the forty-five cities was there any evidence of improvement in the gang situation.[74]

Spergel and colleagues, in developing a model for predicting general effectiveness in dealing with gang problems, stated:

> A final set of analyses across all cities indicate that the primary strategies of community organization and provision of opportunity along with maximum participation by key community actors is predictive of successful efforts at reducing the gang problem.[75]

What this research by Spergel and colleagues has demonstrated is that only an integrated, multidimensional, community-oriented effort is likely to have any long-term effect in preventing and controlling gangs in the United States. This gang prevention and control model must have several components: (1) the community must take responsibility for developing and implementing this model; (2) this structural model must take seriously the hopelessness arising from the unmet needs of underclass children; (3) prevention programs, especially in the first six years of school, must receive a major emphasis; (4) those who support this model must coordinate all the gang intervention efforts taking place in a community; and (5) sufficient financial resources must be available for implementing the model.

SUMMARY

Adolescents finding that their needs are not met in social contacts with family members, teachers, and leaders and participants in churches, school activities, and community organizations, are more likely to be attracted to street gangs and youth gangs. These gangs become quasi-families offering acceptance, status, and esteem.

Youth gangs are now found throughout the United States. Even small towns and rural areas often must contend with the presence of youth gangs. Much is the same and much is new about youth gangs. What is new is the wide use of gun violence, particularly involving automatic and semiautomatic handguns. Drug-trafficking by juveniles takes place now much more than in the past. What is new is that youth gangs have further become street gangs, especially in urban areas. More and more control of these gangs is assumed by adults. In some urban gangs, juveniles are a minority of gang membership.

Gangs have thrived because of the poverty in many urban neighborhoods. The hopelessness of these environments make drug-trafficking attractive and gang membership desirable even with the high possibility of being injured, killed, or imprisoned. Grassroots community groups seem to make the most sense in reducing the spread of gangs, but gang reduction actually depends on providing at-risk children with more positive options than they have today.

WEB SITES OF INTEREST

Many links on gangs can be found at
The National Youth Gang Center can be found at
http://www.iir.com/nygc/
Learn more about street gangs from the Streetgangs web site.
http://www.streetgangs.com/

CRITICAL THINKING QUESTIONS

1. Why are adolescents likely to become involved in youth gangs?
2. How have youth gangs changed through the years?
3. If you had the opportunity to teach a class of high school students, most of whom were in youth gangs, what would you say to them?
4. Why is community participation the most effective means of gang prevention and control?
5. Why do you believe gang participation and membership decreased in the final years of the twentieth century?

NOTES

1. Interviewed in 1995.
2. See Finn-Aage Esbensen, "Preventing Adolescent Gang Involvement," *Juvenile Justice Bulletin* (Washington, DC: Office of Juvenile Justice and Delinquency Prevention, 2000), 2.
3. James C. Howell, *OJJDP Fact Sheet* (Washington, DC: The Office of Juvenile Justice and Delinquency Prevention, 1997), 1.
4. National Youth Gang Center, *1998 National Youth Gang Survey* (Washington, DC: Office of Juvenile Justice and Delinquency Prevention, 2000), xiv.
5. See the section on law-violating behaviors of juveniles for studies supporting these conclusions.
6. Luc Sante, *Low Life: Lures and Snares of Old New York* (New York: Vintage Books, 1991).
7. Robert Redfield, *Folk Culture of Yucatan* (Chicago: University of Chicago Press, 1941).
8. Frederick Thrasher, *The Gang: A Study of 1,313 Gangs in Chicago* (Chicago: University of Chicago Press, 1927).
9. Ibid.
10. See Walter B. Miller, "The Impact of a Total Community Delinquency Control Project," *Social Problems* 10 (Fall 1962), 168–91.
11. John C. Quicker and Akil S. Batani-Khalfani, "Clique Succession among South Los Angeles Street Gangs, the Case of the Crips." Paper presented to the Annual Meeting of the American Society of Criminology, Reno, Nevada (November 1989).
12. Walter B. Miller, *Violence by Youth Gangs and Youth Groups as a Crime Problem in Major American Cities* (Washington, DC: U.S. Government Printing Office, 1975).
13. Walter B. Miller, *Crime by Youth Gangs and Groups in the United States.* A report prepared for the National Institute of Juveniles Justice and Delinquency Prevention, February 1982.

14. See Howell, *OJJDP Fact Sheet.*
15. Carl S. Taylor, *Dangerous Society* (East Lansing: Michigan State University Press, 1990), 4–7.
16. C. Ronald Huff, "Youth Gangs and Public Policy," *Crime and Delinquency* 35 (October 1989), 528–29.
17. Jeffrey Fagan, "The Social Organization of Drug Use and Drug Dealing Among Urban Gangs," *Criminology* 27 (1989), 633–64.
18. Martin Sánchez Jankowski, *Islands in the Streets: Gangs and American Urban Society* (Berkeley: University of California Press, 1991), 5.
19. Ibid., 64–67.
20. Joan Moore, Diego Vigil, and Robert Garcia, "Residence and Territoriality in Chicago Gangs," *Social Problems* 31 (December 1985), 182–94.
21. For more information about drive-by shootings, see William B. Sanders, *Gangbangs and Drive-Bys: Grounded Culture and Juvenile Gang Violence* (New York: Aldine De Gruyter, 1994).
22. Conversations with urban gang chiefs in 1996.
23. Cheryl Maxson, Malcolm W. Klein, and Lea C. Cunningham, "Street Gangs and Drug Sales," Report to the National Institute of Justice (1993).
24. These conversations took place in 1994 and 1995 during prison visits.
25. Law Enforcement Administration, *Crack Cocaine Availability and Trafficking in the United States* (Washington, DC: U.S. Department of Justice, 1988). Ibid.
26. Shay Bilchik, *1997 National Youth Gang Survey* (Washington, DC: Office of Juvenile Justice and Delinquency Prevention, December 1999), 25.
27. Ibid., 24.
28. Ibid., 40.
29. Ibid.
30. C. Ronald Huff and K. S. Trump, "Youth Violence and Gang: School Safety Initiatives in Urban and Suburban School Districts," *Education and Urban Safety* 28 (1996), 5592–5603.
31. Interviewed in 1996.
32. Jeffery Fagan, "Social Processes of Delinquency and Drug Use Among Urban Gangs," in *Gangs in America,* edited by C. Ronald Huff (Newbury Park, CA: Sage, 1990), 199–200.
33. Marvin E. Wolfgang, Terence P. Thornberry, and Robert M. Figlio, *From Boy to Man: From Delinquency to Crime* (Chicago: University of Chicago Press, 1987), 155–56.
34. Ibid., 156–58.
35. See C. Ronald Huff, *Criminal Behavior of Gang Members and At-Risk Youths: Research Preview* (Washington, DC: National Institute of Research, 1998), 1.
36. Ibid., 1–2.

37. Ibid., 1.
38. Terence P. Thornberry, "Membership in Youth Gangs and Involvement in Serious and Violent Offending," in *Serious and Violent Juvenile Offenders: Risk Factors and Successful Intervention,* edited by R. Loeber and D. P. Farrington (Thousand Oaks, CA: Sage Publications, 1998), 147–66.
39. Sara R. Battin-Pearson, Terence P. Thornberry, J. David Hawkins, and Marvin D. Krohn, "Gang Membership, Delinquent Peers, and Delinquent Behavior, "Juvenile Justice Bulletin" (Washington, DC: Office of Justice Programs, Office of Juvenile Justice and Delinquency Prevention, 1998).
40. David Huizinga, "Gangs and the Volume of Crime." Paper presented at the Annual Meeting of the Western Society of Criminology, Honolulu, Hawaii, 1997.
41. Huff, *Criminal Behavior of Gang Members and At-Risk Youths,* 2.
42. Battin, et al., "The Contribution of Gang Membership to Delinquency Beyond Delinquent Friends," 93–115.
43. Finn-Aage Esbensen and David Huizinga, "Gangs, Drugs, and Delinquency in a Survey of Urban Youth," *Criminology* 31 (1993), 565–89.
44. Howell, "Youth Gangs: An Overview," 9.
45. David Curry, Cheryl L. Maxson, and James C. Howell, "Youth Gang Homicides in the 1990s," *OJJDP Fact Sheet* (Washington, DC: Office of Juvenile Justice and Delinquency Prevention, 2001), 1.
46. Howell, "Youth Gangs: An Overview."
47. Ibid.
48. Scott H. Decker, "Collective and Normative Features of Gang Violence," *Justice Quarterly* 13 (1996), 262.
49. Ibid.
50. Howell, "Youth Gangs: An Overview."
51. Beth Bjerregaard and Alan J. Lizotte, "Gun Ownership and Gang Membership," *Journal of Criminal Law and Criminology* 86 (1995), 37–53.
52. Coordinating Council on Juvenile Justice and Delinquency Prevention, *Combating Violence and Delinquency: The National Juvenile Justice Action Plan* (Washington, DC: Juvenile Justice and Delinquency Prevention, 1996), 35.
53. Joseph F. Sheley and James D. Wright, *Youth, Guns and Violence in Urban America*. Paper presented at the National Conference on Prevention Strategies against Armed Criminal and Gang Violence: Federal, State, and Local Coordination, San Diego, CA (Washington, DC: National Institute of Justice, 1992).
54. Scott H. Decker, Tim Bynum, and Deborah Weisel, "A Tale of Two Cities: Gangs as Organized Crime Reports," *Justice Quarterly* 15 (September 1998), 395–425.
55. James McCormick, "The 'Disciples' of Drugs and Death," *Newsweek* (February 5, 1996), 56–57.

56. General Accounting Office, *Nontraditional Organized Crime* (Washington, DC: U.S. Government Printing Office, 1989).

57. Drug Enforcement Administration, *Crack Availability and Trafficking in the United States* (Washington, DC: U.S. Department of Justice, 1988).

58. Robert K. Jackson and Wesley D. McBride, *Understanding Street Gangs* (Costa Mesa, CA: Custom Publishing, 1985), 31–51.

59. Anne Campbell, *The Girls in the Gang: A Report from New York City* (New York: Basil Blackwell, 1984), 5.

60. Jack E. Bynum and William E. Thompson, *Juvenile Delinquency: A Sociological Approach* (Boston: Allyn & Bacon, 1989), 295.

61. Lee Bowker and Malcolm W. Klein, "Female Participation in Delinquent Gang Motivation," *Adolescence* 15 (1980).

62. J. C. Quicker, *Home Girls: Characterizing Chicano Gangs* (San Pedro, CA: International University Press, 1983).

63. G. David Curry, Robert J. Fox, Richard A. Ball, and Darryl Stone, "National Assessment of Law Enforcement Anti-Gang Information Resources." Report to the U.S. Department of Justice, National Institute of Justice (1993).

64. For a review of gang research, including that of emergent gangs, see James C. Howell, "Recent Gang Research: Program and Policy Implications," *Crime and Delinquency* 40 (October 1994), 491–515. For the study in Denver, see Finn-Aage Esbensen and David Huizinga, "Gangs, Drugs, and Delinquency in a Survey of Urban Youth," *Criminology* (1993), 565–89. For the study in Kansas City, Missouri, and Seattle, Washington, see Mark S. Fleisher, "Youth Gangs and Social Networks: Observations from a Long-Term Ethnographic Study," paper presented at the annual meeting of the American Society of Criminology, Miami, Florida (November 1994). For the study in Rochester, New York, see Terence P. Thornberry, Marvin D. Krohn, and Alan J. Lizotte, and Deborah Chard-Wierschem, "The Role of Juvenile Gangs in Facilitating Delinquent Behavior, *Journal of Research in Crime and Delinquency* 30 (1993), 55–87.

65. Howell, "Recent Gang Research."

66. Bing, *Do or Die,* 257.

67. Ibid.

68. Interviewed in 1996.

69. For example, see Felix Padilla's *The Gang as an Ethnic Enterprise* (New Brunswick, NJ: Rutgers University Press, 1992) for the way that youths who traffic drugs for the gang are victimized.

    For a discussion of the destructiveness of gangs to their members, see James F. Short, Jr., "Gangs, Neighborhood, and Youth Crime," *Criminal Justice Research Bulletin* (1990), 3.

70. T. P. Thornberry, "Membership in Youth Gangs and Involvement in Serious and Violent Offending," in *Serious and Violent Offenders: Risk Factors and*

Successful Interventions, edited by R. Loeber and D. P. Farrington (Thousand Oaks, CA: Sage, 1998), 147–166.

71. James C. Howell, "Youth Gang Homicides: A Literature Review," *Crime and Delinquency* 45 (April 1999), 208–41.
72. I. A. Spergel, G. D. Curry, R. A. Ross, and R. Chance, *Survey of Youth Gang Problems and Programs in 45 Cities and 6 Sites.* Tech. report No. 2 National Youth Gang Suppression and Intervention Project (Chicago: University of Chicago, School of Social Service Administration, 1989), 211.
73. Ibid., 212.
74. Ibid., 216.
75. Ibid., 218.

14

THE JUVENILE OFFENDER

OBJECTIVES

1. To classify the various types of juvenile offenders
2. To identify the importance of youth perceptions and their relationship to crime
3. To discuss the interrelationships of problem behaviors

KEY TERMS

chronic offenders
dependent and neglected children
deviant sexual arousal
emotionally disturbed offender
naive offenders
sex offender
sexual assault cycle
situational offenders
status offender
street gang members
teenage prostitution

I returned to Cincinnati when I left TICO [Training Institution, Central Ohio, a maximum security training school of the Ohio Youth Commission] in August 1977. Since I was 18, I opted for independent status and stayed at the Fryar's Club for six months and then moved into my own apartment that I shared with a friend. I had a regular job, both while I was staying at the Fryar's Club and after I moved out. I started college at Thomas More College in Erlanger, Kentucky, in the fall of 1978, and commuted from Cincinnati.

I applied for and received a grant but finally started to run out of money. I majored in chemistry and was hoping to get a job working in a lab. I was not able to find anything local, so after a year and a half at Thomas More, I moved to New Jersey where my mother lived with my two younger sisters. I got a job as a chemist. My mother was able to get me a job at the company she worked for. I had only intended to stay for a year and then return to school. Somehow, that never happened.

I got laid off from the one company and landed a job with another chemical company. After a little over a year and a half, I was in a motorcycle accident and was out of work for three months. When I was ready to return, they had filled my position. I decided that I would go back to school, but I would do it in New Jersey. I went to the local two-year school which was where I met my wife. I then landed a job in chemistry with Colgate-Palmolive, [which] had come recruiting on campus. [It was] located very close to Rutgers, and my intention was to work and go to school at night. School and work proved to be a bit more than I could deal with, so I stopped going to school after about a year.

I stayed at Colgate for about six years, during which time my wife and I were married in May of 1987. I left Colgate and went to work for another chemical company. After being there only a short time, I decided that I was tired of working in a lab, so I went back to school at night for a degree in Information Systems.

My wife and I bought our house in the late fall of 1990. Our daughter was born in April of 1992. I finished my B.S. [Bachelor of Science degree] in the spring of 1993. I was able to make the transition from the lab to IT [information technology] while I was at FMC. That fall I decided to go to graduate school and get an M.B.A. Our son was born in January of 1994. There was a change in management at the company I was with, so I left and joined a consulting firm doing IT consulting. I finished my graduate degree in 1996.

I was promoted and moved to a more senior level position within the consulting firm I was working for. I had started to specialize in pharmaceutical clinical data management systems and was leading a team of six other consultants. I left that firm and joined another consulting firm that I am currently with now. I am currently consulting for a major pharmaceutical company as an IT project manager.

—Former Institutionalized Delinquent[1]

This youth had more than his share of troubles with the law as an adolescent. He ended up being sent to one of the toughest juvenile correctional institutions in the United States. Upon his release at the age of eighteen, this youth could have continued his law-violating activities into his adult years and spent the remainder of his life in and out of prison. Instead, he was motivated to make something of himself. His goals were not always realized in the ways he intended, but he persisted. He earned a bachelor of science degree and eventually was awarded a master of business administration. With his educational achievements came job success, a happy marriage, and the joys of fatherhood.

Unfortunately, not all youthful offenders turn out as well as this young man has. The statistics in Chapter 2 reflect something about the magnitude of the juvenile crime problem but little about the lives of those who commit the crimes. A cursory examination of those who are questioned by the police, petitioned to the courts, placed on probation, confined in juvenile residential facilities, and released to aftercare indicates that a surprising variety of youths are in the system. Although many youths have never violated a law or done anything serious enough to warrant more than a passing glance by, perhaps, an irritated citizen, other youths have committed the most serious and heinous crimes imaginable.

The United States and other industrialized nations have wrestled with their "youth problem" for nearly two centuries. With increasing industrialization and urbanization, as well as the disappearance of the tight-knit family and community social structures, more and more youths find themselves without needed social supports, adequate nurturing from parents, and ability to function satisfactorily in a school context. At the same time, they experience a growing dependency on alcohol and drugs and are attracted to the street gang lifestyle.

Beginning with a general discussion of problem behaviors among adolescents, this chapter examines the various types of juvenile offenders using a classification scheme that considers, among other factors, the perceptions of youths, their gender and race, the frequency of offense, and explanations for their behavior.

WHAT ARE PROBLEM BEHAVIORS AMONG ADOLESCENTS?

Adolescence, generally defined as the period between ages twelve and eighteen, is an exciting time in a youngster's life. In this transitional period, youths experience many biological changes and develop new attitudes, skills, and values to guide them through their young adult years. Youths also experience increased freedom from parental scrutiny, and with this freedom comes greater opportunity to become involved in socially unacceptable behaviors. Furthermore, new tastes, often expensive ones, are acquired, and legitimate means for satisfying these desires may or may not be available. Finally, peers have enormous influence among adolescents, and juveniles' behaviors are frequently dictated by whether their peer group is involved in drugs, gangs, and other forms of antisocial behavior.

Of the nearly forty million adolescents in the United States, one in four is a high risk of engaging in socially unacceptable behaviors. These behaviors include abusing alcohol and drugs, committing delinquent acts, failing academically or dropping out of school, and practicing early, unprotected sexual intercourse. White and male youths make up the majority of high-risk youths and are more frequently involved in offending than are minority youths. Another ten million adolescents, making up 25 percent, practice risky behavior but to a lesser degree and, consequently, are less likely to experience a negative societal reaction. Twenty million, or half the adolescent population, are not presently involved in high-risk behaviors.[2]

High-risk youngsters generally have a number of factors in their lives that contribute to their antisocial behaviors. They are more likely to have problems in school with achievement, behavior, and truancy. They may even have dropped out of school. They also tend to have a less than desirable interaction with parents and peers. This lack of home adjustment frequently contributes to violating curfew, failing to respond to discipline and supervision, and running away from home. Furthermore, high-risk youngsters are frequently rebellious and identify with nonconformity; live in a neighborhood characterized by disorganization, poverty, and multiple social problems; and abuse drugs and alcohol.[3] Finally, they are part of peer groups that are involved in problem behaviors, including truancy and disruption in school, sexual acting-out, delinquency, drug and alcohol use, and gang activities.

The more of these antecedent factors that are present in an adolescent's life, the more likely it is that he or she will become involved in a problem behavior. The accumulation of these factors may also increase the frequency and seriousness of a youth's involvement in a problem behavior. Another important conclusion is that high-risk youths with the accumulation of these factors are likely to participate in multiple problem behaviors.[4]

What this discussion contributes to the understanding of juvenile offending is that the most serious offenders are generally high-risk youths. They have a number of problematic factors in their backgrounds and are usually involved in multiple problem behaviors. They see little future for themselves, at least in terms of using socially acceptable means to achieve success. Yet these hard-core youths still constitute a minority of those who come into contact with the juvenile justice system. Juvenile offenders also come from backgrounds with few problem factors, but, for one reason or another, they become involved typically in minor forms of delinquency but sometimes in violent acts toward others.

In an attempt to depict the diversity of juvenile offending, a classification scheme is presented in this chapter. This classification scheme identifies the various types of juvenile offenders and considers the influence of five factors: (1) the perceptions of offenders; (2) gender; (3) race; (4) frequency of offending; and (5) explanations of this behavior.

The chief types of offenders, according to this classification scheme, are the noncriminal youth, the irresponsible youth, the situational offender, the drug and alcohol abuser, and the chronic offender. Noncriminal youths are further classified as status offenders and dependent and neglected youths; irresponsible youths are divided into naive offenders and emotionally disturbed offenders. The situational offender, whether property or violent offender, may come from any social class, generally commits offenses in the company of peers, and drifts into and out of crime depending on the opportunities

Table 14–1 Types of Juvenile Offenders

Noncriminal youths
Status offenders
Dependent and neglected children
Irresponsible youths
Naive offenders
Emotionally disturbed children
Situational offenders
Property offenders
Violent offenders
Drug and alcohol users
Social or recreational users
Addicts
Chronic offenders
Sex offenders
Prostitutes
Street gang members

available. Drug and alcohol abusers are differentiated by whether they are recreational users or addicts. Chronic offenders include prostitutes and gang members (see Table 14–1).

WHO CAN BE DEFINED AS NONCRIMINAL YOUTHS?

The youthful offenders classified as noncriminal do not consider themselves to be delinquents. They are typically members of multiple-problem families, or they have no families at all. Most of these youths are dependent or neglected, and some are emotionally deprived; others have been abused or battered by parents.

STATUS OFFENDERS

Status offender is a legal description applied to juveniles who commit acts that are law violations only for juveniles. Approximately half of all juvenile arrests each year are for such acts as truancy, waywardness, and running away from home. Many of these behaviors are traced to conflict in the home. A historical look at the development of the status offender concept shows that society long has been interested in the relationship between parents and their children. Indeed, the terms used to connote status offenses, such as predelinquency, incorrigibility, ungovernablity, being beyond control, and waywardness all reflect this concern, as do the labels given to the children themselves, such as minors in need of supervision (MINS), children in need of supervision (CHINS), juveniles in need of supervision (JINS), families in need of supervision (FINS), and persons in need of supervision (PINS).

Originally, the juvenile court movement defined status offenses as delinquency to avoid the notion that delinquency and criminal behavior were alike.[5] See Focus on the Law 14–1.

When the movement began to separate status offenses from delinquent behaviors, each state faced the dilemma of deciding exactly what to define as status offense behavior. Some of the behaviors listed in Focus on the law 14–1 are definite violations of the law. But others are holdovers from earlier religious beliefs that are no longer as powerful as they were in the past. Some acts might harm the offender but no one else. Others might inconvenience or irritate adults but are not harmful or threatening to the offender. Some are merely the normal behaviors of growing children.

Truancy, incorrigibility, ungovernability, unmanageability, being beyond control, curfew violations, and running away are the behaviors most commonly prohibited under the status offense categories in state codes.[6] For example, running away and curfew violation account for about one-quarter of all arrests of adolescent females each year.[7] Yet the vagueness of the statutes has made it difficult to decide which behaviors should be considered status offenses.

The status offender typically has a family-oriented problem that is manifested in negative behavior at home, at school, in the community, or among peers. See Focus on the Offender 14–2.

Status offenders generally place the blame for their problems on parental figures in the home. They frequently feel unloved and unaccepted and claim that their needs for sustenance and support have not been met. The parents, in turn, often view their children as defiant, demanding, and unable to accept limits, and these personal inadequancies often result in status offense behaviors.

The debate over status offenders is one of the most serious debates within the juvenile justice system. The stakes in this debate are high, for a major portion of all youthful misbehavior consists of status offenses. Whether the offenders who commit these offenses remain in or are taken out of the juvenile justice system will have dramatic impact on the cost to the system as well as on the lives of the youths themselves. If these youths remain in the system, society will continue to process many children who have engaged in disapproved of but not criminal behavior. Many citizens and professionals alike fear that processing these youths through the system will harm rather than help them. If these youths are taken out of the system, however, as is being done in some states, youths who need some type of assistance may not receive it. That is, youths who need counseling or simply a roof over their heads may not be able to find the sevices they need. Society must decide whether to handle status offenders differently from delinquent offenders.

Dependent and Neglected Children

Neglect cases usually involve children who are abandoned by parents or whose parents fail to care properly for them. Dependency cases generally concern parents' complete lack of physical, emotional, and financial ability to

FOCUS ON THE LAW 14–1

PROHIBITIVE BEHAVIORS IN EARLY JUVENILE CODES

- Violating any law or ordinance
- Being habitually truant from school
- Associating with vicious or immoral persons
- Being incorrigible
- Demonstrating behavior that is beyond parental control
- Leaving home without consent of parents
- Growing up in idleness or crime
- Participating in behavior that injures or endangers the health, morals, or safety of self or others
- Using vile, obscene, or vulgar language in public
- Entering or visiting a house of ill repute
- Patronizing a place where liquor is sold
- Patronizing a gaming place
- Wandering in the streets at night, not on lawful business (curfew violations)
- Engaging in immoral conduct at school or in other public places
- Smoking cigarettes or using tobacco in any form
- Loitering
- Sleeping in alleys
- Using intoxicating liquor
- Begging
- Running away from a state or charitable institution
- Attempting to marry without consent, in violation of law
- Indulging in sexual irregularities
- Patronizing public pool rooms
- Wandering about railroad yards or tracks
- Jumping a train or entering a train without authority
- Refusing to obey parent or guardian

Critical Thinking Questions:

Which of these offenses do you believe should be defined as delinquent behavior? How many of these behaviors did you engage in when you were a teenager?

FOCUS ON THE OFFENDER 14–2

STATUS OFFENDING

A status offender describes the pressures that various problems place on him. Note the defiance:

They want to stick me in a foster home or something. I told the social worker to forget it. You do that and I'm quitting. I won't do jack shit. No way! If I'm going to be away from my dad and away from the farm, away from my car and all the things I've worked for so far, I won't start over. I just won't.

What does it mean to quit? I don't know, but I don't really want to kill myself. I know that. But if they stick me in a group home or foster home, I'll run. If I keep going back to my home seven or eight times, I think they'll get it in their head that I want to be home.[8]

Critical Thinking Questions:
How would you handle this kid? Is he serious about suicide? Should he be allowed to go home?

provide for their children. These adolescents, whose homes are inadequate or nonexistent, often have not committed any crimes, but they are referred to the juvenile court because there is no other place to send them. They often also have been victims of child abuse.

Dependent and neglected children usually are aware of the unsatisfactory nature of their homes, and, if placed in a foster home, they may resent or even come to hate their parents. Yet many remain hopeful that some day their biological parents will open their arms and homes to them. Frequently such children will run away from a foster placement and return to their parents' home. These youths may become involved in truancy, shoplifting, or other crimes, but they do not consider themselves to be delinquents. They usually blame their problems on lack of parental support or on poor foster parents.

Dependent and neglected children who end up in the juvenile justice system usually have had problems in a number of foster and group homes. The child welfare department, not knowing what to do with them, may turn to the juvenile court and use it as a dumping ground for these "dead endies." A child welfare worker, in Focus on the Offender 14–3, explains why in one case the department had to turn to the juvenile court. The child involved had sex problems and a history of shifting from one home to another.

It is difficult to estimate how many dependent and neglected children are involved in the juvenile justice system. Part of the problem relates to the many different methods of handling these children. For example, forty-one states do not separate dependent and neglected children from delinquents in

FOCUS ON THE OFFENDER 14–3

PLACEMENT

Now we're going downhill. . . . With these tougher kids—hard-to-place kids—you have to place them in a home that may not be the best home, but she [the foster mother] will tolerate him, so he has to be placed there. With a boy like Gino, especially if there are young girls in the family, the foster mother comes to feel he's going to do something to the girls and she can't tolerate it. Hence it becomes almost impossible to find a place that will take the boy.[9]

Critical Thinking Questions:
Why do we have these hard-to-place kids in society? What would you suggest we do with them?

detention facilities, and seventeen states allow these "throwaway children" to be housed with delinquents in juvenile institutions.[10] Some states, such as Illinois, separate the child welfare department from the juvenile court. In other states, juvenile court codes no longer permit the institutionalization of these children.

WHO ARE IRRESPONSIBLE YOUTHS?

Youths classified as irresponsible also do not consider themselves to be delinquent. Naive offenders are included in this category because they lack *mens rea* (criminal intent) or are unable to understand that they have committed an unlawful act. Emotionally disturbed offenders also belong in this category because they find it difficult to control their unlawful impulses.

Naive Offenders

Naive offenders can be divided into three groups of adolescents: youths who are mentally deficient, those who simply are unaware they are violating the law, and those who are naive risk-takers.[11]

Some mentally deficient children have been sent to a state school for the retarded but were then referred to the juvenile justice system because they could not adjust. Others have been referred directly to the justice system because no other resource was available. These youths often had not committed a crime; they were victimized by the fact that no other placement was available. Some mentally deficient children, of course, do break the law. Either alone or with others, they commit serious property and personal crimes.

FOCUS ON THE OFFENDER 14–4

MENTAL DEFICIENCY

One of the authors worked with a naive offender from a rural community in Ohio. He was fishing on a neighbor's property that had signs posted warning against trespassing. This youth with deficient mental skills could not read the signs. Charged with trespassing, the juvenile court adjudicated him as a delinquent, and he was sent to a minimum-security forestry camp. He began a series of institutional runaways that eventually resulted in his being confined with hardened offenders in a maximum-security training school. Not surprisingly, he was a sexual victim in this institutional environment.

Critical Thinking Questions:

Should mentally deficient youths be place in training schools with harder-core delinquents? What should the system do with the mentally deficient?

The number of mentally deficient children processed through the justice system each year is unknown because of the lack of statistics. But even if such statistics were available, a significant problem would arise in identifying these children. Their scores on intelligence tests may vary by several points each time the tests are administered, which makes it difficult to know whether the youths are under or over an arbitrary cutoff point (for example, an I.Q. of 70). See Focus on the Offender 14–4.

Many mentally deficient youths are truly naive offenders, for they do not know when they are doing something wrong. They may suspect that they are doing something wrong, but only on a low level of consciousness. The morals and values of society are not understood by these youths, and, consequently, they are sometimes quite baffled when placed with youthful offenders in the juvenile justice system.

A second group of naive offenders is made up of those of normal intelligence who are simply unaware of the laws they are breaking. For example, one sixteen-year-old boy was having sexual relations with his girlfriend of more than a year when they were caught by her mother. She reported this act to the police, and the young man was charged with statutory rape, was found to be delinquent by the juvenile court, and was sent to the department of youth services. He later reported to his institutional social worker, "I wasn't raping my girlfriend. We had been going together for a year or more. We are going to get married. I wasn't doing nothing wrong. It was just her mother trying to get me."[12]

Another example of a naive offender is a fifteen-year-old male who had never committed a delinquent act before. A friend who had a cool car invited him to go for a ride one night and even asked him to drive. The friend told him to stop at a convenience store and said that he would be right back. He came out shortly thereafter, pulled money out of a sack, and gave the boy what he said was his share. Upon being asked "Why are you giving me this?" the friend said, "I robbed the store. You were out in the car, and you were the driver. You are as much involved in this as I am."[13]

A third group of naive offenders is made up of "naive risk-takers."[14] These youths, according to Thomas Bernard, are naive because "they do not understand that actions have consequences."[15] Without question, many youths are naive in thinking that *their* own actions will not have consequences. They may reason that they will not be caught; even if they are caught, the state cannot prove the case against them; and even if the state could prove its case, the attorney their mother will hire or who is on retainer for the gang will get them off. These youngsters do have *mens rea* and know that what they are doing is illegal, but they refuse to accept the consequences of their actions.

Adolescents can also have naivete in assuming that some larger principle or value is great enough to justify violating the law. One thirteen-year-old boy, who later became a legendary gang leader, was on his way home for supper following a basketball game. Some conflict had occurred on the court, and seemingly out of nowhere, two older teenagers jumped this future gang leader and his friend. They were both badly beaten, and, as they lay on the ground, the two aggressors returned to play more basketball. The thirteen year-old future gang leader quickly came to the decision that he must revenge his respect. He went to a friend's house, got two guns, and brought the guns back; the two younger boys returned to the basketball court and killed their assailants.[16]

Emotionally Disturbed Children

The other type of irresponsible youth is the **emotionally disturbed offender.** The definition of this psychiatric term may vary somewhat, but youths whose emotional problems severely interfere with their everyday functioning and whose behaviors bring them into the justice system are generally included in this broad category. Even if statistics on the number of disturbed youths were available, the vagueness of the term would challenge the validity of such information.

The two most important characteristics of emotionally disturbed offenders are their psychological states and their acting-out behavior, manifested either in persistent behavioral problems or in their involvement in heinous crimes. These youths are labeled emotionally disturbed, prepsychotic, psychotic, or schizophrenic by psychiatrists and clinical psychologists. Psychological evaluations record that they have poor self-concepts, anxiety symptoms, neurotic guilt, little self-awareness, restricted ego capacities, and a high degree of rejection; are unable to control impulses; resist authority; have pathological relationships with family members; have a tendency to act out inadequacies; and have many internal conflicts. See Focus on the Offender 14–12.

Youths with persistent behavioral problems are initially referred to mental health services because they are unable to function in everyday life. They react more negatively than the typical unruly child to the rejection and neglect received at home. They have difficulties relating to and forming friendships with peers. In short, the community looks upon them as a nuisance and sometimes as a danger. They usually are referred for outpatient care in a community mental health facility and may spend some time as patients in psychiatric hospitals. During treatment, they probably receive tranquilizers and are exposed to various types of psychiatric intervention, psychological testing, and casework methods.

Middle-class youths, especially white females, are overrepresented in the category of emotionally disturbed offenders. Instead of being placed in juvenile correctional institutions, they frequently are placed in the mental health system. A few of these emotionally disturbed youths do commit violent and shocking crimes that seem totally out of character. They previously had not been troublemakers; indeed, they may have done well in school, been active in the church and scouts, and been considered fine young people by the community. Nevertheless, these juveniles apparently had been full of repressed rage, and they unleash it one day toward a parent, a sibling, a neighbor, a teacher, or a schoolmate. See Focus on the Offender 14–5.

These youths often do not know what to make of their own behavior. It is, of course, much easier for an adolescent to explain away behavioral problems than it is to dismiss a violent crime. Consequently, disturbed youths who have committed violent crimes frequently react by repressing and denying their actions. Even when there is proof that a youth killed a parent or a friend, the disturbed child may deal with it by blotting it from memory and detaching himself or herself from the event. But such youths seem to be filled with confusion and self-doubt over what they have done. One youth verbalized this when he said, "I don't know why I did that. I hope that I'm not crazy like my father."[19]

Emotionally disturbed youths appear to be distinguished from noncriminal youths by an internal force that causes them to lose control. They are, then, capable of committing horrible and bizarre crimes because they lack internal controls. Neither the disturbed youth nor other types of noncriminal youths, however, perceive themselves to be delinquent or are committed to crime as a way of life. Personal problems, rather than a desire for gain or the wish to please peers, are generally the reason for their presence in the justice system.

WHO ARE SITUATIONAL OFFENDERS?

Neither do **situational offenders** normally look upon themselves as committed to youth crime. They do drift in and out of crime because of boredom, group pressure, or financial need. Yet, except for occasional excursions into

FOCUS ON THE OFFENDER 14–5

EMOTIONAL DISTURBANCE

One example is a junior in high school from an upper-class background who had no previous offenses when she drowned in a bathtub the two children she was baby sitting. When questioned about it, she had no memory of the incident. Another example is a ten-year-old boy who killed both parents after they had repeatedly exposed him to sex acts and pornographic literature. He was diagnosed as suffering from an acute schizophrenic reaction.[17]

Another youth was considered an ideal young man. His teachers thought very highly of him, he had never been in any trouble with the law, and he seemed to have a happy home life. Yet he took a shotgun, shot his parents repeatedly, and then quartered them. The community was shocked. How could this quiet, well-mannered youth from a good middle-class home do such a thing? In working with him, it became abundantly clear to the counselor why he had exploded. Although he had always been polite and compliant, he had been full of rage against his parents. One night he simply lost control of himself. Typical of youngsters who kill their parents, he then repressed the event and dissociated himself from the crime.[18]

Critical Thinking Questions:

Can you think of any ways to reduce the number of mentally ill children in society? Should potential parents be required to undergo parenting classes?

the deviant world, these youths remain law-abiding. But let there be no question about it: They can become involved in serious antisocial behavior such as armed robbery, burglary, auto theft, rape, and even homicide.

David Matza has developed the drift hypothesis to explain the behavior of these youths. The "bind of law," according to Matza, has to be neutralized before the juvenile offender is put into drift. Following the act of giving himself or herself the "moral holiday implicit in drift," the offender must learn from others that the crime is something that is fairly easy to do. Once juveniles are successfully involved in law-violating behavior, they probably have the ability to repeat the crime. Thus, Matza believes that the situational offender is in limbo between convention and crime; influenced by the group, he evades decision and commitment.[20]

Situational offenders may be middle-class adolescents who are simply bored and seeking new thrills. They therefore become involved in drinking, the use of marijuana and other drugs, sexual activity, and destruction of property. Lower-class situational offenders may be on the periphery of gangs or may come from extremely deprived areas. The former tend to commit crimes to gain acceptance of peers, while the latter most often steal to eat, to have clothes, and to have a little money in their pockets. Situational offenses range from armed robbery, burglary, and battery to petty theft, joyriding, and malicious mischief.

Situational offenders seem to be dependent on the peer group. Whether they are affluent middle-class youths destroying property just for kicks, adolescents involved in a drug culture, or lower-class juveniles robbing a liquor store, the group very much influences their behavior. This emotional hold enables them to neutralize the "bind of law," to develop the necessary fatalistic feeling to commit a new infraction, and to activate the will to repeat a crime.[21]

Situational offenders continue to drift in and out of lawbreaking until one of several things happens. They may outgrow the desire to commit crime. They grow up and begin to assume the responsibilities of adults—college, work, marriage, and family. Or they may be apprehended by the police and processed by the juvenile courts; this may either deter them from future antisocial behavior or it may be the start of their being labeled delinquent or bad kids. Evidence exists that youths who are processed by the system and labeled delinquent are apt to continue their negative behavior. Youths who choose to live up to their labels have passed the threshold from situational to chronic offender.

Property Offenders

The majority of property offenders are situational offenders and can be divided into two groups: (1) those who commit only minor property offenses; and (2) those who commit more frequent and more serious property offenses.

Middle-class teenagers often find themselves under suspicion of alcohol or drug-related offenses. (Photo by Stuart Miller.)

FOCUS ON THE OFFENDER 14–6

MINOR PROPERTY CRIMES

A seventeen-year-old, in a fairly representative statement, noted:

We used to do a lot of shit a few years ago. We would break into houses for the hell of it. I remember one time we burned a barn down. On Halloween, we really used to do a lot of stuff, like doing a lot of damage to the houses of people we didn't like. But we never got caught. My parents had no idea what we were doing. I don't do that kind of thing anymore. I plan to go to college next year.[22]

Critical Thinking Questions:

What kinds of things did you do as a kid? What should be done with the kid in the Box? What should have been done with you?

Offenders in the first group are influenced by their peers, tend to have some involvement with alcohol and drug use, and are not specialists in their offenses. This first group also generally is committed more to conforming values than to delinquent values. These youths occasionally become involved in serious property offenses, such as burglary, breaking and entering, auto theft, and arson, but they typically commit minor offenses, for example, destruction of private and school property, vandalism, and "joy-riding." Middle-class offenders are more heavily represented in the first group of property offenders than in the second group, and generally their offenses either do not come to the attention of the authorities or are diverted to nonjudicial agencies. In addition, the offenses of the first group tend to be less goal-oriented than those of the second group. See Focus on the Offender 14–6.

The second group of property offenders seems to have more commitment to delinquency than the first group; that is, these youths appear to be more involved in the spirit of delinquency and to be more alienated from social norms. They also are more deeply involved in drug and alcohol use than are youths in the first group. Furthermore, although their offenses include both minor and serious property offenses, they are more frequently involved in serious property crimes than are juveniles in the first group. In addition, their delinquent behavior tends to be more purposeful than that of those in the first group; they may break into a store simply because they need spending money. The second group of property offenders is more likely than the first group to commit an occasional violent offense. Lower-class offenders tend to be overrepresented in the second group, and, not surprisingly, their more serious offenses are more likely to result in arrest

FOCUS ON THE OFFENDER 14–7

MAJOR PROPERTY CRIMES

A male who appears to fall into this group asserted:

We robbed one place and got $140 cash, and they didn't know about that. We stole $3,000 worth of postage stamps and sold them for $1,000. We ripped off the truck when we stole the stamps. I used the parts for my car. They think I'm a small punk who goes around and takes rinky dink stuff, but the big jobs, I plan them out.[23]

Critical Thinking Questions:

How does this youth's behavior differ from that of the youth in Box 14.6? Should he be on probation? Institutionalized? What?

by the police and a punitive disposition by the court. See Focus on the Offender 14–7.

VIOLENT OFFENDERS

The cohort studies, as stated in Chapter 2, report that **chronic offenders** are more likely to be involved in violent acts than other youthful offenders.[24] Yet, even among chronic offenders, violent offenses are still infrequent in number and seem to be based on an incident taking place in youths' lives.[25] The Columbus cohort study, which examined the records of Columbus, Ohio, juveniles who were born in the years 1956 through 1960 and had been arrested for a violent offense, found that with this group, nonviolent offenses accounted for nearly 70 percent of the reported offenses.[26] Donna Martin Hamparian and colleagues also found that violent offenders as a group did not specialize in the types of crimes committed.[27]

A significant number of violent offenses, including homicides, take place in incidents arising in the lives of those who are first-time offenders or who have very little history of delinquent behaviors. An example is the four midwestern juveniles who took a Chevy Blazer belonging to one of their parents to run away to Canada. None of the four had convictions for more than minor delinquent acts, such as vandalism and smoking marijuana, but one of the youths shot a woman with a .22 rifle they had brought along and then stabbed her thirty-one times.[28]

Clearly, first-time violent offenders (or those with minimal delinquent history) and chronic offenders typically have quite different attitudes toward violence. Chronic offenders who commit acts of violence tend to be lower-class or underclass and frequently are members of a minority. They were

FOCUS ON THE OFFENDER 14–8

VIOLENT CRIMES

A young person who grows up in a ghetto knows that it is necessary to "take care of business if anyone messes with them." This means that it will be necessary to use violent means as a recourse if anyone attempts to violate them in any way. This attitude is illustrated in the comments of several chronic offenders: One said, "I will knife anyone who gets in my way. I've done it before, and I'll do it again."[30] Another, who had made his rounds raping college females on weekends said, "We went around for a couple years on weekends raping college girls. We would drive around the campus, find a girl walking alone, and force her in the car. It was one big blast."[31] A third reported, "We got into robbing stores. One time this guy went for a gun, and I filled his stomach with lead. Man, it was real cool."[32]

Critical Thinking Questions:

What are appropriate "system" reactions to these youths? In this and in previous boxes, are these specific youths who should be dealt with by the balanced and restorative justice model? The medical model? The crime control model? The due process model? What approach would you use with them?

introduced to violence at a young age. A group of gang members told one of the authors that they all had guns pointed at them before they were ten, and most of the group had guns pointed at their heads before they were ten.[29] See Focus on the Offender 14–8.

In contrast, first-time offenders—who may be middle-class or lower-class—usually commit violent acts in an emotional reaction to a stressful situation. They frequently repress this incident and sometimes find it hard to believe that they did it. At other times, they admit that they did it, but it just seems like a bad dream to them.

In another example of a first-time offense, a seventeen-year-old and a friend went shopping in a nearby town. When they left the shopping center and were walking to the car, they both saw a girl they knew. They stopped to talk with her, and two other boys showed up. One of the two got into an argument about the girl with the seventeen-year-old (who played football and was well built). One thing led to another, and the seventeen-year-old struck the rival male in the head. The youth collapsed from the blow and died before he arrived at the hospital. The perpetrator of this act was a White male from a middle-class background who had no delinquent history.

We know a great deal about trends in juvenile homicides. For example, juvenile violent acts appear, for the most part, to be occasional occurrences within a random pattern of delinquent behavior, rather than a "specialty" of juveniles. When committing a violent act, including murder, a youthful offender is more likely to do so in the company of at least one other juvenile than to do so alone. We know that at least 85 percent of juveniles who kill are fifteen, sixteen, or seventeen years of age. Only a small percentage of juveniles kill their parents or stepparents, and only a slightly larger percentage kill other family members. Many juvenile murders take place during the commission of other crimes, and such killings involve weapons such as guns and knives.[33]

WHAT CATEGORIES MAKE UP DRUG AND ALCOHOL USERS?

As indicated by the statistics in Chapter 2, drug use in this country is pervasive and increasing among young people. One group of juveniles includes experimental users; they are curious about drugs and occasionally use them to test the effects. Another group consists of social or recreational users who occasionally take drugs to socialize with friends. In a third group are youths who spend considerable time and money obtaining drugs, and these substances play an important role in the users' lives. Despite heavy and regular use, however, adolescents in this group are still functional and able to meet social and academic responsibilities. The lives of juveniles in a fourth group are dominated by drugs, and the process of securing and using drugs interferes with their everyday functioning. These four groups fit into two clusters: (1) social or recreational users and (2) those whose lives are dominated by drugs—addicts. Some of these are plagued by internal demons. See Focus on the Offender 14–9.

The skinhead with this swastika on his leg was arrested for holding up a restaurant with other skinheads to raise money for their cause.
(Photo courtesy of the North Franklin Police, Washington, Pennsylvania.)

FOCUS ON THE OFFENDER 14–9

DRUGS AND ALCOHOL

My first attempt at easing my inner turmoil with drugs happened when I was in eighth grade. Mom was under a doctor's care for several conditions at the time, and her medicine cabinet housed a row of prescription vials. I knew one of them contained tranquilizers, a pill that could calm you down. My problem was that none of the bottles *said* "tranquilizer." The solution? Try them all, one at a time, until I found the one that made me feel relaxed. Fortunately, I couldn't swallow pills and so had to chew them instead. Chomping down on what I now believe was one of Mom's iron pills, I grimaced, spat, and aborted my mission immediately.

On and on, year, after year, I figured out new ways to buffer the unnamed fear that lived inside me. Surprisingly, though, in terms of alcohol assumption, I was a "late bloomer." I drank my first beer the night I graduated from high school. I liked the effect and drank another, and another, and another. By the time I started college in the fall, I was well acquainted with alcohol-fueled oblivion. For the next seventeen years, "using" was the most important element of my life.

Brenda Medina, "Hell, and How I Got Here" in *Wally Lamb and the Women Of York Correctional Institution.* (United States of America: Regan Books, 2003), pp. 131–132. Reprinted by permission.

Critical Thinking Questions:

"Just say no" is a common saying when it comes to drugs. Will that approach work? Why or why not? Under what conditions will it or will it not work? If this user was a friend of yours, what would you say to her? Would you turn in a friend of yours if you believed you could help him or her? Where would you go for help?

Social or Recreational Users

Adolescents generally prefer substances that are not too costly. Beer and marijuana meet this criterion better than hard drugs do. Availability and potency are also important in drug use, for these substances are likely to be used as means to other ends, especially for achieving excitement. For example, marijuana, alcohol, and other drugs used at football games, rock concerts, parties, outings, dances, and similar activities provide additional excitement already inherent in such activities or, in some cases, produce excitement when it seems to be lacking. In addition to excitement, experience enhancing substances serve the purpose of exploration. They enable the youth to experience new social orbits, mating relations, and unfamiliar places. Narcotic substances are further used to escape or retreat from the external world into an inner and private self.

The fact is that drug and alcohol use among American adolescents is increasing with no good news on the horizon. Alcohol use is continuing to rise among *all* American adolescents, rich as well as poor, nonoffenders as well as offenders. It constitutes a serious social problem that currently is attracting national attention. More bad news is that the use of marijuana has experienced a major increase among American adolescents in the past decade.[34]

Addicts

Too many adolescents' lives are dominated by drugs. Many of these drug dependent youths need speed in the morning, and they require speed in school to make it through the day. Others become intoxicated several evenings a week and may even drink at school. Still others use so much marijuana that they become known to their peers as "pot heads." Even sadder, other youths, especially high-risk ones, have become addicted to crack cocaine. They are likely not to be unable to give up this addiction even if they become pregnant. Further, drug dependent youths typically are multiple drug users.

The factors that make a youth high risk for later substance abuse include the following:

1. Early initiation: use of any substance by the age of ten or twelve.
2. School problems: low expectation that school will be a positive experience, low grades, disruptive behavior in school, and truancy
3. Family problems: lack of parental support and guidance
4. Peer influences: relationships with peers who use substances and an inability to resist their influences
5. Personality: nonconformism, rebellion, or a strong sense of independence[35]

Delbert Elliott and David Huizinga reported that nearly 50 percent of hard-core juvenile offenders were multiple drug users and that 82 percent of these offenders reported use of at least one illegal substance.[36] Indeed, those who work with juvenile offenders argue that rarely is a youth institutionalized or placed on probation who does not have some history of alcohol or narcotics abuse.[37] As one director of guidance noted, "We only have one or two youths a year admitted to this institution who don't have a problem with substance abuse."[38]

The use of drugs, especially on a daily basis, increases the likelihood that a youth will be arrested and referred to the juvenile justice system. Other short-term consequences are vulnerability to other drugs, loss of interest in school, and impaired psychological functioning. Long-term consequences include respiratory problems, drug dependence, chronic depression and fatigue, and social and financial problems. A long-term risk of taking intravenous drugs today is AIDS (acquired immunodeficiency syndrome).[39]

WHO ARE CHRONIC OFFENDERS?

The chronic offender is known by many labels: serious delinquent, repeat offender, violent offender, dangerous offender, hard-core delinquent, and career delinquent. Whatever the label, the predominant characteristics of these youths are their commitment to crime and their involvement in one crime after another, often very serious crimes against persons and property. Their initial participation in crime constitutes the budding of a lifestyle centered on violence and "making it big" in the criminal world. Chronic offenders expect to engage in criminal careers for at least several years, if not for the rest of their lives.

Chronic offenders become committed to criminal careers through one of two routes. In the first, noncriminal and situational offenders move from casual involvement with other offenders on the streets, to being processed with them through the system, to perceiving crime as a way of life, and finally to being willing to stand up for this involvement. Usually these youths have been picked up by the police many times, have been in courts and detention halls several times, and have had one or more institutional stays. The decisions they make at each stage move them closer to a delinquent career.

The second route is quite different. Some youths become absorbed in crime before they have contact with the justice system. These offenders often grow up in a ghetto area and, surrounded by vice and crime, become involved with peers in unlawful acts at an early age. Frequently, they come from impoverished families. They tend to feel that life is a struggle and that only the strong survive; therefore, they are always on guard against being hurt or exploited by others, and they develop a hostile and suspicious view of the world around them. They seem to accept a commitment to crime without any apparent episodes of decision making.

Chronic offenders typically come from lower-class backgrounds and in many cases have grown up in urban pockets of poverty. They most often are minority males who have lived on the streets with insufficient parental support and with a history of failure in social institutions. An inability to function in school either in acceptable academic performance or in satisfactory relationship with teachers and peers characterizes their school experiences. A history of school drop-out is followed by a pattern of unemployment. Part of this inability to find jobs is the lack of marketable skills. These juveniles contribute to the disturbing high rates of unemployment among urban African Americans. See Focus on the Offender 14–10.

The attitudes of chronic offenders, of course, do vary. Some are more bitter or angry than others, and this variation seems to be affected greatly by the

FOCUS ON THE OFFENDER 14–10

CHRONICITY

The attitudes of chronic offenders, especially by the time they are institutionalized, typically can be grouped into several clusters. First, there are attitudes regarding how they see the world as a fearful place, a survival of the fittest where only the strong make it. Chronic offenders commonly express this attitude in such statements as the following.

Man, you're to get them before they get you."

"It is every dog for yourself."

"Weak people are just begging you to get over them."

"I know I may get killed selling drugs, but look at the money I can make."

Second, there are attitudes that reflect a hedonistic but frustrated struggle:

"Don't worry about tomorrow; do your thing today."

"I got tired of being hungry, man."

"My parents didn't have nothing to give me, and so I went to the streets and did my thing."

Third, there are attitudes showing a macho approach to life:

"Be cool."

"Do what is necessary to maintain your image of toughness."

"Never back down."

Finally, there are attitudes concerning the basic unfairness of life:

"The system has always messed over me."

"The cops are out to get me."

"I never had a chance in school."

"You can't trust nobody in life."

Critical Thinking Questions:

What could be done to change the offenders' attitudes? Where would *you* start?

amount of love and acceptance they received at home and the injustices they have experienced. In addition, some chronic offenders have more hope than others. Youths with histories of drug addiction generally do not demonstrate the positive attitudes of those without such histories. Chronic offenders who are closest to institutional release, not surprisingly, are more hopeful than those who face long periods of confinement. Chronic offenders who have developed positive goals for the future are also more hopeful than those who lack such goals. Finally, the more that chronic offenders see life as a "give me" experience, the less they seem able to develop positive relationships with others or to pursue noncrime options.

Several studies have examined the delinquent careers of chronic offenders. Sheldon and Eleanor Glueck drew this conclusion from the follow-up of juvenile delinquent careers: "With the passing of the years there was . . . both a decline in criminality and a decrease in the seriousness of the offenses of those who continued to commit crimes."[40] Marvin Wolfgang, Terence Thornberry, and Robert Figlio's follow-up of a sample of Cohort I found that there was a substantial drop in offensive behavior from the juvenile to the adult period. In this regard, more than half the one-time delinquents (62.4 percent) and the two-time delinquents (55 percent) were never arrested as adults. Furthermore, 45.4 percent of the juveniles arrested three times and 31.8 percent of the juveniles arrested four times were nonoffenders during adulthood.[41] Many official juvenile offenders, then, desisted from offending during their adult years; still, one of the most pertinent findings from this study is "that nondelinquent careers were likely to be followed by noncriminal careers, and delinquent careers were likely to be followed by criminal careers."[42]

Similar to the behavior of other juvenile offenders, the desistance of chronic offenders seems to be strongly related to the maturation process. As they approach the ages of sixteen to eighteen, chronic offenders who desist, or exit from crime, appear to be motivated either by the desirability of pursuing a conventional lifestyle or by the undesirability of continuing unlawful behaviors. The ties to conventional lifestyles are greater for those who have an interest in marrying, in raising a family, in joining the military, or in making their families proud of them.[43]

Chronic juvenile offenders are often involved in prostitution, sex crimes, and street gangs. What prostitution and gang membership have in common is that juveniles may continue these forms of behaviors into adulthood.

WHO ARE JUVENILE SEX OFFENDERS AND WHAT DO WE KNOW ABOUT THEM?

Violent sex crimes often shape the public's perception of sex offenders and sex offending. The view that immediately comes to mind is that of an adult male who by force, guile, or cunning persuades a young person to perform sexual acts deemed inappropriate or illegal by society.[44] These images of adult offenders are assumed to be true of all youthful sex offenders as well; the result is pressure is put on legislators to "pass a law" that somehow will punish youthful sex offenders severely and that will deter others from committing sex offenses. (See Focus on the Law 14.11.) Adolescents who are "growing up," learning how to develop age-appropriate relationships and assimilating the rules of society often become surprised victims of overzealous citizens, legislators, and prosecutors. Given this perspective, just what is the reality of juvenile sex offending, and how accurate is the imagery?

The Uniform Crime Reports indicate that of 17,914 arrests for forcible rape committed in the year 2000, eleven hundred forty-two or 6 percent were

FOCUS ON THE LAW 14–11

THE TEEN SEX OFFENDER

The victims of sex offenders frequently are scarred for life. Coercive or violent rape by family members, friends, serial offenders or members of the same sex devastates victims emotionally. In addition to the physical pain and suffering they experience, these victims wrestle with depression, sleepless nights, and fear of others; many are never able to form normal emotional relationships with others they love. These reasons alone are sufficient to incur society's wrath, but when murder accompanies the act, members of society become particularly incensed, and legislators succumb willingly to public pressures to take up the charge for action. Often knee-jerk reactions take the place of reason and the laws that are passed have unintended consequences.

Teenage boys often are the unwitting victims of legislators' zeal. Not that what the boys do is right, but consider the following: sixteen- and seventeen-year-old boys frequently have sex with their fourteen- and fifteen-year-old girl friends—both of whom intend to marry each other. Some youths engage in "heavy" petting and sexual experimentation with members of the opposite sex on dates. In one case, a boy was dared by his friends at a football game to touch a girl's breast. He did and he, along with the other youths noted above, are now considered sex offenders by their state.

The consequences of this required registration are enormous. Some of these youths may be tried in juvenile or adult courts and remanded to juvenile or adult institutions. They are placed on extended supervision when they get out. Their names are kept on police "watch" lists. People living in their neighborhoods or parents who have children in schools will not want them anywhere near them. The "offenders'" names may be published on informal sex offender lists on the internet and be available to all. Many states publish formal lists and may require youths to register for periods of time ranging from ten to twenty-five years to life. These youths will be unable to get into the military or obtain private security jobs; they cannot become doctors, nurses, school teachers, scout masters, band directors or coach youth sports teams; some companies will not hire them. The youths are labeled for life.

Source: Prepared for this volume by the authors.

Critical Thinking Questions:

In your opinion, is justice served concerning sex offenders? What should be done with boys responding to dares or having sex with their girl friends? Develop a system of classification for sex offenders.

of youths under the age of fifteen and that 2,937 or 16 percent were under the age of eighteen. Of the arrests for "other" sex offenses, 5,933 or 9.7 percent were of youths under the age of fifteen, and 11,399 or 18.6 percent were of youths eighteen or younger.[45] But do these figures account for all points of juvenile sex offending?

An accurate answer to this question is unknown. Much juvenile sexual behavior is concealed in the confines of family, community, and school and remains hidden. Even if discovered, children, parents, and teachers may be confused as to what "really" happened and are often ashamed or embarrassed by their own behavior and by that of their own children, relations, and family friends. Many victims will not report sexual victimization because they believe they deserved what happened, feel guilty, do not want to get others in trouble, or somehow believe that what happened was "normal." Yet, the victims often end up psychologically distraught and damaged; sleeplessness, anxiety, depression, sexual dysfunction, and suicide can result. Damaged emotions and fear destroy their ability to form lasting relationships, and many victims' marriages are filled with violence or do not last. The cost to individuals and society often is perpetuated because many imprisoned adolescent and adult sex offenders report having been abused as youths. The cost of a sex offense early in life often extends into adulthood.

Are all sex offenders alike? No. Their relationships with each other and their personal motives vary widely, making them a diverse lot. The offending behaviors range from noncontact offenses such as voyeurism and exhibitionism to contact offenses such as touching and fondling to sexual penetration with body parts or foreign objects. Most sex offenders also commit nonsexual offenses at rates similar to those of other juvenile offenders. For example, children who experience neglect and physical abuse and who witness family violence are more likely to commit sexual offenses than those who have not, although at an only modestly higher rate.[46] Also, sex offenders who have had prior consensual sexual experiences have higher rates of offending than those without such experience.

In addition to early sexual experience, offenders tend to come from families that are either unstable or dysfunctional, that is, families with problems of neglect or physical, emotional, or sexual abuse.[47] These backgrounds appear to be related to juvenile sex offenders having deficient social skills, relationships with their peers, and being socially isolated. Ferrara and McDonald, in a review of the literature, estimated that one-quarter to one-third of sex offenders have some form of neurological impairment.[48] Other studies document conduct disorder and antisocial traits in juvenile sex offenders. A limited number of studies suggest that pornography plays some role in juvenile offending.[49]

Importantly, a study by Ryan et al., determined that only one-third of juvenile offenders perceive sex as a way to show love and support to another person; 24 percent perceive that sex is a way to feel power and control; 9.4 percent, as a way to get rid of anger; and 8.4 percent, as a means to hurt, degrade, or punish others.[50]

Can Offenders be Classified?

The heterogeneity of sex offenders is problematic to therapists as well as lawmakers. To treat offenders individually is very expensive and time consuming so experts attempt to group offenders into typologies to facilitate residential placement and individual treatment.

Graves analyzed 140 samples containing 16,000 juvenile sex offenders and derived three typologies.[51] *Pedophilic offenders,* who typically molest girls usually at least three years younger than themselves, tend to be socially isolated and lack social confidence. *Sexual assaultists* typically victimize their peers or older females, whereas an *undifferentiated group* commit heterogeneous offenses against victims who vary widely in ages. Undifferentiated offenders engage in hands-off offenses against victims who vary widely in ages; these offenses include exhibitionism and voyeurism as well as deviant arousal. Compared with the other two groups, these latter youths tend to come more frequently from dysfunctional families, are more antisocial with more social and psychological problems and were younger when they began their abusive behavior.

A study by Prentky et al. developed a logically derived system of six categories. Of the major groupings in their sample, 69 percent were child molesters; 12.5 percent, rapists; and 6.25 percent, unclassifiable. Prentky also identified age patterns that differentiated between the offenders and their victims. Other studies found similar results.[52] Becker and Kaplan classify offenders into three categories according to the offender's social skills, family relationships and social environmental factors: these factors may result in the offenders' graduation to further crime, to delinquency or to continued sexual offending.[53] These categories include those who stop offending, continue on a delinquent path, or continue on a sexual interest path, including continued sex offending and often developing deviant sexual arousal patterns. Knight and Prentky studied the difference between adult sex offenders and juvenile sex offenders and found that adults who began offending as juveniles tended to exhibit low social competence, compulsivity, and antisocial behavior. The conclusion these authors draw is that classification schemes developed for adults might be appropriate for juveniles as well.[54] O'Brien and Bera's sevenfold typology includes naive experimenters, undersocialized child exploiters, sexual aggressiveness, sexual compulsion, disturbed impulses, group influences, and the pseudosocialized.[55]

Do Females Commit Sex Offenses?

Yes, some do. But studies of female sex offending are relatively rare and based on insufficient sample sizes. Lane and Lobanov-Rostovsky suggest that females are responsible generally for between 2 and 3 percent of all sex offenses.[56] Righthand et al. found 11 percent of Maine sex offenders were females.[57] English and Ray, studying the Vermont Social Rehabilitation Center Services contend that females account for 8 percent of identified sexual offenders and also found that 9.3 percent of offenders over thirteen years of age were female.[58] Johnson suggests that 21.6 percent of girls between four and twelve years of age who had engaged in inappropriate sexual behavior had been sexually abusive.[59] Most female offenders, 94 percent, were victims of abuse themselves as compared with 85 percent of males; girls also were more likely than boys to have experienced victimization by multiple forms of abuse.[60]

How Do We Treat Sex Offenders?

The "sexual abuse cycle" is referred to frequently throughout the sex offender literature. The assumption behind the concept is that sex offenders engage in a pattern of emotional and thinking processes that lead them to sex offending and which must be broken if offenders are to be helped with their problems. Righthand and Welch describe the cycle as follows:

> The concept is based on the premise that offending is preceded by a negative self-image that contributes to negative coping strategies when the juvenile anticipates negative responses from others, perceives such responses, or both. To avoid such negative anticipated or perceived reactions, the juvenile withdraws, becomes socially isolated, and fantasizes to compensate for resulting feelings of powerlessness and a lack of control. This process culminates in the sex offense, which results in more negative experiences, more feelings of rejection and an increasingly negative self-image; and the cycle continues.

This model is not empirically based and has several limitations. Much abusive behavior such as that committed by "naive experimenters," nonrecidivists, group offenders, and youths who suffer from psychopathological or deviant sexual arousal do not fit easily into the stages of this cycle.

The treatment goals of many programs for sex offenders include breaking the sex offense cycle. Youths are encouraged to assume responsibility for their abusive behavior and to increase their positive and constructive behaviors in both thinking and relations to others. These goals are designed to prevent further sexual misconduct, the emergence of psychosexual problems, and, conversely, to help youths develop appropriate relationships with peers of their own age. Therapists attempt to achieve these goals through individual, group and family interventions. See Focus on the Offender 14–12.

Prostitutes

Teenage prostitution is one form of chronic offending in which females are more involved than males. Although it is difficult to measure the number of youths who are actually involved in prostitution, estimates have ranged from tens of thousands to 2.4 million children annually. It is likely that there are between 100,000 and 300,000 juvenile prostitutes per year.[61]

Mimi S. Silbert and Ayala M. Pines found that 60 percent of the street prostitutes they interviewed had been sexually abused as juveniles.[62]

FOCUS ON THE OFFENDER 14–12

SEXUAL DEVIANCY

A Worst Case Scenario

The following interview was with Domenick A. Lombardo, former Supervisor of Psychological Services, Youth Development Center at New Castle, Pennsylvania.

SM: Let's take a kid who comes in, a severe case. What would he be like in terms of behavior, in terms of morbidity, in terms of psychological problems, in terms of need for cognitive behavioral therapy or chemical therapy? Give us an example.

DL: Here's a seventeen-year-old Caucasian male, with extensive history of psychiatric hospitalization. Although his criminal history is rather mild, he comes to YDC and is committed to a project for emotionally disturbed as a result of aggressive behavior and a result of sexual acting-out; they ask us to evaluate him.

My first concern is whether there is a history. I'm looking for a history of mental illness, a history of drug and alcohol abuse, a history of criminal behavior, because that has something to do in terms of offending. In this kid's case, his extended families also are positive for mental illness on both the mother's and father's sides, including both drug and alcohol abuse.

SM: And by mental illness again you are talking about . . .?

DL: Could be any type of mental illness—could be depression, generalized anxiety disorder, bipolar disorder, schizophrenia, any mental illness.

SM: Does that make a difference in terms of what the kid's going to end up having as to which mental illness that his parents might have? In other words, in terms of the kid's own morbidity?

DL: Oh yes. There's predictive value for problems such as depression and attention deficit hyperactivity disorder. And naturally we are well aware of the biological predisposition for addiction. This person initially was diagnosed with recurrent severe major depression, without psychotic features, learning disability and arrested development, and Pervasive Developmental Disorder. Very obese, anxious, and a history of heart murmur.

SM: Had he been sexually abused?

DL: Let me get to that. The psychosocial factors that are important in looking at this really have to do with abandonment—no contact with father. Placements, frequent changes in schools, ongoing psychiatric and behavior problems. Also, multiple diagnosis was diagnosed after that with Asperger syndrome, bipolar disorder, ADHD [attention deficit/hyperactivity disorder], and oppositional disorder. Most recently, when he came to our facility, our consulting psychiatrists basically saw him with dysthymic disorder, attention deficit/hyperactivity disorder, and generalized anxiety disorder. So now we have all this going on and they ask us to do an evaluation and we do that.

So he was interviewed by me and a staff psychologist who works for me. By the way, this kid was maintained on 500 mg of Depakote and also Adderall at the time of testing. He was rather unkempt, overweight, periods of fidgeting, moving around in the chair shaking his legs, affect relatively flat, very restricted, and a long history of suicide attempts, although he denied this at the time. I focused my inquiry at that time on his sexual history, because this is what we're looking at. He talked about learning about sex when he was five years old.

SM: This is more than kids' normal experimentation?

DL: He was actually molested by a couple of female neighbors, but most of his acting out behavior was in institutions; he was in and out of institutions. He basically acted out sexually with other boys.

SM: Did he act out sexually in the community?

DL: Yes he did. He acted out sexually in the community too. He believes he was molested by his parents when he was a little baby; however, he didn't have a personal recollection of that, that's something we just talked about.

SM: Male or female?

DL: Didn't say. He said he was frequently neglected and exposed to high-risk situations. He said he learned masturbatory behavior in placement. He said that he would frequently get involved with kids and they would have group types of masturbation. Denied any previous intercourse with a female—strictly males.

SM: Had he been the victim of violence himself?

DL: He was also a victim of violence.

SM: What kinds of violence?

DL: He was threatened with violence and raped.

SM: Was he institutionalized at the time?

DL: He was victimized in two other placements by other adolescents.

SM: Had he ever been the subject of violence in the family or community?

DL: He was physically abused.

SM: How about the mother and father relationship, was it extremely violent?

DL: The mother and father relationship—the father wasn't there, he was completely absent and the mother was an addict. He says he was exposed to high-risk situations. One can assume that knowing addiction, with the people coming in and out of the house, that he was exposed to a chaotic environment.

SM: OK, now you mentioned three drugs that he's on when he comes to you. What do you do with this kid?

DL: The first thing is we know he's a severe threat to act out sexually. What he did in placement was learn to associate violence with sex. He was exposed to these behaviors; impulsive young boys in placement would make comments. He admits to rape fantasies. He also admitted to frequent thoughts about rape fantasies.

SM: This is what you consider to be the deviant sexual arousal?

DL: Exactly. He began to verbalize threats of rape toward the African-American female staff when he was down there.

Now what happens with him is that we do the evaluation and identify these problems. We use everything from MMPI to projective drawings; I'm not going to get into details of all these, but there are significant mental health problems. What this all shakes down to is that we have the Abel assessment for sexual interest being positive for preschool females, grade-school females, adolescent females, preschool males, grade school males, adolescent males, adult males. Then there's reported self-arousal to preschool boys, grade school boys. So we have Visual Reaction Time (VRT) scores that are very positive.

SM: So where do you start?

DL: Let's go diagnostically. Diagnostically we see him as conduct disorder, adolescent onset. Type, attention deficit/hyperactivity disorder. Dysthymic disorder is very frequent in terms of criminal behavior with paraphilias, you see a lot of learning disorders, and we diagnose him on Axis 2 with Pervasive Developmental Disorder—NOS by history. Now, what do we want to do with him? We know that the kid is sexually inappropriate towards staff—we know there's danger toward staff. We also know that he has a history of perpetrating against young males, and that he has deviant sexual interests by his own admission, and also by interviewing him. So he's not hiding anything. Basically it all gets progressively more and more out of control. So what we do here, we say, relative to his inappropriateness with objective findings related to sustained sexual interests in children, we say that this kid needs a specific protocol of treatment—sex offense specific treatment.

SM: Why is he going more and more out of control?

DL: He is in an environment with which he is comfortable and is very stimulating. What he's learned to do is have intercourse and sexually act out with males in placement.

SM: Continues if he gets into the community?

DL: And it continues as he gets out into the community. So he's learned this is the place! So here's your main approach to a kid like this. First, you have to appreciate the fact that the person has a mental illness—he's mentally ill. You have to educate him about his mental illness and you have to assist him in becoming stable. Because what's going to happen is the depression will exacerbate the sexual acting out. Second, we know that the kid has been dysthymic for a lot of years, we know he has a history of sexual abuse, so we are going to hypothesize that when this kid begins to feel bad about himself and more and more depressed, then people are more and more at risk. So we need to make sure that we stabilize him and that's done through individual and group cognitive behavioral therapy, that's also done pharmacologically—specific to mental health issues. Thus, we have a person with multiple paraphilias. So now this person has to be exposed to a protocol of treatment which will address his deviant sexual urges and deviant fantasies as necessary to prevent sexual reoffending. He has to address the issues related to emotional and sexual self-regulation.

SM: Can part of this obsessiveness be because of compulsive obsessive-type of disorder or addictive thinking as a result of serotonin imbalances?

DL: No, the literature does not specifically come out and say this.

Now, there is an OCD (obsessive compulsive disorder) spectrum that a lot of people believe some of the paraphiliacs fit into. That means a differentiation does have to be made, because a differentiation really has some implication for treatment.

You know, there's a big difference between a pathological presentation of OCD and a preoccupation with something. That has to be differentiated and there's a lot of people who are preoccupied with having sex who are not OCD.

So, that gets a little tricky, and we try the best we can to discriminate, but the vast majority of what I see is not an OCD driven kind of thing. You have to insist on looking at their past trauma, sexual offending, and past victimization, as re-offense potential. So what you're doing, you're not really beaming in on them as a victim, but you're taking a look at their own victimization.

SM: Your goal, then, is the reduction of the deviant thoughts.

DL: You want to reduce as much as possible the inappropriate urges, fantasies, and behaviors, while simultaneously accelerating age-appropriate sexual fantasies and behaviors. That's the object. Not to make them asexual, but to get them more age-appropriate. And there's a number of other things. You teach them the sexual assault cycle. That has to be done so they understand exactly what goes on with them and how they become more and more out of control.

We use a monitoring system that a resident fills out every day regarding inappropriate sexual urges, fantasies and behaviors as well as appropriate sexual urges, Sexual Arousal Monitoring System (SAMS) developed at New Castle YDC. The youth then talks about them and we have a list of fantasies, targets, that we check off, and then the behaviors. The sexual behaviors, whether they masturbate, touch themselves, watching or staring while they're grooming, all these types of things. We also use a sexual distress index, as I call it, which addresses control and urge. And what they'll do is they'll go from one to five, one being no control, and five being the most control. And they will estimate their level of urges that day, and hence their level of control.

SM: And you say that you try to accelerate proper sexual behavior.

DL: Decelerate interest in deviate sexual behavior and at the same time increase age-appropriate sexual interest.

Comprehensive sexual education is also necessary, emphasizing normal adolescent development. That's imperative.

You have to be teaching people what is normal, and then, skills building. Now you have the other side—you have sex-offense-specific assessments and treatment. Now, what you have to do is you also have to understand there's another side to this, and that's the social skills building, such as self-esteem, social problem-solving skills, relationship enhancement, intimacy training, sexual education, anger management, assertiveness training, adolescent refusal skills.

SM: These are all positive types of things that the kid is doing, whereas in one of our other discussions, you talked about staying away from a deficit model which is punishment oriented.

DL: That's exactly right. The deficit model (can't only focus on deficits), what it really does, is look at the kid's weaknesses. The deficit model looks at the weakness and says don't do this, don't do that, don't do this, don't do that; and when this or that happens, block this, block that, and so forth. Well, you're doing two things here, you want to decelerate, but at the same time, you need to give somebody tools. This person knew how to talk to somebody, but he didn't know anything about dating or relationships or intimacy and so on. If he did, there's a chance that this person might be behaving differently.

SM: Was his treatment all done in group therapy? Or in some cases, in classroom settings; age-appropriate dating behavior, for example.

DL: Oh yes, some of that stuff could go under the general rubric of health.

SM: But most of it would probably be group therapy or group sessions, group conversations?

DL: Group sessions and educational group sessions. It's imperative that this person is cognizant of mental health needs. Its process should be to focus on understanding the relationship between being dysregulated affectively, sexual offenses, and re-offense behavior. He requires ongoing treatment utilizing cognitive behavioral therapy to address mental health symptoms. You have got the traditional sexual offender therapy. If the non-pharmacological method is unsuccessful in reducing deviant urges and fantasy behavior, a trial of SSRI's should be considered.

SM: Okay.

DL: See where we went there? We're going to go here, then we're going to go to the trial of SSRI, and then we talk a little bit about learning disabilities, etc.

SM: Alright.

DL: Now, in this case here, the next step then would be that if this person didn't respond to various SSRI's, several different SSRI's should be tried when treatment failure occurs; the next step would be to convene a meeting and look at the possibility of doing anti-androgen therapy. Discuss its benefits. You have to understand there's a lot of issues in and around young people in terms of bone density, etc. There's a lot of lab work that has to be done. The person has to be medically cleared and the biggest thing to understand is it is not FDA-approved treatment for sex offenders. That's the main thing. This is used very prudently to reduce sexual libido. It does that. There are people who are advocates of Depo and other people who are advocates of oral therapy, it just depends. In this agency and facility we don't use Depo. When anti-androgen therapy is decided, we use oral administration. And that's really the safety feature. So we can control, God forbid, if something happens.

SM: I didn't realize that.

DL: Yes, certainly. Because those shots might be once a month or once every two weeks. So it's really a big-time safety issue. Along with anti-androgen therapy, we use SAMS Forms to monitor treatment response as well as close medical supervision of side effects, blood levels, lab work. The SAMS Forms were developed by a supervisor in the Sex Offenders program and me.

We would like to acknowledge Charlie Chervanik and Joan Lawer of the PA Dept. of Public Welfare; the Office of Children, Youth, and Family Services; and Bob Liggett and Elida Evans at YDC-NC for supporting and financing significant amounts of specialized education, training, and certification in sexual offender evaluation, treatment, and risk predictions.

Critical Thinking Questions:
What issues would you personally have about being a sex offender therapist? Would you want to get involved in this field? Why or why not?

R. J. Phelps and colleagues, in a survey of 192 female youths in the Wisconsin juvenile justice system, discovered that 79 percent (most of whom were in the system for petty larceny and status offenses) had been subjected to physical abuse that resulted in some form of injury.[63] Furthermore, Meda Chesney-Lind and N. Rodriguez's investigation of the backgrounds of adult women in prison underscores the links between childhood victimizations and later criminal careers. Interviews revealed that virtually all were victims of physical and/or sexual abuse as youngsters; more than 60 percent had been sexually abused, and about one-half had been raped.[64]

Silbert and Pines claim that the family background of teenage prostitutes is "surprisingly comfortable,"[65] and Jennifer James documents the increase in juvenile prostitutes from "affluent and overindulged" backgrounds.[66] These authors are clearly describing adolescent prostitutes from middle-class

FOCUS ON THE OFFENDER 14–13

PROSTITUTION

A juvenile probation officer comments about one of these youths on her caseload:

A girl prostitute we had here was adept at telling you what you wanted to hear. She said that prostitution was a great thing and that the only bad thing was you had to work at night. She was involved in heavy drug use and was also involved in sexual abuse with her father. She claimed that she became a prostitute because her father started to see a girlfriend. She ran away and got involved with a pimp. She would still like to live with her father if that other woman would go away.[69]

Critical Thinking Question:

What do you believe causes female prostitution? What approach(es) could be taken to reduce the number of female prostitutes in the United State or elsewhere? Should prostitution remain a criminal offense?

homes. Eleanor M. Miller's *Street Woman,* based on intensive interviews with 64 prostitutes in Milwaukee, argues that street prostitution for Whites was not so much a hustle into which one drifted as it was a survival strategy. For this group, there was often a direct link between prostitution and difficulties with parents, runaway behavior, and contact with the juvenile justice system. Family lives were characterized by interviewees as disorganized, including high levels of violence and abuse. The consequence of running away from these chaotic settings resulted in arrest and lengthy detention as status offenders.[68] See Focus on the Offender 14–13.

Miller argues that for more than one-half her sample, adolescent female prostitution evolves out of the profound social and economic problems confronting these girls, especially young African-American women. For these women, movement into prostitution occurred as a consequence of exposure to deviant street networks. These women, who were recruited by older African-American males with lengthy criminal records, organized themselves into "pseudo families" and engaged in prostitution. Initially attracted by the excitement and money, these women viewed prostitution as an alternative to boring and low-paying jobs, but they soon found that the life was not nearly as glamorous and remunerative as they had anticipated.[70]

Several factors explain why teenage prostitutes are persistent offenders and tend to remain "in the life" at least throughout their adolescent years. First, whether they are adolescents from middle- or lower-class backgrounds, they need money for survival on the streets. Second, many adolescent prostitutes

Runaway teenagers often turn to prostitution to support themselves. Here a 14 year old approaches a driver looking for a 'pickup'. (Photo by Kathryn Miller.)

become addicted to drugs and are reluctant to leave their ready supply of narcotics. Third, most teenage prostitutes are under the control of "pimps," who are known to assault those who leave. Finally, while they may want to "go clean," few adolescent prostitutes have any place to go or any other options.

Street Gang Members

It is estimated that about 40 percent of street gang members in urban areas are juveniles.[71] Nearly all gangs recently emerging in communities across the nation are made up of juveniles. Some imprisoned juveniles have even become involved in prison gangs.

For youths who fail in almost everything they attempt, especially school, gang membership represents acceptance and self-esteem. Gang membership provides excitement and a relief from the boredom of inner-city life. Youths join gangs for the companionship and camaraderie that they perceive as readily available and to fulfill their desire to identify with and belong to a group. Moreover, joining a youth gang also becomes a matter of survival for many juveniles. "Man," one youth responded, "in my neighborhood you didn't have much choice. They put a lot of pressure on you. I played football and that kept me out of the gangs, but many a day, I left school running and didn't stop until I got home."[72]

FOCUS ON THE OFFENDER 14–14

PROFILE OF GANG MEMBERS

The profile of a gang youth often includes some or all of the following indicators:

- Poor progress or achievement in school
- Truancy from school
- Lack of hobbies or something to do with leisure time
- Frequent negative contacts with the police
- Gang signs or insignias
- Problems at home
- Tattoos
- Residence in a neighborhood where gangs exist
- Friends are gang members or "dressed down" in gang attire
- Dressing in traditional gang clothes (i.e., baggy pants or "khakis," oversized T-shirts, bandannas, dark sunglasses)
- Participating in graffiti writing or strikeouts
- Gathering on street corners in groups where gangs are active
- Involvement in some type of illegal activity or violence.[73]

Critical Thinking Questions:
What experiences with gangs have you or your friends had? Are you aware of any non-gang members with these "profile" characteristics? When, in your opinion, does a gang exist?

Juveniles perform a variety of roles in street gangs. In urban gangs, males traffic drugs, stand watch at the entrances of "crack" houses, carry weapons, carry out execution orders, attend meetings, and pay proper respect to gang leaders. Females who are attached to male-oriented gangs do all of the above, and they also frequently perform sexual favors for the male gang members.

WHAT ARE THE LIMITATIONS TO THIS CLASSIFICATION SCHEME?

As with any classification scheme, there are a number of flaws to the one presented in this chapter. First, few juveniles are specialists in the crimes they commit, and a classification scheme seems to suggest that juvenile offending is much more specialized than it actually is. Second, a classification scheme ignores the social reality that juvenile offending may change as youths age. That is, the types of crimes a juvenile commits at age eleven or fifteen may be dramatically different from the socially unacceptable behaviors of this same juvenile at age sixteen or seventeen. Third, a classification scheme neglects the social reality that youthful offenders are typically involved in multiple unacceptable behaviors. It is overly simplistic, then, to attempt to label youths as one type of offender. Fourth, a classification scheme tends to connote that juveniles are divided into "good kids" and "lawbreakers." Self-report studies, especially, are helpful in identifying that juvenile lawbreaking takes place at some point in the lives of most youngsters. What is frequently different in these youths from those in the justice system is that they were lucky enough not to be caught. Fifth, a classification scheme fails to convey the pervasiveness of drugs in the lives of nearly all juvenile offenders. Finally, a classification scheme does not take seriously enough the social definitions of juvenile offending. What is defined as status offenses and delinquent acts vary somewhat from jurisdiction to jurisdiction and from one period of time to another.

Yet, establishing a classification scheme, such as the one presented here, is the first step in understanding the dynamics of youth crime. It is then important to explore a multidimensional analysis of youth crime. For example, what is the relationship between drug use and delinquency? Do drugs cause delinquency, does delinquency lead to drug use, or do some other factors precede both delinquency and the onset of drug use? What best explains the onset and continuing use of illicit drugs? What is the influence of groups on juvenile offending? Do delinquent youths seek out groups to reinforce their values or do they become involved in groups and then are influenced by these groups to become involved in delinquent behavior? What is the relationship between rationality and juvenile offending? That is, how much free will do juvenile lawbreakers actually have?[74]

SUMMARY

Status offenders and chronic offenders receive the most attention from the formal literature on juvenile crime. Clearly, status offenders have sometimes been treated in a scandalous way by the juvenile justice system; there is much debate over how to handle these youths. Chronic offenders, of course, receive more attention because they commit the more frequent and serious crimes among juvenile offenders.

In addition to status and chronic offenders, this chapter considers a variety of other youthful offenders and juveniles who come to the attention of the juvenile justice system. These youths vary from the innocents who simply are unaware they are doing wrong, to those situational offenders who murder a parent, a peer, or an adult who is in the wrong place at the wrong time. At the same time, the misuse of alcohol and drugs occurs in the lives of most youthful offenders, and all juveniles must deal with the influence of peers in their lives. These and other factors, such as gang involvement and problems with school or family, contribute to the unlawful behavior of juveniles.

WEB SITES OF INTEREST

To view research conducted by the National Institute of Mental Health on the factors that contribute to juvenile delinquency, go to

http://www.nimh.nih.gov/publicat/violenceresfact.cfm

CRITICAL THINKING QUESTIONS

1. Why is a consideration of status offenders important in understanding juvenile justice?
2. For the juvenile who kills, should personal pathology or chaotic and victimizing home conditions mitigate the punishment he or she receives?
3. Given their social backgrounds, attitudes, and crimes, what can be done about chronic offenders? Is punishment the only recourse with these youths?
4. Consider each type of offender and decide how this offender should be handled by the juvenile justice system.

NOTES

1. Interviewed in 1999 and used with permission under condition of confidentiality.
2. Joy G. Dryfoos, *Adolescents at Risk: Prevalence and Prevention* (New York: Oxford University Press, 1990), 245–46.
3. For a classification scheme of high-risk youths who abuse drugs, see Richard Dembo, Linda Williams, Jeffrey Fagan, and James Schmeidler, "Development and Assessment of a Classification of High Risk Youth," *Journal of Drug Issues* 24 (1994), 25–53.
4. Ibid., 94–112.
5. Barry Feld, "The Juvenile Court Meets the Principle of Offense: Punishment, Treatment and the Difference It Makes," *Boston University Law Review* 68 (1988), 156–210; and J. R. Sutton, *Stubborn Children: Controlling Delinquency in the United States, 1640–1981* (Berkeley: University of California Press, 1988).
6. See M. A. Bortner, *Delinquency and Justice: An Age of Crisis* (New York: McGraw-Hill, 1988), 96.

7. Meda Chesney-Lind and Randall G. Shelden, *Girls: Delinquency and Juvenile Justice* (Pacific Grove, CA: Brooks/Cole, 1992), 29.
8. Interviewed in 1985 in Iowa.
9. President's Commission on Law Enforcement and Administration of Justice, *Task Force Report: Juvenile Delinquency and Youth Crime* (Washington, DC: Government Printing Office, 1976), 2.
10. Rosemary C. Sarri and Robert D. Vinter, "Justice for Whom? Varieties of Juvenile Correctional Approaches," in *The Juvenile Justice System,* edited by Malcolm Klein (Beverly Hills, CA: Sage Publications, 1976), 190.
11. For the term "naive risk-taker," see Thomas J. Bernard, *The Cycle of Juvenile Justice* (New York: Oxford University Press, 1992), 166–70.
12. The youth reported this to Bartollas in 1979.
13. Interviewed in 1987.
14. Bernard, *The Cycle of Juvenile Justice,* 166–70.
15. Ibid.
16. Unpublished biography on Larry Hoover that Linda Dippold Bartollas wrote.
17. One of the authors is familiar with these cases, which occurred in New Jersey and Virginia.
18. One of the authors worked with this youth in an institutional setting.
19. Interviewed in 1982.
20. The following discussion on delinquency and drift is adapted from David Matza, *Delinquency and Drift* (New York: John Wiley & Sons, 1964), 184–90.
21. Ibid.
22. Interviewed in October 1982.
23. Interviewed in June 1982.
24. Donna Martin Hamparian et al., *The Violent Few: A Study of Dangerous Juvenile Offenders* (Lexington, MA: Lexington Books, 1980), 39.
25. Ibid., 9.
26. Ibid.
27. Ibid.
28. One of the authors was involved in this case.
29. One of the authors worked with this gang in 1990.
30. One of the authors worked with this youth in 1973.
31. Interviewed in 1973.
32. Interviewed in 1987.
33. Ruth-Arlene W. Howe, "A Wake-Up Call for American Society or Have 'The Chickens Just Come Home to Roost?'—Essay Review of Charles Patrick Ewing's "When Children Kill: the Dynamics of Juvenile Homicide," *Nova Law Review* 16 (1992), 848–907. For examinations of juveniles who kill their parents, see Kathleen M. Heide, "Evidence of Child Maltreatment Among

Adolescent Parricide Offenders," *International Journal of Offender Therapy and Comparative Criminology* 38 (Summer 1994), 151–61; Kathleen M. Heide, "Why Kids Kill Parents," *Psychology Today* 25 (September/October 1992), 62–69; Kathleen M. Heide, "Parricide: Incidence and Issues," *The Justice Professional* 4 (Spring 1989), 19–41; and Kathleen M. Heide, "Parents Who Get Killed and the Children Who Kill Them," *Journal of Interpersonal Violence* 8 (December 1993), 531–44.

34. See the statistics for this rise in the use of marijuana in Chapter 2.
35. Dryfoos, *Adolescents at Risk,* 54.
36. Delbert S. Elliott and David Huizinga, "The Relationship Between Delinquent Behavior and ADM Problem Behaviors," paper presented at the ADAMHA/OJJDP State of the Art Research Conference on Juvenile Offenders, Bethesda, Maryland (April 17–18, 1984).
37. A statement made to one of the authors by several training school staff.
38. Interviewed in 1985.
39. Dryfoos, *Adolescents at Risk,* 48.
40. Sheldon Glueck and Eleanor T. Glueck, *Juvenile Delinquents Grown Up* (New York: Commonwealth Fund, 1940), 89.
41. Marvin E. Wolfgang, Terence P. Thornberry, and Robert M. Figlio, eds., *From Boy to Man: From Delinquency to Crime* (Chicago: University of Chicago Press, 1978), 34.
42. Ibid.
43. Alicia Rand, "Transitional Life Events and Desistance from Delinquency and Crime," in *From Boy to Man,* pp. 134–63; James Q. Wilson and Richard Herrnstein, *Crime and Human Nature* (New York: Simon & Schuster, 1985), 126–47.
44. Materials from this section are drawn largely from Sue Righthand and Carlann Welch, *Juveniles Who Have Sexually Offended: A Review of the Professional Literature* (Washington, DC: OJJDP, 2001). Wherever appropriate, the authors of this text refer the reader to the original sources from which Righthand and Welch have drawn their materials.
45. Federal Bureau of Investigation, *Crime in the United States 2000: Uniform Crime Reports* (U.S. Department of Justice 2001), 226.
46. C. Bagley and D. Shewchuk-Dann, "Characteristics of 60 Children and Adolescents Who Have a History of Sexual Assault Against Others: Evidence from a Controlled Study," *Journal of Child and Youth Care* (Fall Special Issue) (1991), 43–52.
47. Sue Righthand and Carlann Welch, "Juveniles Who Have Sexually Offended: A Review of the Professional Literature" (Washington, DC: OJJDP, March, 2001), *Executive Summary,* xi–xiii.
48. M. L. Ferrara and S. McDonald, *Treatment of the Sex Offender: Neurological and Psychiatric Impairments."* (Northvale, NJ: Jason Aronson, 1996.)

49. S. Righthand and Carlann Welch, "Juveniles Who Have Sexually Offended," 8.

50. G. Ryan, T. J. Miyoshi, J. L. Metzner, R. D. Krugman, and G. E. Fryer. "Trends in a National Sample of Sexually Abusive Youths," *Journal of the American Academy of Child and Adolescent Psychiatry* 35(1) (1996), 17–25.

51. Graves as cited in M. Weinrott, *Juvenile Sexual Aggression: A Critical Review* (Boulder, CO: University of Colorado, Institute for Behavioral Sciences, Center for the Study and Prevention of Violence, 1996).

52. R. Prentky, B. Harris, K. Frizzell, and S. Righthand, "An Actuarial Procedure for Assessing Risk in Juvenile Sex Offenders." *Sexual Abuse: A Journal of Research and Treatment* 12(2) (2000), 71–95.

53. J. V. Becker and M. S. Kaplan, "What We Know About the Characteristics and Treatment of Adolescents Who Have Committed Sexual Offenses." *Child Maltreatment* 3(4) (1998), 317–29.

54. R. A. Knight and R. A. Prentky, "Exploring Characteristics for Classifying Juvenile Sex Offenders" in *The Juvenile Sex Offender*, ed. by H. E. Barbaree, W. L. Marshall, and S. M. Hudson (New York: 1993), 45–83.

55. O'Brien and Bera, cited in Weinrott, M. *Juvenile Sexual Aggression: A Critical Review* (Boulder, CO: University of Colorado, Institute for Behavioral Sciences), from Righthand and Welch, *Juveniles Who Have Sexually Offended*.

56. S. Lane and C. Labanov-Rotstovsky, "Special Populations: Children, Families, the Developmentally Disabled and Violent Youth," in *Juvenile Sexual Offending: Causes, Consequences, and Correction*, edited by G. D. Ryan and S. L. Lane (San Francisco, CA: Jossey-Bass Publishers, 1997), 322–59.

57. S. Righthand, R. Hennings, and P. Wigley, *Young Sex Offenders in Maine* (Portland, ME: University of Southern Maine, Public Policy and Management Program, Human Services Development Institute, Committee on Child Sex Abuse: Research Task Force, 1989), in Righthand and Welch.

58. J. A. Ray, and D. J. English, "Comparison of Female and Male Children With Sexual Behavior Problems." *Journal of Youth and Adolescence* 24(4) (1995), 439–51, in Righthand and Welch.

59. Johnson, as cited in S. Lane and C. Lobanov-Rotstovsky, *Juvenile Sexual Offending: Causes, Consequences, and Correction*, 322–59.

60. S. Righthand and C. Welch, *Juveniles Who Have Sexually Offended: A Review of the Professional Literature* (2001), 42, 44. Referring to works by Becker, 1998, Righthand and Welch describe the sex abuse cycle as developed in the works of Ryan and Lane et al., cited in Becker, 1998.

61. Jennifer Williard, *Juvenile Prostitution* (Washington, DC: National Victim Resource Center, 1991).

62. Mimi Silbert and Ayala M. Pines, "Entrance into Prostitution," *Youth and Society* 13 (1982), 476.

63. Cited in Meda Chesney-Lind, "Girls' Crime and Woman's Place: Toward a Feminist Model of Female Delinquency," paper presented at the annual meeting of the American Society of Criminology, Montreal (1987).

64. Ibid, 19.
65. Silbert and Pines, "Entrance into Prostitution."
66. Jennifer James, *Entrance into Juvenile Prostitution* (Washington, DC: National Institute of Mental Health, 1978).
67. Ibid.
68. Eleanor M. Miller, *Street Woman* (Philadelphia: Temple University Press, 1986).
69. Interviewed in 1985.
70. Ibid.
71. Elaine S. Knapp, *Embattled Youth: Kids, Gangs, and Drugs* (Chicago: Council of State Governments, 1988), 13.
72. Interviewed in 1987.
73. "Warning Signs for Parents," mimeographed handout by the Los Angeles Police Department, 1989, 1.
74. For answers to such questions, see Clemens Bartollas, *Juvenile Delinquency*, 6th ed. (Boston: Allyn & Bacon, 2003).

15

INTERNATIONAL JUVENILE JUSTICE

OBJECTIVES

1. To introduce the *Beijing Rules*, their content, and their proposed model rules for juveniles for all nations
2. To describe the basic approach to administering juvenile justice in three industrialized countries—Canada, England, and Australia
3. To examine how four emerging countries—South Africa, China, India, and Brazil—deal with problem youths
4. To illustrate how some countries with extreme population, social, and/or economic difficulties—South Africa, China, India, and Brazil—deal with problem juveniles

KEY TERMS

apartheid
Beijing Rules
capital punishment
common law
corporal punishment
crime control model
developing countries
family conferences
indigenous populations
industrialized countries
jati
nongovernmental organizations (NGOs)
Panchayats
statutory law
traditional cultures
welfare model
Young Offenders Act (YOA)

In Sweden the responsibility for handling young people is shared by the social authorities and the judicial system. In the Swedish language there is no equivalent concept for "juvenile delinquent." Instead they speak of juvenile criminality. This system does not formally recognize status offenses. Such behaviors are dealt with through social welfare measures. All juvenile crime falls under the Swedish Penal Code of 1990. By law juveniles receive special consideration when found committing a crime. Youth[s] under the age of 15 are handled by social authorities rather than the police. Criminal responsibility begins at age 15. [More than] 80 percent of all juvenile crimes are not prosecuted but dealt with informally. Nearly 50 percent are resolved through the use of day fines without a trial procedure being used. Fewer than 10 percent of delinquent youth[s] are placed on probation. The Swedish model is more treatment oriented than most Western countries. But, in recent years the model has been subjected to substantial criticism as youth crime in Sweden has been on the increase and there does not appear to be any empirical support for the treatment oriented programs.

—John A. Winterdyk[1]

One of the most exciting developments in juvenile justice over the past two decades has been a growing international awareness of the problems faced by youths. The world's media, child-care experts, national governments, and international organizations are for the first time looking at the problems of children in a broader context. Their findings, as illustrated by the comments on juvenile justice in Sweden, are both illuminating and sobering. Stark contrasts exist in how countries in different parts of the world and in different stages of economic development treat children. Industrialized and democratized countries, so often held up as models of rational and responsible systems of justice, often fall far short not only of their own ideals but also of those of the international community.

Arguments about what to do about juveniles and juvenile crime in countries around the world are similar to those found in the United States, Canada, and England. Discussed throughout the industrialized world, particularly, are the age of criminal culpability, diversion from the system, due process, the role of the police in dealing with juveniles, the separation of the dependent and neglected from the delinquent and criminal, the severity of sanctions, the efficacy of community-based programs and institutionalization, probation and parole, and the death penalty. Countries vary widely in how they handle these issues. Some governments ignore juveniles totally, while others engage in serious debate and study over what works best. This diversity has a number of sources.

Some of the variation is related to each country's stage of economic, social, and political development. Democratized and **industrialized countries** usually base their criminal and juvenile law on constitutionally derived formal rules and procedures. Well-developed educational systems provide them with trained police, judges, and professional child care workers capable of giving juveniles needed help. **Developing countries** with **indigenous**

populations, however, frequently rely on the internalized and long-standing folkways and mores of **traditional cultures.** Rules in these countries are enforced by parents and by religious and community leaders and very likely are more effective than the formalized methods of democratic nations. Sometimes the two systems collide. Nations colonized by western countries even centuries ago often still experience social strains as traditional ways conflict with modern methods, thereby setting the stage for mistrust, acrimony, and sometimes violent conflict between the governing and the governed.

Attitudes of governmental leaders toward citizens also contribute to the diversity. More than a few countries are governed by political, religious, or ideological despots who care only about wealth, power, and control. Indeed, police, military, and civilian authorities in these countries often engage in beatings, torture, sexual assault, and murder. The methods of suppression used are so horrific that worldwide condemnation is directed at the guilty police, paramilitary security forces, and others. International media, United Nations' White Papers, United States Department of State reports, and **nongovernmental organizations (NGOs)** such as Amnesty International constantly urge those responsible to cease their human rights violations. Yet the leaders of these countries continue to ignore even the most fundamental rights of their citizens. Nevertheless, momentum is building, pushing leaders everywhere to carefully consider their actions and the consequences of their actions before they condone violence against their citizens.

This chapter briefly addresses the first major effort by the United Nations to set standards for the treatment of children—the *Beijing Rules.* Then the focus of the chapter turns to its primary emphasis, justice systems in several other countries. These countries were chosen either for their similarity to the United States, or because their population, culture, or state of socioeconomic development makes them unique. First examined are three "post-industrial" countries, Canada, England, and Australia. The modern, statutory legal systems of these English-speaking countries evolved from English common law; Canada and Australia, as did the United States, disenfranchised their indigenous populations several centuries ago. Four countries, Brazil, China, India, and South Africa, are developing or "emerging" economically. These include three of the world's largest nations in terms of population; all are extremely poor and represent different areas of the world with diverse cultural traditions. In India, South Africa, and Brazil, the laws of colonial nations replaced traditional, native laws of indigenous peoples, usually with **common law.** These common laws were, in turn, replaced by formal **statutory law.** Today, years after the end of colonization, the formal statutory laws remain in place, but long-discarded indigenous practices of native populations are reemerging as challenges to the statutory laws. Brazil has the largest population in South America and a colonial history that includes the disenfranchisement of native populations; its problems are characteristic of many South American countries. China has a huge population, numerous ethnic groups, ideological conflicts, and problems that accompany a changing socioeconomic structure.

India's population matches that of China. India faces abject poverty and has fewer resources. South Africa is still reeling from the consequences of its former apartheid policies.

WHAT ARE THE *BEIJING RULES*?

One outcome of the emerging world order is the setting of international standards for the administration of juvenile justice. The earliest standards, which were developed in 1955 as the United Nations Minimum Rules for the Treatment of Prisoners, did not directly address the issue of children[2] The ***Beijing Rules*** were the first to do this but should be placed alongside two other sets of rules adopted in 1990, the *United Nations Guidelines for the Prevention of Juvenile Delinquency* (the Riyadh Guidelines) and the *United Nations Rules for the Protection of Juveniles Deprived of Their Liberty* (the JDL Rules). These three sets of rules cover the prevention of delinquency, the due process required for processing offenders through justice systems, and the reintegration of offenders into their communities after confinement and/or rehabilitation. The *Beijing Rules* set standards for all countries (see Focus on Policy 15–1).

The fundamental perspective of the *Beijing Rules* is based on the broader human rights movement. The actual rules state "musts" and "shoulds" that sound much like the modern due process requirements of the United States, Canada, England, and Australia. For example, the framers of the *Beijing Rules* emphasize the well-being of all youths as the fundamental principle behind the rules. "Juveniles" include all youths from seven to eighteen, although the age may vary according to local customs. The rules mandate that authorities not overreact to either the offender or the offense and that all youths are presumed innocent until fair hearings are held. Rule 7.1, for example, states:

> Basic procedural safeguards such as the presumption of innocence, the right to be notified of the charges, the right to remain silent, the right to legal representation, the right to the presence of a parent or guardian, the right to call and cross-examine witnesses and the right of appeal to a higher authority shall be guaranteed at all stages of the proceedings."[3]

The rules call for training juvenile justice officials to exercise proper discretion when working with youths. "No intervention" is considered the best policy for many children, and authorities should divert youths from the system at all stages of the proceedings. Youthful offenders should be placed with local families, schools, or agencies capable of providing the youths with appropriate care and protection. If juveniles are taken into custody, authorities must notify the child's parents at the earliest possible moment. Youths have the right to privacy when in custody, and their identities must be kept

FOCUS ON POLICY 15–1

THE BEIJING RULES: FUNDAMENTAL PERSPECTIVES

1. Member States shall seek, in conformity with their respective general interests, to further the well-being of the juvenile and her or his family.
2. Member States shall endeavour to develop conditions that will ensure for the juvenile a meaningful life in the community, which, during that period in life when she or he is most susceptible to deviant behaviour, will foster a process of personal development and education that is as free from crime and delinquency as possible.
3. Sufficient attention shall be given to positive measures that involve the full mobilization of all possible resources, including the family, volunteers and other community groups, as well as schools and other community institutions, for the purpose of promoting the well-being of the juvenile, with a view to reducing the need for intervention under the law, and of effectively, fairly and humanely, dealing with the juvenile in conflict with the law.
4. Juvenile justice shall be conceived as an integral part of the national development process of each country, within a comprehensive framework of social justice for all juveniles, thus, at the same time, contributing to the protection of the young and the maintenance of a peaceful order in society.
5. These Rules shall be implemented in the context of economic, social and cultural conditions prevailing in each Member State.
6. Juvenile justice services shall be systematically developed and coordinated with a view to improving and sustaining the competence of personnel involved in the services, including their methods, approaches, and attitudes.

Source: United Nations, "United Nations Standard Minimum Rules for the Administration of Juvenile Justice: The *Beijing Rules*" (New York: United Nations Department of Public Information, 1986), pp. 1–15.

Critical Thinking Questions:

How does the operation of juvenile justice in the United States fare in terms of the *Beijing Rules?* What changes do you think should be made in terms of juvenile justice in the United States to make it more humane, just, and efficient?

confidential at all stages of the proceedings. A youth should not be confined unless absolutely necessary, and no juvenile should ever be harmed.

The rules go on to state that youths must be permitted to express themselves freely and without fear of recrimination. Juveniles have the right to an attorney and free legal aid; they should have confidence that the courts are informed accurately of their special social, educational, and emotional backgrounds through preadjudicatory and presentencing reports by trained court officers. The courts, additionally, should have access to a wide range of dispositional alternatives including "various care orders, probation, community service orders, compensation to the victim or financial penalties, group counseling and foster care or other educational establishments."[4] Confinement is a last resort, and confined youths must be released as soon as possible and must be placed in programs for reintegrating them back into the community. Corporal punishments are prohibited, and no youth under the age of 18 should be put to death.

Importantly, the laws of all nations "shall be applied to juvenile offenders impartially, without distinction of any kind, for example as to race, colour, sex, language, religion, political or other opinions, national or social origin, property, birth or other status."[5] Few if any nations in the world today meet the standards set by the *Beijing Rules.*

HOW DO INDUSTRIALIZED NATIONS HANDLE JUVENILE CRIME?

This section focuses on three industrialized, English-speaking countries: Canada, England, and Australia. All share a common social, cultural, and legal background.

CANADA

The development of Canadian juvenile justice parallels that of the United States in that juveniles in colonial Canada were tried in the same courts and held in the same prisons as adults. Then, in the early 1800s, some houses of refuge were built, and a few reformatories were constructed in the mid-1800s. Most juveniles were tried in adult courts and confined in adult prisons throughout the nineteenth century. Whether youths had the mental capacity to understand their actions, however, was debated as much then as it is today. Child-savers of the late 1800s maintained that youthful offenders were misdirected children who required assistance more than punishment. Reformers of this era further believed that juveniles needed to be tried in separate juvenile courts and confined in facilities separate from those for adults, a clear shift in thinking from the past.[6]

The consequence was that a Juvenile Delinquents Act (JDA) was passed in 1908 at the federal level, calling for Canada's provinces and territories to implement a new approach to juvenile justice. This law called for a **welfare**

model approach to juvenile justice similar to that of the 1899 act that created the juvenile court in Chicago.[7] Provinces and territories developed their own facilities and set the age of jurisdiction at sixteen, seventeen, or eighteen, depending on the prevailing philosophy in the particular political jurisdiction. The system that was developed called for informal practices with officials free to exercise great amounts of discretion. This approach dominated Canadian juvenile justice until the 1960s, when reformers questioned whether juveniles actually were being rehabilitated.

A 1965 report on juvenile delinquency in Canada criticized the informal and often arbitrary procedures of the 1908 act, but it continued to accept the ideals of the welfare model. After a number of unsuccessful tries, a new reform bill, the ***Young Offenders Act (YOA)***, was passed in 1982. This bill set the age of eighteen as the upper limit of jurisdiction across Canada and called for a modified justice model approach to juvenile crime.[8] Youths began to be held accountable for their crimes, to be provided with many of the same due process rights as adults, and to receive sentences proportionate to their offenses. Nevertheless, the YOA principles calling for welfare services for youths in need remained strong, but they emphasized that these needs should not be addressed in the criminal justice system.[9] Thus, the YOA was a compromise between the welfare and justice models, although the C.19 Bill of 1995 removes some of the treatment objectives of the YOA and strengthens justice and due process responses to serious and violent offenders.[10] These last two changes move Canadian juvenile justice toward a **crime control model** and have implications for all components of the juvenile justice system. See Focus on Practice 15–2 for the "get tough" approach in Canada.

The Police

The police function in Canada is to respond to and investigate youth crime. Upon apprehending a juvenile, police must inform the youth of his or her rights, which include consulting parents or counsel and remaining silent. In the event the juvenile is willing to talk to the police, police must obtain a written statement that the youth agrees to waive these rights before the police are permitted to take a statement or conduct an interview. In some provinces, Crown counsel must approve the police charge before information is sworn. If a youth is put on probation, the police enter his or her status on a national law enforcement computer information network and check the network on a regular basis when investigating juveniles considered suspicious. Police share information with probation officers to facilitate the filing of new charges in the event that a youth violates probation.[11]

Prosecution

The prosecution's role is most comprehensive in British Columbia, Quebec, and New Brunswick, where prosecutors make all decisions relating to intake, diversion, and filing charges; the prosecutor may divert the youth from

FOCUS ON PRACTICE 15–2

PRESENT CONTROVERSY ON JUVENILE JUSTICE IN CANADA

There is evidence that juvenile justice in Canada is presently more controversial now than it has ever been in its century-old existence. This controversy has focused on the issue of youth violence.

Politicians at the municipal, provincial, and federal levels of government are responding in earnest to the growing public and media clamor to "get tough" with youthful offenders in general and violent juveniles in particular. Daily, the media tell of accounts of largely unprecedented horrific and senseless violent acts committed by youthful offenders; of youth gangs operating in suburbs; of drive-by shootings; of home invasions by juveniles in wealthy neighborhoods; of crimes involving "smash and grabs" in large shopping mall jewelry stores in which semiautomatic guns are fired into the ceiling and shoppers are terrorized; of children under 12 years of age committing serious crimes who can be neither arrested nor charged; and of vicious murders by youthful offenders that often result in failed efforts to transfer these cases to adult courts and therefore result in a maximum three-year youth detention sentence. While the homicide rate by youthful offenders in Canada has remained stable over the past 20 years, the charges for violent offenses have more than doubled since 1986.

Some Canadian scholars charge that the fear of youth crime is the unwarranted result of a media-induced "moral panic." They argue that the media sensationalize the few violent acts by a handful of youthful offenders, which greatly exaggerates the (minimal) real threat to the public. Furthermore, they maintain that due to the tremendous spillover of news and entertainment media from the United States, the public projects media images of endemic youth violence in major American cities into the Canadian context. This results in erroneous views of Canadian juvenile offenders who have only superficial parallels with their American counterparts.

Source: Raymond R. Corrado and Alan Markwart, "Canada," in *International Handbook on Juvenile Justice,* edited by Donald J. Shoemaker (Westport, CT: Greenwood Press, 1996), pp. 34–35.

Critical Thinking Questions:

Besides the similarity of the politicians' "get tough" approach on violent youth crime, what other comparisons have you found between juvenile justice in Canada and that in the United States? How much has the media contributed to a "moral panic" against youthful offenders in the United States?

the system if he or she desires.[12] In other provinces, police still are responsible for filing charges, although their charges, the evidence, and the possibility of conviction are reviewed by Crown counsel before the youth is taken to court. In all provinces, Crown counsel must "show cause" before remanding a youth to a juvenile facility before trial.

In addition, Crown counsel makes the decision whether to transfer violent youths to adult court for trial. This decision usually is made on the grounds that youths cannot benefit from the treatment services offered by the juvenile justice system. This area of transfer is pervaded with ambiguous standards because of the conflict between the rehabilitative and crime control models of justice; the ambiguities force Crown counsel into many arguments and appeals over whether transfers should occur.[13] Beyond these roles, the prosecuting attorneys are deeply involved in recommendations to the courts concerning the proper dispositions for youths. Generally, Canada's Supreme Court relies on the "special needs" principle when evaluating appeals concerning the transfer of youths to adult court, and relatively few youths are transferred to adult court as a consequence.

Probation Officers

The probation officer's role has changed considerably since the implementation of the YOA. Probation officers now work closely with prosecution counsel in preparing background reports on youths. In addition, probation officers interview police in preparing their reports and again in supervising youths on probation. Judges, too, expect probation officers to play more of a law enforcement role than under the JDA, where probation officers were expected to employ the welfare model and seek treatment for youths in need. Instead of playing a youth advocacy role as in the past, judges now prefer probation officers to be neutral in the courtroom and in the community. Also, many youths in the past were remanded to hospitals or clinics under "treatment orders recommended by the probation officers." These orders are no longer available to the courts today unless requested by the youth. Indeed, the current emphasis on law enforcement and due process makes it difficult for probation officers to develop comprehensive and integrated case plans for juveniles.[14]

The Courts

Judges' roles also changed with the implementation of the YOA. Whereas judges' discretion was extremely broad and informally administered under the JDA, judge's roles today are restricted in that judges cannot remand younger juveniles to child care agencies nor can they transfer older offenders directly to adult court. Yet judges now may impose determinate sentences, assess whether youths should be placed in open or secure custodial facilities, and release youths from custody early. Judges today may also sentence young offenders to extended terms for murder; offenders now have the responsibility of demonstrating to judges why they should remain in the juvenile system.[15]

Juvenile Facilities

In spite of some changes, the traditions initiated by the JDA and the philosophy of the juvenile court at its beginning continue to influence Canadian juvenile justice today. Community-based corrections are found in all provinces and include community service, intensive supervision, and counseling services. Also used are private-sector programs such as wilderness camps and public-sector initiatives such as foster care, alternative schools, drug and alcohol abuse centers, and counseling centers. With the exception of Quebec and, to a certain degree, Ontario and Saskatchewan, these are not full-service programs, and probation officers remain somewhat frustrated with their inability to implement the welfare model.[16]

Juvenile institutions vary by security level and by province as much as juvenile facilities do in the United States. Some open facilities tend to lack fences and walls while others, depending on the province, have all the security features of a United States maximum-security juvenile facility. Facilities focus on security, health, education, and recreation, with treatment provided when requested by youths. Most treatment is delivered by outside contractors, with the exception of facilities in Quebec, which offer treatment in institutions. Ontario and Quebec try to keep both minor offenders and criminal youths in the juvenile system because the legislators from these provinces believe that both types of offenders face the same fundamental problems.[17] Reports of physical and sexual assault by peers and staff continue to filter out of Canada's juvenile facilities.

Current Concerns

Canada today is experiencing a basic tension among the welfare, due process, and crime control models of justice. Its juvenile justice code is an amalgam of the three, with the welfare model remaining strong but with the crime control and due process models gaining strength. Police particularly resent tenets of the welfare model that call for helping youths. Police further believe their hands are tied when arresting or working with street children and juvenile gangs. In addition, the amount of paperwork has increased as authorities attempt to guarantee fairness to youths. Tensions also exist within the courts as defense attorneys, prosecutors, and judges must perform a balancing act between the principles of the three models.

Many critics of Canada's juvenile justice system question whether the police and courts discriminate against minority youths. Police and court activity does vary from province to province, but evidence exists that Native Indians are prosecuted four times as often as the nonnatives in British Columbia. In other provinces, more than half the confined youths are Native Indians. Government reports state that the discrepancy between natives and nonnatives is the result of widespread discrimination, but some studies find no evidence of such discriminatory practices.

England and Wales

As noted in earlier chapters, English common law helped set the stage for criminal and juvenile law in the United States. The concept of *parens patriae* was of particular importance as it justified the intervention of the king into the lives of, first, all citizens and their families and, later, children. To review, children under the age of seven seldom faced any legal sanctions for misbehavior; children between the ages of seven and fourteen could face criminal sanctions depending on the seriousness of the crime, their intent, and their ability to determine right from wrong.

Children who met one or more of these latter criteria faced the possibility of being punished as adults—often by imprisonment or **corporal punishment** such as whipping and branding. English law also called for **capital punishment** (the death penalty) for close to two hundred offenses as well as for the transportation of youthful offenders to British colonies in Australia, New Zealand, and North America. Many of those sentenced to death were pardoned or transported, but, according to Leon Radzinowicz, eighteen of twenty people executed in London in 1785 were under the age of eighteen.[18]

In the late 1700s, the English and U.S. methods for handling juveniles roughly paralleled each other. The English initiated the use of private homes to house minor offenders, and lower courts were set up to adjudicate minor offenses. In 1847, the Juvenile Offenders Act permitted summary trials of youths under the age of fourteen. Then, in 1854, the first Reformatory Schools Act was passed; this act called for placing youths in reformatories separate from adult prisons. In 1879, summary trials for youths under the age of sixteen were permitted for most offenses, and, in a significant reform, the number of juveniles imprisoned with adults was reduced.

The first juvenile court was established in England under the Children Act, 1908.[19] This court's jurisdiction was over criminal matters for *children* under age fourteen, for *young persons* between fourteen and sixteen, and for civil jurisdiction over youths in need of welfare services.[20] The 1908 Children Act called for abolishing the imprisonment of youths with adults and for placing juveniles in reformatories for treatment.[21]

The early acts did not emphasize special training for judges, nor did the acts focus on the special needs of youths—unless the youth's needs were exceptional. In the Children and Young Persons Act, 1933, the principle that the court "should always act in the best interests of the welfare of the child was affirmed as was the principle of *in loco parentis*."[22] The philosophy behind this act clearly was based on positivism and a welfare model rather than a punishment model of justice. Also established were changes in the ages of youths under the jurisdiction of the courts; "the age of criminal responsibility was raised from seven to eight (Sec. 50) and sixteen-year-olds were placed under the criminal jurisdiction of the juvenile court."[23] Thus, the court had both criminal and civil jurisdiction.

The Children and Young Persons Act, 1969, reemphasized the importance of treating delinquents the same as any other youths in need. The age of minimum responsibility was raised from eight to ten, and juveniles who formerly were treated as criminal were handled through civil proceedings. Police were required to consult social work personnel about decisions concerning youths, and children under the age of seventeen were not to be confined in Borstals or detention centers.[24] Nevertheless, the ideals of the welfare model were not met, and the juvenile court took on the form of a criminal court that emphasized punishment.[25] A hard line emerged in England at this time paralleling the development of a similar hard line in the United States. Even so, the Criminal Justice Act, 1982, empowered magistrates to place delinquent youths in custody, issue care orders with residential requirements, and require community service; this act reflected a blend of both treatment and punishment.[26] In 1989, the Children Act affirmed an existing philosophy that youths should be prosecuted only as a last resort; care cases were transferred to the civil courts.

The Criminal Justice Act, 1991, renamed the juvenile court, the youth court, broadened the court's jurisdiction to include youths as old as seventeen, emphasized individualized sentencing based on the maturity of youths, placed more responsibility on parental responsibility, called for more interagency cooperation in dealing with youths, and developed new procedural guidelines for the police and courts. The 1994 Criminal Justice and Public Order Act was passed. It called for longer custodial sentences and a "secure training order" for juveniles.[27] The hard line was now in place.

The Police

The police departments in England are usually the first formal agencies to make contact with juveniles. Depending on the behavior of youths and the evidence, English Bobbies (police officers) are expected to exercise discretion in determining whether to hold youths for further action. If further action is believed necessary, youths and their parents must go to the police station, where most juveniles are released to their parents. Information about the children is collected by the juvenile bureau and is used by the Chief Inspector to determine whether to prosecute, issue a formal caution, or drop the case. If a formal reprimand is decided on, the juveniles are warned about their behavior and informed that further offenses will result in court action. According to David Farrington and Trever Bennett, "A caution can only be administered if the juvenile admits the offence, if the parents agree that the juvenile should be cautioned, and if the complainant or victim is willing to leave the decision to the police."[28] Cautions are used widely to minimize the penetration of youths into the system.

The ability to issue cautions has resulted in "net widening" in that officers are now bringing increasing numbers of youths into stations to reprimand them. At the court level, the number of youths diverted from the juvenile court increased and the number of youths sentenced to confinement declined.[29]

Police make arrests in England for the following types of offenses: in 1994, some 60 percent of males ages ten to fourteen were arrested for theft and handling stolen goods, 18 percent were arrested for burglary, 10 percent for crimes against the person, and 1 percent for drug violations. Females followed the same pattern, although the male to female arrest ratio was roughly three to one. Also, the youthful crime rate in England is slowly decreasing, as it is in the United States.[30]

Juvenile Courts

Juvenile courts in England usually are presided over by three lay magistrates or, less frequently, one magistrate. These magistrates are lay citizens who are believed to be well-qualified for working with juveniles and who undergo twelve months of special training in courtrooms, in juvenile institutions, and with juvenile probation and parole officers.[31] The court sessions are more informal than adult trials and are conducted by the magistrates at different times and places than the adult courts when possible; court proceedings are closed to the public. As in the United States, juveniles have no right to jury trials. The media may be present but must keep all information about the juveniles confidential. In England, unlike in the United States, juveniles have the right to bail.

Whereas only police officers prosecuted cases in the past, today, either a representative from the Crown Prosecution Service or a police officer may try cases. Whereas in the past the courts relied on the presumed fairness of the police in presenting cases, the system today is moving toward the representation of juveniles by lawyers.

Once in the courtroom, juveniles and their parents must be present as the charges are read. If the magistrate is not convinced that the parent or child understands the charges, the magistrate may enter a "not admit" (not guilty) plea in behalf of the family and throw the burden of proof on the prosecution.[32] The prosecution then presents the information available about the case to the magistrate(s), who asks the youth and his or her parents if the information is accurate. The child's parents or counsel may cross-examine the police officer and any available witnesses.[33] If the youth is found guilty, a predisposition report is prepared, and, once completed, the juvenile and his or her parents are called back before the magistrate for sentencing.

Magistrates, depending on the seriousness of the offense, have a range of sentences available to them. Magistrates may discharge cases, issue fines, require offenders to pay recognizance (which is refunded if the offenders complete their "binding over" successfully), place juveniles under supervision (probation), require community service or the payment of compensation to the victim(s), or defer sentences for six months to see how well the youths behave during that time.[34] Magistrates attempt to avoid imposing the maximum custodial sentence of six months on offenders, although two consecutive sentences of six months each may be handed out if necessary. For more serious offenses, juveniles over the age of 15 may be tried in Crown court where longer sentences, including life sentences for murder, may be handed down.

Juvenile Institutions

Juveniles were housed with adults in local jails, prisons, and galleys in the late 1700s and early 1800s. The violence and disease in these facilities attracted the attention of reformers, who began to look for safer alternative placements for juveniles. One of the first reforms involved putting some juveniles with minor problems into private homes. Then, the Juvenile Offenders

Act, 1847, was passed, and the first reformatories for juveniles under the age of sixteen were built. Not until the early 1900s did the Borstal system develop with a heavy emphasis on aftercare. Borstals lasted until the 1980s, when they were turned into youth custody centers in which sentences were determinate and in which youths received shorter confinements. The other institutions used for juveniles are junior detention centers for youths fourteen to seventeen years of age and senior detention centers for youths seventeen to twenty-one years old. These centers emphasize cleanliness, order, discipline, and hard work.[35] See Focus on Practice 15–3.

FOCUS ON PRACTICE 15–3

THE BORSTAL SYSTEM

The principles of the Borstal system are important to outline because they became influential in setting up similar programs in the United States and in the British overseas dominions. Briefly, the Borstal system called for the lad's reform by "individualization," mentally, morally and physically. There would be physical drills, gymnastics, and technical literacy training. Good conduct would be rewarded. The staff were selected for characteristics that were likely to influence youths of the kind that Borstal had to work with. Soon after the beginning of the program, it was decided that the minimum period of exposure to Borstal should be at least a year.

The Borstal system proceeded on this fairly austere plan until 1921, when the remarkable personality of Alexander Paterson (1884–1997) was added to the Prison Commission. He was one of a kind. The son of an affluent family, he attended a public school and went on to Oxford University like hundreds of others headed for conventional careers in the civil service or politics. At the age of 21, he graduated from Oxford and settled in Bermondsey, one of London's worst slums, as a member of the staff of the Oxford Medical Mission. He lived in Bermondsey for 20 years, organizing boys' clubs and recruiting Oxford students to work with him in the clubs and, later, when he became a prison commissioner, to take on assignments in the Borstal system.

Patterson's work in the Borstal system was notable for at least four achievements. First, so far as possible, he removed the appearances and the procedures of the British prisons from the Borstals. The governor was still called the governor, but the assistant governors were housemasters serving, as far as possible, the roles of housemasters in an English public school. The prison officials were taken out of uniform, and so were the lads, who were allowed to wear civilian clothes instead of the convicts' demeaning uniform.

Second, having removed as many of the earmarks of prison as he could, he went on to bring in young university men to fill the posts of governors and housemasters. To induce scions of the upper and middle classes to choose a career in penology was an astonishing innovation. The governor in one of the largest prisons in England tells how he was recruited to work in the Borstal system. He had worked in Patterson's settlement house in Bermondsey during a university vacation. Shortly after his return to Oxford, there were a knock on the door of his college room, and there was Patterson. He said, "I need you as a housemaster at a new Borstal. I want you to report to my office in London next Monday." The startled young student protested that he was only in his second year at Oxford but perhaps could work during the next vacation. "That's not soon enough," Patterson replied. "I need you full time, beginning next Monday." To the mystification of the college authorities and the dismay of his parents, he left Oxford, reported the following Monday, and continued in the Borstal system and later in the Prison Commission for the succeeding 40 years.

Patterson's third innovation was a training school for prison and Borstal staff at Wakefield in the north of England. The prison staff college was opened in 1935 to train likely candidates for promotion—not a popular new departure among prison officers accustomed to promotion by security. Eventually, the training program was expanded to include a six-week curriculum for all new recruits for prisons and Borstals and a six-month course for new assistant governors and housemasters.

Patterson's fourth and surely his most significant contribution was the Borstal mystique. He had a flair for aphorisms: "You cannot train a man for freedom in conditions of captivity." He added:

> The Borstal System has no merit apart from the Borstal Staff. It is men and not buildings who will change the hearts and ways of misguided lads. Better an institution that consists of two log huts in swamp or desert, with a staff devoted to their task, than a model block of buildings . . . whose staff is solely concerned with thoughts of pay and promotion.

American prison reformers took a considerable interest in the Borstal model. In 1940 the American law Institute made a long and comprehensive study of the problem of delinquency that culminated in a model Youth Correction Authority Act, recommended for adoption by each state; it also called specifically for new institutions patterned on the Borstal system. The system was adopted in California and in modified form by several other states.

Source: Sir Evelyn Ruggles-Brise, *The English Prison System* (London: Macmillan, 1921), 85–100.

Critical Thinking Questions:

Do we need such charismatic and dedicated leaders as Patterson today in juvenile justice in the United States? Can such a person still make a real difference? Do you believe that you can make a difference in juvenile justice in this nation? How?

Current Concerns

A hard-line consensus appears to dominate the thinking of both the Conservative and Labour Parties in England. Nevertheless, critics of the English system continue to argue that detention and other custodial facilities are "schools of crime" and that a return to treatment and the welfare model is in order. On another level, more specific issues are of concern. The murder of a two-year-old boy by two ten-year-old youths in 1993 generated national soul-searching and debate similar to that resulting from the Columbine High School massacres in Colorado in the United States. The emergence of a "rave culture" and the fact that one-half of all males and one-third of all females have tried drugs suggests to many that drug use is increasing among British youths.[36] Particularly disturbing to the middle class is that it is middle-class children, not lower-class children, who are involved with drugs, particularly the drug Ecstasy. Finally, extreme reservations are being expressed about the increased use of guns by disadvantaged youths. Whether a lack of jobs in England will result in problems of violence becoming more endemic and comparable to that in the United States is in the back of many minds. Concern, too, is expressed about reports that British police are using unjustified violence among the immigrant minority populations that make up an increasingly larger part of the British population.

Australia

European settlers arrived in New South Wales in 1788. The age of responsibility was seven, and older youths were tried in the same courts and often confined in the same institutions as adults. Most early attention was directed toward neglected or vagrant youths, and institutions were developed to handle the needs of these children. Later, these same institutions held juvenile offenders. In the latter half of the 1800s, industrial schools were established for neglected youths, and reformatories were created for young offenders, an early effort to distinguish youths in need from criminal or delinquent youths. Magistrates often confined youths in these institutions for indefinite periods of time as well as in institutions for adults.[37] The early efforts to treat juveniles separately from adults set the stage for what was to become a welfare model in Australian juvenile justice.

In the late 1800s and early 1900s, children's courts modeled after the English juvenile courts were adopted throughout Australia.[38] These children's courts were influenced by both United States and English philosophy and were based on the *parens patriae* principle. The age of responsibility for youths in these courts ranged from seven in Tasmania and eight in Australian Capital Territory to seventeen in three states and one territory; the remaining Australian territories and states used the age of eighteen as the minimum age of responsibility.

Panels

Major mechanisms of dealing with juveniles until recently were Children's Aid Panels, mechanisms that reflected Australian thinking that most young offenders should be handled outside the courts. Troublesome youths were diverted to a panel consisting of a social worker and a police officer, who had the options of dropping the case, sending the child to the police for a caution, referring the youth to a Children's Aid Panel, or recommending prosecution.[39] The Children's Aid Panels were heavily criticized for their "net-widening" effect as well as the arbitrariness, coerciveness, and lack of concern for due process. Children's Aid Panels are now being disbanded in favor of a restorative model of juvenile justice as a consequence of 1993 legislation in South Australia. The panels are being replaced by a system of community or family conferences which initially was developed in New Zealand.[40]

Family Conferences

The family conferences vary in form but are designed to overcome the problems of the Children's Aid Panels and to facilitate implementation of the restorative model of justice. These goals are accomplished by police bringing together all members of the community who are affected by an offense to determine the best method of repairing the damage and restoring the victim. People close to both the offender and the offended are invited to the conferences and are called on to help minimize the damage done to the community.[41] Family conference members include a police officer, the offender, and a youth justice coordinator who chairs the hearing. Parents, relatives, or others who know the offender well also may attend, and lawyers are permitted to represent the youth.[42] Youths are required to do anything the conference members believe will benefit them. Options available include requiring the youth to pay restitution, perform community service, or apologize to the victim; conference members may also issue a formal caution. A youth who fails to attend a conference hearing as requested is charged and prosecuted for the offense.

The restorative model currently in effect has several premises: (1) the victim is of central importance, (2) offenders must face consequences for their actions, (3) more sanctions should be developed with which to punish offenders more quickly, (4) the offender's family is partly responsible for the youth's actions, and (5) the police should actively participate in the process. The restorative model's goal is to promote concern for the victim, the payment of restitution by the offender, the facilitation of the healing process, and the restoration of calm to the community.[43] Furthermore, it is important to note that many crime control strategies are called for which focus on a quick response by the police, protection of the community, and more involvement of the police in the juvenile justice process.

The Police

The general philosophy of the Australian police is to arrest only when necessary. The organization of police departments varies considerably by state and territory, and only a few of the state and territorial police forces have special juvenile units. Police are encouraged to use extensively both formal and informal cautioning processes, particularly for first and minor offenders. Informal cautions are given on the streets, and formal cautions are administered in police stations.[44] The cautioning process available to the police today is fairly flexible. Cautions given on the streets typically consist of police warning offenders, telling them to avoid certain individuals, and encouraging youths to find better ways to spend their free time. Nevertheless, a major criticism of the Australian police is that they traditionally have been overzealous in their contacts with Aboriginal youths. See Focus on the Police and the Offender 15–4.

Australia further limits the role of the police through guidelines and rules governing assistance, cautions, arrest, interrogation, searches, the issuance of summons, pretrial detention, photographing, and fingerprinting.[45] The

FOCUS ON THE POLICE AND THE OFFENDER 15–4

AUSTRALIA

"Edith" is a fourteen-year-old Aboriginal girl living in the Northern Territory, Australia. In 1997, when she was twelve years old, she was arrested for stealing to get food for herself and for other hungry and neglected children she was caring for, including a baby. She was kept overnight in an adult cell in the local police station and then released, but ordered to stay with relatives. When she broke the order several times by running away, including to visit the baby in hospital and to see her family, she was rearrested and detained in Don Dale, the only juvenile detention center in the Northern Territory, which is located some fifteen hundred kilometers away from Edith's home. Her case did prompt the welfare authorities to start supplying emergency food to her family.

Since July 1998, Edith has repeatedly been detained for up to three weeks at Don Dale, usually for minor offenses such as stealing and repeatedly breaching court orders. In August 1998 short-term juvenile holding cells for children awaiting court hearings were opened at her home town's Aboriginal Youth refuge. However, earlier this year, Edith was detained for six more weeks at Don Dale for new offences and breaches of court orders. On one occasion, she reportedly ran away to visit a critically ill relative in hospital. She was arrested and detained for two weeks. Aboriginal children make up only about one-third of the child population of the Northern Territory, but account for about 90 percent of its juvenile detainees.

Source: http://www.amnesty.org/ailib/intcam/children/kids99/kidreport.htm. Accessed July 24, 2003.

offending juvenile is supposed to be interviewed by the police in the presence of a parent or independent adult, but the courts have almost unlimited discretion to use evidence gathered in violation of the rules. The police are encouraged to issue summonses, and, in two states, a "court attendance notice" is given to the suspect at the police station. Serious offenders occasionally are held in police cells until their court hearing, although a few offenders in need of detention are held in remand centers run by departments of welfare.

The Courts

Children's courts are presided over by magistrates or judges who can try juveniles for all but most serious indictable offenses such as murder. The states and territories vary considerably according to whether specific offenses are excluded from the jurisdiction of these courts by legislative, judicial, or prosecutorial exclusion. Only Western Australia and Queensland children's courts may try all offenses. Not all states or territories prohibit bystanders in the courtroom, although all do prohibit the publishing of youths' names or relevant identifying information in the media.

Judges select dispositions from a wide range of options once a youth is found guilty of an offense. Cases may be conditionally or unconditionally discharged, and youths reprimanded or placed on regular or intensive probation. In addition, judges may require youths to perform community service such as working alongside members of community organizations. Judges also send youths to community centers in the evenings or weekends, where the youths receive further education, participate in recreational opportunities, undergo counseling, receive vocational training, or acquire assistance in finding jobs. The most serious cases in all states and territories may be placed in detention centers.[46] Courts in three jurisdictions have the power to transfer juveniles over age sixteen to adult prisons if offenders have been sentenced to detention centers; courts in Tasmania, Western Australia, and the Northern Territory have the power to imprison juveniles in adult facilities.

Juvenile Institutions

Training schools are used less frequently than in the past. The programming in these facilities is not particularly rigorous, and youths are held for fairly short periods of time. The institutions of choice are detention centers, which are found in every state and territory. These facilities, like training schools, are primarily for less serious offenders with maximum sentences of two to three years, depending on the age of the juvenile and the political jurisdiction; a parole board determines a juvenile's release date.

Debate is ongoing over the use of the facilities. Although all provide educational and recreational programs as well as trade and vocational training, many serve primarily as warehouses for youths and employ staff who are repressive, brutal, and discipline oriented.[47] Some detention homes, however, pride themselves on the ability of their staff to meet their charges' social and personal needs. Finally, youths convicted of murder or other extremely serious offenses often serve part of their sentences in detention centers and the remainder in adult prisons.

Current Concerns

The direction of juvenile justice in Australia is under considerable debate, and some changes have occurred over the past two decades. While Australia remains committed to a restorative model of juvenile justice, violent crimes in the early 1990s generated a movement to take serious and dangerous offenders off the streets and to give them longer and harsher sentences than in the past, often in adult prisons. Some concern also exists over the role of juvenile institutions. The debate is whether these institutions should be primarily custodial and pay little attention to the needs of their inmates, or should dedicate themselves to a welfare model that tries to meet the personal needs of their residents. Finally, a major issue is the way the juvenile justice system treats Aboriginal children. Evidence exists that in some jurisdictions, these youths are arrested, referred to court, convicted, and confined at much higher rates than the dominant, largely white Australian population. Police in South Australia, for example, appear to favor the use of arrest over the use of cautions when dealing with Aboriginal youths, and Aboriginal juveniles are considerably overrepresented in correctional facilities.[48] These charges of racism are troubling to many in the Australian society.

HOW DO EMERGING NATIONS HANDLE JUVENILE CRIME?

Most nations around the world either have economies based on agriculture or are just beginning to industrialize. Their per capita incomes are extremely low, most citizens are impoverished, and life is a desperate struggle for survival. The four countries discussed here are chosen in part because of the regions of the world they represent; combined, their populations constitute close to one-half of the world's population.

South Africa

The first Europeans in South Africa found stable tribal societies with well-integrated family, religious, and community life. Youths were socialized to accept traditional tribal, social, and other customary laws, and social control was immediate, firm, and harsh when deemed necessary. As Europeans began to achieve dominance over populations and institutions they considered inferior, Western law and legal institutions were substituted for traditional tribal practices.

Europeans treated both youths and adults in trouble quite harshly. Not until 1856 were magistrates allowed to place youths under the care of responsible persons. In 1882, the first reformatory was chartered for the detention and rehabilitation of youths under the age of sixteen. In 1911, an act was passed that permitted the construction of nine different types of reformatories as well as the development of programs for the education of confined youths. These facilities ranged from child care schools to reformatories with very strict regimens but with considerable emphasis on rehabilitation.[49] Reformatories generally were (and are) the last stop before prison. Throughout the 1900s, Whites continued to increase their dominance over the black population.

With the formalization of **apartheid** in 1950, Whites completed the formation of a segregated society. Separate societies were set up with strict social, legal, economic, and political barriers between Whites and suppressed minorities. This separation of Whites and minorities in South Africa continues even today—a decade after the dismantling of the apartheid system in the late 1980s and the implementation of a new constitution in 1993. The result is that, from a native African's perspective, the law remains a "White man's" law that is applied in a racially discriminatory manner. Also, although modernization has resulted in the call for more formal procedures of the type found in industrialized countries, South Africa is only now setting up a juvenile justice system separate from that for adults.[50] The consequence is, in part, that no statistical data are available on juvenile crime.

Even today, nevertheless, many nonwhite South Africans consider the family the primary political unit and rely on traditional law and custom as tools of social control. In addition, the *people* are considered the first and final source of all power, and community elders make decisions on behalf of the community at large.[51] At this level, traditional law and custom often emerge as more important than the formal rules of the modern state when dealing with juveniles in need. Indeed, neither formal rules nor magistrates are respected or trusted by native Africans.

The Police

Police in South Africa are a paramilitary force, many of whose White officers had served as counterinsurgency personnel in the military. This background, combined in the past with the apartheid policies of the white government, resulted in widespread abuses by the police. Confessions extracted by torture and beatings and unjustified shootings of suspects by police death squads undermined public confidence in law enforcement officers. Today, more than fifty percent of the police officers are black, and the government is attempting to develop standards to bring South Africa in line with recommendations of the *Beijing Rules.*[52] Efforts are being made to extend formal training of officers, to limit police powers, to increase the community's role in law enforcement, and to reduce police corruption.[53] Nevertheless, police practices are far from ideal. Most juveniles arrested are street youths who are taken into custody for petty crimes such as loitering, shoplifting, drunkenness, and marijuana use. Even in these minor cases, police often do not follow through on their responsibility to notify the parents of the children of the arrest and/or trial date and, as recently as 1993, some nine thousand to twelve thousand youths were being held in police lockups, jails, and prisons awaiting trial.[54]

The Courts

By law, all persons under eighteen in South Africa are considered children, and those under the age of seven are not considered criminally culpable.[55] Youths between the ages of seven and fourteen may be held culpable, but only if prosecutors can prove beyond reasonable doubt that the child comprehends the nature and consequences of his or her actions, understands that the actions were wrong, and intended to commit the offenses for which he or she was charged. How courts respond to juveniles depends on both the maturity of children and the type of offense when deciding whether and at what level the child should be tried.

Two basic forms of juvenile courts are found in South Africa. Children's courts hear the cases of youths determined to be in need of care. Youths who are abandoned, have no parents, are out of control, keep bad company, beg, engage in street trading, or are in undesirable home conditions come under the jurisdiction of these courts. These courts usually send juveniles to child-care schools. Youths who commit offenses under South African law are, however, tried by criminal courts. Only in larger urban areas are some criminal courts set aside for the trying of delinquent juveniles, although separate children's courts are available for youths in need.[56] Conviction in these courts classifies the offending youth as a criminal and may result in the youth being sent to reform school or prison. Juvenile courts may sentence a youth to corporal punishment (some thirty-five thousand youths were caned annually until 1995). Courts also fine them; place them under the supervision of probation officers, parents, or other suitable persons designated by the courts; or sentence them to reform schools or imprisonment. Youths may not be given the death penalty.[57] These adult courts may convert themselves into a "Children's Court Inquiry" if the court's members decide a juvenile needs care rather than punishment.[58]

Institutions

Facilities for youths include clinic schools, child care schools, reform schools, and prisons. The *clinic schools* cater to youths who are unable to perform well, have behavioral problems, do not respond to counseling, live in dysfunctional families, or are caught breaking the law. The *child care* schools formerly were called industrial schools. These are residential facilities that attempt to reintegrate secondary school students into their communities through psychological and educational services. The *reform schools* accept youths who continue to have difficulty in other placements such as private custody, clinics, children's homes, and child care schools. The juvenile courts also send to reform schools youths who have previous convictions for less serious offenses but who are then arrested for a more serious offense such as a serious assault, rape, robbery, or murder. South Africa's two *juvenile prisons* are reserved for youths who either are troublemakers in the reform schools or are sent directly to prison from the juvenile court.[59] Youths also may be assigned to prison farms for juveniles.[60] Unfortunately, large numbers of youths end up in jails and prisons which, even though the youths are sometimes segregated by age, are extremely dangerous and degrading.[61]

Current Concerns

The South African government is working continually to bring its justice system in line with those in other countries around the world. Tradition dictates that the people, their elders, and the informal courts and councils of the communities are primarily responsible for maintaining order in the community.[62] But the formal law puts more emphasis on governmental control and the courts in judicial decision making than it does on the people. The result is that people lack confidence in the formal system of law, and a gap is widening between the government and the people that could result in future conflict. Another concern is the approximately nine thousand children wandering the streets throughout South Africa as a result of parental alcoholism, abuse, and poverty. The overwhelming majority of these youths are males of African origin who average thirteen years of age.[63]

Importantly, the hold of the local family, religion, and community over youths is weakening as the poverty level remains high and families continue to move to urban areas in the hopes of finding work and a better life. The problems of children also are heightening as the number of AIDS cases increases the frequency of children losing parents and relatives to the epidemic. The South African government is setting up a variety of social programs to combat these various problems as well as to implement the juvenile justice standards of the *Beijing Rules.*

China

The People's Republic of China is the world's most populous nation today, with approximately 1.2 billion people crowded into a land area roughly the size of the United States. Slightly more than 43 percent of China's population is under the age of thirty-four, with 25 percent under the age of eighteen.[64] Whereas China relied historically on traditional family, school, and community structures and processes to control its youths, China today is attempting to shift the responsibility for the social control of juveniles to the state. This shift accompanies a general weakening of local family, neighborhood, and factory controls as China is permitting some horizontal mobility of its citizens and more individual entrepreneurism in its quest for an economically productive and competitive society.

Historical Periods

Children in feudal China were ranked by family, sex, and age. Males were ranked higher than the females, who were raised as child-bearers and servants. Children were expected to serve their families by working on the farms and rice paddies, and their role was one of subservience and helpfulness. The family's responsibility was to ensure the conformity of its children, and when the family failed in its mission, the school and the community intervened. In addition, most eras in Chinese history were replete with such desperate living conditions that social upheaval, unrest, and wars resulted; thousands of children were neglected, abused, and wandering the streets in need of care as a consequence.[65] Not until after World War II did the first serious efforts to aid juveniles occur.

The first era in modern Chinese juvenile justice extends from 1949 to 1965. Following the seizure of control by Mao Zedong and the Communist Party in 1949, the government cracked down on "criminals" left over from pre-Mao days. The government also initiated efforts to improve the welfare of dependent and neglected children by setting up welfare services and institutions for juveniles and to eliminate the one thousand-year-old practice of child labor.[66] The purpose was to rescue millions of children from the sex trade and to provide youths in need with proper care and attention. Emergency shelters, educational facilities, orphanages, and child welfare houses were set up to get children back in their families, adopted, or in foster homes.[67] The primary concern of governmental agencies was with children's needs, their susceptibility to abusive upbringing, and their dependence on others. Particular attention was paid to holding parents responsible for how they raised their children.

The second era, 1966 to 1976, was a period of social chaos as China underwent a "cultural revolution." In this process, Chinese rulers attempted to rid the nation of all enemies of the proletariat class. During this time, the operations of all criminal justice institutions, including those directed toward juveniles, were suspended.

The third era extends from shortly after Mao's death in 1976 to the present. Authorities wrote a new constitution in 1982 and took appropriate steps for strengthening the legal system.[68] Authorities also recognized that its justice institutions were flawed and that the crime rates among the young were increasing. Steps were taken to deal with the problem. Youths who are guilty of minor behavioral problems such as incorrigibility or who commit minor offenses are sometimes required by parents, school teachers, or community leaders to go to work-study schools called *gongdu* schools.[69] Youths guilty of more serious offenses most frequently are confined, without trial, in reformatories or penal institutions that focus on Education through Labor and Reform through Labor.[70] Both types of youths, in other words, are dealt with administratively rather than processed through the system. Although no national statistics are published, available data suggest that 75 percent of all crime in China is committed by individuals under age twenty-five.[71] Chinese youths' problem behaviors cover the spectrum from major to minor, yet numbers of major offenses in China appear to be low compared with those in more industrialized nations.

The Police

Youths receive four chances. The first chance is when the neighborhood faction of the Communist Party comes to the child's home and discusses potential or real problems with his or her parents and asks the parents for their help; neighbors and neighborhood organizations also may be approached. The second chance is when assistance is sought from school teachers and other authorities such as the police. The third chance is when the youth is sent to a work-study school, and the fourth comes when the youth is sent to a reformatory, with or without court action.[72]

On the negative side, police are permitted to use coercion, torture, beatings, and violence against citizens, depending on the situation.[73] On the positive side, the police role is to provide service and order maintenance to communities. Thus, police actually may become aware of a youth's problems at any of the above times and, in fact, counsel, mediate, and negotiate with juveniles and work with the community to help children solve their problems. In this regard, police act more like social workers than crime fighters. When the rare juvenile who does commit a serious crime comes to the attention of the police, he or she is taken into police custody where interrogation must be undertaken within twenty-four hours; remand to the prosecutor's office must occur within four days. By law, police may detain the youth only in juvenile facilities or an adult facility if no juvenile facility is available. As in other countries, police may not release a child's name, address, or photo to the media. See Focus on Practice 15–5.

The Courts

Most juveniles with problems are dealt with by parents, local citizens, and neighborhood groups, but China's central government today is attempting to expand the more formal methods of handling juvenile offenders. The *Beijing Rules* standard of defining juveniles as anyone under age eighteen is now accepted as the age of majority for Chinese youth, although for some purposes the age of majority is age twenty-five. Age, in other words, is a mitigating factor in Chinese juvenile justice. For example, serious offenders under the age of eighteen actually are tried in adult courts, but these are closed to the public in deference to the youth's age. Youths between the ages of fourteen and sixteen may be held criminally liable for crimes, but no youth under the age of eighteen may be executed for a crime unless the crime is extremely serious. Juveniles age sixteen or seventeen who commit a capital crime and who are given the death penalty are held until the age of eighteen before execution.

Crimes in China are classified according to whether they are intentional or negligent and whether the offender violated a criminal law or minor violations not deemed criminal.[74] Once juveniles' cases are turned over to the procurator, the courts must either render a decision or dismiss the cases within thirty days. Typically, the courts decide on the adequacy of police evidence, but juveniles have no rights in the proceedings and are assumed guilty. The state's responsibility, under the inquisitory system, is to prove the guilt of the offenders by presenting the facts of the cases to the judges, one of whom is from the formal court system and two of whom are lay judges from the community. Typically, the courts decide whether the juveniles should be dealt with in the community by their parents or a community agency, given criminal detention in a jail or other

FOCUS ON PRACTICE 15–5

INFORMAL JUSTICE IN CHINA

China is much more oriented toward informal juvenile justice than most industrialized nations. In China, the police's role with juveniles primarily involves either order maintenance or service activities, rather than law enforcement.

The informal role of the police, especially, is oriented toward crime prevention and services. Police precincts assign their officers to different neighborhoods or large dwelling complexes to work closely with the neighborhood committees and schools to oversee the safety and welfare of those neighborhoods. The behavioral problems of children are quickly identified at the first sign of trouble by an informally organized coalition consisting of parents, school teachers, neighborhood committee volunteers, and police officers. The lower expectation for family privacy in the Chinese cultural tradition permits police officers to penetrate the community and family lives. It is not at all unusual for police officers to make casual visits to members to whom children have been adjudicated by the court and have been placed under parents' custody or in which juveniles have been released from juvenile institutions for postrelease supervision.

Most police officers in China carry neither a gun or a baton, therefore they appear more like social workers than police officers. In fact, the police generally devote about 90 to 95 percent of their time and resources to serving the community's various social and human needs. Exercising police discretion to arrest juvenile offenders is rare and considered as a last resort. Only when a juvenile commits a serious crime would he or she be taken into police custody and be adjudicated by the court. Otherwise, police usually work with parents, schools, or neighborhood committees to counsel children in trouble.

Source: Xin Ren, "People's Republic of China," in *International Handbook on Juvenile Justice*, edited by Donald J. Shoemaker (Westport, CT: Greenwood Press, 1996), pp. 63–64.

Critical Thinking Questions:

What would trouble you if the powers of the U.S. police were expanded with children in trouble? What would be the advantages of increasing police control over children? What should the police be doing in the United States that they are not doing to prevent and control juvenile crime?

facility, placed in Institutions of Juvenile Management and Education for Juvenile Offenders, or given a fixed-term imprisonment, life imprisonment, or the death penalty.[75] In recent years, more and more youths are placed on probation in community organizations than confined in institutions, as the Chinese prefer that all youths under the age of fourteen are worked with intensively by parents, neighborhood organizations, local police, and schools.

Institutionalization

Some youngsters are not placed with families or treated by community organizations or schools. These youths are likely to be between the ages of fourteen and sixteen and guilty of serious criminal law violations, or to have parents who are deemed incapable of taking care of them; this latter group includes youths up to the age of twenty-five. Both of these groups of youths are subject to confinement in juvenile facilities such as the *gongdu* schools; some are placed in adult institutions. Yet another classification of youths is sometimes confined, and these are juveniles sentenced by local police, schools, and neighborhood committees for up to three years in educational camps through the Labor Department under what is called "administrative commitment."[76] Educational camps are reformatories guarded by armed guards who march uniformed youths from one assignment to the next in double time.

Two basic types of institutions designated for juveniles exist: community-based facilities and Institutions of Management and Education for Juvenile Offenders. Sixty percent of juveniles are placed in institutions for five years or less. Regardless of length of stay, the emphasis in institutions is on "persuasion and salvation," with reintegration of the youth into their family with a better education and newly developed values.[77]

Current Concerns

China's massive population, limited resources, increasing inflation, and rapidly increasing unemployment rate pose significant problems to all Chinese who want a higher standard of living. Chinese rulers, in an effort to improve productivity and increase the number of jobs, are encouraging individual entrepreneurial activity as well as industrial growth.[78] The consequence is that parents work harder for longer hours and spend less time socializing with their children. In addition, only one-third of today's Chinese high school students are accepted into college, thereby shaming their parents and guaranteeing themselves a bleak economic future; considering these trends, the reasons for juvenile offending become clear.[79] With weakening family, neighborhood, and social controls, youths are freer today than at any time in recent history. All of these factors together result in an increase in delinquency that must be brought under control.

Furthermore, the Chinese central government has stated that it desires to bring the country into compliance with the *Beijing Rules.* Thus, for juveniles at least, it would appear that China is moving slowly away from traditional methods of social control to a more formal system of justice. Still, tradition is strong, and the Chinese place heavy emphasis on informal community services and organizations to keep youths in line. Parents, school teachers, trade union representatives, neighborhood committees, Juvenile Scouts, police officers, special schools, and many others try to rehabilitate youths both in the community and in juvenile institutions. Of considerable interest is the fact that while China seems slowly to be moving *away* from these informal methods of control, many countries in other parts of the world are moving *toward* such methods.[80] Given that much of the industrialized world is trying to reintegrate youths into their families and communities, some question exists whether China is going in the right direction.

Another important consideration is that China is notorious for its human rights violations. Police apparently are permitted to use certain types of torture; charges of abuse are not condemned; investigations of rights violations are not investigated; and youths are tried without being indicted, not permitted effective legal representation, or given fair trials. If the Chinese government is to win the respect of other countries around the world, due process of justice must be developed in all thirty of China's administrative units.

India

India's population is projected to surpass that of China's by the year 2025.[81] Birth rates now hover around to 3.2 children per woman of child-bearing age. Of the projected population of more than 1.4 billion people (in 2025), more than three hundred million will be juveniles. Still, even with more than several hundred million youths, only a tiny fraction of these youths are arrested each year for all national Indian Penal Code violations and local codes combined. The low arrest rates are explained by a combination of factors, including that the crime rate is, in fact, low, and that most offenders are handled informally; a major factor, however, is the extensive police corruption found throughout India.[82]

The first major Indian acts identifying juveniles as a special category of offenders began with the Apprentice Act of 1850 that granted special protection to young people. An 1860s act established the age of responsibility as seven. An 1861 act called for separate trials for youths under age fifteen, and an 1897 act permitted the confinement of males under age fifteen in reformatories in place of exile or confinement in adult prisons.[83] Separate judicial and confinement systems were established for juveniles and adults in the early 1920s.[84] In 1960, a national Children's Act was passed for use by all nationally governed territories and as a model for India's states, a goal that is only partially met.

The most recent major change in Indian juvenile justice law is based on the 1960s national Children's Act. In 1986, some fifty-five political jurisdictions passed laws facilitating the treatment and rehabilitation of neglected and delinquent youths.[85] "Delinquent" and "neglected" were defined in this act, as were the procedures to be used in processing each through the system. In India, a juvenile is any male under the age of sixteen and any female under the age of eighteen. A delinquent, as might be expected, is anyone who violates one of India's codes, and a neglected youth is any youth who might be classified as a status offender in the United States. The act also describes the types of residential and correctional facilities each type of youthful offender is to be confined in and the qualifications of correctional staff. Within the formal system, the first stop for youths is either the welfare boards or courts, although a semi-official agency, the *Panchayat,* recently has reemerged as an agent of social control in Indian society.[86]

An important consideration relates to the traditional methods of social control in Indian society. Custom and tradition enforced by the family long were used to maintain order. Equally as important as a social control factor was the fact that the family's position in the caste or subcaste (or ***jati***) was based on its reputation in that *jati.* Youths who engaged in deviancy of any type threatened the reputation of their families and therefore also threatened the family's ability to obtain jobs, the family's ability to arrange good marriages for their daughters, and the family's overall socioeconomic status. Also important is that a deep distrust still is directed at the police and courts as a result of British rule. Indians today still prefer traditional methods of social control with the consequence that few youths ever come to the attention of the police and courts.[87]

Panchayats

Panchayats are quasi-governmental organizations located at the community level. These groups have their roots in ancient India but were eliminated at the time of British colonization. With the return of the nation to Indian rule, the *Panchayats* have again emerged. They consist of elected members of the community, usually village elders, who understand community traditions and who are able to deal with all aspects of youthful misbehavior. *Panchayats* hear cases, levy fines, order youths to stop associating with others, and, in extreme cases, compel youths to undergo corporal punishment.[88]

The Police

Police in India generally are viewed with suspicion because of the way the British used them to maintain control. Police today continue to control, but often in the name of the upper classes or whoever happens to have power. Thus, child labor and bondage and female and child prostitution are often overlooked by the police in deference to the ruling parties. Police are also known to engage in extralegal beatings, arrests, "disappearances," and, in some parts of the country, rapes, tortures, and murders. Nevertheless, we should point out, police behavior varies widely in the different cities, states, and political jurisdictions throughout India. See Focus on India 15–6.

Police officers have the option of taking juveniles before either the welfare boards or the juvenile courts, depending on the characteristics of the offenders, their situations, and their offenses. Most of the offenses for which police make arrests under the Indian Penal Code are property crimes and gambling, whereas offenses under Local and Special Laws consist primarily of alcohol prohibitions; the number of drug violations is very small. The distrust of police and formal law leads most communities to deal with the problems of the juveniles informally and in *Panchayats.*

FOCUS ON INDIA 15–6

CHILDREN IN CUSTODY

Seema has been tortured, ill-treated and harassed. She is still only 12 years old. The adults responsible for her suffering are police officers, the very people who should protect her form harm. The daughter of a landless labourer, Seema was sent from Bihar to live with her grandparents in a slum in Delhi, India. She found work as a domestic servant, but the day after she got the job, her employer was murdered. Seema was arrested by police on 10 December 1997 and illegally detained for two days. She was never charged but was questioned repeatedly about the events surrounding the murder. She subsequently told members of the South Asia Coalition on Child Servitude that in custody she had been tied with electric cord and thrashed with a ruler. She was also hung upside-down and slapped on her ears. She was not provided with proper food or blankets to keep warm. She was released on the morning of 12 December, but continues to be called to the police station and questioned. On 24 January she filed a complaint with police which remains pending.

Children like Seema are arbitrarily detained, tortured and ill-treated by police and other state authorities in lockups, prisons and army camps throughout South Asia. Far from giving them special protection, their status as children makes them especially vulnerable to abuse. The majority come from extremely poor families or have had to fend for themselves, outside family and social structures, from a very young age. Their poverty brings them into the path of the law, as they are forced into begging, prostitution and exploitative forms of labour in order to survive. Often they are additionally vulnerable because of other aspects of their identity, such as their gender, ethnicity or caste background, for which they are discriminated against by state officials.

Source: http://web.amnesty.org/library/print/ENGASA040011998. Accessed July 24, 2003.

The Courts

Delinquent youths come before special juvenile courts whose membership is mandated by the state to be either metropolitan or judicial magistrates. Each court has a panel of two honorary social workers, one of whom, as in the case of the welfare boards, must be a woman.[89] Citizens appointed to the welfare boards or courts must have some understanding of the psychology and needs of youths. A wide range of sentences is available to judges. Youths may be sent home after consultation, released to parents, placed on probation or with responsible persons in the community, fined, or confined in community facilities, special homes, jails, or prisons.[90]

The Indian point of view is that both the courts and the police are to be avoided at all costs. Nevertheless, police do occasionally bring juveniles before the courts for violation of both the Indian Penal Code and the Local and Special Laws. Court hearings are closed to the public, although either the juvenile or the court may request anyone relevant to the case to appear.

Institutions

Although the Children's Act of 1960 and the Juvenile Justice Act of 1986 state that juveniles may not be held in the same facilities as adults, youths are confined with adults in both jails and prisons across India. The problems of confined youths are undoubtedly increased in that prisoners are classified by their social status. Wealthy prisoners and prominent citizens are classified as Class A prisoners and are held in private rooms and government guest houses and may have their food supplemented by their families. Class B prisoners consist of college students and taxpayers and are held in less auspicious facilities with poorer support services. Class C prisoners often are held in overcrowded cells with dirt floors, no furnishings, and poor-quality food.[91] Juveniles from the lower castes and *jatis* are most frequently found in facilities for Class C prisoners.

Only a small minority of youths are ever confined, as most are either acquitted of the charges, released to their parents or placed under supervision in the community. Some children are placed in observation homes or "places of safety" until their cases are decided. Youths who are considered neglected or incorrigible may be placed in juvenile homes for a period of time up to age twenty for males and age eighteen for females.[92] Children who violate their probation often end up in these special homes.

Current Concerns

India's expanding population, lack of natural resources, and abject poverty characterize the struggle of its citizens for survival. Children growing up under these conditions, especially those in the remnants of the lower castes and *jatis,* find themselves hungry and disease ridden. A nationwide shortage of jobs means that most children have no economically viable future. If they are poor, and most are, children must attempt to survive in any way possible. The options for most are child labor, wandering the streets, prostitution, begging, and crime. Estimates are that India has some five hundred thousand street children nationwide and another three hundred thousand who are bonded, that is, children who are forced to work for others to help pay back their parent's debts. Trafficking in young females for purposes of prostitution and begging is common.[93] Dramatically, an estimated 34 percent of all primary school children drop out of school, many of whom enter the illegal labor markets. Given the economic importance of children to the ruling classes, little incentive exists for the central government to crack down on those who violate child labor laws and even less incentive for police and local authorities to try to dissuade youths or those who exploit them from undesirable activities.

The plight of females in India also must not be overlooked. Already noted is that females are sold into prostitution and frequently are the victims of infanticide. Females also are given as child brides to males in exchange for dowries that are paid to the male's family. When these dowries are considered inadequate, the brides, more than one-half of whom are under the age of sixteen, are often beaten and/or killed. The assumption in India is that any woman under the age of sixteen who dies is the victim of murder by either her husband or his family.

The Indian government is trying to improve its justice system. Nevertheless, the challenge for the government is to generate the financial resources necessary to expand and professionalize its police forces. Resources must also be found to train professionals in child care, rehabilitation, and the administration of justice. Facilities exclusively for juveniles must be built, and staff sensitive to the needs of children hired. Finally, the ethnic and social class divisions found throughout India result in almost unlimited sources of conflict between the rulers and the ruled.

Brazil

Brazil has the largest population of any country in South America and is the fifth most populous nation in the world, with 174 million people.[94] Its legislative history in dealing with children has its roots in European law, particularly the Napoleonic and Rocco Codes, and has long called for differential treatment of juveniles and adults. The Penal Code of the Empire and the First Penal Code of the Republic, for example, differentiate between adults and juveniles by focusing on the ways minors' degree of "moral responsibility" and "discernment" exempt them from criminal culpability. The Penal Code of 1940 established that minors under the age of eighteen lack criminal responsibility entirely, and this assumption was continued through the enactment of a juvenile code in 1979 and the State of the Child and Adolescent (SEA) in 1990. The latter act specifically identifies a "child" as any person up to the age of twelve and an "adolescent" as any youth between the ages of twelve and seventeen.[95] The main thrust of Brazilian laws and codes is on the "protection of fundamental rights to physical, intellectual, emotional, social, and cultural development."[96] In 1988, the Statute of the Child and Adolescent called for the government to protect the rights of children. Reform groups and the government continue to call for human rights for children and for setting up a wide range of social service facilities throughout the country.[97] The first stop for a child in trouble is often a guardianship council.

Guardianship Council

Guardianship councils are composed of five members chosen by local citizens of local communities. The proceedings of these councils begin upon the referral of a youth by a judge to the council. The charge of these agencies is to guarantee that any youth who gets into difficulties receives any of a number of protective measures. The councils may, for example, recommend that children be placed under the care of their parents, basic education schools, government or community programs for youths or their families, hospitals, shelter foster families, or treatment.[98] Adolescents, in addition to being subject to protective measures, may be reprimanded, required to pay restitution or perform community service, or placed on probation. Youths caught committing serious crimes are subject to the deprivation of liberty if approved by the proper judicial authority.[99]

The Police

Police officers vary widely in how they handle juveniles. Reports of police brutality and vigilante murders continue to shock the world as three children are estimated murdered in Brazil each day. A disturbing number of these children are murdered on the streets and in custody by both on- and off-duty police officers.[100] Youths of African descent, mixed parentage, and Native Indian heritage are the primary targets, with males outnumbering females at a ratio of seven to one. Estimates are that many impoverished youths engage in begging, petty theft, shoplifting, loitering, and prostitution in an attempt to supplement family incomes.

In an effort to reduce police arbitrariness in dealing with juveniles, police must take any youth caught in the act of committing a crime directly to a guardianship council or a juvenile court judge as soon as possible. In rural areas, the youth usually is taken to a regular police station and often is confined with adult offenders. Once the police investigate the offense as well as the needs of the minor, the youth may either be released or, if the evidence warrants, sent to the prosecutor.

The Courts

Once a prosecutor decides how to dispose of a case, it is sent to either a juvenile judge, if one is available, or, more likely, to a judge of the adult court who handles the review. This judge then evaluates the characteristics of the juvenile, the juvenile's family situation, and the seriousness of the behavior. If the judge agrees with the prosecutor's procedures and decisions, the judge then calls for the sentence to be carried out. If the judge does not agree, the case is sent back to the chief prosecutor's office for another hearing.

The courts work closely with the guardianship councils to maintain the juvenile's ties to the family and community and to provide juveniles with the proper educational experiences. As with the councils, judges have available to them such mechanisms as enrolling youths and parents in specialized schools and programs in order to assist them in solving their problems.[101]

Institutions

New laws provide for community centers for youths and include Integrated Screening Centers, which are open 24 hours a day and which are available to all street youths who need help. Also available are training centers that operate as day-care centers and shelters that offer children a safe place to sleep. Actual penalties include reprimands, requiring the payment of restitution, performing community service, or, in more extreme instances, depriving youths of their liberty.[102] This latter sanction may involve either semiliberty, in which youths work or go to school during the day and return to a facility at night, or internment, which is confinement in a juvenile institution.

Maximum-security institutions are used only as a last resort for youths who are guilty of particularly serious offenses, who are repeat offenders, and who are capable of understanding and evaluating their own behavior. In fact, all types of youths, including the dependent and neglected, status offenders, and minor offenders, are often institutionalized. Once confined, juveniles are supposed to be evaluated every six months and are confined for no more than three years. In spite of today's welfare orientation, children are beaten, sexually abused, and packed in small cells without bathrooms or ventilation. In a recent riot in a juvenile institution in São Paulo, residents killed four inmates of whom one was beheaded. Forty other people were injured, including sixteen guards.[103] Life in institutions is often as brutal as life on the streets. For a report on Brazilian juvenile facilities, see Focus on Institutions 15–7.

Current Concerns

Brazil is a society of extremes. Industrially and agriculturally based wealth qualify Brazil to be listed in some reports as an emerging nation. Yet Brazil has poverty and discrimination as deep as any country in South America. In addition, wild economic fluctuations over the past several decades have frequently destabilized Brazilian society to the point that few have confidence that their economic status will remain stable for long. The poor do not have these concerns, as their status at the bottom of the Brazilian socioeconomic structure remains unchanging.

Brazil's task in achieving justice for its juveniles is as daunting as that of India or China. While the government's statements and commitments to a better system of justice undoubtedly are genuine and the work of nongovernmental organizations is impressive, historical legacies and economic realities also are impinging and restrictive. Add a police force that only recently has had its repressive tactics challenged, and some of whose members believe literally in "cleaning the streets" by killing children, and Brazil's task becomes clear. More resources must be devoted to the training of all justice personnel. Old structures of justice must be reformed and efforts undertaken to provide an economic base sufficient to support all citizens.

FOCUS ON INSTITUTIONS 15–7

BRAZIL

An international expert on prison conditions, invited to accompany an Amnesty International delegation to Brazil in October 1999, wrote in his report of São Paulo's juvenile detention centers: " I should say as clearly as possible that I have never seen children kept in such appalling conditions . . . In my view the place should be closed down." A few days later, on 24 October, a riot broke out that shocked even those most hardened to the torture and neglect in São Paulo's juvenile detention system, the Foundation for the Well-Being of Minors,[1] FEBEM. Eighteen hours later, four boys were dead, 58 people were injured, including 29 FEBEM staff, dozens of boys had escaped and the complex had been completely destroyed.

FEBEM has been the subject of scrutiny for decades. Thousands of adolescents[2] have passed through FEBEM detention units since the Foundation came into being in 1976. Throughout this time Amnesty International has received denunciations of torture, ill-treatment, and cruel, inhuman and degrading conditions of detention affecting hundreds of adolescents. A number of boys have died in violent circumstances because the São Paulo government has failed to protect their safety.

Throughout the decade since the launch of Brazil's much-fêted Statute of the Child and Adolescent, ECA,[3] public prosecutors, bar associations, parliamentary commissions of inquiry, state human rights councils, guardianship councils, FEBEM staff unions and human rights organizations have all submitted to the São Paulo authorities detailed reports, denouncing the inhuman and dehumanizing conditions in FEBEM detention units. They have all made concrete and detailed recommendations aimed at putting an end to the decades long pattern of violence, riots and escapes, and calling for the outdated repressive model of juvenile detention to be brought into line with Brazil's own Constitution and legislation regarding children and adolescents. Yet the São Paulo authorities have persistently avoided meeting their obligations to reform the juvenile detention system in line with the law, abandoning both FEBEM detainees and FEBEM staff to cope with a situation of violence and chaos.

Source: http://web.amnesty.org/ai.nsf/Index/AMR190142000?OpenDocument&of=COUNTRIES \E... Accessed June 17, 2002.

Critical Thinking Question:

To what extent should the United States develop a formal policy concerning situations such as this in other countries?

SUMMARY

Few if any countries around the world meet the standards set by the *Beijing Rules.* Even democratic, industrialized, and bureaucratic societies such as the United States, Canada, England, and Australia fall short of the ideals accepted as necessary by many of the top justice and human rights advocates in the world. The proposed standards are based on the basic needs of all human children for protracted and protected childhoods that are free of physical, emotional, and sexual abuse and neglect. The guidelines are based on the principle that juveniles up to the age of eighteen are still maturing physically, emotionally, and spiritually; they are grounded in the belief that children need tutoring and guidance and the ability to grow into mature adults capable of making positive contributions to their societies.

Children are among the most powerless of all in society. The *Beijing Rules* and other international treatises on human rights are set up in recognition that children are dependent on others for physical and emotional nurturing until they are ready to take their place as adults in society. Poverty, physical and sexual abuse, neglect, and violence all act to prevent children from reaching their potential as adults. Damaged children become damaged adults who often perpetuate the cycles of violence, abuse, poverty, and neglect they experienced themselves. In recognition of this, the leaders of most countries do accept that very young children, that is, those under the age of seven, need extensive care and protection. Older youths between seven and fourteen, and even those fourteen to eighteen, also need help. Knowing what kind of help works best is not always clear. Nevertheless, as research and theory become more fully developed and informative, professionals in the fields of child development, medicine, social work, and law are slowly moving us toward the types of understanding necessary for just and humane societies.

WEB SITES OF INTEREST

Amnesty International is a human rights organization with an excellent reputation for documenting injustices to individuals who are the victims of persecution in their own countries. Amnesty International's annual report for 1999 discusses human rights violations in 142 countries and territories. See

http://www.amnesty.org

The *United Nations* also has many sites in the area of human rights, children's rights, and criminal and juvenile justice. To get started, see

http://www.un.org

The *United States Department of Justice* has set up the National Institute of Justice, which, in turn, has a web page for the United Nations Online Crime and Justice Clearinghouse (UNOJUST) to assist member criminological institutes around the world in developing their capacity to exchange information electronically. For these different sites, see

http://www.justinfo.net

The *United States Department of State* issues reports on human rights practices in countries around the world. To access the regions site map for 1998, see

http://www.state.gov/www/global/human_rights/1998_hrp_report/98hrp_report_toc.html

CRITICAL THINKING QUESTIONS

1. What are the major differences and similarities between the United States approach to juvenile justice and those of the countries discussed in this chapter?
2. What is the influence of the different historical backgrounds of the countries discussed in this chapter on their delinquency rates and their juvenile justice systems?
3. How are the changing social and economic conditions of the countries discussed in this chapter likely to influence both their delinquency rates and the way they approach juvenile justice?
4. Should the United States try to develop some informal methods of social controls of youths similar to those found in other countries?
5. Should states in the United States follow, or be required to follow, the *Beijing Rules*?
6. Do you believe that the techniques of juvenile justice used by other countries would work in the United States? Why or why not?

NOTES

1. John A. Winterdyk, ed., *Juvenile Justice Systems: International Perspectives* (Toronto: Canadian Scholar's Press, 1997), ix.
2. United Nations, "United Nations Standard Minimum Rules for the Administration of Juvenile Justice: The *Beijing Rules*" (New York: United Nations, 1986), 1–15. For a synopsis of the rules, see Geraldine Van Bueren and Anne-Marie Tootell, "United Nations Standard Minimum Rules for the Administration of Juvenile Justice: *Beijing Rules*," http://childhouse.uio.no/childrens_rights/dci_html, 1–28.
3. United Nations, "United Nations Standard Minimum Rules: *Beijing Rules*," Rule 7.1, 6; see also Van Bueren and Tootell, "United Nations Standard Minimum," 4.
4. Van Bueren and Tootell, "United Nations Standard Minimum Rules," 5.

5. United Nations, "United Nations Standard Minimum Rules: Beijing Rules," Part 1, Rule 2.1.
6. Maureen McGuire, "C.19: An Act to Amend the Young Offenders Act and the Criminal Code—Getting Tougher?" *Canadian Journal of Criminology* 39, no. 2 (April 1997), 186.
7. John A. Winterdyk, "Juvenile Justice and Young Offenders: An Overview of Canada," in *Juvenile Justice Systems,* edited by John A. Winterdyk, 141. See also McGuire, "C.19: An Act to Amend the Young Offenders Act," 186.
8. McGuire, "C.19: An Act to Amend the Young Offenders Act," 186.
9. For a listing of some of the major juvenile justice legislation leading up to the YOA as well as the major tenets of the YOA, see Winterdyk, "Juvenile Justice and Young Offenders," 143–46.
10. McGuire, "C.19: An Act to Amend the Young Offenders Act," 188.
11. Raymond Corrado and Alan Markwart, "Canada," in *International Handbook on Juvenile Justice* (Westport, CT: Greenwood Press, 1996), 44.
12. Ibid., 41.
13. Ibid., 42.
14. Alan W. Leschied, Peter G. Jaffe, Dan Andrews, and Paul Gendreau, "Treatment Issues and Young Offenders: An Empirically Derived Vision of Juvenile Justice Policy," in *Juvenile Justice in Canada: A Theoretical and Analytical Assessment,* edited by Raymond R. Corrado, et al., (Toronto: Butterworth, 1992).
15. McGuire, "C.19: An Act to Amend the Young Offenders Act," 191.
16. Corrado and Markwart, "Canada," 48.
17. Ibid.
18. Leon A. Radzinowicz, *A History of English Criminal Law and Its Administration from 1750–1833* (London: Stevens and Sons, 1948).
19. Chris Cunneen and Rob White, *Juvenile Justice: An Australian Perspective* (Melbourne: Oxford University Press, 1995), 18–20. For a detailed discussion of the history of English juvenile law as it relates to competing British conservative and labor ideologies, see Loraine Gelsthorpe and Mark Fenwick, "Comparative Juvenile Justice: England and Wales," *Juvenile Justice Systems,* edited by John A. Winterdyk, 79–80.
20. William Wakefield and David Hirschel, "England," in *International Handbook on Juvenile Justice* (Westport, CT: Greenwood Press, 1996), 94.
21. Winterdyk, "Overview of the Juvenile Justice System," 79–80; and Cunneen and White, *Juvenile Justice,* 19.
22. Gelsthorpe and Fenwick, "Comparative Juvenile Justice," 79–80.
23. Wakefield and Hirschel, "England," 94.
24. Ibid., 95.
25. Michael Cavadino and James Dignan, *The Penal System* (London: Sage Publications, 1992).

26. Gelsthorpe and Fenwick, "Comparative Juvenile Justice," 96.
27. Wakefield and Hirschel, "England," 97.
28. David P. Farrington and Trever Bennett, "Police Cautioning of Juveniles in London," *British Journal of Criminology* 21 (1981), 123–35.
29. Bryan Gibson, Paul Cavadino, Andrew Rutherford, and John Harding, *The Youth Court: One Year Onwards* (Winchester, England: Waterside Press, 1994).
30. Gelsthorpe and Fenwick, "Comparative Juvenile Justice," 96. For a comparison of crime rates in the United States and England, see Patrick A. Langan and David P. Farrington, "Crime and Justice in the United States and England and Wales: 1981–1996," (Washington, DC: Bureau of Justice Statistics, Executive Summary, 1998).
31. Wakefield and Hirschel, "England," 99–100.
32. B. F. Harrison and A. J. Maddox, *The Work of a Magistrate,* 3d ed. (London: Shaw and Sons, 1975).
33. Wakefield and Hirschel, "England," 101.
34. Ibid., 102–103.
35. Ibid., 104.
36. Gelsthorpe and Fenwick, "Comparative Juvenile Justice," 103–104.
37. Cunneen and White, *Juvenile Justice,* 10.
38. Ibid., 10, 13, 18–20.
39. Ibid., 147.
40. Ibid., 250–51. Cunneen and White note that these "conferences" are known by a variety of names, including Children's Aid Panels, Family Group Conferences, Community Aid Panels, Community Justice Panels, and Koori Justice Programs.
41. David B. Moore, "Transforming Juvenile Justice—Transforming Policing: The Introduction of Family Conferencing in Australia," in *Comparative Criminal Justice: Traditional and Nontraditional Systems of Law and Control,* edited by Charles B. Fields and Richter H. Moore, Jr. (Prospect Heights, IL: Waveland Press, 1996), 583–600.
42. Cunneen and White, *Juvenile Justice,* 250–51.
43. Ibid., 251–53.
44. Ibid., 203–206, 247–48.
45. Ibid., 203–206; John Seymour, "Australia," in *International Handbook on Juvenile Justice* (Westport, CT: Greenwood Press, 1996), 3.
46. Cunneen and White, *Juvenile Justice,* 231–38.
47. See Amnesty International, "Australia: Juvenile Aboriginal Detention a Key Human Rights Concern," January 18, 1996, http://www.amnesty.org/news/1996/31200196.htm.
48. Fay Gale, Rebecca Bailey-Harris, and Joy Wondersitz, *Aboriginal Youth and the Criminal Justice System: The Injustice of Justice* (Cambridge, England: Cambridge University Press, 1990); See also Amnesty International, "Australia."

49. Herman Conradie, "The Republic of South Africa," in *International Handbook,* 287.
50. South African Law Commission, "Issue Paper 9: Juvenile Justice," (Pretoria, South Africa: South African Law Commission), October 20, 1999, http://www.law.wits.ac.za/sale/sale.html, 2.
51. Conradie, "Republic of South Africa," 286–300.
52. Wilfried Scharf and Rona Cochrane, "South Africa," *World Factbook of Criminal Justice Systems,* http://www.Africa.com, 6–10.
53. Mark Shaw, "South Africa: Crime and Policing in Post-Apartheid South Africa," in *War and Peace in Southern Africa: Crime, Drugs, Armies, Trade,* edited by Robert I. Rotberg and Greg Mills (Washington, DC: Brookings Institution Press, 1998), 31, 34–37.
54. Michelle Saffer, "South Africa's Youngest Prisoners," Third-World-Oriented Gemini News Service of London (World Press Review, March 1993), 31.
55. South African Law Commission, "Issue Paper 9, " 9.
56. Ibid., 50–51.
57. Ibid., 59–65.
58. Scharf and Cochrane, "South Africa," 15.
59. Conradie, "Republic of South Africa," 293–94, 297.
60. Scharf and Cochrane, "South Africa," 20–21.
61. Saffer, "South Africa's Youngest Prisoners," 31.
62. Conradie, "Republic of South Africa," 298–99.
63. Johann Le Roux, "Street Children in South Africa: Findings from Interviews on the Background of Street Children in Pretoria, South Africa," *Adolescence* 13, no. 122 (Summer 1996), 423–31.
64. John R. Weeks, *Population: An Introduction to Concepts and Issues,* 7th ed. (New York: Wadsworth, 1999), 14, 461.
65. Xin Ren, "People's Republic of China," in *International Handbook on Juvenile Justice* (Westport, CT: Greenwood Press, 1996), 55–79.
66. Judge Emily Baker, "People's Republic of China Today: A View of Its Juvenile Justice System," *Juvenile and Family Court Journal* (1986), 51; Xin Ren, "People's Republic of China," 57.
67. Ren, "People's Republic of China," 57–59.
68. Dorothy Bracey, "'Like a Doctor to a Patient, Like a Parent to a Child'—Corrections in the People's Republic of China," *Prison Journal* 68, no. 1 (1988), 25.
69. *Gongdu* schools are middle schools that administer to children ages 12–17. For a discussion of these facilities, see Daniel J. Curran and Sandra Cook, "Growing Fears, Rising Crime: Juveniles and China's Justice System," *Crime and Delinquency* 39, no. 3 (July 1993), 296–315.
70. Baker, "People's Republic of China Today," 51–57.
71. Curran and Cook, "Growing Fears, Rising Crime," 302.

72. Baker, "People's Republic of China Today," 54. Curran and Cook, in "Growing Fears, Rising Crime," state that the juveniles face a five-stage hierarchy of control: education assisted by the community, education through work and study, reeducation through labor, reform through labor, and discipline in the reformatory.
73. Amnesty International, "China: Gross Human Rights Violations Continue," *Amnesty International Report* (February 1996), 3.
74. Baker, "People's Republic of China Today," 52.
75. Dorothy H. Bracey, "Like a Doctor to a Patient, Like a Parent to a Child," 24–33.
76. Baker, "People's Republic of China Today," 55.
77. Ibid., 55.
78. Xiaogang Dent and Ann Cordilia, "To Get Rich Is Glorious: Rising Expectations, Declining Control, and Escalating Crime in Contemporary China," *International Journal of Offender Therapy and Comparative Criminology* 43, no. 2 (1999), 211–28. See also Curran and Cook, "Growing Fears, Rising Crime," 307–309.
79. Curran and Cook, "Growing Fears, Rising Crime," 304–305.
80. Ren, "People's Republic of China," 72–75.
81. Weeks, *Population,* 17–23.
82. Arvind Verma, "Cultural Roots of Police Corruption in India," *Policing: An International Journal of Police Strategies and Management* 22, no. 3 (1999), 264–79; see also Clayton Hartjen, "Legal Change and Juvenile Justice in India," *International Criminal Justice Review* 5 (1995), 6.
83. For a listing of acts related to juveniles, see K. S. Shukla, "Role of the Police in Juvenile Justice," *Indian Journal of Criminology* (September 1981), 163.
84. Hartjen, "Legal Change and Juvenile Justice in India," 2–3.
85. Ibid.
86. Clayton A. Hartjen and G. Kethineni, "India," *International Handbook on Juvenile Justice* (Westport, CT: Greenwood Press, 1996), 184–87.
87. Ibid.
88. Ibid., 185.
89. Hartjen, "Legal Change and Juvenile Justice in India," 4.
90. Ibid.
91. U.S. Department of State, "India Report on Human Rights Practices for 1997," Bureau of Democracy, Human Rights and Labor (January 30, 1998), 10.
92. Hartjen, "Legal Change and Juvenile Justice in India," 5.
93. U.S. Department of State, "India Report on Human Rights," 21, 25–26.
94. Weeks, *Population,* 17–23.
95. Annina Lahalle, "Modern Legislation for a Country of Contrasts: The Example of Brazil," in *Juvenile Delinquents and Young People in Danger in an Open*

Environment, edited by Willie McCarney (Winchester, NM: Waterside Press, 1966), 177–83.

96. Lahalle, "Modern Legislation for a Country of Contrasts," p. 180.
97. Chuck Pfister, "Not for Kids," September 1995, http://www.brazil-brazil.com/cvrsep95.htm.
98. Lahalle, "Modern Legislation for a Country of Contrasts," 182.
99. Ibid., 182–88. This legislative act also calls for programs that offer assistance to parents.
100. Vincent A. Keeton and Michael P. McConnell, "Street Children in Brazil: The Policy Issue, Policy Background, and Current Policy and Programs," Chapter 11, PRP Papers, 1994–1995, http://lanic.utexas.edu/project/ppb/papers94–95/mcconnel.html.
101. Lahalle, "Modern Legislation for a Country of Contrasts," 182–83.
102. Keeton and McConnell, "Street Children in Brazil," 16.
103. Reuters, "Brazil Youth Riot Ends with Four Boys Dead," October 25, 1999, http://www.nytimes.com/reuters/international/international-brazil-html.

16

JUVENILE JUSTICE IN THE TWENTY-FIRST CENTURY

OBJECTIVES

1. To review the basic problems in American society that have an impact on juveniles
2. To review the basic problems in the administration of juvenile justice
3. To discuss the individual, systemic, and societal changes necessary for a promising future for juvenile justice

KEY TERMS

habilitation
healing
honor
hope

Kids are kids, not adults. . . . But it troubles me deeply that our focus is on juvenile justice and not juvenile education. It's about trials and not about schools or discipline. It's about punishment and not about mentoring. No, I can't understand it and I don't agree with it. We will never, in my view, solve our problems on the back end with punishment. We will solve our problems only if we are united with a higher purpose of doing better on the front end with day care, preschool, schools, churches, other institutions and yes, families. Kids are our future and we need to invest in them. Treating kids as adults solves very little; it's another quick-fix solution to a complex problem that took years to reach and will take years to resolve.

—Barry Glick and William Sturgeon[1]

Barry Glick and William Sturgeon do not deny that juvenile crime is both a serious matter and a common phenomenon today.[2] Yet they contend that what is needed is more effective front-end programs, including day care, preschool, schools, and community programs. They believe that such an investment in youngsters will have far greater success than punishment programs on the back end.

The long-standing mission of juvenile justice is to correct youthful offenders so that they will neither return to the juvenile justice system nor continue on into the life of an adult criminal. Indeed, the opposite often appears to be true, for once trouble-making youths are processed through the correctional system, the chances of their returning are increased, not reduced. Juvenile corrections often breeds rather than reforms offenders.[3] A more recent mission is to provide justice to juveniles who are referred to the juvenile justice system.[4] As this book repeatedly documents, there is a long way to go to achieve the goals of either rehabilitation or justice.

Many intervention methods have been tried in order to accomplish the mission of rehabilitation. These include diversion, community-based corrections, radical nonintervention, the closing of training schools, mandatory sentencing, punishment, transactional analysis, guided group interaction, positive peer culture, behavior therapy, work release, home furloughs, and coeducational institutionalization. Although we know that some things work in some situations with some offenders, overall, these strategies fall short of accomplishing the goal of preventing youngsters from returning to the system.

As we begin a new century, the juvenile justice system is under attack from all quarters. Few support keeping the juvenile justice system as it has been. Some urge the decriminalization of status offenders; others want to increase the number of youths transferred to the adult court. An increasingly vocal minority even propose the merging of the juvenile system into the adult justice system.

This chapter depicts the problems facing juveniles in their communities and the problems limiting the juvenile justice system; then it recommends a credo for society and for the juvenile justice system that is compatible with this new vision.

HOW DO THE PROBLEMS OF MODERN SOCIETY AFFECT YOUTHS AT RISK?

The problems of juveniles start well before they come to the attention of juvenile justice authorities. Accordingly, for real progress to be made in understanding the problems of high-risk youths, the larger social context of their lives must be examined.

THE FAMILY

The American family has changed rather dramatically in recent decades. Inflation has eroded away the economic support of the traditional family. Even in intact families, both parents often must work to make ends meet. Single parents experience greater financial difficulties because they have only one source of income; some qualify only for unskilled and minimum-wage jobs. The result in too many families is that children find themselves on their own for significant portions of the day as parents attempt to survive financially.

To add to their problems, many children are members of dysfunctional families, in which neglect, emotional abuse, physical abuse, and sexual abuse are regular occurrences. Dysfunctional families also have more than their share of parents who are emotionally disturbed, alcoholics, drug users, or in prison. Children in some dysfunctional families may have no contact with one parent or may not even remember that parent. But even in what appear to be stable family units, parents may be struggling with problems stemming from long-repressed violence, neglect, or sexual or emotional abuse from their own childhood. The result is that many youths never receive the love, affection, and acceptance they need from parents.

THE SOCIOECONOMIC STRUCTURE

The American social class structure has come under increased scrutiny over the past decade. Such headlines as "The Rich Get Richer" and "Income Disparity Between the Rich and Poor Increases" frequently are found in the media. Increased references to a "shrinking middle class" and the "development of the underclass" are also found. These media trends reflect statistics indicating that a rather small percentage (20 percent) of the population controls more than 86 percent of the wealth in the nation and receives more than 45 percent of the income. The bottom 20 percent of the population controls less than 1 percent of the wealth and receives less than 5 percent of the income. The gap between the bottom 20 percent and the top 20 percent is increasing. In addition, the middle class has more people moving down than up in the social class structure.

The rapidly expanding underclass is one of the most serious social problems facing the United States. The underclass is made up of the poorest of the poor. Joblessness pervades the inner cities, as young males find employment increasingly difficult to find. The lack of suitable jobs tends to make the underclass welfare dependent, but its members do not receive enough welfare support to escape the ravages of poverty—high rents, dilapidated and inadequate housing, deteriorated neighborhoods, and ineffective schooling for their children.[5] Another feature of underclass life is the ever increasing trend of adolescent females to have children out-of-wedlock, which only perpetuates the welfare and poverty cycle to another generation. Drugs, especially crack cocaine, is readily available as an escape from this dreary existence.

The Neighborhood

As children reach an age that allows them to spend time outside the home and away from direct supervision of parents or guardians, the neighborhood becomes an important focus of their expectations. For urban children, exploration of the neighborhood brings them in contact with a variety of social groups and institutions. Unfortunately, they find their inner-city neighborhoods too frequently to be battlegrounds where wars are waged among different ethnic groups. The battles are fought for reasons of misunderstandings, imagined slights, and sometimes to protect the markets in which drugs are the sole means of making a living.

These neighborhoods reflect the downside of American society. Residents of such communities are poor, face prejudice, and feel powerless. On a daily basis, they must deal with an absence of jobs, vermin-filled housing, untreated diseases, scarcity of food, unwanted pregnancies, and a lack of community political and social organization. Weighed down with such problems, residents come to believe in fate rather than in their ability to bring positive change to their lives.

The School

Inner-city schools, especially, are under increased criticism. Although such schools have long been targeted as in need of reform, society has yet to take more than a piecemeal approach to the problems of uninterested and bored students, disillusioned and detached teachers, antiquated facilities, and inadequate curriculums. Gang battles of the streets are often carried into the halls of the schools, and innocent youths have been beaten and killed on school steps, hallways, classrooms, and playgrounds. Not surprisingly, these schools have become dens of fear and frustration for the remaining students and teachers. Drugs are frequently available, as police and security staff attempt to bring some semblance of order to the disorder. Too frequently, juveniles caught up in the environments of these schools make poor grades, become disruptive, skip school, are suspended, assault others, join gangs, traffic in drugs, and drop out. These problems help assure that this nation has more uneducated citizens, higher dropout rates, and more people with minimal reading skills than do most of the industrialized countries in the world. African-

American, Hispanic, and Native American students are particularly vulnerable to these problems.

The Gang

Almost all adolescents are members of peer groups. This grouping together with peers is a normal rite of passage to adulthood. What is not normal from society's viewpoint is the weaponry and violence, drug trafficking, and other

Neighborhood centers provide one-on-one help to youths from impoverished areas. (Photo by Kathryn Miller.)

antisocial behaviors of urban and emerging gangs. Measures taken toward these gangs are often repressive and fail to recognize the major functions of the gangs for their members.

Many juveniles, especially those from the inner cities, see gangs as substitutes for their families. Gangs provide their members with roots, respect, and identity, which they can carry either to an early grave or into prison systems—the only futures on the horizons of many gang youths. For the first time in their lives, many feel a sense of respect and belonging they can get nowhere else. The gang gives them a sense of loyalty and an identity marked by the turf of their neighborhood. Finally, the gang offers the belief that only in this social group can they really belong to something and attain what is missing in their lives.

But gang participation is ultimately as self-defeating or destructive as, or perhaps even more than, the family and school have been. Gang involvement thrusts a youth into dangerous and deadly games. Gang members are more likely than nongang members to commit youthful offenses and to become victims. Gang involvement also is one of the best ways for a juvenile to increase the likelihood of confinement in juvenile and adult facilities. Moreover, gangs poorly prepare a youth for marriage, employment, or learning to adapt to an adult world.[6]

Youth Attitudes

Juveniles can be divided into high risk, middle risk, and low risk. High-risk children, making up about one-fourth of the adolescent population, frequently are involved in problem-oriented behaviors. Middle-risk children, making up another one-fourth of the population, occasionally become involved in problem behaviors, especially in minor forms of juvenile lawbreaking, drug and alcohol use, and sexual behaviors. Low-risk children, constituting the other 50 percent of the adolescent population, become involved in few problem behaviors.[7] The high-risk children are those with the most problematic social contexts shaping their lives. Middle-risk children have some problems in their social backgrounds but usually have positive forces balancing the negative ones. Low-risk children tend to have positive social and family backgrounds.

High-risk children frequently come out of their experiences with families, neighborhoods, and schools with the self-concepts of losers. Told all of their lives that they are dumb, worthless, and troublemakers and that they will never amount to anything, they tend to be self-absorbed, look down upon themselves, and resent anyone who confronts them. Once immersed in alcohol and drugs, they may assume that no legitimate avenues of success will ever open to them and that a life of trouble and an early death are their inevitable future. These youngsters blame society and others for their failures and have no confidence in themselves or in their abilities to turn their lives around.

WHY IS IT HARD FOR A JUVENILE OFFENDER TO "GO STRAIGHT"?

The four key words in juveniles' ability to turn their lives around are **habilitation, healing, hope,** and **honor.** These four interrelated concepts go to the heart of why youths at risk feel alienated from modern society. Whether at home, on the streets, or in juvenile correctional institutions, all youths need to feel that they have the capacity to attain their goals.

HABILITATION

In a large gathering of juvenile justice practitioners, a seasoned probation officer raised the question, "How can we rehabilitate kids who have not first been habilitated?"[8] This person went on to say that a juvenile is not likely to be a good citizen if he or she has not learned how to get along with others and is unable to accept responsibility for his or her own behavior.

This reality goes to the heart of the problem facing many youths today. It reflects the fact that impoverished and dysfunctional families have difficulty raising children who will become contributing members of society. Nor are youths from these families likely to receive much positive reinforcement at school, in the workplace, or anywhere else. Accordingly, they do not believe that they have useful social roles to play, and, not surprisingly, they lack any real stake in the system or any basic respect for social norms, values, or institutions.

This discussion leads to several questions. Is it possible to make up for what was lacking at home? Is it possible to make up for deficient social skills, for the inability to function in school, and for the lack of job marketability? These questions continue to come up in working with hard-core delinquents, whether they are violent offenders, gang delinquents, drug-addicted or drug-trafficking offenders, or repetitive property offenders.

Clearly, the place to achieve habilitation is in the home before the child leaves the family. Society needs to support families in such a manner that the habilitation of all children is guaranteed from the very beginning of their lives. Other early possibilities for habilitation include day-care centers, preschools, and Head Start programs. Sensitive teachers and innovative approaches can help the school socialize children. For those children who fail to receive positive socializing influences at home or at school, the task of habilitation falls to neighbors, extended family, staff of community organizations, gang workers, juvenile justice personnel, and social service agencies.

HEALING

Healing is a crucial need in the lives of most youthful offenders because youths at risk frequently have a long litany of painful experiences. Pain, of course, is a normal part of life, but youths today appear to be experiencing pain in unparalleled numbers. Many are reared in one-parent families, in which they have experienced financial and perhaps emotional deprivation. Others have been neglected and/or abused. Incest is especially traumatic and may require a lifetime to overcome its destructiveness. As youths attempt to cope with emotional and/or material deprivations at home, they also face problems in school. Academic success can help ease this pain, but those who lack support from home all too often find school difficult or nonrewarding. Minority youths, particularly those faced with lack of support from home and with a history of failure in school, often are unable to find jobs. But even if youths can locate low-paying jobs in fast-food restaurants or convenience stores, they are aware that this type of employment has no future and may result in ridicule from members of their peer group.

Their painful experiences, not surprisingly, flood these youths with negative emotions. Many react with anger, resentment, rage, guilt, or depression. Some become self-destructive, engaging in prostitution or excessive drug or alcohol use. Their anger may explode toward others as they strike out in homicide, assaultive behavior, or gang violence.

These youths soon discover that painful consequences accompany their acting-out behaviors. Labeled at school, suspended, or perhaps even expelled, some are removed from their homes and placed in foster care or in residential facilities. Others are adjudicated to training schools or are waived to adult courts. Placement in long-term correctional facilities, especially, is extremely painful because of the freedom the youths lose.

The concept of healing is as old as human society. Yet today, the concept is usually limited to problems of physical healing designated to the care of a medical doctor. Emotional healing is left to the psychiatrists, psychologists, professional social workers, and caseworkers of the world. Clergy are sometimes seen as spiritual healers with family counseling offered with a Judeo-Christian emphasis.

Paradoxically, most treatment technologies in juvenile justice are prefaced on the need for healing among correctional clients, yet few treatment modalities are able to reach the inner selves where healing can be effected. A further problem with treatment in juvenile justice is that it is imposed on juveniles. When a receptivity to treatment becomes a necessary prerequisite of release from correctional service or confinement, then treatment will always be viewed as involuntarily imposed on offenders.

Only within the past decade or so has much effort gone into understanding how individuals can open themselves to the healing process. What we have learned is that prevention is the best approach to avoid the pain that arrests self-development. Prevention, as previously suggested, is largely ignored in modern society. Hence, we are left with the necessity of having to heal what we have failed to prevent.

We have also learned that the desire, or impetus, for healing must begin with an individual. For youths to become useful members of society and to experience a turning point, they must overcome the negative emotions of fear, anger, resentment, and hate and must create or experience positive emotions which will help their minds and bodies stay healthy.

Finally, we are aware that this healing process is one in which an individual needs continual reinforcement from a supportive network of significant others. When a juvenile has been going down one street and tries to change and go the other way, which is exactly what needs to happen with many youthful offenders, it requires a much more dependable support system than is typically found in juvenile justice.

HOPE

Hopelessness—the absence of hope—is being experienced by increasing numbers of individuals today. They feel that future possibility is defined by already known limits; in effect, the past exercises absolute tyranny over their future.[9] The absence of hope is especially found among the underclass in this nation. The feeling of hopelessness is generated by a history of poverty without any apparent means to escape in the present or the future. This feeling contributes to high rates of child and spousal abuse and to frequent use of drugs and alcohol. The feeling of hopelessness among the underclass has also contributed to large numbers being sentenced to correctional care and imprisonment.

For juveniles, the feeling of hopelessness is also related to the high rates of teenage pregnancies and unwed motherhood as young girls often have babies in the hope that the babies will love them when no one else has. Hopelessness increases the appeal of drugs, especially crack cocaine. Hopelessness provides the stimulus for the development of drug trafficking gangs, initially in our inner cities and now throughout the nation. It leads to involvement in crime, even though offenders know they face the possibility of incarceration in jail and prison. Finally, the feeling of hopelessness leads to a fatalistic approach to life. For example, gang youths often believe that life will be short, perhaps extending barely into their twenties.

"Where there is no hope," the Old Testament prophet tells us, "the people perish." The dimensions of *hopefulness* include an accurate portrayal of self, an ability to establish realistic goals for the future, the willingness to reach out to positive support systems, and the acknowledgment of one's sense of power. Hope is contained in the desire for some good to be accomplished with the belief that it is obtainable. Hope enables us to trust in the future. It is fostered by a belief in personal freedom based on the choices presented. The philosopher Marcel adds that hope is the radical refusal to calculate the limits of the possible.[10]

Hope gives adolescents something to anticipate—a reason to obey the law, to attend school, to avoid drug involvement, and to stay out of gangs. Those who have hope are more likely to be bonded to society.[11] They are more able to delay gratification. They believe that good things will happen in the future, including employment, education, marriage, and family.

Our challenge is to provide nourishing environments so that young people can be hopeful about their futures. Of course, achieving this with younger children is easier than with older adolescents. Prevention programs must be developed with young children before they become involved in antisocial groups and commit illegal activities. Adolescents pose a more challenging problem, because many may have already been socialized into a deviant lifestyle. For these youngsters to feel hopeful, they must come to believe that (1) they can attain their goals, (2) the future has possibilities for them, and (3) there are others who will support them in attaining their goals.

Honor

Juveniles worry a great deal about their reputation with valued peer groups. Prosocial youngsters want to wear stylish clothing. They try to do what is socially acceptable, and they usually attempt to avoid anything that will bring embarrassment to themselves. Similarly, youngsters who support negative practices, such as satanic worship, pursue the same strategy for peer approval. Their clothing, tattoos, jewelry, and interactions with outsiders must be approved by other youngsters who believe in satanic worship and beliefs.

The need for peer approval, of course, will not change. But what is important are the values of the peer groups to which a youth turns for acceptance and guidance. The aspirations, values, and worldviews of one peer group might lead to confinement in a training school and to a continuation of crime as an adult, whereas another peer group might lend support to positive directions and socially approved goals for its members.

The peer groups to which juveniles turn depend largely on the youths' definitions of self and where they feel they fit in the social fabric. Those who feel powerless, for example, will turn to groups that will provide what they feel they cannot provide for themselves. One problem with seeking for answers "out there" is that many youths join gangs that inevitably lead to drug addiction, to violent gang activity, and to crime as the best or only options for achieving the good life.

An alternative direction for youths to take is to affirm their honor in socially acceptable ways. This affirmation refers to developing a sense of self-worth, of personal dignity, and of meaningful and important lives. Youths must respect themselves and believe they are entitled to achieve their goals.

In sum, habilitation, healing, hope, and honor are the processes that must take place for a juvenile to turn his or her life around from a negative to a positive direction. A youth who is receptive to change or is fed up with the ways of crime needs support from helpful and caring adults to stay on the path to good citizenry.

WHAT PROBLEMS ARE THERE IN THE ADMINISTRATION OF JUVENILE JUSTICE?

The administrative problems facing the juvenile justice system likewise are formidable and extensive. Inadequate funding, fragmentation within the system, the lack of a unifying philosophy, a sharp upsurge in the public's fear of the violent juvenile, poorly developed prevention strategies, and the overuse of intervention constitute some of the many problems that demand solutions if the offending juvenile is to be successfully reintegrated into the daily life of the community.

The meagerness of the funding of juvenile justice sorely handicaps social policy advances. Juvenile justice presently is a relatively marginal area of governmental concern in most states. Regardless of how large certain budget line-items for justice may seem, or how pressing litigation or code revision may be, the dollars involved are almost insignificant compared to the state resources allocated to public education, or to overcoming energy shortages and unemployment, or even to adult corrections. Consequently, it is not surprising to find that juvenile justice has no general backing within most states, that few interest groups regularly support juvenile justice measures, that coalitions of interest groups and political and governmental leaders seldom push for change, and that reports on important events relating to juvenile justice (other than incidents of crime) are usually relegated to the back pages of the newspapers.[12] It becomes much easier to explain why progress does not occur in this area than to trace the reasons for juvenile justice's varying directions and rate of change among the states.[13]

The fragmentation of the juvenile justice system also presents a barrier to those who would bring change to juvenile justice. Fragmentation clearly prevents juveniles from receiving just treatment under the law, because state and local units operate autonomously, with little coordination or cooperation at any level. Furthermore, the policy and program concerns of some states are quite different from those of other states: In fact, the policy, structure, or program solutions chosen by some states are the very ones rejected by other states as unworkable or undesirable.

The lack of a unifying philosophy is another barrier to change. Should our child-saving philosophy be based on the treatment, the justice, the balanced, or the punishment model? Should our strategy with juveniles in trouble be nonintervention, diversion, deinstitutionalization, or institutionalization? If a juvenile must be institutionalized, should our aim be treatment, punishment, or merely warehousing? The net effect of these philosophical differences works to form pressure groups and professional associations. These groups take specific, sometimes narrow, positions as each attempts to convince others that its position is the only one that deserves to be heard. Each stance is defended emotionally, and often more effort goes into argument than into a genuine concern with the needs of children.

Furthermore, a sharp upsurge in the public's fear of juvenile and adult crime has created a national mood of "let's get tough with juvenile criminals." The trilogy of gangs, drugs, and guns is doing much to contribute to this get tough approach. This attitude is producing a rise in the populations of juvenile correctional institutions and a loss of support for community-based corrections and diversionary programs. Determinate sentencing for juveniles has become the established policy in several states, and mandatory sentencing laws for youthful offenders have been adopted throughout the nation. More juvenile offenders are being transferred to the adult courts. In some states, the death penalty may be imposed on sixteen-year-old juveniles who commit what for adults would be a capital offense. Overall, as the crime control, or punishment, model gathered momentum during the 1970s and 1980s, retrenchment rather than innovation became the predominant characteristic of juvenile justice.

The juvenile justice system has too long been a disposal unit for the children of the poor. The lack of social justice for poor and minority groups is a grave indictment of our society. At the same time that the heavy-handed ministrations of the state have harshly processed the poor, the justice system has worked very hard at saving the "saved"—the middle-class youths who have committed minor offenses. These juveniles are usually the ones diverted from the system, placed on probation, and retained in community-based corrections.

When minor offenders and noncriminal youths, such as status offenders, go into the system, they typically stay a long time and have painful experiences; nothing testifies so well to the fact that the juvenile justice system does not work as the tossing of all youths into the same bag, the rapist with the runaway. The reality is that the system too often refuses to sort the youths who come into it.[14] The unfortunate consequence is that youths who either are noncriminal or have committed only minor offenses often end up being confined for months longer than those who have committed violent crimes. In the past, status offenders tended to become the institutional scapegoats and sometimes chose to take their own lives because they could not survive in the institutional context. Today, they are more likely to be sent to private placements where they end up spending two or three times as long as delinquent youths sent to state institutions.

In addition, juvenile institutionalization is for many youngsters a dehumanizing, brutal, and criminogenic experience. Exploitation has reached epidemic proportions in some training schools, where the weak give up everything, including their bodies, to the strong. Some youngsters come out of institutions psychologically devastated; others emerge much more committed to crime as a way of life and further alienated from conventional values and institutions than before their stay.

Prevention strategies are underdeveloped and inefficient.[15] We have not been able to prevent delinquency, and once youngsters become involved in lawbreaking behavior, we have not been able to exercise control. Problems in prevention strategies emerge on at least three fronts: First, although crime prevention must begin in the local community or on the grassroots level, little progress has been made in community organization since the Chicago Area Projects; second, basic concepts in the prevention field are not precise, and few attempts have been made to design programs around theoretical constructs; and third, we have failed to appreciate fully the negative effects of removing juvenile offenders from such mainstream institutions as the home and school to rehabilitate them.

The overuse of intervention has too frequently characterized juvenile justice. Confined youths usually are required to participate in treatment programs because of our desire to help them. Faced with the options of locking up, giving up, or trying harder with certain youths, we have tried harder to treat them. Consequently, a treatment sprawl has resulted, in which these offenders are faced with what must seem like an endless variety of ways to "recycle" them. The treatment goes on and on, sometimes involving contradictory methods.

Closely related to overintervention is the failure of many community-based and diversionary programs to deliver. Too many programs set their goals too high and promise too much in order to obtain federal funding. In effect, each program promises to be the panacea for youth crime. Not only are these programs unable to achieve projected goals, but they also tend to evade accountability for the quality of their work with youths. For example, while these programs may do the necessary evaluation for funding renewal, the follow-up on program effectiveness is not done, with the result that poor programs are sometimes perpetuated rather than allowed to die.

Juvenile justice is in a quandary on what to do with the hard-core or difficult-to-handle juvenile. In the past, isolation, padded cells, Thorazine, handcuffs, and corporal punishment were usually reserved for these youths who were shipped to maximum-security juvenile facilities. Hard-core offenders now face transfer to the adult court, mandatory sentencing, and if they have committed a heinous crime, perhaps even the death penalty. But our strategies and programs are not rehabilitating these youngsters. The public says that hard-core, youthful criminals must be locked up because the innocent deserve protection, but in places of juvenile confinement, these youths become inmate leaders and set the mood and the rules for a violent inmate subculture. In adult prisons and jails, juvenile thugs become the prey of adult predators.

In sum, a critical examination of juvenile justice easily leads the observer to cynicism and to the feeling that nothing can be done. The agencies that run our political system do not provide enough money for the juvenile justice system to be effective. Innovative methods are fought tooth-and-nail by those who benefit from keeping things the way they are. High-risk youths often have too much against them even if the system could be substantially improved. In addition, the skyrocketing growth of gangs across the nation, the lure of drugs and alcohol, the increased use of guns, and the rising number of hate crimes all contribute to rebellion against adult rules and law.

WHAT WILL JUVENILE JUSTICE LOOK LIKE IN THE TWENTY-FIRST CENTURY?

This unsettling review of the present status of juvenile crime in the United States needs to be supplemented by the grim picture of what may take place with juvenile crime in the twenty-first century. Most disturbing, the number of fifteen- to nineteen-year-old males, the group that commits the most crime, is likely to increase by 15 to 20 percent between 2000 and 2015. Most of this population cohort will come from impoverished homes headed by single mothers.[16] If this population growth materializes and jobs remain marginal or nonexistent, the following trends likely will occur:

- The rates of juvenile violence, including homicides, may again spur a growth rate, as it did in the late 1980s and early 1990s.[17]
- The trilogy of gangs, drugs, and guns will become an even greater social problem than it presently is. Youth gangs are likely to expand, become more organized, and extend their base of criminal operations. Yet the issue of gun control may be an even more serious problem facing juvenile justice than are youth gangs.
- Youth bias or hate crimes are likely to increase as jobs available to unskilled youths remain poorly paid. Youths will strike out at those whom they believe to be threats to their futures.
- The dissatisfaction with the juvenile justice system will increase significantly. Those who want to eliminate the juvenile justice system and the juvenile court will be more vocal and will receive much greater support.
- It remains unlikely that this nation will give up anytime in the near future on its century-long experiment with a separate system for juveniles.
- A structural change that will likely be implemented is the removal of serious crimes from the jurisdiction of the juvenile court. What will probably be imposed is some mechanism for the direct referral of juvenile crimes to the adult court.
- State legislatures will become increasingly involved in passing laws related to the social control of juveniles.
- The numbers of juveniles in adult prisons will greatly increase. Wardens and their staffs will view the protection of these youngsters as one of their most difficult management problems.
- The execution of juveniles will probably take place less frequently in the future than it has in the last few years. The evidence is that the nation is beginning to turn away from juvenile death penalties as most were being reversed in the 1990s.
- The juvenile justice system likely will demonstrate less, rather than more, fairness in handling minorities in the juvenile justice system. When it is remembered that the growth of the juvenile population will come from poor youngsters, then this trend becomes even more problematic.
- The widespread feeling today that there are more troubled teenagers than in the past will be even more pronounced in the next

twenty years. Consequently, adolescent psychiatry will be more frequently called on to treat these youths, and more children of the haves will be placed in private hospitals and treatment centers.

WHAT IS A VIABLE CREDO FOR JUVENILE JUSTICE IN THE NEXT ONE HUNDRED YEARS?

Changes to promote the vision of juvenile justice found in this text must take place in terms of systemic changes in the juvenile justice system and structural changes in the wider society.

SYSTEMIC CHANGES IN JUVENILE JUSTICE

Let us turn to the grim reality of the juvenile justice process—a reality that includes drug trafficking, extortion, drive-by shootings, rape, and murder. The fact is that the history of juvenile justice has been filled with individuals who have made a difference in juvenile justice agencies. One of the authors worked with one such person for four years in a maximum-security training school. He had an absolutely astounding positive impact on these older, aggressive offenders.

The administrative system of this "jungle," as residents were fond of calling this institution, did not treat this person well. Nor have many other such individuals been treated well by the justice systems in which they worked. They are sometimes fired. They are often ignored. They are likely to experience burnout. They receive frequent harassment. And they may leave their jobs emotionally broken.

We need to be proud of the fact that some outstanding individuals make the difference they do in the midst of what appears to be overwhelming odds. We need to admire what they achieve but, at the same time, be aware that their contributions frequently are limited and often short-lived because they stand alone. Superior workers need support and encouragement from peers who believe in similar ideas.

The lesson to be learned is that those individuals who want to effect a more humane, just, and effective criminal justice process must establish networks with others. As these individuals develop their networks and express the visions of systemic reform, they will eventually become a critical mass. Interestingly, once certain numbers of supporters are attained—the critical mass—a movement suddenly dramatically increases its power and persuasiveness.

Specifically, the vision of juvenile justice described in this text points to the following systemic emphases to achieve a more hopeful juvenile crime prevention and control strategy.

- Grassroots participation is essential for any hopeful response to prevent and control youth crime; the community must participate in efforts of crime prevention and control.
- The concern for human dignity and wholeness requires that ethical considerations and personal integrity be viewed as essential components of working in the juvenile justice system.
- The spirit of cooperation and assistance of those who work in the juvenile justice system must replace competition, jealousy, and indifference.
- Conflict resolution approaches are much more efficient and effective means to resolve differences among young people. In order to mediate conflict and violence, these approaches can be more widely used at home, in the school and community, and in correctional settings.
- The more that young people's basic needs are met, the less likely it is that they will turn to antisocial behaviors and drug use.
- Upholding the dignity of the human being requires that each person is treated fairly and that discriminatory treatment becomes a relic of the past.
- The more emphasis that is placed on prevention, the more likely it is that negative individual behavior patterns can be avoided before they become fixed and permanent features of personality structure.
- The principle that good people make a difference is readily seen by those who are making a difference in improving systems and in motivating colleagues and offenders to be the best they can be. At a time in which so much powerlessness is evident among the public, youthful and adult offenders, and juvenile justice practitioners, there is increased need for those who have a positive vision for change and are able to lead others toward this vision.

Structural Changes in Modern Society

Modern societies must take positive steps to reduce the problems of society and the juvenile justice system. Whereas the elimination of crime is clearly unrealistic, the possibility that some problems can be reduced, or at least stabilized, does remain. The following are some goals to attain, at least in part, the vision of a better society for youngsters as well as adults.

- Systemwide planning is required to guarantee a social structure that is sensitive to the needs of all people, regardless of their social class.
- The activities of social service agencies must be coordinated to provide integrated services to all families and youths in a caring manner.

- Disorganized and dangerous neighborhoods must be changed to make them safe and secure.
- All families must believe that they have ready access to agencies capable of providing them direction in solving their problems.
- All families must have access to jobs that provide them with the adequate necessities of life.
- Youths must grow up experiencing a positive social and economic milieu that gives them hope for the future.
- Schools must become responsive to the realities faced by youngsters and must attempt to prepare them realistically for life after graduation.

SUMMARY

Our intent in this final chapter is to map uncharted territory. Our experience in working with juvenile offenders, in researching juvenile justice publications, and in writing about the rhetoric and reality of juvenile justice operations has convinced us that a new direction is needed. We hope that you share some of our enthusiasm and aspirations about the possibility of creating a better day for youngsters in our society.

The challenge in juvenile justice is great at this time. If we care for children, we will increase our efforts to diminish the negative effects of the hardline and punitive approaches to corrections. If we care for children, we will see to it that our ideas are presented forcefully and clearly to policymakers. And if we care for children, we will not wait until the system finally works, but instead, we will reach out and help those youths seeking to find themselves.

CRITICAL THINKING QUESTIONS

1. Is it possible to have hope in the midst of our hopelessness?
2. What is needed to improve juvenile justice in the United States?
3. What is the present status of juvenile corrections in social policy?
4. What is the most serious problem in developing a new vision for juvenile corrections?

NOTES

1. Barry Glick and William Sturgeon, *No Time to Play: Youthful Offenders in Adult Correctional Systems* (Lanham, MD: American Correctional Association, 1998), 10.

2. Refer to the self-report and cohort studies found in Chapter 2.
3. See Lyle Shannon, *Assessing the Relationships of Adult Criminal Careers to Juvenile Careers* (Washington, DC: Government Printing Office, 1982); and Donna Martin Hamparian et al., *The Violent Few: A Study of Dangerous Juvenile Offenders* (Lexington, MA: Lexington Books, 1980).
4. See David Fogel, *We Are the Living Proof: The Justice Model for Corrections* (Cincinnati: Anderson, 1975); and David Fogel and Joe Hudson, eds., *Justice as Fairness: Perspectives on the Justice Model* (Cincinnati: Anderson, 1981).
5. Recent welfare legislation promises to make it even more difficult for the underclass.
6. James F. Short, Jr., "Exploring Integration of Theoretical Levels of Explanation: Notes on Gang Delinquency," in *Theoretical Integration,* edited by S. F. Messner, M. D. Krohn, and A. E. Liska (Albany: State University of New York Press, 1989), 3.
7. Joy G. Dryfoos, *Adolescents at Risk: Prevalence and Prevention* (New York: Oxford University Press, 1990).
8. Statement made in a conference one of the authors attended in 1978.
9. Sam Keen, *Apology for Wonder* (New York: Harper and Row, 1969), 174.
10. Cited in ibid.
11. Travis Hirschi, *Causes of Delinquency* (Berkeley: University of California Press, 1969).
12. Cited in Rosemary C. Sarri and Robert D. Vinter, "Justice for Whom? Varieties of Juvenile Correctional Approaches," in *The Juvenile Justice System,* edited by Malcolm W. Klein (Beverly Hills, CA: Sage Publications, 1976), 169.
13. Sources that explore the many directions of juvenile corrections include Barry Krisberg and Ira Schwartz, "Rethinking Juvenile Justice," *Crime and Delinquency* (July 1983); Barry Krisberg, Ira Schwartz, Paul Litsky, and James Austin, "The Watershed of Juvenile Justice," *Crime and Delinquency* 23 (January 1986); and Dennis Maloney, "The Challenge for Juvenile Corrections: To Serve Both Youths and the Public," *Corrections Magazine* (August 1989).
14. Ira M. Schwartz, *(In)justice for Children: Rethinking the Best Interests of the Child* (Lexington, MA: Lexington Books, 1989), 167.
15. Richard J. Lundman, *Prevention and Control of Juvenile Delinquency* (New York: Oxford University Press, 1984); Richard J. Lundman, Paul T. McFarlane, and Frank R. Scarpitti, "Delinquency Prevention: A Description and Assessment of Projects Reported in the Professional Literature," *Crime and Delinquency* 22 (July 1976).
16. Marie Simonetti Rosen, "A LEN Interview with Professor Albert Blumstein of Carnegie Melon University," *Law Enforcement News* 21 (April 30, 1995), 10.
17. Howard N. Snyder and Melissa Sickmund, *Juvenile Offenders and Victims: A Focus on Violence* (Pittsburgh: National Center for Juvenile Justice, 1995), 7.

NAME INDEX

SUBJECT INDEX